ABC's OF
RELATIONSHIP SELLING

The Irwin/McGraw-Hill Series in Marketing

SIXTH EDITION

ABC's OF RELATIONSHIP SELLING

CHARLES M. FUTRELL
TEXAS A & M UNIVERSITY

Irwin
McGraw-Hill

Boston   Burr Ridge, IL   Dubuque, IA   Madison, WI
New York   San Francisco   St. Louis
Bangkok   Bogotá   Caracas   Lisbon   London
Madrid   Mexico City   Milan   New Delhi   Seoul
Singapore   Sydney   Taipei   Toronto

To my wife Sue—the lady who role-played
as my buyer when I carried the sales bag

Irwin/McGraw-Hill

*A Division of The **McGraw-Hill** Companies*

ABC's OF RELATIONSHIP SELLING

This book is printed on acid-free paper.

domestic   1 2 3 4 5 6 7 8 9 0 QPD/QPD 9 0 9 8 7 6 5 4 3 2 1 0 9

ISBN 0-07-229727-1

Vice president/Editorial-in-chief: *Michael W. Junior*
Publisher: *Gary Burke*
Sponsoring editor: *Karen Westover Black*
Editorial assistant: *Katharine Norwood*
Senior marketing manager: *Colleen J. Suljic*
Project manager: *Pat Frederickson*
Production supervisor: *Kari Geltemeyer*
Cover designer: *Michael Warrell*
Cover illustrator: *Nicholas Wilton*
Photo research coordinator: *Sharon Miller*
Photo researcher: *Corrine L. Johns*
Compositor: *GAC Indianapolis*
Typeface: *10/12 Times Roman*
Printer: *Quebecor Printing Book Group/Dubuque*

Library of Congress Cataloging-in-Publication data

Futrell, Charles.
    ABC's of relationship selling / Charles M. Futrell.—6th ed.
        p.   cm.
    Includes index.
    ISBN 0-07-229727-1 (paperbound)
    1. Selling.   I. Title.
HF5438.25.F868   2000
658.85—dc21   99–12833

Charles M. Futrell is the Federated Professor of Marketing at Texas A&M University in College Station, Texas. He has a B.B.A., M.B.A., and Ph.D. in marketing. Dr. Futrell is a former salesperson turned professor. Before beginning his academic career, Professor Futrell worked in sales and marketing capacities for eight years with the Colgate Company, the Upjohn Company, and Ayerst Laboratories.

Dr. Futrell serves as a frequent reviewer for several academic journals. He is on the editorial board of the *Journal of Personal Selling & Sales Management* and the editorial advisory board of the *Journal of Marketing Theory and Practice.* His research in personal selling, sales management, research methodology, and marketing management has appeared in numerous national and international journals, such as the *Journal of Marketing* and the *Journal of Marketing Research.* An article in the summer 1991 issue of the *Journal of Personal Selling & Sales Management* ranked Charles as one of the top three sales researchers in America. He was also recognized in *Marketing Education,* Summer 1997, as one of the top 100 best researchers in the marketing discipline. His work has earned him several research awards and has resulted in his being associated with such groups as the national Bank Marketing Association's Sales and Professional Development Council, and the Direct Selling Education Foundation's board of directors.

Professor Futrell served as the American Marketing Association's Chair of the Sales and Sales Management Special Interest Group (SIG) for the 1996–1997 academic year. He was the first person elected to this position. Charles was elected Finance Chair for the Sales SIG's 1998–99 term. In spring 2000, Dr. Futrell serves as the Fulbright-Flad Chair in Marketing at the Portuguese Catholic University, Lisbon.

Dr. Futrell has written or cowritten eight successful books for the college and professional audience. Three of the most popular books are—*Sales Management: Teamwork, Leadership, and Technology,* sixth edition, The Dryden Press; *Fundamentals of Selling: Customers for Life,* sixth edition, and *ABC's of Relationship Selling,* sixth edition, both published by Irwin/McGraw-Hill publishers. These books are used in hundreds of American and international schools. Over 300,000 students worldwide have benefited from Professor Futrell's books.

Professor Futrell has more than 25 years of teaching experience. Noted for being an excellent classroom instructor, he has developed numerous innovative instructional materials, including computer simulations, computerized classroom materials, video and CD-ROM exercises, and Web sites and sales internet exercises.

TAMU's College of Business Administration and Graduate School of Business is one of the largest business programs in America, with more than 6,000 full-time business majors. Approximately 50 percent of the Marketing Department's 800 majors are in Charles's personal selling and/or sales management classes. He has worked with close to 10,000 students in sales-related classes.

Professor Futrell's books, research, and teaching are based upon his extensive work with sales organizations of all types and sizes. This broad and rich background has resulted in his being invited to be a frequent speaker, researcher, and consultant to industry.

The 21st-century business world will unquestionably be a dynamic and changing place. The rapid growth in technology, the globalization of business, and increasing competition make sales and relationship skills more important than ever. In the sixth edition of *ABC's of Relationship Selling,* my goal is to give students the information that they need to compete in the 21st century. This edition has been updated to include more examples of selling in a global environment, more information about the technology available to every salesperson, and most importantly, the ABC's of relationship selling.

ABC's is written by a salesperson turned teacher. For eight years I worked in sales with Colgate, Upjohn, and Ayerst. As an academic, I have taught selling to thousands of college students, businesspeople, and industry sales personnel, developing and using the strategies, practices, and techniques presented in this textbook. Moreover, each year I continue to spend time in field work with sales personnel. In my classes and programs, I stress "learning by doing" examples and exercises and videotape role-playing of selling situations. This book is the result of these experiences.

When students ask me why I moved out of sales, I always reply, "I really haven't. I'm just selling a different product in a different industry." We are all selling, whether it's a product, an idea, our parents, a friend, or ourselves—as when interviewing for a job.

ABC's Approach

ABC's was conceived as a method of providing ample materials for readers to construct their own sales presentations after studying the text. This allows the instructor the flexibility of focusing on the "how-to-sell" approach within the classroom. Covering the basic foundations for understanding the concepts and practices of selling in a practical, straightforward, and readable manner, it provides students with a guide to use in preparing sales presentations and role-playing exercises.

The Philosophy behind This Text

The title should help you understand the philosophy of this book. A student of sales should understand the ABC's—the basics—of personal selling. All of them. I do not advocate one way of selling as the best route to success! There are many roads to reaching one's goals.

I *do* feel a salesperson should have an assortment of selling skills and should be very knowledgeable, even an expert, in the field. Based on the situation faced, the salesperson determines the appropriate actions to take for a particular prospect or customer. No matter what situation is faced, however, the basic fundamentals of selling can be applied.

There is no place in our society for high-pressure, manipulative selling. The salesperson is a problem solver, a helper, and an advisor to the customer. If the customer has no need, the salesperson should accept that and move on to help another person or firm. If the customer has a need, however, the salesperson should and must go for the sale. All successful salespeople I know feel that once they determine that the customer is going to buy someone's product—and that their product will satisfy that customer's needs—it is their job to muster all their energy, skill, and knowhow to make that sale. That is what it's all about!

It is my sincere hope that after the reader has studied this book, he or she will say, "There's a lot more to selling than I ever imagined." I hope many people will feel that this material can help them earn a living and that selling is a great occupation and career.

At the end of the course, I hope all the students will have learned how to prepare and give a sales presentation by visually, verbally, and nonverbally communicating their message. I know of no other marketing course whose class project is so challenging and where so much learning takes place.

Finally, I hope each student realizes that these new communication skills can be applied to all aspects of life. Once learned and internalized, selling skills can help a person be a better communicator throughout life.

Basic Organization of the Text

The publisher and I worked hard to ensure that *ABC's of Relationship Selling* would provide students with the basic foundation—the fundamentals—for understanding all major aspects of selling. The 15 chapters in the text are divided into four parts:

- **Selling as a Profession.** Emphasizes the career, rewards, and duties of the professional salesperson and illustrates the importance of the sales function to the organization's success. It also examines the social, ethical, and legal issues in selling.

- **Preparation for Relationship Selling.** Presents the background information that salespeople use to develop their sales presentations.

- **The Relationship Selling Process.** At the heart of this text, this part covers the entire selling process from prospecting to follow-up. State-of-the-art selling strategies, practices, and techniques are presented in a "how-to" fashion.

- **Careers in Selling.** The importance of the proper use of managing one's time and sales territory are given thorough coverage. This part also discusses the selling challenge and the excellent career opportunities available in retailing and organizational selling. Coverage of services and nonprofit selling are new to this edition.

What's New

Lots! But the basic core of our sales process remains because reviewers, users, and especially students love it. Added is more about

- World Wide Web
- ACT! Customer Contact
- Technology in selling
- Sales careers
- Relationship selling
- Total quality selling
- Global selling
- The multicultural workplace
- Ethics
- Small business
- Services and nonprofit selling
- Role plays
- Experiential exercises

The following features have been expanded or are new to this edition:

World Wide Web. Throughout the book, these Web exercises introduce prospective salespeople to the use of the WWW.

ACT! Customer Contact. Using software for keeping in contact with customers and prospects is a necessity in the 21st century.

Student Application Learning Exercises (SALE). Chapters directly related to creating the role play have SALEs that aid students in better understanding how to construct this popular class project. These were first used in Professor Futrell's classes in the fall of 1997. Students unanimously felt they were great in helping them correctly construct their role-play.

Sales Careers. Career information has been expanded throughout so students will better understand that there are sales jobs in *all* organizations—business, service, and nonprofit.

Selling Experiential Exercises. These end-of-chapter exercises help students to better understand themselves and/or the text material. Many can be done within class or completed outside and discussed within class.

Selling Globally. Many of these new box items were written by friends and colleagues from countries around the world.

Technology in Selling. A central theme within each chapter shows the use of technology and automation in selling and servicing prospects and customers.

Sales World Wide Web Directory. This brand new resource contains the URLs for the Sales World Wide Web Exercises found at the end of each chapter and for organizations with the largest sales forces in the United States.

Text and Chapter Pedagogy

Many reality-based features are included in the sixth edition to stimulate learning. One major goal of this book is to offer better ways of using it to convey sales knowledge to the reader. To do this, the book includes numerous special features:

Photo Essays. The book features many photographs accompanied by captions that describe sales events and how they relate to chapter materials.

Chapter Topics and Objectives. Each chapter begins with a clear statement of learning objectives and an outline of major chapter topics. These devices provide an overview of what is to come and can also be used by students to see whether they understand and have retained important points.

Sales Challenge/Solution. The text portion of each chapter begins with a real-life challenge faced by sales professionals. The challenge pertains to the topic of the chapter and will heighten students' interest in chapter concepts. The challenge is resolved at the end of the chapter, where chapter concepts guiding the salespersons' actions are highlighted.

Making the Sale. These boxed items explore how salespeople, when faced with challenges, use innovative ideas to sell.

Selling Tips. These boxes offer the reader additional selling tips for use in developing their role plays.

Artwork. Many aspects of selling tend to be confusing at first. "What should I do?" and "How should I do it?" are two questions frequently asked by students in developing their role plays. To enhance students' awareness and understanding, many exhibits have been included throughout the book. These exhibits consolidate key points, indicate relationships, and visually illustrate selling techniques. They also make effective use of color to enhance their imagery and appeal.

Chapter Summary and Application Questions. Each chapter closes with a summary of key points to be retained. The application questions are a complementary learning tool that enables students to check their understanding of key issues, to think beyond basic concepts, and to determine areas that require further study. The summary and application questions help students discriminate between main and supporting points and provide mechanisms for self-teaching.

Key Terms for Selling/Glossary. Learning the selling vocabulary is essential to understanding today's sales world. This is facilitated in three ways. First, key concepts are boldfaced and completely defined where they first appear in the text. Second, each key term, followed by the page number where it was first introduced and defined, is listed at the end of each chapter. Third, a glossary summarizing all key terms and definitions appears at the end of the book for handy reference.

Ethical Dilemma. These challenging exercises provide students an opportunity to experience ethical dilemmas faced in the selling job. Students should review Chapter 3's definition and explanation of ethical behavior before discussing the ethical dilemmas.

Further Exploring the Sales World. These projects ask students to go beyond the textbook and classroom to explore what's happening to the real world. Projects can be altered or adapted to the instructor's school location and learning objectives for the class.

Cases for Analysis. Each chapter ends with several brief but substantive cases for student analysis and class discussion. These cases provide an opportunity for students to apply concepts to real events and to sharpen their diagnostic skills for sales problem solving.

As you see, the publisher and I have thoroughly considered how best to present the material to readers for maximizing their interest and learning. Teacher, reviewer, and student response to this revision has been fantastic. They are pleased with the readability, reasonable length, depth, and breadth of the material. You will like this edition better than the last one.

Teaching and Learning Supplements

Irwin/McGraw-Hill has spared no expense to make *ABC's* the premier text in the market today. Many instructors face classes with limited resources, and supplementary materials provide a way to expand and improve the students' learning experience. Our learning package was specifically designed to meet the needs of instructors facing a variety of teaching conditions and for both the first-time and veteran instructor.

Tutor Software. This Windows program allows students to test themselves. It is organized by chapter and offers true/false, multiple-choice, and matching questions.

ProSelling Video. Several hours of student role plays, exercises, examples of selling techniques, and industry sales training programs show students how to prepare their role plays and how course content relates to the sales world.

Instructor's Manual. Loaded with ideas on teaching the course, chapter outlines, commentaries on cases, answers to everything—plus much more—the *Instructor's Manual* is a large, comprehensive time-saver for teachers.

Test Bank. The most important part of the teaching package is the *Test Bank*. The *Test Bank* was given special attention during the preparation of the sixth edition because instructors desire test questions that accurately and fairly assess student competence in subject material. Prepared by Dr. Thomas K. Pritchett, Dr. Betty M. Pritchett of Kennesaw State University and myself, the *Test Bank* provides hundreds of multiple choice and true/false questions. Professor Tom Pritchett also uses the book for his selling classes. The test items have been reviewed and analyzed by Texas A & M University's Measurement and Testing Center and class tested to ensure the highest quality. Each question is keyed to chapter learning objectives, has been rated for level of difficulty, and is designated either as factual or application so that instructors can provide a balanced set of questions for student exams.

Computerized Test Bank. A *Computerized Test Bank* for the IBM PC is available free to adopters. The *Computerized Test Bank* allows instructors to select and edit test items from the printed *Test Bank* and to add their own questions. Various versions of each test can be custom printed.

TeleTest. A favorite of the author, *TeleTest* allows the instructor to select test questions, call Irwin/McGraw-Hill, and have the test typed out and mailed to the instructor. Irwin/McGraw-Hill can supply various versions of the same questions and can randomly select questions for a chapter by difficulty level.

Transparency Masters. The *Instructor's Manual* contains masters of materials within and outside of the book to create transparencies for overhead projection or photocopies for distribution to students.

Acknowledgments

Working with the dedicated team of professionals at Irwin/McGraw-Hill, who were determined to produce the best personal selling book ever, was a gratifying experience.

In overseeing this revision, Developmental Editor Katharine Norwood worked enthusiastically to ensure a quality product. Sharon Miller, Photo Research Coordinator, oversaw the selection of appropriate new photographs for this edition. Project Manager Patricia Frederickson ably guided the manuscript and page proof through the production process.

Another group of people who made a major contribution to this text were the sales experts who provided advice, reviews, answers to questions, and suggestions for changes, insertions, and clarifications. I want to thank each of these colleagues for their valuable feedback and suggestions:

- Glen Abke
  Owens Community College
- James M. Arnold
  North Central Technical College
- Ramon A. Avila
  Ball State University

Ed Bashaw
University of Arkansas at Little Rock

Gerald Baumgardner
Pennsylvania College of Technology

Chris Beloin
University of Wisconsin–Stevens Point

Stanley Belostock
Newbury College

Joseph Bonnici
Bryant College

George W. Boulware
Lipscomb University

Nancy J. Boykin
Tarleton State University

David J. Burns
Youngstown State University

Richard Cassel
Fullerton Community College

Tom Castle
Mount Mercy College

Brent Cunningham
Union University

Ellen P. Daniels
Kent State University

R. Selby Downer
University of Mississippi

Cathie Elliot
Western State College

Richard J. English
San Diego State University

Patrick D. Fountain
Methodist College

Amy Gehrig
Lakeshore Technical College

Jim Gilliland
Idaho State University

Jeff D. Gordon
San Joaquin Valley College

Karen Gore
Ivy Tech State College

Kenneth M. Hadge
Newbury College

LeeAnna Harrah
Marion Technical College

Hal Harris, Jr.
Bevill State Community College

Jon M. Hawes
University of Akron

Joe Jaboor
Missouri College

Laurence Jacobs
University of Hawaii

Kenneth R. Jones
University of Houston

Karen Kennedy
University of South Florida

Patricia Kishel
Cypress College

James M. Kohut
Youngstown State University

Daniel Kraska
North Central Technical College

Jean Kujawa
Lourdes College

Doug LaBahn
California State University–Fullerton

Dr. Michael Luthy
Bellarmine College

Steven Lysonski
Marquette University

Karl Mann
Tennessee Technical University

James W. Marco
Wake Technical Community College

John A. Marino
Kent State University–Trumbull

Wendy Martin
Judson College

Theresa Mastriani
Kingsborough Community College

Chip E. Miller
Pacific Lutheran University

James R. Muluihill
SCTC

Rebecca J. Oliphant
Stetson University

Cliff Olson
Southern Adventist University

John O'Malley, Jr.
Virginia Tech

Jill Padget
Arizona Western College

Jack Partlow
Northern Virginia Community College

Kari Roach
Davenport College

John E. Robbins
Winthrop University

John Rooney
American Intercontinental University

Terry E. Rumker
Ohio State ATI

Lynn Anderson Schramm
Ohio State ATI

Gary L. Selden
Kennesaw State University

Donald Shifter
Fontbonne College

Craig T. Snider
Southwest Baptist University

Nancy Strohbusch
Southwest Wisconsin Technical College

■ Dennis B. Tademy
Cedar Valley College

■ S. Stephen Vitucci
University of Central Texas

■ Homer Warren
Youngstown State University

■ Alan S. Weiser
Bryant and Stratton Business Institute

■ Brent M. Wren
University of Alabama–Huntsville

I also want to again thank those people who contributed to earlier editions, because their input is still felt in this sixth edition. They were

Ramon A. Avila, *Ball State University;* Duane Bachmann, *Central Missouri State University;* Ames Barber, *Adirondack Community College;* John R. Beem, *College of DuPage;* Milton J. Bergstein, *Pennsylvania State University;* Marjorie Cooper, *Baylor University;* Norman Cohn, *Milwaukee Tech;* Gerald Crawford, *University of North Alabama;* William H. Crookston, *California State University–Northridge;* Gary Donnelly, *Casper College;* Sid Dudley, *Eastern Illinois University;* Earl Emery, *Baker Junior College of Business;* O. C. Ferrell, *Colorado State University;* Myrna Glenny, *Fashion Institute of Design and Merchandising;* Ric Gorno, *Cypress College;* Deborah Jansky, *Milwaukee Area Technical College;* Albert Jerus, *Northwestern College;* Donna Kantak; Deborah Lawe, *San Francisco State University;* James E. Littlefield, *Virginia Polytechnic Institute & State University;* Lynn J. Loudenback, *New Mexico State University;* Leslie E. Martin Jr., *University of Wisconsin–Whitewater;* Brian Meyer, *Mankato State University;* Ken Miller, *Kilgore College;* Harry Moak, *Macomb Community College;* Dick Nordstrom, *California State University–Fresno;* Roy Payne, *Purdue University;* Robert Piacenza, *Madison Area Technical College;* Jeff Sager, *University of North Texas;* Donald Sandlin, *East Los Angeles College;* Camille P. Schuster, *Xavier University;* Dee Smith, *Lansing Community College;* Robert Smith, *Illinois State University;* Ed Snider, *Mesa Community College;* William A. Stull, *Utah State University;* Albert J. Taylor, *Austin Peay State University;* James L. Taylor, *University of Alabama;* Rollie Tilman, *University of North Carolina at Chapel Hill;* John Todd, *University of Tampa;* Glenna Urbshadt, *British Columbia Institute of Technology;* Bruce Warsleys, *Trend Colleges;* Dan Weilbaker, *Northern Illinois University;* Timothy W. Wright, *Lakeland Community College;* and George Wynn, *James Madison University.*

I would also like to thank the many Texas A & M students who have used the book in their classes and provided feedback. Thanks also to the many instructors who call me each year to discuss the book and what they do in their classes. While we have never met face-to-face, I feel I know you. Your positive comments, encouragement, and ideas have been inspirational to me.

Additionally, salespeople and sales managers have provided photographs, selling techniques, answers to end-of-chapter exercises and cases, and other industry materials that enrich the reader's learning experience. They are:

Kim Allen, *McNeil Consumer Products Company;* Alan Baker, *Noxell Corporation;* Michael Bevan, *Parbron International of Canada;* Richard Ciotti, *JC Penney Company;* John Croley, *The Gates Rubber Company;* Terry and Paul Fingerhut, *Steamboat Party Sales, Inc., Tupperware;* Bill Frost, *AT&T Communications;* Steve Gibson, *Smith Barney;* Gary Grant, *NCR;* Jerry Griffin, *Sewell Village Cadillac—Sterling, Dallas;* Martha Hill, *Hanes Corporation;* Debra Hutchins, *Sunwest Bank of Albuquerque;* Mike Impink, *Aluminum Company of America (ALCOA);* Bob James, *American Hospital Supply Corporation;* Morgan Jennings, *Richard D. Irwin, Inc.;* Patrick Kamlowsky, *Hughes Tool Company;* Cindy Kerns, *Xerox Corporation;* Alan Killingsworth, *FMC Corporation;* Santo Laquatra, *SmithKline Beecham;* Stanley Marcus; Gerald Mentor, *Richard D. Irwin, Inc.;* Jim Mobley, *General Mills, Inc.;* George Morris, *The Prudential Insurance Company of America;* Vikki Morrison, *First Team Walk-In Realty, California;* Greg Munoz, *The Dow Chemical Company;* Kathleen Paynter, *Campbell Sales Company;* Bruce Powell, *Richard D. Irwin, Inc.;* Jack Pruett, *Bailey Banks & Biddle;* Emmett Reagan, *Xerox Corporation;* Bruce Scagel, *Scott Paper Company;* Linda Slaby-Baker, *The Quaker Oats Company;* Sandra Snow, *The Upjohn Company;* Matt Suffoletto, *International Business Machines (IBM);* Ed Tucker, *Cannon Financial Group, Georgia.*

For the use of their selling exercises and sales management cases, I am especially grateful to

■ Gerald Crawford, Keith Absher, Bill Stewart
University of North Alabama

■ Dick Nordstrom
California State University–Fresno

■ James L. Taylor
University of Alabama

■ George Wynn
James Madison University

Finally, I wish to thank the sales trainers, salespeople, and sales managers who helped teach me the art of selling when I carried the sales bag full time. I hope I have done justice to their great profession of selling.

I hope you learn from and enjoy the book. I enjoyed preparing it for you. Readers are urged to forward their comments on this text to me. I wish you great success in your selling efforts. Remember, it's the salesperson who gets the customer's orders that keeps the wheels of industry turning. America cannot do without you.

Charles M. Futrell
c-futrell@tamu.edu
http://futrell-www.tamu.edu

Contents in Brief

Contents

PART II

PREPARATION FOR RELATIONSHIP SELLING

CHAPTER 3

The Psychology of Selling: Why People Buy   66

CASES

CHAPTER 4

Communication for Relationship Building: It's Not All Talk   104

PART III

THE RELATIONSHIP SELLING PROCESS

CHAPTER 6

Prospecting—The Lifeblood of Selling   172

CHAPTER 7

Planning the Sales Call Is a Must!   200

CHAPTER 8

Carefully Select Which Sales Presentation Method to Use   224

CHAPTER 9

Begin Your Presentation Strategically   248

PART IV

CAREERS IN SELLING

CHAPTER 14

Time, Territory, and Self-Management: Keys to Success   398

CHAPTER 15

Retail, Business, Services, and Nonprofit Selling   422

PART I

SELLING AS A PROFESSION

This introductory part of *ABC's of Relationship Selling* is an overview of the sales profession. First, we examine the sales job; then we review the essential social, ethical, and legal sales issues involved in being a professional salesperson. Included in this part are:

1. The Life, Times, and Career of the Professional Salesperson
2. Social, Ethical, and Legal Issues in Selling

1

The Life, Times, and Career of the Professional Salesperson

LEARNING OBJECTIVES

This chapter introduces you to the professional and rewarding career of selling. After studying this chapter, you should be able to:

- Define and explain the term *selling*.

- Explain why everyone sells, even you.

- Discuss the reasons people might choose a sales career.

- Enumerate some of the various types of sales jobs.

- Describe the job activities of salespeople.

- Define the characteristics that are needed for success in building relationships with customers.

- List and explain the 10 steps in the sales process.

Debra Hutchins majored in French, with a minor in English literature, at Washington University in St. Louis. After graduation she began work as a secretary in the marketing department at Sunwest Bank in Albuquerque, New Mexico.

"I had never considered a sales job while in school, and sales didn't appeal to me when I began work at the bank. I always felt you would have to be an extrovert. I'm more the shy, intellectual type. I don't see myself in the role of a salesperson."

"Someday I *do* want a more challenging job. I'm a very hard worker; long hours don't bother me. I've always had a need to achieve success. One of the things I like about being a secretary is helping customers when they call the bank. It is important to carefully listen to their problems or what they want in order to provide good customer service. Maybe one day I'll find a job that has more challenge, professionalism, and reward."

If you were in Debra's position, what would you do? What types of jobs would you recommend she consider?

Debra Hutchins is like many people in that while she was in school a career in sales did not seem like the thing to do. Most people are unfamiliar with what salespeople do.

As you learn more about the world of sales, a job selling goods or services may become appealing. The salesperson makes valuable contributions to our quality of life by selling goods and services that benefit individuals and industry. Red Motley, former editor of *Parade* magazine, once said, "Nothing happens until somebody sells something." Selling brings in the money and causes cash registers across the country to ring. For centuries, the salespeople of the world have caused goods and services to change hands.

More than ever, today's salespeople are a dynamic power in the business world. They generate more revenue in the U.S. economy than workers in any other profession. The efforts of salespeople directly impact such diverse areas as:

- The success of new products.
- Keeping existing products on the retailer's shelf.
- Constructing manufacturing facilities.
- Opening businesses and keeping them open.
- Generating sales orders that result in the loading of trucks, trains, ships, airplanes, and pipelines that carry goods to customers all over the world.

The salesperson is engaged in a highly honorable, challenging, rewarding, and professional career. In this chapter, you are introduced to the career, rewards, and duties of the salesperson. The chapter begins by examining why people choose sales careers.

WHAT IS SELLING?

Many people consider *selling* and *marketing* synonymous terms. However, selling is actually only one of many marketing components. In business, **personal selling** refers to the personal communication of information to persuade a prospective customer to buy something—a good, service, idea, or something else—that satisfies that individual's needs.

EXHIBIT 1–1

In personal selling, a salesperson can tailor a presentation to the needs of an individual customer.

This definition of selling involves a person helping another person. The salesperson often works with prospects or customers to examine their needs, provide information, suggest a product to meet their needs, and provide after-the-sale service to ensure long-term satisfaction.

The definition also involves communications between seller and buyer. The salesperson and the buyer discuss needs and talk about the product relative to how it will satisfy the person's needs. See, for example, Exhibit 1–1. If the product is what the person needs, then the salesperson attempts to persuade the prospect to buy it.

Everybody Sells!   If you think about it, everyone sells. From an early age, you develop communications techniques for trying to get your way in life. You are involved in selling when you want someone to do something. For example, if you want to get a date, ask for a pay increase, return merchandise, urge your professor to raise your grade, or apply for a new job, you are selling. You use personal communication skills to persuade someone to act. Your ability to communicate effectively is a key to success in life.

This is why so many people take sales courses. They want to improve their communication skills to be more successful in both their personal and business lives. The skills and knowledge gained from a selling course can be used by a student who plans to go into virtually any field, such as law, medicine, journalism, the military, or their own business.

Selling is not just for salespeople; it is a must for everyone. In today's competitive environment, where good interpersonal skills are so valued, the lack of selling capability can put anyone at a disadvantage. So as you read this book and progress through the course, think about how you can use the material both personally and in business.

WHY CHOOSE A SALES CAREER?

Five major reasons for choosing a sales career are (1) the wide variety of sales jobs available; (2) the freedom of being on your own; (3) the challenge of selling; (4) the opportunity for advancement in a company; and (5) the rewards from a sales career.

A Variety of Sales Jobs Are Available

As members of a firm's sales force, salespeople are a vital element in the firm's effort to market goods and services profitably. Personal selling accounts for major expenditures by most companies and presents a large number of career opportunities. It is estimated that American firms spend over $180 billion on their salespeople, which equals the amount spent on sales promotion and advertising. There are some 16.3 million people employed in selling jobs in the United States. By the year 2005, employment is projected to grow over 30 percent to over 21 million sales jobs.[1]

Selling Power, a leading magazine for sales professionals, published a list of the 125 largest U.S. manufacturing and 125 largest service organizations' sales forces.[2] The 250 organizations had 967,000 salespeople. These salespeople and their companies generated a whopping $2.4 trillion in sales. (Retail store sales personnel are not included.) The breakdown is as follows:

- Top 125 manufacturing companies: 342,000 salespeople, $1.3 trillion in sales.
- Top 125 service companies: 625,000 salespeople, $1.1 trillion in sales.
- Big 3 automobile dealers: 166,000 salespeople, $359 billion in sales.

It is astonishing to realize that a grand total of 967,000 salespeople contribute up to $2.5 million per salesperson. Given the average ratio of $200,000 in sales per employee, it would take 10 million nonsales employees to produce the same $2 trillion in business. As these numbers attest, the profession of selling is not merely a spoke in the wheel of American business—it is the wheel that moves the U.S. economy.

According to *Personal Selling*'s research, there are approximately 6 million companies in the United States that create close to 90 million jobs. More than 14 million Americans are working in manufacturing or service full-time sales positions, and there are half as many who work in part-time sales jobs. It is interesting to note that the 250 organizations with large sales forces represent only 0.003 percent of America's 6 million businesses, yet they employ 10 percent of the business-to-business sales force. According to *Selling Power* these 967,000 salespeople are creating jobs for 9,188,422 employees. Every salesperson creates enough sales revenue to pay for nine other jobs within the company.

Retail sales are not included in this listing or in the above numbers. The number of full-time retail salespeople is estimated to be between two and four times the number of full-time business-to-business salespeople. Thus, retail salespeople will number between 28 to 56 million.

Direct sellers sell face-to-face to consumers—typically in their homes—who use the products for their personal use. Sales in international markets, such as Europe and Asia, are exploding. This rapid sales growth will require millions more new salespeople for this industry alone in the next few years.[3]

Retail vehicle sales is another industry hiring several hundred thousand salespeople. The manufacturers, such as Ford and General Motors, have large sales forces, as do their retail dealers. There are almost 200,000 people selling new automobiles. And that does not include the hundreds of thousands of people selling used cars and trucks.

What do those sales personnel numbers mean to you? There are millions of sales jobs and there is a high probability that at one time during your life you will have a sales job.

EXHIBIT 1–2

Profile of the American
salesperson

- 33 years old
- 71% male
- 29% female
- 18% black, Hispanic, Asian
- 81% some college or degree
- 9% graduate degree
- Most likely to leave after 4.3 years
- Average length of service—6.3 years
- Mostly paid:
  20% salary
  30% commission
  50% combination
- Trainee makes $33,000; experienced makes $80,000
- Costs $22,000 to train

- Length of training—3 months
- Sales call cost—$95.00 to $400.00
- Sales calls per day—6.5
- Number of calls to close—5
- Field expenses cost—$30,000
- Value of benefits—$16,000
- Average sales volume—$600,000
- Spends 41 hours per week in selling activities within the territory
- Spends 10 hours per week in nonselling activities, such as paperwork and planning sales calls
- Turnover rate: 20% a year

Exhibit 1–2 provides a glimpse of the American salesperson.[4] The data represent estimates of these characteristics and are not meant to be totally accurate but to provide general information. For example, a recent population census reports 68,694 women in product sales (other than retail sales) out of a total of 433,496 salespeople, or slightly less than 16 percent of the total. However, the service sector of the economy and other nonmanufacturing industries have high percentages of females. For example, the financial, publishing, real estate, and cosmetic industries are traditionally made up of 40 to 50 percent women.

The Exhibit 1–2 profile indicates that the sales position is professional in nature. Salespeople are well-educated, young, loyal, well-trained, and receive above-average pay. We also see that it is costly to operate a sales force. Salespeople work long hours. Often salespersons must visit customers numerous times to determine their needs before being able to close sales.

The Sales Force of the Future

Marketers mapping long-range sales strategies through the year 2010 and beyond are dealing with a sales force whose complexion is changing markedly.[5] Mostly, marketers can expect to have a more diverse sales force calling on prospects and accounts. They are also benefiting from healthy productivity gains by their salespeople and experiencing considerable challenges in hiring younger trainees.

These trends are triggered by the aging of the baby boom generation and the baby bust group that followed it. The effects of this maturation process are at the core of the federal government's new long-range projections developed by the Bureau of Labor Statistics' Office of Economic Growth and Employment Projections (OEGEP), which covers the economy, labor force, industry, and occupations.

As the total labor force (people with jobs plus people looking for work) increases, two-thirds of the newcomers are women. Considering that the total number of salespeople is projected to increase at a faster-than-average rate of 30 percent, this rapid growth implies that marketers will have to hire greater numbers of women to keep expanding their sales forces.

Marketers can be encouraged by the changed age mix of tomorrow's work force. Nearly three-fourths of the labor force in the year 2010 will be in the prime working ages (25 to 54 years), compared with *two-thirds* in 1984. In fact, prime-age workers will swell to 24 million, while younger (16 to 24) and older (55 and up) workers will decline to 3.7 million and 1.6 million, respectively.[6]

Thus, the sales force of the 21st century will be older, include more females and minorities, and be more productive. Plus, there will be an above-average growth rate in the number of hired salespeople.

Types of Sales Jobs—Which Is for You?

While there are numerous specific types of sales jobs, most salespeople work in one of three categories: either as a retail salesperson, a wholesaler's salesperson, or as a manufacturer's sales representative. These categories are classified according to the type of products sold and the salesperson's type of employer.

Selling in Retail.   A **retail salesperson** sells goods or services to consumers for their personal, nonbusiness use. Three common types of sellers who sell at retail are the (1) in-store salesperson, (2) direct seller who sells face-to-face away from a fixed store location, and (3) telephone salesperson.

More than 2.8 million retail stores compete for business in the United States. Yearly retail sales in 1996 totaled over $2.5 trillion.[7] By any measure, more people are employed in retail selling than in any other type of sales. Look back at the definition of a retail salesperson. Think of all the different types of retail organizations selling something—retailers such as bakeries, banks, caterers, clothes, electronics, flowers, food, furniture, hotels, video stores, and travel agents. See Exhibit 1–3. Each customer contact person takes your money and provides a good or service in return. This is personal selling.

Millions of salespeople sell directly to consumers. An organization could have one salesperson or hundreds of thousands of people, like Mary Kay Cosmetics, selling their products directly to consumers in their homes. Retail selling is so important to a society that this book has a chapter on retail selling, mainly because retailers use somewhat different approaches than other types of sellers.

As in any type job—including accountants, mechanics, and politicians—some retail salespeople do very little to help their customers. However, many retail salespeople are highly skilled professionals, commanding exceptionally high incomes for their ability to service their customers. I personally know retail salespeople earning $40,000 a year selling shoes; $80,000 selling furniture; $110,000 selling jewelry; and $150,000 selling automobiles.

Selling for a Wholesaler.   Wholesalers (also called distributors) buy products from manufacturers and other wholesalers and sell to other organizations. A **wholesale salesperson** sells products to parties for:

- Resale, such as grocery retailers buying items and selling to consumers.
- Use in producing other goods or services, such as a home builder buying electrical and plumbing supplies.
- Operating an organization, such as your school buying supplies.

Firms engaged in wholesaling are called wholesaling middlemen. Classifying wholesaling middlemen is difficult because they vary greatly in (1) products they sell, (2) markets to which they sell, and (3) methods of operation. Thus, the discussion of types of wholesalers is beyond the scope of this book as there are so many different types.

At last count in 1996 there were about 480,000 wholesaling establishments in the United States. They employ several million inside and outside salespeople. The total annual sales volume of wholesaling middlemen is more than $3 trillion.[8]

Selling for a Manufacturer. Manufacturers' salespeople work for organizations producing the product. The types of **manufacturer's sales representative** positions range from people who deliver milk and bread, to the specialized salesperson selling highly technical industrial products. Working for the firm that manufactures a salesperson's products is the most prestigious sales job available. The salesperson working for a manufacturer may sell to other manufacturers, wholesalers, retailers, or directly to consumers. There are five main types of manufacturer sales positions:

An account representative calls on a large number of already established customers in—for example—the food, textile, and apparel industries. This person asks for the order.

A detail salesperson concentrates on performing promotional activities and introducing new products rather than directly soliciting orders. The medical detail salesperson seeks to persuade doctors, the indirect customers, to specify a pharmaceutical company's trade name product for prescriptions. The actual sale is ultimately made through a wholesaler or is made directly to pharmacists and hospitals who fill prescriptions.

EXHIBIT 1–3

Retail salespeople are becoming well-rewarded professionals.

A sales engineer sells products that call for technical know-how and an ability to discuss technical aspects of the product. Expertise in identifying, analyzing, and solving customer problems is another critical factor. This type of selling is common in the oil, chemical, machinery, and heavy equipment industries because of the technical nature of their products.

Greg Munoz, a sales engineer for the Dow Chemical Company, says, "Our sales technique typically takes the team approach. Several of Dow's finest staff (technical, production, marketing, and support) and I work in unison to address the customer's specific needs. I am responsible for building the business relationship with the customer and directing resources and information toward securing a customer's plastic-resin business. Market managers and district sales managers coordinate pricing and positioning as the customer relates to the industry as a whole. Dow technicians engineer materials to meet or exceed the requirements specified for the application and work with the customer's production department to see that they perform accordingly. Customer service representatives handle order placement and product delivery logistics while servicing the customer's information needs. Once the sale is closed, I follow up and maintain our profile while serving as the first line of communication and interface for the customer."

An industrial products salesperson, nontechnical, sells a tangible product to industrial buyers. No high degree of technical knowledge is required. Packaging materials manufacturers and office equipment sales representatives are nontechnical salespeople.

A service salesperson, unlike the four preceding types of manufacturing salespeople, must sell the benefits of intangible or nonphysical products such as financial, advertising, or computer repair services. See Exhibit 1–4. Services, like goods, are either technical or nontechnical in nature.

EXHIBIT 1–4

Selling services offers excellent career opportunities; banks, hotels, airlines, and travel agencies are industries that need professional salespeople.

Selling services is ordinarily more difficult than selling tangibles. The salesperson can show, demonstrate, and dramatize tangible products. With intangible products, the salesperson cannot do this. Intangibles often are difficult for the prospect to comprehend. People cannot feel, smell, see, hear, or taste intangible products. This makes them more challenging to sell.

Order-Takers versus Order-Getters.   Sales jobs vary widely in their nature and requirements. See Exhibit 1–5. Some sales jobs require the salesperson only to take orders. **Order-takers** may ask what the customer wants or wait for the customer to order. They do not have a sales strategy and use no sales presentation. Order-takers must be employed to bring in additional business that the employer probably would not obtain without their efforts. Many never attempt to close the sale. They perform useful services. However, few truly *create* sales.

On the other hand, the creative selling of tangible goods or intangible services in highly competitive lines (or where the product has no special advantages) moves merchandise that cannot be sold in equal volume without a salesperson. These people are **order-getters.** They get new and repeat business using a creative sales strategy and a well-executed sales presentation. The salesperson has an infinitely more difficult selling situation than that faced by the order-taker. In this sense, the individual is a true salesperson, which is why this person usually earns so much more than the order-taker.

This salesperson has two selling challenges. First, the salesperson must often create discontent with what the prospect already has before beginning to sell constructively. Second, the salesperson often has to overcome the most powerful and obstinate resistance. For example, the prospect may never have heard of the product and, at the outset, may have no desire whatsoever to purchase it. The prospect may even be prejudiced against it and may resent the intrusion of this stranger. In other instances, the prospect may want it, but may want competing products more. Frequently, the prospect cannot afford it. To meet such sales situations successfully requires creative selling of the highest order.

Creative salespeople often are faced with contacting numerous people to get one order. This is the most difficult selling situation because the representative may have to win over not only the decisionmaker, the one who can say yes, but also other persons who cannot approve the order but each of whom has the power to veto.

Freedom of Action: You're on Your Own

A second reason people choose a sales career is the freedom it offers. A sales job provides possibly the greatest relative freedom of any career. Experienced employees in outside sales usually receive little direct supervision and may go for days, even weeks, without seeing their bosses.*

Job duties and sales goals are explained by a boss. Salespeople are expected to carry out their job duties and achieve goals with minimum guidance. They usually leave home to contact customers around the corner or around the world.

Job Challenge Is Always There

Working alone with the responsibility of a territory capable of generating thousands (sometimes millions) of dollars in revenue for your company is a personal challenge. This environment adds great variety to a sales job. Salespeople often deal with

---

*Outside sales usually are made off the employer's premises and involve person-to-person contact. Inside sales occur on the premises, as in retail and telephone contact sales.

EXHIBIT 1-5

The complexity and difficulty of these seven sales job categories increase as they move left to right.

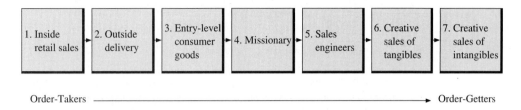

Order-Takers ────────────────────────────────→ Order-Getters

hundreds of different people and firms over time. It is much like operating your own business, without the burdens of true ownership.

Opportunities for Advancement Are Great

Successful salespeople have many opportunities to move into top management positions. In many instances, this advancement comes quickly. For example, General Mills and Quaker Oats may promote successful salespeople to managerial positions such as district sales managers after they have been with the company for only two years.

A sales personnel **career path,** as Exhibit 1–6 depicts, is the upward sequence of job movements during a sales career. Occasionally, people without previous sales experience are promoted into sales management positions. However, 99 percent of the time, a career in sales management begins with an entry-level sales position. Firms believe that an experienced sales professional has the credibility, knowledge, and background to assume a higher position in the company.

Most companies have two or three successive levels of sales positions, beginning at the junior or trainee level. Beginning as a salesperson allows a person to:

- Learn about the attitudes and activities of the company's salespeople.
- Become familiar with customer attitudes toward the company, its products, and its salespeople.
- Gain firsthand knowledge of products and their application, which is most important in technical sales.
- Become seasoned in the business world.

When asked why they like their jobs, first-line sales managers say it is because of the rewards. By rewards, they mean both financial rewards and nonfinancial rewards, such as the great challenge and the feeling of making a valuable contribution to their salespeople and the company. Managers also frequently mention that this position represents their first major step toward the top. They have made the cut and are on the management team. Instead of having responsibility for $1 million in sales like a salesperson, the manager is responsible for $10 million.

With success, many jobs throughout the sales force and in the corporate marketing department open up. This can include sales training, sales analysis, advertising, and product management. Frequently, traveling the upward career path involves numerous moves from field sales to corporate sales, back to the field, then to corporate, back to the field, and so on. However, sales experience prepares people for more responsible jobs in the company.

SELLING GLOBALLY

When in Rome, Do What the Romans Do

Imagine American salesperson Harry Slick starting out on his overseas business trip. The following events occur on his trip:

1. In England, he phones a long-term customer and asks for an early breakfast business meeting so that he can fly to Paris at noon.
2. In Paris, he invites a business prospect to have dinner at La Tour d'Argent and greets him with, "Just call me Harry, Jacques."
3. In Germany, he arrives ten minutes late for an important meeting.
4. In Japan, he accepts the business cards of his hosts and, without looking at them, puts them in his pocket.

How many orders is Harry Slick likely to get? Probably none, although his company will face a pile of bills.

International business success requires each businessperson to understand and adapt to the local business culture and norms. Here are some rules of social and business etiquette that managers should understand when doing business in other countries.

France: Dress conservatively, except in the south where more casual clothes are worn. Do not refer to people by their first names—the French are formal with strangers.

Germany: Be especially punctual. An American businessman invited to someone's home should present flowers, preferably unwrapped, to the hostess.

During introductions, greet women first and wait until they extend their hands before extending yours.

Italy: Whether you dress conservatively or go native in a Giorgio Armani suit, keep in mind that Italian businesspeople are style conscious. Make appointments well in advance. Prepare for and be patient with Italian bureaucracies.

United Kingdom: Toasts are often given at formal dinners. If the host honors you with a toast, be prepared to reciprocate. Business entertaining is done more often at lunch than at dinner.

Saudi Arabia: Although men kiss each other in greeting, they never kiss a woman in public. An American woman should wait for a man to extend his hand before offering hers. When a Saudi offers refreshment, accept; declining it is an insult.

Japan: Don't imitate Japanese bowing customs unless you understand them thoroughly—who bows to whom, how many times, and when. It's a complicated ritual. Presenting business cards is another ritual. Carry many cards, present them with both hands so your name can be easily read, and hand them to others in descending rank. Expect Japanese business executives to take time making decisions and to work through all of the details before making a commitment.[9]

Success also brings financial rewards. The larger a company's revenues, the heavier the responsibility of the chief executive, and the larger the compensation. Today, it's common for a CEO of a large national corporation to receive compensation totaling more than $1 million annually.

Leaving aside compensation at the top echelons, both corporate and field sales managers typically receive higher salaries than others (such as production, advertising, product, or personnel managers) at the same organizational level. Salary is just one part of compensation. Many firms offer elaborate packages that include extended vacation and holiday periods; pension programs; health, accident, and legal insurance programs; automobiles and auto expenses; payment of professional association dues; educational assistance for themselves and sometimes for their families; financial planning assistance; company airplanes; home and entertainment expenses; and free country club membership. The higher the sales position, the greater the benefits offered. In addition to performance, salary typically is related to:

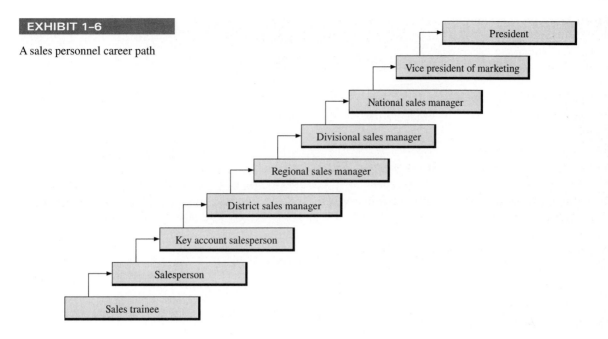

EXHIBIT 1–6

A sales personnel career path

- Annual sales volume of units managed.
- Number of salespeople managed.
- Length of experience in sales.
- Annual sales volume of the firm.

Rewards: The Sky's the Limit

As a salesperson, you can look forward to two types of rewards—nonfinancial and financial.

Nonfinancial Rewards

Sometimes called psychological income or intrinsic rewards, nonfinancial rewards are generated by the individual, not given by the company. You know the job has been done well—for instance, when you have skillfully delivered a sales presentation.

Successfully meeting the challenges of the job produces a feeling of self-worth: you realize your job is important. Everyone wants to feel good about a job, and a selling career allows you to experience these good feelings and intrinsic rewards daily. Salespeople often report that the nonfinancial rewards of their jobs are just as important to them as financial rewards.

After training, a salesperson is given responsibility for a sales territory. The person then moves into a regular sales position. In a short time, the salesperson can earn the status and financial rewards of a senior sales position by contacting the larger, more important customers. Some companies refer to this function as a key account sales position.

There Are Two Career Paths

Don't let Exhibit 1–6 mislead you—many salespeople prefer selling to managing people. They want to take care of themselves rather than others. In some companies, a salesperson may even earn more money than the manager.

	Compensation*	Travel and Entertainment Expenses†	Total
Sales Trainee			
Consumer goods	$30,100	$11,400	$41,500
Industrial goods	35,000	13,300	48,300
Services	33,000	10,611	43,611
Mid-level Salesperson			
Consumer goods	45,000	15,820	60,820
Industrial goods	50,000	15,600	65,600
Services	47,000	13,448	60,448
Top-level Salesperson			
Consumer goods	80,000	16,606	96,606
Industrial goods	110,000	16,880	126,880
Services	85,000	15,000	100,000
Sales Superior			
Consumer goods	82,000	26,000	108,000
Industrial goods	112,000	29,200	141,200
Services	87,000	28,198	115,198

*Compensation includes base salary, commission, and bonus.
†Expenses include travel, entertainment, food, and lodging.

Many companies have recognized the value of keeping some salespeople in the field for their entire sales career. They do a good job, know their customers, and love what they are doing—so why promote them if they do not want to move up within the organization? However, many other people work hard to move into management.

You Can Move Quickly into Management

The first managerial level is usually the district sales manager's position. It is common for people to be promoted to this position within two or three years after joining the company. From district sales manager, a person may move into higher levels of sales management.

Financial Rewards

Many are attracted to selling because in a sales career financial rewards are usually based solely on performance. Many professional salespeople have opportunities to earn large salaries. Their salaries average even higher than salaries for other types of workers at the same organizational level.

Exhibit 1–7 shows the findings of a large survey determining compensation and job-related expenses paid by consumer, industrial, and service organizations.[10] These dollar figures are averages for the several hundred firms participating in the survey. Remember, however, that many salespeople make more or less than the earnings shown. These high salaries indicate that organizations recognize the importance of their salespeople and are willing to pay for results.

IS A SALES CAREER RIGHT FOR YOU?

It may be too early in life to determine if you really want to be a salesperson. The balance of this book will aid you in investigating sales as a career. Your search for any career begins with *you*. In considering a sales career, be honest and realistic. Ask yourself questions such as:

- What are my past accomplishments?
- What are my future goals?
- Do I want to have the responsibility of a sales job?
- Do I mind travel? How much travel is acceptable?
- How much freedom do I want in the job?
- Do I have the personality characteristics for the job?
- Am I willing to transfer to another city? Another state?

Your answers to these questions can help you analyze the various types of sales jobs and establish criteria for evaluating job openings. Determine the industries, types of products or services, and specific companies in which you have an interest.

College placement offices, libraries, and business periodicals offer a wealth of information on companies as well as sales positions in them. Conversations with friends and acquaintances who are involved in selling, or have been in sales, can give you realistic insight into what challenges, rewards, and disadvantages the sales vocation offers. To better prepare yourself to obtain a sales job, you must understand what companies look for in salespeople.

A Sales Manager's View of the Recruit

The following discussion of what sales managers consider when hiring a salesperson is based on a summary of a talk given by a sales manager to a sales class. It is reasonably representative of what companies look for when hiring salespeople.

> We look for outstanding applicants who are mature and intelligent. They should be able to handle themselves well in the interview, demonstrating good interpersonal skills. They should have a well-thought-out career plan and be able to discuss it rationally. They should have a friendly, pleasing personality. A clean, neat appearance is a must. They should have a positive attitude, be willing to work hard, be ambitious, and demonstrate a good degree of interest in the employer's business field. They should have good grades and other personal, school, and business accomplishments. Finally, they should have clear goals and objectives in life. The more common characteristics on which applicants for our company are judged are (1) appearance, (2) self-expression, (3) maturity, (4) personality, (5) experience, (6) enthusiasm, and (7) interest in the job.

People often consider sales careers because they have heard that persons can earn good salaries selling. They think anyone can sell. These people have not considered all of the facts. A sales job has high rewards because it also has many important responsibilities. Companies do not pay high salaries for nothing. As you will see in this book, a sales career involves great challenges that require hard work by qualified individuals. Let us review the characteristics of a successful salesperson.

SUCCESS IN SELLING—WHAT DOES IT TAKE?

Throughout this book you will read comments from salespeople about their jobs. Over the years, I have asked thousands of salespeople the question, What makes a salesperson successful? The nine most frequently mentioned characteristics were (1) love of their job; (2) willingness to work hard; (3) need to achieve success; (4) optimistic outlook; (5) knowledge of their job; (6) careful use of selling time;

(7) ability to ask questions and listen to customers; (8) customer service; and (9) being physically and mentally prepared for life and the job. Each of these characteristics is described more fully next.

Love of Selling

The successful salesperson is an individual who loves selling, finds it exciting, and is strongly convinced that the product being sold offers something of great value. Prudential Life Insurance salesperson John Young stated it best by saying, "To be successful you need a very deep commitment to your product and what it will do." In selling her Amway products, Bernice Hansen emphasizes that she "has wonderful products that everyone needs. . . . If you believe in what you are doing as strongly as I do, you have the self-confidence to be successful."

To be sure, a love of selling itself is one characteristic of successful salespeople. Other salespeople quoted throughout this book make similar comments about how their enthusiasm for their work helps them to be successful. They possess an eagerness to do the job well, which causes them to work hard at selling.

Willingness to Work Hard, Work Smart, Then Work Some More

There is one word that means everything to a person's success in life. That word turns the dull mind into a bright mind. It turns the bright mind into a brilliant mind. It turns the brilliant person into a steadfast person. That word opens doors for you. That word rolls out red carpets for you. That word connects you to some of the most beautiful and powerful people in the world. That word gives every person success. That miracle magic word **is W-O-R-K.** A positive attitude toward work works wonders! Successful people are often described as lucky. However, they spell luck **W-O-R-K.** The harder they work, the luckier they get.

Successful salespeople say that even though they enjoy it, selling requires long hours of hard work, day in and day out, to reach personal goals. "You need to work at least one-half of each day to be successful in sales," says Linda Franklin of General Electric. "I don't care which 12 hours of the day you work, but it takes that much effort and commitment to be a top seller these days." A 10- to 12-hour workday is common—including many Saturdays and Sundays. It is their love of work and their need for success that motivate the really top sellers—the sellers who make the really big bucks!

Matt Suffoletto of IBM once said, "If you would make each sales call, presentation, or proposal as if it were the single event from which you will gain quota attainment, recognition, or promotion, you will always be miles in front of your competition." Underlying a tolerance for hard work is often a desire for success in life.

Need to Achieve

Each of us has a desire to be successful; yet some individuals seem to have a higher desire for success. Successful salespeople have, as part of their personalities, a strong work ethic and a high need to strive for success. If people love their work, are willing to work hard, and have a strong desire to achieve success, do you think they will be successful?

Steve Gibson, a stockbroker for Smith Barney, finds "being second best is not good enough. I am personally challenged to be my customers' best broker. I want to excel. I've found that asking myself the simple question 'Did I do my best?' at the end of each business day is important." "Second is not good enough," "Go beyond the call of duty," and "Make that second effort" are frequent comments of successful salespeople like Steve Gibson.

The need to achieve involves persistence. Consider former U.S. president Calvin Coolidge's famous comments:

MAKING THE SALE

Don't Quit

When things go wrong, as they sometimes will,
When the road you're trudging seems all uphill,
When the funds are low and the debts are high,
And you want to smile, but you have to sigh,
When care is pressing you down a bit—
Rest if you must, but don't you quit.
Life is queer with its twists and turns,
As every one of us sometimes learns,
And many a person turns about
When they might have won had they stuck it out.

Don't give up though the pace seems slow—
You may succeed with another blow.
Often the struggler has given up
When he might have captured the victor's cup;
And he learned too late
When the night came down,
How close he was to the golden crown.
Success is failure turned inside out—
So stick to the fight when you're hardest hit—
It's when things seem worst that you mustn't quit.

Nothing in this world can take the place of *persistence.* Talent will not. Nothing is more common than unsuccessful men with talent. Genius will not. Unsuccessful genius is almost a proverb. Education will not. The world is full of educated derelicts. Persistence and determination alone are omnipotent. The slogan "press on" has solved and always will solve the problems of the human race.

With persistence often comes the ability to go beyond normal limits. Only our self-imposed limitations can hold us back. If we fail to realize success or if our success is limited, it is often due to preconceptions that throw an invisible barrier across our path. The following puzzle illustrates how we can be held back from breaking through. The challenge is to connect all nine dots with four straight lines, without lifting your pencil from the paper. Try it!

It seems impossible to intersect all nine dots with four straight lines. But how do you move something from the impossible to the possible? *Go beyond the limits.*

When you go beyond the limits, the impossible becomes possible. When you go beyond the limits, you can connect all nine dots with four straight lines.

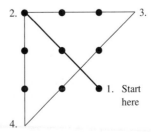

Successful salespeople break through their self-imposed limitations. No one said when you drew four straight lines that they couldn't go beyond the dots. That was a limitation you imposed. When you impose limitations, the puzzle becomes unsolvable. You can break away from self-imposed limits when you think bigger.

A student came into my office at the beginning of the term and said, "Professor Futrell, I need to make an 'A' in your personal selling class to graduate. My grade point is below a 2.0. The only 'A' I've ever made was in a PE course. I'm not sure I can do it."

I said, "It's up to you—not me—what grade you make in this course. It may seem and sound impossible to you today. If you want the 'A' badly enough, you can earn it. Be prepared for every class period as if I am giving a test that day. Outline every chapter; memorize every key word's definition; and know examples of each definition, concept, and selling technique. Begin today collecting the information needed to give your in-class sales presentation. Talk with no less than two salespeople who sell your product and two buyers of that product. Have the presentation developed two weeks before it's due so that you can practice, practice, practice. Remember, the grade you want tomorrow is based on what you do today!"

He made a 72 on the first test. The class average was 79.5. He dropped the course shortly afterward—as he should have since he frequently missed class. It was sad because he set his own limits.

Successful people don't wall themselves in by refusing to stretch their boundaries. Stretching one's boundaries will probably require some tough, blind faith. Faith is leaping over the fence. It's crossing the mountains. It's going beyond the boundaries. It's breaking through the limitations that you and others have set. It's seeing around the corner to a bright new beginning and a beautiful new tomorrow.

Have an Optimistic Outlook

Salespeople credit a positive attitude toward their companies, products, customers, themselves, and life as major reasons for their success. Successful salespeople are enthusiastic, confident, and constantly think of themselves as successful. Sure, salespeople have times when things do not go as they wish. Yet their positive mental attitude helps overcome periodic problems. They continually look for methods to improve their attitudes.

Successful salespeople say that their greatest enemy is procrastination. The biggest obstacle is inertia. The most dangerous temptation is delaying. Getting started is the hardest part. Breaking loose and beginning is their toughest job. Top sales professionals realize that postponing can wipe out the opportunity to make a sale.

Successful salespeople don't use the word *someday*. They realize that what you do today determines your tomorrows. Thus, *tomorrow* is today! They always think of today as a new opportunity in their lives.

> Today Is a New Day!
>
> The sun is shining, the sky is blue!
> There's a new day dawning for me and you.
> With every dawning of the sun
> New possibilities have just begun.
> With every breaking of the morn
> Fresh opportunities are newly born.
>
> *Robert Frost*

The early bird gets the worm: successful salespeople know it. They are do-it-now people. They pick up the phone, mail a letter, or make a sales call today to be successful tomorrow. In no other career is the need to think positively more important than in sales. As a salesperson, examine your inner self, commonly referred to as your self-concept, and make sure you have a positive, enthusiastic attitude toward yourself, your work, and your customers. This involves:

- Believing in yourself.
- Thinking of yourself as a success.
- Being positive in your outlook on life and the job.

Optimism and hard work are building blocks for success. In addition, top salespeople believe job and product knowledge also are necessary for success in a sales career.

Be Knowledgeable

Successful salespeople place great emphasis on being thoroughly knowledgeable in all aspects of their business. This helps them to project a professional image and to build customer confidence. Take, for example, the comments of Smith Barney's Steve Gibson:

> Successful salespeople gain a broad knowledge of their business through reading and observation. Learning through study, such as reading, does not end after college—it begins! Many professionals have extensive personal libraries. In general, sales professionals often are not coached or motivated by their companies to read enough. You may have to do it on your own. Subscribe to such publications as your industry's trade magazines, *The Wall Street Journal* and *Business Week*. Routinely visit your local bookstores and public and college libraries. Keep abreast of local, state, national, and international news. Take an evening course at a local college.

As goods and services become more complex, companies place greater emphasis on training their salespeople and on salespeople training themselves. It is no wonder that corporate recruiters seek above-average individuals to fill their entry-level sales positions.

Knowledge also includes awareness of the most up-to-date ideas concerning selling skills. Successful salespeople are experts at developing and presenting talks that sell their products. They constantly educate themselves on methods to better determine customers' needs and to effectively communicate the benefits of their products to satisfy their needs.

Salespeople read books and magazine articles on selling and attend sales training courses to learn how to sell their products better. See Exhibit 1–8. This knowledge is incorporated into their sales presentations that are rehearsed until they sound like a natural conversation between seller and buyer. Remember that knowledge is power, but enthusiasm pulls the switch. Another characteristic found in good salespeople is the careful use of time.

Be Ruthless about Time

The most successful people are ruthless about guarding their time. In daily activities, they instinctively understand the powerful secret to success that is called the Pareto principle.

The Pareto principle is named after the 19th-century economist Vilfredo Pareto, who found that in any human activity, the biggest results usually arise from a small number of factors. For example, studies have shown that most people spend 80 percent of their time on the least important 20 percent of their jobs . . . and only 20 percent doing the work that yields 80 percent of their bottom-line results.

Successful salespeople define the specific results that practically guarantee success. Then, they ruthlessly arrange daily priorities to invest 80 percent of their time behind the 20 percent of work with the greatest results payout. Since there is only so much time in the day for contacting customers and there are so many demands on their time,

EXHIBIT 1-8

Salespeople work hard in becoming experts on their products and those of their competitors. Only then can they effectively use selling skills to provide information that helps customers.

successful salespeople value time and use it wisely by carefully planning their day's activities. Effective time management is a must. What customer will be called on, what product will be presented, and how to present it must be planned carefully.

Ask Questions and Then Listen to Uncover Customer Needs

Joe Gandolfo, who sold more than *$1 billion* of life insurance in a single year, has a sign on his office wall that reads, "God gave you two ears and one mouth, and He meant for you to do twice as much listening as talking."

Good salespeople are good listeners. They ask questions to uncover prospects' needs and then listen as prospects answer the questions and state their needs. Then, they show how their products' benefits will fulfill these needs. The ability to identify and meet customer needs separates the successful salesperson from the average salesperson. To meet customers' needs successfully, you must provide service.

Serve Your Customer

The most important characteristic for establishing a lasting sales relationship with a customer is willingness to provide service. Customers must believe that you care about them and their welfare. Successful salespeople respect their customers, treat them fairly, like them, and develop a good working relationship with them like a partnership. They provide outstanding service to each person.

These factors help them earn the respect of customers and to be considered professional businesspeople with ethics. Steve Gibson says, "I've found the Golden Rule of 'Do unto others . . .' always to be a basis of earning respect."

Be Physically and Mentally Prepared

With physical preparedness comes mental strength. Exercise elevates the mood by increasing energy and simultaneously secreting adrenaline-like substances in the body that act as stimulants and antidepressants, according to the medical community. This increased feeling of well-being transmits itself to the body and mind.

Knowing that you are in shape to deal with today and tomorrow is an important component of being successful. Being in shape is a mental and physical process. Remember, the mind is like a muscle in one respect: It deteriorates if unused.

MAKING THE SALE

What Is Your Value?

Top-performing salespeople are always striving to be the best they can be. Each of us has control of our destiny. We will be what we want to be. Consider, for example, a plain bar of iron that is worth about $5. Made into a horseshoe, it's worth about $11; made into screwdrivers, it's worth about $15; made into needles, it's worth about $3,500. The same is true for another kind of material—YOU! Your value is determined by what you decide to make of yourself.

Confidence and enthusiasm persuade us to engage our minds and bodies. That kind of mood is bound up, in turn, in how we feel about ourselves physically.

"Get into an exercise program," says salesperson Jay Firestone. "Join a gym or do it on your own at home." If you cannot seem to wedge a 30- to 60-minute exercise period three or five times a week into your busy schedule—no problem. Medical studies have found that catching 10 minutes of aerobic exercise here and there can improve cardiovascular fitness.

Newspapers, television, radio, and magazines continually have information on the positive aspects of exercise. They also discuss diet. What we choose to eat, drink, and smoke directly influences our physical and mental processes. Learn about the dietary and physical aspects of your body. You need everything at your disposal to succeed in today's competitive marketplace. The status of one's body, mind, and soul directly influences your performance level.

RELATIONSHIP SELLING

Salespeople are no longer adversaries who manipulate people for personal gain. They want to be consultants, partners, and problem-solvers for customers. Their goal is to build a long-term relationship with clients. Salespeople seek to benefit their employer, themselves, and customers.

In recent years, the distinction between a salesperson and a professional has blurred because the salesperson of today is a pro. Many salespeople know more about their field and product than the buyer. This expertise enables the seller to become the buyer's partner, a counselor on how to solve problems. Today's salesperson professionally provides information that helps customers make intelligent actions to achieve their short- and long-term objectives. Service and follow-up are then provided to ensure satisfaction with the purchase. This builds *customer loyalty*—a relationship.

Exhibit 1–9 shows the four main elements in the customer relationship process used by salespeople to build relationships. They analyze customers' needs, recommend a solution and gain commitment for the purchase, implement the recommendation, and maintain and grow the relationship.

SALES JOBS ARE DIFFERENT

As you can see, sales jobs are different from other jobs in several ways. Here are some major differences:

- Salespeople represent their companies to the outside world. Consequently, opinions of a company and its products are often formed from impressions left

MAKING THE SALE

What Is a Customer?

- Customers are the most important people in any business.
- Customers are not dependent on us. We are dependent on them.
- Customers are not an interruption of our work. They are the purpose of it.
- Customers do us a favor in doing business with us. We aren't doing customers a favor by waiting on them.
- Customers are part of our business—not outsiders. Customers are not just money in the cash register. Customers are human beings with feelings, and they deserve to be treated with respect.

- Customers are people who come to us with needs and wants. It is our job to fill them.
- Customers deserve the most courteous attention we can give them.
- Customers are the lifeblood of this and every business. Customers pay your salary. Without customers we would have to close our doors.
- Don't ever forget it!

by the sales force. The public ordinarily does not judge a firm by its office or factory workers.

- Other employees usually work under close supervisory control, whereas the outside salesperson typically operates with little or no direct supervision. Moreover, to be successful, salespeople must often be creative, persistent, and show great initiative—all of which require a high degree of motivation.
- Salespeople probably need more tact, diplomacy, and social poise than other employees in an organization. Many sales jobs require the salesperson to display considerable emotional and social intelligence in dealing with buyers.
- Salespeople are among the few employees authorized to spend company funds. They spend this money for entertainment, transportation, and other business expenses.
- Some sales jobs frequently require considerable traveling and time spent away from home and family. At times, salespeople deal with customers who seem determined not to buy the sellers' products. These challenges, coupled with the physical demands of long hours and traveling, require mental toughness and physical stamina rarely demanded in other types of jobs.

Selling is hard work! It requires intelligence, the desire to achieve, and the ability to overcome difficulties.

WHAT DOES A PROFESSIONAL SALESPERSON DO?

The salesperson's roles or activities can vary from company to company, depending on whether sales involve goods or services, the firm's market characteristics, and the location of customers. For example, a salesperson selling Avon products performs similar, but somewhat different, job activities than the industrial salesperson making sales calls for General Electric.

Most people believe that a salesperson only makes sales presentations, but there is much more to the job than person-to-person selling. The salesperson functions as a **territory manager**—planning, organizing, and executing activities that increase sales and profits in a given territory. A sales territory comprises a group of customers assigned within a geographical area. Exhibit 1–10 indicates a few typical activities of

Main elements in the customer
relationship process

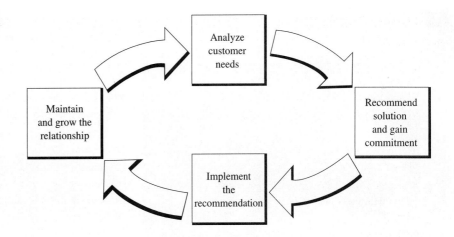

a salesperson. As manager of a territory, the salesperson performs the following nine
functions:

1. **Creates New Customers.** In order to increase sales and replace customers that
will be lost over time, many types of sales jobs require a salesperson to prospect.
Prospecting is the lifeblood of sales because it identifies potential customers. Salespeople locate people and/or organizations that have the potential to buy their products. The salespeople need the ability to close, or make, the sale.

2. **Sells More to Present Customers.** Tomorrow's sales come from selling to new
customers and selling present customers again . . . and again . . . and again.

3. **Builds Long-Term Relationships with Customers.** Earning the opportunity to
sell a present customer more product means the salesperson must have a positive,
professional business relationship with people and organizations who trust the salesperson and the products purchased.

4. **Provides Solutions to Customer's Problems.** Customers have needs that can be
met and problems that can be solved by purchasing goods or services. Salespeople
seek to uncover potential or existing needs or problems and show how the use of
their products or services can satisfy needs or solve problems.

5. **Provides Service to Customers.** Salespeople provide a wide range of services,
including handling complaints, returning damaged merchandise, providing samples,
suggesting business opportunities, and developing recommendations on how the customer can promote products purchased from the salesperson.

   If necessary, salespeople may occasionally work at the customer's business. For
example, a salesperson selling fishing tackle may arrange an in-store demonstration
of a manufacturer's products and offer to repair fishing reels as a service to the retailer's customers. Furthermore, a manufacturer may have its salespeople sell to distributors or wholesalers. Then, the manufacturer's representative may make sales
calls with the distributor's salespeople to aid them in selling and providing service
for the distributor's customers.

6. **Helps Customers Resell Products to Their Customers.** A major part of many
sales jobs is for the salesperson to help wholesalers and retailers resell the products
that they have purchased. The salesperson helps wholesale customers sell products to
retail customers and helps retail customers sell products to consumers.

EXHIBIT 1–10

A professional salesperson . . .

. . . helps meet the needs and solve the problems of the customer.

. . . makes presentations to new and current customers.

. . . sells to wholesalers and distributors.

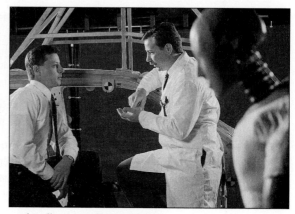

. . . handles customer complaints.

Consider the Quaker Oats salesperson selling a product to grocery wholesalers. Not only must the wholesaler be contacted but also grocery retailers must be called on, sales made, and orders written up and sent to the wholesaler. In turn, the wholesaler sells and delivers the products to the retailers. The Quaker Oats salesperson also develops promotional programs to help the retailer sell the firm's products. These programs involve supplying advertising materials, conducting store demonstrations, and setting up product displays.

7. **Helps Customers Use Products after Purchase.** The salesperson's job is not over after the sale is made. Often, customers must be shown how to obtain full benefit from the product. For example, after a customer buys an IBM computer system, technical specialists help the buyer learn how to operate the equipment.

8. **Builds Goodwill with Customers.** A selling job is people-oriented, entailing face-to-face contact with the customer. Many sales are based, to some extent, on friendship and trust. The salesperson needs to develop a personal, friendly, businesslike relationship with everyone who may influence a buying decision. This

EXHIBIT 1–11

What does a professional
salesperson do?

1. Creates new customers.
2. Sells more to present customers.
3. Builds long-term relationships with customers.
4. Provides solutions to customer's problems.
5. Provides service to customers.
6. Helps customers resell products to their customers.
7. Helps customers use products after purchase.
8. Builds goodwill with customers.
9. Provides company with market information.

ongoing part of the salesperson's job requires integrity, high ethical standards, and a
sincere interest in satisfying customers' needs.

9. **Provides Company with Market Information.** Salespeople provide information
to their companies on such topics as competitors' activities, customers' reactions to
new products, complaints about products or policies, market opportunities, and their
job activities. This information is so important for many companies that their salespeople are required to send in weekly or monthly reports on activities of the firm's
competition in their territory. Salespeople are a vital part of their employers' information retrieval system.

Reflect Back   Review the nine functions shown in Exhibit 1–11 to see what they mean and if you
could do any or all of them. Carefully think about the second and third functions. To
be successful, a salesperson must close sales and build relationships with the same
person and/or organization in order to sell more. To do both is challenging to any person. It requires the salesperson to do the other functions: solve problems, provide service, help resell, teach how to use the purchase, build goodwill, and keep your
employer up-to-date on customers' needs and feelings towards product and service.

Your book is about these nine functions and much more. When combined and
properly implemented, these nine job activities produce increased sales for the organization and more rewards for the salesperson. An example of how a salesperson
integrates these activities helps to better understand the sales job. See the box "A
Typical Day for a Xerox Salesperson."

**RELATIONSHIP
MARKETING**

Organizations today have targeted new and present customers. The emphasis is shift-
ing from selling customers *today* to creating customers for *tomorrow.* Thus, business
is finally beginning to think more long term than short term.

Relationship marketing is the creation of customer loyalty. Organizations use
combinations of products, prices, distribution, promotions, and service to achieve
this goal. Relationship marketing is based on the idea that important customers need
continuous attention.

An organization using relationship marketing is not seeking a simple sale or transaction. It has targeted a major customer that it would like to sell now and in the future. The company wants to demonstrate to the customer that it has the capabilities to
serve the account's needs in a superior way, particularly if a *committed relationship*

A Typical Day for a Xerox Salesperson

You are responsible for sales coverage, time, and budget. Help is available and you'll have plenty of marketing and service support; but you're expected to work independently, without constant direction.

Your day is devoted primarily to customer contact. Potential customers may phone the branch and ask to see a Xerox representative. More likely, however, you will acquire customers by making appointments or by visiting businesses to meet the decision-makers, discuss their needs, and offer solutions to their problems. As part of your position, you'll make product presentations, either at the Xerox branch office or at the customer's office. You will also spend a fair amount of time on the telephone following up leads, arranging appointments, and speaking with managers in a variety of businesses and organizations.

In working with customers, you'll need to solve a number of problems. What Xerox product best fits the customer's needs? How do Xerox products compare with the competition? Should the machine be purchased or leased? What's the total cash outlay—and per-copy cost—for the machine and its service? How should the product be financed? Where should the machine be placed for maximum efficiency? What training is needed for employees? How can Xerox products meet future office needs?

You'll also be engaged in a number of customer support activities, such as expediting product deliveries, checking credit, writing proposals, and training customer employees in the use of the product. You also might refer customers to other Xerox sales organizations and make joint calls with representatives from these organizations.

Each day will bring you new challenges to face and problems to solve. Your days will be busy and interesting.[11]

can be formed. The type of selling needed to establish a long-term collaborative relationship is complex. General Motors, for example, prefers suppliers who can sell and deliver a coordinated set of goods and services to many locations, who can quickly solve problems that arise in their different locations, and who can work closely with them to improve products and processes.

Most companies, unfortunately, are not set up to meet these requirements. Today, the level of customer relationships varies. Many organizations still sell customers and then forget them. Other organizations develop a close relationship—even a partnership—with their customers.

LEVELS OF RELATIONSHIP MARKETING

What type of relationships should an organization have with its customers? Is the cost of keeping a relationship worth it? To answer these questions, let's define the three general levels of selling relationships with customers:

- **Transaction selling:** customers are sold and not contacted again.
- **Relationship selling:** the seller contacts customers after the purchase to determine if they are satisfied and have future needs.
- **Partnering:** the seller works continually to improve its customers' operations, sales, and profits.

Most organizations focus solely on the single transaction with each customer. When you go to McDonald's and buy a hamburger, that's it. You never hear from them again unless you return for another purchase. The same thing happens when you go to a movie, rent a video, open a bank checking account, visit the grocery store, or have your clothes cleaned. Each of these examples involves low-priced, low-profit products. Also involved are a large number of customers who are geographically dispersed. This makes it very difficult and quite costly to contact customers. The business is forced to use transactional marketing.

Relationship marketing focuses on the transaction—making the sale—along with follow-up and service after the sale. The seller contacts the customer to ensure satisfaction with the purchase. The Cadillac Division of General Motors contacts each buyer of a new Cadillac to determine the customer's satisfaction with the car. If that person is not satisfied, General Motors works with the retailer selling the car to make sure the customer is happy.

Partnering is a phenomenon of the 1990s. Businesses' growing concerns over the competition not only in America but also internationally revitalized their need to work closely with important customers. The familiar **80/20 principle** states that 80 percent of sales often come from 20 percent of a company's customers. Organizations now realize the need to identify their most important customers and designate them for their partnering programs. The organization's best salespeople are assigned to sell and service these customers.

Selling Is for Large and Small Organizations

Many textbook examples are from big business. This is typically because readers recognize the Ford Motor Company or McDonald's. Even though America's large organizations are easily recognizable and extremely important to our prosperity, it is easy to overestimate the importance of big business because of its greater visibility. Small businesses seem dwarfed by such corporate giants as General Motors (748,000 employees) and IBM (more than $6 billion annual profits). Yet small firms, even though less conspicuous, are a vital component of our economy.

Small business contributes significantly to our economy. The Small Business Administration classifies approximately 98 percent of all business in the United States—sole proprietorships, partnerships, corporations, part-time businesses, and unincorporated professional activities—as small businesses.

Small enterprises run the gamut from a corner news vender to a developer of optical fibers. Small business people sell gasoline, flowers, and coffee to go. They publish magazines, haul freight, teach languages, and program computers. They make wines, motion pictures, and high-fashion clothes. They build new homes and restore old ones. They repair plumbing, fix appliances, recycle metals, and sell used cars. They drive taxicabs, run cranes, and fly helicopters. They drill for oil, quarry sand and gravel, and mine exotic ores. They forge, cast, weld, photoengrave, electroplate, and anodize. They also invent antipollution devices, quality control mechanisms, energy-saving techniques, microelectronic systems—a list would go on for volumes.

Often, small business entrepreneurs cannot compete head-to-head with giant firms. However, most large firms started small, and then prospered by using many of the concepts, ideas, and practices discussed in your textbook. Due to this fact, we use small business as examples throughout your textbook.

THE PLAN OF YOUR TEXTBOOK

Personal selling and the sales job are much more than you might have imagined. The plan of your textbook provides you with the *fundamentals* of what selling is all about. Some of the major topics you will study include:

- The role of the sales force in the firm's marketing efforts.
- The social, ethical, and legal issues in selling.
- Why people and organizations buy what they do.
- Verbal and nonverbal communications.
- The importance of knowing your and your competition's products.

Mexico, Here I Come

As you come to the end of your presentation, you realize one of your best customers—John Adams—may not buy. John and you have become friends over the last three years. Losing this sale will result in your missing out on a $500 bonus, forfeiting a chance to win a trip to Mexico, and failing to reach your sales quota for the year.

When you finish, John says, "We can't buy." You then explain your situation to John. He says, "Well, why don't you ship the merchandise to me. After the contest is over but before it's time to pay for it, I will ship it back to your company or you can transfer it in small quantities to several of your customers. That way you'll get credit for the sale." You know your boss will not mind because if you reach your sales quota he will also look good and be rewarded.

What do you do?

- An in-depth discussion of the selling process.
- Self, time, and sales territory management.
- Retail, business, services, and nonprofit selling.

Salespeople are managers of the sales generated from their customers. There is much to know if you want to be a successful sales professional.

BUILDING RELATIONSHIPS THROUGH THE SALES PROCESS	Much of your course will revolve around the sales process. The **sales process** refers to a sequential series of actions by the salesperson that leads toward the customer taking a desired action and ends with a follow-up to ensure purchase satisfaction. This desired action by a prospect is usually buying, which is the most important action. Such desired actions also can include advertising, displaying, or reducing the price of the product.

Although many factors may influence how a salesperson makes a presentation in any situation, there is a logical, sequential series of actions that, if followed, can greatly increase the chances of making a sale. This selling process involves 10 basic steps as briefly listed in Exhibit 1–12. The following chapters discuss each of these steps in greater detail.

Before a sales presentation is attempted, several important preparatory activities should occur. This involves prospecting and planning the sales presentation. Steps 3 through 9 compose the sales presentation itself. Step 10 involves the important follow-up phase of the selling process to ensure customer satisfaction.

Before discussing the selling process, Chapter 2 considers the social, ethical, and legal issues in selling. With this background, we are ready to examine what is involved in preparing to meet the customer, followed by an in-depth discussion of how to develop the sales presentation. |
| **SUMMARY OF MAJOR SELLING ISSUES** | Personal selling is an old and honorable profession. It has helped improve this country's standard of living and provided benefits to individual buyers through the purchase of products. Millions of people have chosen sales careers because of the |

EXHIBIT 1–12

Ten important steps in the customer relationship selling process

1. *Prospecting.* Locating and qualifying prospects.
2. *Preapproach.* Obtaining interview; determining sales call objective; developing customer profile, customer benefit program, and sales presentation strategies.
3. *Approach.* Meeting prospect and beginning customized sales presentation.
4. *Presentation.* Further uncovering needs; relating product benefits to needs using demonstration, dramatization, visuals, and proof statements.
5. *Trial close.* Asking prospects' *opinions* during and after presentation.
6. *Objections.* Uncovering objections.
7. *Meet objections.* Satisfactorily answering objections.
8. *Trial close.* Asking prospect's *opinion* after overcoming each objection and immediately before the close.
9. *Close.* Bringing prospect to the logical conclusion to buy.
10. *Follow-up and service.* Serving customer after the sale.

availability of sales jobs, the personal freedom sales provides, its challenge, the multitude of opportunities for success, and its nonfinancial and financial rewards.

A person can become a successful salesperson through company and personal training and by properly applying this knowledge while developing skills and abilities that benefit customers. Also important are believing in the product or service being sold, working hard, wanting to succeed, and maintaining a positive outlook toward both selling and oneself. In addition, a successful salesperson should be knowledgeable, be able to plan, and use selling time wisely. Effective salespeople are good listeners who provide service to customers. En route to success, salespeople develop a range of skills through study and practice, enhancing their ability to think strategically, relate to others, and understand the technical aspects of their business.

The remainder of this book expands on these topics to provide you with the background either to improve your present selling ability or to help you decide if a sales career is right for you.

MEETING A SALES CHALLENGE

As a secretary in Sunwest Bank's marketing department, Debra Hutchins worked closely with their outside salespeople and sales manager. When a sales job opened up, both Alex Romero, the director of marketing, and Rick Mather, the sales manager, asked her if she wanted the job. Debra had seen what salespeople do, so she said, "OK, I'll give it a shot."

Debra was so good as a salesperson she was promoted and now is sales manager, managing three men and one woman. "It's the best decision I've ever made," she says. "If you have not considered a sales career, I highly recommend it."

KEY TERMS FOR SELLING

personal selling   03
direct sellers   05
retail salesperson   07
wholesale salesperson   07
manufacturer's sales representative   08
order-taker   10
order-getter   10
career path   11

territory manager   22
relationship marketing   25
transaction selling   26
relationship selling   26
patnering   26
80/20 principle   27
sales process   28

SALES APPLICATION QUESTIONS

1. The term *salesperson* refers to many types of sales jobs. What are the major types of sales jobs available?

2. Chapter 1 described characteristics of several successful salespeople currently selling goods and services for national companies. Describe those characteristics and then discuss whether or not those same characteristics also are needed for success in other types of jobs.

3. People choose a particular career for many reasons. What are the five reasons someone might give for choosing a sales career?

4. What is meant by the term *career path?* What are the various jobs to which a salesperson might be promoted in a company?

SALES WORLD WIDE WEB EXCERSICE

Find out about a Career in sales

Looking for a job? Would you consider a sales job? Want to find out more about a sales career? The answers to these questions are found on the WWW. In fact there is so much career information on the Web that one wonders where to send you.

The easiest place to start is to enter the word "career" into your favorite Web search engine. The term **search engine** is computer lingo for a Universal Resource Locator (URL) site you can use to perform a keyword search by developer or subject name. As with everything on the Internet, these search tools change daily and new features are constantly added. Here are several URLs for the major search engines:

www.el.com	www.infoseek.com
www.yahoo.com	www.lycos.com
www.altavista.com	www.search.com
www.excite.com	

If you still need to find out more about a career in sales you can try URLs created specifically to help people looking for a job. These include:

www.salesstaffers.com	www.monster.com
www.careersite.com	www.occ.com
www.careermosaic.com	www.careerpath.com
www.hotjobs.com	

Take a look at your school's home page. Many schools refer you to career opportunities. You should also go to the Web site of a specific company. Many companies have hyperlinks from their home page to their job openings. Try finding career opportunities for several of the organizations listed in the Sales World Wide Web directory located at the back of your book.

FURTHER EXPLORING THE SALES WORLD

1. Interview one or more salespeople and write a brief report on what they like and dislike about their jobs; why they chose a sales career; what activities they perform; and what they believe it takes to succeed in selling their products.

2. Contact your college placement office and report on what they believe firms - recruiting people for sales positions look for in applicants.

EXHIBIT A

Items	Step 1 Your Individual Ranking	Step 2 The Team's Ranking	Step 3 Survival Expert's Ranking	Step 4 Difference Between Steps 1 and 3	Step 5 Difference Between Steps 2 and 3
Compress kit					
Ball of steel wool					
Cigarette lighter					
.45-caliber pistol					
Newspaper					
Compass					
Ski poles					
Knife					
Sectional air map					
Piece of rope					
Chocolate bars					
Flashlight					
Whiskey					
Shirt and pants					
Shortening					
Totals (The lower the score the better)				Your Score (Step 4)	Team Score (Step 5)

		Team Number					
Please complete the following steps and insert the scores under your team's number.		1	2	3	4	5	6
Step 6	Average Individual Score—Add up all the individual team members' scores (Step 4) and divide by the number on the team.						
Step 7	Team Score (Step 5 above)						
Step 8	Gain (Loss) Score—The difference between the Team Score and the Average Individual Score. If the Team Score is lower than Avg. Ind. Score, gain is "+"; if higher, gain is "−".						
Step 9	Percentage Change—Divide the gain (loss) by the Average Individual Score.						
Step 10	Lowest Individual Score—on the team.						
Step 11	Number of Individual Scores—lower than the team score.						

SALES TEAM BUILDING EXERCISE

You and your sales team were flying from Chicago, Illinois, to Fairbanks, Alaska, when your plane crash-landed in the woods somewhere in the Canadian Yukon. It is 10 A.M. in January. The single-engine plane and the bodies of the pilot and co-pilot were completely destroyed except for the airplane's frame. No one in your sales team was injured.

The plane was struck by lightning causing it to crash instantly. The pilot was unable to radio for help. The storms in the region caused the plane to change course several times. Immediately before the plane was struck by lightning, the pilot announced the plane was about 90 miles from the nearest town.

You are in a wooded area with numerous lakes, rivers, and mountains. It is –10 degrees now and night-time temperatures are expected to be –30. The group is dressed in casual clothes appropriate for living in a city—jeans, shirts, street shoes, and overcoats.

Before the plane caught fire your group was able to salvage the 15 items listed in Exhibit A. You are to rank these 15 items in order of their importance to your survival, starting with "1" as the most important to "15" as the least important.

You can assume the number of survivors is the same as the number on your team; the team has agreed to stick together; and all items are in good condition.

Assignments

- First, on their own, each member of the sales team is to individually rank each item in order of importance to survival.
- Second, rank each item as a team. It is critical no one changes their individual rankings once discussion starts within the group.

SELLING EXPERIENTIAL EXERCISE

Are You a Global Traveler?

Our global environment requires that American sales personnel learn to deal effectively with people in other countries. The assumption that foreign business leaders behave and negotiate in the same manner as Americans is false. How well prepared are you to live with globalization? Consider the following items, writing the numbers reflecting your views on another sheet of paper.

Are you guilty of:	Definitely No				Definitely Yes
1. Being impatient? Do you think "Time is money" or "Let's get straight to the point"?	1	2	3	4	5
2. Having a short attention span, bad listening habits, or being uncomfortable with silence?	1	2	3	4	5
3. Being somewhat argumentative, sometimes to the point of belligerence?	1	2	3	4	5
4. Being ignorant about the world beyond your borders?	1	2	3	4	5
5. Having a weakness in foreign languages?	1	2	3	4	5
6. Placing emphasis on short-term success?	1	2	3	4	5
7. Believing that advance preparations are less important than negotiations themselves?	1	2	3	4	5

Are you guilty of:	Definitely No				Definitely Yes
8. Being legalistic and believing a deal is a deal, regardless of changing circumstances?	1	2	3	4	5
9. Having little interest in seminars on the subject of globalization, failing to browse through international topics in libraries or magazines, or not interacting with foreign students or employees?	1	2	3	4	5
				Total Score _____	

Add up your score. If you scored less than 27, congratulations. You have the temperament and interest to do well in a global company. If you scored more than 27, it's time to consider a change. Regardless of your score, go back over each item and make a plan of action to correct deficiencies indicated by answers of 4 or 5 to any question.[12]

CASE 1–1

What They Didn't Teach Us in Sales Class*

Rick Lester was depressed. He was cold and damp from the rain as he sat in his van in the parking lot of a Food World supermarket. He had just telephoned the Nabisco division sales office and talked with Helen, the office secretary. Rick had asked her, "What are we supposed to do when it rains like this?" Rick could hear her repeat the question to Mr. Brown, the division sales manager, who just happened to be in the office. Rick could hear the reply in the background, "Tell him to buy a raincoat!" When Helen repeated the response, Rick replied to her, "OK, have a nice day" with a slightly embarrassed tone in his voice. As he hung up the pay phone and sat back in his van he thought, "What a heck of a way to make a living."

As a new salesman, it was clear that Rick had much to learn. He had only been on the job for one month, but he had about decided that it was no "piece of cake." It had all seemed so much easier when he watched Mr. Brown make calls during his two-week on-the-job training period. Now that he was making calls on his own, it was quite different and much more difficult. Interestingly, the sales class Rick had taken at the University of Alabama at Birmingham the previous year had covered many reasons to go into selling, but few disadvantages of pursuing a career in sales. Rick was now learning about these firsthand.

Rick's family—his parents and two younger sisters—had lived in Birmingham for many years. Mr. Lester was a salesman, and Mrs. Lester was a homemaker. Rick was an average student in high school, where he really majored in athletics and cheerleaders. After high school he accepted a partial athletic scholarship to Northwest Mississippi Junior College. His grades in college were about average overall but were low in basic math classes. The chief reason he selected business as his major was that it required no algebra. Following two years in Mississippi, Rick transferred to the University of Alabama at Birmingham and continued to work toward a B.S. degree in marketing. He met a nice girl there, and they later married when he graduated from UAB. There had been three specific job opportunities, all in sales, but he chose the job with Nabisco because it was a big company with many benefits. He also thought highly of Mr. Brown, the local recruiter and division sales manager.

*This case was written by Gerald Crawford and R. Keith Absher, Professors of Marketing, and William S. Stewart, Professor of Management, University of North Alabama, Florence, Alabama 35632.

Rick started to work on September 1. The first week was spent reviewing sales training manuals and completing employment paperwork. He also stocked his new van with merchandise, advertising materials, and displays. The following two weeks were spent "working the trade" with Mr. Brown, who made most of the calls while Rick learned by observing. Toward the end of the third week of employment, Rick was starting to make the sales presentations while Mr. Brown observed. They would discuss each call after they returned to the van. During the fourth week, Rick worked alone. The present week had been difficult . . . there was so much he didn't know. On Friday it rained, and this was not helpful. It was about two o'clock when he called the office and was told to buy a raincoat.

As he sat in the van waiting for the rain to let up, he began thinking about the situation in which he now found himself, and it was depressing. The rain was not the only reason for his low morale. He thought about his wife and how she had told her friends that Rick was in public relations rather than sales. Although they had not discussed it, Rick assumed that she did not particularly like the title *salesman*. Somewhere in the back of Rick's thoughts, there was clearly an image that selling has low occupational status. Maybe it came from his father. He couldn't remember. Another troublesome aspect of the new job was the calloused way that some retailers treat all salespeople. Others simply try to brush them off or avoid them altogether. This job, Rick thought, certainly does not build up one's ego.

There are other negative aspects of being in sales. One is that selling is physically demanding. It is a requirement to carry the sales bag into all calls. Properly loaded, Rick's sales bag weighed 38 pounds and contained advertising materials, new products, sample merchandise, a stapler, and the selling portfolio. Additionally, in some calls, salespeople must transport cases of merchandise from the storage area to the shelves. A great deal of bending and lifting is simply a part of the routine workday. By quitting time each day, Rick's clothing was wrinkled and damp from perspiration. Yesterday he had snagged a hole in the trousers of his new suit.

At the end of each day, Rick had to prepare reports and mail them to the home office. It was also necessary to reorganize and restock the van for the next day's work. Sometimes there were telephone calls that had to be made. By the time these chores were completed, it was almost bedtime. There was not much time left to spend with his new wife, and she had mentioned this a time or two.

The last annoying concern involved the knowledge that a good part of his success, or lack of it, depended on events over which he had no control. In several calls this week, a competitor had persuaded dealers to reduce shelf space for Nabisco products. These dealers reported that the competitor had a special promotion going on and the deal was just too good to pass up. There was no way that Rick could recover the lost shelf space in those calls. This did not look good on the salesperson's daily report.

As the rain continued to come down, Rick felt very alone. Mr. Brown was not there to help or provide answers. The physical and emotional obstacles just seemed too big to overcome. The only way out of this mess, it seemed, was to quit this job and try to find another one that was not this depressing. "Maybe I could get a job in a bank, where customers are always nice and the work is easier," Rick thought. As he started his van and drove away toward the division office, he felt relieved that he would soon be free of this impossible responsibility.

Questions

1. Should Rick Lester "turn in his keys"?
2. How should Mr. Brown handle this situation? What should he say to Rick?
3. How can firms reduce high turnover among new sales personnel?
4. What can firms do to increase salesperson status?
5. What can professors do to better prepare students in sales classes?

2

Social, Ethical, and Legal Issues in Selling

MAIN TOPICS

Management's Social Responsibilities

What Influences Ethical Behavior?

Management's Ethical Responsibilities

Ethics in Dealing with Salespeople

Salespeople's Ethics in Dealing with Their Employers

Ethics in Dealing with Customers

The International Side of Ethics

Managing Sales Ethics

LEARNING OBJECTIVES

This chapter is one of the most important in this text. Social, ethical, and legal issues for sales personnel are often personal and technical in nature, yet they are essential for understanding how to be an outstanding professional. After studying this chapter, you should be able to:

- Describe management's social responsibilities.

- Explain what influences ethical behavior.

- Define management's ethical responsibilities.

- Discuss ethical dealings among salespeople, employers, and customers.

- Describe the international side of ethics.

- Explain what is involved in managing sales ethics.

As the sales manager of a printing company, you are about to invest in a car leasing program that involves 18 company cars for your sales staff. Together with your comptroller, you have examined several leasing programs. You have narrowed down your selection to two leasing companies that offer very similar terms. You are meeting with the president of Equilease, a company with which you have never done business before. You know from your own prospect files that one of your sales representatives has tried to call on the purchasing manager of Equilease before to get some of their printing business; however, he could not sell the account.

As you meet with the president for lunch, you gently steer the conversation in the direction of printing services. Since he is very knowledgeable about printing services and prices, you ask him about ballpark prices charged by his existing supplier. You believe you could provide his company with higher-quality service at a better price.

Since the president of Equilease is in a good mood, you think about setting up a win-win situation. You are considering making this offer: Let's make this a double win. I'll give you 100 percent of our leasing business if you'll consider giving us 50 percent of your printing business. Fair enough?

Is there an ethical conflict in this situation? Would it be ethical to propose such a deal?

Sales personnel constantly are involved with social, ethical, and legal issues. Yet if you think about it, everyone is—including you. If you found a bag full of $100 bills lying on the side of the road, would you keep it? Would you say you were sick to get extra time off work? Would you use the company car to run a personal errand? Have you ever broken the speed limit? Have you ever gone home with one of your employer's pens in your jacket pocket?

These sorts of questions may be difficult for the average person to answer. Some people will respond with an unequivocal yes or no. Others may mull it over awhile. Still others may feel compelled to say "it depends" and qualify their response with a "yes, but . . ." or a "no, but . . ." Maybe that was what you did with the Facing a Sales Challenge feature.

Newspapers, radio, and television frequently have news stories of individuals and organizations involved in both good and bad practices. This chapter addresses many of the important social, ethical, and legal issues in selling. It begins by discussing management's social responsibilities. Then it examines ethical behavior followed by the ethical issues involved in dealing with salespeople, employers, and consumers. The chapter ends by presenting ways an organization can help its sales personnel follow ethical selling practices.

MANAGEMENT'S SOCIAL RESPONSIBILITIES

In one sense, the concept of corporate social responsibility is easy to understand; it means distinguishing right from wrong and doing right. It means being a good corporate citizen. The formal definition of **social responsibility** is management's obligation to make choices and take actions that contribute to the welfare and interests of society as well as to those of the organization.

As straightforward as this definition seems, social responsibility can be a difficult concept to grasp, because different people have different opinions as to which actions improve society's welfare. To make matters worse, social responsibility covers a range of issues, many of which have ambiguous boundaries between right and wrong.

EXHIBIT 2–1

Major stakeholders in the
organization's performance

Organizational Stakeholders

One reason for the difficulty in understanding social responsibility is that managers must confront the question, Responsibility to whom? The organization's environment consists of several sectors both inside and outside the organization. From a social responsibility perspective, enlightened organizations view the internal and external environment as a variety of stakeholders.

A **stakeholder** is any group within or outside the organization that has a stake in the organization's performance. Each stakeholder has a different interest in the organization.

Exhibit 2–1 illustrates eight important stakeholders. These are represented by the acronym **CCC GOMES.** The first *C* refers to customers and the last *S* refers to suppliers. Owners', creditors', and suppliers' interests are served by managerial efficiency—that is, the use of resources to achieve profits. Managers and salespeople expect work satisfaction, pay, and good supervision. Customers are concerned with decisions about the quality and availability of goods and services.

Other important stakeholders are the government and the community. Most corporations exist under the proper charter and licenses and operate within the limits of the laws and regulations imposed by the government, including safety laws and environmental protection requirements. The community includes local government, the natural and physical environments, and the quality of life provided for residents. Socially responsible organizations pay attention to all stakeholders affected by their actions.

An Organization's Main Responsibilities

Once a company is aware of its stakeholders, what are its main responsibilities to them? There are four types: (1) economic, (2) legal, (3) ethical, and (4) discretionary. See Exhibit 2–2.

Economic Responsibilities

The business institution is, above all, the basic economic unit of society. Its responsibility is to produce the goods and services that society wants and to maximize profits for its owners and shareholders.

Quite often, corporations are said to operate solely to maximize profits. Certainly, profits are important to a firm, just as a grade point average is important to a student. Profit provides the capital to stay in business, to expand, and to compensate for the risks of conducting business. There is a responsibility to make a profit to serve society. Imagine what would happen to our society if large corporations (e.g., AT&T,

EXHIBIT 2–2

An organization's main
responsibilities

General Motors) did not make a profit and went out of business. Thousands of people and the U.S. economy would be affected.

Legal Responsibilities

All modern societies lay down ground rules, laws, and regulations that organizations are expected to follow. Legal responsibility defines what society deems as important with respect to appropriate corporate behavior. Organizations are expected to fulfill their economic goals within the legal framework. Legal requirements are imposed by local town councils, state legislators, and federal regulatory agencies.

Failure to abide by legal responsibilities can be expensive for a company. In 1996, John Hancock Mutual Life Insurance Company paid $1 million to the New York State Insurance Department for improper sales practices. Among other violations, the insurance company had engaged in *churning,* which is the creation of new policies paid with proceeds of old policies without customer signatures.[1]

Ethical Responsibilities

Ethical responsibility includes behaviors that are not necessarily codified into law and may not serve the corporation's direct economic interests. To be ethical, organizational decisionmakers should act with equity, fairness, and impartiality; respect the rights of individuals; and provide different treatment of individuals only when relevant to the organization's goals and tasks. Unethical behavior occurs when decisions enable an individual or company to gain at the expense of society.

Discretionary Responsibilities

Discretionary responsibility is purely voluntary and guided by a company's desire to make social contributions not mandated by economics, law, or ethics. Discretionary activities include generous philanthropic contributions that offer no monetary return to the company and are not expected. In 1992, IBM needed to reduce the size of its sales force due to the recession. Instead of firing people, they stopped hiring, offered early retirements, and let normal turnover decrease sales force size.

Discretionary responsibility is the highest criterion of social responsibility, because it goes beyond societal expectations to contribute to the community's welfare. For example, Baxter International, a manufacturer and marketer of medical products, is using its environmental knowledge to help its customers set up pollution-reduction and recycling programs. Baxter has even set up an alliance with Waste Management to better assist customers in handling environmental problems. Baxter also has studied its own products and packing to find ways to reduce waste. By reducing the waste created by its products, Baxter reduces the environmental problems of its customers.[2]

How to Demonstrate Social Responsibility

A corporation can demonstrate social responsibility in numerous ways. Actions that can be taken by all organizations include:

1. Taking corrective action before it is required.
2. Working with affected constituents to resolve mutual problems.
3. Working to establish industrywide standards and self-regulation.
4. Publicly admitting mistakes.
5. Getting involved in appropriate social programs.
6. Helping correct environmental problems.
7. Monitoring the changing social environment.
8. Establishing and enforcing a corporate code of conduct.
9. Taking needed public stands on social issues.
10. Striving to make profits on an ongoing basis.

Economic, legal, ethical, and discretionary responsibilities to stakeholders are important concerns organizations must face in the 1990s and beyond. Society is demanding more responsible action of organizations, particularly regarding their ethical conduct.

Companies that do not maintain ethical standards face tangible costs. In 1994, for example, Metropolitan Life's revenue from new business plummeted 52.5 percent when the company was the subject of negative publicity concerning deceptive sales practices and churning.[3]

Some corporations, however, are using their positions to benefit society. For example, Procter & Gamble has assisted community projects by supplying expertise in areas such as marketing and training.[4] Actions such as these help to improve a company's image in the community and demonstrate its responsibility to society.

WHAT INFLUENCES ETHICAL BEHAVIOR?

Organizations are composed of individuals. These individuals' morals and ethical values help shape those of the organization. Critical to making decisions in an ethical manner is the individual integrity of the organization's managers, especially those in top management positions. Thus, two major influences on the ethical behavior of sales personnel are employees and the organization itself.

The Individual's Role

All of us, employees and managers alike, bring certain ethical values to a job. Personality, religious background, family upbringing, personal experiences, and the situation faced are examples of factors that guide people in making decisions. Individuals usually can be placed into one of the following levels of moral development:

- **Level One: Preconventional.** At the **preconventional moral development level,** an individual acts in one's own best interest and thus follows rules to avoid punishment or receive rewards. This individual would break moral and legal laws.
- **Level Two: Conventional.** At the **conventional moral development level,** an individual conforms to the expectations of others, such as family, friends, employer, boss, society and upholds moral and legal laws.
- **Level Three: Principled.** At the **principled moral development level,** an individual lives by an internal set of morals, values, and ethics. These are upheld regardless of punishments or majority opinion. The individual would disobey orders, laws, and consequences to follow what he or she believes is right.

The majority of sales personnel, as well as people in general, operate at the conventional level. However, a few individuals are at level one, and it is estimated that less than 20 percent of individuals reach level three.

The Organization's Role

If the vast majority of people in our society are at the preconventional or conventional levels, it seems that most employees in an organization would feel they must "go along to get along"; in other words, they go along to keep their jobs. At most, they only follow formal policies and procedures.

How will sales personnel handle ethical dilemmas? What if there are no policies and procedures pertaining to some sales practices and a person is directed to do something by a superior that appears unethical? It is no wonder that radio, television, and newspaper reports frequently feature unethical business practices. Following the hear-no-evil, see-no-evil, speak-no-evil philosophy can create a preconventional or conventional organizational climate.

MANAGEMENT'S ETHICAL RESPONSIBILITIES

The concept of ethics, like social responsibility, is easy to understand. However, ethics is difficult to define in a precise way. In a general sense, **ethics** is the code of moral principles and values that govern the behaviors of a person or a group with respect to what is right or wrong. Ethics sets standards as to what is good or bad in conduct and decision making.[5]

Many companies and their sales personnel get into trouble by making the mistaken assumption that if it's not illegal, it must be ethical. Ethics and moral values are a powerful force for good that can regulate behaviors both inside and outside the sales force. As principles of ethics and social responsibility are more widely recognized, companies can use codes of ethics and their corporate cultures to govern behavior, thereby eliminating the need for additional laws governing right and wrong.

What Is Ethical Behavior?

Sales personnel are frequently faced with ethical dilemmas. **Ethical behavior** refers to treating others fairly. Specifically, it refers to:

- Being honest.
- Maintaining confidence and trust.
- Following the rules.
- Conducting yourself in the proper manner.
- Treating others fairly.
- Demonstrating loyalty to company and associates.
- Carrying your share of the work and responsibility with 100 percent effort.

The definition of ethical behavior, while reasonably specific and easy to understand, is difficult to apply in every situation. In real life, there are always conflicting viewpoints, fuzzy circumstances, and unclear positions. Though difficult, it is critically important to cut through the smoke screen that sometimes exists in such a situation and use 20/20 vision to make an ethical choice.

What Is an Ethical Dilemma?

Because ethical standards are not codified, disagreements and dilemmas about proper behavior often occur. An ethical dilemma arises in a situation when each alternative choice or behavior has some undesirable elements due to potentially negative ethical or personal consequences. Right or wrong cannot be clearly identified. Consider the following examples:

- Your boss says he cannot give you a raise this year because of budget constraints, but because of your good work this past year, he will look the other way if your expense accounts come in a little high.
- Stationed at the corporate headquarters in Chicago, you have 14 salespeople in countries all over the world. A rep living in another country calls to get approval to pay a government official $10,000 to OK an equipment purchase of $5 million. Such payoffs are part of common business practice in that part of the world.
- An industrial engineer, who is your good friend, tells you three of your competitors have submitted price bids on his company's proposed new construction project. He suggests a price you should submit and mentions certain construction specifications his boss is looking for on this job.

Managers must deal with these kinds of dilemmas and issues that fall squarely in the domain of ethics. Because of their importance, an Ethical Dilemma feature appears at the ends of Chapters 1 through 15. In answering them, refer both to this chapter and to the chapter in which each feature appears.

Now let's turn to the three main ethical areas most frequently faced by sales personnel. These involve:

1. Salespeople
2. Employer
3. Customers

Although not all-inclusive, our discussion gives you a feel for some of the difficult situations faced by sales personnel.

ETHICS IN DEALING WITH SALESPEOPLE

Sales managers have both social and ethical responsibilities to sales personnel. Salespeople are a valuable resource; they are recruited, carefully trained, and given important responsibility. They represent a large financial investment and must be treated in a professional manner. Yet, occasionally, a company may place managers and/or salespeople in positions that force them to choose among compromising their ethics, not doing what is required, or leaving the organization. The choice depends on the magnitude of the situation. At times, situations arise wherein it is difficult to say whether a sales practice is ethical or unethical. Many sales practices are in a gray area somewhere between completely ethical and completely unethical. Five ethical considerations faced by the sales managers are the level of sales pressure to place on a salesperson, decisions concerning a salesperson's territory, whether or not to be honest with the salesperson, what to do with the ill salesperson, and employee rights.

EXHIBIT 2–3

How much pressure should a manager place on salespeople to increase sales?

Level of Sales Pressure

What is an acceptable level of pressure to place on salespeople? Should managers establish performance goals that they know a salesperson has only a 50–50 chance of attaining? Should the manager acknowledge that goals were set too high? If circumstances change in the salesperson's territory—for example, a large customer goes out of business—should the manager lower sales goals? See Exhibit 2–3.

These are questions all managers must consider. There are no right or wrong answers. Managers are responsible for group goals. There is a natural tendency to place pressure on salespeople so that the managers' goals are reached. Some managers motivate their people to produce at high levels without applying pressure while others place tremendous pressure on salespeople to attain sales beyond quotas. However, managers should set realistic and obtainable goals. They must consider individual territory situations. If this is done fairly and sales are still down, then pressure may be applied.

Decisions Affecting Territory

Management makes decisions that affect sales territories and salespeople. For example, the company might increase the number of sales territories, which often necessitates splitting a single territory. A salesperson may have spent years building the territory to its current sales volume only to have customers taken away. If the salesperson has worked on commission, this would mean a decrease in earnings.

Consider a situation of reducing the number of sales territories. What procedures would you use? Several years ago, a large manufacturer of health and beauty aids (shaving cream, toothpaste, shampoo) reduced the number of territories to lower selling costs. So, for example, three territories became two. Here is how one of the salespeople described it:

> I made my plane reservation to fly from Dallas to Florida for our annual national meeting. Beforehand, I was told to bring my records up to date and bring them to the regional office in Dallas; don't fly, drive to Dallas. I drove from Louisiana to Dallas with my bags packed to go to the national meeting. I walked into the office with my records under my arm. My district and regional managers were there. They told me of the reorganization and said I was fired. They asked for my car keys. I called my wife, told her what happened, and then

caught a bus back home. There were five of us in the region that were called in that day. Oh, they gave us a good job recommendation—it's just the way we were treated. Some people had been with the company for five years or more. They didn't eliminate jobs by tenure but by where territories were located.

Companies must deal with the individuals in a fair and straightforward manner. It would have been better for managers of these salespeople to go to their home-towns and explain the changes personally. Instead, they treated the salespeople unprofessionally.

One decision affecting a territory is what to do with extra-large customers, some-times called *key accounts*. Are they taken away from the salesperson and made into house accounts? Here, responsibility for contacting the accounts rests with someone from the home office (house) or a key-account salesperson. The local salesperson may not get credit for sales to this customer even though the customer is in the sales-person's territory. A salesperson states the problem:

> I've been with the company 35 years. When I first began, I called on some people who had one grocery store. Today, they have 208. The buyer knows me. He buys all of my regular and special greeting cards. They do whatever I ask. I made $22,000 in commis-sions from their sales last year. Now, management wants to make it a house account.

Here, the salesperson loses money. It is difficult to treat the salesperson fairly in this situation. The company does not want to pay large commissions, and 90 percent of the 208 stores are located out of the salesperson's territory. They should carefully ex-plain this to the salesperson. Instead of taking the full $22,000 away from the sales-person, they could pay a one-time bonus as a reward for building up the account.

To Tell the Truth?

Should salespeople be told they are not promotable, that they are marginal perform-ers, or that they are transferred to the poorest territory in the company so that they will quit? Good judgment must prevail. Sales managers prefer to tell the truth.

Do you tell the truth when you fire a salesperson? If a fired employee has tried and has been honest, many sales managers will tell prospective employers that the person quit voluntarily rather than being fired. One manager put it this way: "I feel he can do a good job for another company. I don't want to hurt his future."

The Ill Salesperson

How much help do you give to an alcoholic, drug-addicted, or physically or mentally ill salesperson? Many companies require salespeople to seek professional help for substance abuse, and, if they improve, offer support and keep them in the field. Yet, there is only so far the company can go. The firm cannot have an intoxicated or high salesperson calling on customers. Once the illness has a negative effect on business, the salesperson is taken out of the territory. Sick leave and workers' compensation of-ten cover expenses until the salesperson recovers. The manager who shows a sincere, personal interest in helping the ill salesperson greatly contributes to the person's chances of recovery.

Employee Rights

The sales manager must be current on ethical and legal considerations regarding employee rights and must develop strategies for the organization in addressing those rights. Here are several important questions that all managers should be able to answer:

- Under what conditions can an organization fire sales personnel without com-mitting a violation of the law?
- What rights do and should sales personnel have regarding the privacy of their employment records and access to them?

■ What can organizations do to prevent sexual and racial harassment and other forms of bias in the workplace?

Employee rights are rights desired by employees regarding their job security and the treatment administered by their employers while on the job, irrespective of whether or not those rights are currently protected by law or collective bargaining agreements of labor unions. Let's briefly examine three employee-rights questions.

Termination-at-Will

Early this century, many courts were adamant in strictly applying the common law rule to terminate at will. For example, the **termination-at-will rule** was used in a 1903 case, *Boyer* v. *Western Union Tel. Co.* [124 F 246, CCED Mo. (1903)], in which the court upheld the company's right to discharge its employees for union activities and indicated that the results would be the same if the company's employees were discharged for being Presbyterians.

Later on, in *Lewis* v. *Minnesota Mutual Life Ins. Co.* [37 NW 2d 316 (1940)], the termination-at-will rule was used to uphold the dismissal of the life insurance company's best salesperson—even though no apparent cause for dismissal was given and the company had promised the employee lifetime employment in return for his agreement to remain with the company.

In the early 1980s, court decisions and legislative enactments moved the pendulum of protection away from the employer and toward the rights of the individual employee through limitations on the termination-at-will rule.

Although many employers claim that their rights have been taken away, they still retain the right to terminate sales personnel for poor performance, excessive absenteeism, unsafe conduct, and poor organizational citizenship. It is crucial, however, for employers to maintain accurate records of these events for employees and to inform employees on where they stand. To be safe, it is also advisable for employers to have an established grievance procedure for employees to ensure that due process is respected. These practices are particularly useful in discharge situations that involve members of groups protected by Title VII, the Rehabilitation Act, or the Vietnam Era Veterans Act.

Privacy

Today it is more important than ever to keep objective and orderly personnel files. They are critical evidence that employers have treated their employees fairly and with respect, and have not violated any laws. Without these files, organizations may get caught on the receiving end of a lawsuit.

Although there are several federal laws that influence recordkeeping, they are primarily directed at public employers. However, many private employers are giving employees the right to access their personnel files and to prohibit the file information from being given to others without their consent. In addition, employers are casting from their personnel files any non-job-related information and ending hiring practices that solicit such information.

Sexual Harassment

Cooperative acceptance refers to the right of employees to be treated fairly and with respect regardless of race, sex, national origin, physical disability, age, or religion while on the job (as well as in obtaining a job and maintaining job security). Not only

The EEOC and Sexual Harassment

Sexual harassment in the workplace wasn't recognized as a legal issue until the 1970s. In 1980, the Equal Employment Opportunity Commission (EEOC) guidelines identified two types of sexual harassment: The first type is quid pro quo; an employee who refuses to submit to a superior's sexual advances is threatened with dismissal or other sanctions. The second type is hostile environment harassment; it occurs when jokes, graffiti, and other behavior are directed at persons of the opposite sex. The landmark ruling came in 1986, when the Supreme Court held unanimously that sexual harassment violates Title VII of the 1964 Civil Rights Act if it is unwelcome and "sufficiently severe or pervasive to alter the conditions of the victim's employment and create an abusive working environment."

Some executives believe the courts are being unreasonable about their definitions of sexual harassment. The issue is often awkward or embarrassing to discuss, and no clear-cut definitions of what constitutes offensive behavior exist. For example, a comment about clothing might be considered a compliment by the giver but harassment by the receiver. For these and other reasons, some companies are unwilling to spend time or money educating employees about this issue.

The problem continues to be serious. In 1990, the EEOC received about 5,600 sexual harassment complaints. And new forms of harassment, such as obscene software on company computers and suggestive electronic mail and answering machine messages, keep appearing.

Fortunately, DEC, Honeywell, Corning, CBS, and a number of other companies have long been concerned about sexual harassment. They distribute booklets that describe inappropriate behavior to employees. They hire consultants or conduct in-house training sessions that include films and role playing. The EEOC has published guidelines to help people understand liability. A key factor in determining liability is whether the employer has an effective internal grievance procedure that allows employees to bypass immediate supervisors (who are often the offenders).[6]

does this mean that employees have the right not to be discriminated against in employment practices and decisions, but it also means that employees have the right to be free of sexual and racial harassment.

Today, the right to not be discriminated against is generally protected under Title VII, the Age Discrimination in Employment Act, the Rehabilitation Act, the Vietnam Era Veterans Readjustment Assistance Act, and numerous court decisions and state and local government laws. Though the right to be free of sexual harassment is found explicitly in fewer laws, it has been made a part of the 1980 EEOC guidelines, which state that sexual harassment is a form of sex discrimination. The designation of sexual harassment as a form of sex discrimination under Title VII also is found in numerous court decisions.

It is necessary for employers to prevent racial and sexual harassment. This can be done with top management support, grievance procedures, verification procedures, training for all employees, and performance appraisal and compensation policies that reward persons who practice antiharassment behavior and punish persons who do not.

Companies realize that sexual harassment can be expensive. For example, in a landmark decision, a federal judge in Madison, Wisconsin, approved a damages award of $196,500 to a man who said he was demoted because he resisted the sexual advances of his female supervisor. This was the first time a man ever won a sexual harassment case against a woman. The man also received $7,913 in back pay and $21,726 in attorney's fees in addition to the damages award approved by U.S. Judge John Shabaz.[7]

Companies must recognize these important strategic purposes served by respecting employee rights:

- Providing a high quality of work life.
- Attracting and retaining good sales personnel. This makes recruitment and selection more effective and less frequent.
- Avoiding costly back-pay awards and fines.
- Establishing a match between employee rights and obligations and employer rights and obligations.

Here, both organizations and employees benefit from antibias measures. Organizations benefit from reduced legal costs, since not observing employee rights is illegal; and their image as a good employer increases, resulting in enhanced organizational attractiveness. This makes it easier for the organization to recruit a pool of qualified applicants. And, although it is suggested that expanded employee rights, especially job security, may reduce needed management flexibility and profitability, it may be an impetus for better planning, resulting in increased profitability.

Increased profitability also may result from the benefits employees receive when their rights are observed; employees may experience feelings of being treated fairly and respectfully, increased self-esteem, and a heightened sense of job security. Employees who have job security may be more productive and committed to the organization than those who do not. As employees begin to see the guarantees of job security as a benefit, organizations also gain through reduced wage-increase demands and greater flexibility in job assignments.

SALESPEOPLE'S ETHICS IN DEALING WITH THEIR EMPLOYERS

Salespeople, as well as sales managers, may occasionally misuse company assets, moonlight, or cheat. Such unethical practices can affect co-workers and need to be prevented before they occur.[8]

Misusing Company Assets

Company assets most often misused are automobiles, expense accounts, samples, and damaged-merchandise credits. All can be used for personal gain or as bribes and kickbacks to customers. For example, a credit for damaged merchandise can be given to a customer when there has been no damage, or valuable product samples can be given to a customer.

Moonlighting

Salespeople are not closely supervised and, consequently, they may be tempted to take a second job—perhaps on company time. Some salespeople attend college on company time. For example, a salesperson may enroll in an evening M.B.A. program but take off in the early afternoon to prepare for class.

Cheating

A salesperson may not play fair in contests. If a contest starts in July, the salesperson may not turn in sales orders for the end of June and lump them with July sales. Some might arrange, with or without the customer's permission, to ship merchandise that is not needed or wanted. The merchandise is held until payment is due and then returned to the company after the contest is over. The salesperson also may overload the customer to win the contest.

Affecting Other Salespeople

Often, the unethical practices of one salesperson can affect other salespeople within the company. Someone who cheats in winning a contest is taking money and prizes

EXHIBIT 2–4

This salesperson can easily download company data and take it with him to his next employer

from other salespeople. A salesperson also may not split commissions with co-workers or may take customers away from co-workers.

Technology Theft   Picture this. A salesperson or sales manager quits, or is fired, and takes the organization's customer records to use for his or her or a future employer's benefit. (See Exhibit 2–4.) How is that possible? Well, it's getting easier to do these days because more and more companies provide their sales personnel with computers, software, and data on their customers.

ETHICS IN DEALING WITH CUSTOMERS

"We have formal, ethical policies called *business conduct guidelines,*" says FMC's Alan Killingsworth. "These guidelines thoroughly discuss business conduct and clearly state what is proper conduct and how to report improper conduct. All sales personnel review them and even sign a statement that they understand the guidelines."

Numerous ethical situations may arise in dealing with customers. All sales organizations may create specific business conduct guidelines, such as FMC's. Some common problems faced by sales personnel include bribes, misrepresentation, price discrimination, tie-in sales, exclusive dealership, and sales restrictions.

Bribes   A salesperson may attempt to bribe a buyer.[10] Money, gifts, entertainment, and travel opportunities may be offered. At times, there is a thin line between good business and misusing a bribe or gift. A $10 gift to a $10,000 customer may be merely a gift, but how do we define a $4,000 ski trip for buyers and their spouses?

Many companies forbid their buyers to take gifts of any size from salespeople. However, bribery does exist. The U.S. Chamber of Commerce estimates that bribes and kickbacks account for $27 billion of the annual $50 billion in white-collar crime.

Buyers may ask for cash, merchandise, or travel payments in return for placing an order with the salesperson. Imagine that you are a salesperson working on a 5 percent commission. The buyer says, "I'm ready to place a $20,000 order for office supplies with you. However, another salesperson has offered to pay my expenses for a weekend in Las Vegas in exchange for my business. You know $500 tax-free is a lot of money." You quickly calculate that your commission is $1,000. You still make $500. Would it be hard to pass up that $500?

SELLING GLOBALLY

Customer Gift Giving in Japan

The highly ritualized practice of exchanging presents is paramount to cultivating long-lasting relationships in Japan. Gifts are exchanged with customers, between companies doing business together, and between employees and superiors within Japanese companies. As important as the gifts may be, so are the decorative wrappings and even the stores where the items are purchased.

As for presents, IBM's Vince Matal rules "the more lavish the better." Matal claims that he learned his lesson the hard way after returning from a few buying missions with totally inappropriate items, such as books, which are generally deemed too practical or unimpressive for the gift swap. Matal finds luxuries to be more on target, such as French chocolates, fine wine, or hard-to-come-by treats, such as the honeydew melon he once presented to a client. "It was a $55 melon," Matal says, "It was an imported melon from—possibly California—I don't know. But they sure don't grow them in Japan. It came in a beautiful wooden crate. And then we gave them a beautiful bottle of very nice sake. Another $90. So we gave a $150 gift, easily, and that was regular." [9]

Many large companies have taken steps to control giving and receiving gifts. Bull H. N. Information Systems, a Massachusetts computer manufacturer, prohibits employees from accepting "money, favors, or anything of significance." This does not include, however, bar bills, meals, entertainment, or other small items given as tokens of appreciation. [10]

Misrepresentation

Today, even casual misstatements by salespeople can put a company on the wrong side of the law. Most salespeople are unaware that they assume legal obligations—with accompanying risks and responsibilities—every time they approach a customer. However, we all know that salespeople sometimes oversell. They exaggerate the capabilities of their products or services and sometimes make false statements just to close a sale.

Often, buyers depend heavily on the technical knowledge of salespeople along with their professional integrity. Yet, sales managers and staff find it difficult to know just how far they can go with well-intentioned sales talk, personal opinion, and promises. They do not realize that by using certain statements they can embroil their companies in a lawsuit and ruin the business relationship they are trying to establish.

When a customer relies on a salesperson's statements, purchases the product or service, and then finds that it fails to perform as promised, the supplier can be sued for **misrepresentation** and **breach of warranty.** Companies around the United States have been liable for million-dollar judgments for making such mistakes, particularly when their salespeople sold high-ticket, high-tech products or services.

You can avoid such mistakes, however, if you're aware of the law of misrepresentation and breaches of warranty relative to the selling function, and if you follow strategies that keep you and your company out of trouble. Salespeople must understand the difference between sales puffery (opinions) and statements of fact—and the legal ramifications of both. There are preventive steps to follow; salespeople must work closely with management to avoid time-consuming delays and costly legal fees.

What the Law Says

Misrepresentation and breach of warranty are two legal causes of action; that is, theories on which an injured party seeks damages. These two theories differ in the proof

MAKING THE SALE

Keep Your Sense of Humor

"It was my first call as a district manager in Washington, D.C.," says Alan Lesk, senior vice president of sales and merchandising at Maidenform. "One of the major department stores was not doing a lot of business with Maidenform, and we were looking for more penetration in the market. Surprisingly, the sale took only two sales calls.

"The first person I approached was a buyer. He was completely uncooperative. On the way out of the store, I popped my head into his boss's office and we set up a meeting with some higher level executives later in the week.

"So there I was, a young kid facing a committee of nine tough executives, and I had to make my presentation. I was in the middle of my pitch when the executive vice president stopped me. He told me that this was going to be a big program, about $500,000, and asked me point blank how much of a rebate I was willing to give him to do business with their store, over and above the normal things like co-op ad money. He was actually asking me for money under the table!

"I had to make a decision fast. I stood up and said, 'If this is what it takes to do business here, I don't want anything to do with it.' I then turned to walk out the door, and the guy started cracking up. I guess he was just testing me to see what lengths I'd go to in order to get my sales program into the store.

"This one incident taught me some very important things: You can't compromise your integrity, and you can't let people intimidate you. Most importantly, don't lose your sense of humor. Needless to say, we got the program into the store, and today we do more than $2 million worth of business a year with them."[11]

required and the type of damages awarded by a judge or jury. However, both theories arise in the selling context and are treated similarly for our purposes. Both examples arise when a salesperson makes erroneous statements or offers false promises regarding a product's characteristics and capabilities.

Not all statements have legal consequences, however. When sales personnel loosely describe their product or service in glowing terms ("Our service can't be beat; it's the best around"), such statements are viewed as opinions and generally cannot be relied on by a customer, supplier, or wholesaler. Thus, a standard defense used by lawyers in misrepresentation and breach of warranty lawsuits is that a purchaser cannot rely on a salesperson's puffery because it's unreasonable to take these remarks at face value.

When a salesperson makes claims or promises of a factual nature regarding a product's or service's inherent capabilities (that is, the results, profits, or savings that will be achieved; what it will do for a customer; how it will perform; etc.), the law treats these comments as statements of fact and warranties.

There is a subtle difference between sales puffery and statements of fact; they can be difficult to distinguish. No particular form of words is necessary; each case is analyzed according to its circumstances. Generally, the less knowledgeable the customer, the greater the chances that the court will interpret a statement as actionable. The following is an actual recent case that illustrates this point:

An independent sales rep sold heavy industrial equipment. He went to a purchaser's construction site, observed his operations, then told the company president that his proposed equipment would "keep up with any other machine then being used," and that it would "work well in cooperation with the customer's other machines and equipment."

The customer informed the rep that he was not personally knowledgeable about the kind of equipment the rep was selling, and that he needed time to study the rep's report. Several weeks later, he bought the equipment based on the rep's recommendations.

MAKING THE SALE

Is This Man Really Dying to Make a Sale?

"He made his sales pitch over the phone, and he was good. There existed a little-known but glistening investment opportunity, and if I got into it early I could make an awesome profit.

"Then I said, 'Sounds good to me. I will buy several million shares.' There was a gasp from the other end of the line. 'How many?' he said. 'Several million,' I said, in my coolest manner. By now he was panting. And I felt guilty. He was just trying to make a living.

"On the other hand, he was trying to gouge me out of my net worth. So I offered him a deal. 'I will go for it if you will sign a paper.' 'What kind of paper?' he asked. 'I would like you to sign a piece of paper saying that if this investment fails, you will kill yourself. Or, if you can't fulfill your end of it, I can terminate you.'

"He sounded stunned. 'You expect me to kill myself?' 'It seems reasonable to me,' I said. 'You are asking me to risk the food on my family's table, the roof over their heads. So it seems to me that if this is a foolproof investment, the least you can do is put your life on the line.'

"The man actually stuttered. You don't hear many stutterers these days. He said, 'You have to be kidding.' I told him, in a most grave tone: 'No, I am not kidding. It seems reasonable to me that if this is a good deal and if I can't lose money on it, and if you are so kind as to offer this opportunity to a total stranger rather than to your friends and loved ones, the least you can do is stake your life on it.'

"There was a long pause on the other end. Then he said, 'That's the most ridiculous thing I've ever heard.' Now my feelings were hurt. Here was a man trying to persuade me to put my blood, meaning the rewards of my labors, into an investment, and he was quibbling over a petty deal.

" 'You won't agree to kill yourself?' I asked. 'That is ridiculous,' he said. 'So is your pitch,' I said. He hung up. I knew he wasn't sincere. Odds are that he didn't ask his grandmother to put her dough into that stock. So my advice to any potential investors is this: Ask them if they will leap off a bridge if you lose money. If they refuse, it isn't a good deal."

After a few months, he sued the rep's company, claiming that the equipment didn't perform according to the representations in sales literature sent prior to the execution of the contract and to statements made by the rep at the time of sale. The equipment manufacturer defended itself by arguing that the statements made by the rep were nonactionable opinions made innocently by the rep, in good faith, with no intent to deceive the purchaser.

The court ruled in favor of the customer, finding that the rep's statements were "predictions" of how the equipment would perform; this made them more than mere sales talk. The rep was held responsible for knowing the capabilities of the equipment he was selling; his assertions were deemed statements of fact, not opinions. Furthermore, the court stated that it was unfair that a knowledgeable salesperson would take advantage of a naive purchaser.[12]

Suggestions for Staying Legal

The following suggestions cover ways that management and sales staff can minimize exposure to costly misrepresentation and breach of warranty lawsuits. Salespeople must always do the following:

1. Understand the distinction between general statements of praise and statements of fact made during the sales pitch (and the legal consequences). For example, the following statements, taken from actual cases, were made by salespeople and were determined legally actionable as statements of fact:

MAKING THE SALE

Conflict of Interest?

The real estate salesperson assured the young couple that she would work hard to find them the right house. "Consider me your scout," she said. "I'll find you the best house for the least money." The couple was reassured, and on the way home they talked about their good fortune. They had a salesperson working just for them. With prices so high, it was nice to think they had professional help on their side.

The family selling the house felt the same way. They carefully chose the broker because, they observed, with home prices all over the lot these days, they hoped a good salesperson might win them several thousand dollars more. They had another reason to choose carefully: At today's prices, the 6 percent sales commission is a lot of money. "If we have to pay it," they reasoned, "we're better off paying it to the best salesperson."

It happens all the time, and it can have serious consequences. How can both parties expect the best deal? How can a salesperson promise the seller the most for the money and then make the same promise to the buyer?

In the same vein, how can a salesperson whose commission rises or falls with the price of the house being sold be expected to cut into her income? Isn't her total allegiance with the person paying her?

Confusion of this sort has existed in the marketplace for so long that critics are sometimes confounded that regulators haven't made greater efforts to clarify matters.

Two explanations are sometimes offered. First, it is more a human than a legal problem; even if warned, buyers will continue to assume that salespeople work solely for them, rather than for the seller, who pays the salesperson a commission.

Second, a good salesperson sometimes can come close to serving the desires of both parties. The point is arguable, but the justification offered is that the salesperson's compromises may be necessary to save a sale from falling through.

A somewhat similar situation exists in the stock market, where many small investors view their stockbroker as a confidant and adviser.

- This refrigerator will preserve foods in the warmest weather.
- This tractor has live power-take-off features.
- Feel free to prescribe this drug to your patients, doctor. It's nonaddicting.
- This mace pen is capable of instantaneous incapacitation for a period of 15 to 20 minutes.
- This is a safe, dependable helicopter.

2. Thoroughly educate all customers before making a sale. Salespeople should tell as much about the specific qualities of the product as possible. The reason is that when a salesperson makes statements about a product in a field in which his or her company has extensive experience, the law makes it difficult for the salesperson to claim it was just sales talk.

This is especially true for products or services sold in highly specialized areas to unsophisticated purchasers who rely entirely on the technical expertise of the salesperson. However, if the salesperson deals with a customer experienced in the trade, courts are less likely to find that the salesperson offered an expressed warranty, since a knowledgeable buyer has a duty to look beyond the assertions of a salesperson and investigate the product individually.

3. Be accurate when describing a product's capabilities. Avoid making speculative claims, particularly with respect to predictions concerning what a product will do.

EXHIBIT 2-5

This salesperson must be careful about the claims made in the sales presentation. If he says, "This equipment will increase production 2 percent" and if it doesn't, the salesperson and his company may find themselves in court.

4. Know the technical specifications of the product. Review all promotional literature to ensure that there are no exaggerated claims. Keep abreast of all design changes as well. The W.W. Grainger salesperson shown in Exhibit 2–5, for example, carefully and honestly explains the technical aspects of his product to his industrial buyers.

5. Avoid making exaggerated claims about product safety. The law usually takes a dim view of such affirmative claims, and these remarks can be interpreted as warranties that lead to liability.

For example, the Minnesota Court of Appeals recently ruled that a salesperson's assurances that a used car had a rebuilt carburetor and was a "good runner" constituted an expressed warranty of the vehicle's condition. Someone had bought the car based on the salesperson's assurance of its good quality. The carburetor jammed, causing the car to smash into a tree and injuring the purchaser, who recovered sizable damages.[13]

6. Know federal and state laws regarding warranties and guarantees.

7. Know the capabilities and characteristics of your products and services.

8. Keep current on all design changes and revisions in your product's operating manual.

9. Avoid offering opinions when the customer asks what results a product or service will accomplish unless the company has tested the product and has statistical evidence.

Statements such as, "This will reduce your inventory backlog by 40 percent" can get the company in trouble if the system fails to achieve the promised results. Stay away from that kind of statement. If you don't know the answer to a customer's question, don't lead her on. Tell her you don't know the answer but will get back to her promptly with the information.

10. Never overstep authority, especially when discussing prices or company policy. Remember, a salesperson's statements can bind the company.

One final point: it's generally easy for customers to recover damages on the grounds of misrepresentation and breach of warranty. In many states, this holds even when a salesperson's statement is made innocently.

Price Discrimination

Some customers may receive price reductions, promotional allowances, and support while others do not, even though, under certain circumstances, this violates the **Robinson-Patman Act** of 1936. The act allows sellers to grant what are called *quantity discounts* to larger buyers based on savings in manufacturing costs.

Individual salespeople or managers may practice **price discrimination** to improve sales. *Price discrimination* refers to selling the same quantity of the same product to different buyers at different prices. This can be illegal if it injures or reduces competition. It is certainly unethical and no way to treat customers.

Tie-in Sales

To buy a particular line of merchandise, a buyer may be required to buy other, unwanted products. This is called a **tie-in sale** and is prohibited under the **Clayton Act** when it substantially lessens competition. For example, the salesperson of a popular line of cosmetics tells the buyer, "I have a limited supply of the merchandise you want. If all of your 27 stores will display, advertise, and push my total line, I may be able to supply you. That means you'll need 10 items you have never purchased before." Is this good business? No—it's illegal.

Exclusive Dealership

When a contract requires that a wholesaler or retailer purchase products from one manufacturer, it is an *exclusive dealership.* If it lessens competition, it is prohibited under the Clayton Act.

Reciprocity

The salesperson says, "I can get my company to buy all of our office supplies from your company if you buy lighting fixtures, supplies, and replacement parts from us." Is this a good business practice?

Reciprocity refers to buying a product from someone if the person or organization agrees to buy from you. The Federal Trade Commission and the Department of Justice consider such a trade agreement illegal if it results in hurting or eliminating competition. Most purchasing agents find this practice offensive. Because reciprocal sales agreements may be illegal, if not unethical, buyers often are afraid to even discuss this with sellers.

Sales Restrictions

To protect consumers against the sometimes unethical sales activities of door-to-door salespeople, there is legislation at the federal, state, and local levels. The Federal Trade Commission and most states have adopted **cooling-off laws.** They provide a cooling-off period (usually three days) in which the buyer may cancel the contract, return any merchandise, and obtain a full refund. The law covers sales of $25 or more made door-to-door. It also states that the buyer must receive from the seller a written, dated contract and/or receipt of the transaction and be told there is a three-day cancellation period.

Many cities require persons selling directly to consumers to be licensed by the city in which they do business if they are not residents and to pay a license fee. A bond also may be required. These city ordinances often are called **Green River ordinances** because the first legislation of this kind was passed in Green River, Wyoming, in 1933. This type of ordinance protects consumers and aids local companies by making it more difficult for outside competition to enter the market.

Both the cooling-off laws and the Green River ordinances were passed to protect consumers from salespeople using unethical, high-pressure sales tactics. These statutes and others were necessary because some salespeople used unethical practices in sales transactions.

THE INTERNATIONAL SIDE OF ETHICS

Often guidelines for conducting international business are not the same as ours or, in many cases, are nonexistent.* The laws are quite different, and you could find yourself competing with foreign companies allowed to do things considered unethical by U.S. standards.

It is a serious mistake to think that laws for U.S. companies end at our borders. Each and every employee of a U.S. company is subject to U.S. law regardless of the country in which the business takes place. Even the agents or the distributors are subject to U.S. law, and you are responsible, as a manager, for their actions. It's important to be up to date on the law and aware of how authorized representatives are conducting business.

The American position on business ethics is well known throughout the business world. FMC's Alan Killingsworth says:

> In my tenure internationally, I never lost an order because we refused to compromise our ethics. I will say we had to sell a little harder in some cases and had to continue to focus the customer on the benefits and features of our product, services, and company. We sold to an organization and not to an individual. This limited any attempt by an individual making a purchasing decision to evaluate FMC on anything but our features and benefits.
>
> Don't let these statements mislead you. The vast majority of international companies you will deal with have high ethical standards. The ones that don't cannot be defined by geographic location or culture. Awareness of your customer will lead you, early on, to feel comfortable in dealing with the people making the buying decisions. You'll learn to recognize quickly if you are being treated fairly and evaluated on the merits of your company.
>
> Ethics relating to employees and community are often more difficult to understand. We have to remember we are guests in a country and not there to impose our ideas on their culture. Often, we are confronted with situations that seem strange and unfair. All we can do in such cases is to lead by example. We should treat our international community and personnel with the same respect we give people back in the good old U.S.A.

MANAGING SALES ETHICS

Over the years, a number of surveys to determine managers' views of business ethics have found the following:

- All managers feel they face ethical problems.
- Most managers feel they and their employers should be more ethical.
- Managers are more ethical with their friends than with people they do not know.
- Even though they want to be more ethical, some managers lower their ethical standards to meet job goals.
- Managers are aware of unethical practices in their industry and company ranging from price discrimination to hiring discrimination.
- Business ethics can be influenced by an employee's superior and company environment.

*This section was written by Alan Killingsworth of FMC's petroleum equipment group. He has spent more than 18 years in sales overseas and is now stationed in Asia.

Organizations are concerned about how to improve their social responsiveness and ethical climate. Managers must take active steps to ensure that the company stays on ethical ground. Management methods for helping organizations to be more responsive include: (1) top management taking the lead, (2) carefully selecting leaders, (3) establishing and following a code of ethics, (4) creating ethical structures, (5) formally encouraging whistle-blowing, (6) creating an ethical sales climate, and (7) establishing control systems.

Follow the Leader

The organization's chief executive officer, president, and vice presidents should clearly champion the efforts for ethical conduct. (See Exhibit 2–6.) Others will follow their lead. Their speeches, interviews, and actions need to constantly communicate the ethical values of the organization. The Business Roundtable, an association of chief executives from 250 large corporations, issued a report on ethics policy and practice in companies such as Boeing, Chemical Bank, General Mills, GTE, Xerox, Johnson & Johnson, and Hewlett-Packard. The report concluded that no point emerged more clearly than the crucial role of top management in guiding the social and ethical responsibilities of their organization.

Leader Selection Is Important

Since so few individuals are at the principled level of moral development, it is critical to carefully choose managers. Only people who have the highest level of integrity, standards, and values should assume leadership positions.

Establish a Code of Ethics

A **code of ethics** is a formal statement of the company's values concerning ethics and social issues. It states those values or behaviors that are expected and those that are not tolerated. These values and behaviors must be backed by management's action. Without top management support, there is little assurance that the code will be followed.

The two types of codes of ethics are principle-based statements and policy-based statements. Principle-based statements are designed to affect corporate culture,

Top-level management sets the climate for ethical behavior in the sales force

define fundamental values, and contain general language about company responsibilities, quality of products, and treatment of employees. General statements of principle are often called *corporate credos.* Examples are GTE's "Vision and Values," Johnson & Johnson's "The Credo," and Hewlett-Packard's "The HP Way."

Policy-based statements generally outline the procedures to be used in specific ethical situations. These situations include marketing practice, conflicts of interest, observance of laws, proprietary information, political gifts, and equal opportunities. Examples of policy-based statements are Boeing's "Business Conduct Guidelines," Chemical Bank's "Code of Ethics," GTE's "Code of Business Ethics" and its "Anti-Trust and Conflict of Interest Guidelines," and Norton's "Norton Policy on Business Ethics."

Create Ethical Structures

An **ethical committee** is a group of executives appointed to oversee company ethics. The committee provides rulings on questionable ethical issues. The ethics committee assumes responsibility for disciplining wrongdoers. This responsibility is essential if the organization is to directly influence employee behavior. An **ethical ombudsman** is an official given the responsibility of corporate conscience who hears and investigates ethical complaints and informs top management of potential ethical issues. For example, companies like IBM, Xerox, and Procter & Gamble have ethics committees reporting directly to the CEO.

Encourage Whistle-Blowing

Employee disclosure of illegal, immoral, or illegitimate practices on the employer's part is called *whistle-blowing.* Companies can provide a mechanism for whistle-blowing as a matter of policy. All employees who observe or become aware of criminal practices or unethical behavior should be encouraged to report the incident to their superiors, to a higher level of management, or to an appropriate unit of the organization, such as an ethics committee. Formalized procedures for complaining can encourage honest employees to report questionable incidents. For example, a company could provide its employees with a toll-free number that they may call to report unethical activities to top management. This silent witness program could be successful because it allows employees to report incidents without actually having to confront personnel. This program is especially valuable if the employee's own manager is involved in unethical practices. However, with programs such as these, careful verification then becomes necessary to guard against the use of such means to get even with managers or other employees.

Create an Ethical Sales Climate

The single most important factor in improving the climate for ethical behavior in a sales force is the action taken by top level managers. Sales managers must help develop and support their codes of ethics. They should publicize the code and their opposition to unethical sales practices to their subordinate managers and their salespeople. A stronger level of ethical awareness can be achieved during sales meetings, training sessions, and when contacting customers while working with salespeople.[14]

Establish Control Systems

Finally, control systems must be established. Methods should be employed to determine whether salespeople give bribes, falsify reports, or pad expenses. For example, sales made from low bids could be checked to determine whether procedures have been followed correctly. Dismissal, demotion, suspension, reprimand, or withholding of sales commissions would be possible penalties for unethical sales practices.

Overall, management must make a concerted effort to create an ethical climate within the workplace to best serve customer and organizational goals.

ETHICAL DILEMMA

Have You Lost the Sale?

You have been working for two months on an industrial account to obtain a firm commitment for a $185,000 computer system. If you can land the order today, you will become eligible for a quarterly performance bonus of $2,500. To meet your competitor's lower price, your manager decides to give you special authorization to offer your client a $9,000 package consisting of free software, specialized operating training, and extended service-contract terms. Similar incentives have been offered on special occasions in the past. You feel that this sweetened offer will bring you below your competitor's rock-bottom price. You know that your customer is a price buyer.

As you drive to your customer, you get tied up in a huge traffic jam. You call your client from your car phone and ask her secretary if it would be OK to come about 30 minutes later than scheduled. He tells you not to worry.

As you are ushered into the buyer's office, you greet your customer with a smile, ready to announce the good news. She informs you that she signed a contract with your competitor just 10 minutes ago. Upon your insistence, she shows you the bottom line on the signed contract. You realize that by purchasing your system, she could have saved as much as $12,000.

What do you do?

SUMMARY OF MAJOR SELLING ISSUES

Ethics and social responsibility are hot topics for managers. Ethical behavior pertains to values of right and wrong. Ethical decisions and behavior are typically guided by a value system. For an individual manager, the ability to make correct ethical choices will depend on both individual and organizational characteristics. An important individual characteristic is one's level of moral development. Corporate culture is an organizational characteristic that influences ethical behavior.

Corporate social responsibility concerns a company's values toward society. How can organizations be good corporate citizens? The model for evaluating social performance uses four criteria: economic, legal, ethical, and discretionary.

Social responsibility in business means profitably serving employees and customers in an ethical and lawful manner. Extra costs can accrue because a firm takes socially responsible action, but this is a part of doing business in today's society and it pays in the long run.

Salespeople and managers realize that their business should be conducted in an ethical manner. They must be ethical in dealing with their salespeople, their employers and their customers. Ethical standards and guidelines for sales personnel must be developed, supported, and policed. In the future, ethical selling practices will be even more important to conducting business profitably. Techniques for improving social responsiveness include leadership, codes of ethics, ethical structures, whistle-blowing, and establishing control systems. Finally, research suggests that socially responsible organizations perform as well as—and often better than—organizations that are not socially responsible.

MEETING A SALES CHALLENGE

In essence, the sales manager was seeking reciprocity. The contemplated deal is clearly unethical. In some cases, such a deal may even be unlawful. Companies aware of their legal and ethical responsibilities protect themselves and their employees from unnecessary exposure.

For example, IBM marketing representatives are urged to follow the specific steps set forth in IBM's "Business Conduct Guideline"—a policy-based code of ethics—which states,

"You may not do business with a supplier of goods or services." Reasonable? *Yes.* Important? *Absolutely.*

Remember that your career and the future of your company depend on creating values that last. This objective depends on making decisions we can live with tomorrow, not on what we might get away with today.

KEY TERMS FOR SELLING

social responsibility 37	misrepresentation 49
stakeholder 38	breach of warranty 49
CCC GOMES 38	Robinson-Patman Act 54
discretionary responsibility 39	price discrimination 54
preconventional moral development level 41	tie-in sale 54
conventional moral development level 41	Clayton Act 54
principled moral development level 41	reciprocity 54
ethics 41	cooling-off laws 54
ethical behavior 41	Green River ordinances 54
employee rights 45	code of ethics 56
termination-at-will rule 45	ethical committee 57
cooperative acceptance 45	ethical ombudsman 57

SALES APPLICATION QUESTIONS

1. Which of the following situations represents socially responsible actions by firms?
   a. Creating recreation facilities for sales personnel.
   b. Paying for college courses associated with an M.B.A. program.
   c. Allowing sales personnel to buy company products at a discount.
   Do managers feel business ethics can be improved? Describe ethical situations that sales managers may face in dealing with salespeople.

2. Imagine that you are being encouraged to inflate your expense account. Do you think your choice would be most affected by your individual moral development or by the cultural values of the company for which you worked? Explain.

3. Have you ever experienced an ethical dilemma? Evaluate the dilemma with respect to its impact on other people.

4. Discuss the difference between sales puffery and misrepresentation and how to avoid making mistakes that may prove costly to the firm.

5. Lincoln Electric considers customers and employees to be more important stakeholders than shareholders. Is it appropriate for management to define some stakeholders as more important than others? Should all stakeholders be considered equal?

6. Do you think a code of ethics combined with an ethics committee would be more effective than leadership alone for implementing ethical behavior? Discuss.

SALES WORLD WIDE WEB EXERCISES

What Is Ethical in the World of Sales?

Ethical behavior refers to treating others fairly. This is an easy definition to understand. Yet what seems ethical to one person may not seem ethical to another person. Salespeople must deal with various job dilemmas and issues that fall squarely in the domain of ethics. Beginning with your favorite WWW search engines listed in the Sales World Wide Web Directory at the back of the book and in Chapter One's Sales World Wide Web exercise—research the topic of ethics. Also see if these URLs have information:

Business Ethics Magazine: Online
www.condor.depaul.edu/ethics/bizethics.html

Marketing Ethics: Ethics, Associations, Organizations and Institutions of Interest
www.lan.unt.edu/mktg/faculty/pelton/mesig/other.html

Association for Practical and Professional Ethics
www.ezinfo.ucs.indiana.edu/~appe/home.html

Corporate Watch
www.corpwatch.org

American Marketing Association Code of Ethics for Marketing on the Internet
www.ama.org/ethcode.html

Center for Applied Ethics
www.ethics.ubc.ca/papers/business.html

National Association of Sales Professionals
www.nasp.com

Sales & Marketing Management Magazine
www.salesandmarketing.com

The Better Business Bureau
www.bbb.org

Your computer search should turn up names of organizations mentioned in articles. Go directly to several of the companies to see if they have

1. A code of ethics.
2. An ethics committee.
3. An ethical ombudsman.
4. Procedures for whistle-blowing.

Look in the telephone directory to see if any of these companies have an office close to you. Call up the sales manager and arrange for an interview to discuss their ethics procedures and anything you turned up in your computer search.

FURTHER EXPLORING THE SALES WORLD

1. Contact your local Better Business Bureau and prepare a report on local laws regulating the activities of salespeople.

2. The *Journal of Public Policy & Marketing* has a "Legal Developments in Marketing" section. Report on several legal cases in this section that are related to a firm's personal selling activities.

3. Talk to a sales manager about the social, ethical, and legal issues involved in the job. Does the manager's firm have
   a. A code of ethics?
   b. An ethics committee?
   c. An ethical ombudsman?
   d. Procedures for whistle-blowing?
   Get a copy of any materials relating to topics discussed in this chapter. Report on your findings.

SELLING EXPERIENTIAL EXERCISE

Ethical Work Climates

On a separate sheet of paper answer the following questions by writing down the number that best describes an organization for which you have worked:

	Disagree				Agree
1. Whatever is best for everyone in the company is the major consideration here.	1	2	3	4	5
2. Our major concern is always what is best for the other person.	1	2	3	4	5
3. People are expected to comply with the law and professional standards over and above other considerations.	1	2	3	4	5
4. In this company, the first consideration is whether a decision violates any law.	1	2	3	4	5
5. It is very important to follow company rules and procedures here.	1	2	3	4	5
6. People in this company strictly obey company policies.	1	2	3	4	5
7. In this company, people are mostly out for themselves.	1	2	3	4	5
8. People are expected to do anything to further the company's interests, regardless of the consequences.	1	2	3	4	5
9. In this company, people are guided by their own personal ethics.	1	2	3	4	5
10. Each person in this company decides for himself or herself what is right and wrong.	1	2	3	4	5

Total Score _____

Add up your score. These questions measure the dimensions of an organization's ethical climate. Questions 1 and 2 measure caring for people, questions 3 and 4 measure lawfulness, questions 5 and 6 measure rules adherence, questions 7 and 8 measure emphasis on financial and company performance, and questions 9 and 10 measure individual independence. Questions 7 and 8 are reverse scored. (That is, if you answered "five," your actual score to write down is "one"; a "four" is really a "two," etc.) A total score above 40 indicates a very positive ethical climate. A score from 30 to 40 indicates above-average ethical climate. A score from 20 to 30 indicates a below-average ethical climate, and a score below 20 indicates a very poor ethical climate.

Go back over the questions and think about changes that you could have made to improve the ethical climate in the organization. Discuss with other students what you could do as a manager to improve ethics in future companies you work for.[15]

CASE 2–1
Fancy Frozen Foods*

Last Friday, Bill Wilkerson of Fancy Frozen Foods (FFF) was confronted with a situation that he has not resolved successfully. Grady Bryan, a purchasing agent for Smith Supermarket Chain, Inc., made it apparent to Bill that if he wanted to retain

*This case was prepared by Bill A. Wilkerson, a salesperson, as a basis for classroom discussion and not to illustrate either effective or ineffective handling of an administrative position. Company names have been changed. Wilkerson changed jobs two years after he prepared this case.

the company's business in frozen food sales, special action would be necessary. In a telephone conversation, Grady suddenly got onto the subject of his new fishing boat and how much better it would perform with an 80-horsepower, inboard-outboard Evinrude motor. Bill and Grady have been fairly friendly, having done business together for the past four years. However, a conversation of this kind seemed out of the ordinary to Bill, especially during a long-distance call for which he was paying. What got Bill's attention was Grady's subtle mention of a competitor, Specialty Frozen Foods, whose territorial sales representative had stopped in to price some outboard motors after lunch with Grady. This alerted Bill to the complicated situation he faced. He realized it would take a tricky strategy to enable his company to retain Smith's exclusive business.

Fancy Frozen Foods

Fancy Frozen Foods (FFF) operates in Texas and Louisiana, with Dallas and New Orleans being the two largest markets. They carry a complete line of frozen foods that they manufacture and wholesale, enabling them to undercut most wholesalers' prices. The company presently employs 20 salespeople. Their territories are divided according to geographic size, keeping salespeople's travel time to a minimum. Salespeople are paid a set salary of $12,000 yearly and commission of 3 percent for everything above a designated quota. Quotas differ by territory. They are set according to the relative potential of each market.

The company has no formal written policy regarding gift-giving and entertainment. However, in the past, the president emphasized that customers may not receive gifts worth more than $25. In addition to this, FFF owns a ranch in West Texas. They invite each of their customers for a three-day vacation, involving hunting and other outdoor activities.

Smith Supermarket Chain

Smith has 13 supermarkets in Dallas and 15 outlets in Houston. All of these accounts are currently serviced exclusively by FFF. Grady Bryan, in one of his various duties as warehouse ordering agent in the Dallas area for Smith, selects sellers of frozen foods. The 13 store managers call in their weekly frozen food orders to Grady, who then compiles the orders and calls this order into Bill Wilkerson of FFF. This type of system is employed to obtain lower prices than if each individual outlet made an order. The order is sent to the central warehouse, where it is broken down for individual outlets and scheduled for delivery in an efficient fashion.

What to Do?

Bill is confronted with a situation that he has never faced. He has, in the past, given Grady modest Christmas gifts in line with the president's wishes and occasionally takes Grady to lunch. The company-sponsored hunting trips are another form of entertainment. However, none of these things, at least to Bill, indicated that Bill would succumb to a suggested bribe of this proportion. The crux of the matter is not that Bill's previous practices have indicated he would comply with this request but that Bill's competition has shown a blatant willingness to employ unethical tactics to gain Smith's frozen food sales. The question is, should Bill take the chance of losing the 13 accounts by not offering the bribe, or should he succumb to the bribe and avoid the risk?

Questions

1. What is the main problem presented in this case?
2. What must Bill do?

"I'm glad you came in, Marge. I've been wanting to talk with you." Anne Jackson, sales manager for the Southwest region of Sports Shirts, Inc., greeted one of her salespeople, Marge Phillips, as she entered the office. The company marketed a line of sports clothing consisting primarily of three styles of running suits.

"What about?" asked Marge.

"You know, since you've been with us, I've always considered you one of our top salespeople. You always meet quotas. You always find new accounts. But I've got a problem that we need to discuss. I got a letter from one of your customers. He claims he couldn't sell the goods you sold him even if he tried all year. And he's also claiming that our running suits aren't worth a dime—that they fall apart soon after the customer buys them. He included some sales data that seemed to point to the fact that he always has a large quantity of our merchandise left at the end of the season. Now, normally, I would just pass this off as a store's sour grapes because of declining sales, but this isn't the first time this has happened. I've received several such letters recently. What do you think the problem might be?"

"I don't see that we really have a problem. I do get complaints about the quality of the merchandise, but that's not my problem. Besides, I just concentrate on the profit-potential figures for the retailers, and quality seems a secondary consideration in that context. You give me a quota, and I meet it. What am I supposed to do, refuse to sell them as much as they will take? It's not my fault if they overbuy! I guess I'm just a top-notch salesperson."

The facts certainly indicated that Marge was a good salesperson. Some of her co-workers had said that she could sell snow to Eskimos. They call her "Load 'em down Marge." In three years with the company, she has already worked her way up to being the top salesperson in the company. Her sales figures are shown in Exhibit A.

EXHIBIT A

Sales Data

Year	Quota (000)	Sales (000)	New Accounts
1	$400	$450	20
2	440	460	23
3	480	800	30

The running suits Marge sells are made from one of the several combinations of materials and labor that resulted in suits of different durability. Cost and durability data are summarized in Exhibit B. The company chose the second alternative of the three listed.

There were many complaints about the quality of the running suits that the firm marketed. Seams came apart after only a few washings, consumers complained. "We sell good running suits, but you can't expect them to last forever," was management's reply.

The manager had other concerns about Marge. However, she was doing such an excellent selling job and was making the company so much money that the manager did not want to have a confrontation. In fact, sales for the entire region had increased 17 percent this year. Much of the increase was due to Marge's influence on other salespeople. They applied many of her selling techniques. There were rumors that she was considering buying into a partnership and becoming a manufacturers' agent specializing in high-fashion clothing. It would affect sales if Marge left the company. In fact, Jackson was concerned that Marge would hire away the firm's better salespeople.

Jackson remembered when Marge was hired. She had always wanted to sell in the clothing industry, but no one would give her the opportunity. So, on graduation from

EXHIBIT B

Relative Cost of Merchandise

	Cost		
Year	Material	Labor	Rating*
A	$1.28	$2.00	5
B	1.45	3.00	10
C	1.95	4.00	20

*The durability rating was basically a measure of the number of washings garments could go through and still look good.

college, Marge went to work for a large department store chain. In two years, she moved from manager of the women's clothing department in one of the smaller stores to head buyer of women's wear for the entire chain. Marge said she wanted more out of life than what a $25,000-a-year job could give. So Jackson hired her on a straight commission of 10 percent on sales up to quota and 15 percent on all sales after quota. This year Marge would earn $98,000, with a sales increase of over 40 percent.

Jackson did not believe Marge had worked less than 12 hours a day since she began. She had always been a ball of fire. She plowed back much of her earnings into customer goodwill and it appeared to have helped her sales. Gifts and entertainment were a large overhead expense item for her. The only expense the company paid was an amount up to 1 percent of a salesperson's actual sales, and this had to go for entertaining. Marge said she spent over $15,000 on her customers in addition to the $4,600 the firm paid.

During the recent year-end performance appraisal session, Jackson was surprised when Marge accepted her next year's $1 million sales quota so calmly. Marge said it would be no problem. In fact, she estimated that her sales would increase to between $1.5 and $2 million. When asked why, Marge said a friend of hers was now buyer for the retail chain for which she once worked. The buyer had worked for Marge until Marge quit to begin working at Sports Shirts. Marge recalled discovering that her friend was receiving kickbacks of over $5,000 in cash, merchandise, and vacation trips. Marge said nothing to the chain's management, mainly because she was doing the same thing, which her friend did not know. So Marge was sure she could sell this buyer her entire line of running suits. Further, last year Marge began requiring many of her customers to buy all of the styles and sizes she sold in order to receive the best-selling models.

However, Marge did ask for an additional 1 percent in entertainment expenses. Last summer, she gave a party with a live band and professional female and male escorts for buyers. Marge felt this greatly increased sales and wanted to continue the practice. However, it was quite expensive.

Corporate management had begun to ask about Marge's management capabilities. They felt that if she could train salespeople as well as she sold, she would make a great sales manager.

Questions

1. How would you describe Marge Phillips' success?
2. Is she a good salesperson? Do her sales results justify her methods of selling?
3. What should Anne do?

PART II

PREPARATION FOR RELATIONSHIP SELLING

This part of your book deals with the main sales knowledge needed by salespeople. Being knowledgeable about buyer behavior, communication skills, and such things as products, prices, distribution, promotion, and competition are essential to sales success. Included in this part are

3. The Psychology of Selling: Why People Buy

4. Communication for Relationship Building: It's Not All Talk

5. Sales Knowledge: Customers, Products, Technologies

3

The Psychology of Selling: Why People Buy

LEARNING OBJECTIVES

What do people really buy? They buy the benefits of a product. This chapter examines why and how individuals buy. It emphasizes the need for salespeople to stress benefits in their presentations. After studying this chapter, you should be able to:

- Explain the difference between a feature, an advantage, and a benefit.

- Be able to construct a SELL Sequence.

- Know when and how to use a trial close.

- Explain why people buy benefits rather than features or advantages.

- Enumerate techniques for determining a customer's needs.

- List factors that influence the customer's buying decision.

- Show why buying is a choice decision.

Five years ago John Salley graduated with a computer science degree from MIT. One year later, he earned his MBA from Texas A & M University with a perfect "A" average. John was on every campus recruiter's list as an outstanding applicant. He had the brains, personality, looks, and motivation of a winner. IBM convinced him to take a sales job.

John was at the top of his class in the IBM sales-training program. However, his first two years in sales resulted in an average performance. He could not understand why, because his knowledge of the products was outstanding. John could discuss in great depth the most technical aspects of his products. He was not used to being average. John loved sales but felt things had to change.

If you were in John's position, what would you do?

John Salley is like many people in that they do everything it takes to be successful in sales. Yet for some reason, they never reach their maximum performance potential. To be successful, salespeople need to be knowledgeable, even experts, on everything discussed in Part II, "Preparation for Relationship Selling."

Chapter 3 examines why and how an individual buys. There are numerous influences involved in why people buy one product over another. We discuss these reasons and apply them to the various steps in the customer's buying process. This chapter presents selling techniques that will aid you later in developing your sales presentation. They also can help John Salley in his efforts to improve his sales performance. He needs to know why people buy.

WHY PEOPLE BUY—THE BLACK BOX APPROACH

The question of why people buy has interested salespeople for many years. Salespeople know that some customers buy their product after the presentation, yet they wonder what thought process resulted in the decision to buy or not to buy. Prospective buyers are usually exposed to various sales presentations. In some manner, a person internalizes or considers this information and then makes a buying decision. This process of internalization is referred to as a **black box** because we cannot see into the buyer's mind—meaning that the salesperson can apply the stimuli (a sales presentation) and observe the behavior of the prospect but cannot witness the prospect's actual decision-making process.

The classic model of buyer behavior shown in Exhibit 3–1 is called a **stimulus–response** model. A stimulus (sales presentation) is applied resulting in a response (purchase decision). This model assumes that prospects respond in some predictable manner to the sales presentation. Unfortunately, it does not tell us why they buy or do not buy the product. This information is concealed in the black box.

Salespeople seek to understand as much as they can about the mental processes that yield the prospects' responses. We do know:

EXHIBIT 3–1

Stimulus–response model of buyer behavior.

- That people buy for both practical (rational) and psychological (emotional) reasons.
- That salespeople can use specific methods to help determine the prospects' thoughts during sales presentations.
- That buyers consider certain factors in making purchase decisions.

This chapter introduces these three important topics. Each topic emphasizes the salesperson's need to understand people's behavior.

PSYCHOLOGICAL INFLUENCES ON BUYING

Since personal selling requires understanding human behavior, each salesperson must be concerned with a prospective customer's motivations, perceptions, learning, attitudes, and personality. Furthermore, the salesperson should know how each type of behavior might influence a customer's purchase decision.

Motivation to Buy Must Be There

Human beings are motivated by needs and wants. These needs and wants build up internally, which causes people to desire to buy a product—a new car or a new duplicating machine. People's **needs** result from a lack of something desirable. **Wants** are needs learned by the person. For example, people need transportation—but some want a Cadillac while others prefer a Ford Mustang.

This example illustrates that both practical or rational reasons (the need for transportation) and emotional or psychological reasons (the desire for the prestige of owning a Cadillac) influence the buying decision. Different individuals have different reasons for wanting to buy. The salesperson must determine a prospect's needs and then match the product's benefits to the particular needs and wants of the prospect. See Exhibit 3–2.

Economic Needs: The Best Value for the Money

Economic needs are the buyer's need to purchase the most satisfying product for the money. Economic needs include price, quality (performance, dependability, durability), convenience of buying, and service. Some people's purchases are based primarily on economic need. However, most people consider the economic implications of all their purchases along with other reasons for buying.

EXHIBIT 3–2

Customers are motivated to buy by both practical and emotional needs.

This salesperson must first determine the customer's needs and then find the shoes that will do what is needed.

Many salespeople mistakenly assume that people base their buying decisions solely on price. This is not always correct. A higher product price relative to competing goods often can be offset by such factors as service, quality, better performance, friendliness of the salesperson, or convenience of purchase.

Whatever a person's need might be, it is important for a salesperson to uncover it. Once you determine the individual's need, you are better prepared to develop your sales presentation in a manner relating your product's benefits to that particular need. This is not always easy to do, since people may not be fully aware of their needs.

Awareness of Needs: Some Buyers Are Unsure

You have seen that people purchase products to satisfy various needs. Often, however, these needs are developed over such a long period that people may not be fully conscious of their reasons for buying or not buying a product. The buying decision can be complicated by their awareness level of needs. Three levels of need awareness have been identified—conscious, preconscious, and unconscious.

At the first level, the **conscious need level,** buyers are fully aware of their needs. These are the easiest people to sell to because they know what products they want and are willing to talk about their needs. A customer might say to the salesperson, "I'd like to buy a new car and I want a Cadillac loaded with accessories. What can you show me?"

At the second level, the **preconscious need level,** buyers may not be fully aware of their needs. Needs may not be fully developed in the conscious mind. They know what general type of product they want but may not wish to discuss it fully. For example, a buyer may want to buy a certain product because of a strong ego need yet be hesitant about telling you. If you don't make a sale and ask why, this buyer may present false reasons, such as saying your price is too high, rather than revealing the real motivation. Falsification is much easier than stating the true reasons for not buying your product—thus getting into a long conversation with you, arguing with you, or telling you that your product is unsatisfactory. You must avoid this brush-off and determine a buyer's real needs first and then relate your product's benefits to these needs.

At the third level, the **unconscious need level,** people do not know why they buy a product—only that they do buy. When people say, "I really don't know what I want to buy," it may be true. Their buying motives might have developed years earlier and may have been repressed. In this case, the salesperson needs to determine the needs that are influential. Often, this is accomplished by skillful questioning to draw out prospective buyers' unconscious needs. An awareness of the types of needs that buyers may have will allow you to present your product as a vehicle for satisfaction of those needs. Several methods of presenting a product's benefits are available.

A FABULOUS APPROACH TO BUYER NEED SATISFACTION

A most powerful selling technique used by successful salespeople today is **benefit selling.** In benefit selling, the salesperson relates a product's benefits to the customer's needs using the product's features and advantages as support. This technique is often referred to as the *FAB selling technique* (*F*eature, *A*dvantage, and *B*enefit).* These key terms are defined as follows:

- A product **feature** is any *physical characteristic* of a product.
- A product **advantage** is the *performance characteristic* of a product that describes how it can be used or will help the buyer.

*Some companies train their salespeople using only features and benefits. They would see an advantage and benefit as one and the same. Most companies use FAB. This section plus the trial close and SELL Sequence sections are very important for you to learn and use in your sales presentation.

- A product **benefit** is a favorable *result* the buyer receives from the product because of a particular advantage that has the ability to satisfy a buyer's need.

The Product's Features: So What?

All products have features or physical characteristics such as the following:

■ Size	■ Terms	■ Packaging
■ Color	■ Quantity	■ Flavor
■ Taste	■ Price	■ Service
■ Quality	■ Shape	■ Uses
■ Delivery	■ Ingredients	■ Technology

Descriptions of a product's features answer the question, What is it? Typically, when used alone in the sales presentation, features have little persuasive power since buyers are interested in specific benefits rather than features.

When discussing a product's features *alone,* imagine the customer is thinking, "So what? So your product has this shape or quality; how does it perform and how will it benefit me?" That is why you have to discuss the product's advantages as they relate to the buyer's needs.

The Product's Advantages: Prove It!

Once a product feature is presented to the customer, the salesperson normally begins to discuss the advantages provided by that product's physical characteristics. This is better than discussing only its features. The chances of making a sale are increased by describing the product's advantages, how a product can be used, or how it will help the buyer. Examples of product advantages (performance characteristics) follow:

- It is the fastest-selling soap on the market.
- You can store more information and retrieve it more rapidly with our computer.
- This machine will copy on both sides of the pages instead of only one.

How does the prospective customer know that your claims for a product are true? Imagine a prospect thinking, "Prove it!" Be prepared to substantiate any claims you make.

Companies typically train their salespeople thoroughly on the product's physical and performance characteristics. A salesperson may have excellent knowledge of the product yet be unable to describe it in terms that allow the prospect to visualize the benefits of purchasing it. This is because many salespeople present only a product's features and advantages—leaving the buyer to imagine its benefits.

While your chances of making a sale increase when you discuss both the features and the advantages of your product, you must learn how to stress product benefits that are important to the prospect in your presentation. Once you have mastered this selling technique, your sales will increase.

The Product's Benefits: What's in It for Me?

People are interested in what the product will do for them. Emphasizing benefits appeals to the customer's personal motives by answering the question, What's in it for me? In your presentation, stress how the prospect will benefit from the purchase rather than the features and advantages of your product as shown in Exhibit 3–3.

To illustrate the idea of buying benefits instead of only features or advantages, consider four items: (1) a diamond ring, (2) camera film, (3) STP motor oil, and (4) movie tickets. Do people buy these products or services for their features or advantages? No; people buy the product's benefits such as:

EXHIBIT 3-3

Discuss benefits to fulfill people's needs and to increase sales.

Industrial salespeople work closely with customers to design products and systems that fit their needs.

Consumer goods salespeople can show customers how to increase sales by setting up strategic merchandise displays.

- A diamond ring—image of success, investment, or to please a loved one.
- Camera film—memories of places, friends, and family.
- STP motor oil—engine protection, car investment, or peace of mind.
- Movie tickets—entertainment, escape from reality, or relaxation.

As you can see, people are buying benefits—not a product's features or advantages. These benefits can be both practical, such as an investment, and psychological, such as an image of success. The salesperson needs to discuss benefits to answer the prospect's question, What's in it for me?

Example:
Vacuum-cleaner salesperson to householder: "This vacuum cleaner's high speed motor (feature) works twice as fast (advantage) with less effort (advantage), which saves you 15 to 30 minutes in cleaning time (benefit) and the aches and pains of pushing a heavy machine (benefit)."

Notice that the benefit specifically states favorable results of buying the vacuum cleaner, which answers the buyer's question, What's in it for *me?* You can see the benefits are specific statements and not generalizations. Instead of saying "This vacuum cleaner will save you time," also say, "you will save 15 to 30 minutes."

Notice that a benefit can result in a further benefit to the prospect. For example, "By saving cleaning time (a benefit), you reduce the aches and pains of pushing a heavier machine (a benefit of a benefit) because the high speed motor (advantage) pulls it (advantage)." Examples of product benefits include:

- Greater profit
- Time savings
- Increased sales

- Cost reductions
- More customers drawn into retail store
- Elimination of out-of-stock merchandise

Not only are benefits important, but the order in which you introduce product benefits during the presentation, along with the product's features and advantages, is also necessary to plan.

Order Can Be Important

Some salespeople prefer to state the benefit first and then state that the feature or advantage makes the benefit possible, such as, "The *king-size* (feature) Tide will bring you *additional profits* (benefits) because it is the *fastest-selling size* (advantage)." In this example, the advantage supports the statement of derived customer benefits.

While stating the benefit first is preferable, you do not always have to discuss the three parts of the FAB formula in particular order, as these examples show:

> Air conditioning salesperson to customer: "This air conditioner has a high energy-efficiency rating (feature) that will save you 10 percent on your energy costs (benefit) because it uses less electricity (advantage)."

> Sporting goods salesperson to customer: "With this ball, you'll get an extra 10 to 20 yards on your drives (advantage) helping to reduce your score (benefit) because of its new solid core (feature)."

> Salesperson to buyer of grocery store health and beauty aids: "Prell's economy size (feature) sells the best of all brands (advantage) in stores like yours. You can increase store traffic 10 to 20 percent (benefit) and build your sales volume by at least 5 percent (benefit) by advertising and reducing its normal price (feature) in next Wednesday's ad."

New salespeople frequently are not accustomed to using feature, advantage, and benefit phrases. To use them regularly in your sales conversation, a standardized *FAB Sequence* can be used as follows:

> The . . . (feature) . . . means you . . . (advantage) . . . with the real benefit to you being . . . (benefit). . . .

The FAB Sequence allows you to easily remember to state the product's benefit in a natural, conversational manner. For example, "*The* new solid core center of the Gunshot Golf Ball *means you* will have an extra 10 or 20 yards on your drives, *with the real benefit to you being* a lower score." You can substitute any features, advantages, and benefits between these transition phrases to develop FAB sequences. Several sequences can be used one after another to emphasize your product's benefits.

Try it. Outloud, read the golf ball FAB Sequence. Then do it again using your own phrasing. Create several variations until finding one you would feel comfortable using in a conversation.

Why should you emphasize benefits? There are two reasons (see Exhibit 3–4). First, they fulfill a person's needs or solve a problem. That is what buyers want to know about. Second, your sales will increase. Stressing benefits in your presentation, rather than features or advantages, will bring success.

Given that people make a buying decision based on whether they believe a product's benefits will satisfy their needs, how can you uncover a buyer's needs?

HOW TO DETERMINE IMPORTANT BUYING NEEDS—A KEY TO SUCCESS

Your initial task when first meeting the customer is to differentiate between important buying needs and needs of lesser or no importance. Exhibit 3–4 illustrates the concept that buyers have both important needs and needs that are not major reasons for buying a product (relatively unimportant buying needs).

Determine buyers' important needs and concentrate on emphasizing product benefits that will satisfy these needs. Benefits that would satisfy buyers' unimportant needs should be de-emphasized in the sales presentation. Suppose your product had

EXHIBIT 3–4

Match buyer's needs to product's benefits and emphasize them in the sales presentation.

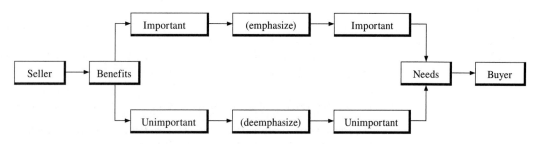

benefits involving service, delivery, time savings, and cost reductions. Is the buyer interested in all four benefits? Maybe not. If you determine that delivery is not important, concentrate on discussing service, time savings, and cost reductions.

This selling strategy is important to your success in selling. One of the things low-performance salespeople do that loses more sales is to discuss benefits of little or no interest to the prospect.

Elmer Wheeler, a famous sales speaker, said, "Sell the sizzle, not the steak!" Wheeler is saying that people buy for reasons other than what the product will actually do or its price. They have both practical (rational) and psychological (emotional) reasons for buying. Customers may not buy the product to solve the rational need that the salesperson perceives as important. They may buy to satisfy an emotional need not easily recognized. It is important to understand this sales concept and learn to determine the buyer's important buying needs. A list of common psychological buying needs includes:

- Fear
- Vanity (keep up with the Joneses)
- Desire for gain
- Security
- Love of family

- Personal pleasure
- Desire to succeed
- Comfort or luxury
- Self-preservation
- Prevention of loss

You must determine the buying needs that are most important to the customer. How can you do this? Several methods are frequently used to uncover important needs. These methods create the acronym **L-O-C-A-T-E:**

Listen:	Prospects may drop leading remarks like, "I wish I had a television like this one."
Observe:	Look at prospects; study their surroundings. Experienced salespeople can determine much about people by observing the way they dress or where they live and work.
Combine:	A skillful salesperson may talk to others, listen to a prospect, probe with questions, make careful observations, and empathize—all in an effort to uncover the prospect's needs.
Ask questions:	Questions often bring out needs that the prospect would not reveal or does not know. The salesperson asks, "Is a quiet ceiling fan important to you?" "Yes, it is," says the buyer. "If I could provide you with the quietest ceiling fan on the market, would you be interested?"

Talk to others: Ask others about a prospect's needs. For instance, ask an office manager's secretary about the manager's satisfaction with a copy machine.

Empathize: Look at the situation from the customer's point of view.[1]

Once the major buying need is determined, you are ready to relate the person's needs to your product's benefits. Like the television camera that transmits images to the television receiver, buyers picture desired products in their minds. Before the picture is focused, buyers often need to be turned on and tuned in. Once you find their real reasons for wanting a particular product or identify major problems that they want to solve, you have uncovered the key to selling to them.

Uncovering these important buying needs is pushing the button that turns on a machine. You have just pushed the customer's hot button. You have awakened a need, and customers realize that you understand their problems. *Basically, this is what selling is all about—determining needs and skillfully relating your product's benefits to show how its purchase will fulfill customers' needs.*

This is not always easy. As we have seen, people have a multitude of different needs and may not understand or see their unconscious needs or problems. In this situation, your challenge is to convert customers' apparently unconscious needs into recognized and understood needs. One of the best ways to uncover needs is to ask questions at certain times during the sales presentation. This question is referred to as a trial close.

THE TRIAL CLOSE—A GREAT WAY TO UNCOVER NEEDS AND SELL

The **trial close** is one of the best selling techniques to use in your sales presentation. It checks the pulse or attitude of your prospect toward the sales presentation. The trial close should be used at these four important times:

1. After making a strong selling point in the presentation.
2. After the presentation.
3. After answering an objection.
4. Immediately before you move to close the sale.

The trial close allows you to determine (1) whether the prospect likes your product's feature, advantage, or benefit (the strong selling point); (2) whether you have successfully answered the objection; (3) whether any objections remain; and (4) whether the prospect is ready for you to close the sale. It is a powerful technique to induce two-way communication (feedback) and participation from the prospect. The Selling Tips box gives examples of trial closes. Learn these—you'll use them throughout the course.

If, for example, the prospect says little while you make your presentation, and if you get a no when you come to the close, you may find it difficult to change the prospect's mind. You have not learned the real reasons why the prospect says no. To avoid this, salespeople use the trial close to determine the prospect's attitude toward the product throughout the presentation.

The trial close asks for the prospect's *opinion,* not a decision to buy. It is a direct question that can be answered with few words.* Look at the trial close examples shown in Selling Tips.

Remember the prospect's positive reactions. Use them later to help overcome objections and in closing the sale. Also, remember the negative comments. You may

---

*See Chapter 9 for other uses and examples of direct questions.

SELLING GLOBALLY

Respecting the Traditions of India

Lisa Hendrick walked briskly through the low door; the sound of her heels was muffled by the soft, thick rugs on the floor. She greeted her customer, Babu Jagjivan, with a wide smile and an outstretched hand. Babu Jagjivan was clad in a long, khaki cotton shirt with swirls of white cloth wrapped around his legs. He took her hand rather tentatively and gestured her to take a seat. Hendrick sat on the nearest available chair and crossed her legs. She was ready to negotiate prices with the help of her interpreter, who spoke Hindi. However, Babu Jagjivan did not appear ready to conduct business. Instead, he summoned a boy with a clap of his hands. Immediately, the boy brought two steel containers filled with hot, steaming tea. Being a hot, summer day with temperatures soaring to the 100s, Hendrick declined the tea. Babu Jagjivan seemed to be extremely reluctant to talk, let alone negotiate a deal. Hendrick was puzzled. She had thought she was adjusting to India very well. Only yesterday, she had negotiated a good contract with Mr. Rajan in Bangalore, a large metropolitan city in south India. But here, in Kanpur (a major city in north India), she was not meeting with much success. Hendrick wondered what could be wrong.

In India, customers vary from Westernized, urban sophisticates like Mr. Rajan to the earthy Babu Jagjivan. Although people always seek to maximize economic benefits from a contract, the subtleties of negotiation and social mores cannot be overlooked. Babu Jagjivan was uncomfortable dealing with a woman. In the more traditional areas of India, it is not customary to shake hands with women—the traditional gesture of folding one's hands in respect (*namaste*) is the norm. The golden rule is to give the customer the pleasure of playing host, by accepting his tea and indulging in social pleasantries before getting down to business. Salespersons in India, as elsewhere, try to adapt to their customers by identifying with their customs. Hence, in urban India, the preferred language for business is English and customers are more apt to be familiar with Western customs. In smaller towns, customers are more comfortable in the regional language (there are 15 official languages in India). People would be distrustful of salespersons who do not respect their customs. Certain weekdays (usually Fridays) are considered auspicious for signing business contracts, although this may vary from one region to another. For instance, even though people in many parts of south India would not commence new business on Tuesdays, this may not be true in the north.[2]

---

need to offset the negatives with the positives later in the presentation. Generally, however, you will not discuss the negative again.

Here is an example of using the prospect's positive comments to ask for the order. Assume that during the presentation you have learned from the prospect that she likes the product's profit margin, fast delivery, and credit policy. You can summarize these benefits in a positive manner such as:

Salesperson: Ms. Stevenson, you say you like our profit margin, fast delivery, and credit policy. Is that right? [Summary and trial close.]

Prospect: Yes, I do.

Salesperson: With the number of customers coming into your store and our expected sales of the products due to normal turnover, along with our marketing plan, I *suggest you buy* . . . [State the products and their quantities.] This will provide sufficient quantities to meet customer demand for the next two months, plus provide you with the profit you expect from your products. I can have the order to you early next week. [Now wait for her response.]

Note that the prospect has said there are three things she likes about what you are selling. She has committed herself. It will be hard for her to say no.

SELLING TIPS

Using Trial Closes

The trial close is an important part of the sales presentation. It asks for the prospect's opinion concerning what you have just said. The trial close does not ask the person to buy directly. Here are examples:

- How does that sound to you?
- What do you think?
- Are these the features you are looking for?
- That's great—isn't it?
- Is this important to you?
- Does that answer your concern?

- I have a hunch that you like the money-saving features of this product. Did I guess right?
- It appears that you have a preference for this model. Is this what you had in mind?
- I can see that you are excited about this product. On a scale from one to ten, how do you feel it will fit your needs?
- I notice your smile. What do you think about . . . ?
- Am I on the right track with this proposal?

If the prospect responds favorably to your trial close, then you are in agreement or you have satisfactorily answered an objection. Thus, the prospect may be ready to buy. However, if you receive a negative response, do not close. Either you have not answered some objection or the prospect is not interested in the feature, advantage, or benefit you are discussing. This feedback allows you to better uncover what your prospect thinks about your product's potential for satisfying needs.

SELL SEQUENCE   One way to remember to incorporate a trial close into your presentation is the **SELL Sequence.** Exhibit 3–5 shows how each letter of the word *sell* stands for a sequence of things to do and say to stress benefits important to the customer. By remembering the word *sell,* you remember to *show the feature, explain the advantage, lead into the benefit, and then let the customer talk by asking a question about the benefit (trial close).*

> EXAMPLE:
> Industrial salesperson to industrial purchasing agent: "This equipment is made of stainless steel [feature], which means it won't rust [advantage]. The real benefit is that it reduces your replacement costs, thus saving you money [benefit]! That's what you're interested in—right [trial close]?

> EXAMPLE:
> Beecham salesperson to consumer goods buyer: "Beecham will spend an extra $1 million in the next two months advertising Cling Free fabric softener [feature]. Plus, you can take advantage of this month's $1.20 per dozen price reduction [feature]. This means you will sell 15 to 20 percent more Cling Free in the next two months [advantage], thus making higher profits and pulling more customers into your store [benefits]. How does that sound [trial close]?

Once you use a trial close, carefully listen to what the customer says and watch for nonverbal signals to determine if what you said has an impact. If you have a positive response to your trial close, you are on the right track.

EXHIBIT 3-5

The SELL Sequence: Use it throughout your presentation.

S	E	L	L
Show feature	Explain advantage	Lead into benefit	Let customer talk

EXHIBIT 3-6

Examples of features, advantages, benefits, and trial closes that form the SELL Sequence.

Features (physical characteristic)	Advantages (performance characteristic)	Benefits (result from advantage)	Trial Closes (feedback questions)
1. Nationally advertised consumer product	1. Will sell more product	1. Will make you a high profit	1. What do you think?
2. Air conditioner with a high energy efficiency rating	2. Uses less electricity	2. Saves 10 percent in energy costs	2. Is this important to you?
3. Product made of stainless steel	3. Will not rust	3. Reduces your replacement costs	3. How does that sound to you?
4. Supermarket computer system with the IBM 3651 Store Controller	4. Can store more information and retrieve it rapidly by supervising up to 24 grocery check-out scanners and terminals and look up prices on up to 22,000 items	4. Provides greater accuracy, register balancing, store ordering, and inventory management	4. That's great—isn't it?
5. Five percent interest on money in bank checking NOW account	5. Earns interest that would not normally be received	5. Gives you one extra bag of groceries each month	5. Do you want to earn extra money?
6. Golf clubhead aerodynamically designed titanium steel	6. Increased clubhead speed, longer drives	6. Lower scores	6. And that's what counts—right?

Remember, the trial close does not ask the customer to buy or make any type of purchase decision. It asks only for an opinion. The trial close is a trial question to determine the customer's opinion toward the salesperson's proposition to know if it is time to close the sale. Thus, its main purpose is to induce feedback from the buyer.

Exhibit 3–6 presents six examples of SELL Sequences composed of features, advantages, benefits, and trial closes of products. The first column lists features or product characteristics such as size, shape, performance, and maintenance data. The second column shows advantages that arise from respective features. These are the performance characteristics or what the product will do. The third column contains benefits to the customer of these features and advantages.

The last column shows a question—or trial close—related to what was said by the salesperson. The trial close acts as a feedback method to determine the buyer's opinion about the feature, advantage, and/or benefit. It helps uncover what is important, and what is not important, to the other person. Try using the trial close in your everyday conversations with friends, co-workers, and family members. It works!

For each major product feature, you should develop the resulting advantage and benefit. Then create a trial close to induce feedback for the buyer. The SELL Sequences should be used throughout your presentation.

YOUR BUYER'S PERCEPTION

Why would two people have the same need but buy different products? Likewise, why might the same individual at different times view your product in diverse ways? The answers to both questions involve how the person perceives your product.

Perception is the process by which a person selects, organizes, and interprets information. The buyer receives the salesperson's product information through the senses: hearing, touch, taste, and smell. These senses act as filtering devices that information must pass through before it can be used.

Each of the three perception components plays a part in determining buyers' responses to you and to your sales presentation. Buyers often receive large amounts of information in a short period, and they typically perceive and use only a small amount of it. Some information is ignored or quickly forgotten because of the difficulty of retaining large amounts of information. This process is known as **selective exposure** because only a portion of the information an individual is exposed to is selected to be organized, interpreted, and allowed into awareness.

Why does some information reach a buyer's consciousness while other information does not? First, the salesperson may not present the information in a manner that assures proper reception. For example, there may be too much information given at one time. This causes confusion, and the buyer tunes out. In some cases, information may be haphazardly presented, which causes the buyer to receive it in an unorganized manner. See Exhibit 3–7.

A sales presentation that appeals to the buyer's five senses helps to penetrate perceptual barriers. It also enhances understanding and reception of the information as you present it. Selling techniques such as asking questions, using visual aids, and demonstrating a product can force buyers to participate in the presentation. This helps determine if they understand your information.

Second, buyers tend to allow information to reach consciousness if it relates to needs they recognize and wish to fulfill. If, for example, someone gives you reasons for purchasing life insurance and you do not perceive a need for it, there is a good chance that your mind will allow little of this information to be perceived. However, if you need life insurance, chances are you will listen carefully to the salesperson. If you are uncertain about something, you will ask questions to increase your understanding.

EXHIBIT 3–7

The questions asked by this salesperson help him understand the buyer's perceptions, attitudes, and beliefs.

MAKING THE SALE

Find the F's

Count the number of F's in the sentence below. How many did you find the first time you read the sentence?

> FEATURE FILMS ARE
> THE RESULT OF YEARS
> OF SCIENTIFIC STUDY
> COMBINED WITH THE
> EXPERIENCE OF YEARS

We often miss what may be right under our noses, such as buying signals. How many F's are there? There are six, but three are part of the word *of* which has a different sound. You would be surprised at the number of people who miss the answer.

A buyer's perceptual process also may result in **selective distortion** or the altering of information. It frequently occurs when information is received that is inconsistent with a person's beliefs and attitudes. When buyers listen to a sales presentation on a product that they perceive as low quality, they may mentally alter the information to coincide with present beliefs and attitudes, thereby reinforcing themselves. Should buyers believe that the product is of high quality, even when it is not, they may change any negative information about the product into positive information. This distortion can substantially lessen the intended *effect* of a salesperson attempting to compare a product to the product currently used by the individual.

Selective retention can also influence perception. Here, buyers may remember only information that supports their attitudes and beliefs, and forget what does not. After a salesperson leaves, buyers may forget the product's advantages stressed by the salesperson because they are not consistent with their beliefs and attitudes.

These perceptions help explain why a buyer may or may not buy. The buyer's perceptional process acts as a filter by determining what part of the sales message is heard, how it is interpreted, and what product information is retained. Therefore, two different sales messages given by two different salespeople, even though they concern similar products, can be received differently. A buyer can tune out one sales presentation, tune in the other presentation, and purchase the perceived product.

While you cannot control a buyer's perceptions, often you can influence and change them. To be successful, you must understand that perceptual barriers can arise during your presentation. You must learn to recognize when they occur and how to overcome them.

PERCEPTIONS, ATTITUDES, AND BELIEFS

You make a sales presentation concerning a product's features, advantages, and benefits. Your goal is to provide information that makes the buyer knowledgeable enough to make an educated purchase decision. However, a person's perceptual process may prevent your information from being fully utilized. Understanding how people develop their perceptions can help you be more successful in selling. See Exhibit 3–7.

Perceptions are learned. People develop their perceptions through experience. This is why **learning** is defined as acquiring knowledge or a behavior based on past experiences.

Successful salespeople must help buyers learn about them and their products. If buyers have learned to trust you, they listen and have faith in what you say, therefore increasing the chance of making sales. If your products perform as you claim they will, buyers will repurchase them more readily. If your presentation provides the information necessary to making a decision, your probability of making the sale increases. Product knowledge influences the buyer's attitude and beliefs about your product.

A person's **attitudes** are learned predispositions toward something. These feelings can be favorable or unfavorable. If a person is neutral toward the product or has no knowledge of the product, no attitude exists. A buyer's attitude is shaped by past and present experience.

Creating a positive attitude is important, but it alone does not result in your making the sale. To sell it to someone, you also must convert a buyer's belief into a positive attitude. A **belief** is a state of mind in which trust or confidence is placed in something or someone. The buyer must believe your product will fulfill a need or solve a problem. A favorable attitude toward one product rather than another comes from a belief that one product is better.

Also, a buyer must believe that you are the best person from whom to buy. If you are not trusted as the best source, people will not buy from you. Assume, for example, that someone decides to buy a 19-inch, portable, RCA color television. Three RCA dealers are in the trading area and each dealer offers to sell at approximately the same price. Chances are that the purchaser will buy from the salesperson believed to be best, even though there is no reason not to trust the other dealers.

If buyers' perceptions create favorable attitudes that lead them to believe your product is best for them and that they should buy from you—you make sales. Often, however, people may not know you or your product. Your job is to provide information about your product that allows buyers to form positive attitudes and beliefs. Should their perception, attitudes, and beliefs be negative, distorted, or incorrect, you must change them. As a salesperson, you spend much time creating or changing people's learned attitudes and beliefs about your product. This is the most difficult challenge a salesperson faces.

Example of a Buyer's Misperceptions

Assume, as an example, that a woman is shopping for a ceiling fan for her home. The three main features of the product she is interested in are price, quality, and style. While shopping around, she has seen two brands, the Hunter and the Economy brand. The information she received on these two brands has caused her to conclude that all ceiling fans are basically alike. Each brand seems to offer the same features and advantages. Because of this attitude, she has formed the belief that she should purchase a low-price fan, in this case, the Economy ceiling fan. Cost is the key factor influencing this purchase decision.

She decides to stop at one more store that sells Casablanca fans. She asks the salesperson to see some lower-priced fans. These fans turn out to be more expensive than either the Hunter or Economy models. Noting their prices, she says to the salesperson, "That's not what I had in mind." She walks away as the salesperson says, "Thanks for coming by."

What should the salesperson have done? When the customer walked into the store, the salesperson knew her general need was for a ceiling fan. However, the customer had wrongly assumed that all brands are alike. It was the salesperson's job to first ask fact-finding questions of the customer such as: "Where will you use the fan?" "What color do you have in mind?" "Is there a particular style you are interested in?" "What features are you looking for?" and "What price range would you like to see?" These questions allow the salesperson to determine the customer's specific needs and her attitudes and beliefs about ceiling fans.

Learning the answers to these questions enables the salesperson to explain the benefits of the Casablanca fan as compared to the Hunter and Economy brands. The salesperson can show that fans have different features, advantages, and benefits, and why there are price differences among the three fans. The buyer can then make a decision as to which ceiling fan best suits her specific needs. Knowledge of a buyer's learned attitudes and beliefs can make sales; with this information, a salesperson can alter the buyer's perceptions or reinforce them when presenting the benefits of the product.

THE BUYER'S PERSONALITY SHOULD BE CONSIDERED

People's personalities also can affect buying behavior by influencing the types of products that fulfill their particular needs. **Personality** can be viewed as the individual's distinguishing character traits, attitudes, or habits. While it is difficult to know exactly how personality affects buying behavior, it is generally believed that personality has some influence on a person's perceptions, attitudes, and beliefs, and thus on buying behavior.

Self-Concept

One of the best ways to examine personality is to consider a buyer's **self-concept,** the view of the self. Internal or personal self-evaluation may influence a buyer's attitude toward the products desired or not desired. Some theorists believe that people buy products that match their self-concept. According to self-concept theory, buyers possess four images:

1. The **real self**—people as they actually are.
2. The **self-image**—how people see themselves.
3. The **ideal self**—what people would like to be.
4. The **looking-glass self**—how people think others regard them.

As a salesperson, you should attempt to understand the buyer's self-concept, for it may be the key to understanding the buyer's attitudes and beliefs. For example, if a man is apparently unsatisfied with his self-image, he might be sold through appeals to his ideal self-image. You might compliment him by saying, "Mr. Buyer, it is obvious that the people in your community think highly of you. They know you as an ideal family man and good provider for your family [looking-glass self]. Your purchase of this life insurance policy will provide your family with the security you want [ideal self]." This appeal is targeted at the looking-glass self and the ideal self. Success in sales is often closely linked to the salesperson's knowledge of the buyer's self-concept rather than the buyer's real self.

ADAPTIVE SELLING BASED ON BUYER'S STYLE

While it is important to know a buyer's self-concept, you also should attempt to uncover any additional aspects of the prospect's personality that might influence a decision to buy so that you can further adjust your sales approach. One way to do this is through the study of personality types.

Personality Typing

Carl Gustav Jung (1875–1961), with Sigmund Freud, laid the basis for modern psychiatry. Jung divided human awareness into four functions: (1) feeling, (2) sensing,

(3) thinking, and (4) intuiting.* He argued that most people are most comfortable behaving in one of these four groups. Each group, or personality type, has certain characteristics formed by past experiences.

Exhibit 3–8 shows some guidelines you can use to identify someone's personality style. You can determine styles by identifying the key trait, focusing on time orientation, and identifying the environment, and by what people say. Imagine that four of your buyers say the following things to you:

a. "I'm not interested in all of those details. What's the bottom line?"

b. "How did you arrive at your projected sales figure?"

c. "I don't think you see how this purchase fits in with our whole operation here."

d. "I'm not sure how our people will react to this."

How would you classify their personality styles?†

Adapt Your Presentation to the Buyer's Style

The major challenge is to adapt your personal style to best relate to the people you deal with. For example, if you consider the customer (or person) that you best relate to, the one that you find it easiest to call on, the odds are that his or her primary personality style is similar to yours. The other side of the coin states that the person hardest for you to call on usually has a primary style that differs from yours.

The objective is to increase your skill at recognizing the style of the people you deal with. Once the basic style of a buyer is recognized, for example, it is possible to modify and adapt your presentation to the buyer's style to achieve the best results. While this method is not foolproof, it does offer an alternative way of presenting material if you are not succeeding. Let's examine a suggested tailored selling method based on the prospect's personality type preferences.

The Thinker Style

This person places high value on logic, ideas, and systematic inquiry. Completely preplan your presentation with ample facts and supporting data and be precise. Present your material in an orderly and logical manner. When closing the sale be sure to say, "Think it over, Joe, and I'll get back to you tomorrow," whenever the order does not close on the spot.

The Intuitor Style

This person places high value on ideas, innovation, concepts, theory, and long-range thinking. The main point is to tie your presentation into the buyer's big picture or overview of this person's objectives. Strive to build the buyer's concepts and objectives into your presentation whenever possible. In presenting your material, be sure you have ample time.

In closing the sale, stress time limitations on acting. A good suggestion is to say, "I know you have a lot to do—I'll go to Sam to get the nitty-gritty handled and get this off the ground."

---

*There are numerous methods of personality typing. Each is due to the conceptual theory used by the method. Currently, personality typing is a popular sales training technique. I use Jung's classification because of his scientific reputation.

†Answers: (a) Senser, (b) Thinker, (c) Intuitor, and (d) Feeler.

EXHIBIT 3–8

Guidelines to identifying personality style.

Guideline	Thinker	Intuitor	Feeler	Senser
How to describe this person	A direct, detail-oriented person. Likes to deal in sequence on *his/her time*. Very precise, sometimes seen as a nitpicker. Fact oriented.	A knowledgeable, future-oriented person. An innovator who likes to abstract principles from a mass of material. Active in community affairs by assisting in policy making, program development, etc.	People oriented. Very sensitive to people's needs. An emotional person rooted in the past. Enjoys contact with people. Able to read people very well.	Action-oriented person. Deals with the world through his/her senses. Very decisive and has a high energy level.
The person's strengths	Effective communicator, deliberative, prudent, weighs alternatives, stabilizing, objective, rational, analytical, asks questions for more facts.	Original, imaginative, creative, broad-gauged, charismatic, idealist, intellectual, tenacious, ideological, conceptual, involved.	Spontaneous, persuasive, empathetic, grasps, traditional values, probing, introspective, draws out feelings of others, loyal, actions based on what has worked in the past.	Pragmatic, assertive, directional results oriented, technically skillful, objective—bases opinions on what he/she actually sees, perfection seeking, decisive, direct and down to earth, action-oriented.
The person's drawbacks	Verbose, indecisive, overcautious, overanalyzes, unemotional, nondynamic, controlled and controlling, overserious, rigid nitpicking.	Unrealistic, fantasy-bound, scattered, devious, out-of-touch, dogmatic, impractical, poor listener.	Impulsive, manipulative, overpersonalizes, sentimental, postponing, guilt-ridden, stirs up conflict, subjective.	Impatient, doesn't see long-range, status-seeking, self-involved, acts first then thinks, lacks trust in others, nitpicking, impulsive, does not delegate to others.
Time orientation	Past, present, future	Future	Past	Present
Environment				
Desk	Usually neat	Reference books, theory books, etc.	Personal plaques and mementos, family pictures	Chaos
Room	Usually has a calculator and computer runs, etc.	Abstract art, bookcases, trend charts, etc.	Decorated warmly with pictures of scenes or people. Antiques.	Usually a mess with piles of papers, etc. Action pictures or pictures of the manufacturing plant or products on the wall.
Dress	Neat and conservative.	Trendy or rumpled.	Current styles or informal.	No jacket; loose tie or functional work clothes.

The Feeler Style

This person places high value on being people oriented and sensitive to people's needs. The main point to include in your presentation is the impact on people that your idea will have. The feeler likes to small talk with you, so engage in conversation and wait for this person's cue to begin your presentation. The buyer will usually ask, "What's on your mind today?" or something similar. Use emotional terms and words, such as, "We're *excited* about this!"

In your presentation, start with something carried over from your last call or contact. Keep the presentation on a personal note. Whenever possible, get the buyer away from the office (lunch, snack, etc.) on an informal basis; this is how this person prefers to do business. Force the close by saying something such as, "OK, Joe, if there are no objections, let's set it up for the next week." Even if the buyer says "No," you are not dead. The key with a feeler is to push the decision.

The Senser Style

This person places high value on *action*. The key point with a senser is to be brief and to the point. Graphs, models, and samples help as the senser can visualize your presentation. With a senser, verbal communication is more effective than written communication.

In presenting, start with conclusions and results and have supporting data to use when needed. Suggest an action plan—"Let's move *now*"—the buyer has to feel you know what to do.

In closing, give one best way. Have options, but do not present them unless you have to. An effective senser close is, "I know you're busy; let's set this up right *now*."

Watch for Clues

Exhibit 3–9 shows two buyers' environments. Look at the environment guidelines listed in Exhibit 3–8 to identify each buyer's personality style.

The neatness of the desk and dress of the buyer on the left indicates he may be a thinker, whereas the buyer on the right appears to be a senser. The salesperson should alternate the presentation to fit each person's style. However, determining a buyer's personality style is not always as easy as the example shown in Exhibit 3–9.

Determining Style Can Be Difficult

Each of the four styles is present, in some degree, in all of us. However, one primary style is usually dominant, and another complementary style is used as a backup. The primary style employed by an individual often remains the same in both normal and stress situations, while the secondary style is likely to vary.

Some individuals do not have a primary or secondary style, but have a personal style comprising all four types. Dealing with this individual requires strong rapport to isolate the prospect's strong personal likes and dislikes.

EXHIBIT 3-9

Environment provides clues to the buyer's style. What are the personality styles of the buyers who sit at these desks?

YOU CAN CLASSIFY BUYING SITUATIONS

Some people may appear to make up their minds quickly and easily either to buy or not to buy. This is not always the case. The quickness and ease of deciding the product to buy typically depends on the buying situation. Purchasing a gallon of milk is quite different from buying an automobile. People have more difficulty in selecting, organizing, and interpreting information in purchasing an automobile. Also, their attitudes and beliefs toward the automobile may not be well formed.

True, a few people have the type of personality (and resources) that allows them to quickly purchase an expensive product like an automobile, but this is unusual. When purchasing some types of products, most people carefully compare competing brands. They talk to salespeople. As information is collected, attitudes and beliefs are formed toward each product. People must decide which product has the most desirable features, advantages, and benefits. When considering several brands, people may seek information on each one. The more information collected, the greater the difficulty they may have in deciding which product to buy.

Purchase decisions can usually be classified as to the difficulty involved in deciding which product to buy. The purchase decision is viewed as a problem-solving activity falling into one of three classifications shown in Exhibit 3–10. These situations are routine decision making, limited decision making, and extensive decision making.

Some Decisions Are Routine

Many products are purchased repeatedly. People are in the habit of buying a particular product. They give little thought or time to the routine purchase; they fully realize the product's benefits. These are called low-involvement goods because they involve a routine buying decision. People's attitudes and beliefs toward the product are already formed and are usually positive. Milk, cold drinks, and many grocery items often are purchased through **routine decision making.**

For a customer making a routine purchase decision, reinforce that this is a correct buying decision. It is important to have the product in stock. If you do not have it, the customer may go to another supplier.

For someone not currently using your product, the challenge is to change this person's product loyalty or normal buying habits. The features, advantages, and benefits of your product should be directly compared to the buyer's preferred brand. Of course, not all purchase decisions are routine.

Some Decisions Are Limited

When buyers are unfamiliar with a particular product brand, they seek more information in making a purchase decision. In this case, there is **limited decision making**—a moderate level of actual buyer involvement in the decision. The general qualities of goods in the product class are known to the buyer. However, buyers are not familiar with each brand's features, advantages, and benefits. For example, they may perceive that Xerox, 3M, and Canon copiers are the same in performance.

These buyers have more involvement in buying decisions in terms of shopping time, money, and potential dissatisfaction with the purchase than in the routine purchase decision. They seek information to aid them in making the correct decision. A sales

EXHIBIT 3–10

The three classes of buying situations.

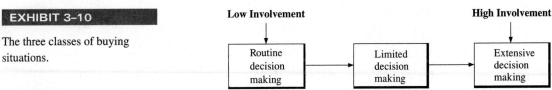

presentation should be developed that provides buyers with the necessary knowledge to make brand comparisons and to increase their confidence that the purchase of your product is the correct decision. Occasionally, the purchase of some products requires prospective buyers to go one step further and apply extensive decision making.

Some Decisions Are Extensive

Buyers seeking to purchase products such as insurance, a home, or an automobile are highly involved in making the buying decision. They may be unfamiliar with a specific brand or type of product and have difficulty in making the purchase decision. This kind of purchase requires more of an investment in time and money than the limited decision. This situation demands **extensive decision making** and problem-solving activities.

In making extensive decisions, buyers believe that much more is at stake relative to other buying decisions. They may become frustrated during the decision-making process, especially if a large amount of information is available. They may become confused—not knowing what product features they are interested in because of unfamiliarity with the products. Buying an automobile or a life insurance policy, for example, entails potentially confusing purchase decisions.

Determine all possible reasons why buyers are interested in a product. Then, in a simple, straightforward manner, present only enough information to allow the buyer to make a decision. At this time, product comparisons can be made, if necessary. You also can help the buyer evaluate alternative products.

In summary, your job is to *provide buyers with product knowledge that allows them to develop positive beliefs that your products fulfill their needs.* Determining the type of decision process a buyer is engaged in is critical to you as a salesperson.

TECHNOLOGY PROVIDES INFORMATION

Technology provides information for customer decision making and service. With enormous amounts of data and sophisticated computer programs at their fingertips, salespeople can serve customers faster and better.

The salesperson shown in Exhibit 3–11, for example, looks at the architect's specifications while reviewing his products on a laptop computer to see which best meet

EXHIBIT 3–11

This salesperson has seen automation increase his quality of service to his customers.

the customer's needs. At the same time, he is talking to his warehouse to determine inventory status and product cost. Once satisfied that the salesperson's product satisfies his needs and is available at a reasonable cost, the construction foreman approves the purchase.

The salesperson asks his warehouse when the product would arrive at the construction site and then tells the warehouse to ship it. Technology allowed the salesperson to sell his customer the right product, at the right price, in the quantity needed and have it delivered in a timely manner.

VIEW BUYERS AS DECISION MAKERS

Buyers, whether private consumers or industrial purchasing agents, are constantly exposed to information about various products. What steps do people go through in making a purchase decision?

Typically, the buying decision involves the five basic steps shown in Exhibit 3–12. Buyers recognize a need, collect information provided by the salesperson, evaluate that information, decide to buy, and after the purchase determine whether they are satisfied with the purchase. This sequence reveals that several events occur before and after the purchase, all of which should be considered by the salesperson.

As seen in Exhibit 3–12, numerous forces influence a consumer's buying behavior. Rich people or older people, for example, often view purchases differently than lower income or younger consumers. Psychological factors such as past experience with a salesperson—good or bad—certainly influence buying decisions. Have you ever had a friend or family member cause you to buy one product rather than another? We all have. Thus, whether we realize it or not, numerous factors influence why someone buys something.

Need Arousal

Remember from the first part of this chapter that buyers may experience a need, or the need can be triggered by the salesperson; this is called **need arousal.** It could be psychological, social, or economic; it could be a need for safety, self-actualization, or ego fulfillment. You must determine a person's needs to know what product information to provide. This information should relate the product's benefits to the person's needs.

Collection of Information

If buyers know which product satisfies a need, they buy quickly. The salesperson may need only approach them; they already want to buy the product.

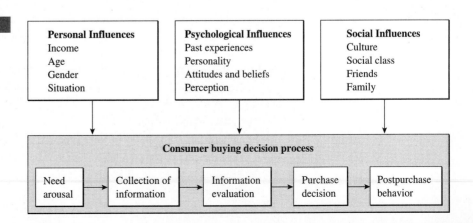

EXHIBIT 3–12

Personal, psychological, and social forces that influence consumers' buying behavior.

However, when buyers are faced with limited or extensive problem solving, they may want to **collect information** about the product. They might visit several retail stores and contact several potential suppliers. They may talk with a number of salespeople about a product's price, advantage, size, and warranty before making a decision.

Information Evaluation

A person's product **information evaluation** determines what will be purchased. After mentally processing all the information about products that will satisfy a need—and this may or may not include your product—a buyer matches this information with needs, attitudes, and beliefs, as discussed earlier, in making a decision. Only then will a **purchase decision** be made.

This evaluation process includes rating preferences on factors such as price, quality, and brand reputation. Attitudes on different products are based on either psychological or rational reasons.

At this stage, a salesperson can be effective. Providing information that matches product features, advantages, and benefits with a buyer's needs, attitudes, and beliefs increases the chances of a favorable product evaluation. So, the salesperson is responsible for uncovering the person's needs, attitudes, and beliefs early in the discussion to match the product with the person's needs.

One way to get such information is to determine not only needs, beliefs, and attitudes but also the type of information a person needs before making a decision. Here are some questions you need to know how to answer:

- Which product attributes are important in this decision—price, quality, service?
- Of these attributes, which are *most* important?
- What are the prospect's attitudes toward your products?
- What are the prospect's attitudes toward your competitor's products?
- Which level of satisfaction is expected from buying the product?

This type of questioning tells you not only about the customer's needs but also involves the customer in the presentation and may convey the idea that you are truly interested in his or her needs. This attitude toward you is enough to create positive attitudes about your product.

Armed with this knowledge about the customer, the salesperson is in a better position to provide the information necessary for a decision and also to help the customer evaluate information in favor of your product. The information should be provided simply, clearly, and straightforwardly. It should seek to correct any negative information or impression about your product. Matching information with a customer's needs may enable you to:

- Alter the person's beliefs about your product, for example, by convincing the customer that your product is priced higher than the competition because it is a quality product.
- Alter the person's beliefs about your competitor's products.
- Change the amount of importance a person attaches to a particular product attribute, for example, by having the customer consider quality and service rather than price alone.
- Show unnoticed attributes of your product.
- Change the search for the ideal product into a more realistic pursuit, such as by substituting a $100,000 home for a $200,000 home, or showing a man whose height is 6 feet, 10 inches a midsize car rather than a compact.

A company has no better promotional device than having its sales force help prospects and customers to evaluate products on the market—and not merely their products. The two-way communication between buyer and seller is exceptionally effective in providing the information needed to make the sale on the one hand, and to evaluate the product on the other. Salespeople provide knowledge to aid people in their decision-making process. In many respects, salespeople are teachers (professors, if you will) who provide helpful information.

Purchase Decision   Is the sale made once the prospect states an intention to buy? No. Do not consider the sale final until the contract is signed or until you have the buyer's money, because there is still a chance for a change of mind. Even after a customer has selected a product, purchase intentions can be changed by these four basic factors:

1. The attitude of significant others, such as a relative, spouse, friend, or boss. Consideration should be given to both the intensity of another person's attitude and the level of motivation the buyer has to comply with or to resist this other person's attitude. See Exhibit 3–13.
2. The perceived risk of buying the product—will it give a return on the money?
3. Uncontrollable circumstances, such as not being able to finance the purchase of a house or to pass the physical examination for a large life insurance policy.
4. The salesperson's actions after the decision has been reached—sometimes it is unwise to continue to talk about a product after this point; something could change the customer's mind.

The third factor, uncontrollable circumstances, is self-explanatory. However, how can attitudes of others influence a sale? A man may want to buy a dark, conservative

EXHIBIT 3–13

Other people can influence the prospect's decision to purchase.

This pharmaceutical rep must service and meet the needs of technicians, physicians, and buyers in hospitals that use his company's products.

This salesperson should sell to both people in the discussion. Otherwise, one person could talk the other out of buying the product.

business suit, whereas his wife wants him to buy a sport coat and slacks. The buyer's original favorable attitude toward the business suit may have been changed by his wife. In industrial selling, others in the buyer's firm can influence the sale. Be sure and tell your story.

Since buyers may not always be sure that they will be satisfied with a purchase, they may perceive a risk; they may experience tension and anxiety after buying your product. Haven't we all asked ourselves, Have I made the correct decision? The levels of tension and anxiety people experience are related to their perceptions of and attitudes about the products they had to choose from. Uncertainty about differences between your product and those of your competitors can create anxiety, especially if both products' benefits appear similar, or if your product is more expensive yet promises better benefits. Prospects might see little difference between products, or may like them all—and thus can fairly easily change their minds several times before buying.

Finally, many sales have been lost after a buyer has said, "I will buy," and the salesperson continues to talk. Additional information sometimes causes buyers to change their minds. It is important to finalize the sale as quickly as possible after the buyer makes a decision. Once the prospect decides, stop adding information, pack up your bag, and leave.

Postpurchase

No, the decision process does *not* end with the purchase—not for the buyer at least! A product, once purchased, yields certain levels of satisfaction and dissatisfaction. **Purchase satisfaction** comes from receiving benefits expected, or greater than expected, from a product. If buyers' experiences from the use of a product exceed expectations, they are satisfied, but if experiences are below expectations, customers are dissatisfied.

The buyer can experience **purchase dissonance** after the product's purchase. Dissonance causes tension over whether the right decision was made in buying the product. Some people refer to this as *buyer's remorse*. Dissonance increases with the importance of the decision and the difficulty of choosing between products. If dissonance occurs, buyers may get rid of a product by returning it or by selling it to someone else. Alternatively, they may seek assurance from the salesperson or friends that the product is a good one and that they made the correct purchase decision (positively reinforcing themselves).

You can help the buyer to be satisfied with the product and lower the level of dissonance in several ways. First, if necessary, show the buyer how to use the product properly, as shown in Exhibit 3–13. Second, be realistic in claims made for the product. Exaggerated claims may create dissatisfaction. Third, continually reinforce buyers' decisions by reminding them how well the product actually performs and fulfills their needs. Remember, in some situations buyers can return the product to the seller after purchase. This cancels your sale and hurts your chances of making future sales to this customer. Fourth, follow up after the sale to determine if a problem exists. If so, help correct it. This is a great way to increase the likelihood of repeat business.

In summary, seek to sell a product that satisfies the buyer's needs. In doing so, remember the sale is made only when the actual purchase is complete, and that you should continue to reinforce the buyer's attitudes about the product at all times, even after the sale. This practice reduces the perceived risk of making a bad buy, which allows buyers to listen to and trust your sales message even though some of your proposals may be out of line with their purchase plans. It also can reduce the buyers' postpurchase dissonance. Buyers who have developed a trust in your product claims believe that you will help them properly use the product.

SATISFIED CUSTOMERS ARE EASIER TO SELL

It is easier to sell a customer than a stranger—especially a satisfied customer! That's why building a relationship—keeping in touch after the sale—is so important to a salesperson's success. Sally Fields of California Office Supply says:

> It took me five tough years to build up my customer base. Now selling is easy and fun. But the first months were terrible. Calling only on strangers got old, but I hung in there. I was going to succeed—no matter how hard I had to work.
>
> The more strangers I sold, the more friends (customers) I had. It is easy to sell a friend. So in the mornings I contacted possible new customers and in the afternoons I visited customers to make sure they were happy with their purchases and sell them more office supplies. Today, 80 percent of my monthly sales comes from customers. I still make cold calls to keep sharp. By next year my goal is to have 95 percent sales come from customers. To do that I must do all I can to make sure customers are happy plus find new customers. The relationships I build today will take care of my tomorrow!

Fields owes her success to doing everything she can to ensure her customers are happy with their purchases and her organization's service. Her yearly income is now more than $100,000. She has built her business through hard work, selling, and service. More on follow-up and service later in the book.

TO BUY OR NOT TO BUY—A CHOICE DECISION

Salespeople realize that people buy a product because of a need, and that need can be complex due to the influence of perceptions, attitudes, beliefs, and personality. Furthermore, perceptions, attitudes, and beliefs may differ from one purchase situation to another. How is it possible to state why people buy one product and not another?

Salespeople do not have to be psychologists to understand human behavior. Nor do they need to understand the material covered in courses taken by a psychology major. Furthermore, the average salesperson cannot know all that is involved in the psychological and practical processes that a buyer goes through in making a purchase decision.

What the salesperson *does* need to understand are the various factors that can influence the buying decision, the fact that buyers actually examine various factors that influence these decisions, that buyers actually go through various steps in making decisions, and how to develop a sales presentation that persuades buyers to purchase the product to satisfy needs. To do this, the salesperson should consider the following questions before developing a sales presentation:

- What type of product is desired?
- What type of buying situation is it?
- How will the product be used?
- Who is involved in the buying decision?
- What practical factors may influence the buyer's decision?
- What psychological factors may influence the buyer's decision?
- What are the buyer's important buying needs?

Again, it seems necessary to know a great deal about a person's attitudes and beliefs to answer these questions. Can this be made simpler? Yes. Simply stated, to buy or not to buy is a choice decision. The person's choice takes one of two forms: First, a person has the choice of buying a product or not. Second, the choice can be between competing products. The question salespeople should ask themselves is,

ETHICAL DILEMMA

Sock It to Her!

Selling new cars often was difficult, but Linda Martin felt she had a new Cadillac sold. A woman called and said she wanted to buy a new Cadillac exactly like the one that was parked outside of Linda's office. Linda had another one the same color, but it was fully loaded with the latest high-tech equipment and cost $6,000 more.

The buyer, a 68-year-old widow, listened as Linda described both cars, emphasizing the higher-priced Cadillac.

The buyer seemed to become confused over how to work options such as the disc stereo system and cellular telephone. Suddenly the buyer said, "Linda, you seem like a nice person. Which car do you think I should buy?"

What would you do?

"How can I convince a person to choose my product?" The answer to this question involves five things; each is necessary to make the sale. People will buy if:

1. They perceive a need or problem.
2. They desire to fulfill a need or solve a problem.
3. They decide there is a high probability that your product will fulfill their needs or solve their problems better than your competitor's products.
4. They believe they should buy from you.
5. They have the resources and authority to buy.

What do you do if you know your product can reduce a prospect's manufacturing costs, saving the firm $5,000 a year, for a cost of $4,000, and the prospect says, "No thanks, I like my present equipment"? This buyer does not perceive a need, and will not buy. Suppose you make your point about reducing operating costs, but for some reason the prospect is not interested in reducing costs? Chances are, this person will not buy no matter how persuasively you present your product's benefits—because high costs are not seen as an important problem.

Furthermore, even customers who want to solve a problem, but do not like your product, will not buy. But, if you have convinced them, if they want to solve a problem, and if they perceive your product as solving this problem, the question is still: Will these customers buy from you? They will, if they believe you represent the best supplier. If they would rather buy from another supplier, you have lost the sale. Your job is to provide the necessary information so that customers say yes to each of the five statements.

SUMMARY OF MAJOR SELLING ISSUES

As a salesperson, be knowledgeable about factors that influence your buyer's purchase decision. You can obtain this knowledge, which helps to increase the salesperson's self-confidence and the buyer's confidence in the salesperson, through training and practice.

A firm's marketing strategy involves various efforts to create exchanges to satisfy the buyer's needs and wants. The salesperson should understand the characteristics of the target market (consumer or industrial) and how these characteristics relate to the buyer's behavior to better serve and sell to customers.

The individual goes through various steps or stages in the three buying situations of routine decision making, limited decision making, and extensive decision making. Uncover who is involved in the buying decision and the main factors that influence the decision. These factors include various psychological and practical buying influences.

Psychological factors include the buyer's motives, perceptions, learning, attitudes, beliefs, and personality—all of which influence the individual's needs and result in a search for information on what products to buy to satisfy them. Established relationships strongly influence buying decisions, making satisfied customers easier to sell to than new prospects. The information is evaluated, which results in the decision to buy or not to buy. These same factors influence whether the buyer is satisfied or dissatisfied with the product.

Realize that all prospects will not buy your products, at least not all of the time, due to the many factors influencing their buying decisions. You need to uncover buyers' needs, solve buyers' problems, and provide the knowledge that allows them to develop personal attitudes toward the product. These attitudes result in positive beliefs that your products fulfill their needs. Uncovering prospects' needs is often difficult, since they may be reluctant to tell you their true needs or may not really know what and why they want to buy. You can usually feel confident that people buy for reasons such as to satisfy a need, fulfill a desire, and obtain a value. To determine these important buying needs, you can ask questions, observe prospects, listen to them, and talk to their associates about their needs.

MEETING A SALES CHALLENGE

John Salley took the advice of Joe Gandolfo who has reportedly sold more life insurance than any other person in the world. Joe's philosophy is that "selling is 98 percent understanding human beings and 2 percent product knowledge." Do not let that statement mislead you, for Joe holds the Charter Life Underwriter (CLU) designation as a member of the American College of Life Underwriters. He is extremely knowledgeable about insurance, tax shelters, and pension plans. In fact, he spends several hours a day studying recent changes on pensions and taxation. "But," Joe says, "I still maintain that it's not product knowledge but understanding of human beings that makes a salesperson effective."

John had his sales region's training director work with him two days a week for a month. John's sales presentations were analyzed and found to concentrate almost entirely on the technical features and advantages of the products. The training director contacted six of John's customers. Each said they often did not understand him because he was too technical. John immediately began emphasizing benefits and discussing features and advantages in nontechnical terms. Slowly his sales began to improve. Today, John Salley is a true believer in the phrase, "It's not what you say, but how you say it."

KEY TERMS FOR SELLING

black box 67	*FAB* selling technique 69
stimulus–response 67	feature 69
needs 68	advantage 69
wants 68	benefit 70
economic needs 68	L-O-C-A-T-E 73
conscious need level 69	trial close 74
preconscious need level 69	SELL Sequence 76
unconscious need level 69	perception 78
benefit selling 69	selective exposure 78

SALES APPLICATION QUESTIONS

1. What three types of buying situations may the buyer be in when contacted by a salesperson? Briefly describe each type.

2. What are the psychological factors that may influence the prospect's buying decision?

3. While you do not have to be a psychologist or understand exactly how the buyer's mind works, you do need to uncover the buyer's motives.
   a. What techniques can be used to uncover the buyer's motives?
   b. The prospect's intention to buy can be influenced by several things. What information does the salesperson need to obtain concerning the prospect's buying intentions before developing a sales presentation?

4. In the following statements, write down each idea that is a benefit:
   a. Counselor talking to a student: "To improve your science grade, Susie, you must establish better study habits."
   b. Construction supervisor talking to a worker: "That job will be a great deal easier, Joe, and you won't be as tired when you go home nights if you use that little truck over there."
   c. Father talking to his son: "You will make a lot of friends, Johnny, and be respected at school, if you learn how to play the piano."
   d. Banker talking to customer: "If you open this special checking account, Ms. Brown, paying your bills will be much easier."

5. In the following statements, determine what parts of each statement are features, advantages, or benefits.
   a. Hardware sales representative to homeowner: "Blade changing is quick and easy with this saw because it has a push-button blade release."
   b. Consumer sales representative to grocery store buyer: "The king-size package of Tide will bring in additional profits because it is the fastest-selling, most economical size."
   c. Clothing salesperson to customer: "For long wear and savings on your clothing costs, you can't beat these slacks. All the seams are double-stitched and the material is 100 percent Dacron."

6. Indicate which of the following statements are a feature, advantage, or benefit. Write your answer on a sheet of paper.
   a. Made of pure vinyl.
   b. Last twice as long as competing brands.
   c. It's quick-frozen at 30° below zero.
   d. Available in small, medium, and large sizes.
   e. New.
   f. No unpleasant aftertaste.

    g. Saves time, work, and money.

    h. Approved by Underwriters' Laboratory.

    i. Gives 20 percent more miles to the gallon.

    j. Contains XR-10.

    k. Baked fresh daily.

    l. Includes a one-year guarantee on parts and labor.

    m. Is packed 48 units or eight 6-packs to the case.

    n. Guaranteed to increase your sales by 10 percent.

    o. Adds variety to your meal planning.

7. Consider the following information:

    The DESKTOP XEROX 2300 copier is a versatile model that delivers the first copy in six seconds. It is also the lowest-priced new Xerox copier available. The 2300 is designed as a general purpose office copier and occupies less than half the top of a standard desk. The new unit copies on a full range of office materials as large as 8 ½ by 14 inches. A special feature is its ability to reproduce 5 ½ by 8 ½-inch billing statements from the same tray used for letter-size or legal-size paper. Selling price of the 2300 will be as low as $3,495 and rentals as low as $60 a month on a two-year contract without a copy allowance.

    What are the features, advantages, and benefits of the DESKTOP XEROX 2300 copier? What are additional benefits of the copier: List two additional features, advantages, and benefits that a Xerox salesperson could use in presenting the new copier to a prospective buyer.

8. Several features of a car are listed below. Match each feature with its corresponding benefit(s):

    a. Low hoodline:

      1. Better visibility.

      2. Economy.

      3. Quick startup.

    b. Tinted glass:

      1. Reflects sunlight.

      2. Reduces eyestrain.

      3. Reduces glare from sun.

    c. Rear window defroster:

      1. Clears rear windshield, and thus reduces the danger of driving on a cold, foggy day.

      2. Rear windshield can be deiced or defogged automatically so you do not have to do it yourself.

      3. Increases the cost of the car by $250.

    d. Whitewall tires:

      1. Provide better handling and a more stable ride.

      2. More appealing to the eye.

      3. Increase the life of your tires.

9. To convince the customers that your product's benefits are important, show how the product benefits will meet their needs. Suppose the customer says: "I need some kind of gadget that will get me out of bed in the morning." Which of the following statements best relates your product feature, the GE clock radio's snooze alarm, to this customer's need?

    a. "Ms. Jones, this GE radio has a snooze alarm that is very easy to operate. See, all you do is set this button and off it goes."

    b. "Ms. Jones, the GE radio is the newest radio on the market. It carries a one-year guarantee and you can trade in your present radio and receive a substantial cut in the price."

c. "Ms. Jones, since you say you have trouble getting up in the morning, you want an alarm system that will make sure you wake up. Now, GE's snooze alarm will wake you up no matter how often you shut the alarm off. You see, the alarm goes off every seven minutes until you switch off the special 'early bird' knob."

10. A salesperson says: "You expect a pencil sharpener to be durable. Our sharpener is durable because it's constructed with titanium steel bearings. Because of these bearings, our sharpener will not jam up and will last a long time."

   a. In this example, the titanium steel bearings are a (an):
      1. Benefit.
      2. Feature.
      3. Need.
      4. Advantage.

   b. "Will not jam up" is a (an):
      1. Benefit.
      2. Feature.
      3. Need.
      4. Advantage.

   c. In the statement, "will not jam up," the salesperson has:
      1. Converted a product feature into an advantage.
      2. Converted benefits into a product feature.
      3. Related a product feature to the customer's need via benefits.
      4. Numbers (1) and (2) are correct.
      5. Numbers (1) and (3) are correct.

   d. The statement, "will last a long time," is a (an):
      1. Benefit.
      2. Feature.
      3. Need.
      4. Advantage.

11. For each of the following products, determine a potential benefit based on their advantages:

Product	Feature	Advantage
Sony stereo turntable	Direct-drive turntable	More dependable, fewer moving parts
Tab	Only one calorie per 16 oz. serving	Will not increase your body weight when you drink it
Bic erasable ink pen	Erasable ink	Can erase mistakes
Ceiling fan	Hangs from ceiling, high efficiency	Out of the way, uses less electricity
Sheer panty hose	No dark patches	Looks like real skin
Drilling an oil well	One of our engineers for the entire job	Better service
Hefty trash bags	2-ply	Puncture proof, can overstuff it

12. As a salesperson for Procter & Gamble's soap division, you have been asked by your sales manager to determine the features, advantages, and benefits for Tide detergent and to discuss using Tide's benefits in a sales presentation at the next sales meeting. You have determined the following four features of Tide;

listed underneath each feature are your ideas of factors that might interest retail grocery buyers. For each feature, determine the benefit that you would emphasize:

a. Number one selling detergent:
   1. Best traffic-pulling detergent.
   2. Great brand loyalty.
   3. High percent of market share.
b. Four sizes:
   1. Increases your total detergent sales.
   2. Boxes are standard sizes.
   3. Case cost is the same.
c. Heaviest manufacturer-advertised detergent:
   1. Continue to attract new customers to your store.
   2. More customers remember this brand's advertising.
   3. Produces high repeat business.
d. Distinctive, colorful package:
   1. Speeds shopping—easy for shoppers to locate on shelves.
   2. High visual impact stimulates impulse purchases when on special display.
   3. Familiar package design easy to recognize in store ads.

SALES WORLD WIDE WEB EXERCISES

What Is Your Personality?

Salespeople need to be good communicators. Communication skills help people do a better job of relating product benefits to customer needs. This increases the salesperson's productivity. An essential part of having good communication skills is to better understand your own personality.

To better understand yourself, first complete the selling experiential exercise at the end of this chapter. It is entitled "What's Your Style—Senser, Intuitor, Thinker, Feeler?" This exercise uses an adaptation of the Myers-Briggs Temperament Indicator. The Keirsey Temperament Sorter URL below has you complete a more comprehensive Myers-Briggs type indicator.

To further your understanding of the real you, go to these sites and complete several of the personality exercises you feel are important for salespeople:

www.2h.com (IQ, personality and entrepreneurial)

www.keirsey.com/cgi-bin/keirsey/newkts.cgi (the Keirsey Temperament Sorter)

www.el.com (type in *personality test*)

www.yahoo.com (type in *emotional intelligence*)

Write up a short report summarizing what the personality tests uncovered about you. Do you feel the tests accurately assessed your personality and the real you?

FURTHER EXPLORING THE SALES WORLD

1. Keep a diary of your purchases for two weeks. Select five or more of the products you purchased during that period and write a short report on why you purchased each product and what you feel are the features, advantages, and benefits of each product.

2. This week examine the television advertisement of three different products or services and report on the features, advantages, and benefits used in the commercial to persuade people to buy each product.
3. Go shop for a product costing over $100. Report on your experience. Find out if the salesperson is on a commission pay plan.

STUDENT APPLICATION LEARNING EXERCISES (SALES)

(Part 1 of 7)

At the end of appropriate chapters beginning with Chapter 3, you will find Student Application Learning Exercises (SALES). SALES are meant to help you construct the various segments of your sales presentation. SALES build upon one another so that after you complete each, you will have constructed the majority of your sales presentation.

Now you are ready to begin developing your sales presentation. To make Sale 1:
1. State what you will sell.
2. Briefly describe the individual and/or organization to which you will sell.
3. List three features of your product, including each feature's main advantage and benefit. Refer back to Chapter 3 for FAB definitions. FABs should discuss your product, not your marketing plan or business proposition. We'll do that later.

Feature	Advantage	Benefit
a.		
b.		
c.		

4. Now create a SELL Sequence for each FAB (see pages 74–77). Label each of the components of the SELL Sequence using brackets as shown on page 76.

SELLING EXPERIENTIAL EXERCISE

What's Your Style—Senser, Intuitor, Thinker, Feeler?

Individuals differ in the way they interact with others and the way they go about gathering and evaluating information for problem solving and decision making. As discussed in the chapter, four psychological functions identified by Carl Jung are related to this process: sensation, intuition, thinking, and feeling.[3]

Before you read further, complete the Problem-Solving Diagnostic Questionnaire (Exhibit A), then check the scoring key that appears in Exhibit B.[4] There are no right or wrong answers; just read each item carefully, then respond with your answer.

According to Jung, gathering information and evaluating information are separate activities. People gather information either by *sensation* or *intuition* but not by both simultaneously. People using *sensation* would rather work with known facts and hard data and prefer routine and order in gathering information. People using *intuition* would rather look for possibilities than work with facts and prefer solving new problems and using abstract concepts.

Information evaluation involves making judgments about the information a person has gathered. People evaluate information by *thinking* or *feeling*. These represent the extremes in orientation. *Thinking* individuals base their judgments on impersonal analysis, using reason and logic rather than personal values or emotional aspects of the situation. *Feeling* individuals base their judgments more on personal feelings such as harmony and tend to make decisions that result in approval from others.

Indicate your responses to the following questionnaire on a separate sheet of paper. There are no
right or wrong responses to any of these items.

Part I. Write down the number and letter of the response that comes closest to how you usually feel
or act.

1. I am more careful about
   a. People's feelings.
   b. Their rights.
2. I usually get on better with
   a. Imaginative people.
   b. Realistic people.
3. It is a higher compliment to be called
   a. A person of real feeling.
   b. A consistently reasonable person.
4. In doing something with many people, it appeals more to me
   a. To do it in the accepted way.
   b. To invent a way of my own.
5. I get more annoyed at
   a. Fancy theories.
   b. People who do not like theories.
6. It is higher praise to call someone
   a. A person of vision.
   b. A person of common sense.
7. I more often let
   a. My heart rule my head.
   b. My head rule my heart.
8. I think it is a worse fault
   a. To show too much warmth.
   b. To be unsympathetic.
9. If I were a teacher, I would rather teach
   a. Courses involving theory.
   b. Fact courses.

Part II. Write down the letters of the words in the following pairs that appeal to you more.

10. *a.* compassion   *b.* foresight
11. *a.* justice   *b.* mercy
12. *a.* production   *b.* design
13. *a.* gentle   *b.* firm
14. *a.* uncritical   *b.* critical
15. *a.* literal   *b.* figurative
16. *a.* imaginative   *b.* matter-of-fact

According to Jung, only one of the four functions—sensation, intuition, thinking, or feeling—is dominant in an individual. However, the dominant function is usually backed up by one of the functions from the other set of paired opposites. Exhibit C shows the four problem-solving styles that result from these match-ups.[5]

Questions

1. Look back at your scores. What is your personal problem-solving style? Read the action tendencies. Do they fit?

EXHIBIT B

Scoring key to determine
your style.

The following scales indicate the psychological functions related to each item. Use the point value columns to arrive at your score for each function. For example, if you answered a to the first question, your *1a* response in the feeling column is worth zero points when you add up the point value column. Instructions for classifying your scores follow the scales.

Sensation	Point Value	Intuition	Point Value	Thinking	Point Value	Feeling	Point Value
2 b___	1	2 a ___	2	1 b ___	1	1 a ___	0
4 a___	1	4 b ___	1	3 b ___	2	3 a ___	1
5 a___	1	5 b ___	1	7 b ___	1	7 a ___	1
6 b___	1	6 a ___	0	8 a ___	0	8 b ___	1
9 b___	2	9 a ___	2	10 b ___	2	10 a ___	1
12 a___	1	12 b ___	0	11 a ___	2	11 b ___	1
15 a___	1	15 b ___	1	13 b ___	1	13 a ___	1
16 b___	2	16 a ___	0	14 b ___	0	14 a ___	1
Maximum point value:	(10)		(7)		(9)		(7)

Classifying total scores:
- Write *intuition* if your intuition score is equal to or greater than your sensation score.
- Write *sensation* if your sensation score is greater than your intuition score.
- Write *feeling* if your feeling score is greater than your thinking score.
- Write *thinking* if your thinking score is greater than your feeling score.

EXHIBIT C

The four styles and their
tendencies

Personal Style	Action Tendencies
Sensation-thinking	■ Emphasizes details, facts, certainty
	■ Is decisive, applied thinker
	■ Focuses on short-term, realistic goals
	■ Develops rules and regulations for judging performance
Intuitive-thinker	■ Shows concern for current, real-life human problems
	■ Is creative, progressive, perceptive thinker
	■ Emphasizes detailed facts about people rather than tasks
	■ Focuses on structuring organizations for the benefit of people
Sensation-feeling	■ Prefers dealing with theoretical or technical problems
	■ Is pragmatic, analytical, methodical, and conscientious
	■ Focuses on possibilities using interpersonal analysis
	■ Is able to consider a number of options and problems simultaneously
Intuitive-feeling	■ Avoids specifics
	■ Is charismatic, participative, people oriented, and helpful
	■ Focuses on general views, broad themes, and feelings
	■ Decentralizes decision making, develops few rules and regulations

2. Studies show that the sensation-thinking (ST) combination characterizes many managers in Western industrialized societies. Do you think the ST style is the best fit for most jobs in today's society?
3. Also look back at Exhibit 3–8, Guidelines to identifying personality style. Compare yourself and others you know to the guidelines. Is there a match between you and the individual style? What about your roommate, spouse, parents, or your brother or sister?
4. How can you use this information to improve your communication ability?

CASE 3–1
Economy Ceiling Fans, Inc.

As a salesperson for Economy Ceiling Fans, you have been asked to research and determine customers' attitudes and beliefs toward your brand of ceiling fans. With this information you will determine if your company has the correct product line and suggest selling points for the company's salespeople when discussing fans with customers who come into their chain of retail stores.

You decide to hold an open house on a Sunday in one of your typical stores located in an upper-income neighborhood and advertise your special prices. During that time, you ask everyone to be seated, thank them for coming, and ask them to discuss their attitudes toward your company and ceiling fans.

Some people felt that ceiling fans should be shopped for without considering brands, but once a brand is selected, they go to the stores carrying that particular brand and buy from the store with the best price. Most people had collected information on fans from personal sources (such as friends), commercial sources (such as advertising, salespeople, company literature), and public sources (such as consumer rating organizations). Sixty percent had narrowed their choice to fans from Hunter, Casablanca, and Economy, and they seemed to look for three things in a ceiling fan: price, quality, and style.

Question

Given this information on why people buy ceiling fans, what should salespeople be instructed to do when a customer enters their store?

CASE 3–2
McDonald's Ford Dealership

The used-car salesperson for McDonald's Ford, John Alexander, approaches a woman, June Miller, in the car lot and says:

Seller: Can I help you?

Buyer: 20,000 miles on this one—I'll bet a little old lady owned this lemon! What was it, really, before you set it back?

Seller: That is the actual mileage. Hi, I'm John Alexander and you are . . . [*He waits for reply.*]

Buyer: June Miller.

Seller: June, what can I help you with?

Buyer: Oh, I don't know. Something that runs and will get me around.

Seller: Do you travel out of town or just drive back and forth to work?

Buyer: I drive everywhere! I'm even getting in a car pool with my boss.

Seller: Good mileage is important then.

Buyer: Sure is. [*She walks over and looks at a full-size, four-door Ford.*] Say, I like this one! $6,500! You have to be kidding.

Seller: Do you need that much room?

Buyer: Not really, there is just me.

Seller: June, are you saying you need a car that is dependable, gets good gas mileage, not too big, and not too expensive?

Buyer: How did you guess?

Seller: Follow me . . . . [*He shows her five cars that he feels have those features. Then he asks:*] Which one of these do you like?

Buyer: Well, they are OK, but I really don't like them. Thanks for your time. I'll shop around a little more. Give me your card and I'll get back to you later.

Questions

1. Describe the situation and the buyer's apparent needs.
2. What should the seller do now that the buyer has said no to the cars he has shown her and is about to leave the car lot?

4

Communication for Relationship Building: It's Not All Talk

MAIN TOPICS

Communication: It Takes Two

Nonverbal Communication: Watch for It

Barriers to Communication

Master Persuasive Communication to Maintain Control

LEARNING OBJECTIVES

The ability to effectively communicate both verbally and nonverbally is crucial to sales success. This chapter introduces this important sales skill. After studying this chapter, you should be able to:

■ Present and discuss the salesperson–buyer communication process.

■ Discuss and illustrate the importance of using nonverbal communication when selling.

■ Define and recognize acceptance, caution, and disagreement nonverbal signals.

■ Review barriers to effective sales communication.

■ Explain ways of developing persuasive communication.

Amos Skaggs, purchasing agent, stands as a salesperson enters his office. "Hi, Mr. Skaggs," the salesperson says, offering his hand. Skaggs returns a limp, one-second handshake and sits down behind his desk. He begins to open his afternoon mail, almost as though no one else was in the room.

The salesperson sits down and begins his canned sales talk by saying, "Mr. Skaggs, I'm here to show you how your company can lower manufacturing costs by 10 percent." Skaggs lays his mail down on his desk, leans back in his chair, crosses his arms, and with a growl says: "I'm glad to hear that. You know something, young fellow; pretty soon it won't cost us anything to manufacture our products." "Why is that?" the salesman mumbles, meekly looking down to the floor. "Well, you are the ninth person I've seen today who has offered to save us 10 percent on our costs."

Skaggs stands up, leans over the table and while peering over his glasses says slowly, "I believe I've heard enough sales pitches for one day." The initially enthusiastic salesperson now apologetically says, "If this is not a good time for you, sir, I can come back at a later date."

The problem facing this salesperson is common. The buyer has been seeing salespeople all day. Basically, they say the same thing: "Buy from me and I'll save you money." The buyer has communicated his feelings toward the salesperson both verbally and nonverbally. What message has Skaggs sent to the salesperson? If you were the salesperson, what might you do now?

While many other factors are crucial to sales success, the ability to communicate effectively is of prime importance. To convincingly convey this important sales skill, this chapter directly applies a basic communication model to the buyer–seller interaction. We describe several factors influencing communication, along with possible barriers to effective communication. Also examined is the often ignored—though always critical—topic of nonverbal communication. The balance of this chapter relates some techniques to improve sales communication.

COMMUNICATION: IT TAKES TWO

Communication, in a sales context, is the act of transmitting verbal and nonverbal information and understanding between seller and buyer. This definition presents communication as an exchange process of sending and receiving messages with some type of response expected between seller and buyer.

Communication during the sales presentation takes many forms. Ideas and attitudes can be effectively communicated by media other than language. Actually, in a normal two-person conversation, less than 35 percent of the social meaning utilizes verbal components. Said another way, much of the social meaning in a conversation is conveyed nonverbally.

Research has found that face-to-face communication is composed of *verbal, vocal,* and *facial* communication messages. One equation presents the total impact of communicated messages as equal to 7 percent verbal, 38 percent tone of voice, and 55 percent nonverbal expressions.[1] If one recognizes these findings as a reasonable approximation of the total communicative process, then uninformed salespeople actually ignore a major part of the communication process that occurs during buyer–seller interaction. How the sales message is given can be as important to making the sale as what is said. Thus, nonverbal communications are important in

SELLING TIPS

Say What You Mean

There are at least six messages involved in the communication process:

1. What you mean to say.
2. What you really say.
3. What the other person hears.
4. What the other person thinks is heard.
5. What the other person says about what you said.
6. What you think the other person said about what you said.

It gets complicated, doesn't it? Sue and I were looking at a gorgeous moon together under romantic circumstances. As we shared the moment, how was I actually feeling? I was feeling romantic. If we followed the six messages, that incident would have looked something like this:

1. What you mean to say.   ("The moon puts me in a romantic mood.")

2. What you really say.   ("Isn't that a brilliant moon?")

3. What the other person hears.   ("The moon is bright.")

4. What the other person thinks she hears.   ("Yes, it's bright enough for a walk.")

5. What the other person says about what you said.   ("Yes, it's bright enough to hit a golf ball by.")

6. What you think the other person said about what you said.   ("I don't feel romantic.")

We can miss each other's wavelengths completely by the time the six messages are completed without even realizing what has happened. All of us are constantly in the process of encoding and decoding messages.

We need to learn to ask questions, or restate the point for clarification of meaning. To say what we mean straightforwardly must be our constant goal in order for those around us to discard all decoding devices.

communication between buyer and seller. An awareness of nonverbal communication is a valuable tool in successfully making a sale.

Vocal communication includes such factors as voice quality, pitch, inflection, and pauses. Radio newscaster Paul Harvey is famous for how he broadcasts the news. His vocal pauses and inflections are masterfully used to obtain and hold the attention of his radio audience. A salesperson's use of vocal factors can aid in sales presentation, too. Along with verbal, vocal, and facial communication, many other elements also are involved in sales communication.

Salesperson–Buyer Communication Process Requires Feedback

A basic communication model that depicts how the salesperson–buyer communication process works is shown in Exhibit 4–1. Basically, communication occurs when a sender transmits a message through some type of medium to a receiver who responds to that message. Exhibit 4–1 presents a model that contains eight major communication elements. Each of these elements is defined as follows:

- **Source.** The source of communication (also called the communicator); in our case, it's the salesperson.
- **Encoding process.** The conversion by the salesperson of ideas and concepts into the language and materials used in the sales presentation.
- **Message.** The information conveyed in the sales presentation.
- **Medium.** The form of communication used in the sales presentation and discussion; most frequently words, visual materials, and body language.
- **Decoding process.** Receipt and translation (interpretation) of the information by the receiver (prospective buyer).

EXHIBIT 4–1

The basic communication model has eight elements.

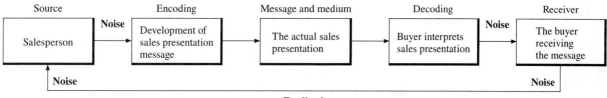

Source		Encoding	Message and medium	Decoding		Receiver
Salesperson	Noise	Development of sales presentation message	The actual sales presentation	Buyer interprets sales presentation	Noise	The buyer receiving the message

Noise ←——————————————————————————————————→ Noise

Feedback

- **Receiver.** The person the communication is intended for; in our case, it's the prospect or buyer.
- **Feedback.** Reaction to the communication as transmitted to the sender. This reaction may be verbal, nonverbal, or both.
- **Noise.** Factors that distort communication between buyer and seller. Noise includes barriers to communication, which we discuss later.

This model portrays the communication process. A salesperson should know how to develop a sales presentation (encoding) so that the buyer obtains maximum understanding of the message (decoding). Communication media that most effectively communicate a specific sales message should be used. Clear verbal discussion, employment of visual aids such as pictures or diagrams, and development of models or samples of the product are several types of media a salesperson might use in communicating a sales message.

One-way communication occurs when the salesperson talks and the buyer only listens. The salesperson needs a response or feedback from the buyer to know if communication occurs. Does the buyer understand the message? Once feedback or interaction and understanding between buyer and seller exists in a communication process, two-way communication has been established.

Two-way communication is essential to make the sale. The buyer must understand your message's information to make a buying decision. Two-way communication gives the salesperson the ability to present a product's benefits, instantly receive buyer reactions, and answer questions. Buyers usually react both verbally and nonverbally to your presentation.

NONVERBAL COMMUNICATION: WATCH FOR IT

Recognition and analysis of nonverbal communication in sales transactions is relatively new. Only in the past 10 to 15 years has the subject been formally examined in detail. The presence and use of nonverbal communication, however, has been acknowledged for years. In the early 1900s, Sigmund Freud noted that people cannot keep a secret even if they do not speak. A person's gestures and actions reveal hidden feelings about something.

People communicate nonverbally in several ways. Four major **nonverbal communication** channels are the physical space between buyer and seller, appearance, handshake, and body movements.

Concept of Space

The concept of **territorial space** refers to the area around the self a person will not allow another person to enter without consent. Early experiments in territorial space dealt with animals. These experiments determined that higher-status members of a group often are afforded a freedom of movement that is less available to those of lower status. This idea has been applied to socially acceptable distances of space that human beings keep between themselves in certain situations. Territorial space can easily be related to the selling situation.

Space considerations are important to salespeople because violations of territorial space without customer consent may set off the customer's defense mechanisms and create a barrier to communications. A person (buyer) has four main types of distances to consider—intimate (up to 2 feet); personal (2 to 4 feet); social (4 to 12 feet); and public (greater than 12 feet).

Intimate space of up to two feet, or about arm's length, is the most sensitive zone, since it is reserved for close friends and loved ones. To enter intimate space in the buyer–seller relationship, for some prospects, could be socially unacceptable—possibly offensive.

During the presentation, a salesperson should carefully listen and look for signs that indicate the buyer feels uncomfortable, perhaps that the salesperson is too close. A buyer may deduce from such closeness that the salesperson is attempting to dominate or overpower the buyer. This feeling can result in resistance to the salesperson. If such uneasiness is detected, the salesperson should move back, which reassures the customer.

Personal space is the closest zone a stranger or business acquaintance is normally allowed to enter. Even in this zone, a prospect may be uncomfortable. Barriers, such as a desk, often reduce the threat implied when someone enters this zone.

Social space is the area normally used for a sales presentation. Again, the buyer often uses a desk to maintain a distance of four feet or more between buyer and seller. Standing while facing a seated prospect may communicate to the buyer that the salesperson seems too dominating. Thus, the salesperson should normally stay seated to convey a relaxed manner.

A salesperson should consider beginning a presentation in the middle of the social distance zone, six to eight feet, to avoid the prospect's erecting negative mental barriers. This is especially true if the salesperson is not a friend of the prospect.

Public space can be used by the salesperson making a presentation to a group of people. It is similar to the distance between teacher and student in a classroom. People are at ease and thus easy to communicate with at this distance, since they do not feel threatened by the salesperson.

Space Threats   The territorial imperative causes people to feel that they should defend their space or territory against **space threats.** The salesperson who pulls up a chair too close, takes over all or part of the prospect's desk, leans on or over the desk, or touches the objects on the desk runs the risk of invading a prospect's territory. Be careful not to create defensive barriers. However, should you sense a friendliness between yourself and the prospect, use territorial space to your benefit.

Space Invasion.   The prospect who allows you to enter or invade personal and intimate space is saying, "Come on into my space; let's be friends." Now you can use space to your advantage.

In most offices, the salesperson sits directly across the desk from the prospect. The prospect controls the space arrangement. This defensive barrier allows the prospect to control much of the conversation and remain safe from **space invasion.** Often, seating is prearranged and it could be a space threat if you moved your chair when calling on a prospect for the first time.

EXHIBIT 4–2

Office arrangements and
territorial space.

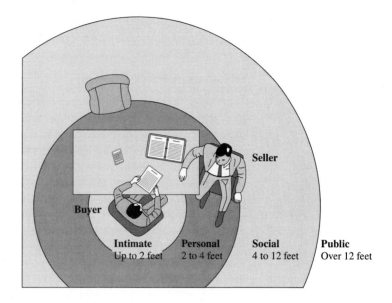

| Intimate | Personal | Social | Public |
| Up to 2 feet | 2 to 4 feet | 4 to 12 feet | Over 12 feet |

However, if you have a choice between a chair across the desk or beside the desk, take the latter seat, as shown in Exhibit 4–2. Sitting beside the prospect lowers the desk communication barrier. If you are friends with the buyer, move your chair to the side of the desk. This helps create a friendly, cooperative environment between you and the buyer.

Communication through Appearance and the Handshake

Other common methods of nonverbal communication are signals conveyed by a person's physical appearance and handshake. Once territorial space has been established, general appearance is the next medium of nonverbal communication conveyed to a customer by a salesperson. Appearance not only conveys information such as age, sex, height, weight, and physical characteristics but it also provides much data on personality. For instance, hairstyle is one of the first things a buyer notices about a salesperson.

Style Hair Carefully

Hairstyle traditionally has been important in evaluating personal appearance. Today's salespeople must consider the type of customer they call on and adjust their hairstyles accordingly.

Though recently decreasing somewhat in popularity, facial hair is worn by some salesmen. For several decades, American males did not sport beards and moustaches to any great extent, but that trend reversed in the 1960s and '70s. A research study in the early 1970s asked people their opinion of facial hair and came up with two very different opinions. One group felt that bearded men are perceived as more sensitive, more masculine, more intelligent, and warmer than clean-shaven men. The other group felt that men with beards are perceived as more deviant, radical, independent, and introverted.[2]

Salespeople should carefully consider their grooming and its impact on customers' perceptions. Some companies ask male salespersons to be clean shaven and wear conservative haircuts. Their female salespersons are asked to choose a simple, businesslike, shoulder-length hairstyle. Other companies leave grooming up to each individual. Your grooming objective is to eliminate communication barriers. Your grooming can convey a favorable first impression. Should your company not have a policy on grooming, examine your customers' grooming before deciding on your style.

Dress as a Professional

Wardrobe has always been a major determinant of sales success, and today it is emphasized as never before. A variety of books and articles have appeared on proper dress for businesspeople. These books espouse the doctrine that men and women sales representatives should wear conservative, serious clothing that projects professionalism, just the right amount of authority, and a desire to please the customer. Sporty clothing is believed to accentuate sales aggressiveness, which can place a purchasing agent on the defensive and result in lost sales.

Many companies believe that decision rules exist for every major clothing item and accessory, but these are derivatives of one basic commandment—dress in a simple, elegant style. Xerox, IBM, and other large companies have incorporated these ideas into their sales training and daily policies. These firms encourage sales personnel to wear dark, conservative clothing. This practice is designed to project a conservative, stable corporate image to both customers and the general public.

Exhibit 4–3 illustrates several key considerations for appropriate dress and grooming. If you are uncertain about what to do, visit several retailers. Make sure at least one retailer is a specialty store. They will have the latest styles and spend time with you. Tell the salespeople what you are looking for and see what they say. Think of this as an investment in yourself because it is expensive to build a wardrobe. However, you are worth it!

Clothes, accessories, and shoes are important, but do not forget personal grooming, such as skin care and hairstyle. Women and men should visit a hairstylist. Learn to recognize image symbols in business dress and use them to your advantage. Be cautious in becoming too individualistic—the unspoken message in most companies is that freedom in dress may be a privilege of rank. Remember, too, that these guides for dress, including the remainder of the chapter, apply to selling yourself in job interviews.

The nonverbal messages that salespeople emit through appearance should be positive in all sales situations. Characteristics of the buyer, cultural aspects of a sales territory, and the type of product being sold all determine a mode of dress. In considering these aspects, create a business wardrobe that sends positive, nonverbal messages in every sales situation. Once you have determined appropriate dress and hairstyle, the next nonverbal communication channel to consider is your contact with a prospect through the handshake.

Shake Hands Firmly and Look People in the Eye

The handshake is said to have evolved from a gesture of peace between warriors. By joining hands, two warriors were unable to bear arms against one another (assuming that a shield—not a weapon—was held in the other hand).

Today, a handshake is the most common way for two people to touch one another in a business situation, and some people feel that it is a revealing gesture. A firm handshake is more intense and is indicative of greater liking and warmer feelings. A prolonged handshake is more intimate than a brief one, and it could cause the customer discomfort, especially in a sales call on a new prospect. A loosely clasped, cold, or limp handshake is usually interpreted as aloof and unwilling to become involved. This cold fish handshake is also perceived as unaffectionate and unfriendly.

EXHIBIT 4–3

To look sharp, be sharp, and feel sharp the correct clothes, grooming, attitude, and physical conditioning are required. This applies to your career, to interviewing, and to your life.

Choose a suit that means business.

Natural fibers, a good fit, and current styles are important.

Physical conditioning produces the stamina and positive mental attitude necessary to be a success.

First impressions are crucial. Remember that you are representing your organization—and your customer's perception of that organization begins with you.

General rules for a successful handshake include extending your hand first—if appropriate. (Also see Exhibit 4–4.)[3] Remember, however, a few people may be uncomfortable shaking hands with a stranger. At times, you may want to allow your customer to initiate the gesture. Maintain eye contact with the customer during the handshake, gripping the hand firmly. These actions allow you to initially establish an atmosphere of honesty and mutual respect—starting the presentation in a positive manner [4]

Body Language Gives You Clues

From birth, people learn to communicate their needs, likes, and dislikes through nonverbal means. The salesperson can learn much from a prospect's raised eyebrow, a smile, a touch, a scowl, or reluctance to make eye contact during a sales presentation. The prospect can communicate with you literally without uttering a word. An ability to interpret these signals is an invaluable tool to the successful sales professional. In conjunction with interpretation of body language, the salesperson's skillful use and control of physical actions, gestures, and overall body position also are helpful.

The buyer can send nonverbal signals via five communication modes. They are the body angle, facial expression, arm movement or position, hand movements or

EXHIBIT 4–4

Five tips for international handshaking.

1. International protocol dictates that you shake hands with everyone in a room—omissions are noticed, and are considered a rejection.

2. Women should initiate handshakes, and shake hands with other women and men. Not extending her hand to a European male will cause an American businesswoman to lose credibilty.

3. Western and Eastern Europeans reshake hands whenever they're apart for even a short period of time (e.g., lunch).

4. French and Japanese businespeople shake hands with one firm gesture. In Japan, the handshake may be combined with a slight bow, which should be returned.

5. In Arab countries, handshakes are a bit limp and last longer than typical American handshakes. Latin Americans also tend to use a lighter, lingering handshake. In all cases, don't pull your hand away too soon; such a gesture will be interpreted as a rejection.

position, and leg position. (Exhibit 4–5 shows examples.) These modes generally send three types of messages: (1) acceptance, (2) caution, and (3) disagreement.

Acceptance signals indicate that your buyer is favorably inclined toward you and your presentation. These signals give you the green light to proceed. While this may not end in a sale, at the least the prospect is saying, "I am willing to listen." What you are saying is both acceptable and interesting. Some common acceptance signals are:

- *Body angle.* Leaning forward or upright at attention.
- *Face.* Smiling, pleasant expression, relaxed, eyes examining visual aids, direct eye contact, positive voice tones.
- *Hands.* Relaxed and generally open, perhaps performing business calculations on paper, holding on as you attempt to withdraw a product sample or sales materials, firm handshake.
- *Arms.* Relaxed and generally open.
- *Legs.* Crossed and pointed toward you or uncrossed.

Salespeople frequently rely only on facial expressions as indicators of acceptance. This practice may be misleading since buyers may consciously control their facial expressions. Scan each of the five key body areas to verify your interpretation of facial signals. A buyer who increases eye contact, maintains a relaxed position, and exhibits positive facial expressions gives excellent acceptance signals.

Acceptance signals indicate that buyers perceive that your product might meet their needs. You have obtained their attention and interest. You are free to continue with your planned sales presentation.

Caution signals should alert you that buyers are either neutral or skeptical toward what you say. Caution signals are indicated by:

- *Body angle.* Leaning away from you.
- *Face.* Puzzled, little or no expression, averted eyes or little eye contact, neutral or questioning voice tone, saying little, and then only asking a few questions.
- *Arms.* Crossed, tense.
- *Hands.* Moving, fidgeting with something, clasped, weak handshake.
- *Legs.* Moving, crossed away from you.

Caution signals are important for you to recognize and adjust to for two main reasons. First, they indicate blocked communication. Buyers' perceptions, attitudes, and beliefs regarding your presentation may cause them to be skeptical, judgmental, or

EXHIBIT 4–5

Which of the five communication modes can a salesperson look for with these two customers?

uninterested in your product. They may not recognize that they need your product or that it can benefit them. Even though you may have their attention, they show little interest in or desire for your product.

Second, if caution signals are not handled properly, they may evolve into disagreement signals, which causes a communication breakdown and makes a sale difficult. Proper handling of caution signals requires that you:

■ Adjust to the situation by slowing down or departing from your planned presentation.

■ Use open-ended questions to encourage your buyers to talk and express their attitudes and beliefs. Have you ever been interested in improving the efficiency of your workers? or What do you think about this benefit? are examples of open-ended questions.

■ Carefully listen to what buyers say and respond directly.

■ Project acceptance signals. Be positive, enthusiastic, and smile. Remember, you are glad to be there to help buyers satisfy their needs. Refrain from projecting caution signals even if a buyer does so. If you project a positive image in this situation, there is greater probability that you will change a caution light to a green one and make the sale.

Your objective in using these techniques is to change the yellow caution signal to the green go-ahead signal. If you continue to receive caution signals, proceed carefully with your presentation. Be realistic, alert to the possibility that the buyer may begin to believe that your product is not beneficial and begin sending disagreement or red-light signals.

Disagreement signals tell you immediately to stop the planned presentation and quickly adjust to the situation. Disagreements, or red-light signals, indicate that you are dealing with a person becoming uninterested in your product. Anger or hostility may develop if you continue the presentation. Your continuation can cause a buyer to feel an unacceptable level of sales pressure resulting in a complete communication breakdown. Disagreement signals may be indicated by:

■ *Body angle.* Retracted shoulders, leaning away from you, moving the entire body back from you, or wanting to move away.

■ *Face.* Tense, showing anger, wrinkled face and brow, little eye contact, negative voice tones, or may become suddenly silent.

■ *Arms.* Tense, crossed over chest.

- *Hands.* Motions of rejection or disapproval, tense and clenched, weak handshake.
- *Legs.* Crossed and away from you.

You should handle disagreement signals as you did caution signals, by using open-ended questions and by projecting acceptance signals. There are four additional techniques to use. First, stop your planned presentation. There is no use in continuing until you have changed disagreement signals into caution or acceptance signals. Second, temporarily reduce or eliminate any pressure on the person to buy or to participate in the conversation. Let the buyer relax as you slowly move back to your presentation. Third, let your buyer know you are aware that something upsetting has occurred. Show that you are there to help, not to sell at any cost. Finally, use direct questions to determine a buyer's attitudes and beliefs such as, "What do you think of . . . ?" or "Have I said something you do not agree with?"

Body Guidelines

Over time, you will know customers well enough to understand the meaning of their body movements. Although a prospect may say no to making a purchase, body movements may indicate uncertainty. As Richard Dreyfuss says in the movie *The Goodbye Girl,* "Your lips say *no, no, no,* but your eyes say *yes, yes, yes!*" This phrase sometimes holds true for selling.

Exhibit 4–6 relates some common nonverbal signals that buyers may give off.[5] The interpretation of most body language is obvious. Be cautious in interpreting an isolated gesture, such as assuming that little eye contact means the prospect is displeased with what you are saying. Instead, concentrate on nonverbal cues that are part of a cluster or pattern. Let's say your prospect begins staring at the wall. That is a clue that may mean nothing. You continue to talk. Now, the prospect leans back in the chair. That is another clue. By itself, it may be meaningless, but in conjunction with the first clue, it begins to take on meaning. Now, you see the prospect turn away, legs crossed, brow wrinkled. You now have a cluster of clues forming a pattern. It is time to adjust or change your presentation.

In summary, remember that nonverbal communication is well worth considering in selling. A salesperson ought to:

- Be able to recognize nonverbal signals.
- Be able to interpret them correctly.
- Be prepared to alter a selling strategy by slowing, changing, or stopping a planned presentation.
- Respond nonverbally and verbally to a buyer's nonverbal signals.

Effective communication is essential in making a sale. Nonverbal communication signals are an important part of the total communication process between buyer and seller. Professional salespeople seek to learn and understand nonverbal communication to increase their sales success.

BARRIERS TO COMMUNICATION

Like the high hurdler, a salesperson often must overcome a multitude of obstacles. These obstacles are more aptly called *barriers to communication.* Consider this example:

Salesperson Joe Jones heard that the XYZ Company buyer, Jake Jackson, was displeased with the company's present supplier. Jones had analyzed XYZ's operation

EXHIBIT 4–6

What nonverbal signals are these buyers giving to you?

1. When you mention your price, this purchasing agent tilts her head back, raises her hands and assumes a rigid body posture. What nonverbal signals is she communicating and how would you move on with the sale?

2. As you explain your sales features, this buyer looks away, clasps his hands, and crosses his legs away from you. What nonverbal signals is he communicating and how would you move on with the sale?

3. As you explain the quality of your product, this company president opens his arms and leans toward you. What nonverbal signals is he communicating and how would you move on with the sale?

Answers

1. Your buyer is sending red signals. That means you are facing nearly insurmountable barriers. You've got to stop what you are doing, express understanding, and redirect your approach.
2. This buyer is sending yellow signals that warn you to exercise caution. Your own words and gestures must be aimed at relaxing the buyer or the prospect may soon communicate red signals.
3. This buyer is sending green signals that say everything is "go." With no obstacles to your selling strategy, simply move to the close.

and knew that his product could save the company thousands of dollars a year. Imagine Jones' surprise when Jackson terminated the visit quickly with no sale and no mention of a future appointment.

Jones told his boss about the interview: "Jackson kept asking me where I went to school, whether I wanted coffee, and how I liked selling while I was trying to explain to him the features, advantages, and benefits of our product. Suddenly, Jackson stopped the interview." Jones asked the boss, "What did I do wrong? I know he needed our product."

The buyer was sending Jones signals that he likes doing business with people he knows. He was a "feeler," as discussed in Chapter 3. The buyer did not want to get down to business immediately. He wanted to visit for a while. There was never any true communication established between Jackson and Jones, which caused Jones to misread the customer and incorrectly handle the situation.

Salespeople, as illustrated in this example, often lose sales by failing to recognize communication barriers between buyer and seller. The main reasons communication breaks down in the sales situation are

1. **Differences in perception.** If the buyer and seller do not share a common understanding of information contained in the presentation, communication breaks down.

SELLING GLOBALLY

Wanted: Global Sales Managers and Salespeople

A new minority is in demand in corporate America and overseas. Colgate-Palmolive Company calls these people *globalites*. In Europe, they are known as *Euromanagers*. Regardless of the name, corporations around the world are scrambling to locate and nab the brightest and best candidates for global management.

Competition is intense. Colgate-Palmolive's program, introduced in 1987, attracts 15,000 applicants for 15 slots. The need for global managers also has spawned several successful executive search firms. Top international headhunters such as Korn/Ferry; Egon Zehnder International; and Russell Reynolds Associates, Inc., recruit multilingual executives with wide experience and the ability to deal with other cultures.

Could you qualify? Do you have enough international knowledge to answer these questions? A smiling fish is (*a*) a term used in the Middle East or (*b*) a dish served in China. During meals in Belgium, you should (*a*) keep your hands off the table or (*b*) keep your hands on the table. Eye contact and gestures of openness are important when discussing business in (*a*) Mexico or (*b*) Saudi Arabia. When they're talking, Americans stand closer than do South Americans or Africans: (*a*) true or (*b*) false. In England, to table an issue

means to (*a*) put it aside or (*b*) bring it up for discussion. (The correct answer for each question is *b*.)

Global corporations have initiated and promoted management programs to help employees overcome their cultural blunders. A program at General Electric's aircraft engine unit encourages foreign language and cross-cultural training for midlevel managers and engineers. American Express regularly transfers junior managers to overseas units. PepsiCo, Raychem, Honda of America, and GM are among the growing number of companies with global management training programs. As one international human resource manager pointed out, "Knowing how to conduct business in foreign cultures and to grasp global customers' different needs is the key to global business."

Multilingual skills aren't enough; corporations seek candidates with highly developed human skills. "We tend to look for people who can work in teams and understand the value of cooperation and consensus," said the chairman of Unilever. Successful globalization requires teamwork and overcoming national, racial, and religious prejudice. That minority of managers who quickly grasp global skills will increasingly find themselves on the fast track to success.[6]

The closer a buyer's and seller's perceptions, attitudes, and beliefs, the stronger communication will be between them. Cultural differences are easily misperceived by buyers and sellers. See, for example, the Selling Globally box.

2. **Buyer does not recognize a need for product.** Communication barriers exist if the salesperson is unable to convince the buyer of a need, and/or that the salesperson represents the best supplier to buy from.

3. **Selling pressure.** There is a fine line between what is acceptable sales pressure or enthusiasm and what the buyer perceives as a high-pressure sales technique. A pushy, arrogant selling style can quickly cause the prospect to erect a communication barrier.

4. **Information overload.** You may present the buyer with an excess of information. This overload may cause confusion, perhaps offend, and the buyer will stop listening. The engineer making a presentation to a buyer who is not an engineer may concentrate on the technical aspects of a product but the buyer only wants a small amount of information.

5. **Disorganized sales presentation.** Sales presentations that seem unorganized to the buyer tend to cause frustration or anger. Buyers commonly expect you to understand their needs or problems and to customize your sales presentation to their individual situations. If you fail to do this, communication can fall apart.

6. **Distractions.** When a buyer receives a telephone call or someone walks into the office, distractions occur. A buyer's thoughts may become sidetracked, and it may be difficult to regain attention and interest.

7. **Poor listening.** At times, the buyer may not listen to you. This often occurs if you do all or most of the talking—not allowing the buyer to participate in the conversation.

8. **Not adapting to buyer's style.** Sitting in on a sales call with a young salesperson selling high-priced industrial equipment, it became clear that the two were not communicating. The salesperson, who preferred telling to showing, kept talking about the product. But the visually oriented client wanted to see a picture of it. Eventually, the conversation deteriorated into a show versus tell confrontation. It was the classic sales miscommunication. Amazingly, the rep had product brochures in his briefcase. But he didn't bring them out because he was locked into his own form of communication. It is critical for salespeople to use different communication styles as discussed in Chapter 3. Most successful salespeople have learned to match their customer's communication styles.

The eight barriers to communication just listed are not the only ones that may occur. As in the example of Joe Jones, the buyer may actually need the product and the salesperson may have excellent product knowledge and believe that a good sales presentation was made, yet because of communication barriers, the buyer rejects the salesperson and the product. As a salesperson, constantly seek ways to recognize and overcome communication barriers, and identify and satisfy buyer needs through persuasive communication.

MASTER PERSUASIVE COMMUNICATION TO MAINTAIN CONTROL

To become a better communicator, consider two major elements of communication. First, always strive to improve the message delivered in the sales presentation. You need to be a capable encoder. Second, improve your ability to determine what the buyer is communicating to you. Therefore, you need to be a good listener or decoder. A good sales communicator knows how to effectively encode and decode during a presentation.

Salespeople want to be good communicators to persuade people to purchase their products. **Persuasion** means the ability to change a person's belief, position, or course of action. The more effective you are at communicating, the greater your chances of being successful at persuasion.

The chapters on the selling process go into greater detail on specific persuasion techniques. For now, let's review several factors to develop persuasive communications. These factors relate to several components of the communication model shown in Exhibit 4–1: feedback, empathy, simplicity, listening, attitude, and proof statements.

Feedback Guides Your Presentation

Learn how to generate feedback to determine whether your listener has received your intended message. Feedback does not refer to any type of listening behavior by the buyer but to a recognizable response from the buyer. A shake of the head, a frown, or an effort to say something are all signals to the salesperson. If the salesperson fails to notice or respond to these signals, no feedback can occur, which means faulty or incomplete communication. A salesperson's observation of feedback is like an auto racer's glances at the tachometer. Both aid in ascertaining a receiver's response.

Often, feedback must be sought openly because the prospect does not always give it voluntarily. By interjecting into the presentation questions that require the customer

SELLING TIPS

Don't Complicate Things

How can you simplify the following statements?

1. A mass of concentrated earthly material perennially rotating on its axis will not accumulate an accretion of bryophytic vegetation.

2. Individuals who are perforce constrained to be domiciled in vitreous structures of patent frangibility should on no account employ petrous formations as projectiles.

3. A superabundance of talent skilled in the preparation of gastronomic concoctions will impair the quality of a certain potable solution made by immersing a gallinaceous bird in embullient Adam's ale.

Answers

1. A rolling stone gathers no moss.
2. People who live in glass houses shouldn't throw stones.
3. Too many cooks spoil the broth.

to give a particular response, you can stimulate feedback. Questioning, sometimes called probing, allows the salesperson to determine the buyer's attitude toward the sales presentation. **Probing** refers to gathering information and uncovering customer needs using one or more questions.

MCI Communications included this type of feedback in their sales training sessions. MCI sales trainers suggested to their salespeople that they use questions in their presentations. Some of the questions were:

- Do you think you are paying too much for telecommunications equipment?
- Are you happy with the service now being provided?
- Are you happy with the equipment your present supplier has installed for your company?

These questions were intended to draw negative responses from the customers concerning the relationship with their present supplier. They provided the MCI salespeople with a method of determining how the prospect felt about the competitor. These responses allow the salesperson to discuss the specific features, advantages, and benefits of MCI products relative to the products presently used by the prospect. Future chapters will fully discuss questioning techniques to use during your presentation.

Remember the Trial Close

In planning your presentation, it is important to predetermine when and what feedback-producing questions to ask. Remember to use the trial close as part of your SELL Sequence, as discussed in Chapter 3. The use of a question after discussing a benefit is a great method of obtaining feedback. Another way of creating positive feedback is through empathy.

Empathy Puts You in Your Customer's Shoes

Empathy is the ability to identify and understand the other person's feelings, ideas, and situation. As a salesperson, you need to be interested in what the buyer is saying—not just in giving a sales presentation. Many of the barriers to communication mentioned earlier can be overcome when you place yourself in the buyer's shoes. Empathy is saying to a prospect, "I'm here to help you," or asking, "Tell me your problems and needs so I can help *you*." Empathy is also evidenced by a salesperson's display of sincerity and interest in the buyer's situation.

This may mean acknowledging at times that a prospect may not need your product. Take, for example, the Scott Paper Company salesperson who finds that the customer still has 90 percent of the paper towels purchased three months ago. There is no reason to sell this customer more paper towels. It is time to help the customer sell the paper towels now on hand by suggesting displays, price reductions, and formats for newspaper advertisements. It is always wise to adopt your customer's point of view to meet the customer's needs best.

Keep It Simple

The new salesperson was sitting in a customer's office waiting for the buyer. His boss was with him. As they heard the buyer come into the office, the sales manager said, "Remember, a **KISS** for him." No, he was not saying to give the buyer a kiss, but to use the old selling philosophy of **k**eep **i**t **s**imple, **s**alesperson.

The story is told of a little old lady who went into a hardware store. The clerk greeted her and offered her some help. She replied that she was looking for a heater. So the clerk said, "Gee, are you lucky! We have a big sale on these heaters, and a tremendous selection. Let me show you." So after maybe 30 or 45 minutes of discussing duothermic controls, heat induction, and all the factors involved with how a heater operates, including the features and advantages of each of the 12 models, he turned to the little old lady and said, "Now, do you have any questions?" To which she replied, "Yes, just one, Sonny. Which one of these things will keep a little old lady warm?"

An overly complex, technical presentation should be avoided when it is unnecessary. Use words and materials that are understood easily by the buyer. The skilled salesperson can make a prospect feel comfortable with a new product or complex technology through the subtle use of nontechnical information and a respectful attitude.

Creating Mutual Trust Develops Friendship

Salespeople who develop a mutual, trusting relationship with their customers cannot help being successful. This type of relationship eventually results in high source credibility and even friendship.

The buyer realized that in the past she was sold products that performed to expectations; the products were worth their price; and the salesperson did everything promised. Building mutual trust is important to effective long-run communication.

Listening Clues You In

Hearing refers to being able to detect sounds. **Listening** is deriving meaning from sounds that are heard. Not everything you hear is worth your undivided attention; for the salesperson, however, listening is a communication skill critical to success.

Salespeople often believe that their job is to talk rather than to listen. If they both talk *and* listen, their persuasive powers increase. Since people can listen (about 400 words per minute) roughly twice as fast as the average rate of speech, it is understandable that a person's mind may wander while listening to a salesperson's presentation or that the salesperson may tune out a prospect. To keep the buyer listening, ask questions, get the buyer involved in the conversation, and show visual aids. Once you ask a question, carefully listen to what is said.

Listen to Words, Feelings, and Thoughts

This may seem obvious, but when someone speaks to you, the person is expressing thoughts and feelings. Despite the logic of this statement, most of us listen only to the words. Spoken language is an inexact form of communication, but it is the best we have in this stage of human evolution. If you come back 2,000 years from now, perhaps you will communicate with your prospects via mental telepathy. For now, given the limitations of words, look beyond them to hear the entire story.

MAKING THE SALE

Do You Have Any of These Listening Habits?

No one is perfect. We all have some bad listening habits that we get away with when we talk to our family and friends. In a business context, however, leave these bad habits behind and practice active listening. To gain insight into your listening habits, read through this list of common irritating listening habits and be honest with yourself; notice what you are guilty of and use this awareness to begin eliminating them:

1. You do all the talking.
2. You interrupt when people talk.
3. You never look at the person talking or indicate that you are listening.
4. You start to argue before the other person has a chance to finish.
5. Everything that is said reminds you of an experience you've had, and you feel obligated to digress with a story.
6. You finish sentences for people if they pause too long.
7. You wait impatiently for people to finish so that you can interject something.
8. You work too hard at maintaining eye contact and make people uncomfortable.
9. You look as if you are appraising the person talking to you, looking him or her up and down as if considering the person for a modeling job.
10. You overdo the feedback you give—too many nods of your head and "uh-huh's."

Listen *behind* the words for the emotional content of the message. This is conveyed in the nuances of voice and body language. Some people, such as sensors (discussed in Chapter 3), give you little emotional information. That's all right, because you deal with them in a factual, business-only style. Feelers, on the other hand, reveal their emotions, and in turn, they appreciate your acknowledgement of their feelings. It is appropriate to discuss their feelings and treat them more as friends than as strict business associates.

You can hear the emotions behind the words in several ways. First, look for changes in eye contact. After establishing a comfortable and natural level of eye contact, any sudden deviations from the norm tip you off to emotional content in the message. People tend to look away from you when they talk about something embarrassing. When this happens, make a quick mental note of what it pertained to and treat that subject delicately. Also, give a person the courtesy of looking away momentarily yourself—as if you are saying, "I respect your privacy."

Listen *between* the words for what is not said. Some people reveal more in what they don't say. Part of this is due to the emotional content of the message and part is due to the information they give you. A story illustrates this point.

A salesperson was talking to the president of a large paper mill. "I simply asked him what kind of training he had for his salespeople. He went into a long discourse on all the seminars, training films, videotapes, and cassettes they had from the parent company, suppliers, industry associations, and in-house programs. I sat, listened, and took notes. At the end of his speech I said to him, 'I noticed you didn't mention anything about time management for salespeople.' He raised his voice and emphatically said, 'You know, just this morning I was talking to a guy and I told him we have to have some time-management training for our salespeople'."

The lesson here is to get the prospect talking and listen actively—concentrate. Take notes, look for clues to emotions, and don't interrupt or start thinking about your next question. See Exhibit 4–7.

EXHIBIT 4–7

Active listening is important to your sales success. Concentrate, take notes, look for clues, don't interrupt!

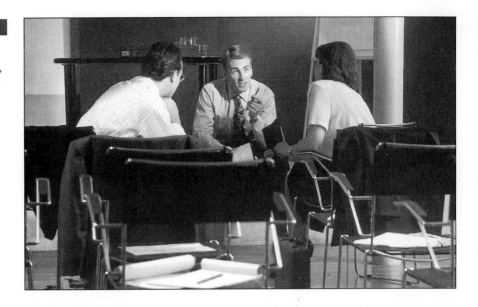

The Three Levels of Listening

Whenever people listen, they are at one of three basic levels of listening. These levels require various degrees of concentration by the listener. As you move from the first to the third level, the potential for understanding and clear communication increases.

Marginal Listening. Marginal listening, the first and lowest level, involves the least concentration, and typically listeners are easily distracted by their thoughts. During periods of marginal listening, a listener exhibits blank stares, nervous mannerisms, and gestures that annoy the prospect and cause communication barriers. The salesperson hears the message but it doesn't sink in. There is enormous room for misunderstanding when a salesperson is not concentrating on what is said. Moreover, the prospect cannot help but feel the lack of attention, which may be insulting and diminishes trust. It may be funny when family members continually patronize each other with, "Yes, dear," regardless of what is said. In real life, however, it is not funny:

> **Prospect:** What I need, really, is a way to reduce the time lost due to equipment breakdowns.

> **Salesperson:** Yeah, OK. Let's see, uh, the third feature of our product is the convenient sizes you can get.

Salespeople of all experience levels are guilty of marginal listening. Beginners who lack confidence and experience may concentrate so intensely on what they are supposed to say next that they stop listening. Old pros, by contrast, have heard it all before. They have their presentations memorized and want the prospect to hurry and finish talking so the important business can continue. These traditional salespeople forget that the truly important information lies in what the prospect says.

Evaluative Listening. Evaluative listening, the second level of listening, requires more concentration and attention to the speaker's words. At this level, the listener actively tries to hear what the prospect says but isn't making an effort to understand the

Listening Guidelines

Here are several things to do to improve your listening skills:

- Stop talking.
- Show the prospect you want to listen.
- Watch for nonverbal messages and project positive signals.

- Recognize feelings and emotions.
- Ask questions to clarify meaning.
- If appropriate, restate the prospect's position for clarification.
- Listen to the full story.

intent. Instead of accepting and trying to understand a prospect's message, the evaluative listener categorizes the statement and concentrates on preparing a response.

The evaluative listening phenomenon is a result of the tremendous speed at which a human can listen and think. It is no surprise that evaluative listening is the level of listening used most of the time. Unfortunately, it is a difficult habit to break, but it can be done with practice.

Prospect: What I need, really, is a way to reduce the time lost due to equipment breakdown.

Salesperson: (defensively) We have tested our machines in the field, and they don't break down often.

In this example, the salesperson reacted to one aspect of the prospect's statement. Had the salesperson withheld judgment until the end of the statement, he could have responded more objectively and informatively.

In evaluative listening, it is easy to be distracted by emotion-laden words. At that point, you aren't listening to the prospect. Instead, you are obsessed with the offensive word and wondering what to do about it. This is a waste of time for both you and the prospect. It increases personal and relationship tension and throws your communication off course. To avoid the problems of marginal and evaluative listening, practice active listening.

Active Listening. Active listening is the third and most effective level of listening. The active listener refrains from evaluating the message and tries to see the other person's point of view. Attention is not only on the words spoken but also on the thoughts, feelings, and meaning conveyed. Listening in this way means the listener puts herself into someone else's shoes. It requires the listener to give the other person verbal and nonverbal feedback.

Prospect: What I need is a way to reduce the time lost due to equipment breakdowns.

Salesperson: Could you tell me what kind of breakdowns you have experienced?

In this example, the salesperson spoke directly to the prospect's concerns—not around them. Her desire to make a presentation was deferred so she could accomplish a more important task—effectively communicate with the prospect.

Active listening is a skill that takes practice in the beginning, but after a while, it becomes second nature. The logic behind active listening is based on courtesy and concentration.

Active listening is sometimes difficult to do, especially for the novice salesperson. The novice may continue to talk about a particular situation or problem. However, the salesperson must *learn to listen*. It is a key to sales success. People like and appreciate a listener as this poem says so well:

> His thoughts were slow,
> His words were few,
> And never made to glisten,
> But he was a joy
> Wherever he went.
> You should have heard him listen.
>
> —*Author Unknown*

Technology Helps to Remember

A distinction must be drawn between listening and remembering. Listening is the process of receiving the message the way the speaker intended to send it. **Memory** is recall over time. Listening and time have profound effects on memory. An untrained listener is likely to understand and retain only about 50 percent of a conversation. After 48 hours, the retention rate drops to 25 percent. Think of the implications. Memory of a conversation that occurred more than two days ago may be incomplete and inaccurate.

After you leave the prospect's office, take a few minutes to write down, or log in your computer, what occurred during the sales call (see Exhibit 4–8). This is valuable information for doing what you promised and planning the next sales call. Chapter 5 will discuss much more about the use of technology in communicating with customers.

EXHIBIT 4–8

Computers help you remember.

Computers are great tools for recording what was discussed in the sales call.

ETHICAL DILEMMA

It's Party Time!

You are part of a sales district containing six sales-people. At least once a month, everyone gets together for dinner and sometimes entertainment. This is an ag-gressive group, very spirited in their discussion of any topic.

Tonight you sit listening to one of the salespeople maliciously and wrongfully attack your company and your boss. You can tell that this person is serious and has strong feelings about what was being said.

What would you do?

Your Attitude Makes the Difference

While a variety of methods and techniques exist in selling, truly effective sales per-suasion is based on the salesperson's attitude toward the sales job and customers. The most important element of this attitude is the salesperson's degree of interest and en-thusiasm in helping people to fulfill their needs. This is the foundation for building effective communication techniques. **Enthusiasm** is a condition in which an indi-vidual is filled with excitement toward something. Excitement does not mean an ag-gressive attitude, but rather a positive view toward solving the customers' problems.

Sell yourself *on* yourself and *on* being a salesperson. The highly successful sales-person goes all out to help customers. Strive to make the buyer feel important. Show the buyer that you are there solely as a problem-solver. Do this by developing meth-ods of expressing true interest such as asking questions instead of talking at the buyer. This attitude will benefit you by allowing you to look at the sales situation from the buyer's viewpoint (empathy).

Salespeople who have established **credibility** with their customers through con-tinued empathy, willingness to listen to specific needs, and continual enthusiasm to-ward their work and customers' business can make claims that their customers treat as gospel in some cases. Enthusiasm combined with proof statements greatly im-prove a salesperson's persuasive ability.

Proof Statements Make You Believable

Salespeople have known for years that using highly credible sources can improve the persuasiveness of the sales presentation message. **Proof statements** are statements that substantiate claims made by the salesperson. Pharmaceutical companies often quote research studies done by outstanding physicians at prestigious medical schools to validate claims of product benefits. These proof statements add high credibility to a sales message.

Salespeople sometimes quote acknowledged experts in a field on the use of prod-ucts. By demonstrating that other customers or respected individuals use the prod-ucts, they encourage customer belief in the validity of information presented in a sales presentation. People place greater confidence in a trustworthy, objective source (particularly one not associated with the salesperson's firm) and are therefore more receptive to what is said by the salesperson.

SUMMARY OF MAJOR SELLING ISSUES

Communication is defined as transmission of verbal and nonverbal information and understanding between salesperson and prospect. Modes of communication com-monly used in a sales presentation are words, gestures, visual aids, and nonverbal communication.

A model of the communication process is composed of a sender (encoder) who transmits a specific message via some media to a receiver (decoder) who responds to that message. The effectiveness of this communication process can be hampered by noise that distorts the message as it travels to the receiver. A sender (encoder) can judge the effectiveness of a message and media choice by monitoring the feedback from the receiver.

Barriers, which hinder or prevent constructive communication during a sales presentation, may develop or already exist. These barriers may relate to the perceptional differences between the sender and receiver, cultural differences, outside distractions, or how sales information is conveyed. Regardless of their source, these barriers must be recognized and either overcome or eliminated if communication is to succeed.

Nonverbal communication has emerged as a critical component of the overall communication process within the past 10 or 15 years. Recognition of nonverbal communication is essential for sales success in today's business environment. Awareness of the prospect's territorial space, a firm and confident handshake, and accurate interpretation of body language are of tremendous aid to a salesperson's success.

Overall persuasive power is enhanced through development of several key characteristics. The salesperson who creates a relationship based on mutual trust with a customer by displaying true empathy (desire to understand the customer's situation and environment), a willing ear (more listening, less talking), and a positive attitude of enthusiastic pursuit of lasting solutions for the customer's needs and problems increases the likelihood of making the sale.

MEETING A SALES CHALLENGE

In this imaginary sales call, buyer and seller communicated both verbal and nonverbal messages. Here, nonverbal messages conveyed both parties' attitudes better than the actual verbal exchange. The salesperson's negative reactions served to increase Amos Skaggs's hostile attitude. He could sense that the salesperson did not understand his problem and was there only to sell him something—not to solve his problem. This impression caused a rapid breakdown in communication. The end result, as in this case, is usually **NO SALE.**

The salesperson may have reacted correctly to Skaggs. Since he is in a bad mood, coming back another day may be best. If the salesperson cannot come another day, then the salesperson needs to stop the planned presentation and let the buyer know he understands. He should show that he is there to help. But most of all, he must project a positive attitude and not be frightened by Skaggs.

KEY TERMS FOR SELLING

communication 105	territorial space 107	persuasion 117
source 106	intimate space 108	probing 118
encoding process 106	personal space 108	empathy 118
message 106	social space 108	KISS 119
medium 106	public space 108	hearing 119
decoding process 106	space threats 108	listening 119
receiver 107	space invasion 108	memory 123
feedback 107	acceptance signals 112	enthusiasm 124
noise 107	caution signals 112	credibility 124
nonverbal	disagreement	proof statements 124
communication 107	signals 113	

SALES APPLICATION QUESTIONS

1. Draw the salesperson–buyer communication process. Describe each step in the process. Why is a two-way communication important in this process?

2. This chapter outlined several forms of nonverbal communication.
   a. Give an example of a salesperson making a good first impression through the proper use of an introductory handshake.
   b. What signals should the salesperson look for from a buyer's body language? Give several examples of these signals.

3. A salesperson may spend hours developing a sales presentation and yet the buyer does not buy. One reason for losing a sale is that the salesperson and the buyer do not communicate. What barriers to communication may be present between seller and buyer during a sales presentation?

4. When two people are talking, they want the listener to understand what they are saying. They both want to be effective communicators. The same is true of the salesperson who wants the buyer to listen to a sales presentation. What can the salesperson do to help ensure that the buyer is listening?

5. You arrive at the industrial purchasing agent's office on time. This is your first meeting. After you have waited five minutes, the agent's secretary says, "She will see you." After the initial greeting, she asks you to sit down. For each of these three situations determine:
   a. What nonverbal signals is she communicating?
   b. How would you respond nonverbally?
   c. What would you say to her?
      (1) She sits down behind her desk. She sits up straight in her chair. She clasps her hands together and with little expression on her face says, "What can I do for you?"
      (2) She sits down behind her desk. She moves slightly backwards in her chair, crosses her arms, and while looking around the room says, "What can I do for you?"
      (3) She sits down behind her desk. She moves slightly forward in her chair, seems hurried, yet she is relaxed toward your presence. Her arms are uncrossed. She looks you squarely in the eye, and with a pleasant look on her face says, "What can I do for you?"

6. In each of the following selling situations determine:
   a. What nonverbal signals is the buyer communicating?
   b. How would you respond nonverbally?
   c. What would you say?
      (1) The buyer seems happy to see you. Because you have been calling on him for several years, the two of you have become business friends. In the middle of your presentation, you notice the buyer slowly lean back in his chair. As you continue to talk, a puzzled look comes over his face.
      (2) As you begin the main part of your presentation, the buyer reaches for the telephone and says, "Keep going; I need to tell my secretary something."
      (3) As a salesperson with only six months' experience, you are somewhat nervous about calling on an important buyer who has been a purchasing agent for almost 20 years. Three minutes after you have begun your presentation, he rapidly raises his arms straight up into the air and slowly clasps his hands behind his head. He leans so far back in his chair that you think he is going to fall backward on the floor. At the same time, he crosses his legs away from you and slowly closes his eyes. You keep on

talking. Slowly the buyer opens his eyes, uncrosses his legs, and sits up in his chair. He leans forward, placing his elbows on the desk top, propping his head up with his hands. He seems relaxed as he says, "Let me see what you have here." He reaches his hand out for you to give him the presentation materials you have developed.

(4) At the end of your presentation, the buyer leans forward, his arms open, and he smiles as he says, "You really don't expect me to buy that piece of junk, do you?"

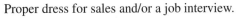

SALES WORLD WIDE WEB EXERCISES

Make a Sale and Get a Job!

The ability to effectively communicate both verbally and nonverbally is crucial to sales success. It is also very important in the process of getting a job.

Look at the Sales World Wide Web exercise in Chapter 1. Examine these URLs to find out helpful information on such topics as:

Proper dress for sales and/or a job interview.

Nonverbal communication techniques in sales and/or a job interview.

Job interview procedures and techniques.

Write a brief report to your boss on your finding. Compare and contrast findings for interviewing for a job versus being "dressed for success" in a sales job.

FURTHER EXPLORING THE SALES WORLD

Using questions is an effective method for a salesperson to obtain feedback from a buyer. This statement applies to conversation between two people. For the next two days, try using questions in your conversations with other people and report on your results. These questions should reflect an interest in the person you are conversing with and the topic being discussed. Use of the words "*you*" and "*your*" should increase feedback and create an atmosphere of trust.

For example, questions such as "What do you mean?" "What do you think?" "How does that sound?" can be used in your conversation to have other people participate and to help determine how they feel toward the topic of conversation.

Asking people's opinions also can result in a positive response, since they may feel flattered that you care about their opinion. Questions can help you guide the direction of topics discussed in conversation. Try to determine people's reactions to your questions and report your findings in class.

SELLING EXPERIENTIAL EXERCISE

Instructions: Read the following questions and write *yes* or *no* for each statement on a separate sheet of paper. Mark each answer as truthfully as you can in light of your behavior in the last few meetings or gatherings you attended.

Listening Self-Inventory

	Yes	No
1. I frequently attempt to listen to several conversations at the same time.	_____	_____
2. I like people to give me only the facts and then let me make my own interpretation.	_____	_____
3. I sometimes pretend to pay attention to people.	_____	_____

4. I consider myself a good judge of nonverbal communications.   _____ _____

5. I usually know what another person is going to say before he or she says it.   _____ _____

6. I usually end conversations that don't interest me by diverting my attention from the speaker.   _____ _____

7. I frequently nod, frown, or whatever to let the speaker know how I feel about what he or she is saying.   _____ _____

8. I usually respond immediately when someone has finished talking.   _____ _____

9. I evaluate what is being said while it is being said.   _____ _____

10. I usually formulate a response while the other person is still talking.   _____ _____

11. The speaker's delivery style frequently keeps me from listening to content.   _____ _____

12. I usually ask people's points of view.   _____ _____

13. I make a concerted effort to understand other people's points of view.   _____ _____

14. I frequently hear what I expect to hear rather than what is said.   _____ _____

15. Most people believe that I have understood their points of view when we disagree.   _____ _____

According to communication theory, the correct answers are as follows: No for questions 1, 2, 3, 5, 6, 7, 8, 9, 10, 11, 14; and Yes for questions 4, 12, 13, 15. If you missed only one or two questions, you strongly approve of your own listening habits, and you are on the right track to becoming an effective listener in your role as a salesperson. If you missed three or four questions, you have uncovered some doubts about your listening effectiveness, and your knowledge of how to listen has some gaps. If you missed five or more questions, you probably are not satisfied with the way you listen, and your friends and co-workers may not feel you are a good listener either. Work on improving your active listening skills.[7]

| CASE 4–1 |
| Skaggs Manufacturing |

John Andrews arrived promptly for his 10 A.M. meeting with Martha Gillespie, the buyer for Skaggs Manufacturing. At 10:15, when she hadn't arrived, John asked her secretary if she was out of the office for the morning. The secretary smiled and said, "She'll probably be a few minutes late." John resented this delay and was convinced that Martha had forgotten the appointment.

Finally, at 10:20, Martha entered her office, walked over to John, said hello, and promptly excused herself to talk to the secretary about a tennis game scheduled for that afternoon. Ten minutes later, Martha led John into her office. At the same time, a competing salesperson entered the office for a 10:30 appointment. With the door open, Martha asked John, "What's new today?" As John began to talk, Martha began reading letters on her desk and signing them. Shortly after that, the telephone began to ring, whereupon Martha talked to her husband for 10 minutes.

As she hung up, Martha looked at John and suddenly realized his frustration. She promptly buzzed her secretary and said, "Hold all calls." She got up and shut the door. John again began his presentation when Martha leaned backward in her chair, pulled her golf shoes out of a desk drawer, and began to brush them.

About that time, the secretary entered the office and said, "Martha, your 10:30 appointment is about to leave. What should I tell him" "Tell him to wait; I need to see him." Then she said, "John, I wish we had more time. Look, I think I have enough of your product to last until your next visit. I'll see you then. Thanks for coming by."

John quickly rose to his feet, did not shake hands, said "OK," and left.

Questions

1. What nonverbal cues did the salesperson, John Andrews, experience when contacting Martha Gillespie?
2. If you were John Andrews, how would you have handled the situation?

CASE 4–2

Alabama Office Supply

Judy Allison sells cellular telephones for Alabama Office Supply in Birmingham. Today she is calling on Bill Taylor, purchasing agent for a large manufacturing firm. Two weeks earlier, she had made her first sales call and had left a demonstrator for the company executives to try out. The previous evening, Bill had called Judy and asked her to come in so he could give her an order. After their initial hellos, the conversation continued:

Buyer: Judy, thanks for coming by today. Our executives really like your equipment. Here is an order for four phones. When can you deliver them?

Salesperson: Is tomorrow too soon?

Buyer: That is perfect. Leave them with Joyce, my secretary. Joyce [*Bill says over the intercom*], Judy will deliver the phones tomorrow. Joyce, I want you to go ahead and take them to Sally, Anne, and Sherri. Women sure understand the use of modern equipment.

Salesperson: Bill, thanks for your help.

Buyer: Forget it Judy, I wish I could have helped more. Your cellular phones can reduce the "telephone tag" we play with each other and customers. Customers are leaving us because they can't reach our salespeople when they are out on the road contacting customers.

Salesperson: You're right; many of my customers are going to them for that very reason.

Buyer: I know, but some executives still feel they don't want them. They don't want their phone to ring when they're in with a customer. Plus, the cancer scare has them worried. I wish the men in our company felt the same way the women do about using these things.

Question

Analyze and describe the conversation between Judy Allison and Bill Taylor. What should Judy do now?

5

Sales Knowledge: Customers, Products, Technologies

LEARNING OBJECTIVES

Successful salespeople are knowledgeable individuals. Many salespeople are experts in their field. After studying this chapter, you should be able to:

- Explain why it is so important to be knowledgeable.

- Discuss the major body of knowledge needed for increased sales success.

- Illustrate how to use this knowledge during the sales presentation.

- Explain the main technologies used by salespeople.

You are proud of the products you sell and tell everyone they are the Cadillac of the industry, the best on the market, light years ahead of the competition. Of course you have only worked for the company two weeks. But the sales training course you took last week clearly convinced you that your products are much better than any others on the market. During one presentation on a new detergent for the washing machine, you concentrated on discussing the quality of the product: how well it cleans; its environmental safety factor; how much users like its pleasant scent on their clothes. The grocery store buyer said, "I could care less about the quality of your products."

Why did the buyer respond in a negative way to you? What is the buyer interested in?[1]

Salespeople need to know many things. Features, advantages, and benefits are important to discuss, but which FABs are of interest to the buyer? The above situation is a sales challenge faced by all salespeople. The salesperson was apparently talking about the wrong things. What would be of interest to a retailer, wholesaler, manufacturer, or consumer? Chances are they are interested in similar, but also different, FABs. This chapter examines the basic body of knowledge essential to the success of all salespeople.

SOURCES OF SALES KNOWLEDGE

Knowledge for selling is obtained in two ways: First, most companies provide some formal sales training. This information is taught through preliminary training programs and sales meetings. Second, the salesperson learns by being on the job. Experience is the best teacher for the beginning salesperson.

Sales training is the effort put forth by an employer to provide the opportunity for the salesperson to receive job-related culture, skills, knowledge, and attitudes that result in improved performance in the selling environment.

Successful companies thoroughly train new salespeople and maintain ongoing training programs for their experienced sales personnel. Companies are interested in training primarily to increase sales volume, salesperson productivity, and profitability.

Like many professional careers, selling is a skill that is truly developed only through *experience.* Sales knowledge obtained through education, reading, formalized sales training, and word-of-mouth is helpful in enhancing overall sales ability, but actual experience is the critical source of sales knowledge. Some sales managers hire only experienced people to fill entry-level selling slots. Indeed, some corporations do not allow people to fill marketing staff positions unless they have had field sales experience with the company or a major competitor.

Sales experience improves a salesperson's abilities by showing how buyers perceive a product or product line; revealing unrecognized or undervalued product benefits or shortcomings; voicing a multitude of unanticipated protests and objections; showing a great number of prospect moods and attitudes over a short period; and generally providing a challenge that makes selling a skill that is never mastered, only improved.

No author or sales trainer can simulate the variety of situations that a salesperson confronts over the span of a career. Authors and trainers can provide only general guidelines as a framework for action. Actual selling experience alone gives a person direct feedback on how to function in a specific selling situation. The sales knowledge gained through periodic sales training and actual experience benefits the salesperson, the firm, and its customers.

KNOWLEDGE BUILDS RELATIONSHIPS	Salespeople today must be knowledgeable to be effective in their jobs. Three important reasons for the salesperson to have selling knowledge are (1) to increase the salesperson's self-confidence, (2) to build the buyer's confidence in the salesperson, and (3) to build relationships. These reasons are, for the salesperson, the major need for acquiring sales knowledge.

Knowledge Increases Confidence in Salespeople . . .

Salespeople who call on, for example, computer systems engineers, university professors, or aerospace experts may be at a disadvantage. In many cases, they have less education and experience than prospects in their fields of expertise.

Imagine making a sales call on Dr. Michael DeBakey, the distinguished heart surgeon. Can you educate him in the use of your company's synthetic heart valves? Not really, but you can offer help in supplying product information from your firm's medical department. This personal service, your product knowledge, and his specific needs are what will make the sale. Knowledge about your company, its market, and your buyer enables you to acquire confidence in yourself, which results in increased sales.

. . . and in Buyers

Furthermore, prospects and customers want to do business with salespeople who know their business and the products they sell. When a prospect has confidence in the salesperson's expertise, a sales presentation becomes more acceptable and believable to the prospect.

Strive to be the expert on all aspects of your product. Knowledge of your product and its uses also allows you to confidently answer questions and field objections raised by prospects. You can explain better how a product suits a customer's needs. But product knowledge alone may not be enough to convince every buyer.

Relationships Increase Sales

Often within minutes buyers can tell if salespersons know what they are talking about. You have experienced it yourself. You ask questions and quickly form an impression of a salesperson. A relationship begins to build; knowledge builds relationships and means sales and money for the seller. Typically, the more knowledge you have, the higher your sales.

KNOW YOUR CUSTOMERS	How can you match up your product's benefits with a buyer's needs if you don't know your customers? If you are selling to someone you've never seen before—such as in a retail store—you have to ask about the buyer's needs. Business-to-business selling also requires asking numerous questions, sometimes spending weeks with a customer. More on this important topic later in your book.

KNOW YOUR COMPANY	Knowledge of your firm usually aids you in projecting an expert image to the prospect. Company knowledge includes information about the history, policies, procedures, distribution systems, promotional activities, pricing practices, and technology that have guided the firm to its present status.

The type and extent of company knowledge to be used depends on the company, its product lines, and the industry. (See Exhibit 5–1.) In general, consumer-goods salespeople require little information about the technical nature of their products; however, selling high-technology products (computers, rocket-engine components,

SELLING GLOBALLY

A Typical Sales Day in China: What to Expect

- The workday begins around 8:15 or 8:30 A.M. Men wear suits and ties; women wear appropriate business attire.

- Travel is by taxi to most appointments. Many use bicycles for personal transportation but chaotic traffic makes this hazardous.

- Mostly you call on men; women hold about 10 percent of the senior advisory or management positions.

- Use English on most business calls (it's the international business language) although Mandarin or Cantonese (in the southern part of China) are required on some. It's not necessary for foreigners to know the many Chinese regional dialects.

- When taking taxis, get someone to write out directions to your destination in Chinese. Negotiate the fare before you leave. If your prospect's office is off the beaten path, or if your call is late in the day, pay extra to have the taxi wait for you. On-call taxis take hours to arrive and you may have a long hike back to a main street to flag one down.

- Expect to conduct business at your client's office or at your office and after hours on the golf course, over cocktails, or at dinner. If you must conduct business at your office, send a car to call for your prospect or customer. However, if your customers prefer meeting in your office, sending a car is not necessary.

- Appearances can be deceiving; senior managers may show up at a trade show wearing overalls. One-on-one sales calls are not the norm. Expect to meet with two or more people. The Chinese are genuinely curious about your company and product line. They all want to learn more.

- Get right down to business. While meetings can begin with personal discussions about your experiences in Asia, the Chinese are not prone to idle chitchat.

- Meals are important and can include 12 courses. If you plan to meet through lunch, you will likely send out for (surprise!) Chinese. Evening meals are divided equally between Asian and Continental cuisine.

- Sales calls usually last from 30 to 45 minutes; depending on the industry, they can last up to several hours. Because of traffic, four calls a day—two in the morning and two in the afternoon—make a great day. Group your calls geographically.

- Companies used to doing business with the West or Japan are fully automated with computers, faxes, albeit much older models than you are used to seeing. Not too many people carry portable phones or pagers but this is changing almost hourly.

- Show your company is serious about staying in China by printing bilingual order forms. Shaking hands and thanking the customer for the order are normal. Bowing is not required unless your customer is Japanese.

- The business of business cards is serious. Take your customer's card in both hands, look at it carefully, remark on something you see. Offer your card first at the beginning of the meeting. If you will be in China for longer than one meeting, print bilingual business cards. If you smoke, offer a cigarette. If the meeting is at your office, offer tea or coffee immediately.

- Business hours end at 6:30 P.M. but days end around 10 or 11 P.M. with dinner and then time at a club. Understand your customer's normal routine. Customers may transport key personnel to and from work in a company bus or other scheduled transportation. Don't get caught at closing with two-thirds of your meeting hurrying out to catch their group ride home.

- Be patient, with yourself and the host country. Study before you go so you won't be caught with egg foo yung on your face.[2]

complex machinery, etc.) to highly knowledgeable industrial buyers requires extensive knowledge.

General Company Information

All salespeople need to know the background and present operating policies of their companies. These policies are your guidelines, and you must understand them to do your job effectively. Information on company growth, policies, procedures, production, and service facilities often is used in sales presentations. Here are four examples:

EXHIBIT 5-1

What would you need to know for selling . . .

. . . clothing to consumers?   . . . shipping containers to a distributor?

Company Growth and Accomplishment

Knowledge of your firm's development since its origin provides you with promotional material and builds your confidence in the company. An IBM office products salesperson might say to a buyer:

> In 1952, IBM placed its first commercial electronic computer on the market. That year, our sales were $342 million. Currently, our sales are projected to be over $80 billion. IBM has reached these high sales figures because our advanced, technological office equipment and information processors are the best available at any price. This IBM "Star Trek I" system I am showing you is the most advanced piece of equipment on the market today. It is five years ahead of any other computer!

Policies and Procedures

To give good service, be able to tell a customer about policies: how an order is processed; how long it takes for orders to be filled; your firm's returned goods policy; how to open a new account; and what to do in the event of a shipping error. When you handle these situations quickly and fairly, your buyer gains confidence in you and the firm.

Production Facilities

Many companies require their new salespeople to tour their production facilities to give them a firsthand look at the company's operations. This is a good opportunity to gain product knowledge. For example, the Bigelow-Sanford Carpet Company salesperson can say, "When I was visiting our production plant, I viewed each step of the carpet-production process. The research and development department allowed us to watch comparison tests between our carpets and competitors' carpets. Our carpets did everything but fly . . . and they are working on that!"

Service Facilities

Many companies, such as Intel, Xerox, and 3M, have both service facilities and service representatives to help customers. Being able to say, "We can have a service representative there the same day you call our service center," strengthens a sales presentation, especially if service is important for the customer (as it is in the office copier and computer industries).

KNOW YOUR PRODUCT

Knowledge about your company's product and your competitors is a major component of sales knowledge. Become an expert on your company's products. Understand how they are produced and their level of quality. This type of product knowledge is important to the buyer. Product knowledge may include such technical details as:

- Performance data.
- Physical size and characteristics.
- How the product operates.
- Specific features, advantages, and benefits of the product.
- How well the product is selling in the marketplace.

Many companies have their new salespeople work in the manufacturing plant (for example, on the assembly line) or in the warehouse (filling orders and receiving stock). This hands-on experience may cost the salesperson a lot of sweat and sore muscles for a couple of weeks or months, but the payoff is a world of product knowledge and help in future selling that could not be earned in any other way. International Paper, for example, has its new salespeople spend several weeks in a production plant. Often, new salespeople in the oil and gas industry roughneck and drive trucks for Exxon and Shell Oil during the first few months on the job. Also, a sales representative for McKesson Chemical spends the first two or three weeks on the job in a warehouse unloading freight cars and flatbed trucks and filling 55-gallon drums with various liquid chemicals.

Much is learned at periodic company sales meetings. At sales meetings, a consumer-goods manufacturer, such as Frito-Lay, may concentrate on developing sales presentations for the products to receive special emphasis during the company sales period. Company advertising programs, price discounts, and promotional allowances for these products are discussed. Although little time is spent on the technical aspects of consumer products, much time is devoted to discussing the marketing mix for these products (product type, promotion, distribution, and price).

Sales managers for firms selling technical products, such as Merck, Alcoa, and Emerson Electric, might spend as much as 75 percent of a sales meeting discussing product information. The remaining time might be allotted to sales techniques.

KNOW YOUR RESELLERS

It is essential to understand the channel of distribution used by your company to move its products to the final consumer. Knowledge of each channel member (also called reseller or middleman) is vital. Wholesalers and retailers often stock thousands of products, and each one may have hundreds of salespeople from a multitude of companies calling on its buyers. Know as much about each channel member as possible. Some important information you will need includes:

- Likes and dislikes of each channel member's customers.
- Product lines and the assortment each one carries.
- When each member sees salespeople.
- Distribution, promotion, and pricing policies.
- What quantity of which product each channel member has purchased in the past.

While most channel members will have similar policies concerning salespeople, keep abreast of the differences.

ADVERTISING AIDS SALESPEOPLE

Personal selling, advertising, publicity, and sales promotion are the main ingredients of a firm's promotional effort. Companies sometimes coordinate these promotional tools in a promotional campaign. A sales force may be asked by the corporate marketing manager to concentrate on selling Product *A* for the months of April and May. Meanwhile, Product *A* is simultaneously promoted on television and in magazines, and direct mail samples or cents-off coupons for Product *A* are sent to consumers.

Keeping abreast of your company's advertising and sales promotion activities is a must. By incorporating this data into your sales presentation, you can provide customers with a world of information that they probably know little about, and that can secure the sale. Exhibit 5–2 illustrates the type of advertising and sales promotion to use when making a sales presentation for a mouthwash called Fresh Mouth. Suppose Fresh Mouth was a new product that just emerged from the test market. As a lead-in to the information in Exhibit 5–2, you might say:

> Ms. Buyer, Fresh Mouth was a proven success in our Eastern test markets. Fresh Mouth had a 9.8 percent market share only nine months after the start of advertising. Laboratory tests proved that the Fresh Mouth formula is superior to the leading competition. Consumer panels significantly preferred Fresh Mouth to leading competing brands. There was a repurchase rate of 50 percent after sampling. The trade (retailers) gave enthusiastic support in the test-market areas.

Next, you would discuss the information contained in Exhibit 5–2.

Types of Advertising Differ

The development and timing of an advertising campaign for a product or service are handled by a firm's advertising department or by an outside advertising agency. The result of this effort is the television commercial, radio spot, print media (newspaper or magazine), or other form of advertisement (billboard, transit placard, etc.). Following development of the ad, the firm must establish and coordinate a plan for tying in sales force efforts with the new ad campaign. There are six basic types of advertising programs that a company can use: national, retail, cooperative, trade, industrial, and direct-mail advertising.

National advertising is advertising designed to reach all users of the product, whether consumers or industrial buyers. These ads are shown across the country. In some cases, national advertisers may restrict their expenditures to the top 100 markets. Top 100 refers to the 100 largest major metropolitan areas where most of the U.S. population is concentrated. Therefore, the advertiser gets more punch per ad

Advertising and sales promotion
information the salesperson tells
the buyer

1. **Massive Sampling and Couponing:**
   - There will be blanketing of the top 300 markets with 4.4-oz. samples plus eighty-cents-off coupons. Your market is included.
   - There will be a 75 percent coverage of homes in the top 100 markets. Your market is included.

2. **Heavy Advertising:**
   - Nighttime network TV.
   - Daytime network TV.
   - Saturation spot TV.
   - Newspapers.
   - The total network and spot advertising will reach 85 percent of all homes in the United States five times each week based on a four-week average. This means that in four weeks, Fresh Mouth will have attained 150 million home impressions—130 million of these impressions will be women.
   - There will be half-page, two-color inserts in local newspapers in 50 markets, including yours. This is more than 20 million in circulation. Scheduled to tie in with saturation sampling is a couponing program.
   - $80 million will be spent on promotion to ensure consumer acceptance.

3. **TV Advertising Theme**—the salesperson would show pictures or drawings of the advertisement:
   - The commercial with POWER to sell!
   - "POWER to kill mouth odor—POWER to kill germs—POWER to give FRESH MOUTH."
   - The commercial shows a young man, about 20 years of age, walking up to a young woman saying, "Hi, Susan!" They kiss and she says, "My, you have a fresh mouth, Bill!" He looks at the camera with a smile and says, "It works!" The announcer closes the commercial by saying, "FRESH MOUTH—it has the POWER!"

4. **Display Materials:**
   - Shelf display tag.
   - Small floor stand for end-of-aisle display—holds 24 12-oz. bottles.
   - Large floor stand—holds 48 12-ounce bottles.

dollar. Giant marketing companies like Procter & Gamble, IBM, Ford, Holiday Inn, and Coca-Cola commonly use national advertising.

Retail advertising is used by a retailer to reach customers within its geographic trading area. Local supermarkets and department stores regularly advertise nationally distributed brand products. National-brand advertising may be totally paid for by the retailer or partially paid by the manufacturer.

Cooperative, or **co-op, advertising** is advertising conducted by the retailer with cost paid for by the manufacturer or shared by the manufacturer and retailer. It is an attractive selling aid for the salesperson to give the buyer an advertising allowance to promote a firm's goods. An advertising agreement between a retailer and a manufacturer often provides for:

- The duration of the advertisement. How long the advertisement will appear.
- The product(s) to be advertised.
- The amount of money paid to the retailer for advertising purposes.
- The type of advertising—radio, television, newspaper, magazine.

■ Proof by the retailer that the product has been advertised as agreed (a copy of the advertisement).

Generally, national and retail advertising are aimed at the final consumers. Trade and industrial advertising are aimed at other members in the channel of distribution and other manufacturers.

Trade advertising is undertaken by the manufacturer and directed toward the wholesaler or retailer. Such advertisements appear in trade magazines serving only the wholesaler or retailer. (The Appendix exhibit 5A–1 is an example of manufacturer advertising to retail pharmacies in the popular trade magazine *American Druggist*.)

Industrial advertising is aimed at individuals and organizations who purchase products for manufacturing other products. General Electric may advertise small electric motors in magazines read by buyers employed by firms such as Whirlpool or Sears.

Direct-mail advertising is mailed directly to the consumer or industrial user; it is an effective method of exposing these users to a product or it reminds that the product is available to meet a specific need. Often, trial samples or coupons accompany direct-mail advertising.

Direct-mail advertising can solicit a response from a current user of a product. For example, the user may be asked to fill out and mail in a questionnaire. In return, the manufacturer sends the user a sample of the product or information about the product.

Why Spend Money on Advertising?

Why would a company spend millions of dollars on advertising? Companies advertise because they hope to:

■ Increase overall sales and sales of a specific product.

■ Give salespeople additional selling information for sales presentations.

■ Develop leads for salespeople through mail-ins, ad response, and so on.

■ Increase cooperation from channel members through co-op advertising and promotional campaigns.

■ Educate the customer about the company's products.

■ Inform prospects that a product is on the market and where to buy it.

■ Reduce cognitive dissonance over the purchase.

■ Create sales or presell customers between a salesperson's calls.

Advertising serves various purposes depending on the nature of a product or industry. The majority of top advertisers are well-known manufacturers of consumer goods. This indicates that advertising dollars are lavished on consumer items. However, as industrial advertising has more specified channels of communication (such as trade periodicals and trade shows) and a smaller number of potential customers, advertising costs tend to be lower. In either case, carefully employed advertising benefits both a firm and its sales force. Sales promotion is another potential aid to a company and its sales force.

SALES PROMOTION GENERATES SALES

Sales promotion involves activities or materials other than personal selling, advertising, and publicity used to create sales for goods or services. Sales promotion can be divided into consumer and trade sales promotion. **Consumer sales promotion** includes free samples, coupons, contests, and demonstrations to consumers. **Trade sales promotion** encourages resellers to purchase and aggressively sell a manufacturer's products by offering incentives like sales contests, displays, special purchase prices, and free merchandise (for example, buy 10 cases of a product and get 1 case free).

The company's promotional efforts can be a useful sales tool for an enterprising salesperson. Sales promotion offers may prove to the retailer or wholesaler that the selling firm will assist actively in creating consumer demand. This, in turn, improves the salesperson's probability of making the sale. Next, we discuss some popular sales promotion items: point-of-purchase displays, shelf positioning, and consumer and dealer premiums such as contests and sweepstakes.

Point-of-Purchase Displays: Get Them out There

Point-of-purchase (POP) displays allow a product to be seen easily and purchased. A product POP display may include photographs, banners, drawings, coupons, a giant-sized product carton, aisle dumps, counter displays, or floor stands. POP displays greatly increase product sales. It is up to the salesperson to obtain the retailer's cooperation to allow the POP display in the store. People are attracted to displays. They catch the customer's attention and make products easy to purchase, which results in increased product sales.

In-store product demonstrations, sampling programs, and cross-merchandising are also popular. My Albertson's grocery frequently has samples of food and drink. They particularly like to cross-merchandise, such as placing cookies in the dairy section. Employees at Neiman Marcus, Foley's, and Dillard's department stores offer to spray men and women with fragrances as they shop. Each of these methods is effective to sell products.

Shelf Positioning Is Important to Your Success

Another important sales stimulator is the shelf positioning of products. **Shelf positioning** refers to the physical placement of the product within the retailer's store. **Shelf facings** are the number of individual products placed beside each other on the shelf. Determine where a store's customers can easily find and examine your company's products and place products in that space or position with as many shelf facings as the store allows. See Exhibit 5–3.

The major obstacle faced when attempting to obtain shelf space for products is limited space. A retail store has a fixed amount of display space and thousands of products to stock. You compete for shelf space with other salespeople and with the retailer's brands.

EXHIBIT 5–3

Sales reps know that good shelf positioning and shelf facings boost sales.

It is often up to the salesperson to sell the store manager on purchasing different sizes of a particular product. Also, the salesperson may want a product displayed at several locations in the store. A Johnson & Johnson salesperson may want their baby powder and baby shampoo displayed with baby products and adult toiletries.

Premiums

The premium has come a long way from being just a trinket in a Cracker Jack box. Today, it is a major marketing tool. American businesses spend billions of dollars on consumer and trade premiums and incentives. Premiums create sales.

A **premium** is an article of merchandise offered as an incentive to the user to take some action. The premium may act as an incentive to buy, to sample the product, to come into the retail store, or to stir interest so the user requests further information. Premiums serve a number of purposes: to promote consumer sampling of a new product; to introduce a new product; to encourage point-of-purchase displays; and to boost sales of slow products. Three major categories of premiums are contests and sweepstakes, consumer premiums, and dealer premiums.

WHAT'S IT WORTH? PRICING YOUR PRODUCT

An important part of a comprehensive marketing strategy for a product is establishing its price. **Price** refers to the value or worth of a product that attracts the buyer to exchange money or something of value for the product. A product has some want-satisfying attributes for which the prospect is willing to exchange something of value. The person's wants assign a value to the item offered for sale. For instance, a golfer who wants to purchase a dozen golf balls already has conceived some estimated measure of the product's value. Of course, the sporting goods store may have set a price higher than estimated. This could diminish *want* somewhat, depending on the difference between the two. Should the golfer then find the same brand of golf balls on sale at a discount store, at a price more in line with a preconceived idea of the product's value, the want may be strong enough to stimulate a purchase.

Many companies offer customers various types of discounts from normal prices to entice them to buy. These discounts become an important part of the firm's marketing effort (see Exhibit 5–4). They are usually developed at the corporate level by the firm's marketing managers. Immediately before the sales period when the product's promotion begins, the sales force is informed of special discounts that they may offer to customers. This discount information becomes an important part of the sales presentation. It is important for salespeople to familiarize themselves with the company's price, discount, and credit policies so that they can use them to competitive advantage and enhance their professional image with the buyer.[3]

At the back of this chapter is a further discussion of the various pricing issues salespeople should be able to explain to their buyers. Appendix A, entitled "Sales Arithmetic and Pricing," has information useful to your developing a sales presentation for your class project role-play.

KNOW YOUR COMPETITION, INDUSTRY, AND ECONOMY

What would the retail salesperson shown in Exhibit 5–5 need to know about his competition? He needs to be knowledgeable about his products, his firm's service and credit policies, and the price of the products. He also needs to know what his competition is doing in each of these areas.

Today's successful salespeople understand their *competitors'* products, policies, and practices as well as their own. It is common for a buyer to ask a salesperson,

EXHIBIT 5-4

Examples of prices and discounts salespeople discuss in their sales presentations.

Reseller

| Retail selling price | $20 |

minus

| Merchandise costs | $10 |

equals

| Gross margin | $10 |

minus

Earned discounts and allowances	.70¢
• Cash discount	.20¢
• Quantity discount	.50¢

equals

| Salesperson's price | $9.30 |

End User

| Product cost | $5,000 |

minus

Earned discounts and allowances	$150
• Cash discount	$100
• Quantity discount	$50

equals

| Salesperson's price | $4,850 |

EXHIBIT 5-5

What does this salesperson need to know about his products and competition?

"How does your product compare to the one I'm presently using?" If unable to confidently answer such a question, a salesperson will lose ground in selling. A salesperson needs to be prepared to discuss product features, advantages, and benefits in comparison to other products and confidently show why the salesperson's product will fulfill the buyer's needs better than competitive products.

One method to obtain information on competitors is through advertisements. From a competitor's advertising, Joe Mitchell, a salesperson representing a small business machines firm, developed a chart for comparing the sales points of his machines against the competition. Joe does not do this for fun, nor does he name the competitive equipment on the chart. Instead, he calls them Machine *A,* Machine *B,* and Machine *C.* When he finds a claimed benefit in one of the other machines that his product does not have, he works to find a better benefit to balance it.

"Maybe the chart isn't always useful," Joe says, "but it certainly has prepared me to face a customer. I know just what other machines have—and what they do not have—that my prospect might be interested in. I know the principal sales arguments used in selling these machines and the benefits I must bring up to offset and surpass competition. Many times a prospect will mention an advertisement of another company and ask about some statement or other," Joe says. "Because I've studied those ads and taken the time to find out what's behind the claims, I can give an honest answer and I can demonstrate how my machine has the same feature or quality and then offer additional benefits. Of course, I never run down a competitor's product. I just try to run ahead of it."

The salesperson selling industrial goods and an industrial buyer work for different companies but are both in the same industry. The industrial buyer often seeks information from salespeople on the *industry* itself, and how economic trends might influence the industry *and* both of their companies. Thus, the salesperson should be well-informed on the industry and the economy. The salesperson can find this information in the company records, newspapers, television, radio, *The Wall Street Journal,* industrial and trade periodicals, and magazines such as *Business Week* and *U.S. News & World Report.* The salesperson who is well informed is more successful than the poorly informed salesperson.

PERSONAL COMPUTERS AND SELLING

The growing use of personal computers (PCs) by sales personnel indicates the need to learn about computers and their use. To the nontechnical person—and that includes many of us—the PC may cause an uncomfortable feeling at first. There is often apprehension about being able to use the PC and its software properly. However, computer manufacturers, software suppliers, and company training programs are quickly and effectively training people and providing easy-to-use computer software. For example, DuPont Merck Pharmaceutical has combated computer apprehension head-on by developing training programs that are humorous and easy to use. The interactive software incorporates games, allowing the users to work from their PC and move at their own pace.[4]

Sales personnel find PCs a valuable tool for increasing productivity within the sales force. The 10 most widely used applications of PCs are shown in Exhibit 5–6. Here are several major reasons for salespeople to use a PC:

- More effective management of sales leads and better follow-through on customer contacts. Computerization provides a permanent lead file.

- Improves customer relations due to more effective follow-ups. This leads to greater productivity.

- Improves organization of selling time. PCs help reps monitor and organize everything.

- Provides more efficient account control and better time and territory management. There is a better awareness of each account's status. This provides more time for customer contacts.

EXHIBIT 5-6

Top 10 PC applications

PC applications are focused on the customer. Here are the top 10 applications in order of use:

1. Customer/prospect profile.
2. Lead tracking.
3. Call reports.
4. Sales forecasts.
5. Sales data analysis.

6. Sales presentation.
7. Time/territory management.
8. Order entry.
9. Travel and expense reports.
10. Checking inventory/shipping status.

EXHIBIT 5-7

The PC has numerous applications.

This salesperson uses his PC to analyze customer data while developing his sales presentation.

- There is an increased number and quality of sales calls.
- Faster speed and improved accuracy in finishing and sending reports and orders to the company.
- Helps develop more effective proposals and persuasive presentations (see Exhibit 5–7).

If you have little knowledge about the computer—start learning! Computers are here to stay. In your readings, look for how the computer is or can be used in your industry. Take a beginning computer course at a college or through your local public school's continuing education program. It is never too late to learn.

KNOWLEDGE OF TECHNOLOGY ENHANCES SALES AND CUSTOMER SERVICE

Computers are at the heart of salespeople's ability to provide top-quality customer service by receiving and sending out information.[5] Computers are impacting technology, advancing it at a rapid pace, and affecting people—including salespeople—in all aspects of their lives. Exhibit 5–8 shows how the use of technology to provide quality customer service is rapidly increasing the productivity of salespeople.

A new wave of technology is going to sweep away computers as we know them and provide the ultimate in user-friendly tools that behave as associates. Within the next decade, many salespeople will have electronic secretaries similar to the one in the Making the Sale box, The Computer as a Sales Assistant. This scenario illustrates

EXHIBIT 5-8

Use technology to provide quality customer service and increase sales productivity.

Her laptop allows this salesperson to sell and service customers no matter where her location.

how a computer can help handle the job that sales is all about—building and solidifying relationships.

Power is what stands between today's user and tomorrow's systems—the ability to process vast amounts of data in a very short time. Today's portable computers simply can't do the calculations needed to take dictation or listen to voice commands, understand most handwriting, or even run most multimedia applications smoothly. A few more generations of technology should change all that.

In today's environment, sales force technology is already at work providing detailed timely information resulting in increased levels of productivity. Once, companies used computers as a way of setting themselves apart; now it is a required part of business to remain competitive.

Sales force technology and automation comes in a variety of sizes and applications. With technology doubling every six months, the desktop computer from a couple of years ago has become the notebook of today. But for those who prefer larger screens and keyboards for comfort, manufacturers are now including docking stations in desktop computers. These ports enable downloading files in laptops to full-size, full-function computers after returning to the office.

Technology helps salespeople increase their productivity effectiveness and allows them to gather and access information more efficiently. You can use computer technology to improve communication to the home office, with others on your sales force, and with customers. Salespeople also use technology to create better strategies for targeting and tracking clients. Sales force automation breaks down into three broad areas of functionality covering (1) personal productivity, (2) communications, and (3) order processing and customer service.

Personal Productivity

Many programs can help a salesperson increase **personal productivity** through more efficient data storage and retrieval, better time management, and enhanced presentations. Let's discuss five of the most popular, beginning with contact management programs.

MAKING THE SALE

The Computer as a Sales Assistant

It's 7:30 A.M., and you're getting ready to leave your hotel room. You turn to your computer and say, "System on."

"Good morning," the machine responds. "Are you ready to review your appointment calendar?"

"Sure. First, summarize e-mail traffic. I didn't have a chance to scan last night because I got in so late."

"You have received 37 messages in the past 24 hours. Twenty are low priority and have been filed in your home machine for review when your trip is over. Ten are medium priority and are stored in my memory for review at your convenience today. I suggest you scan the seven high-priority messages before you begin the day's activities."

"First, let's go over my day's schedule. I remember I had six appointments. Are they still on?"

"One was canceled. During the newswire scan you requested, I picked up serious traffic problems that should be resolved by late afternoon, so I contacted the electronic agents of two of your appointments and rescheduled. They have confirmed the new times. I interfaced with your car's mapping system yesterday, and the preferred routes are available in my memory."

"Any hot points I should remember?"

"Two of your appointments have had birthdays within the past two weeks. Winston of United Products sent a letter of complaint about a delayed shipment four months ago. My records state the issue was resolved to their satisfaction. A special promotion we began last week for American International appears to already have had a positive impact."

"Good. Let's sit down and go over the trends and analysis for each meeting. Sound off. I'll remember better if I just read the text."

Contact Management

Contact management is a listing of all the customer contacts that a salesperson makes in the course of conducting business. This file is like an electronic Rolodex and should include such information as the contact's name, title, company, address, phone number, fax number, and e-mail address. It also may include additional information such as the particular industry, date of last order, name of administrative assistant, birthday, and so on.

A sales force automation system allows you to easily retrieve this information in a variety of formats. You can sort contacts according to any one of the pieces of information you are tracking. For instance, you may be going to Dallas and want a list of those area contacts that have made a purchase in the last six months. Though you could sort this information manually, it would be extremely time consuming. Another example of sorted information that you may require is a list of customers by zip code for mailing labels, or perhaps a list of your clients with birthdays in October. All of this detail is available and readily accessible through automation.

Calendar Management

As a salesperson, the most vulnerable asset you have to manage is time. Improvement of time management directly increases productivity. Electronic **calendar management,** as a part of sales force automation, can make time management easier and less prone to errors or oversights.

When a salesperson schedules appointments, telephone calls, or to-do lists on an electronic calendar, the system automatically checks for conflicts, eliminating the need for rescheduling. An electronic calendar can assign a relative priority to each item. It also can create an electronic link between a scheduled event and a particular contact or account so that the appointment or call information is accessible as both part of the salesperson's calendar, and part of the contact or account history. This makes the information contained in the calendar much more useful, once it can be viewed from different perspectives.

For the sales manager, electronic calendar management automatically consolidates information concerning the whereabouts of the entire sales force. Weekly or monthly calendars, which quickly become outdated, have been improved. Now information can be automatically generated when salespeople schedule their appointments. The system also allows salespeople to instantly update their appointments and schedules directly from the field.

Automated Sales Plans, Tactics, and Ticklers

Sales strategies often fall in a sequence of events that can be identified and plotted. A traditional example involves a thank-you letter sent immediately after an initial sales call and a follow-up telephone call three days later. In the real world, it may be difficult for busy salespeople to track all the details. As a result, important follow-up items sometimes get overlooked. If this happens, a salesperson's diligent prospecting efforts become wasted and valuable prospects are squandered.

A sales force automation system begins working as soon as the initial meeting is entered into the system. A few simple commands tell it to remind you to send a thank-you letter and schedule a follow-up phone call. It also can notify the sales manager if these things are not done.

Another sales situation might call for a regular follow-up every year or two after the sale, depending on the itch cycle associated with your product. It is particularly easy for follow-up calls like this to be neglected because of the long lead time involved. The problem becomes more apparent if the salesperson who made the original sale leaves the company or is promoted. When that happens, the customer often falls through the cracks, becoming an orphan. Automated sales tactics and ticklers prevent this from happening.

Geographic Information Systems

A **geographic information system** allows salespeople to view and manipulate customer and/or prospect information on an electronic map. This may be extremely useful if you are visiting an area for the first time. It also can be helpful in a familiar area. Customer information can be accessed directly from contact-management data and sorted accordingly, allowing you to plan sales calls geographically and make the most efficient use of your time. Also, customer buying patterns that otherwise may not be apparent may be revealed.

Computer-Based Presentations

The computer can be a powerful presentation tool. With sales force automation, dramatic and interactive **computer-based presentations** can be easily created at relatively low costs. Moreover, once created, they can be customized for a particular customer or prospect or to take advantage of a particular sales opportunity.

CD-ROM (compact disk–read only memory) is a piece of added technology enhancing computer presentations. For example, real estate agents once confined to flipping pages of a Multiple Listing Service book are now using CDs to search the listing library for homes. Customers can prioritize about 30 different criteria and view the resulting locations in color. Convenience is a large factor because the

MAKING THE SALE

The Salesperson's Business Card—Telephone, Fax, Beeper, E-mail, and the Web

Today's business cards often show multiple phone numbers; many now have more than one address. The technology-driven trend has fax, cellular, and beeper numbers, as well as e-mail and Web addresses on many cards.

E-mail addresses already are standard fare in the high-tech, communication, and academic fields. Other professions are beginning to add them as more and more people sign onto national and international on-line services that offer e-mail at home or office.

Rocko Mitera, the marketing manager at Wace the Imaging Network, a graphics services company in Chicago, doesn't leave home without e-mail access or without the business cards that point the way to his electronic residence. "I've always maintained an electronic mail address," said Mitera, adding that it made him more accessible to business contacts and friends.

"When you travel, you can receive and respond to messages very quickly," said Mitera, who finds people respond faster to electronic mail.

Mitera uses a laptop to communicate with his office from out-of-town hotels; by using e-mail, he can send documents and file reports. Mitera believes that without e-mail, the minute you walk out the door, you lose your efficiency. E-mail beats phone tag, he contends and predicts it will soon be a regular part of business communications.

While an e-mail address may be the next step in having a well-dressed business card, it's not without its detractors. Steven Buckman, a Chicago marketing consultant, has e-mail, but wouldn't use it for his professional contacts. "E-mail is recreational, the fax is professional." Buckman says. "I'm in sales; I have to talk to [clients]."[6]

presentations can take place almost anywhere: in the agent's office, the client's home, or even in the car on the way to a house. In addition, the CDs are updated weekly as opposed to the book, which is updated monthly.

Communications with Customers and Employer

As we move into the 21st century, a company's success hinges on its ability to deliver information quickly to customers and employees. Today's most popular sales force automation systems involve word processing, e-mail, and faxes.

Word Processing

Written communication plays a large part in the lives of most salespeople. Particularly important is the need for written communication with customers. A thank-you letter mailed immediately after an initial sales call often can make the difference between a favorable impression and one that is not as favorable. Sometimes it can make or break a sale. In spite of its potential impact, this simple task frequently is overlooked because the salesperson lacks an easy way to get it done. There always seem to be other, more pressing things to do. A **word processing** system can abbreviate the time it takes to accomplish this task to no more than a minute or two, the time it takes to execute a few keystrokes.

Electronic Mail

Electronic mail (e-mail) allows messages to be sent electronically through a system that delivers them immediately to any number of recipients. Correspondence is typed into the computer and sent via telephone, cable, or satellite to an e-mail address, such as a telephone number. It is very easy to send or receive messages from almost any location in the world and much more efficient than playing phone tag. For instance, when you are trying to contact a customer temporarily out of town, e-mail may be your best bet. E-mail also could be the mode of choice to send a quick note updating your manager and other salespeople on your team when you have only a few minutes to spare. This technology is having profound effects on corporate culture. If you truly want to be close to your customers, electronic mail can have a tremendous impact. Remarkably, this is as true in a sales environment where salespeople rarely leave the confines of the office as it is when they are based in the field.

Fax Capabilities and Support

Next to the telephone, the fax machine is the most important piece of communication equipment in business. Notebook computers, equipped with fax modems, offer salespeople unique time-savers while in the field. Options include the ability to prepare and fax a document—from your car perhaps—without having to print a hard copy. You can receive documents in the same manner. This represents a convenient, inexpensive way to handle the great majority of salesperson's written communication from the road.

Customer Order Processing and Service Support

The process of obtaining, generating, and completing an order is much more complicated than it may actually sound. The many steps involved in a manual system may take a number of days or even weeks to complete and confirm. Automated systems shorten the sales-and-delivery cycle. While in the office with your customer, you can use a modem to access information and make things happen more efficiently. You can check the inventory status of merchandise on the sales order, receive approval for your client's credit status, and begin the shipping process immediately. Salespeople's automated order entries directly update the company computer without having to be reentered back at the home office.

Salespeople's Mobile Offices

Salespeople have begun installing small offices directly into their vehicles, such as minivans. For those salespeople who need to be constantly in touch with their clients, these minivans are a perfect solution for working through dead time. A vehicle can be equipped with a fully functional desk, swivel chair, light, computer, printer, fax machine, cellular phone, satellite dish, and remote phone. In their **mobile offices,** salespeople can stay in constant touch with their customers even when driving between cities or states. Jeff Brown, an agent manager with U.S. Cellular, uses a mobile office at least three or four times a week. "If I arrive at a prospect's office and they can't see me right away," Brown says, "then I can go outside to work in my office until they're ready to see me."[7]

SALES INTERNET AND THE WORLD WIDE WEB

The Internet provides salespeople access to research, data, people, and vast amounts of information. Presently there is so much to learn about the use of the Internet (Net) that its explanation is beyond the scope of this textbook. Sales organizations are spending millions of dollars on software, hardware, and training for their salespeople to use the Net. It is a great sales tool—if they can only learn how to fully use it. And the Net is constantly changing. You find a Web site you like one day and the next day it is gone, changed or someone is charging for its use. Let's briefly discuss the Internet.

The Internet

The **Internet,** often referred to as the Net, is a global network of computers. It is a worldwide, self-governed network, connecting thousands of smaller networks, and millions of computers and people, to megasources of information. It reaches every country in the world; similar in some ways to the telephone system. Just as you can call people anywhere in the world, so too can you contact their computers as long as they are connected to the Net.

World Wide Web

The Internet and the World Wide Web are often thought of as the same—they are not. The Internet refers to the physical infrastructure of the interconnected global computer network. The Net is just a giant mass of cables and computers. The **World Wide Web** (more affectionately known as the Web or W3) is a part of the Internet that houses "Web sites" that provide text, graphics, video, and audio information on millions of topics. Individuals, companies, government agencies, schools, or other types of organizations develop informational Web sites.

A distinctive characteristic of the Web is that every screenful of information (commonly called a **Web page**) usually has a number of pointers to other pages of information out in the Web. (See Exhibit 5–9.) These pointers, or **links,** are what give the Web its name; all of the links together form a web of information that spans the globe. **Surfing the Internet** is actually exploring the different sites found within this web of links.

At appropriate places throughout your textbook, you will find Web exercises related to sales. The "Globe" icon points to the sales Web exercises. Try them out. Get used to using the Web. Your author's Web site is: http://www.tamu.edu/cba. Click on Marketing Faculty. Then scroll to my name. Visit my Web site any time. Please sign my guest book before leaving the Web site. You can use the "Ask Professor Futrell" feature to contact me using e-mail or e-mail me directly: c-futrell@tamu.edu.

To learn, you need to read, study, and experience the activity. To learn—use the Web. Here are a few sites to visit:

- **http//www.weather.com** Find out the weather forecast for anywhere in the world.
- **http//www.mapquest.com** Get driving directions city-to-city.
- **http//www.lookupusa.com** Locate people and businesses. Try finding yourself.

Over time, using the World Wide Web will become fun. It can be a great learning experience for you. There is no doubt that as a businessperson you need to know how to use sales technology such as the Web.

EXHIBIT 5–9

Web sites can provide valuable information to salespeople.

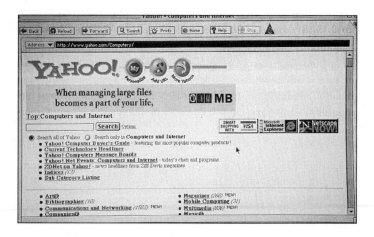

ETHICAL DILEMMA

Advertising Will Close the Deal

Earl George is a new salesperson for a small specialty goods manufacturer, Aggie Novelty Company. One of his products is a new plastic toy car for children ages three to six. In the course of a sales call, the buyer for a small toy chain asks about the extent of the advertising support the company would provide. In the past, the buyer has stressed the importance of advertising support in the chain's product line addition decisions. Because Aggie is small, it does very little TV advertising and no magazine advertising. If George tells the buyer this, he may lose the account. He knows they will buy if Aggie will advertise the product. George may get away with overstating the amount of TV advertising that Aggie will actually run (the chain may not take the time to check the ads).

What would you do in George's position?

GLOBAL TECHNOLOGY PROVIDES SERVICE

The ability to access information is a valuable asset. We are in an era where corporate strategy relies on efficiency; it can make or break a business. When salespersons travel far from home, the need for the right information, at the right time, in the right place becomes critical. Increased worldwide interaction requires access and exchange of data on a global basis.

As technology solves problems, it presents new opportunities. For example, advances in mobile data collection and wireless data communications have dramatically increased the amount of data that needs to be collected, managed, stored, and accessed. Organizations that harness this information can maximize the level of service they offer, resulting in increased sales.

A salesperson in Europe, for example, can send information to America by satellite transmission. The information is stored in the organization's main computer database. A salesperson in Florida has access to the information and can send additional data to the database. Even a Texas salesperson in a customer's office can send and receive information to and from the same database using a telephone modem transmission or wireless communication.

SUMMARY OF MAJOR SELLING ISSUES

Company knowledge includes information on a firm's history, development policies, procedures, products, distribution, promotion, and pricing. A salesperson also must know the competition, the firm's industry, and the economy. This knowledge can even be used to improve one's self-concept. A high degree of such knowledge helps the salesperson build a positive self-image and feel thoroughly prepared to interact with customers.

Wholesalers and retailers stock thousands of products, which often makes it difficult to support any one manufacturer's products as wanted by the manufacturer. This situation may result in conflicts between members of the channel of distribution. To reduce these conflicts and aid channel members in selling products, manufacturers offer assistance in advertising, sales promotion aids, and pricing allowances. In addition, many manufacturers spend millions of dollars to compel consumers and industrial buyers to purchase from channel members and the manufacturer.

National, retail, trade, industrial, and direct-mail advertising create demand for products and are a powerful selling tool for the salesperson in sales presentations. Sales promotion activities and materials are another potential selling tool for the salesperson to use in selling to consumer and industrial buyers. Samples, coupons, contests, premiums, demonstrations, and displays are effective sales promotion techniques employed to help sell merchandise.

Price, discounts, and credit policies are additional facts the salesperson should be able to discuss confidently with customers. Each day, the salesperson informs or answers questions posed by customers in these three areas. Customers always want to know the salesperson's list and net price, and if there are any transportation charges. Discounts (quantity, cash, trade, or consumer) represent important buying incentives offered by the manufacturer to the buyer. The buyer wants to know the terms of payment. The salesperson needs to understand company credit policies to open new accounts, see that customers pay on time, and collect overdue bills. See the appendix at the end of this chapter for additional discussions on pricing.

Finally, success in sales requires knowledge of the many technologies used to sell and service customers. Computers, word processing, e-mail, faxes, pagers, cellular phones, the Internet, and the World Wide Web have quickly become part of the professional's sales kit.

MEETING A SALES CHALLENGE	To be successful, salespeople need to be knowledgeable about many things. However, being an expert on the product is only part of what it takes to be a top performer. You also need to know how to use good communication and selling skills.
	Sure, this grocery buyer wants to sell his customers a good product, but the reseller is possibly more interested in whether he can sell the product once he buys it, and how much money he will make. Resellers are "bottom-line" oriented; because they want to know what's in it for them, they concentrate on discussing return on investment.

KEY TERMS FOR SELLING

SALES APPLICATION QUESTIONS

1. A salesperson's knowledge needs to extend into many areas such as: general company knowledge; product knowledge; knowledge of upcoming advertising and promotional campaigns; knowledge about company price, discount, and credit policies; and knowledge about the competition, the industry, and the economy. These are all vital for sales success. For each of these categories,

explain how a salesperson's knowledge can lay the groundwork for successful selling.

2. How do salespeople generally acquire their sales knowledge?

3. Explain how a salesperson's knowledge can be converted into selling points used in the sales presentation. Give two examples.

4. A salesperson must have a good understanding of the competition, customers, and everything connected with the company. Why, however, should a salesperson take time to be up-to-date on facts about the economy and the industry?

5. What is the difference between a product's shelf positioning and its shelf facings? How can a salesperson maximize both shelf positioning and shelf facings? Why is this important?

6. Companies use numerous premiums in their efforts to market products. Why? What types of premiums do they use? How can a salesperson use a premium offer in a sales presentation to a wholesaler or a retailer?

7. What are the major types of advertising that a manufacturer might use to promote its products? How can a salesperson use information about the company's advertising in a sales presentation?

8. Before firms such as General Foods and Quaker Oats introduce a new consumer product nationally, they frequently place the product in a test market to see how it will sell. How can a salesperson use test information in a sales presentation?

9. What is cooperative advertising? Explain the steps involved.

10. Why do companies advertise?

11. Consumer sales promotion and trade sales promotion try to increase sales to consumers and resellers respectively. Several promotional techniques follow; classify each item as a consumer or trade promotional technique and give an example for each one. Can any of the promotions be used for both consumers and the trade?

   a. Coupons on or inside packages.

   b. Free installation (premium).

   c. Displays.

   d. Sales contests.

   e. Drawings for gifts.

   f. Demonstrations.

   g. Samples.

SALES WORLD WIDE WEB EXERCISES

Business Intelligence: Can the Web Help?

On its way to transforming the world of sales, the World Wide Web is triggering a revolution: It is having a radical effect on the way marketers get the business intelligence they need. There are whole new categories of information available now. A few clicks of the mouse can provide an avalanche of free—but priceless—information about competitors. Useful Web sites include:

Society of Competitive Intelligence Professionals
www.scip.org

Fuld & Company
www.fuld.com

Farcast
www.farcast.com

Hoover's Online
www.hoovers.com

Individual Inc.
www.individual.com

Deja News	**NewsTracker**
www.dejanews.com	nt.excite.com
Newsworks	**Companies Online**
www.newsworks.com	www.companiesonline.com
NewsBot	**SEC's EDGAR file**
www.newsbot.com	www.sec.gov/cgi-bin/srch-edgar

Research one or more companies you have an interest in working for or that you know or have worked for in the past.

FURTHER EXPLORING THE SALES WORLD

To complete this project, you will need to visit two places. First, visit your local library. Examine magazines such as the *American Druggist, Incentive Marketing, Journal of the American Medical Association, Purchasing,* and *Sales & Marketing Management,* and report on the type of promotions companies offer their customers. Second, visit local retailers such as a supermarket and report on merchandising techniques used to promote individual products. Once you have collected information on several products, pick one product and describe how this information could become part of a sales presentation.

SELLING EXPERIENTIAL EXERCISE

How Is Your Self-Confidence?

You may think you have a good attitude for sales, but if you do not have the confidence to meet customers and prospects you do not know, all is lost. This exercise can help you measure your self-confidence. Read each statement and then, on a separate sheet of paper, write the number you believe best fits you.

	High				Low
I can convert strangers into friends quickly and easily.	5	4	3	2	1
I can attract and hold the attention of others even when I do not know them.	5	4	3	2	1
I love new situations.	5	4	3	2	1
I'm intrigued with the psychology of meeting and building a good relationship with someone I do not know.	5	4	3	2	1
I would enjoy making a sales presentation to a group of executives.	5	4	3	2	1
When dressed for the occasion, I have great confidence in myself.	5	4	3	2	1
I do not mind using the telephone to make appointments with strangers.	5	4	3	2	1
Others do not intimidate me.	5	4	3	2	1
I enjoy solving problems.	5	4	3	2	1
Most of the time, I feel secure.	5	4	3	2	1

Total Score _____

Add up the numbers to get your score. If you scored more than 40, you are self-confident enough to consider selling as a profession. If you rated yourself between 25 and 40, you need more experience in dealing with people. A score of less than 25 indicates that you need to build your self-confidence, and another type of job probably would be better for you.[8]

Chapter 5 Appendix:
Sales Arithmetic and Pricing

Salespeople want to exchange something for something—usually their products for the customer's money. Organizations, consumers (and even you) want the answer to the question "How much is this going to cost?" Salespeople have to be prepared to discuss all aspects of costs and prices. Consequently, some knowledge of the rudiments of sales arithmetic and pricing is essential for you.

Since most students taking this course will create a sales presentation as their class project, this information will benefit you. Some students will have had a course in accounting, marketing, or retailing, and so therefore this information is intended as a review. This appendix discusses sales arithmetic and pricing concepts that are useful in sales to (1) resellers, such as wholesalers and retailers, and (2) end users, such as businesses and nonprofit organizations.

TYPES OF PRICES

While a firm may engage in many pricing practices, all companies have a list price, net price, and prices based on transportation terms. Five of the most common types of prices are

- **List price**—the standard price charged to customers.
- **Net price**—the price after allowance for all discounts.
- **Zone price**—the price based on geographical location or zone of customers.
- **FOB shipping point**—FOB (free on board) means the buyer pays transportation charges on the goods—the title to goods passes to the customer when they are loaded on shipping vehicles.
- **FOB destination**—the seller pays all shipping costs.

These prices are established by the company. Normally, the salesperson is not involved in pricing the product. This type of pricing allows the salesperson to quote prices according to company guidelines.

Selling the same quantity of similar products at different prices to two different industrial users or resellers is illegal. Laws such as the Robinson-Patman Act of 1936 forbid price discrimination that injures competition in *interstate* commerce. While the law does not apply to sales within a state (intrastate sales), a majority of states have similar laws.

A company can justify different prices if it can prove to the courts that its price differentials do not substantially reduce competition. Often, companies justify price differentials by showing the courts one of two things. First, take the case of one customer buying more of a product than another. For the customer purchasing larger quantities, a firm can manufacture and market the products at a lower cost. These lower costs are passed on to the customer in reduced prices. Second, price differentials can be justified when a company must lower prices to meet competition. Thus, if justified, companies can offer customers different prices. They typically do this through discounts.

DISCOUNTS LOWER THE PRICE

Discounts are a reduction in price from the list price. In developing a program to sell a product line over a specified period, marketing managers consider discounts along with the advertising and personal selling efforts engaged in by the firm. The main types of discounts allowed to buyers are quantity, cash, trade, and consumer discounts.

Quantity Discounts: Buy More, Pay Less

Quantity discounts result from the manufacturer's saving in production costs because it can produce large quantities of the product. As shown in Exhibit 5A–1, these savings are passed on to customers who buy in large quantities using discounts. Quantity discounts are either noncumulative or cumulative.

EXHIBIT 5A–1

Various promotional allowances available to resellers

GREAT NEW DEAL!
Four double-strength sizes to strengthen your profits!

	Promotional Allowances				Promotional Support
Free-Goods Allowance*	Plus Advertising Allowance†		Plus Merchandising Allowance		
	Option A	Option B‡	Reduced Price Feature	Display	
12 oz. liquid 8 ⅓% off invoice	Up to $1.25 per dozen	$1.00 per dozen	$.75 per dozen reduced price feature	$.75 per dozen floor or end cap display	Direct to consumer national TV promotion . . . 1.705 GRPs
5 oz. liquid 8 ⅓% off invoice	Up to $.75 per dozen	$.50 per dozen	$.50 per dozen reduced price feature	$.50 per dozen floor or end cap display	88% reach 1.7 billion impressions
60s tablets 8 ⅓% off invoice	Up to $1.25 per dozen	$1.00 per dozen	$.75 per dozen reduced price feature	$.75 per dozen floor or end cap display	Year-round physician detailing and sampling
24s tablets 8 ⅓% off invoice	Up to $.75 per dozen	$.50 per dozen	$.50 per dozen reduced price feature	$.50 per dozen floor or end cap display	Major trade and medical journal advertising support

Also available—up to 2% billback allowance for four-color roto advertising or consumer coupon programs.
Unlimited purchases allowed for claiming billback allowances.
Retail buy-in period: July 15 through August 30, 2000.
Advertising performance period: July 15 through November 8, 2000.
Claim deadline: 45 days following appearance of ad.
Contact your representative for complete details.

*Through participating wholesaler.

†All ads should feature both liquid and tablets.

‡Provided advertising coverage is in at least 75% of the applicant's trading area.

One-time reductions in prices are **noncumulative quantity discounts,** which are commonly used in the sale of both consumer and industrial goods. The Schering salesperson might offer the buyer of Coricidin D a 16.6 percent price reduction. The Colgate salesperson may offer the retailer 2 dozen king-size Colgate tubes of toothpaste free for every 10 dozen purchased.

The salesperson is expected to use these discounts as inducements for the retailer to buy in large quantities. The sales goal is to have the prospect display and locally advertise the product at a price lower than normal. Ideally, the retailer's selling price should reflect the price reduction allowed because of the quantity discount.

Cumulative quantity discounts are discounts received for buying a certain amount of a product over a stated period, such as one year. Again, these discounts reflect savings in manufacturing and marketing costs.

To receive a 10 percent discount, a buyer may have to purchase 12,000 units of the product. Under the cumulative discount, the buyer would not be required to purchase the 12,000 units at the same time—say 1,000 units each month, for example. As long as the agreed-on amount is purchased within the specified time, the 10 percent discount on each purchase applies. A cumulative discount allows the buyer to purchase the products as needed rather than in a single order.

Cash Discounts: Entice the Customer to Pay on Time

Cash discounts are earned by buyers who pay bills within a stated period. For example, if the customer purchases $10,000 worth of goods on June 1 and the cash discount is 2/10 net 30, the customer pays $9,800 instead of $10,000. Thus, 2/10 net 30 translates into a 2 percent discount if the bill is completely paid within 10 days of the sale. If the payment is not made within 10 days, the full $10,000 is due in 30 days. See Selling Tip box's discussion on the cash discount. Buyers should understand that 2 percent can mean extra money.

Trade Discounts Attract Channel Members' Attention

The manufacturer may reduce prices to channel members (middlemen) to compensate them for the services they perform. These are **trade discounts.** The trade discount is usually stated as a percentage off the list retail price. A wholesaler may be offered a 50 percent discount and the retailer offered a 40 percent discount off list price. The wholesaler's price to its retail customers is 10 percent above its cost or 40 percent off the list price. The wholesaler earns a 10 percent gross margin on sales to retail customers. Channel members are still eligible to earn the quantity and cash discounts.

Consumer Discounts Increase Sales

Consumer discounts are one-time price reductions passed on from the manufacturer to channel members or directly to the consumer. Cents-off product labels are price reductions passed directly to the consumer. A package marked 15 cents off each product or $1.80 a dozen uses a consumer discount. See Exhibit 5A–2.

The manufacturer expects channel members to reduce the price from their normal price. A mass merchandiser might normally sell a product with a list price of $2.50 for $1.98. The manufacturer would want salespeople to persuade the retailer to price the product 15 cents lower than the $1.98, or at a price of $1.83.

Cents-off coupons that the consumer brings to the retail store are another example of a temporary price discount. In both the cents-off label and coupon examples, the manufacturer ensures that the price reduction is passed on to the consumer. This occurs because channel members may not have promoted the product or reduced the price, keeping the quantity or off-invoice savings for themselves. An offer of a cents-off product label and coupons is used by the salesperson to sell larger quantities to customers. For a summary of discounts and examples of each, see Exhibit 5A–2.

To Take or Not Take the Cash Discount

To take or not take the cash discount is a question many buyers ask themselves and salespeople. After all it is only 2 percent, or is it?

Say you are a buyer for a manufacturing firm. Your credit terms are 2/10, net 30. If you make your payment within the first 10 days on a purchase of $100,000, your discount would be $2,000 ($100,000 – (.02) (100,000) = $2,000)

If your level of purchases is $100,000 each month, your cash discounts for the year would total:

■ $2,000 × 12 months = $24,000

■ The firm pays $120,000 – $24,000 = $96,000

If the firm does not take the discount and instead pays the bill 30 days after the sale, it pays the full amount ($100,000). In essence, the firm is paying $2,000 for the ability to pay their bill 20 days later. (Whether or not the company pays on day 11 or day 30, they still have lost the discount.) Therefore, the company is financing its purchase for 20 days at a 2 percent rate of interest. Certainly 2 percent does not sound like a large amount of interest. Yet, think about what the 2 percent means. This 2 percent is for 20 days only, not for 360 days or a whole year. To figure out a comparable annual interest rate, you would

■ Divide 360 days by 20 days to see how many 20-day periods are in a year. (360 ÷ 20 = 18.)

■ Therefore, 18 20-day periods are in a year.

■ Multiply 2 percent by 18 = *36 percent,* to determine the annual interest rate.

If you purchase $100,000 each month and pay after the cash discount period has passed (day 11 to day 30), you pay:

■ 120,000 – 96,000 = $24,000 a year

■ In this case, the saving is $1 - \dfrac{\$96,000}{120,000} = 20\%$. All from a 2 percent cash discount!

Types and examples of discounts

Types of Discounts	Discount Examples
Quantity discount	• Buy 11 dozen, get 1 dozen free.
Noncumulative	• 20 percent off on all purchases.
(one-time)	• $5 off invoice for each floor-stand purchase.
Cumulative	• 5 percent discount with purchase of 8,000 units.
(yearly purchases)	• 8 percent discount with purchase of 10,000 units.
	• 10 percent discount with purchase of 12,000 units.
Cash discounts	• 2/10 end-of-month.
	• 2/10 net 30.
Trade discounts	• 40 percent off to retailers.
	• 50 percent off to wholesalers.
Consumer discounts	• 15 cents off regular price marked on product's package.
	• 10-cents-off coupon.

RESELLERS: MARKUP AND PROFIT

Markup is the dollar amount added to the product cost to determine its selling price. Markup often is expressed as a percentage and represents gross profit, not net profit. **Gross profit** is the money available to cover the costs of marketing the product, operating the business, and profit. **Net profit** is the money remaining after the costs of marketing and operating the business are paid.

Exhibit 5A–3 presents an example of markup based on a product's selling price for each channel-of-distribution member. Each channel member has a different percentage markup. The product that costs the manufacturer $3 to produce eventually

EXHIBIT 5A–3

Example of markup on selling price in channel of distribution.

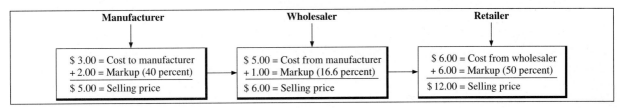

Manufacturer	Wholesaler	Retailer
$ 3.00 = Cost to manufacturer + 2.00 = Markup (40 percent) $ 5.00 = Selling price	$ 5.00 = Cost from manufacturer + 1.00 = Markup (16.6 percent) $ 6.00 = Selling price	$ 6.00 = Cost from wholesaler + 6.00 = Markup (50 percent) $ 12.00 = Selling price

costs the consumer $12. The manufacturer's selling price represents the wholesaler's cost. Price markups enable the wholesaler to pay business operating costs, to cover the product's cost, and to make a profit. The wholesaler's selling price of $6 becomes the retailer's cost. In turn, the retailer marks up the product to cover its cost, the associated costs of doing business (such as stocking the product and allocation of fixed costs per square foot), and to maintain a desired profit level.

The percentage markup is based on either the product's selling price or its cost. It is important to know the method of determining markup. Using a manufacturer's cost of $3, a markup of $2, and a selling price of $5 shown in Exhibit 6A–3, the methods of determining percentage markup can have different results:

$$\text{Percentage markup on selling price} = \frac{\text{Amount added to cost}}{\text{Selling price}} = \frac{\$2.00}{\$5.00} = 40 \text{ percent}$$

$$\text{Percentage markup on cost} = \frac{\text{Amount added to cost}}{\text{Cost}} = \frac{\$2.00}{\$3.00} = 66.6 \text{ percent}$$

Channel members want to buy goods at low prices and establish selling prices at a competitive level that allows for a reasonable profit. Such objectives result in retailers having different markups on different goods. For example, a retailer may have markups of 10 percent on groceries, 30 percent on cameras, and 50 percent on houseware items. Based on the type of store (discount—high volume; specialty—low volume; department—high service), markups may vary greatly depending on the volume of sales and degree of service rendered.

In preparing the sales presentation for an individual customer, the salesperson should consider all the discounts available to suggest a promotional plan for the retailer. For example, the advertisement shown in Exhibit 5A–1 illustrates several of the discounts a retailer can receive with the purchase of three decongestants. The salesperson can use these discounts in the sales presentation by suggesting that the retailer advertise the products at a reduced price and place the promotional displays by each of the store's cash registers.

Markup and Unit Price

Sellers, especially consumer goods salespeople, like to talk in terms of the cost and profits earned from an individual unit. However, wholesalers and retailers do not buy one product at a time. Depending on customer's size, manufacturers may sell resellers several dozens or thousands of dozens at a time. The cost and profits of an individual unit may not be useful for wholesalers, but it becomes extremely important to retailers, since their customers buy the product one at a time.

EXHIBIT 5A–4

Example of using unit cost

Consumer goods salespeople often break down costs and talk of unit costs and profits. Here is the arithmetic one salesperson used in her presentation:

$1.80	=	Regular cost of each unit
−.53	=	Special promotional allowance
$1.27	=	Deal cost
$2.29	=	Manufacturer's suggested selling price
$2.19	=	Normal retail selling price
18%	=	Retailer's normal profit ($2.19 – $1.80 5 39¢ markup) (39¢ 4 $2.19 5 18% markup)
$1.39	=	3-day special price suggested for retailer to advertise product.
8.6%	=	3-day sale profit margin ($1.39 – $1.27 5 12¢) (12¢ 4 $1.39 5 8.6% markup)
$1.89	=	2-week special price suggested for in-store promotion.
33%	=	After-sale profit margin ($1.89 – $1.27 5 .62) (.62 4 $1.89 5 33% markup)
18%	=	Normal profit ($2.19 – 1.80 5 39¢) (39¢ 4 $2.19 5 18%)

The above information (except for the arithmetic in parentheses) was on a sheet of paper with the buyer's company name at the top. The seller showed how the buyer could purchase a large quantity and make 8.6 percent profit by selling each item for $1.39 instead of the normal $2.19. The retailer's customers save 80¢ ($2.19 – $1.39 = 80¢). After the three-day sale, the retailer increases the price to $1.89 for two weeks and makes 33 percent instead of the 18 percent markup.

Here is how it works: Assume you are selling a consumer product to a large chain of grocery stores. As shown in Exhibit 5A–4, each unit normally costs $1.80 and the retailer sells it for $2.19, 10¢ less than the manufacturer's $2.29 suggested selling price. This gives a normal profit of 39¢ or an 18 percent markup [($2.19 – $1.80 = 39¢) then divide by $2.19 (39¢ ÷ $2.19 = 18 percent)]. Subtracting the 53¢ promotional allowance gives a deal cost of $1.27.

The normal profit, or markup, is 18 percent. If the product is sold at $1.89 for an additional two weeks, the markup reflecting the 53¢ promotional allowance equals 33 percent. If the retailer buys the product and does not reduce the price, the manufacturer is throwing away 53¢ a unit or $6.36 a dozen.

What are the salesperson's objectives? To have the retailer: (1) buy a larger quantity than normal; (2) reduce the price for a three-day $1.39 advertised promotion; and (3) run a two-week, in-store promotion at $1.89. The retailer's sale price of $1.39 would provide an 8.6 percent profit and the $1.89 produces a 33 percent profit margin. The manufacturer, retailer, and the retailer's customers all win in this deal.

Markup and Return on Investment

Consumer goods salespeople also can use return on investment (ROI) in their presentations. **Return on investment (ROI)** refers to an additional sum of money expected from an investment over and above the original investment. ROI often is expressed as a percentage; however, a dollar return on investment also can be used by salespeople. The information shown in Exhibit 5A–5 illustrates the actual ROI used by a salesperson. Continuing the previous example shown, the salesperson wants the customer to have a three-day advertised special and a two-week in-store price reduction and to buy a large quantity for normal stock. The purchasing agent buys for a chain of 100 grocery stores.

Normally, the chain averages selling 1,500 dozen during a six-week period. The salesperson feels the promotion and price reduction will increase sales to 3,000 dozen. As seen in Exhibit 5A–5, the salesperson asks the retailer to invest $45,720 ($7,620 + $15,240 + $22,860). Sales are projected to be $70,440 ($8,340 + $22,680 + $39,420)

EXHIBIT 5A–5

Profit forecaster for Granola Bars shown to buyer

	3-Day Special	2-Week Special	Normal
Total stores	100	100	100
Deal dates	June 1 through June 30		
Regular cost per dozen	$21.60	$21.60	$21.60
Less allowance ($.53)	–6.36	–6.36	
Deal cost per dozen	$15.24	$15.24	$21.60
Feature price	1.39	1.89	2.19
Cases purchased	500[a]	1,000	1,500
Total investment	$7,620[b]	$15,240	$22,860
Total gross sales	$8,340[c]	$22,680	$39,420
Total gross profit	$ 720[d]	$ 7,440	$16,560
Return on investment (ROI)	8.6%[e]	33%	42%

[a]5 cases per store
[b]$500 \times 15.24 = \$7,620$
[c]$500 \times 12 = 6,000; 6,000 \times \$1.39 = \$8,340$
[d]$\$8,340 - \$7,620 = \$720$
[e]$\$720 \div \$8,340 = 8.6\%$

with profits of $24,720 ($720 + $7,440 + $16,560). The retailer's return on investment is 35 percent, as shown here:

$$\$70,440 = \text{total gross sales}$$
$$\underline{-45,720} = \text{total investment}$$
$$\$24,720 = \text{total gross profit}$$
$$35\% = \text{ROI } (\$24,720 \div \$70,440)$$

Discounts, payment plans, markups, unit prices, and return on investment are important for salespeople to understand thoroughly. Customers are extremely interested in listening to this information during the salesperson's presentation.

ORGANIZATIONS: VALUE AND ROI

Business salespeople often include a value analysis in the sales presentation. A **value analysis** determines the best product for the money. It recognizes that a high-priced product may sometimes be a better value than a lower-priced product. Many firms routinely review a value analysis before deciding to purchase a product. See Exhibit 5A–6.

The value analysis evaluates how well the product meets the buying company's specific needs. It addresses such questions as:

- How do your product's features, advantages, and benefits compare to the product currently used?
- Can your product do the same job as your buyer's present product at a lower price?
- Does the buyer's current equipment perform better than required? (Is equipment too good for present needs?)
- On the other hand, will a higher-priced, better-performing product be more economical in the long run?

EXHIBIT 5A–6

These truck salespeople at a Kenworth dealership use a value analysis to help customers determine the best buy for their money.

As you can see from the examples in this chapter, frequently you must analyze the buyer's present operation carefully before suggesting how your product might improve efficiency, enhance the quality or quantity of the product produced, or save money.

In discussing how to present a value analysis to a buyer, Patrick Kamlowsky, who sells drilling bits for oil and gas wells, said:

> It's not as simple as it may appear to make a recommendation and have the oil company adhere to it. You must be thorough in the presentation and present the facts in an objective manner. After all, their money is at stake. The presentation must be logical and based on facts that are known; it must be made with as little speculation as possible.
>
> What is difficult is presenting a recommendation to one who has spent 30 or more years in the oil field and has drilled all over the world. I am confronted with the challenge of explaining to this man that the methods he has employed for years may not be the best application where he is currently drilling. The presentation of the recommendation must therefore be thorough and to the point. When talking to him, I do not imply that his method is outdated or wrong, but that I believe I can help him improve his method. To be successful, I must establish two things very quickly—his respect and my credibility. Showing him my proposal and supporting evidence, and permitting him the time to evaluate it are vital. I don't wish to come on to him too strong, just show him that I genuinely want to help.

A salesperson can develop numerous types of value analyses for a prospective buyer. Three types frequently used are (1) product cost versus true value, (2) unit cost, and (3) return on investment.

Compare Product Costs to True Value

All buyers want to know about costs. The value analysis developed for a customer should present cost in a simple, straightforward manner. A product's costs are always relative to something else; thus, cost must be judged in value and results. The base cost of your product should never be the determining factor of the sale. Buying a product solely on cost could cause a customer to lose money.

Never discuss costs until you have compared them to the *value* of a product. In this manner, the customer intelligently compares the true worth of the proposed investment in your product to its true monetary cost. In effect, a good purchase involves more than initial cost; it represents an investment and you must demonstrate that what you sell is a good investment.

	Product C	Product X
EXHIBIT 5A–7		
Cost versus value of a small copier		
Initial cost	$2,695	$3,000
Type of paper	Treated paper	Plain paper
Copy speed	12 copies per minute	15 copies per minute
Warm-up time	Instant	Instant
Cost of each copy	3¢ a copy	1¢ a copy
Monthly cost (assuming 10,000 copies)	$300	$100

Conclusion: The difference in the purchase price of the two copiers is $305 ($3,000 – $2,695). Product X saves $200 on monthly copy costs. The savings on monthly copy costs pays for the higher-priced Product X in one and one-half months. In 15 months, savings on the monthly copy equal the purchase price of Product X. Therefore, Product X is less expensive in the long run.

Exhibit 5A–7 provides an example of how a salesperson might compare the cost of a copier (Product X) with a competitive copier (Product C). It illustrates how you can demonstrate to a buyer that your product is a better value than one would think from looking only at purchase price. Another value analysis technique is to further break down a product's price to its unit cost.

Unit Costs Break Price Down

One method of presenting a product's true value to a buyer is to break the product's total costs into several smaller units or the **unit cost.** Assume you sell a computer system that costs $1,000 per month and processes 50,000 transactions each month. The cost per transaction is only 2 cents.

Return on Investment Is Listened To

Return on investment refers to an additional sum of money expected from an investment over and above the original investment. Buyers are interested in knowing the percentage return on their initial investment. Since the purchase of many business products is an investment in that it produces measurable results, salespeople can talk about the percentage return that can be earned by purchasing their products. See Exhibit 5A–8.

Again, assume you sell computer equipment requiring a $10,000 per month investment. Benefits to the buyer are measured in hours of work saved by employees, plus the resulting salary saving. First, have the buyer agree on an hourly rate, which includes fringe benefit cost; let's say salaries average $5 an hour for employees. The hours saved are then multiplied by this hourly rate to obtain the return on investment. If hours saved amounted to 2,800 per month, it is a savings of $14,000 per month (2,800 hours × $5 hourly rate). You could develop a table to show the potential return on investment:

Value of hours saved	$14,000 per month
Cost of equipment	–10,000 per month
Profit	$ 4,000 per month
Return on investment ($14,000 ÷ $10,000)	140 percent

Subtracting the $10,000 cost per month from the return of $14,000 per month provides a $4,000 a month profit or a 140 percent return on investment. This is taken one step further by considering return on investment after taxes—calculated like this:

$$\frac{\$14,000\ (1 - \text{Tax rate})}{\$10,000}$$

This return on investment presents the buyer with a logical reason to buy. Remember to let the customer make the cost estimates. The buyer must agree with the figures used for this to be effective in demonstrating the real value of buying your product.

KEY TERMS FOR SELLING

list price   155
net price   155
zone price   155
FOB shipping point   155
FOB destination   155
noncumulative quantity discount   157
cumulative quantity discount   157
cash discount   157

trade discount   157
consumer discount   157
markup   158
gross profit   158
net profit   158
return on investment (ROI)   160
value analysis   161
unit cost   163

SALES APPLICATION QUESTIONS

1. Many companies offer customers various discounts from their normal or list price to entice them to buy. Discuss the main types of discounts offered.
2. Should the salesperson mention a discount at the beginning, middle, or end of a sales presentation? Why?
3. It cost a company $6 to manufacture a product that it sold for $10 to a wholesaler who sold it to a retailer for $12. A customer of the retailer bought it for $24. What was the markup on selling price for each member of this product's channel of distribution?
4. Determine the markup of a product that costs your customer $1 with the following potential suggested resell prices: $1.25, $1.50, $2. How much profit would the wholesaler or retailer make selling your product at each of the three suggested resell prices?

5. Assume you sell hardware supplies to grocery, drug, and hardware retailers. Tomorrow, you plan to call on the ACE Hardware chain—your largest customer. To reach your sales quota for this year, you must get a large order. You know they will buy something; however, you want them to purchase an extra amount. Furthermore, you know they are 120 days overdue on paying for what you shipped them months ago, and your company's credit manager will not ship them more merchandise until they pay the bill. How would you handle the sales call? Include in your answer where you would discuss the overdue bill problem in your sales presentation. Also include what you would do if the buyer said, "I haven't paid for my last order yet! How can I buy from you today?"

6. List and define five commonly quoted types of prices.

7. The following examples are several types of discounts. In each situation: (*a*) explain what type of discount is used, (*b*) determine by what percentage the *cost* of the product has been reduced, as well as savings per unit, and (*c*) answer other questions asked for each situation.

   a. Bustwell Inc., a regional business computer firm, is attempting to sell a new computer-operated gasoline pump meter to a convenience store chain, Gas 'N' Go. The device will help reduce gasoline theft, give an accurate record of each sale, and aid in determining when Gas 'N' Go should order more gasoline. Gus Gas, of the convenience chain, seems interested in your initial proposal but believes the price may be too high. The cost of each computer is $1,000, but you could sell Gas 50 computers for $45,000. The Gas 'N' Go chain owns 43 stores and is building eight more that will open in about one month.

   b. The Storage Bin Warehouse in your territory has reported a number of break-ins in the past three months. As a salesperson for No-Doubt Security Products, you believe your extensive line of alarm systems and locks could benefit the warehouse greatly. You make an appointment with the manager at the Storage Bin for early next week. During your preparation for the sales call, you discover that the warehouse presently uses poor quality locks and has no security system. You plan to offer the manager a security package consisting of 150 Sure-Bolt dead bolt locks (for their 150 private storage rooms) at a price of $10 each, and a new alarm system costing $5,000. The terms of the sale are 2/10 net 30. How would the total cost change if the terms of the alarm system alone were changed to 5/10 net 30 (and the locks remained 2/10 net 30)? What is the cost of the security package if the Storage Bin takes 25 days to pay for the purchase?

   c. You are a salesperson for Madcap Arcade Games, selling video games and pinball machines. A local business wants to open an arcade, and would like to buy a new game about every two weeks. A new game costs $3,000. You can offer a 5 percent discount (an end-of-year rebate) if at least 25 games are purchased from you during the next year. What will the discount be in dollars?

   d. The XYZ company is having its year-end sales push. As a salesperson for XYZ, a manufacturer of consumer goods like toothpaste, shampoo, and razor blades, you have been instructed to give a "buy eleven get one free" discount to half of your accounts. The remainder of your accounts, because of their small volume, are offered 10 percent off on all purchases. Compare the two situations. Which is the better deal?

8. As a salesperson for the Electric Generator Corporation, you have decided to attempt to sell your EG 600 generator to the Universal Construction Corporation. The EG 600 costs about $70,000. You estimate that operating and maintenance costs will average $3,000 a year and that the machine will operate

satisfactorily for 10 years. You can offer a $65,000 price to Universal, if they purchase 10 to 20 machines. Should they purchase more than 21 machines, their cost would be $58,000 per generator. The generators currently used originally cost $65,000, have a life of seven years, and cost $5,000 each year to operate. As far as you know, their present supplier cannot offer them a quantity discount.

    a. Develop a value analysis table comparing the two generators.

    b. In your presentation, what are the selling points you would stress?

9. Value analysis is an effective sales tool. Define value analysis and describe its use in a selling situation.

STUDENT APPLICATION LEARNING EXERCISES (SALES)

(Part 2 of 7)

At the end of appropriate chapters beginning with Chapter 3, you will find Student Application Learning Exercises (SALES). SALES are meant to help you construct the various segments of your sales presentation. SALES build upon one another so that after you complete each, you will have constructed the majority of your sales presentation.

An important part of your presentation is the discussion of price to your buyer. To make **Sale 2** first study pages 156–163, and Exhibits 5–4 and 12–11 in Chapter 12. It will be helpful if you understand Exhibits 5A–4, 5A–5, and 5A–7 and how to calculate markup before coming to class.

    Your assignment is to construct one or more pages that show the prices you will discuss with your buyer. This page, or pages, will serve as a visual aid that you show your buyer during the presentation.

CASE 5A–1

Claire Cosmetics

Jane Thompson was hired recently by a national cosmetics manufacturer. She just graduated from college. Having no previous work experience, she always felt nervous about making sales presentations. Her large customers make her especially nervous. However, for the month she was in her territory, Jane only took orders, which relieved much of the pressure, and the salespeople whom Jane replaced did an excellent job; customers seemed to accept Jane because of this.

    In today's mail, Jane receives information on products the company wants the sales force to emphasize next month. She is instructed to review the material and come to next week's sales meeting prepared to discuss the information. Of the four products to concentrate on, one product will receive special emphasis. Claire Super Hold hair spray will have the following sales promotion aids and price allowances:

- Floor stand containing 12 8-ounce and 36 12-ounce sizes.
- Counter display containing 6 8-ounce and 6 12-ounce sizes.
- $1 floor stand and counter display off-invoice allowance.
- 10 percent co-op advertising allowance requiring proof of advertising.
- 10 percent off-invoice discount for each dozen of each size purchased.

The 8-ounce size has a suggested retail price of $1.39 and has a normal invoice cost of 83 cents or $9.96 a dozen. The more popular 12-ounce size retails for $1.99 and costs $1.19 each or $14.28 a dozen. Jane knows that she, like each salesperson, will be called on at the meeting to give her ideas on how to sell this product in front of the 10 salespeople in her district. Her boss will be there and, it is rumored, the national sales manager will be in the area and may attend. This makes her really nervous.

Questions

1. What can Jane do to prepare herself for the meeting to reduce her nervousness?
2. If you were attending the meeting, what ideas would you present?

CASE 5A–2
McBath Women's Apparel

Getting a new, improved product into a chain of stores that has never carried her line of women's apparel is a new experience for Lynn Morris. Lynn has been promoted to key account sales representative for McBath Women's Apparel in the past month.

She has worked for McBath since graduating from college three years earlier. As a novice salesperson in a large metropolitan market, she inherited a sales territory where all of the major department stores in her area carried the popular McBath line. By displaying a service attitude, Lynn kept all her original accounts and managed to help several outlets increase sales of McBath products, but she was never given the opportunity to sell to new accounts.

Now, she has accepted the key account (a key account is one that generates a large volume of sales for the company) sales position in another region of the country. Also, she has the responsibility of selling to a large chain of department stores (Federale) that has never carried McBath products. Maurice Leverett, vice president of marketing at McBath, is counting heavily on adding the Federale chain because James McBath, the company's president, is intent on continuing McBath's rapid sales growth.

Lynn firmly believes that her products are the best on the market. She is concerned, however, about the sales interview she has scheduled with the chief purchasing agent at Federale, Mary Bruce. Despite McBath's high-quality image and its reputation for having a dependable, hard-working sales force, Mary Bruce has turned down other McBath salespeople several times over the past six years, saying, "We already stock four manufacturers' lingerie. We are quite happy with the lines we now carry and with the service their salespeople provide us. Besides, we only have so much floor space to devote to lingerie and we don't want to confuse our customers with another line."

Lynn has decided to make her company's new display system her major selling point for several reasons:

- Several high-ranking McBath executives (including vice president of marketing Maurice Leverett) are strong backers of the new display and want it in all retail outlets.
- The stores currently using the display for test marketing purposes have shown an increase in sales for McBath products of 50 percent.
- Federale will not have to set aside much space for the new system, and it can be installed, stocked, and ready for use in less than one hour.
- The display will increase shopping convenience by allowing shoppers easy access to the well-known, trusted line of McBath products with the aid of clear, soft-shell plastic packaging and easy-to-understand sizing.

■ A new advertising campaign will start in a few weeks and will emphasize the revolutionary display. Other promotions, such as coupons and special introductory sales, will also be tried.

Questions

1. Lynn believes a good presentation will be critical for her to sell Bruce the new display. How should she structure her presentation? What are the key selling points to discuss?

2. Assume you are Maurice Leverett (vice president of marketing for McBath). Give an example of each of the four major types of discounts discussed in this chapter that your salespeople could use to help put the new display into retail stores. What type of discount will be most effective, and least effective? Explain your reasoning.

3. How can Lynn use quantity (cumulative and noncumulative), cash, trade, and consumer discounts to her advantage?

CASE 5A–3
Electric Generator Corporation

The Electric Generator Corporation was founded in the early 1970s to develop and market electrical products for industrial and commercial markets. Recently, the company has developed a new electric generator, the EGI, with a revolutionary design. While its initial cost is $2,000 higher than any competing generator, reduced maintenance costs will offset the higher purchase price in 18 months. The Electric Generator sales force has been instructed to concentrate all effort on selling this new generator as the company believes it has a sales potential of $500 million.

Sandy Hart, their South Texas salesperson, has as her main customer the E. H. Zachary Construction Company of San Antonio, which is the largest nonunion construction firm in the world. Because of the importance of potential Zachary purchases of the EGI (estimated at $1 million), Sandy's boss asks her to take two days off and develop a plan for contacting and selling to Zachary. Monday morning, she is expected at the Houston regional sales office to present this plan to her boss, the regional sales manager, and the divisional sales manager. These two people will critique the presentation, and then the four of them will finalize a sales plan that Sandy will present to Zachary's buying committee.

Questions

1. If you were Sandy, what would be your suggested sales plan?
2. How would a value analysis enter into your presentation?

CASE 5A–4

Frank's Drilling Service

Frank's Drilling Service specializes in drilling oil and gas wells. Scott Atkinson, one of their salespeople, was preparing to contact the drilling engineer at Oilteck, an independent oil company. Scott has learned they plan to drill approximately 12 new wells in the next six months.

Scott estimates that each oil well will require a drilling depth of approximately 10,000 feet. The drilling service the company uses charges 90 cents a foot, plus $1,200 per hour for personnel to operate the equipment. They take about 16 days to drill each well.

Frank's charges $1,200 per hour for personnel and their costs are $1 a foot. Scott believes his drilling crews save customers time and money because they can drill a 10,000 foot well in 12 days.

Questions

1. Using the above information, develop a value analysis that Scott could use to sell to his customer.
2. What are several features, advantages, and benefits Scott should discuss with Oilteck's drilling engineer?

PART III

THE RELATIONSHIP SELLING PROCESS

The selling skills used by successful salespeople are discussed in this part of the book. Selling skills involve prospecting, planning, presenting, handling objections, closing, follow-up, and servicing after the sale. Included in this part are:

6

Prospecting—The Lifeblood of Selling

MAIN TOPICS

The Sales Process Has 10 Steps

Steps before the Sales Presentation

Prospecting—The Lifeblood of Selling

Prospecting Guidelines

The Prospect Pool

The Referral Cycle

Call Reluctance Costs You Money!

Obtaining the Sales Interview

Wireless E-mail Helps You Keep in Contact and Prospect

LEARNING OBJECTIVES

Here we begin to discuss the steps within the sales process. This chapter examines the first step—prospecting. After studying this chapter, you should be able to:

■ Define the sales process; list and describe its 10 steps in the correct sequence.

■ State why it is important to prospect.

■ Describe the various prospecting methods.

■ Ask for a referral anywhere during the referral cycle.

■ Make an appointment with a prospect or customer in person or by telephone.

Larry Long, John Alexander, and Kathryn Reece just sat down for their weekly sales meeting when Larry said, "Selling Apple's new Power Mac personal computer in our market will not be easy for us. The city only has 200,000 people; the county has 275,000. Yet there are 20 or more companies selling personal computers in the area. Radio Shack, IBM, Digital, and the others are tough competitors. I'm not sure where to begin."

"Larry, our best prospects and the ones to begin seeing this afternoon are our present customers—not only the ones presently using our Apple PCs, but customers who buy our equipment and office supplies," said John. "These people know us and already have accounts set up."

"That's OK for you," replied Kathryn; "however, many of my present customers already have PCs. So, I'm not sure I can count on selling many to them. I'm going to have to explore new territories, knock on doors, and dial-for-dollars to even come up with leads."

Larry broke in with, "Let's go after the IBM customers. IBM has the biggest market share in our area. We need to hit them head-on."

"No way," replied John, "we could get creamed if we got into a war by attacking IBM or any of our other competitors."

"But with all of our advertising," Larry continued, "the company's service, and our fair price on a state-of-the-art PC, we can regain our market share."

"Hold it, hold it," Kathryn said. "Let's start over and develop a plan that will allow us to uncover as many prospects as quickly as we can. After all, we need to push this new product and get the competitive edge before competition knows what hit 'em."

If you were one of these salespeople, how would you respond? What would be your sales plan?

The first two parts of this book give much of the background a salesperson needs for making an actual presentation. However, you can be the most knowledgeable person on topics such as buyer behavior, competitors, and product information, yet still have difficulty being a successful salesperson unless you are thoroughly prepared for each part of the sales call. Part III of this book examines the various elements of the sales process and sales presentation. Let's begin by explaining what is meant by the sales process. Then we discuss methods of prospecting that may help Larry Long, John Alexander, and Kathryn Reece plan their sales program.

THE SALES PROCESS HAS 10 STEPS

As discussed in Chapter 1, the **sales process** refers to a sequential series of actions by the salesperson that leads toward the customer taking a desired action and ends with a follow-up to ensure purchase satisfaction. Although many factors may influence how a salesperson makes a presentation in any one situation, there does exist a logical, sequential series of actions that, if followed, can greatly increase the chances of making a sale. This selling process involves 10 basic steps, as listed in Exhibit 6–1. Steps one and two are discussed in this chapter, and all steps are discussed in greater detail in the following chapters. Steps three through nine compose the sales presentation itself. Before a sales presentation can be attempted, several important preparatory activities should be carried out.

EXHIBIT 6-1

The selling process has
10 important steps.

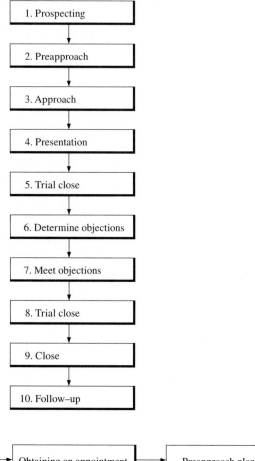

1. Prospecting

2. Preapproach

3. Approach

4. Presentation

5. Trial close

6. Determine objections

7. Meet objections

8. Trial close

9. Close

10. Follow–up

EXHIBIT 6-2

Before the sales presentation

Prospecting → Obtaining an appointment → Preapproach planning

STEPS BEFORE THE SALES PRESENTATION

As indicated in Exhibit 6–2, a successful salesperson is involved in prospecting; this involves obtaining an appointment with the prospect and planning the sales interview prior to ever actually meeting with the prospect. Like a successful lawyer, the salesperson does a great amount of background work before meeting the judge—the prospect. One rule of thumb states that a good sales process involves 20 percent presentation, 40 percent preparation, and 40 percent follow-up, especially when selling large accounts. However, even that varies from account to account. At Xerox, the national account manager will spend up to 18 months preparing a detailed description of a potential national account. This report, which can easily end up being 50 pages, is basically a business plan for selling the prospect. Thus preparation time for this sales call would be greater than the 40 percent rule of thumb.[1] As in most professions, success in selling often requires as much or more preparation before and between calls than is involved in actually making the calls themselves.

In Chapter 1, we said, "Nothing happens until someone sells something." However, even selling requires a preceding step: Nothing happens until someone does some prospecting.

| **PROSPECTING— THE LIFEBLOOD OF SELLING** | Prospecting is the first step in the selling process. A **prospect** is a qualified person or organization that has the potential to buy your product or service. **Prospecting** is the lifeblood of sales because it identifies potential customers. There are two reasons that a salesperson must look constantly for new prospects: |

1. To increase sales.
2. To replace customers that will be lost over time.

A prospect should not be confused with a lead. The name of a person or organization that might be a prospect is referred to as a **lead.** A lead can also be referred to as a suspect, indicating the person or organization is suspected of being a prospect. Once the lead has been qualified, the lead becomes a prospect.[2] As a salesperson, you can ask yourself three questions to determine if an individual or organization is a **qualified prospect:**

1. Does the prospect have the **m**oney to buy?
2. Does the prospect have the **a**uthority to buy?
3. Does the prospect have the **d**esire to buy?

A simple way to remember this qualifying process is to think of the word **MAD.** A true prospect must have the financial resources, money or credit, to pay and the authority to make the buying decision. The prospect also should desire your product. Sometimes an individual or organization may not recognize a need for your product. As later chapters show, your challenge is to create a desire for the product.

Locating leads and qualifying prospects are important activities for salespeople. Take, for example, computer salesperson Matt Suffoletto's comments on prospecting:

> Prospecting is the process of acquiring basic demographic knowledge of potential customers for your product. Lists that are available from many vendors break down businesses in a given geography by industry, revenue, and number of employees. These lists can provide an approach to mass marketing, via either mailings or telephone canvassing. That canvassing is either done by the salesperson or through an administrative sales support person. No matter who performs the canvas or how it is done, it is an important element in increasing sales productivity. The next step of qualifying the potential customer is often included in the prospecting process. Qualification is a means of quickly determining two facts. First, is there a potential need for your product? Second, is the prospect capable of making a purchase decision? Specifically, does he or she have the decision authority and the financial ability to acquire your product?

| **Where to Find Prospects** | Sources of prospects can be many and varied or few and similar, depending on the service or good sold by the salesperson. Naturally, persons selling different services and goods might not use the same sources for prospects. A salesperson of oil-field pipe supplies would make extensive use of various industry directories in a search for names of drilling companies. A life insurance salesperson would use personal acquaintances and present customers as sources of prospects. A pharmaceutical salesperson would scan the local newspaper looking for announcements of new physicians |

EXHIBIT 6–3

Many salespeople prefer to contact prospects having similar characteristics to themselves.

and hospital, medical office, and clinical laboratory openings, whereas a sales representative for a company such as General Mills or Quaker Oats would watch announcements of construction for new grocery stores and shopping centers.

Top real estate salesperson Vikki Morrison feels that prospecting, which for her means knowing people in her neighborhood, has greatly aided her in becoming a successful salesperson. She strives to become her prospect's friend.

"In my area, most of the people I see are wives—and any woman who tried to farm in this tract in high heels and a dress, dripping with jewelry, would never make it," she believes. "I'm not trying to impress anybody. These people either know me or they know about me from the neighbors. I'm no threat—especially in my tennies, pants, and T-shirt!

"Usually, I never meet the husband until the actual listing—then he wants to meet me to find out if I really know what I'm doing in real estate. As far as he's concerned, I'm just a friend of his wife's. These are the people I care about," she explains. "If someone needs a plumber or babysitter or a dentist, they call me. If I need a closing gift and someone on the block does creative things, I call them. We're all in this together!"

Planning a Prospecting Strategy

Frequently salespeople, especially new ones, have difficulty prospecting. Meeting strangers and asking them to buy something can be uncomfortable for people. As illustrated in Exhibit 6–3, many salespeople prefer to see others who have similar characteristics to themselves—although in most cases, the similarity need not go this far! For most of us, that takes little time. To be successful, prospecting requires a strategy. Prospecting, like other activities, is a skill that can be constantly improved by a dedicated salesperson. Some salespeople charge themselves with finding X number of prospects per week. Indeed, Xerox (a large manufacturer of copiers and other types of business equipment) asks its sales force to allocate a portion of each working day to finding and contacting several new prospects. A successful salesperson continually evaluates prospecting methods, comparing results and records with the mode of prospecting used in pursuit of a prospecting strategy that will result in the most effective contact rate.[3]

Prospecting Methods

The actual method by which a salesperson obtains prospects may vary. Several of the more popular prospecting methods are shown in Exhibit 6–4.

EXHIBIT 6-4

Prospecting methods that work!

Prospecting is the lifeblood of selling. While some salespeople don't have to prospect, most rely on prospecting to increase sales and make money. Here are 12 popular methods:

- Cold canvasing
- Endless chain—customer referral
- Orphaned customers
- Sales lead clubs
- Prospect lists
- Get published

- Public exhibitions and demonstrations
- Center of influence
- Direct mail
- Telephone and telemarketing
- Observation
- Networking

Which methods use referrals from customers and other people?

Cold Canvasing

The **cold canvas prospecting method** is based on the law of averages. For example, if past experience reveals that 1 person out of 10 will buy a product, then 50 sales calls could result in five sales. Thus, the salesperson contacts in person, by phone, and/or by mail as many leads as possible, recognizing that a certain percentage of people approached will buy. There is normally no knowledge about the individual or business called on. This form of prospecting relies solely on the volume of cold calls made.

The door-to-door and the telephone salesperson both employ cold canvas prospectors. For example, each summer The Southwestern Company hires college students to sell its books and other educational publications. These salespeople go into a town and knock on the door of every person living on each block they work, often contacting up to 75 people each day. They frequently ask people if they know of others who might like to purchase their products. Many office supply salespeople do the same thing, going from one business to another. Real estate, insurance, and stock brokerage firms are other businesses that use cold calls.

Endless Chain—Customer Referral

Cold calling is tough! Contacting strangers day after day is challenging even for the most motivated of individuals. Yet, many new salespeople have to begin their sales careers cold calling to get customers. Once someone is sold, the salesperson has two possibilities for future sales.

First, satisfied customers are likely to buy again from the salesperson. That is why I stress the importance of building a relationship with the customer. It is critical to your success. Second, the customer often refers the salesperson to someone she knows. This is known as the **endless chain referral method** of prospecting. This is a very effective method for finding customers. *Customers* and *customer referrals* are the two best sources of future sales, with repeat sales from customers being better. A **referral** is a person or organization recommended to you by someone who feels that this person or organization could benefit from you or your product.

Don't ask current customers, "Do you know anyone else who could use my product?" Rarely are clients eager to judge whether colleagues are prepared to make a purchase. Instead, ask whether your customer knows any other individuals or organizations who might be interested in finding out about your product.

If you sense hesitation from customers to give out referrals, it's probably because they are afraid that their associates may not want to be pestered. Say, "Let me tell you what I'm going to do with any names you give me. I will make one phone call to

SELLING GLOBALLY

Little Cold Calling in Japan

Since it's customary in Japanese companies for a sales representative to be formally introduced to a prospect, the purpose of initial calls is understood but not discussed. The decision to do business together, if it occurs, results from the subtlety and patience of relationship building. "In America," says Chuck Laughlin, co-author of *Samurai Selling: The Ancient Art of Service in Sales,* "we may be into the middle of the sales process within days, hours . . . where a Japanese selling person can spend a year building the relationship before he begins to introduce his product."

"It's all a matter of time," says IBM's Vince Matal. Then, after thinking again, he adds, "Proportion, I guess is what I'm saying. Where we might be 20 percent relationship, rapport, that kind of thing, and 80 percent selling the product, they're the opposite."

Now back in the United States as a consulting marketing representative for IBM in Raleigh, North Carolina, Matal remembers the rules from his early days in sales. "You always try to develop a relationship and service your customers," he says; "but [the Japanese] do it to the exclusion—in my opinion—of actually trying to sell the product."

With years of relationship building before any deals get done, how do salespeople earn a living? The answer—a flat

salary—is unusual in the United States, but standard procedure in Japan. This compensation arrangement, which goes hand-in-hand with the tradition of lifetime employment, was the inspiration for the term *salarymen,* the unglamorous description of employees in a work force that was once predominantly male.[4]

each party, indicate that you were nice enough to give me their names and give them a brief outline of what we do.

"If they express an interest, we will get together and I will give them the same professional service I've given you. If, on the other hand, they express no interest, I will thank them for their time and never call them again." This approach puts your customers at ease and moves solid, new prospects onto your lead list.

Don't forget your prospects are friends, neighbors, relatives—anyone and everyone you know or come into contact with. They may know people who are looking for your product and the great service you provide your customers. Everyone is a prospect!

Orphaned Customers

Salespeople often leave their employers to take other jobs; when they do, their customers are **orphaned.** These orphans are great prospects. A salesperson should quickly contact such customers to begin developing relationships. You can turn orphans into a lead-generating gold mine.

In addition, if you've been selling for a while you've surely built up a backlog of inactive accounts. Weed out the names who for whatever reason will never buy. The rest are solid prospects. Call them again and find out why they're not buying from you anymore. What would it take to change that? They may have stopped ordering your type of product altogether, or they may have gone with a competitor because of a special one-time offer, or there may have been a management change and therefore a change in buying patterns. You have to determine why the customer stopped buying from you. After you do that, reestablishing contact and turning that prospect into a customer again is standard sales procedure (SSP).

Examples.   One of my most respected role models is John Young, a former student who sells life insurance. He chose selling life insurance and other financial services as a career because he had analyzed the poor quality of the salespeople selling life insurance; he saw a golden opportunity to excel in a career with minimal competition and great financial rewards. Young convinced his prospects that he was doing a *free* estate plan analysis and they weren't obligated to buy *anything* from him, because (here is the genius of the guy) he had analyzed the entire process of life insurance sales and had come to this conclusion: "In order for me to sell the amount of life insurance I have set as a goal for myself this month, I know I must do 36 free estate plan analyses, from which I will get a dozen invitations to submit life insurance proposals. From these 12, I will historically write the amount of insurance I have set as a goal. So you can see it's not important that you," he tells his prospects, "must buy life insurance from me because I have done this valuable free estate plan for you. You are part of a master plan which guarantees my success because you are a part of the statistics that make up this plan! However, if I do a good job, I do expect you to refer me to someone you know who could benefit from a free estate plan." To do 36 analyses, Young must contact 10 present customers and 60 to 75 prospects. In 1998 John Young earned $260,000.[5]

"Of course, simply making a lot of calls and contacts without serious training and commitment will only serve to run up the telephone bill and waste a lot of time. The more you learn, the more you will earn. The more calls you make, the more you will sell!" says Young.

Dale Morgan, a salesperson for 12 years at a Buick, Hyundai, and GMC dealer in Dallas, sold Janet and Bill Williams a 1992 Buick Skylark in October 1991. In September 1997, the Williamses bought a 1998 Buick from Morgan. This wasn't luck! The sale was in the making from the moment the Williamses left the showroom in 1991. That's because Morgan is an expert in maintaining owner loyalty. Over 80 percent of his sales are from repeat customers and customer referrals.

Morgan stays in touch with all of his customers, making periodic contact by mail, phone, and in person, when possible. He made it a point to know how the Williamses' Skylark was behaving, making sure they were well satisfied during their entire ownership period. Whenever the Buick needed service, for example, they called Morgan, who then set up an appointment with the service department. Morgan visited with Janet Williams when she brought in the car. He made sure she was satisfied with the service. Occasionally he had someone drive a loaner to the Williamses' home and pick up their car for service.

When they reentered the market at the beginning of the '98 model year, they turned to Morgan to help them into another new Buick. In the last eight years, the Williamses bought two new cars plus one GMC Suburban van and one used car for their son—all from Dale. They also sent Dale 11 customers who bought 33 vehicles during that same period.

Sales personnel turnover is high in the car business. Which is good for Morgan. When a salesperson quits, Morgan frequently asks his sales manager for a list of orphaned customers.

Does Dale Morgan wait for people to come to his dealership? Is it luck that earned him more than $140,000 in 1998 selling over 300 vehicles? No way! He understands the importance of customer retention, customer referrals, contacting orphans, and prospecting. Both John Young and Dale Morgan are successful because they build long-term relationships with their customers. For them *luck* is spelled *work* and they go about it in a very professional, smart manner.

Sales Lead Clubs

Organize a group of salespeople in related but noncompetitive fields to meet twice a month to share leads and prospecting tips. To get started, write a formal mission statement, charge dues to ensure commitment, and grant membership to only one salesperson from each specific field. Next, set up administrative procedures and duties to keep the club on track and committed to its stated mission.

Finally, establish guidelines for what constitutes a good lead and track prospect information and effectiveness. Group leads by effectiveness so members can better understand which leads can help the rest. You may even have every member who closes a lead contribute to a kitty. Each month the winner can be the member who provided the most closed leads.

Get Lists of Prospects

Make a list of what your ideal prospect looks like. Ask yourself the following questions:

- Who are my ideal prospects?
- Which economic bracket do they usually fall into?
- What kinds of organizations do they belong to?
- What characteristics do most of my existing customers share?
- Are they married, single, widowed, or divorced?
- Do they have children?
- Do they have particular political leanings?
- Do they have similar occupations, educations, hobbies, illnesses, transportation needs, or family concerns?

And the key question:

- Where am I most likely to find the greatest conglomeration of people who fit my prospects profile?

List Number One. Take the information you have accumulated and apply it. Go to the library and look up the Standard Industrial Classification (SIC) code number for your ideal prospects' businesses. Ask a librarian for help if you need it. Every type of business has a specific SIC code. Related industries have similar numbers; scan the directory to locate the numbers that fit the profile. This should provide you with an excellent prospect list. In addition, literally hundreds of other business directories can help you generate lists based on corporate profiles.

List Number Two. What kinds of publications do your ideal prospects likely read? Find out whether these publications sell lists of subscribers. If a publication's readership matches your prospect profile well enough, this list should be well worth the cost.

List Number Three. Go to the Standard Rate and Data Service's directory of firms that sell lists. These companies offer a variety of criteria that you can use to generate a quality prospect list. Dun & Bradstreet is an example of such a company. For your convenience, the information may even be available on computer disk.

Become an Expert—Get Published

Although you may give your services as a writer away for free, the residual benefits make your efforts well worth the time. Submit articles about your field or industry to journals, trade magazines, and newspapers. Your submissions don't have to be glossy and expensive; just fill them with information that people can genuinely use, then make sure you have no spelling or grammatical mistakes. Instead of getting paid, ask the publication to include your address and telephone number at the end of the article and to write a little blurb about your expertise.

By convincing an editor that you're an expert in your field, you become one. Once prospects think of you as an expert you'll be the one they contact when they're ready to buy. In addition, prospects who call you for advice can come to depend on you and your product. Thus, you attract prospects without having to go out prospecting.

Public Exhibitions and Demonstrations

Exhibitions and **demonstrations** frequently take place at trade shows and other types of special interest gatherings. Many times, related firms sponsor a booth at such shows and staff it with one or more salespeople.[6] As people walk up to the booth to examine the products, a salesperson has only a few minutes to qualify leads and get names and addresses in order to contact them later at their homes or offices for demonstrations. Although salesperson–buyer contact is usually brief, this type of gathering gives a salesperson extensive contact with a large number of potential buyers over a brief time. Remember, however, that success at trade shows stems from preparation. Here are several things to do:

- Set up an interesting display to get people's attention. A popcorn machine, juggler, or expensive giveaway are good ideas.
- Write down your message so that it fits on the back of a business card.
- Practice communicating two or three key points that get your message across succinctly. Get it down pat but don't memorize your sales pitch to make it sound overly canned.
- Make a list of the major buyers at the show you want to pursue for contacts.
- Set up to maximize your display's visibility based on the flow of traffic.
- Be assertive in approaching passers-by. Instead of the common "Hello" or "How are you?" try "Do you use [product or service] in your operations?" or "Have you seen [product or service]? If I can show you how to be more profitable, would you be interested?" Next offer them a sample to handle, but not to keep. Don't let them take the item and move on without talking to you.
- Use lead cards to write down prospect information for efficient and effective postshow follow-up.
- Be prepared for rejection. Some buyers will ignore you. Don't take it personally. Be brief but professional. Your time is too valuable to waste on nonprospects.

MAKING THE SALE

Successful Selling Secrets: Vikki Morrison

"There are no secrets to successful selling. There is only hard work from 7:00 in the morning to 10:00 at night. The biggest secret is total honesty at all times with all parties. You should act with integrity and treat clients with the same respect you want from them.

"Never call clients with anything but calm assurance in your voice, because if they feel you are panicked, they will become panicked. Your walk, speech, mannerisms, and eye-to-eye contact say more about you than you'll ever know, so practice all forms of your presentation every day in every way. I suppose a secret is to save the best house for last. I just try to do the best job for the client, even when it means turning them over to another agent who would have a more suitable property in a different area."

Morrison does not work alone; she uses her available resources in selling. A computer terminal in her office gives her up-to-date information on listings and an analysis of proposed transactions. She personally employs three assistants to help her keep up with the listings and shoppers. Vikki Morrison knows the value of the real estate in her area and can give free market analysis with less than one hour's notice.

"An important part of my job is providing customers personal service via constant follow-up, before the appointment, during, and after the sale. I have periodic follow-ups to see how they like their new home or investments. Anniversary flowers and cards on their birthday are a specialty of mine. I try to eliminate any and all of their buying fears when I can, and be available to reassure them.

"I sell on emotional appeal. No matter what the facts, most people still buy based on emotion. The triggers for someone's emotional side can be quite varied. For example, for some men, their families are their hot button; for others, the greed appeal of a good deal is more important. Every person is different and should be handled as the very important individual that they are.

"Another factor in my selling is that I care about my clients. They know it, I know it, and they feel it when I'm working with them and long after the escrow is closed. These people are my good friends and we have fun together."

Center of Influence

Prospecting via the **center of influence method** involves finding and cultivating people in a community or territory who are willing to cooperate in helping to find prospects. They typically have a particular position that includes some form of influence over other people, as well as information that allows the salesperson to identify good prospects. For example, a person who graduates from a college and begins work for a local real estate firm might contact professors and administrators at his alma mater to obtain the names of teachers who have taken a job at another university and are moving out of town. He wants to help them sell their homes.

Clergy, salespeople who are selling noncompeting products, officers of community organizations like the chamber of commerce, and members of organizations such as the Lions Club or a country club are other individuals who may function as a center of influence. Be sure to show your appreciation for this person's assistance. Keeping such influential persons informed on the outcome of your contact with the prospect helps to secure future aid.

Direct Mail

In cases where there are a large number of prospects for a product, **direct-mail prospecting** is sometimes an effective way to contact individuals and businesses. Direct-mail advertisements have the advantage of contacting large numbers of people, who may be spread across an extended geographical area, at a relatively low

EXHIBIT 6-5

The processing system within a telemarketing center

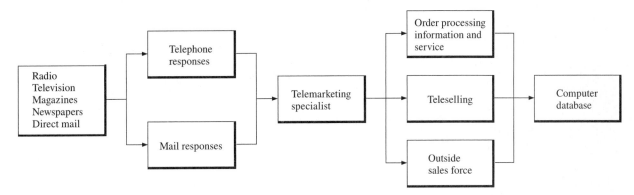

cost compared to using salespeople. People who request more information from the company subsequently are contacted by a salesperson.

Telephone and Telemarketing

Like direct marketing, use of **telephone prospecting** to contact a large number of prospects across a vast area is far less costly than use of a canvasing sales force, though usually more costly than mailouts.[7]

This person-to-person contact afforded by the telephone allows for interaction between the lead and the caller—enabling a lead to be quickly qualified or rejected. Salespeople can even contact their local telephone company for aid in incorporating the telephone into the sales program.

One example of telephone prospecting is the aluminum siding salesperson who telephones a lead and asks two questions that quickly determine if that person is a prospect. The questions are

Telephone Salesperson: Sir, how old is your home?

Lead: One year old.

Telephone Salesperson: Is your home brick or wood?

Lead: Brick!

Telephone Salesperson: Since you do not need siding, would you recommend we contact any of your neighbors or friends who can use a high-quality siding at a competitive price? [Endless chain technique]

A big sale buzzword today is **telemarketing.** Telemarketing is a marketing communication system using telecommunication technology and trained personnel to conduct planned, measurable marketing activities directed at targeted groups of consumers.

The internal process of a telemarketing center is shown in Exhibit 6–5. Many firms initiate telemarketing ventures by featuring an 800 phone number in some advertisement. In print ads, a coupon may be made available for the reader. When the coupon response or a telephone call comes into the center, a trained specialist handles it. This person may take an order (in the case of a telephone call) or transfer the person to a telephone selling or *teleselling unit.* The specialist may provide information

EXHIBIT 6–6

Reports from a telemarketing center to other marketing groups within the firm

Advertising
- Inquiries per advertisement
- Profiles of respondents
- Sales-conversion rates per advertisement

Market Management
- Segment analyses
- Marginal-account identification

Marketing Research
- Demographic data
- Image and attitude
- Forecasting data

Physical Distribution
- Consumers' orders
- Distributors' orders
- Tracing and dispatching
- Shipment requirements
- Inventory requirements
- Product return needs
- Customer-service needs

Product Management
- Sales per product
- Questions and complaints
- Consumer profiles

Sales Management
- Lead qualification
- Marginal-account status

or service. The specialist also can determine whether the customer has sufficient potential to warrant a face-to-face sales call. The duties of a telemarketing specialist are based on the type of product being sold and to whom it is sold.

From thousands of such contacts with the public, a firm can develop a valuable database that produces many informational reports. Many companies use telemarketing centers in this way. Exhibit 6–6 describes some of their informational reports.

As an example, the Westinghouse Credit Corporation uses telemarketing to qualify leads and develop live prospects for its field sales force. Specialists at the Westinghouse telemarketing center call prospects to determine interest level and to verify addresses. Having qualified a number of prospects, they call in the leads to the various sales branch offices.

Observation

A salesperson often can find prospects by constantly watching what is happening in the sales area—the **observation method.** Office furniture, computer, and copier salespeople look for new business construction in their territories. New families moving into town are excellent leads for real estate and insurance salespeople. No matter what prospecting method is used, you must always keep your eyes and ears open for information on who needs your product.

Networking

For many salespeople, prospecting never ends. They are always on the lookout for customers. Everyone they meet may be a prospect or that person may provide a name that could lead to a sale. The term given to making and using contacts is **networking.**

Of the many ways to find new prospects, networking can be the most reliable and effective. People want to do business with, and refer business to, people they know, like, and trust. The days of the one-shot salesperson are over; the name of the game today is relationship building.

Building a network is important, but cultivating that network brings sales. The key is positioning, not exposure. The goal of cultivating your network is to carve a solid niche in the mind of each of your contacts so when one of those contacts, or someone he or she knows, needs your type of product or service, you are the *only* possible resource that would come to mind.

Here are several tips for cultivating your network to dramatically increase your referral business:

1. Focus on meeting *center-of-influence* people. These people have established a good reputation and have many valuable contacts. A few places to find the key people in your industry are trade association meetings, trade shows, or any business-related social event.

2. Ninety-nine percent of your first conversation with a networking prospect should be about his or her business. People want to talk about their business, not yours.

3. Ask open-ended, feel-good questions like, "What do you enjoy most about your industry?"

4. Be sure to ask, "How would I know if someone I'm speaking with would be a good prospect for you?" If you're on the lookout to find this person new business, he will be more inclined to do the same for you.

5. Get a networking prospect's business card. It's the easiest way to follow up with your new contact.

6. Send a handwritten thank-you note that day: "It was nice meeting you this morning. If I can ever refer business your way, I certainly will."

7. When you read newspapers and magazines, keep the people in your network in mind. If you find an article one of your contacts could use or would enjoy, send it.

8. Stay on your contacts' minds by sending them something every month; notepads with your name and picture are perfect. They will keep these pads on their desks and be constantly reminded of you and your product or service.

9. Send leads. The best way to get business and referrals is to give business and referrals.

10. Send a handwritten thank-you note whenever you receive a lead, regardless of whether it results in a sale.

When meeting someone, tell them what you sell. Ask what they do. Exchange business cards and periodically contact the person. Eventually, you may build a network of people talking to each other, sharing ideas, and exchanging information. Also, you can use several of the previously discussed methods of prospecting to build your network such as the endless chain or center of influence methods.

PROSPECTING GUIDELINES

Like many other components of the selling process, prospecting methods should be chosen in light of the major factors defining a particular selling situation. As in most other optional situations discussed in this text, there is no one optimal mode of prospecting to fit all situations. Generalizations can be made, however, regarding the criteria used in choosing an optimal prospecting method for a particular selling situation. Three criteria that should be used in developing the best prospecting method should have you:

1. *Customize* or choose a prospecting method that fits the specific needs of your individual firm. Do not copy another company's method; however, it's all right to adapt someone's method.

2. Concentrate on *high potential* customers first, leaving for later prospects of lower potential.

3. Always *call back* on prospects who did not buy. With new products, do not restrict yourself to present customers only. A business may not have purchased your present products because they did not fit their present needs; however, your new product may be exactly what they need.

Always keep knocking on your prospect's and customer's door to help them solve problems through the purchase of your product. Only in this way can you maximize your long-term sales and income.

Referrals Used in Most Prospecting Methods

Referrals can be directly used in (1) cold canvasing, (2) endless chain–customer referrals, (3) orphaned customers, (4) sales lead clubs, (5) public exhibitions and demonstrations, (6) center of influence, (7) telephone, and (8) networking. Eight of the 12 popular prospecting methods directly ask someone if they know others who might be interested in their product.

Many salespeople using these methods are reluctant to ask for referrals. Yet if they would, sales would increase. Try it! If done correctly, people will give referrals. Here are some ideas on getting referrals who make up the prospect pool.

THE PROSPECT POOL

Referrals come from prospects. Different sources of prospects form the prospect pool. The **prospect pool** is a group of names gathered from various sources. Your source, for example, may be a mailing list, telephone book, referrals, orphans, or existing customers. As shown in Exhibit 6–7, a prospect pool is usually created from four main sources.[8]

1. **Leads**—people and organizations you know nothing, or very little, about.

2. **Referrals**—you frequently know very little about these people or organizations other than what you learned from the referral.

Components of the prospect pool

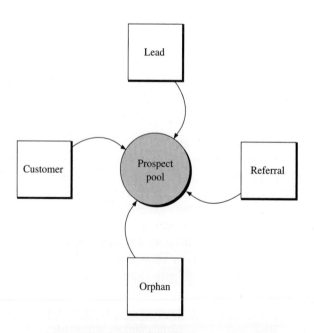

3. **Orphans**—company records provide your only information about these past customers.

4. **Your customers**—the most important prospects for future sales.

Most salespeople required to create customers through prospecting do not like to cold call. They have the goal of their prospect pool being composed of customers, referrals, and, when available, orphans. The secret to reaching this goal is the referral cycle.

THE REFERRAL CYCLE

Obtaining referrals is a continuous process without beginning or end. The salesperson is always looking for the right opportunity to find a referral. The **referral cycle** provides guidelines for a salesperson to ask for referrals in four commonly faced situations experienced by salespeople as shown in Exhibit 6–8.

If you have a sales presentation at 10 A.M., you can begin the referral cycle in the presentation phase. If you are delivering a product to a client, you can start the cycle in the product delivery phase. If you are planning on making telephone calls to leads, referrals, orphans, or customers tonight, you can begin in the preapproach phase.

Regardless of where you are in the referral cycle, you can begin at that point. Perfect your techniques so that you will be working on every phase of the cycle simultaneously. Any contact with the prospect must be geared toward presenting yourself and your product in such a way as to overcome any objections you could face later when asking for referrals and, of course, when making a sale.

The Parallel Referral Sale

Salespeople must sell the product, plus sell the prospect on providing referrals. This is referred to as the **parallel referral sale.** Equal emphasis must be given to both the product sale and the referral sale. You must nurture a parallel referral sale from the time of the initial contact, such as when making an appointment. The referral sale should receive equal importance, effort, and emphasis as the product sale. This is the key to the referral cycle.

The referral cycle: When to ask for referrals

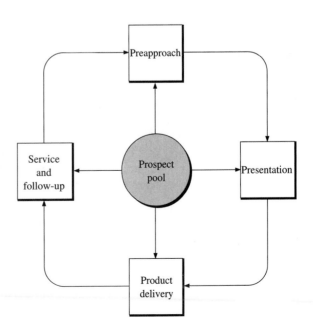

The Secret Is to Ask Correctly

Many salespeople do not ask for referrals. If they do ask, it's often done infrequently and incorrectly. It must be understood that if others—even customers—never had objections to giving referrals there would be no problem in getting them. A salesperson could simply ask for referrals and live happily ever after. Unfortunately, this is not the case. Here are examples why some clients may not wish to give referrals.

- Clients are afraid of upsetting friends and relatives.
- Clients do not want friends to think they're being talked about.
- Clients may believe in the product but not in the salesperson.
- Clients fear the salesperson may not be around years down the road.
- Clients do not feel they can benefit from giving the salesperson referrals.

It is absolutely essential that these objections be considered in asking for referrals. By doing so, you will obtain more referrals, get more appointments, and make more sales.

When to Ask

Properly asking for referrals can greatly improve a person's sales. Sounds simple doesn't it?! All one needs to do is ask others for referrals. Well it's simple, but not as simple as it first sounds. It is important to professionally ask at each phase of the referral cycle.

The Preapproach

Great care must be taken during the preapproach contact phase of the referral cycle. Whether the initial contact is face-to-face or via telephone, the effectiveness of your approach will be the deciding factor in determining whether or not you are given the opportunity to make a sales presentation.

Many prospects will hang up the phone as soon as they suspect an attempt is being made to sell them something. If, in the first several seconds, you fail to overcome their initial feelings of discomfort and intrusion, your chances of developing a relationship are slim.

Mentioning that a firm or business acquaintance of theirs recommended that you call helps alleviate some of the initial anxiety in overcoming quick objections. This is one of the reasons why working on referrals is so effective. Certainly, people are willing to listen a bit longer if they know a person whom they trust has caused this personal contact to occur. Here's an example:

> Hello, is this John? . . . Hi, John, my names is Charles Futrell from Merrill Lynch. George and Barbara Smith are clients of mine. I met with them last week and helped them set up their retirement program. They were really pleased with both my products and service. *And since I work primarily through referrals,* they were kind enough to mention that you might be interested in learning about the value I have to offer.
>
> I'd like to set up a time to stop by your home or office and share some ideas that you may find of great benefit. *It's not really important to me that we do business;* all I ask is if you appreciate the time we share together, if you feel that you benefit from the time we spend together, and, most important, if you respect my integrity, *you would be willing to pass my name on to a friend or business associate who may also benefit from my services,* just as George and Barbara did. Is that fair enough?

We have begun the process of selling the prospect—and hopefully customer—on giving us one or more referrals. We are telling John that it is not important for me to make a sale. We are asking if he feels it is reasonable, if and only if he is happy with me, that he pass my name on just as his friends did. It is easy for John to answer yes.

I have presented my offer in a nonthreatening manner that was endorsed by his friends George and Barbara.

To say "it's not really important to me that we do business" is very unusual. People are not accustomed to hearing a salesperson say that it is not important to make a sale.

The Presentation

Motivator

1. money

Security

Depending upon the particular industry you represent, the situation in which you present your product for sale may be called by a variety of names. It could be a meeting, appointment, interview, or presentation. Hereafter, it is referred to as the presentation.

During the presentation you have the greatest opportunity to influence your prospect. It is important to understand that your prospect will scrutinize everything you say and do, whether it be through words, expressions, or body language. During this presentation you also must be conscious of presenting your desire to get referrals.

The presentation phase of the referral cycle actually begins when you sit down with your prospects for the purpose of making a sales presentation. As comfortably as possible, you should make a conscious effort to mention the referring person. This may be a remark as simple as: "George told me that you like to golf. Did you get a chance to get out this week?" or "Barbara mentioned that you like to garden. Did the last frost we had affect your plants at all?"

This initial contact plants the seed for the beginning of the parallel referral sale. During the next 10 or 15 minutes there should be no discussion about the product or service being offered. This time is best used to build rapport and help break down any barriers between the prospects and their perception of you as a salesperson. To accelerate this process you should mention the referring person as often as possible. It is easy to tell when the barriers begin to come down. The walls of resistance have fallen when you begin to feel comfortable with your prospects. If you do not feel comfortable with your prospects, they certainly will not feel comfortable with you.

One you establish rapport, you should take a moment to explain to your prospects what will occur during the time you will be together. It doesn't matter what good or service you are selling; this approach should be used regardless. Then when appropriate mention the referrals. Here are two examples:

> John and Nonnie, if you're happy with my service, I hope you will be willing to pass my name on to other people who would appreciate the same honesty and integrity I have extended to you. I don't do this because I'm a good guy, or because I'm a good Christian; I do it because it makes good business sense. If I take care of you, you'll take care of me. And my livelihood depends on getting referrals.

> My success and the success of my business is totally dependent upon getting quality referrals from my client. I realize that you will introduce me to your friends, family, and business associates only if the quality and integrity of the service I provide surpasses that to which you've grown accustomed. This I pledge.

Product Delivery

Almost every selling profession has some type of product delivery phase. The delivery phase is more obvious with some products than others. For example, in the life insurance industry it involves the agent physically handing the policy to the client. In real estate, it would be the day the sale closes on the home or property. With computers, it would be the day that the system is installed and useable. In advertising, it would be the day that the ad runs in the publication. Automobile buyers go to the dealership or have the vehicle delivered to them by the salesperson. Whatever your profession, you should identify the precise moment that your product becomes of value to your customer, and at this point the product delivery phase begins. Here's an example of how to make the referral sale:

> I'm sure by now, John, you realize that I work strictly through referrals. I am constantly striving to bring my clients even greater service by improving my business. I have a very important question for you and would appreciate your giving this some thought. Is there any one thing that you would like to see me change or improve upon that would increase the likelihood of my getting referrals from you in the future?

This is only an example to get you thinking about how to properly ask for the referral. And you do need to always ask!

Service and Follow-Up

Customer service is the performance of any helpful or professional work or activity for a person, family, or organization. The service and follow-up phase of the referral cycle provides you with ongoing opportunities to maintain contact with your clients. Anytime that you have contact with your clients you encounter the possibility of getting more referrals. The quality and quantity of service will help enhance the quality and quantity of the referrals you receive. High-quality service helps create a very professional and caring image that clients are not afraid of sharing with their friends, family, and business associates; a high quantity of service helps keep you and your product fresh in the minds of clients.

For many salespeople, the product delivery phase represents the end of the relationship with their clients. There are three reasons why this happens. First, the nature of the business may not require any additional service. Second, although there may be a need for continued service, salespeople are so preoccupied with prospecting or selling that they cannot devote adequate time providing adequate service. Third, salespeople may not realize that providing their clients with quality service can benefit them in expanding the quality and quantity of their business. What it comes down to is no need, no time, or no benefit. Here is an example of what might be said during a typical annual follow-up:

> Hello, John. This is Charles Futrell. As I promised when we first did business, this is my "official" once-a-year call to let you know that I am thinking about you. Do you have any questions? Is there anything I can do for you? . . . I also want to make sure you and Nonnie have received your birthday cards and quarterly newsletters. What do you think of my newsletters? . . . Terrific. I'll let you go now. Don't forget, you've got my number if you need any help. Please keep me in mind when talking to your friends and business associates. As you know, John, I depend on quality clients like you and Nonnie to keep me in business. One of the reasons I work so hard to help my customers is because of the people you refer to me. Your referrals are really appreciated. (Pause) John, is there anyone you or Nonnie feel I should help? (Pause) Thank you very much! I look forward to seeing you soon. Goodbye.

The secret of obtaining referrals is to always professionally ask people. The main times to ask for referrals are shown in Exhibit 6–8.

Don't Mistreat the Referral

One final thought on referrals—don't mistreat them! The salesperson who mistreats a referral can lose the referring customer and the prospect. Like dropping a rock into a pool of water—it can have a ripple effect. Be sure to treat the referral in a professional manner. Always follow through on what you have told the referral.

Once you have sold the referral, and gotten more referrals, ask the *new* customer to contact the *referring* customer on her experience with the salesperson. Now you have two customers giving your referral. This can create an *endless chain* of referrals, helping to quickly fill your prospect pool with only customers and referrals.

Tracking Referrals

Keeping track of referrals is just as important as staying in contact with customers. Whether you use index cards or a computerized contact system, it's important to keep detailed records on all information you collect on the prospect/customer. (See Chapter 7's discussion of the customer profile and Chapter 5's review of computerized customer contact programs.)

CALL RELUCTANCE COSTS YOU MONEY!

What good is knowing how to prospect if you won't prospect? All salespeople seem to have call reluctance from time to time. An estimated 40 percent of all salespeople suffer a career-threatening bout of call reluctance at some point. In its milder forms, call reluctance keeps countless salespeople from achieving their potential. Research indicates that 80 percent of all first-year salespeople who don't make the grade fail because of insufficient prospecting.

Call reluctance refers to not wanting to contact a prospect or customer. This tricky demon assumes a dozen faces and comes disguised as a salesperson's natural tendencies. See Exhibit 6–9 to find out if you might occasionally be 1 of the 12 types.[9]

Countermeasures are numerous and depend on the type of call reluctance a salesperson has. But the initial step is always the same: "You must admit you have call reluctance and that your call reluctance is keeping you from earning what you're worth." For many salespeople, owning up to call reluctance is the most difficult part of combating it.

OBTAINING THE SALES INTERVIEW

Given a satisfactory method of sales prospecting and an understanding of the psychology of buying, a key factor in the selling process that has yet to be addressed is obtaining a sales interview. Although cold calling (approaching a prospect without prior notice) is suitable in a number of selling situations, industrial buyers and some other types of individuals may have neither the time nor the desire to consult with a sales representative who has not first secured an appointment.

The Benefits of Appointment Making

The practice of making an appointment before calling on a prospect can save a salesperson hours in time wasted in traveling and waiting to see someone who is busy or even absent, as seen in Exhibit 6–10. When an appointment is made, a buyer knows you are coming. People are normally in a more receptive mood when they expect someone than when an unfamiliar salesperson pops in. Appointment making is often associated with a serious, professional image and is sometimes taken as an outward gesture of respect toward a prospect.

From the salesperson's point of view, an appointment provides a time set aside for the buyer to listen to a sales presentation. This is important, since adequate time to explain a proposition improves the chance of making the sale. In addition, a list of appointments aids a salesperson in optimally allocating each day's selling time. Appointments can be arranged by telephone or by contacting the prospect's office personally.

Telephone Appointment

For obvious reasons of time and cost, salespersons usually phone to make sales appointments. Though seemingly a simple task, obtaining an appointment over the

EXHIBIT 6–9

The 12 faces of call reluctance

Think you might suffer from call reluctance? See if you fit 1 of the 12 classic types identified by researchers George Dudley and Shannon Goodson. They're listed in order from most common to least common.

1. **Yielder**
   Fears intruding on others or being pushy.

2. **Overpreparer**
   Overanalyzes, underacts.

3. **Emotionally unemancipated**
   Fears loss of family approval, resists mixing business and family.

4. **Separationist**
   Fears loss of friends, resists prospecting among personal friends.

5. **Hyper-pro**
   Obsessed with image, fears being humiliated.

6. **Role rejector**
   Ashamed to be in sales.

7. **Socially self-conscious**
   Fears intruding on others or being pushy. Intimidated by upmarket customers.

8. **Doomsayer**
   Worries, won't take risks.

9. **Telephobic**
   Fears using the telephone for prospecting or selling.

10. **Stage fright**
    Fears group presentations.

11. **Referral aversions**
    Fears disturbing existing business or client relationships.

12. **Oppositional reflex**
    Rebuffs attempts to be coached.

How to Conquer the Fear

- First and foremost, you must admit to having call reluctance. Acknowledgment is a major step toward recovery, but it's not an easy move. Denial is the most frequent companion of call reluctance, and the problem is sometimes hard to identify. Salespeople "typically know something is wrong, but they may not know what it is," says behavioral scientist and call reluctance expert George Dudley. "Many who do know they are experiencing sales call reluctance don't feel secure admitting it to management, because many sales organizations still tend to feature cultlike, unrealistic emphasis on maintaining a positive attitude," Dudley explains.

- Second, determine your call reluctance type and adopt appropriate countermeasures. The numerous prescriptions often involve clearly and specifically identifying your fears or negative thoughts. Then you can tackle them head-on, one at a time. In a sense, curbing call reluctance is like breaking a bad habit. Some salespeople find token reward systems helpful; others use relaxation techniques. In one countermeasure known as thought zapping, you place a rubber band around your wrist. When a negative thought intrudes, you snap the rubber band sharply and immediately conjure up a positive mental image of yourself—recalling, for example, a time when you did well in a similar situation.

- Third, follow up, keep plugging, make calls. Taming call reluctance is work, and for many salespeople it takes continuous effort. "Don't confuse a change in your outlook with a change in the number of contacts you initiate with prospective buyers," Dudley warns. If you're call reluctant, take heart in the knowledge that your problem actually may be a sign of commitment to selling. "Salespeople who are not motivated or goal-focused can never be considered call reluctant," says Dudley. Salespeople with authentic call reluctance care very much about meeting prospecting goals. "You simply cannot be reluctant to get something you don't want in the first place."

telephone is frequently difficult. Business executives generally are busy and their time is scarce. However, these practices can aid in successfully making an appointment over the telephone:

- Plan and write down what you will say. This helps you organize and concisely present your message.

- Clearly identify you and your company.

EXHIBIT 6–10

Major stakeholders in the organization's performance

This salesperson saves time by scheduling and then confirming next week's appointments by phone.

- State the purpose of your call and briefly outline how the prospect may benefit from the interview.
- Prepare a brief sales message, stressing product benefits over features. Present only enough information to stimulate interest.
- Do not take no for an answer. Be persistent even if there is a negative reaction to the call.
- Ask for an interview so that you can further explain product benefits.
- Phrase your appointment request as a question. Your prospect should be given a choice, such as: "Would nine or one o'clock Tuesday be better for you?"

Successful use of the telephone in appointment scheduling requires an organized, clear message that captures interest quickly. Before you dial a prospect's number, mentally or physically sketch out exactly what you plan to say. While on the telephone get to the point quickly (as you may have only a minute), disclosing just enough information to stimulate the prospect's interest. For example:

> Mr. West, this is Sally Irwin of On-Line Computer Company calling you from Birmingham, Alabama. Businessmen such as yourself are saving the costs of rental or purchase of computer systems, while receiving the same benefits they get from the computer they presently have. May I explain how they are doing this on Tuesday at nine o'clock in the morning or would one o'clock in the afternoon be preferable?

One method for obtaining an appointment with anyone in the world is for you to have someone else make it for you. Now, that sounds simple enough, doesn't it?

MAKING THE SALE

Getting an Appointment Is Not Always Easy

The owner of an oil field supply house in Kansas City was Jack Cooper's toughest customer. He was always on the run, and Jack had trouble just getting to see him, much less getting him to listen to a sales presentation. Jack would have liked to take him to lunch so he could talk to him, but the owner never had time. Every day he called a local hamburger stand and had a hamburger sent to his office so he wouldn't have to waste time sitting down to eat.

Jack wanted to get the owner interested in a power crimp machine that would enable him to make his own hose assemblies. By making them himself, the owner could save about 45 percent of his assembly costs—and Jack would make a nice commission.

The morning Jack was going to make his next call, his wife was making sandwiches for their children to take to school. Jack had a sudden inspiration. He asked his wife to make two deluxe bag lunches for him to take with him.

Jack arrived at the supply house just before lunchtime. "I know you're too busy to go out for lunch," he told the owner, "so I brought it with me. I thought you might like something different for a change."

The owner was delighted. He even took time to sit down and talk while they ate. After lunch, Jack left with an order for the crimper—plus a standing order for hose and fittings to go with it!

However, do not just have anyone make the appointment. It should be a satisfied customer. Say, "Listen, you must have a couple of people who could use my product. Would you mind telling me who they are? I'd like you to call them up and say I'm on my way over." Or, "Would you just call them up and ask them if they would meet with me?" This simple technique frequently works. In some situations, an opportunity to make an appointment personally arises or is necessitated by circumstances.

Personally Making the Appointment

Many business executives are constantly bombarded with an unending procession of interorganizational memos, correspondence, reports, forms and *salespeople*. To use their time optimally, many executives establish policies to aid in determining whom to see, what to read, and so on. They maintain gatekeepers (secretaries or receptionists) who execute established time-use policies by acting as filters for all correspondence, telephone messages, and people seeking entry to the executive suite. Successful navigation of this filtration system requires a professional salesperson who: (1) is determined to see the executive and believes it can be done; (2) develops friends within the firm (many times including the gatekeepers); and (3) optimizes time by calling only on individuals who make or participate in the purchase decision.

Believe in Yourself. As a salesperson, believe that you can obtain interviews because you have a good offer for prospects. Develop confidence by knowing your products and by knowing prospects—their business and needs. Speak and carry yourself as though you expect to get in to see the prospect. Instead of saying, "May I see Ms. Vickery," you say, while handing the secretary your card, "Could you please tell Ms. Vickery that Ray Baker from XYZ Corporation is here?"

Develop Friends in the Prospect's Firm. Successful salespeople know that people within the prospect's firm often indirectly help in arranging an interview and influence buyers to purchase a product. A successful Cadillac salesperson states:

SELLING TIPS

Customer Call Reluctance—Your Own Worst Enemy

According to a study by Behavioral Sciences Research Press, the problem of call reluctance in sales is widespread and costly.[10] Among the findings of the Dallas research and sales training firm:

■ Some 80 percent of all new salespeople who fail within their first year do so because of insufficient prospecting activity.

■ Forty percent of all sales veterans experience one or more episodes of call reluctance severe enough to threaten their continuation in sales. It can strike at any time.

■ The call-reluctant salesperson loses more than 15 new accounts per month to competitors.

■ Call-reluctant stockbrokers acquire 48 fewer new accounts per year than brokers who have learned to manage their fear.

■ In some cases, the call-reluctant salesperson loses $10,800 per month in gross sales.

■ In others, call reluctance costs the salesperson $10,000 in lost commissions per year.

To do business with the boss, you must sell yourself to everyone on his staff. I sincerely like people—so it came naturally to me. I treat secretaries and chauffeurs as equals and friends. Ditto for switchboard operators and maids. I regularly sent small gifts to them all. An outstanding investment.

The little people are great allies. They can't buy the product. But they can kill the sale. Who needs influential enemies? The champ doesn't want anyone standing behind him throwing rocks. In many cases, all you do is treat people decently—an act that sets you apart from 70 percent of your competitors.

Matt Suffoletto, the computer salesperson mentioned earlier, says it another way:

I have observed one common distinction of successful salespeople. They not only call on the normal chain of people within the customer's organization, but they have periodic contact with higher level decision makers to communicate the added value which their products and services have provided. This concept, when exercised judiciously, can have a tremendous impact on your effectiveness.

Respect, trust, and friendship are three key elements in any salesperson's success. Timing is also important.

Call at the Right Time on the Right Person. Both gatekeepers and busy executives appreciate salespeople who do not waste their time. Using past sales call records or by calling the prospect's receptionist, a salesperson can determine when the prospect prefers to receive visitors. Direct questions, such as asking the receptionist, "Does Mr. Smith purchase your firm's office supplies?" or "Whom should I see concerning the purchase of office supplies?" can be used in determining whom to see.

Do Not Waste Time Waiting. Once you have asked the receptionist if the prospect can see you today, you should: (1) determine how long you will have to wait, and whether you can afford to wait that length of time; (2) be productive while waiting by reviewing how you will make the sales presentation to the prospect; and (3) once an acceptable amount of waiting time has passed, tell the receptionist, "I have another appointment and must leave in a moment." When politely approached, the receptionist will usually attempt to get you in. If still unable to enter the office, you can ask for an appointment as follows: "Will you please see if I can get an appointment for 10 on Tuesday?" If this request does not result in an immediate interview, it implies the establishment of another interview time. If you establish a positive relationship with a prospect and with gatekeepers, waiting time normally decreases while productivity increases.

WIRELESS E-MAIL HELPS YOU KEEP IN CONTACT AND PROSPECT

No one needs constant contact with the home office, customers, and prospects more desperately than a sales representative. While e-mail is one of the best ways to accomplish that, adapting e-mail to meet the requirements of the itinerant sales reps has never been simple.

This is the problem that Jeff Pruss, a sales rep for Hewlett-Packard's Computer Products Organization in Pleasanton, California, faces every day. His sales team's solution is to use WyndMail for Windows to keep in touch with co-workers, customers, and prospects. "We're not very often at our desks, nor do we necessarily have a phone jack," Pruss says. "Wireless e-mail helps keep us mobile."

Pruss explains that his team chose WyndMail for several reasons. One reason was very simple: It was the only wireless e-mail program for Windows on the market at the time. A more important reason, he adds, was that Wynd Communications "was very responsive to our particular needs." For example, the first version of the address book didn't operate the way the team wanted it to—it always sorted by last name. Wynd very quickly addressed that issue, he says. "In the new version, WyndMail enables each of us to open our address books in our own preferred sort order. It feels the way we like it to feel," says Pruss.

To connect to the outside world, WyndMail uses the RAM Mobile Data network and the Internet. Some of his peers questioned WyndMail's apparently high costs, but Pruss says his co-workers "don't know what they're missing. It's worth the money."

The only "problem" with WyndMail's service, according to Pruss, is that there is only one place where the coverage hasn't been good: Lake Tahoe. "This is a good thing," he commented wryly, "because when I'm skiing, I want to relax."

SUMMARY OF MAJOR SELLING ISSUES

The sales process involves a series of actions beginning with prospecting for customers. The sales presentation is the major element of this process. Before making the presentation, the salesperson must find prospects to contact, obtain appointments, and plan the entire sales presentation.

Prospecting involves locating and qualifying the individuals or businesses that have the potential to buy a product. A person or business that might be a prospect is a *lead*. These questions can determine if someone is qualified: Is there a real need? Is the prospect aware of that need? Is there a desire to fulfill the need? Does the prospect believe a certain product can be beneficial? Does the prospect have the finances and authority to buy? and Are potential sales large enough to be profitable to me?

Several of the more popular prospecting methods are cold canvas and endless chain methods, public exhibitions and demonstrations, locating centers of influence, direct mailouts, and telephone and observation prospecting. To obtain a continual supply of prospects, the salesperson should develop a prospecting method suitable for each situation.

Once a lead has been located and qualified as a prospect, the salesperson can make an appointment with that prospect by telephone or in person. At times, it is difficult to arrange an appointment, so the salesperson must develop ways of getting to see the prospect. Believing in yourself and feeling that you have a product needed by the prospect are important.

ETHICAL DILEMMA

What an Offer! Or Is It?

You are a new life insurance agent and have just made a sale to an old family friend who is the personnel manager for a large manufacturing company in your town. To help you in your prospecting, he offers you a large file of personal data on the employees of the company, including income, family size, phone numbers, and addresses.

This information would be very valuable. You are sure to make 5 to 10 sales from this excellent prospect list. As he hands you the material, you notice it is stamped, "Not for Publication, Company Use Only!"

What would you do?

Developed by Richard T. Brown.

MEETING A SALES CHALLENGE

The proposed prospecting systems were fairly well analyzed by Larry Long, John Alexander, and Kathryn Reece. Old customers are easy to see and know the company. However, there are people who will quickly point out that just because a firm buys one thing from a company does not mean that it will buy another. Xerox learned that lesson in marketing its line of word processors. Companies often are fooled by their corporate egos into thinking that their existing customers will buy just about anything they make.

Going after IBM seems to scare John for some reason. However, think a minute. Exactly what will IBM do that they won't do competitively anyway? They have some competition from all sides by many firms. If the company has a good cost story to tell, then go after the big users to whom the cost savings will be significant.

In short, all the systems have virtues and none should be excluded from consideration. New blood is needed. You can't stay in business by just relying on one set of customers. So much depends on a particular territory. The sales rep must be governed by the territory. In some, there may be few old customers or few IBM users. The salesperson must adapt to the characteristics of the territory.

KEY TERMS FOR SELLING

sales process 173	direct-mail prospecting 182
prospect 175	telephone prospecting 183
prospecting 175	telemarketing 183
lead 175	observation method 184
qualified prospect 175	networking 184
cold canvas prospecting method 177	prospect pool 186
endless chain referral method 177	referral cycle 187
referral 177	parallel referral sale 187
orphaned customers 178	customer service 190
exhibitions and demonstrations 181	call reluctance 191
center of influence method 182	

SALES APPLICATION QUESTIONS

1. What is the difference between a lead and a prospect? What should you, as a salesperson, do to qualify a potential customer?

2. This chapter termed prospecting the *lifebood of selling.*
   a. Where do salespeople find prospects?
   b. List and briefly explain seven prospecting methods discussed in this chapter. Can you think of other ways to find prospects?

3. Assume that you have started a business to manufacture and market a product line selling for between $5,000 and $10,000. Your primary customers are small retailers. How would you uncover leads and convert them into prospects without personally contacting them?

4. Assume you had determined that John Firestone, vice president of Pierce Chemicals, was a prospect for your paper and metal containers. You call Mr. Firestone to see if he can see you this week. When his secretary answers the telephone, you say, "May I speak to Mr. Firestone, please?" and she says, "What is it you wish to talk to him about?" How would you answer her question? What would you say if you were told, "I'm sorry, but Mr. Firestone is too busy to talk with you?"

5. You are a new salesperson. Next week, your regional sales manager will be in town to check the progress you have made in searching for new clients for your line of industrial chemicals. You have learned that Big Industries, Inc., a high-technology company, needs a supplier of your product. Also, a friend has told you about 12 local manufacturing firms that could use your product. The sales potential of each of these firms is about one-tenth of Big Industries. Knowing that your sales manager expects results, explain how you will qualify each lead (assuming the 12 smaller firms are similar).

SALES WORLD WIDE WEB EXERCISES

Research a Company of Your Choice!

Pick an organization for which you would like to work. Research it using the World Wide Web.

Write a report that summarizes such things as the organization's: (1) history, (2) sales for the last five years, (3) customers and markets, (4) products, and (5) future plans. Determine the geographic location of the national headquarters. If you were asked to go to the national headquarters for a job interview, how would you get to its location? Using a URL such as www.mapquest.com or www.tripquest.com, locate the address and print out a map showing how to drive to the location once you are in that city.

FURTHER EXPLORING THE SALES WORLD

Contact several salespeople in your community and ask them to discuss their prospecting system plus the steps they use in planning their sales calls. Write a short paper on your results and be prepared to discuss it in class.

SELLING EXPERIENTIAL EXERCISE

Your Attitude toward Selling

To measure your attitude toward selling, complete this exercise. On another sheet of paper write a 5 to indicate your attitude could not be better in this area; write a 1 to indicate you definitely do not agree. Write a 2, 3, or 4 if you are saying something in between disagree and agree.

	Disagree				Agree
1. There is nothing demeaning about selling a good or service to a prospect.	1	2	3	4	5
2. I would be proud to tell friends selling is my career.	1	2	3	4	5
3. I can approach customers, regardless of age, appearance, or behavior, with a positive attitude.	1	2	3	4	5
4. On bad days—when nothing goes right—I can still be positive.	1	2	3	4	5
5. I am enthusiastic about selling.	1	2	3	4	5

6.	Having customers turn me down does not cause me to be negative.	1	2	3	4	5
7.	The idea of selling challenges me.	1	2	3	4	5
8.	I consider selling to be a profession.	1	2	3	4	5
9.	Approaching strangers (customers) is interesting and usually enjoyable.	1	2	3	4	5
10.	I can always find something good in a customer.	1	2	3	4	5

Total Score _____

Add up your score. If you scored more than 40, you have an excellent attitude toward selling as a profession. If you rated yourself between 25 and 40, you appear to have serious reservations. A rating under 25 indicates that another type of job is probably best for you.[11]

CASE 6–1
Canadian Equipment Corporation

You work for the Canadian Equipment Corporation selling office equipment. Imagine entering the lobby and reception room of a small manufacturing company. You hand the receptionist your business card and ask to see the purchasing agent. "What is this in reference to?" the secretary asks, as two other salespeople approach.

Question

Which of the following alternatives would you use and why?

a. Give a quick explanation of your equipment, ask whether the secretary has heard of your company or used your equipment, and again ask to see the purchasing agent.

b. Say, "I would like to discuss our office equipment."

c. Say, "I sell office equipment designed to save your company money and provide greater efficiency. Companies like yours really like our products. Could you help me get in to see your purchasing agent?"

d. Give a complete presentation and demonstration.

CASE 6–2
Montreal Satellites

As a salesperson for Montreal Satellites, you sell television satellite dishes for homes, apartments, and businesses. After installing a satellite in Jeff Sager's home, you ask him for a referral. Jeff suggests you contact Tom Butler, his brother-in-law.

Mr. Butler is a well-known architect who designs and constructs unique residential homes. Your objective is to sell Mr. Butler a satellite for his office and home in hopes he would install them in the homes he builds. Certainly he is a center of influence and a good word from him to his customers could result in numerous sales. Thus, another objective is to obtain referrals from Mr. Butler.

Questions

1. After eight attempts, you now have Mr. Butler on the telephone. What would you say in order to get an appointment and set the stage for getting referrals?

2. You get the appointment and are now in Mr. Butler's office trying to get him to buy a satellite for his home and office. Sometime during the presentation you are going to ask for a referral. What would you say?

3. Mr. Butler buys a satellite for his home but not his office. You install the satellite yourself and then spend 15 minutes showing Mr. and Mrs. Butler and their two teenagers how to use it. Before you leave, how would you ask for a referral?

4. Three months after the installation you are talking to Mr. Butler. How would you ask for a referral?

7

Planning the Sales Call Is a Must!

LEARNING OBJECTIVES

Planning the sales call is the second step in the selling process. It is extremely important to spend time planning all aspects of your sales presentation. After studying this chapter, you should be able to:

- Explain the importance of sales call planning.
- List the four planning steps in order and understand them.
- Develop a customer benefit plan.
- Describe the prospect's five mental steps in buying.

After being hired, trained, and assigned a sales territory, you have been assigned by your boss to work with three of your company's salespeople. You immediately notice they are not doing what you've been trained to do. They walk into an office, introduce themselves, and ask if the customer needs anything today. Prospects rarely buy, and customers tell them what they need. This doesn't seem like selling to you. It's order taking, and that type of job is not for you.

The problem is—how do you get someone to listen to you? How do you know what they think of your product? How do you know when they're ready to buy? Next Monday, you call on your first customer. What are you going to do?

Your job as a salesperson is to find prospects who need your product and convince them your product will satisfy their need. Walking into a prospect's office and asking if they need anything is "order taking" not "order getting." This chapter introduces you to the importance of planning each sales call. It often takes hours to plan a sales presentation and minutes to make, but without preparation your sales will suffer.

STRATEGIC CUSTOMER SALES PLANNING—THE PREAPPROACH

Once the prospect has been located, or the salesperson determines which customer to call on, the salesperson is ready to plan the sales call. Planning is often referred to as the preapproach (see Exhibit 7–1). This chapter discusses the many aspects of planning a sales call. Let's begin by learning why salespeople should consider the customer's needs in order to recommend a creative solution that will benefit both the buyer and seller.

High performing salespeople tend to be strategic problem solvers for their customers. **Strategic** refers to programs, goals, and problems of great importance to customers. The top salespeople who are effective strategic problem solvers have the skills and knowledge to be able to:

- Uncover and understand the customer's strategic needs by gaining an in-depth knowledge of the customer's organization.
- Develop solutions that demonstrate a creative approach to addressing the customer's strategic needs in the most efficient and effective manner possible.
- Arrive at a mutually beneficial agreement.

These key terms—strategic needs, creative solutions, and mutually beneficial agreements—are critical to strategic problem solving. Properly done by the salesperson, they create a **strategic customer relationship** or a formal relationship with the customer the purpose of which is joint pursuit of mutual goals. Strategic goals for a customer typically include reducing costs and/or increasing productivity, sales, and profits. The sales organization has goals of increasing sales and profits.

Strategic Needs

The salesperson who understands the full range of the customer's needs is in a much better position to provide a product solution that helps the customer progress more efficiently and effectively toward achieving his or her organization's strategic goal. "The top salespeople have an in-depth understanding of our needs," said one business purchasing agent. "They can match up their products with these needs to help us reach our goals."

201

EXHIBIT 7-1

The preapproach involves planning the sales presentation.

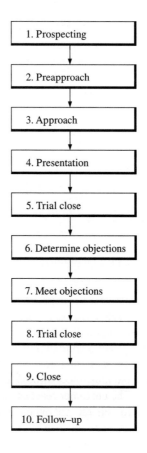

1. Prospecting

2. Preapproach

3. Approach

4. Presentation

5. Trial close

6. Determine objections

7. Meet objections

8. Trial close

9. Close

10. Follow–up

Creative Solutions

For each customer, a salesperson is often faced with a specific, unique set of problems to solve. As a result, each customer requires a specific solution from the sales organization. The ability of a salesperson to tailor a "custom" solution for each customer is critical today. The salesperson needs to use creative problem solving to identify the specific solution that meets each customer's needs. Instead of one product, the salesperson often must create the solution from a mix of goods and services. Usually, the solution represents either one of two options:

1. A customized version or application of a product and/or service that efficiently addresses the customer's specific strategic needs.
2. A mix of goods and services—including, if appropriate, competitors' products and services—that offers the best possible solution in light of the customer's strategic needs.

The better a salesperson is at creatively marshalling all available resources to address a customer's strategic need, the stronger the customer relationship becomes. Today's salespeople need to be **creative problem solvers** who have the ability to develop and combine nontraditional alternatives to meet the specific needs of the customer.

Mutually Beneficial Agreements   Salespeople and customers say that a significant shift has occurred in their expectations of the outcome of sales agreements—from the adversarial "win–lose" to the more collaborative "win–win" arrangement. To achieve a mutually beneficial agreement, salespeople and customers must work together to develop a common understanding of the issues and challenges at hand.

EXHIBIT 7–2

Consultative selling—customer relationship model

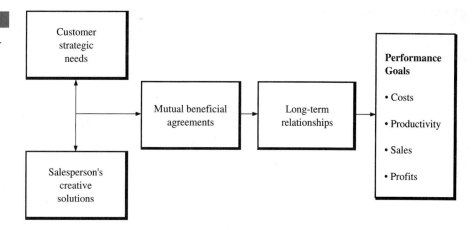

Information about an organization's business strategies and needs is often highly confidential. But more and more customers, in the interest of developing solutions that will help achieve their strategic goals, are willing to let salespeople cross the threshold of confidentiality.

The Customer Relationship Model

The customer relationship model shown in Exhibit 7–2 brings together the main elements of consultative selling. It shows the customers have strategic needs salespeople must meet through creative solutions. In doing so, both buyer and seller benefit. The customer reaches its goal, as does the seller. This results in the seller being able to sell the customer again, again, and again—building a long-term relationship. Strategic customer sales planning is extremely important to the success of today's salespeople. Let's examine the important aspects of the second step in our customer relationship process called the preapproach. The **preapproach** refers to planning the sales call on a customer or prospect.

Reasons for Planning the Sales Call

Planning the sales call is the key to success. See Exhibit 7–3. While salespeople say there are numerous reasons for planning the sales call, four of the most frequently mentioned reasons are planning aids in building confidence, it develops an atmosphere of goodwill between the buyer and seller. It reflects professionalism, and it generally increases sales.

Builds Self-Confidence

In giving a speech before a large group of people, most people are nervous. This nervousness can be greatly reduced and self-confidence increased by planning what to say and practicing your talk. The same is true in making a sales presentation. By carefully planning your presentation, you increase confidence in yourself and your ability as a salesperson. This is why planning the sales call is especially important.

Develops an Atmosphere of Goodwill

The salesperson who understands a customer's needs and is prepared to discuss how a product will benefit the prospect is appreciated and respected by the buyer. Knowledge of a prospect and concern for the prospect's needs demonstrate a sincere interest in a prospect that generally is rewarded with an attitude of goodwill from the prospect. This goodwill gradually aids in building the buyer's confidence and results in a belief that the salesperson can be trusted to fulfill obligations.

Planning is the key to success.

The sales team rehearses an upcoming sales call.

Creates Professionalism

Good business relationships are built on your knowledge of your company, industry, and customer's needs. Show prospects that you are calling on them to help solve their problems or satisfy their needs. These factors are the mark of a professional salesperson who uses specialized knowledge in an ethical manner to aid customers.

Increases Sales

A confident salesperson who is well prepared to discuss how products solve particular needs always will be more successful than the unprepared salesperson. Careful planning ensures that you have diagnosed a situation and have a remedy for a customer's problem. Planning assures that a sales presentation is well thought out and appropriately presented.

Like other beneficial presales call activities, planning is most effective (and time efficient) when done logically and methodically. Some salespeople try what they consider planning, later discarding the process because it took too much time. In many cases, these individuals were not aware of the basic elements of sales planning.

Elements of Sales Call Planning

Exhibit 7–4 depicts the four facets considered in **sales planning.** These facets are (1) determining the sales call objective; (2) developing or reviewing the customer profile; (3) developing a customer benefit plan; and (4) developing the individual sales presentation based on the sales call objective, customer profile, and customer benefit plan.

Steps in the preapproach: planning the sale

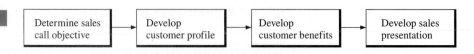

Determine sales call objective → Develop customer profile → Develop customer benefits → Develop sales presentation

Always Have a Sales Call Objective

The **sales call objective** is the main purpose of a salesperson's contact with a prospect or customer.

Is it possible to make a sales call without having a sales call objective in mind? Why can't salespeople just go in and see what develops? They can: in fact, a survey call is a legitimate sales technique. However, when all the calls that salespeople make are survey calls, they should be working exclusively for the market research department.

The Precall Objective

Selling is not a very complex process. It's just difficult to do on a consistent basis. That's why, whether you regard it as an art or a science, the discipline of selling starts with setting a precall objective.

If anyone doubts this, remember that, by definition, a sales call must move systematically toward a sale. Often, we're not talking about elaborate planning. Sometimes it only takes a few seconds before a call. But on every occasion, it's vital for the sales representative to answer one simple question: "If this call is successful, what will result?"

Taking the time to do this starts the selling process in motion. Before every sales call, ask yourself, "What am I going in here for? What is the result I'm trying to make happen? If they give me the opportunity, what am I going to recommend?"

Focus and Flexibility

Writing down your precall objective increases the focus of your efforts. Given today's rising costs, this focus is essential. If salespeople are just going around visiting customers to see what develops, they are merely well-paid tourists. If they are professional sales representatives, they should be moving their customers in the direction of a predetermined goal.

Knowing where you are going definitely increases the likelihood of getting there. Obviously, if the precall objective turns out to be inappropriate as the sales call develops, it's easy to switch tactics. Often, such changes involve a simple redirection.

Making the Goal Specific

When asked the purpose of a call, some salespeople say enthusiastically, "It's to get an order. Let's go!" Of course, everyone's in favor of getting orders, but that's more likely to happen if salespersons stop and ask themselves questions such as: What need of this prospect can I serve? Which product or service is best for this account? How large an order should I go for? The more specific the objective, the better.

Moving toward Your Objective

Just because a salesperson isn't making a formal presentation doesn't mean that the call shouldn't be planned. Sometimes the sales call has a limited objective. Guiding the customer in the direction of that preplanned outcome is what I see experienced salespeople doing on most sales calls. They do it with such simple questions as:

- If we can meet the spec, can you set up a trial?
- How soon will the vice president be available to make a decision?
- Can you schedule a demonstration before the end of the month?

Set an Objective for Every Call

Don't let anyone tell you that selling is so repetitive that the next step becomes a matter of rote. Knowing where you are going may be rote, but getting there requires thinking and skill. Set a **SMART** call objective that is

Specific—to get an order is *not* specific.

Measurable—quantifiable (number, size, etc.).

Achievable—not too difficult to fulfill.

Realistic—not too easy to fulfill.

Timed—at this call or before the end of the financial year.

It's amazing how often even veteran salespeople skip the precall objective step in favor of just seizing whatever opportunities present themselves. As a professional, it's your responsibility to head off this kind of behavior. Commit to having an objective for every call, and after a call check your results against that objective. This is a simple truth that the best sales professionals have known all along. Often the most important step in a sale takes place without the customer even being there.

In addition, the sales call objective should be directly beneficial to the customer. For example, the Colgate salesperson might have the objectives of checking all merchandise, having the customer make a routine reorder on merchandise, and selling promotional quantities of Colgate toothpaste.

The Colgate salesperson might call on a chain store manager with the multiple objectives of making sure that Colgate products are placed where they sell most rapidly; replenishing the store's stock of Colgate products so that customers will not leave the store disgruntled due to stockouts, and aiding the manager in deciding how much promotional Colgate toothpaste and Rapid Shave shaving cream should be displayed.

Industrial salespeople develop similar objectives to determine if customers need to reorder or to sell new products.

Customer Profile Provides Insight

A customer profile sheet, such as shown in Exhibit 7–5, can be a guide for determining the appropriate strategy to use in contacting each customer. As much relevant information as possible should be reviewed regarding the firm, the buyer, and the individuals who influence the buying decision—before a sales call is made—to properly develop a customized presentation. The material discussed in Chapter 3 concerning why the buyer buys needs to be considered by the salesperson at this time. A **customer profile** should tell you such things as:

- Who makes the buying decisions in the organization—an individual or committee?
- What is the buyer's background? The background of the buyer's company? The buyer's expectations of you?
- What are the desired business terms and needs of the account, such as delivery, credit, technical service?
- What competitors successfully do business with the account? Why?
- What are the purchasing policies and practices of the account? For example, does the customer buy special price offer promotions, or only see salespeople on Tuesday and Thursday?

EXHIBIT 7-5

Information used in a profile and
for planning

Customer Profile and Planning Sheet

1. Name: _____
    Address: _____
2. Type of business:_____
    Name of buyer: _____
3. People who influence buying decision or aid in
    using or selling our product: _____
4. Buying hours and best time to see buyer: _____
5. Receptionist's name: _____
6. Buyer's profile: _____
7. Buyer's personality style: _____
8. Sales call objectives: _____
9. What are customer's important buying needs: _____
10. Sales presentation: _____
    a. Sales approach: _____
    b. Features, advantages, benefits: _____
    c. Method of demonstrating FAB: _____
    d. How to relate benefits to customer's needs: _____
    e. Trial close to use: _____
    f. Anticipated objections: _____
    g. Trial close to use: _____
    h. How to close this customer: _____
    i. Hard or soft close: _____
11. Sales made—product use/promotional plan agreed on: _____
    _____
12. Post sales call comments (reason did/did not buy; what to do on next call;
    follow-up promised): _____

■ What is the history of the account? For example, past purchases of our products, inventory turnover, profit per shelf foot, our brand's volume sales growth,
payment practices, and attitude toward resale prices.

Determine this information from a review of records on the company or through
personal contact with the company.

Customer Benefit Plan: What It's All About!

Beginning with your sales call objectives and what you know about your prospect,
you are ready to develop a **customer benefit plan.** The customer benefit plan
contains the nucleus of the information used in your sales presentation; thus it should
be developed to the best of your ability. Creating a customer benefit plan can be
approached as a four-step process:

Step 1:

Select the features, advantages, and benefits of your product to present to your
prospect. (See Chapter 3.) This addresses the issue of why your product should be
purchased. The main reason your product should be purchased by your prospect is

EXHIBIT 7–6

Examples of topics contained in the marketing plan segment of your sales presentation

Resellers	End Users
1. Advertising	1. Availability
■ Geographical	2. Delivery
—National	3. Guarantee
—Regional	4. Installation
—Local	■ Who does it?
—Co-op	■ When?
■ Type	■ How?
—Television	5. Maintenance/service
—Radio	6. Training on use
—Direct-mail	7. Warranty
—Internet	
2. Sales Promotion	
■ Contests	
■ Coupons	
■ Demonstrations	
■ Samples	
■ Sweepstakes	
■ POP displays	
3. Sales Force	
■ Working with their salespeople	
4. Trade Shows	

that its benefits fulfill certain needs or solve certain problems. Carefully determine the benefits you wish to present.

Step 2:

Develop your marketing plan. If selling to wholesalers or retailers, your marketing plan should include how, once they buy, they will sell your product to their customers. An effective marketing plan includes suggestions on how a retailer, for example, should promote the product through displays, advertising, proper shelf space and positioning, and pricing. For an end user of the product, such as the company who buys your manufacturing equipment, computer, or photocopier, develop a program showing how your product is most effectively used or coordinated with existing equipment.

Exhibit 7–6 has other examples of topics often discussed in the marketing plan segment of your sales presentation. Many of these topics were discussed in Chapter 5.

Step 3:

Develop your business proposition, which includes items such as price, percent, markup, forecasted profit per square foot of shelf space, return on investment, and payment plan. Value analysis is an example of a business proposition for an industrial product. Other examples of topics discussed in the business proposition segment of your sales presentation are shown in Exhibit 7–7.

EXHIBIT 7-7

Examples of topics contained in the business proposition segment of your sales presentation

Resellers	End Users
1. List price	1. List price
2. Shipping costs	2. Shipping costs
3. Discounts	3. Discounts
■ Cash	■ Cash
■ Consumer	■ Quantity
■ Quantity	4. Financing
■ Trade	■ Payment plans
■ Financing	■ Interest rates
—Payment plans	5. ROI
—Interest rate	6. Value analysis
4. Markup	
5. Profit	

Step 4:

Develop a suggested purchase order based on a customer benefit plan. A proper presentation of your customer needs analysis and your product's ability to fulfill these needs, along with a satisfactory business proposition and marketing plan, allows you to justify to the prospect what product and/or how much to purchase. This suggestion may include, depending on your product, such things as what to buy, how much to buy, what assortment to buy, and when to ship the product to the customer.

Visual aids should be developed to effectively communicate the information developed in these four steps. The visuals should be organized in the order you discuss them. Your next step is to plan all aspects of the sales presentation.

The Sales Presentation Is Where It All Comes Together

It is now time to plan your **sales presentation** from beginning to end. This process involves developing steps 3 to 9 of the sales presentation described earlier in Exhibit 7–1: the approach, presentation, and trial close method to uncover objections; ways to overcome objections; additional trial closes; and the close of the sales presentation. Each step is discussed in the following chapters.

New salespeople often ask their sales trainers to be more specific on how to construct the sales presentation. In addition to the ten steps in the selling process shown in Exhibit 7–1, they ask, "What's involved in the presentation itself?" Exhibit 7–8 summarizes the major phases within the sales presentation. Before briefly discussing them, let's review a few things.

Before developing your presentation, you need to determine the prospect or customer to call on; make an appointment; and then plan the sales call. This process is shown in Exhibit 6–2. The steps in planning the call are shown in Exhibit 7–4. Now that we know whom we will call on and what our objective will be, it's time to plan out and prepare the sales presentation itself.

The major phases within the presentation are shown in Exhibit 7–8. Please understand Exhibit 7–8 is more specific than Exhibit 7–1 in showing the selling process steps. You should plan out everything that is included in Exhibit 7–8. You should also do each phase in the exact order shown in Exhibit 7–8 in order to create a well organized presentation.

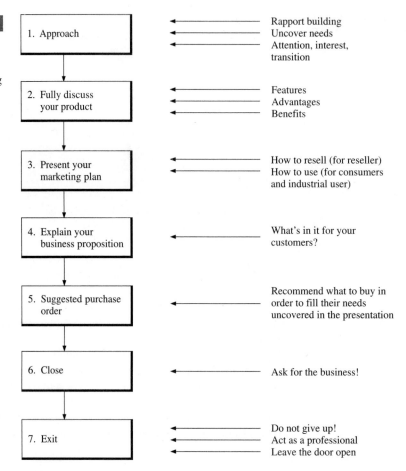

EXHIBIT 7–8

Major phases in your presentation: a sequence of events to complete in developing a sales presentation

1. Approach — Rapport building / Uncover needs / Attention, interest, transition

2. Fully discuss your product — Features / Advantages / Benefits

3. Present your marketing plan — How to resell (for reseller) / How to use (for consumers and industrial user)

4. Explain your business proposition — What's in it for your customers?

5. Suggested purchase order — Recommend what to buy in order to fill their needs uncovered in the presentation

6. Close — Ask for the business!

7. Exit — Do not give up! / Act as a professional / Leave the door open

Here's what you do in creating the presentation. Based upon the homework you have done on the prospect or customer, create the opening (approach) of the presentation. This is discussed in Chapter 9. Then prepare your FABs, marketing plan, and business proposition. They were discussed earlier in this chapter and in previous chapters. Based upon what you feel the customer should buy, prepare a suggested purchase order and choose a closing method that feels natural for you to use when asking for the business. Should you make the sale or not make the sale, it is important to know how to exit the buyer's office. Closing the sale and the exit are discussed in Chapter 12.

Visual aids and demonstrations should be used to help create an informative and persuasive sales presentation. As mentioned earlier, the *last step* in planning your sales call is the development and rehearsal of the sales presentation.

In developing the sales presentation, think of leading the prospect through the five steps or phases that salespeople believe constitute a purchase decision. These phases are referred to as the prospect's mental steps.

THE PROSPECT'S MENTAL STEPS

In making a sales presentation, quickly obtain the prospect's full attention, develop interest in your product, create a desire to fulfill a need, establish the prospect's conviction that the product fills a need, and finally, promote action by having

EXHIBIT 7-9

The prospect's five mental steps in buying

Attention → Interest → Desire → Conviction → Purchase

the prospect purchase the product. As in Exhibit 7–9, these steps occur in the following order:

Attention   From the moment you begin to talk, quickly capture and maintain the prospect's **attention.** This may be difficult at times because of distractions, pressing demands on the prospect's time, or lack of interest. Carefully plan what to say and how to say it. Since attention-getters have only a temporary effect, be ready to quickly move to Step 2, sustaining the prospect's interest.

Interest   Before meeting with prospects, determine their important buying motives. These can be used in capturing **interest.** If not, you may have to determine them at the beginning of your presentation by asking questions. Prospects enter the interest stage if they listen to and enter into a discussion with you. Quickly strive to link your product's benefits to prospects' needs. If this link is completed, prospects usually express a desire for the product.

Desire   Using the FAB formula (Chapter 3), strive to bring prospects from lukewarm interest to a boiling **desire** for your product. Desire is created when prospects express a wish or wanting for a product like yours.

To better determine if the product should be purchased, prospects may have questions for you and may present objections to your product. Anticipate prospects' objections and provide information to maintain their desire.

Conviction   While prospects may desire a product, they still have to be convinced that your product is best for their needs and that you are the best supplier of the product. In the **conviction** step, strive to develop a strong *belief* that the product is best suited to prospects' specific needs. Conviction is established when no doubts remain about purchasing the product from you.

Purchase or Action   Once the prospect is convinced, plan the most appropriate method of asking the prospect to buy or act. If each of the preceding steps has been implemented correctly, closing the sale is the easiest step in the sales presentation.

OVERVIEW OF THE SALES PROCESS   We have briefly discussed the various steps in the selling process, reviewed the sales presentation, and examined the five mental steps a prospect moves through while purchasing a product. Each step will be examined in more depth later, along with methods and techniques that successful salespeople use to lead the prospect to make the correct purchase decision. Exhibit 7–10 presents an overview of the selling process and gives corresponding examples of the prospect's mental stages and questions that may be posed at various points during the presentation.

The approach used is to get the prospect's attention and interest by having the prospect recognize a need or problem, and stating a wish to fulfill the need or solve the problem. The presentation constantly maintains interest in the information you present and generates desire for the product.

EXHIBIT 7–10

The selling process and examples of prospect's mental thoughts and questions.

Steps in the Selling Process	Prospect's Mental Steps	Prospect's Potential Verbal and Mental Questions

1. Prospecting
   Salesperson locates and qualifies
   prospects		

2. Preapproach
   Salesperson determines sales call
   objective, develops customer
   profile, customer benefit program,
   and selling strategies. Customer's
   needs are determined.		

3. Approach
   Salesperson obtains interview,
   meets prospect, and begins
   individualized sales presentation.
   Needs are further uncovered.
	Attention due to arousal of potential need or problem.
	
	Interest due to recognized need or problem and the desire to fulfill the need or solve the problem.
		Should I see salesperson?
		Should I continue to listen, interact, devote much time to a salesperson?
		What's in it for me?

4. Presentation
   Salesperson relates product benefits
   to needs, using demonstration,
   dramatizations, visuals, and proof
   statements.
	Interest in information that provides knowledge and influences perceptions and attitude.
	
	Desire begins to develop based on information evaluation of product features, advantages, and benefits. This is due to forming positive attitudes that product may fulfill need or solve problem. Positive attitudes brought about by knowledge obtained from presentation.
		Is the salesperson prepared? Are my needs understood? Is the seller interested in my needs?
		Should I continue to listen and interact?
		So what? (to statements about features)
		Prove it! (to statements about advantages)
		Are the benefits of theis product the best to fulfill my needs?

5. Trial Close
   Salesperson asks prospect's opinion
   on benefits during and after
   presentation.
	Desire continues based on information evaluation.	

6. Objections Salesperson uncovers objections.	*Desire* continues based on information evaluation.	Do I understand the salesperson's marketing plan and business proposition? I need more information to make a decision. Can you meet my conditions?

7. Meet Objections
   Salesperson satisfactorily answers
   objections.
	Desire begins to be transformed into belief.
	Conviction established due to belief the product and salesperson can solve needs or problems better than competitive products.
	Appears ready to buy.
		Let me see the reaction when I give the salesperson a hard time.
		I have a minor/major objection to what you are saying.
		Is something nonverbal being communicated?
		Did I get a reasonable answer to my objection?

ETHICAL DILEMMA

The Boss Told Me to Do It!

The prospect must have delivery of the product in four weeks to meet a national advertising rollout. They have big bucks invested in the ad campaign. After beating the production people about the head and shoulders, the best delivery your company can promise is six weeks. The boss orders you to promise the customer delivery within a four-week deadline.

What do you do?

EXHIBIT 7–10

(concluded)

Steps in the Selling Process	Prospect's Mental Steps	Prospect's Potential Verbal and Mental Questions
8. Trial Close Salesperson uses another trial close to see if objections have been overcome; or if presentation went smoothly before the close, to determine if the prospect is ready to buy.	*Conviction* becomes stronger.	Can I believe and trust this person? Should I reveal my real concerns?
9. Close Salesperson has determined prospect is ready to buy and now asks for the order.	*Action* (purchase) occurs based on positive beliefs that the product will fulfill needs or solve problems.	I am asked to make a buying decision now. If I buy and I am dissatisfied, what can I do? Will I receive after-the-sale service as promised? What are my expectations toward this purchase? Why don't you ask me to buy? Ask one more time and I'll buy.
10. Follow-Up Salesperson provides customer service after the sale.	*Satisfaction—Dissatisfaction*	Did the product meet my expectations? Am I experiencing dissonance? How is the service associated with this product? Should I buy again from this salesperson?

Uncovering and answering the prospect's questions and revealing and meeting or overcoming objections results in more intense desire. This desire is transformed into the conviction that your product can fulfill the prospect's needs or solve problems. Once you have determined the prospect is in the conviction stage, you are ready for the close.

SUMMARY OF MAJOR SELLING ISSUES

Most salespeople agree that careful planning of the sales call is essential to success in selling. Among many reasons why planning is so important, four of the most frequently mentioned are: that planning builds self-confidence, develops an atmosphere of goodwill, creates professionalism, and increases sales. By having a logical and methodical plan, you can decide what to accomplish and then later measure your accomplishments with your plan.

There are four basic elements of sales call planning. First, you must always have a sales call objective—one that is specific, measurable, and beneficial to the customer. Second, as a salesperson, also develop or review the customer profile. By having relevant information about your customer, you can properly develop a customized presentation. Information on the background, needs, and competitors of your potential buyer can be fund by reviewing your company's records or by personally contacting the buyer and the company.

The third step in planning your sales call involves developing your customer benefit plan. To do this, look at why your product should be purchased and develop a marketing plan to convey those reasons and the benefits to your prospect. Then, develop a *business proposition* by listing your price, percent markup, return on investment, and other quantitative data about your product in relation to your prospect. Lastly, develop a *suggested purchase order* and present your analysis, which might include suggestions on what to buy, how much to buy, what assortment to buy, and when to ship the product.

Finally, plan your whole sales presentation. Visual aids can help make your presentation informative and creative. In making your call, think in terms of the phases that make up a purchase decision—the mental steps. The steps involved are capturing the prospect's attention, determining buying motives, creating desire, convincing the person that your product is best suited to her or his needs, and then closing the sale.

By adhering to these guidelines for planning your sales presentation, you may spend more time than on the actual sales call. However, it will be well worth it.

MEETING A SALES CHALLENGE

The purpose of your sales presentation is to provide information so the prospect can make a rational, informed buying decision. You provide this information using your FABs, marketing plan, and business approval.

The information you provide allows the buyer to develop positive personal *beliefs* toward your product. The beliefs result in *desire* (or *need*) for the type of product you sell. Your job, as a salesperson, is to convert that need into a want and into the *attitude* that your product is the best product to fulfill a certain need. Furthermore, you must convince the buyer not only that your product is the best, but that you are the best source to buy from. When this occurs, your prospect has moved into the *conviction* stage of the mental buying process. Listen and watch for it.

When a real need is established, the buyer will want to fulfill that need, and there is a high probability that he or she will choose your product. Whether to buy or not is a "choice decision," and you provide the necessary information so that the customer chooses to buy from you.

When you are prepared, the prospect or customers recognizes it. This gives you a better chance of giving your presentation and thus increases your sales, because the more presentations given, the more people sold. Veteran salespeople have a tendency to not prepare. Many get lazy and fall into a bad habit of "winging it." Top sales professionals rarely are unprepared. Do you want to be an order-taker or an order-getter? Your success is entirely up to you!

KEY TERMS FOR SELLING

strategic   201
strategic customer relationship   201
creative problem solvers   202
preapproach   203
sales planning   204
sales call objective   205
customer profile   206
customer benefit plan   207

sales presentation   209
prospect's mental steps   210
attention   211
interest   211
desire   211
conviction   211
purchase or action   211

SALES APPLICATION QUESTIONS

1. What are the elements to consider when planning a sales call? Explain each one.
2. An important part of planning a sales call is the development of a customer benefit plan. What are the major components of the customer benefit plan? What is the difference in developing a customer benefit plan for a General Foods salesperson selling consumer products versus an industrial salesperson selling products for a company such as IBM?
3. Many salespeople feel a prospect goes through several mental steps in making a decision to purchase a product. Discuss each one of these steps.
4. Outline and discuss the sequence of events in developing a sales presentation.
5. Some salespeople feel a person should not be asked to buy a product until the prospect's mind has entered the conviction step of the mental process. Why?
6. What is the difference, if any, between the selling process and the sales presentation?
7. Define the term *the selling process.* Second, list the major steps in the selling process on the left side of a page of paper. Third, beside each step of the selling process, write the corresponding mental step that a prospect should experience.
8. Below are 13 situations commonly faced by salespeople. For each situation, determine the mental buying stage that your prospect is experiencing. Give a reason for why the prospect is at that stage.
   a. "Come on in; I can only visit with you for about five minutes."
   b. "That sounds good, but how can I be sure it will do what you say it will?"
   c. "Yes, I see your copier can make 20 copies a minute and copy on both sides of the page. Big deal!"
   d. The buyer thinks, "Will the purchase of this equipment help my standing with my boss?"
   e. "I didn't know there were products like this on the market."
   f. The buyer thinks, "I'm not sure if I should listen or not."
   g. "I wish my equipment could do what yours does."
   h. "Well, that sounds good, but I'm not sure."
   i. "What kind of great deal do you have for me today?"
   j. "When can you ship it?"
   k. You discuss your business proposition with your buyer, and you receive a favorable nonverbal response.
   l. "I like what you have to say. Your deal sounds good. But I'd better check with my other suppliers first."
   m. You have completed your presentation. The buyer has said almost nothing to you, including asking no questions and giving no objections. You wonder if you should close.
9. Think of a product sold through one of your local supermarkets. Assume you were recently hired by the product's manufacturer to contact the store's buyer to

purchase a promotional quantity of your product and to arrange for display and advertising. What information do you need for planning the sales call, and what features, advantages, and benefits would be appropriate in your sales presentation?

You've recently acquired a significant lead on a possible sale to Dell Computer Corporation. Being your company's top sales rep of novelty items, such as sweatshirts, T-shirts, and sports gear, you have been chosen to pursue the account.

It was just pure luck that at a computer convention yesterday in Las Vegas, the national sales manager for Dell stopped by your booth and mentioned she wanted to have a company create a motivational program that centers around sportswear and gear. She asks you to be in her office next Wednesday at 3:00 P.M.

At this time, though, your secretary is on vacation and you are responsible for making your own travel arrangements. Your secretary has told you that there are Web sites where you can make travel arrangements from your computer and not have to make any phone calls. To make your airline reservations, hotel arrangements, and car rental all in one stop, visit the following sites:

www.previewtravel.com	www.americanair.com
www.expedia.com	www.flycontinental.com
www.expedia.msn.com	www.iflyswa.com
www.air-fare.com	

But hey! Where are the headquarters for Dell Computer? You have heard the name Dell Computer and you know they make computers, but that is about all. First things first. Check out www.dell.com. Click on company information, then investor information, and finally contact information to find their geographical location. You need to go to your favorite search engine(s) and research Dell. Also search the sites:

www.mfginfo.com	www.bigbook.com
www.companiesonline.com	www.EL.com
www.bigyellow.com	

You saw an article in the October 1997 issue of *Sales & Marketing Magazine*, www.salesandmarketing.com, entitled "The Dell Way." You had better read it.

Since you may be driving your own rental car, you will need specific directions so as not to get lost. Go to:

www.mapquest.com	www.tripquest.com
www.lookupusa.com	
www.el.com (click on phone/address and review travel)	

Also check out the weather forecast at: www.weather.com. Finally, check the correct time at www.el.com by scrolling down to references, then clicking on USNO at "Clock." Then write up a memo to your boss outlining your travel schedule. Print out appropriate URL screens and place in the appendix of your memo.

FURTHER EXPLORING THE SALES WORLD

Ask a buyer for a business in your community about what salespeople should do when calling on a buyer. Find out if the salespeople that this buyer sees are prepared for each sales call. Ask why or why not something is purchased. Do salespeople use the FAB method as discussed in this chapter? Does the buyer think privately, "So what?" "Prove it!" and "What's in it for me?" Finally, ask what superiors expect of a buyer in the buyer's dealing with salespeople.

SELLING EXPERIENTIAL EXERCISE **Plan Your Appearance—It Projects Your Image!**	The most successful people in customer contact jobs claim that being sharp mentally means communicating a positive self-image. Like an actor or actress, interacting with others requires you to be on stage at all times. Creating a good first impression is essential. Also important is understanding the direct connection between your attitude and how you look to yourself. The better your self-image when you encounter customers, clients, or guests, the more positive you are.

On a separate sheet of paper, rate yourself on each of the following grooming areas. If you write 5, you are saying that improvement is not required. If you write a 1, or 2, you need considerable improvement. Be honest.[1]

	Excellent	Good	Fair	Weak	Poor
▪ Hairstyle, hair grooming (appropriate length and cleanliness)	5	4	3	2	1
▪ Personal cleanliness habits (body)	5	4	3	2	1
▪ Clothing and jewelry (appropriate to the situation)	5	4	3	2	1
▪ Neatness (shoes shined, clothes clean, well-pressed, etc.)	5	4	3	2	1
▪ General grooming: Does your appearance reflect professionalism on the job?	5	4	3	2	1

When it comes to appearance on the job, I would rate myself:

☐ Excellent   ☐ Good   ☐ Need improvement

STUDENT APPLICATION LEARNING EXERCISES (SALES) **(Part 3 of 7)**	At the end of appropriate chapters beginning with Chapter 3, you will find Student Application Learning Exercises (SALES). SALES are meant to help you construct the various segments of your sales presentation. SALES build upon one another so that after you complete each, you will have constructed the majority of your sales presentation. In planning the sales presentation, it is necessary to create a marketing plan. Review the section beginning on page 207 entitled "Customer Benefit Plan: What It's All About." The marketing plan is described in Step 2 on page 208. Stop your study on page 210. Carefully study Exhibit 7–6. Review the advertising and sales promotion sections contained in pages 136–140. To make **Sale 3:**

1. List three **FABs** you could discuss in your marketing plan.

Feature	Advantage	Benefit
a.		
b.		
c.		

2. Write out one **SELL Sequence** using the **FABs.** Label each of the components of the **SELL Sequence** using parentheses as shown on page 76.

Picture yourself as a Procter & Gamble salesperson who plans to call on Ms. Hansen, a buyer for your largest independent grocery store. Your sales call objective is to convince Ms. Hansen that she should buy the family-size Tide detergent. The store now carries the three smaller sizes. You believe your marketing plan will help convince her that she is losing sales and profits by not stocking Tide's family size.

You enter the grocery store, check your present merchandise, and quickly develop a suggested order. As Ms. Hansen walks down the aisle toward you, she appears to be in her normal grumpy mood. After your initial greeting and handshake, your conversation continues:

Salesperson: Your sales are really up! I've checked your stock in the warehouse and on the shelf. This is what it looks like you need. [You discuss sales of each of your products and their various sizes, suggesting a quantity she should purchase based on her past sales and present inventory.]

Buyer: OK, that looks good. Go ahead and ship it.

Salesperson: Thank you. Say, Ms. Hansen, you've said before that the shortage of shelf space prevents you from stocking our family-size Tide—though you admit you may be losing some sales as a result. If we could determine how much volume you're missing, I think you'd be willing to make space for it, wouldn't you?

Buyer: Yes, but I don't see how that can be done.

Salesperson: Well, I'd like to suggest a test—a weekend display of all four sizes of Tide.

Buyer: What do you mean?

Salesperson: My thought was to run all sizes at regular shelf price without any ad support. This would give us a pure test. Six cases of each size should let us compare sales of the various sizes and see what you're missing by regularly stocking only the smaller sizes. I think the additional sales and profits you'll get on the family size will convince you to start stocking it regularly. What do you think?

Buyer: Well, maybe.

Questions

1. Examine each item you mentioned to Ms. Hansen, stating what part of the customer benefit plan each of your comments is concerned with.
2. What are the features, advantages, and benefits in your sales presentation?
3. Examine each of Ms. Hansen's replies stating the mental buying step she is in at that particular time during your sales presentation.
4. At the end of the conversation, Ms. Hansen said, "Well, maybe." Which of the following should you do now?
   a. Continue to explain your features, advantages, and benefits.
   b. Ask a trial close question.

c. Ask for the order.

d. Back off and try again on the next sales call.

e. Wait for Ms. Hansen to say, "OK, ship it."

CASE 7–2

Machinery Lubricants, Inc.

Ralph Jackson sells industrial lubricants to manufacturing plants. The lubricants are used to lubricate the plant's machinery. Tomorrow, Ralph plans to call on the purchasing agent for Acme Manufacturing Company.

For the last two years, Ralph has been selling Hydraulic Oil 65 in drums to Acme. Ralph's sales call objective is to persuade Acme to switch from purchasing oil in drums to a bulk oil system. Last year, Acme bought approximately 364 drums or 20,000 gallons at a cost of $1.39 a gallon or $27,800. A deposit of $20 was made for each drum. Traditionally, many drums are lost, and one to two gallons of oil may be left in each drum when returned by customers. This is a loss to the company.

Ralph wants to sell Acme two 3,000-gallon storage tanks at a cost of $1,700. He has arranged with Pump Supply Company to install the tanks for $1,095. Thus, the total cost of the system will be $2,795. This system reduces the cost of the oil from $1.39 to $1.25 per gallon, which will allow it to pay for itself over time. Other advantages include having fewer orders to process each year, a reduction in storage space, and less handling of the oil by workers.

Question

If you were Ralph, how would you plan the sales call?

Chapter 7 Appendix: ACT!
To Create Customers for Life!

ACT! is a top-rated, best-selling, contact manager. It is software that allows you to manage your business relationships. It stores information on all of your customers, such as your previous business conversations, calls to make, meetings to attend, and action items to complete. In addition to data entry, ACT! allows you to write letters, e-mail, fax, use calendars, and organize contact groups.

ACT! is a product of Symantec. Symantec maintains an excellent Web site which allows you to review and order their products. Also available is an excellent demonstration disc of ACT! The demonstration disk allows you to do everything the complete software does at no cost. The only restriction with the disk is you can only have data of 25 contacts or fewer, versus the hundreds of contacts with the software you buy.

Why Review and Learn ACT!?

Most companies have their salespeople use some type of customer software, such as ACT! When you interview for a sales job, it is a selling point for you if you mention to the recruiter that you are familiar with ACT! If you are in sales now, you probably need to be using contact manager software. This is a great way of determining if ACT! can help you be more productive.

How to Obtain the ACT! Software

To use the ACT! demonstration disk, you need to have a computer with a hard drive. ACT! is downloaded onto the hard drive. Once loaded onto your computer's hard drive, you can use the software.

You can obtain a copy of the ACT! demonstration disk by writing Symantec or using their Web site. Their mailing address is Symantec Corporation, 10201 Torre Avenue, Cupertino, California 95014-2132.

If you have some knowledge of using a computer, it is easiest to get a copy of the ACT! demonstration disk by downloading it from Symantec's Web site. Companies are always changing their Web site offerings and instructions. At the time of this book's writing, here are the instructions for downloading the ACT! 4.0 Windows 95/NT demonstration disk from the Web site: http://www.symantec.com.

The software that you will download is a compressed version. This software needs to be installed (loaded) onto the hard drive of a computer before you can use it. Once it is installed in a computer you can start using the 25 entries study data included along with it.

Instructions for Downloading ACT! 4.0 Windows 95/NT

Here are the instructions for downloading the ACT! demonstration disk. If instructions are different on Symantec's Web site look for instructions related to trial software. Remember that you need a hard drive to store and use the software.

Computer System Requirements

- Windows 95, Windows 98, Windows NT 4.0

- 486 or higher PC compatible computer
- 8 MB RAM
- 30 MB available hard disk space for minimum installation
- Mouse or any other pointing device

Finding the Site for Downloading

- The software for downloading is available on the Symantec Web page. To go to this site you need to enter this address: http://shop.symantec.com/trialware/
- This will take you to *Trialware.*

Under this you will find the authorized beta program version of ACT! for use with Windows 95/98/NT.

4.0 Updated version—English 14.8MB ***(click on the one under 95)***

- This will take you to *ACT! 4.0 for Windows 95 Trial.* Complete the form given. Enter your full name. Then, instead of the company name, select "Jr./Sr./Sophomore/ . . . Student" followed by the name of your school. Then read the License Agreement. If you accept the terms, click on *"Accept."*
- This will take you to *ACT! 4.0 for Windows 95.* Download the file, as follows.
- As you will be downloading the version for Windows 95, you will need to double-click on act40t.exe (14.8 MB), which is next to *Download from the FTP server:*
- Once done, it will give you the message *"Opening act40t.exe"* and ask what you would like to do with this file. Highlight *"Save it to disk"* and click on *"OK."* It will ask you the path of the file you have already created. Give the path and click on *"Save."* This process will take some time. The total file size here will be 14.8 MB.

Instructions for Installing the Trial Version of ACT! 4.0

- Once this is done, open the file where you have downloaded the program. Once there, double-click on act40t.exe to unzip it.
- It will ask if you wish to install ACT! 4.0 Click on *"Yes."* It will then start the setup for ACT! Trial Size.
- It will then give you the Online License Agreement. Read it and click on *"Yes."*
- On the form that follows, enter your full name. Again, instead of the company name, enter whether you are Jr./Sr./ . . . and your school name. Click on *"Next."*
- This will give you the program destination location. Click on *"Browse"* to select the path where you have downloaded the act40t.exe file. After doing so, click *"OK."*
- It will now tell you the path you have selected. Click on *"Next."*
- Now select your respective country version.
- For *"Select Program Folder,"* click *"Next"* with the default selections.
- The system will start installing the ACT! 4.0 files.
- Now it will ask you to "Register Now." Select the Respective Country and the Method as Internet and click on *"Next."*
- Fill out the small form. Click on *"Myself"* to get the product registered in your name. Then click on *"Next."*

- Then fill out the displayed form and click on *"Next."* This will display the message, *"Ready to process your registration."* Click on *"Start"* to process the registration.
- Once the setup is done, it will give you a screen with the message *"Thank you for registering."* Click on *"Finish."*
- Now, it will give you a window entitled *"Setup Complete."* Here, select the box before *"Place Shortcut icons to ACT! and SideACT! on your desktop."* Click on *"Finish"* to complete setup.

Once ACT! has been loaded onto your computer and is ready to use, start the program by clicking on the *"ACT! 4.0 Trial Size"* icon on the desktop. Enter the necessary information as prompted for initial setup. For help on how to use ACT! go to the Help menu located on the task bar at the top of the screen.

8

Carefully Select Which Sales Presentation Method to Use

MAIN TOPICS

Sales Presentation Strategy

Sales Presentation Methods—Select One Carefully

Sales Presentations Go High Tech

LEARNING OBJECTIVES

To know the best way to begin the sales presentation, first determine the type of sales presentation to use for each prospect or customer. After studying this chapter, you should be able to:

- State why you first select a sales presentation method and then select the approach.

- Describe the different sales presentation methods; know their differences; and know the appropriate situation for using a particular method.

- Better understand how to give a presentation to a group of prospects.

- Understand why negotiations can be an important part of the presentation.

It took you four hours to plan, prepare, and practice your sales presentation to the largest manufacturer in your sales territory. Although they have never purchased before, you feel your product will benefit them. You arrive on time for your appointment with Juan Gomez.

Mr. Gomez's secretary takes you into a large conference room, saying, "They'll be with you in a few minutes." "They," you think. "Who is coming?" you ask. "The head of accounting, production, and two engineers—and the president wants us to call her once the meeting gets under way." As she leaves, you become dizzy, your stomach gets upset, and you feel weak in the knees. "I've never given a presentation to a group—let alone experts. And the president of the company. Oh, my—what am I going to do?" What would you do?

Salespeople, sales trainers, and sales managers agree that the most challenging, rewarding, and enjoyable aspect of the buyer–seller interaction is the **sales presentation.** An effective sales presentation completely and clearly explains all aspects of a salesperson's proposition as it relates to a buyer's needs. Surprisingly, attaining this objective is not as easy as you might think. Few successful salespeople will claim that they had little trouble developing a good presentation or mastering the art of giving the sales presentation. How then can you, as a novice, develop a sales presentation that will improve your chances of making the sale?

You must first select a sales presentation method according to your prior knowledge of the customer, your sales call objective, and your customer benefit plan. Once it is selected, you are ready to develop your sales presentation. The particular sales presentation method that you select will make an excellent framework upon which to build your specific presentation.

Once you select the presentation method for a specific prospect or customer, determine how to open or begin the sales presentation. The sales opener, or approach, as shown in Exhibit 8–1, is the first major step in the sales presentation—Steps 3 through 9. The approach is discussed in Chapter 9.

This chapter discusses the four different sales presentation methods including how to conduct a group presentation. Negotiations are also introduced in this chapter, since they are often necessary regardless of the presentation method used.

SALES PRESENTATION STRATEGY

Salespeople work with customers in different ways. As discussed in Chapter 1, salespeople may be involved in transactional, relationship, or partnering selling. Thus, salespeople face numerous situations such as:

- **Salesperson to buyer:** A salesperson discusses issues with a prospect or customer in person or over the phone.
- **Salesperson to buyer group:** A salesperson gets to know as many members of the buyer group as possible.
- **Sales team to buyer group:** A company sales team works closely with the members of the customer's buying group.
- **Conference selling:** The salesperson brings company resource people to discuss a major problem or opportunity.
- **Seminar selling:** A company team conducts an educational seminar for the customer company about state-of-the-art developments.

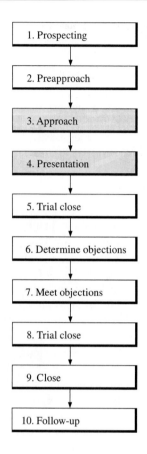

EXHIBIT 8–1

The third step in the sales process is the first step in the sales presentation. The sales presentation method determines how you open your presentation.

Each customer contact represents a unique challenge for the salespeople. Thus, the salesperson needs to understand the various sales presentation methods.

SALES PRESENTATION METHODS— SELECT ONE CAREFULLY

The sales presentation involves a persuasive vocal and visual explanation of a business proposition. Of the many ways of making a presentation, four methods are presented here to highlight the alternatives available to help sell your products.

As shown on the continuum in Exhibit 8–2, the four sales presentation methods are: memorized, formula, need-satisfaction, and problem-solution selling methods.[1] The basic difference in the four methods is the percentage of the conversation controlled by the salesperson. In the more structured memorized and formula selling techniques, the salesperson normally has a monopoly on the conversation, while the less structured methods allow for greater buyer–seller interaction; both parties participate equally in the conversation. Transactional selling generally is more structured, whereas partnering requires a more customized presentation, with relationship selling typically somewhere in between. See Exhibit 8–2.

The Memorized Sales Presentation

The **memorized presentation** is based on either of two assumptions: that a prospect's needs can be stimulated by direct exposure to the product, via the sales presentation, or that these needs have already been stimulated because the prospect has made the effort to seek out the product. In either case, the salesperson's role is to develop this initial stimulus into an affirmative response to an eventual purchase request.

EXHIBIT 8–2

The structure of sales presentations

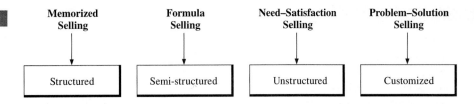

Memorized Selling	Formula Selling	Need–Satisfaction Selling	Problem–Solution Selling
↓	↓	↓	↓
Structured	Semi-structured	Unstructured	Customized

EXHIBIT 8–3

Participation time by customer and salesperson during a memorized sales presentation

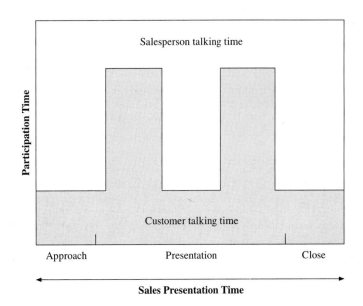

The salesperson does 80 to 90 percent of the talking during a memorized sales presentation, only occasionally allowing the prospect to respond to predetermined questions, as shown in Exhibit 8–3. Notably, the salesperson does not attempt to determine the prospect's needs during the interview, but gives the same canned sales talk to all prospects. Since no attempt is made at this point to learn what goes on in the consumer's mind, the salesperson concentrates on discussing the product and its benefits, concluding the pitch with a purchase request. The seller hopes that a convincing presentation of product benefits will cause the prospect to buy.

National Cash Register Co. (now AT&T Global Information Solutions) pioneered the use of canned sales presentations. During the 1920s, an analysis of the sales approaches of some of its top salespeople revealed to NCR that they were saying the same things. The firm prepared a series of standardized sales presentations based on the findings of their sales approach analysis, ultimately requiring its sales force to memorize these approaches during sales calls. The method worked quite well for NCR and was later adopted by other firms. Canned sales presentations are still used today, mainly in telephone and door-to-door selling.

Actually parts of any presentation may be canned, yet linked with freeform conversation. Over time, most salespeople develop proven selling sentences, phrases, and sequences in which to discuss information. They tend to use these in all presentations.

Despite its impersonal aura, the canned or memorized sales presentation has distinct advantages, as seen in Exhibit 8–4.[2]

- It ensures that the salesperson gives a well-planned presentation and that the same information is discussed by all of the company's salespeople.
- It both aids and lends confidence to the inexperienced salesperson.

EXHIBIT 8-4

Dyno Electric Cart memorized presentation

Situation: You call on a purchasing manager to elicit an order for some electric cars (like a golf cart) to be used at a plant for transportation around the buildings and grounds. The major benefit to emphasize in your presentation is that the carts save time; you incorporate this concept in your approach. For this product, you use the memorized stimulus–response presentation.

Salesperson: Hello, Mr. Pride, my name is Karen Nordstrom and I'd like to talk with you about how to save your company executives' time. By the way, thanks for taking the time to talk with me.

Buyer: What's on your mind?

Salesperson: As a busy executive, you know time is a valuable commodity. Nearly everyone would like to have a few extra minutes each day and that is the business I'm in, selling time. While I can't actually sell you time, I do have a product that is the next best thing . . . a Dyno Electric Cart—a real time-saver for your executives.

Buyer: Yeah, well, everyone would like to have extra time. However, I don't think we need any golf carts. [First objection.]

Salesperson: Dyno Electric Cart is more than a golf cart. It is an electric car designed for use in industrial plants. It has been engineered to give comfortable, rapid transportation in warehouses, plants, and across open areas.

Buyer: They probably cost too much for us to use. [Positive buying signal phrased as an objection.]

Salesperson: First of all, they only cost $2,200 each. With a five-year normal life, that is only $400 per year plus a few cents electricity and a few dollars for maintenance. Under normal use and care, these carts only require about $100 of service in their five-year life. Thus, for about $50 a month, you can save key people a lot of time. [Creative pricing—show photographs of carts in use.]

Buyer: It would be nice to save time, but I don't think management would go for the idea. [Third objection, but still showing interest.]

Salesperson: This is exactly why I am here. Your executives will appreciate what you have done for them. You will look good in their eyes if you give them an opportunity to look at a product that will save time and energy. Saving time is only part of our story. Dyno carts also save energy and thus keep you sharper toward the end of the day. Would you want a demonstration today or Tuesday? [Alternative close.]

Buyer: How long would your demonstration take? [Positive buying signal.]

Salesperson: I only need one hour. When would it be convenient for me to bring the cart in for your executives to try out?

Buyer: There really isn't any good time. [Objection.]

Salesperson: That's true. Therefore, the sooner we get to show you a Dyno cart, the sooner your management group can see its benefits. How about next Tuesday? I could be here at 8:00 and we could go over this item just before your weekly management group meeting. I know you usually have a meeting Tuesdays at 9:00 because I tried to call on you a few weeks ago and your secretary told me you were in the weekly management meeting. [Close of the sale.]

Buyer: Well, we could do it then.

Salesperson: Fine, I'll be here. Your executives will really be happy! [Positive reinforcement.]

- It is effective when selling time is short, as in door-to-door or telephone selling.
- It is effective when the product is nontechnical—such as books, cooking utensils, and cosmetics.

As may be apparent, the memorized method has several major drawbacks:

- It presents features, advantages, and benefits that may not be important to the buyer.
- It allows for little prospect participation.
- It is impractical to use when selling technical products that require prospect input and discussion.
- It proceeds quickly through the sales presentation to the close, requiring the salesperson to close or ask for the order several times, which may be interpreted by the prospect as high-pressure selling.

The story is told of the new salesperson who was halfway through a canned presentation when the prospect had to answer the telephone. When the prospect finished the telephone conversation, the salesperson had forgotten the stopping point and started over again. The prospect naturally became angry.

In telling of his early selling experiences, salesperson John Anderson remembers that he was once so intent on presenting his memorized presentation that halfway through it the prospect yelled, "Enough, John, I've been waiting for you to see me. I'm ready to buy. I know all about your products." Anderson was so intent on giving his canned presentation, and listening to himself talk, that he did not recognize the prospect's buying signals.

For some selling situations, a highly structured presentation can be used successfully. Examine its advantages and disadvantages to determine if this presentation is appropriate for your prospects and products.

Some situations may seem partially appropriate for the memorized approach but require a more personal touch. Such circumstances warrant the examination of formula selling.

The Formula Presentation

The **formula presentation,** often referred to as the *persuasive selling presentation,* is akin to the memorized method: it is based on the assumption that similar prospects in similar situations can be approached with similar presentations. However, for the formula method to apply, the salesperson must first know something about the prospective buyer. The salesperson follows a less structured, general outline in making a presentation, allowing more flexibility and less direction.

The salesperson generally controls the conversation during the sales talk, especially at the beginning. Exhibit 8–5 illustrates how a salesperson should take charge during a formula selling situation.[3] For example, the salesperson might make a sales opener (approach), discuss the product's features, advantages, and benefits, and then start to solicit comments from the buyer using trial closes, answering questions, and handling objections. At the end of the participation curve, the salesperson regains control over the discussion and moves in to close the sale.

The formula selling approach obtains its name from the salesperson using the attention, interest, desire, and action (AIDA) procedure of developing and giving the sales presentation. We earlier added conviction (C) to the procedure because the prospect may want or desire the product, yet not be convinced this is the best product or the best salesperson from whom to buy.

Straight rebuy and modified rebuy situations, especially with consumer goods, lend themselves to this method. Many prospects or customers buy because they are

EXHIBIT 8-5

Participation time by a customer
and salesperson during a formula
sales presentation

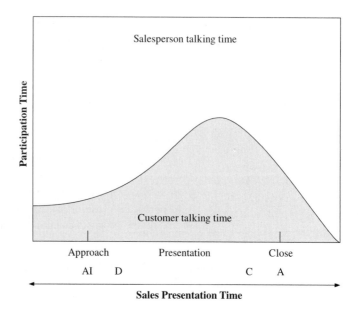

familiar with the salesperson's company. The question is how can a salesperson for
Quaker Oats, Revlon, Gillette, Procter & Gamble, or any other well-known manufacturer develop a presentation that convinces a customer to purchase promotional
quantities of a product, participate in a local advertising campaign, or stock a new,
untried product?

Beecham Products, a consumer goods manufacturer, has developed a sequence, or
formula, for its salespeople to follow. They refer to it as the *10-step productive retail
sales call.* The Beecham salesperson sells products such as Cling Free Sheets, Aqua-
Fresh toothpaste, Aqua Velva, and Sucrets. The 10 steps and their major components
are shown in Exhibit 8–6.

Formula selling is effective for calling on customers who currently buy and for
prospects about whose operations the salesperson has learned a great deal. In such
situations, formula selling offers significant advantages:

- It ensures that all information is presented logically.
- It allows for a reasonable amount of buyer–seller interaction.
- It allows for smooth handling of *anticipated* questions and objections.

When executed in a smooth, conversational manner, the formula method of selling has no major flaws, as long as the salesperson has correctly identified the
prospect's needs and wants. The Procter & Gamble formula sales presentation given
as an example in Exhibit 8–7 can be given to any retailer who is not selling all available sizes of Tide (or of any other product). In this situation, a formula approach is
used in calling on a customer the salesperson has sold to previously. If, on the other
hand, the salesperson did not know a customer's needs and used this Tide presentation, chances are customer objections would arise early in the presentation—as they
sometimes do with the memorized sales presentation method. Still, the formula technique is not adaptable to a number of complex selling situations. These require other
sales presentations.

The Need-Satisfaction Presentation

The **need-satisfaction presentation** is different from the memorized and the formalized approach; it is designed as a flexible, interactive sales presentation. It is the
most challenging and creative form of selling.

EXHIBIT 8–6

The 10-step productive retail sales call

Step No.	Action
1. Plan the call.	■ Review the situation
	■ Analyze problems and appointments.
	■ Set objectives.
	■ Plan the presentation.
	■ Check your sales materials.
2. Review plans.	■ Before you leave your car to enter the store, review your plans, sales call objectives, suggested order forms, and so on.
3. Greet personnel.	■ Give a friendly greeting to store personnel.
	■ Alert the store manager for sales action.
4. Check store conditions.	■ Note appearance of stock on shelf.
	■ Check distribution and pricing.
	■ Note out-of-stocks.
	■ Perform a quick fix by straightening shelf stock.
	■ Report competitive activity.
	■ Check back room (storeroom):
	Locate product to correct out-of-stocks.
	Use reserve stock for special display.
	■ Update sales plan if needed.
5. Approach.	■ Keep it short.
6. Presentation.	■ Make it logical, clear, interesting.
	■ Tailor it to dealer's style.
	■ Present it from dealer's point of view.
	■ Use sales tools.
7. Close.	■ Present a suggested order (ask for the order).
	■ Offer a choice.
	■ Answer questions and handle objections.
	■ Get a real order.
8. Merchandising.	■ Build displays.
	■ Dress up the shelves.
9. Records and reports.	■ Complete them immediately after the call.
10. Analyze the call.	■ Review the call to spot strong and weak points. How could the sales call have been improved? How can the next call be improved?

The salesperson typically starts the presentation with a probing question like: "What are you looking for in investment property?" or "What type of computer needs does your company have?" This opening starts a discussion of the prospect's needs and also gives the salesperson an opportunity to determine whether any of the products being offered might be beneficial. When something the prospect has said is not understood by the salesperson, it can be clarified by a question or by restating what the buyer has said. The need-satisfaction format is especially suited to the sale of industrial and technical goods with stringent specifications and high price tags.

Often, as shown in Exhibit 8–8, the first 50 to 60 percent of conversation time (referred to as the **need-development** phase) is devoted to a discussion of the buyer's needs.[4] Once aware of the prospect's needs (the **need-awareness** phase), the salesperson begins to take control of the conversation by restating the prospect's needs to clarify the situation. During the last stage of the presentation, the **need-fulfillment** (or need-satisfaction) phase, the salesperson shows how the product will satisfy

EXHIBIT 8–7

A formula approach sales presentation

Formula Steps	Buyer–Seller Roles	Sales Presentation
Summarize the situation for *attention* and *interest*.	**Salesperson:**	Ms. Hanson, you've said before that the shortage of shelf space prevents you from stocking our family-size Tide—though you admit you may be losing some sales as a result. If we could determine *how much* volume you're missing, I think you'd be willing to *make* space for it, wouldn't you? [Trial close.]
State your marketing plan for *interest*.	**Buyer:**	Yes, but I don't see how that can be done.
	Salesperson:	Well, I'd like to suggest a test—a weekend display of all four sizes of Tide.
	Buyer:	What do you mean?
Explain your marketing plan for *interest* and *desire*.	**Salesperson:**	My thought was to run all sizes at regular shelf price *without* any ad support. This would give us a pure test. Six cases of each size should let us compare sales of the various sizes and see what you're missing by regularly stocking only the smaller sizes. I think the additional sales and profits you'll get on the family size will convince you to start stocking regularly. [Reinforce key benefits.] What do you think? [Trial close.]
Buyer appears to be in *conviction* stage.	**Buyer:**	Well, maybe. [Positive reaction to trial close.]
Suggest an easy next step or *action*.	**Salesperson:**	May I enter the six cases of family-size Tide in the order book now? [Close.]

EXHIBIT 8–8

Participation time by customer and salesperson during need-satisfaction and problem–solution sales presentations

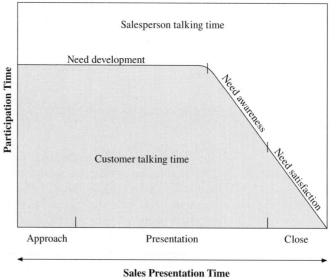

mutual needs. As seen in Exhibit 8–9, the salesperson selling the Dyno Electric Cart begins the interview with the prospect by using the planned series of questions to un-cover problems and to determine whether the prospect is interested in solving them.[5]

Should you have to come back a second time to see the prospect, as is often the case in selling industrial products, you would use the formula sales presentation

EXHIBIT 8–9

A need-satisfaction presentation

Salesperson: Mr. Pride, you really have a large manufacturing facility. How large is it?

Buyer: We have approximately 50 acres under roof, with our main production building almost 25 acres under one roof. We use six buildings for production.

Salesperson: How far is it from your executives' offices to your plant area? It looks like it must be two miles over to there.

Buyer: Well, it does, but it's only one mile.

Salesperson: How do your executives get to the plant area?

Buyer: They walk through our underground tunnel. Some walk on the road when we have good weather.

Salesperson: When they get to the plant area, how do they get around in the plant?

Buyer: Well, they walk or catch a ride on one of the small tractors the workers use in the plant.

Salesperson: Have your executives ever complained about having to do all that walking?

Buyer: All the time!

Salesperson: What don't they like about the long walk?

Buyer: Well, I hear everything from "It wears out my shoe leather," to "It's hard on my pacemaker." The main complaints are the time it takes them and that some older executives are exhausted by the time they get back to their offices. Many people need to go to the plant but don't.

Salesperson: It sounds as if your executives are interested in reducing their travel time and not having to exert so much energy. By doing so, doesn't it seem they would get to the plant as they need to, saving them time and energy and saving the company money?

Buyer: I guess so.

Salesperson: Mr. Pride, on the average, how much money do your executives make an hour?

Buyer: Maybe $30 an hour.

Salesperson: If I could show you how to save your executives time in getting to and from the plant, would you be interested?

Buyer: Yes, I would. [Now the salesperson moves into the presentation.]

method in calling on the same prospect. You might begin with a benefit statement such as:

> Mr. Pride, when we talked last week, you were interested in saving your executives time and energy in getting to and from your plant, and you felt the Dyno Electric Cart could do this for you. (You could pause to let him answer or say, "Is that correct?")

From the buyers' response to your question, you can quickly determine what to do. If an objection is raised, you can respond to it. If more information is asked for, you can provide it. If what you have said about your product has pleased the buyer, you simply ask for the order.

Be cautious when uncovering a prospect's needs. Too many questions can alienate the prospect. Remember, initially many prospects do not want to open up to salespeople. Actually, some salespeople are uncomfortable with the need-satisfaction approach because they feel less in control of the selling situation than with a canned or formula presentation. A good point to remember is that you are not a performer on a stage, but that rather, your job is to meet your prospect's needs—not your own. Eventually, you can learn to anticipate customer reactions to this presentation and learn to welcome the challenge of the interaction between you and the buyer.

The Problem–Solution Presentation

In selling highly complex or technical products such as insurance, industrial equipment, accounting systems, office equipment, and computers, salespeople often are required to make several sales calls to develop a detailed analysis of a prospect's needs. After completing this analysis, the salesperson arrives at a solution to the prospect's problems and usually uses both a written analysis and an oral presentation. The **problem–solution presentation** usually consists of six steps:

1. Convincing the prospect to allow the salesperson to conduct the analysis.
2. Making the actual analysis.
3. Agreeing on the problems and determining that the buyer wants to solve them.
4. Preparing the proposal for a solution to the prospect's needs.
5. Preparing the sales presentation based on the analysis and proposal.
6. Making the sales presentation.

The problem–solution presentation is a flexible, customized approach involving an in-depth study of a prospect's needs, and requires a well-planned presentation. Often, the need-satisfaction and problem–solution presentations are used when it is necessary to present the proposal to a group of individuals.

The Group Presentation

At times you will meet with more than one decision maker for a group presentation.[6] Many group presentation elements are similar to other types of presentations. The primary difference is that either you or your team present the proposal to a group of decision makers.

The group presentation, depending on size, may be less flexible than a one-on-one meeting. The larger the group, the more structured your presentation. It would not work if everyone jumped in with feedback and ideas simultaneously, so a semblance of order has to be arranged. As the salesperson in charge, you can structure the presentation and provide a question-and-answer period at the end of or during the presentation.

The ideal situation is to talk with most or all of the decision makers involved during the analysis phase. That way, they will have contributed to determining what is needed. The points you discuss will hit on thoughts they have expressed regarding the problems at hand. In the initial part of the presentation, you should accomplish the following:

Give a Proper Introduction

State your name, company, and explain in a clear, concise sentence the premise of your proposal. For example, your statement might sound like this: Good morning. I'm Jeff Baxter from International Hospitality Consultants. I'm here to share my findings, based on research of your company and discussions with Mary Farley, that suggest my company can help increase your convention bookings by 15 to 30 percent."

Establish Credibility

Give a brief history of your company that includes the reason the business was started, the company philosophy, its development, and its success rate. Mention a few companies that you have worked with in the past, especially if they are big names. This reassures the client by letting the group know who you are and the extent of your experience and credibility.

Provide an Account List

Have copies of an account list available for everyone in attendance. It would be monotonous to say each company that you've worked with. Instead, hand out copies either in advance or while you talk. This list shows the various sizes, locations, and types of companies you've helped in the past.

State Your Competitive Advantages

Right up front you can succinctly tell the group where your company stands relative to the competition. Don't get into a detailed analysis of comparative strengths and weaknesses; make it clear that you can do better than the competition.

Give Quality Assurances and Qualifications

Get the group on your side by stating guarantees in the beginning. This shows pride in your product and that you don't skirt the issue of guarantees. Also, give your company's qualifications and credentials. For example, "We are certified by the United States government and licensed in 48 states to treat or move toxic waste," or "I have copies of the test reports from an independent lab." If your company has an impressive money-back guarantee or an extended warranty, mention it.

Cater to the Group's Behavioral Style

Every group comprises individuals with personal styles. However, a group also exhibits an overall or dominant style; that is, it has a decision-making mode that characterizes one of the four behavioral styles. (See Chapter 3.) If you can quickly determine the group style, you will hold their attention and give them what they want more effectively. Some people are more impatient than others. If you don't address their needs, you will lose their attention.

After establishing the credibility of your company, involve the group in the presentation. The first thing to do is go around the room asking for everyone's input into the decision-making criteria for making the purchase. Preface this with, "I spoke to Fred, Sally, and Sue and learned their views on what your company would like to see changed in this area. In my research, I discovered it would also benefit you to have X, Y, and Z improved. I'd like to hear all of your thoughts on this matter." Ask each person to add to the list of benefits and the decision-making criteria. Take notes, perhaps on a flip chart, of what everyone says to help shape your presentation.

After everyone has had a chance to speak, go through your presentation exactly as in a one-on-one presentation. The primary difference is that you want to answer all the questions, fears, and concerns in the group. Meet each person's specific needs with a specific proposal.

When using this method, it is essential during your preparation to brainstorm all possible concerns and questions the decision makers may have. This information comes from talking to people within the company, other salespeople, and people in the industry. Be so well prepared that there is nothing they could come up with as decision-making criteria that you haven't already thought of and answered.

When you prepare for a group, write a proposal document that ranges from one page to an entire notebook with data, specifications, reports, and solutions to specific problems. The proposal document is a reference source that tells your customer what she bought if she said yes and what she didn't buy if the answer was no. This document addresses everything you and your prospect discussed in the analysis phase: problems, success criteria, decision-making criteria, and how your product or service answers each. At the end, include relevant documents and copies of testimonial letters from satisfied customers.

During your presentation, do not read from the document. It is not the presentation; it is strictly a resource of facts to give your prospect after a decision is made. In addition, when making your presentation, do not expect to cover every point in the proposal unless you are brief. Your presentation will focus on the issues that relate to the customer's specific need gap; tangential information should be left in the document. Remember that proposal documents don't sell products; people sell products. The document is no substitute for a first-rate presentation.

The best way to present a proposal document is without prices. There are several reasons for this. First, some people will go directly to the prices without reading through the document. Second, prices tend to prejudice non-decision makers—who should not be concerned with prices. If the decision maker asks why the prices are missing, tell him, "I thought you would prefer the flexibility of showing the document to other people without their knowing prices. It's a matter of confidentiality." The third reason is politics. Imagine a board of directors that has not had a raise in two years looking at a document that proposes a $2 million computer for the company. This may stir up problems.

Make it clear that you are not trying to hide the prices and that you would be more than happy to talk about them with the appropriate people, the decision makers. It is important to present prices in the proper perspective and context.

When you share the proposal, address each problem and give specific information about your solutions. Make sure you discuss features, advantages, and benefits—and get feedback from the group. Ask trial closes like:

- "Can you see any other advantages to this?"
- "How do you feel about that? Do you think that would solve the problem?"

At the end, summarize your proposal by giving a benefits summary: "Here is what you will get if you accept my proposal." Talk about how the benefits will address their specific problems.

Before your presentation, find out from your primary contact in the company if the group will make a decision while you are there or if they will discuss it and inform you later. You also should know if they are responsible for dealing with the financial aspects of the purchase. If so, you will have to talk about the costs and the benefits they will receive in relation to the costs. If they will not be concerned with prices, don't discuss them.

When you have completed the benefits summary, solicit impressions from the group. Ask if they agree that the solution you proposed would solve their problem or meet their needs. Without asking for it, get a feeling for the disposition of the group. If you are working with one person, it is easier to ask for an impression.

At the end of your summary, ask if there are any questions. At this point, you are close to the end of your allotted time. When someone asks a question that is

MAKING THE SALE

Characteristics for Successful Negotiation

The following 10 personal characteristics necessary to successful negotiation can help you determine the potential you already possess and also identify areas where improvement is needed. On a separate piece of paper, write the number that best reflects where you fall on the scale. The higher the number the more the characteristic describes you. When you have finished, total the numbers.

1. I am sensitive to the needs
   of others.   1 2 3 4 5 6 7 8 9 10

2. I will compromise to solve
   problems when necessary.   1 2 3 4 5 6 7 8 9 10

3. I am committed to a win/
   win philosophy.   1 2 3 4 5 6 7 8 9 10

4. I have a high tolerance for
   conflict.   1 2 3 4 5 6 7 8 9 10

5. I am willing to research
   and analyze issues fully.   1 2 3 4 5 6 7 8 9 10

6. Patience is one of my
   strong points.   1 2 3 4 5 6 7 8 9 10

7. My tolerance for stress is
   high.   1 2 3 4 5 6 7 8 9 10

8. I am a good listener.   1 2 3 4 5 6 7 8 9 10

9. Personal attack and ridicule
   do not unduly bother me.   1 2 3 4 5 6 7 8 9 10

10. I can identify bottom line
    issues quickly.   1 2 3 4 5 6 7 8 9 10

If you scored 80 or more, you have characteristics of a good negotiator. You recognize what negotiating requires and seem willing to apply yourself accordingly. If you scored between 60 and 79, you should do well as a negotiator but have some characteristics that need further development. If your evaluation is less than 60, you should go over the items again carefully. You may have been hard on yourself, or you may have identified some key areas on which to concentrate as you negotiate. Repeat this evaluation again after you have had practice negotiating.[7]

answered in your proposal document, refer him to the appropriate section of the document and assure him that a complete answer is provided.

Negotiating So Everyone Wins

No matter what type of presentation method used, or whether you talk to one person or a group of people, be prepared to negotiate. Many salespeople negotiate during the confirming phase of the sale. Their products or services are big-ticket items with many negotiable details. The negotiating process during the sale confirmation becomes a critical point that can affect the business relationship.

There are many negotiating styles with various names. For example, there are cooperative, competitive, attitudinal, organizational, and personal modes of negotiating. Most inexperienced negotiators operate in the competitive mode because they mistakenly think the shrewd businessperson is one who wins at the other's expense. With a win–lose attitude in mind, they "don't show all their cards" and use other strategies to gain the upper hand. Often this is done at the expense of the business relationship.

If you see prospects as adversaries rather than business partners, you will have short-term, adversarial relationships. The tension, mistrust, and buyer's remorse created are not worth the small gains you may win using this negotiating style. There is a better way.

Professional salespeople negotiate in a way that achieves satisfaction for both parties. They rely on trust, openness, credibility, integrity, and fairness. Their attitude is not, "How can I get what I want out of this person?" It's "There are many options to explore that will make both of us happy. If two people want to do business, the

SELLING GLOBALLY

Chinese Culture: Don't Shy Away from Negotiating

To the Chinese, negotiation can be sport. "Negotiating? It's not esoteric," says former U.S. Ambassador to China James Lilley, who is now a business consultant. "There's no arcane world of Chinese deviousness. Once you figure out what they want—and they telegraph their punches—you can make your deal. You've got to be willing to go to the brink. You've got to be willing to use them against each other. You've got to be willing to come in on top and bring pressure to bear." (In other words, use high-level pressure developed through relationships.)

The tough-love approach is suggested again and again: Be respectful; don't fly off the handle, but be resolute. Jim Stepanek, who spent years negotiating in China for Honeywell and other U.S. companies, says: "The only universal language is pain and anger. When they push down your price, and you calmly say no, they are going to delay the meeting another day and push you some more. When you finally get upset, and you ask to leave the room to control yourself because your blood vessels are popping out, and you come back a half hour later with steam still coming out your ears, then they know it is your lowest price."

There are advantages to negotiating in China rather than Japan, suggests Craig McLaughlin. "When you are negotiating with a Japanese organization, even when what you are presenting is totally unacceptable to the individual or company, they may not tell you. That is not a problem in China. They will be very direct. They're more likely to try and get you to negotiate against yourself. Instead of giving you a counterproposal they say, `Go home and think about it, and come back with a better offer.'

"Another trait," continues McLaughlin, "is that quite often the people with whom you are negotiating do not have

the authority to reach a compromise. The delegation of authority in China is not totally spelled out. Your best move? Tell them that there is little point in going further with the meeting unless they are willing to reveal their chain of command. They may not necessarily give you a straight answer, and sometimes they may not even know themselves, but it is a step in the right direction."[8]

details will not stand in the way." It is important *not* to negotiate the details before your customer has made a commitment to your solution.

Phases of Negotiation

If your product or service requires negotiating on a regular basis, set the stage for negotiation early in the sales process. There are things you can do to prepare for negotiation from the beginning.

Planning. The number one asset of a strong negotiator is preparation. During the planning phase, after completing a competition analysis, you know how your

---

SELLING TIPS

Negotiating

- When you give something up, try to gain something in return. When you give something for nothing, there is a tendency for people to want more. In all fairness to you and your prospect, therefore, balance what you give and receive. For example, "I'll lower the price if you pay in full within 30 days," or "I'll give you 10 percent off, but you will be charged for additional services such as training."

- Look for items other than price to negotiate. For example, gain some flexibility by offering: better terms, payment plans, return policies, and delivery schedules; lower deposits or cancellation fees; or implementation and

training programs. Often these items are provided for less than your company would lose if you lowered the price.

- Do not attack your prospect's demand; look for the motive behind it. Never tell a prospect his demand is ridiculous or unreasonable. Remain calm and ask for the reason behind the desire.

- Do not defend your position; ask for feedback and advice from the prospect. If you meet resistance to an offer, don't be defensive. Say something like, "This is my thinking. What would you do if you were in my position?"

---

company compares to the competition for price, service, quality, reputation, and so on. This knowledge is important at negotiation time. You may be able to offer things the competition cannot. It is advantageous to point these advantages out to your prospect when the time is right.

Before you make a proposal to a client, search your company's sales records to find any reports of previous sales to your prospect or similar businesses. If these records documented the successes and failures of negotiating, you will learn from other salespeople's experience. For this reason, your call reports should include details of what transpired during any negotiation. The knowledge gained from these records is not a strategy per se but insight into the priorities of this market segment. For example, businesses in a certain industry segment may value service more than price, or they may care more about help in training and implementation than a discount.

During your preparation, review the various bargaining chips available to you. Some of the questions to answer are:

- What extra services can you offer?
- How flexible is the price or the payment plan?
- Are deposits and cancellation fees negotiable?
- Is there optional equipment you can throw in free?
- Can you provide free training?
- What items in the negotiation will be inflexible for you?
- How can you compensate for these items?

Meeting. When you meet a prospect, you start building the relationship by proving you are someone who is credible, trustworthy, and hopefully the type of person your prospect likes to do business with. If you are all of these things, you will eliminate tension from the relationship and thereby ease the negotiation process.

As proof of this concept, imagine selling your car to a friend. Now imagine selling it to a stranger. Who would be easier to negotiate with? The friend, of course. For both of you, the top priority is the relationship; the secondary priority is the car deal.

MAKING THE SALE

Matt Suffoletto of IBM Uses the Problem–Solution Presentation Method

"A successful salesperson has expertise in the products he or she sells, as well as an in-depth knowledge of the customer's business. The salesperson often makes recommendations which alter the mainstream of the customer's business process. Recognizing the requirement for business skills, IBM provides training in both the technical aspects of our products, as well as their industrial application.

"My territory consists of manufacturing customers; hence, I pride myself in understanding concepts such as inventory control, time phased requirements planning, and shop floor control. Typically, I work with customer user department and data processing people to do application surveys and detailed justification analysis. After the background work is completed, I make proposals and presentations to educate the chain of decision makers on the IBM recommendations.

"Selling involves the transformation of the features of your product into benefits for the customer. The principal vehicles for that communication are the sales call, formal presentations, and proposals. The larger the magnitude of the sale, the more time and effort is spent on presentations and proposals. A proposal may range from a simple one-page letter and attachment with prices, terms, and conditions, to multivolume binders with detailed information on the product, including its use, detailed justification, implementation schedules, and contracts. The wide range of comprehensiveness implies an equal range in time commitment of the salesperson.

"Very few sales are made in a single call. At the first sales call, the salesperson generally searches for additional information that needs to be brought back, analysis that needs to be done, or questions to be answered. These are opportunities to demonstrate responsiveness to the customer. Getting back to the customer in a very timely and professional manner is a way to build trust and confidence into a business relationship."

Studying. When you study a prospect's business, look at the big picture. As mentioned earlier in the book, don't focus on features; look for benefits you can provide. Look behind a prospect's demands for reasons. You can ask, "What are you trying to accomplish by asking for this?" After you are told, you may be able to say, "We can accomplish that another way. Consider this alternative . . ." The more options for providing benefits, the more flexible the negotiation.

During this phase, you must find out what other company's products or services your prospect is considering. This gives insight into what they are looking for and willing to pay. If you are selling a half-million-dollar CAT scanner and your prospect is also considering a three-quarter-million-dollar CAT scanner, you know your product is not priced too high. If, however, your prospect is looking at a lot of lower-priced units, it may be an uphill struggle to get the prospect to spend what you're asking. Knowing who your competitors are will help you assess bargaining strengths and weaknesses.

Every purchase is made with decision-making criteria in mind, either consciously or unconsciously. Find out what they are for your prospect and the prospect's company. Within those criteria, there are usually three levels of desire: must have, should have, and would be nice to have. Be clear about these levels and how they create limits for negotiations. Obviously, "must haves" are much less flexible than "would be nice to have."

Proposing. Proposing is another phase that indirectly affects subsequent negotiations. What you do in the presentation sets the stage for what may come later. During your presentation, tie features and advantages to benefits and emphasize unique benefits. In this way, your product or service and company are

ETHICAL DILEMMA

Ship It to Russia

Before there's an available sample, you've given the prospect—a Fortune 100 company—a spec sheet on your company's new PC. The spec sheet lists an operating speed of 20 megahertz and a 100 megabyte hard drive. After the product is purchased, you learn that the spec sheet was printed incorrectly. The operating speed is 18 megahertz and the hard disk has 90 megabytes. That same afternoon, there's an order in the mail from the Fortune 100 company for 100 units. They are to be delivered from your U.S. plant to a subsidiary of the ordering company located in Russia.

What do you do?

positioned above the rest. It is important to position yourself as well. Don't be afraid to let your prospect know she is getting you and everything you have promised to do after the sale.

The successful resolution of a negotiation starts with a commitment to do business together. It is then necessary for both parties to maintain common interests and resolve any conflicts cooperatively. The key to selling and negotiating is to always seek a win–win solution in which both buyer and seller are happy.[9]

What Is the Best Presentation Method?

Each of these sales presentation methods is the best one when the method is properly matched with the *situation.* For example, the stimulus–response method can be used where time is short and the product is simple. Formula selling is effective in repeat purchases or when you know or have already determined the needs of the prospect.

The need-satisfaction method is most appropriate where information needs to be gathered from the prospect as is often the case in selling industrial products. Finally, the problem-solving presentation is excellent for selling high-cost technical products or services, and especially for system selling involving several sales calls and a business proposition. To help improve sales, the salesperson should understand and be able to use each method based on each situation.

SALES PRESENTATIONS GO HIGH TECH

Videos, CD ROMs, satellite conferencing, plus computer hardware and software are increasingly being used in sales presentations. Whether in transactional, relationship, or partnering situations, salespeople are finding high-tech sales presentations effective in providing customers the necessary information for them to make informed decisions. Chapter 10 discusses these important selling tools further.

Select the Presentation Method, Then the Approach

Before developing the presentation, you must know which presentation method you will use. Once you determine which presentation method is best for your situation, plan what you will do when talking with your prospect. Your initial consideration should be how to begin your sales presentation.

SUMMARY OF MAJOR SELLING ISSUES

To improve your chances of making a sale, you must master the art of giving a good sales presentation. An effective presentation will work toward specifically solving the customer's problems. The sales presentation method selected should be based on prior knowledge of the customer, your sales call objective, and your customer benefit plan.

Because prospects want to know how you and your product will benefit them and the companies they represent, you must show that you have a right to present your product because it has key benefits for them. Many different sales presentation methods are available. They differ from one another depending on what percentage of the conversation is controlled by the salesperson. The salesperson usually does most of the talking in the more structured memorized and formula selling techniques, while there is more buyer–seller interaction in the less structured methods.

In the memorized presentation, or stimulus–response method, the salesperson does 80 to 90 percent of the talking, with each customer receiving the same sales pitch. Although this method ensures a well-planned presentation and is good for certain nontechnical products, it is also somewhat inflexible, allowing little prospect participation. The formula presentation, a persuasive selling presentation, is similar to the first method, but it takes the prospect into account by answering questions and handling objections.

The most challenging and creative form of selling uses the need-satisfaction presentation. This flexible method begins by raising questions about what the customer specifically needs. After you are aware of the customer's needs, you can then show how your products fit these needs. You must be cautious because many people don't want to open up to the salesperson.

When selling highly complex or technical products like computers or insurance, a problem-solution presentation consisting of six steps is a good sales method. This method involves a detailed analysis of the buyer's specific needs and problems and designing a proposal and presentation to fit these needs. This customized method often uses a selling team to present the specialized information to the buyer.

In comparing the four presentation methods, there is no one best method. Each one must be tailored to meet the particular characteristics of a specific selling situation or environment.

MEETING A SALES CHALLENGE

Don't panic! You've done everything you could have done. You have worked hard on this presentation, and you are prepared. This will be a challenge you can handle. As all pros know, on any sales call you have to be prepared to adapt to the situation. They must be very interested, or they would not have these executives attend the meeting.

This presentation is similar to the one-on-one you practiced but less flexible. Once the group has assembled, they will ask you to begin—so first introduce yourself and explain in a clear, concise sentence the premise of your proposal. Follow the remaining five group-presentation suggestions in this chapter. Invite everyone to ask questions throughout your talk.

KEY TERMS FOR SELLING

sales presentation 225	need development 231
memorized presentation 226	need awareness 231
formula presentation 229	need fulfillment 231
need-satisfaction presentation 230	problem–solution presentation 234

SALES APPLICATION QUESTIONS

1. What are the four sales presentation methods discussed in this chapter? Briefly explain each method; include any similarities and differences in your answer.

2. One salesperson profiled in this text stated that he concentrates on the need-fulfillment phase of the sales presentation. Is he correct in his approach? Why or why not?

3. Assume that a salesperson already knows the customer's needs. Instead of developing the customer's needs as a part of the sales presentation, he goes directly to the close. What are your feelings on this type of sales presentation?

4. To properly use the formula sales presentation, what information does the seller need?

5. What steps are required to develop and use the need-satisfaction presentation?

6. Assume you are selling a product requiring you to typically use the problem-solving sales presentation method. You have completed your study of a prospect's business and are ready to present your recommendation to her. What is your selling strategy?

FURTHER EXPLORING THE SALES WORLD

Assume that you are a salesperson selling a consumer item such as a wristwatch. Without any preparation, make a sales presentation to a friend. If possible, record your sales presentation on a tape recorder. Analyze the recording and determine the approximate conversation time of your prospect. On the basis of your analysis, which of the four sales presentation methods discussed in Chapter 8 did you use? How early in the sales presentation did your prospect begin to give you objections?

SELLING EXPERIENTIAL EXERCISE

You have learned much about selling so far in this course. Let's find out how much, and at the same time better understand your attitude toward selling. *Three* of the 10 statements are false. Which are the false statements? Please first cover answers.

Is Selling for You?

1. Dealing with customers is less exciting than the work involved in most other jobs.

2. Selling brings out the best in your personality.

3. Salespeople are made, not born; if you don't plan and work hard, you'll never be exceptional at selling.

4. Attitude is more important in selling positions than most other jobs.

5. Those good at selling often can improve their income quickly.

6. Learning to sell now will help you succeed in *any* job in the future.

7. In your first sales job, what you learn can be more important than what you earn.

8. Selling is less demanding than other jobs.

9. You have less freedom in most selling positions.

10. A smile uses fewer muscles than a frown.[10]

False statements: 1, 8, and 9.

SALES WORLD WIDE WEB EXERCISES

Can You Improve Your Presentation?

The most challenging, rewarding, and enjoyable aspect of the sales job is the sales presentation. An effective presentation completely and clearly explains all aspects of a salesperson's proposition as it relates to a buyer's needs. To learn more about effective presentations, visit your favorite search engine(s) and some or all of the following URLs:

Presenting Solutions—The Art of Communicating Effectively
www.presentingsolutions.com

Fast Company Magazine
www.fastcompany.com/09/beforetalk.html
www.fastcompany.com/07/130crash.html

CommWeb	**Sharing Ideas**
www.commweb.com	www.speaking.com
Professional Speaker	**High Impact Speech Writing**
www.nsaspeaker.org	www.speechwriting.com

It is often not what you say but how you say it that influences someone to buy from you. Salespeople are using more multimedia presentations to convey their message. See what you can find out about methods, equipment, and the effectiveness of using multimedia in a sales presentation.

CASE 8-1
Cascade Soap Company

Mike Bowers sells soap products to grocery wholesalers and large retail grocery chains. The following presentation occurred during a call he made on Bill Reese, the soap buyer for a grocery store.

Salesperson: Bill, you have stated several times that the types of promotions or brands that really turn you on are ones that carry the best profit. Is that right?

Customer: Yes, it is. I'm under pressure to increase my profit-per-square-foot in my department.

Salesperson: Bill, I recommend that you begin carrying the king size of Cascade. Let's review the benefits and economics of this proposal. King-size Cascade would cost you 86.8¢ a box. The average resale in this market is 99¢. That means that you would make 12.2¢ every time you sell a box of king-size Cascade. Based on my estimated volume for your store of $40,000 per week, you would sell approximately two cases of king-size Cascade per week. That is $19.80 in new sales and $2.44 in new profits per week for your store. As you can see, the addition of Cascade 10 to your automatic dishwashing detergent department will increase your sales and, even more importantly, increase your profits—and this is what you said you wanted to do, right?

Customer: Yes, I am interested in increasing profits.

Salesperson: Do you want me to give this information to the head stock clerk so that she can make arrangements to put Cascade 10s on the shelf? Or would you like me to put it on the shelf on my next call?

Questions

1. What sales presentation method was Mike using?
2. Evaluate Mike's handling of this situation.

CASE 8–2

A Retail Sales Presentation

A customer is looking at a display of Cross gold pens and pencils.

Customer: I'm looking for a graduation gift for my brother, but I'm not necessarily looking for a pen and pencil set.

Salesperson: Is your brother graduating from college or high school?

Customer: He is graduating from college this spring.

Salesperson: I can show you quite a few items that would be appropriate gifts. Let's start by taking a look at this elegant Cross pen and pencil set. Don't they look impressive?

Customer: They look too expensive. Besides, a pen and pencil set doesn't seem like an appropriate gift for a college graduate.

Salesperson: You're right, a Cross pen and pencil set *does* look expensive. Just imagine how impressed your brother will be when he opens your gift package and finds these beautiful writing instruments. Even though Cross pen and pencil sets look expensive, they are actually quite reasonably priced, considering the total value you are getting.

Customer: How much does this set cost?

Salesperson: You can buy a Cross pen and pencil set for anywhere from $15 to $300. The one I am showing you is gold-plated and costs only $28. For this modest amount you can purchase a gift for your brother that will be attractive, useful, last a lifetime, and will show him that you truly think he is deserving of the very best. Don't you think that is what a graduation gift should be?

Customer: You make it sound pretty good, but frankly I hadn't intended to spend that much money.

Salesperson: Naturally, I can show you something else. However, before I do that, pick up this Cross pen and write your name on this pad of paper. Notice that in addition to good looks, Cross pens offer good writing. Cross is acclaimed widely as one of the best ball-point pens on the market. It is nicely balanced, has a point that allows the ink to flow on the paper smoothly, and rides over the paper with ease.

Customer: You're right, the pen writes really well.

Salesperson: Each time your brother writes with this pen, he will remember that you gave him this fine writing instrument for graduation. In addition, Cross offers prestige. Many customers tell us that Cross is one of the few pens they have used that is so outstanding that people often comment on it by brand name. Your brother will enjoy having others notice the pen he uses is high in quality.

Customer: You're right. I do tend to notice when someone is using a Cross pen.

Salesperson: You can't go wrong with a Cross pen and pencil set for a gift. Shall I wrap it for you?

Customer: It's a hard decision.

Salesperson: Your brother will be very happy with this gift.

Customer: Okay. Go ahead and wrap it for me.

Salesperson: Fine. Would you like me to wrap up another set for you to give yourself?

Customer: No, one is enough. Maybe someone will buy one for me someday.

Questions

1. Describe the selling techniques being used by the retail salesperson.
2. Evaluate the salesperson's handling of this situation.

CASE 8–3
Negotiating with a Friend

Barney wants to buy a car. He spotted a high-quality used car on a dealer's lot over the weekend. He would buy it immediately if he had more cash. The dealer will give him only $1,200 on a trade for his current automobile. The car Barney wants is really great, and chances are good it will be sold in short order. Barney has planned carefully and decided he can swing the deal if he can sell his present vehicle to a private party for around $2,000. This would give him $1,500 for a down payment and $500 for accessories he wishes to add. The car is in good condition except for a couple of minor dents in the fender. The snow tires for his current car won't fit the new one but can probably be sold; that will help. Barney can remove the new stereo system he installed last month and place it in the new car.

Billie, one of Barney's co-workers, heard that Barney wants to sell his car and plans to talk to him about it. Her daughter is graduating from college in three months and will need a car to drive to work. Billie can only afford about $1,800 including any repairs that might be required, and she needs to reserve enough money for snow tires. Her daughter has seen the car and thinks it's sporty, especially with the stereo. Billie checked the blue book price for the model of Barney's car, and she knows the average wholesale price is $1,200 and the average retail price is $1,950.

Questions

1. What are Barney's objectives?
2. What are Billie's objectives?
3. What are likely to be the points of conflict?
4. What power does Barney have?
5. What power does Billie have?
6. How important is time to Barney?
7. How important is time to Billie?
8. What are some possible points of compromise?

9

Begin Your Presentation Strategically

MAIN TOPICS

The Right to Approach

The Approach—Opening the Sales Presentation

Technology in the Approach

Using Questions Results in Sales Success

Is the Prospect Still Not Listening?

Be Flexible in Your Approach

LEARNING OBJECTIVES

You have selected your prospect, planned the sales call, and determined the appropriate presentation method. Now, you must determine how to begin the sales presentation. This step in the selling process is called the *approach*. After studying this chapter, you should be able to:

■ Explain the importance of using an approach and provide examples of approaches.

■ Illustrate why the approach should have a theme that is related to the presentation and the prospect's important buying motives. What is an example?

■ Present four types of questioning techniques for use throughout the presentation and give an example of each technique.

■ Understand the importance of being flexible in your approach.

You are making a cold call on the office manager of a local bank—Citizen's National. You assume one of the manager's responsibilities consists of ordering office supplies. Based on your experience with other banks, you suspect the volume of orders would be small but steady throughout the year.

As a salesperson for University Office Supplies, you especially want to sell your new equipment for mailing out bank statements, along with the paper and other products associated with this job. Since this is a small bank, you decide to go in cold, relying on your questioning ability to uncover potential problems and make the prospect aware of them.

You are now face-to-face with the manager. You have introduced yourself, and after some small talk you feel it is time to begin your presentation. Many salespeople face this situation several times each day. What would you do? What type of presentation would you use? How would you begin the presentation?

Have you ever been told, "You get only one opportunity to make a good first impression"? If the first minute of talking with a prospect creates a bad impression, it can take hours to overcome it—if you ever do. Many times, salespeople get only one chance to sell a prospect.

The approach—or beginning—of your presentation is essential to the prospect's allowing you to discuss your product. If done incorrectly the prospect may stop you from telling your sales story. You need to have a good beginning in order to have a good ending to your sales presentation.

This chapter introduces you to the *dos* and *don'ts* of beginning your sales presentation. Many salespeople are nervous in contacting prospects. Let's begin our discussion of the approach by seeing why you have the right to talk with a prospect.

THE RIGHT TO APPROACH

You have the right (or duty) to present your product if you can show that it will definitely benefit the prospect. In essence, you have to prove *you* are worthy of the prospect's time and serious attention. You may earn the right to this attention in a number of ways:

- By exhibiting specific product or business knowledge.
- By expressing a sincere desire to solve a buyer's problem and satisfy a need.
- By stating or implying that your product will save money or increase the firm's profit margin.
- By displaying a service attitude.

Basically, prospects want to know how you and your product will benefit *them* and *the companies* they represent. Your sales approach should initially establish, and thereafter concentrate on, your product's key benefits for each prospect.

This strategy is especially important during the approach stage of a presentation because it aids in securing the prospect's interest in you and your product. At this point, you want this unspoken reaction from the prospect: "Well, I'd better hear this salesperson out. I may hear something that will be of use to me." Now that you have justified your right to sell to a prospect, determine how to present your product.

EXHIBIT 9-1

Making sure your attitude is
positive

Dizziness

Tiny brain

Fear of memory lapse
and brain disconnecting
from mouth

Small ears making
hearing difficult

Mouth programmed
to say "No" and
"Price too high"

Dryness in mouth

Adam's apple that
won't work

Small heart

Leather windbags
for lungs

Rapid heartbeat

Upset stomach

Cold fish hands

Sweating palms

Trembling hands

Big stomach to
hold free meals

Weakness in knees

THE APPROACH— OPENING THE SALES PRESENTATION

Raleigh Johnson spent days qualifying the prospect, arranging for an appointment, and planning every aspect of the sales presentation; and in the first 60 seconds of the sales presentation, he realized his chance of selling was excellent. He quickly determined the prospect's needs and evoked attention and interest in his product because of the technique he used to begin the sales interview.

A buyer's reactions to the salesperson in the early minutes of the sales presentation are critical to a successful sale. This short period is so important that it is treated as an individual step in selling referred to as the approach. Part of any approach is the prospect's first impression of you.

Your Attitude during the Approach

As shown in Exhibit 9–1, it is common for a salesperson to experience tension in various forms when contacting a prospect. Often this is brought on when the salesperson has preconceived ideas that things may go wrong during the sale. Prospects may be viewed as having negative characteristics that make the sales call difficult.

All salespeople experience some degree of stress at times. Yet successful salespeople have learned a relaxation and concentration technique called **creative imagery** that allows them to cope with stress. The salesperson envisions the worst that can happen. Then preparation is made to react to it and even accept it if need be. The best that can happen is also envisioned, as seen in Exhibit 9–2. Furthermore, contingency plans are mentally prepared should the planned sales talk need to be abandoned.

The last question the salesperson should ask herself is, "What are the chances that things will go wrong?" Chances are the answer involves a low probability. Usually, there is less than a 1 percent chance that things will go wrong, especially when careful planning has taken place before the sales call. A greater than 99 percent probability that things will go as planned should dim fears of the most worrisome salespeople.

Creative imagery is a great way to relax while psyching yourself up before seeing your prospect.

Picture worst and best that can happen, plus success.

The First Impression You Make Is Critical to Success

When you meet your prospect, the initial impression you make is based on appearances. If this impression is favorable, your prospect is more likely to listen to you; if it is not favorable, your prospect may erect communication barriers that are difficult to overcome.

The first impression is centered on the image projected by your (1) appearance and (2) attitude. Here are some suggestions for making a favorable first impression:

- Wear business clothes that are suitable and fairly conservative.
- Be neat in dress and grooming.
- Refrain from smoking, chewing gum, or drinking when in your prospect's office.
- Keep an erect posture to project confidence.
- Leave all unnecessary materials outside the office (overcoat, umbrella, or newspaper).
- If possible, sit down. Should the prospect not offer a chair, ask, "May I sit here?"
- Be enthusiastic and positive toward the interview.
- Smile, always smile! (Try to be sincere with your smile; it will aid you in being enthusiastic and positive toward your prospect.)
- Do not apologize for taking the prospect's time.
- Do not imply that you were just passing by and that the sales call was not planned.
- Maintain eye contact with the prospect.

Five ways to remember
prospect's name

1. Be sure to hear the person's name and use it: "It's good to meet you, Mr. Firestone."
2. Spell it out in your mind, or if it is an unusual name, ask the person to spell the name.
3. Relate the name to something you are familiar with, such as relating the name Firestone to Firestone automobile tires.
4. Use the name in the conversation.
5. Repeat the name at the end of the conversation, such as "Goodbye, Mr. Firestone."

- If the prospect offers to shake hands, do so with a firm, positive grip while maintaining eye contact.
- If possible, before the interview, learn how to pronounce your prospect's name correctly and use it throughout the interview. Should the prospect introduce you to other people, remember their names by using the five ways to remember names shown in Exhibit 9–3.

Like an actor, the salesperson must learn how to project and maintain a positive, confident, and enthusiastic first impression no matter what mood the prospect is in when first encountered by the salesperson.

The following factors must be examined and assigned a degree of importance before entering your customer's office.

- Your sales call *objective.*
- The *type of approach* that will be well received by the customer.
- Your *customer benefit plan.*

This approach selection process can greatly aid in making a satisfactory impression.

Approach Techniques and Objectives

Approach techniques are grouped into three general categories: (1) opening with a statement; (2) opening with a demonstration; and (3) opening with a question or questions.

Your choice of approach technique depends on which of the four sales presentation methods you have selected based on your situation and sales presentation plan. Exhibit 9–4 presents one way of determining the approach technique to use. Using questions in a sales approach is feasible with any of the four presentation methods, whereas statements and demonstrations typically are reserved for either the memorized or formula sales presentation methods. Because of their customer-oriented nature, the need-satisfaction and problem–solution sales presentation methods

The approach techniques for
each of the four sales
presentation methods

Sales Presentation Methods	Approach Technique		
	Statement	Demonstration	Questions
Memorized (canned)	✔	✔	✔
Formula (persuasive selling)	✔	✔	✔
Need-satisfaction			✔
Problem-solving			✔

always employ questions at the outset. This chapter reviews each of the approach techniques with examples of their uses and benefits.

Both the statement and demonstration approach techniques have three basic objectives:

1. To capture the *attention* of the prospect.
2. To stimulate the prospect's *interest*.
3. To provide a *transition* into the sales presentation.

Imagine the prospect silently asking three questions: (1) "Shall I see this person?" (2) "Shall I listen, talk with, and devote more time to this person?" and (3) "What's in it for me?" The answers to these questions help determine the outcome of the sale. If you choose to use either of these two approaches, create a statement or demonstration approach that causes the prospect to say yes to each of these three questions.

Small Talk Warms 'Em Up

In most, if not all, sales calls the approach consists of two parts. First is usually a "small talk" or rapport-building phase. You might talk about the weather, sports, or anything. This is especially true when calling on a prospect who has a feeler, intuitor, or thinker personality style.* The senser, however, may want to get directly to business.

The second part of the approach is the planned, formal selling technique used as a lead-in to the upcoming discussion of the product. It consists of using either a statement, demonstration, or one or more questions. Which of these three to use is based on the situation.

The Situational Approach

The situation you face determines which approach technique you use to begin your sales presentation. The situation is dictated by a number of variables that only you can identify. Some of the more common situational variables are

- The type of *product* you are selling.
- Whether this is a *repeat call* on the same person.
- Your degree of knowledge about the *customer's needs*.
- The *time* you have for making the sales presentation.
- Whether the customer is *aware of a problem*.

The sales approach can be a frightening, lonely, heart-stopping experience. It can easily lead to ego-bruising rejection. Your challenge is to move the prospect from an often cold, indifferent, or sometimes even hostile frame of mind to an aroused excitement about the product. By quickly obtaining the prospect's attention and interest, the conversation can make a smooth transition into the presentation that greatly improves the probability of making the sale by allowing you to lead quickly into the sales presentation, shown in Exhibit 9–5.

EXHIBIT 9-5

The approach leads quickly into the sales presentation.

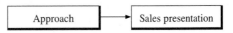

---

*Refer back to Chapter 3 for the discussion on personality styles.

EXHIBIT 9–6

Approach techniques for opening the presentation

Statements	Demonstrations	Questions
■ Introductory	■ Product	■ Customer Benefit
■ Complimentary	■ Showmanship	■ Curiosity
■ Referral		■ Opinion
■ Premium		■ Shock
		■ Multiple Question (SPIN)

In addition to creating attention, stimulating interest, and providing for transition, using questions in your approach includes the following objectives:

1. To *uncover* the needs or problems *important* to the prospect.
2. To determine if the prospect wishes to *fulfill* those needs or *solve* these problems.
3. To have the prospect *tell you* about these needs or problems, and the intention to do something about them.

Since people buy to fulfill needs or solve problems, the use of questions in your approach is preferable to statements or demonstrations. Questions allow you to uncover needs, whereas statements and demonstrations are used when you assume knowledge of the prospect's needs. However, all three approach techniques can be used by the salesperson in the proper situation. Exhibit 9–6 shows the three basic approach techniques and examples of each technique you will study, beginning with opening statements.

Opening with Statements

Malika W. Shabazz

Opening statements are effective if properly planned, especially if the salesperson has uncovered the prospect's needs before entering the office. Four statement approaches frequently used are (1) the introductory approach; (2) the complimentary approach; (3) the referral approach; and (4) the premium approach.

The **introductory approach** is the most common and the least powerful because it does little to capture the prospect's attention and interest. It opens with the salesperson's name and business: "Hello, Ms. Crompton, my name is John Gladstone, representing the Pierce Chemical Company."

The introductory approach is needed when meeting a prospect for the first time. In most cases, though, the introductory approach should be used in conjunction with another approach. This additional approach could be the complimentary approach.

Everyone likes a compliment. If the **complimentary approach** is sincere, it is an effective beginning to a sales interview:

■ Ms. Rosenburg, you certainly have a thriving restaurant business. I have enjoyed many lunches here. While doing so, I have thought of several products that could make your business even better and make things easier for you and your employees.

■ Mr. Davidson, I was just visiting with your boss who commented that you were doing a good job in keeping your company's printing costs down. I have a couple of ideas which may help you further reduce your costs!

Sometimes a suitable compliment is not in order or cannot be generated. Another way to get the buyer's attention is to mention a mutual acquaintance as a reference. See Exhibit 9–7.

The use of another person's name, the **referral approach,** is effective if the prospect respects that person; it is important to remember, however, that the referral approach can have a negative effect if the prospect does not like the person:

EXHIBIT 9–7

The referral approach

Angie was creative in using the referral approach. A friend of the buyer allowed her to tape a brief introductory message. She put the tape recorder on his desk and let the buyer listen. It was a great way to open her presentation.

- Ms. Rosenburg, my name is Carlos Ramirez, with the Restaurant Supply Corporation. When I talked to your brother last week, he wanted me to give you the opportunity to see Restaurant Supply's line of paper products for your restaurant.
- Hello, Mr. Gillespie—Linda Crawford with the Ramada Inn suggested that I contact you concerning our new Xerox table copier.

One salesperson tells of taking the customer to tape-record a brief introduction to a friend. When calling on the friend, the salesperson placed the recorder on the desk and said, "Amos McDonald has a message for you, Ms. James . . . let's listen."

Few people can obtain a reference for every prospect they intend to contact (this may be especially true for a beginning salesperson). Even if you don't know all the right people, you can still get on track by offering the buyer something for nothing—a premium.

A **premium approach** is effective because everyone likes to receive something free. When appropriate, use free samples and novelty items in a premium approach.

- Early in the morning of her first day on a new campus, one textbook salesperson makes a practice of leaving a dozen doughnuts in the faculty lounge with her card stapled to the box. She claims that prospects actually come looking for her!
- Mr. Jones, here is a beautiful desk calendar with your name engraved on it. Each month I will place a new calendar in the holder which, by the way, will feature one of our products. This month's calendar, for example, features our lubricating oil.
- Ms. Rogers, this high-quality Fuller hair brush is yours, free, for just giving me five minutes of your time.
- Ms. McCall [handing her the product to examine], I want to leave samples for you, your cosmetic representative, and your best customers of Revlon's newest addition to our perfume line.

Creative use of premiums is an effective sales approach. Demonstrations also leave a favorable impression with a prospect.

MAKING THE SALE

A Successful Salesperson's Approach

Sheila Fisher, a middle-aged widow, lived in California for 25 years before returning to her native England three years ago. Now she wanted to move back to California and buy a home of her own. She had some cash available for a down payment, but her income was fixed and she was not sure what she could make if she went back to work as a hair stylist. However, she knew what she did not want. "I don't want exotic financing," Sheila told Vikki Morrison. "I want to keep my life simple. I don't want to get in a situation where, in three years, I'll have to sell."

This encounter was their first face-to-face meeting. Vikki has a formula for such situations. From a previous telephone conversation, she had a rough idea of what Sheila wanted: a three-bedroom home with a formal dining room and assumable financing that would keep her monthly payments at or below $600 after a $50,000 down payment.

Before the meeting, Vikki had combined the multiple listing book for condominiums that matched Sheila's needs and compiled a list of addresses. If she had viewed the home before, she simply called the owners to warn them she would be dropping in. If she hadn't visited the home, Vikki put it on the list of homes to screen before Fisher's arrival.

By the time the two women met, Vikki had mapped out a tour of five homes, building up to a spacious condominium with a $144,000 price tag that the realtor thought was the best of the lot. But she didn't really expect to sell any of them that day.

"This is our getting-acquainted day," Vikki told Sheila as she turned into traffic on busy Golden West Avenue. "So be very blunt, very upfront. That's the only way I can learn your tastes. Okay?"

Sheila agreed. She had already decided that she liked Vikki Morrison, the fourth real estate agent whom she had consulted.

"I think she's listening to me," she confided in Vikki's absence. "I think she understands."

Demonstration Openings

Opening using demonstrations and dramatics are effective because of their ability to force the prospect into participating in the interview. Of the two methods discussed here, the product approach is more frequently used by itself or in combination with statements and questions.

In the **product approach,** the salesperson places the product on the counter or hands it to the customer, saying nothing. The salesperson waits for the prospect to begin the conversation. The product approach is useful if the product is new, unique, colorful, or if it is an existing product that has changed noticeably.

If, for example, Pepsi-Cola completely changed the shape of its bottle and label, the salesperson would simply hand the new product to the retail buyer and wait for a reaction. In marketing a new pocket calculator for college students, the Texas Instruments salesperson might simply lay the product on the buyer's desk and wait. It is possible to effectively combine the product approach with the showmanship approach.

The **showmanship approach** involves doing something unusual to catch the prospect's attention and interest; this should be done carefully so that the approach does not backfire, which can happen if the demonstration does not work or is so flamboyant that it is inappropriate for the situation.

- "Ms. Rosenburg, our paper plates are the strongest on the market, making them drip-free, a quality your customers will appreciate." [The salesperson places a paper plate on her lap and pours cooking grease or motor oil onto it while speaking to the prospect.]
- As she hands the buyer a plate from a new line of china, she lets it drop to the floor. It does not break. While picking it up, she says, "Our new breakthrough in treating quality china will revolutionize the industry. Your customers, especially newlyweds, will love this feature. Don't you think so?"

- The salesperson selling Super Glue would repeat the television advertisement for the prospect. In the prospect's office, the salesperson glues two objects together, such as a broken handle onto a coffee cup, waits one minute, hands the cup to the buyer for a test, and then begins the sales presentation. The mended cup can be left with the buyer as a gift and a reminder.

- The life insurance salesperson hands the prospect a bunch of daisies, saying, "Steve, when you're pushing daisies, what will your family be doing?" [This is probably too tactless to use on anyone except a close friend, but you get the picture.]

Opening with Questions

Questions are the most common openers because they allow the salesperson to better determine the prospect's needs and force the prospect to participate in the sales interview. The salesperson should use only questions that experience and preplanning have proven receive a positive reaction from the buyer, since a negative reaction is hard to overcome.

Like opening statements, opening questions can be synthesized to suit a number of selling situations. In the following sections, several basic questioning approaches are introduced. This listing is by no means exclusive, but introduces you to a smattering of questioning frameworks. With experience, a salesperson develops a knack for determining what question to ask what prospect.

Customer Benefit Approach

Using this approach, the salesperson asks a question that implies the product will benefit the prospect; if it is their initial meeting, the salesperson can include both his (her) and the company's name:

- Hi. I'm Charles Foster of ABC Shipping and Storage Company! Mr. McDaniel, would you be interested in a new storage and shipping container that will reduce your transfer costs by 10 to 20 percent?

- Would you be interested in saving 20 percent on the purchase of our IBM computers?

- Ms. Johnson, did you know that several thousand companies—like yours—have saved 10 to 20 percent of their manufacturing cost as described in the *Newsweek* article? [Continue, not waiting for a response.] They did it by installing our computerized assembly system! Is that of interest to you?

Your **customer benefit approach** statement should carefully be constructed to anticipate the buyer's response. However, always be prepared for the unexpected, as when the salesperson said, "This office machine will pay for itself in no time at all." "Fine," the buyer said; "As soon as it does, send it to us."

A customer benefit approach also is implemented through the use of a direct statement of product benefits. While the customer benefit approach begins with a question, it can be used with a statement showing how the product can benefit the prospect. The three customer benefit questions shown earlier can be converted into benefit statements:

- Mr. McDaniel, I want to talk with you about our new storage and shipping container, which will reduce your costs by 10 to 20 percent.

- I'm here to show you how to save 20 percent on the purchase of our IBM computers.

EXHIBIT 9–8

The curiosity approach

"Ms. Thompson, do you know why 300 banks use our customer information system?"

■ Ms. Johnson, several thousand companies—like yours—have saved 10 to 20 percent on their manufacturing cost by installing our computerized assembly system! I'd like 15 minutes of your time to show how we can reduce your manufacturing costs.

Benefit statements are useful in situations where you know the prospect's or customer's critical needs and have a short time to make your presentation. However, to assure a positive atmosphere, statements can be followed by a short question—"Is that of interest to you?"—to help ensure that the benefits are important to the buyer. Even if you know of the buyer's interest, a positive response—"Yes"—to your question is a commitment: the buyer will listen to your presentation because of the possible benefits offered by your product.

Furthermore, you can use the buyer's response to this question as a reference point throughout your presentation. A continuation of an earlier example illustrates the use of a reference point:

■ Mr. McDaniel, earlier you mentioned interest in reducing your shipping costs. The [now mention your product's feature] enables you to [now discuss your product's advantages]. And the benefit to you is reduced manufacturing costs.

Sometimes, salespeople have to prepare an approach that temporarily baffles a prospect. One common method of baffling entails the exploration of human curiosity.

Curiosity Approach

The salesperson asks a question or does something to make the prospect curious about the product or service. See Exhibit 9–8. For example, a salesperson for Richard D. Irwin, the company that publishes this text, might use the **curiosity approach** by saying:

■ Do you know why college professors such as yourself have made this [as she hands the book to the prospect] the best-selling book about how to sell on the market?

■ Do you know why a recent *Newsweek* article described our new computerized assembly system as revolutionary? [The salesperson briefly displays the *Newsweek* issue, then puts it away before the customer can request to look at the article. Interrupting a sales presentation by urging a prospect to review an article would lose the prospect's attention for the rest of the interview.]

One manufacturer's salesperson sent a fax to a customer saying, "Tomorrow is the big day for you and your company." When the salesperson arrived for the interview, the prospect could not wait to find out what the salesperson's message meant.

In calling on a male buyer who liked to smoke cigars, a saleswoman set a cigar box on the buyer's desk. After some chatting, the buyer said, "What's in the box?" The salesperson handed the box to the buyer and said, "Open it." Inside was a product she wanted to sell. After he bought, she gave him the cigars. Selling can be fun, especially if the salesperson enjoys being creative.

Opinion Approach

People are usually flattered when asked their opinion on a subject. Most prospects are happy to discuss their needs if asked correctly. Here are some examples:

■ I'm new at this business, so I wonder if you could help me? My company says our Model 100 copier is the best on the market for the money. What do you think?

■ Mr. Jackson, I've been trying to sell you for months on using our products. What is your honest opinion about our line of electric motors?

The **opinion approach** is especially good for the new salesperson because it shows that you value the buyer's opinion. Opinion questioning also shows that you will not challenge a potential buyer's expertise by spouting a memorized pitch.

Shock Approach

As its title implies, the **shock approach** uses a question designed to make the prospect think seriously about a subject related to the salesperson's product. For example:

■ Did you know that you have a 20 percent chance of having a heart attack this year? (Life insurance)

■ Did you know that home burglary, according to the FBI, has increased this year by 15 percent over last year? (Alarm system)

■ Shoplifting costs store owners millions of dollars each year! Did you know that there is a good chance you have a shoplifter in your store right now? (Store cameras and mirrors)

This type of question must be used carefully, as some prospects may feel you are merely trying to pressure them into a purchase by making alarming remarks.

Multiple Question Approach (SPIN)

In many selling situations, it is wise to use questions to determine the prospect's needs. A series of questions is an effective sales interview opener. Multiple questions force the prospect to immediately participate in the sales interview and quickly develop two-way communication. Carefully listening to the prospect's needs aids in determining what features, advantages, and benefits to use in the sales presentation. See Exhibit 9–9.

EXHIBIT 9-9

The SPIN approach first
determines needs.

In the SPIN approach, the sales rep uses a specific sequence of
questions to effectively open a sales interview.

A relatively new method of using multiple questions is the **multiple question approach (SPIN),** which involves using a series of four types of questions in a specific sequence.[1] SPIN stands for: (1) *S*ituation, (2) *P*roblem, (3) *I*mplication, and (4) *N*eed–payoff questions. Since SPIN requires questions asked in their proper sequence, its parts are carefully described in the following four steps.

Step 1

*S*ituation questions. Ask about the prospect's general situation as it relates to your product.

> *Industrial examples:* Dyno Electric Cart salesperson to purchasing agent: "How large are your manufacturing plant facilities?"
>
> IBM computer salesperson to purchasing agent: "How many secretaries do you have in your company?"
>
> *Consumer examples:* Real estate salesperson to prospect: "How many people do you have in your family?"
>
> Appliance salesperson selling a microwave oven to prospect: "Do you like to cook?" "Do you and your family eat out much?"

As the name of this question implies, the salesperson first asks a situation question that helps provide a general understanding of the buyer's needs. Situation questioning allows the salesperson to move smoothly into questions on specific problem areas. Also, beginning an approach using specific questions may make the prospect uncomfortable and unwilling to talk to you about problems, and may even deny them. There are warm-up questions enabling you to get a better understanding of the prospect's business.

Step 2

*P*roblem questions. Ask about specific problems, dissatisfactions, or difficulties perceived by the prospect relative to your situation question.

Industrial examples: Dyno Electric Cart salesperson to purchasing agent: "Have your executives ever complained about having to do so much walking in and around the plant?"

IBM computer salesperson to purchasing agent: "Do your Canon word processors do all that your secretaries want them to do?" (You may have previously asked the secretaries this question and know that they are dissatisfied.)

Consumer examples: Real estate salesperson to prospect: "Has your family grown so that you need more space?"

Appliance salesperson selling microwave oven to prospect: "Are you happy with your present oven?" "Are there times when you must quickly prepare meals?"

Problem questions are asked early in the presentation to bring out the needs or problems of the prospect. Your goal is to have the prospect admit, "Yes, I do have a problem."

To maximize your chance of making the sale, determine which of the prospect's needs or problems are important (explicit needs) and which are unimportant. The more explicit needs you can discover, the more vividly you can relate your products' benefits to areas the prospect is actually interested in, and thus, the higher your probability of making the sale.

An important or explicit need or problem is recognized as such by the prospect. There is a desire to fulfill the need or solve the problem. Problem questions are useful in developing explicit needs.

If the prospect should state a specific need after your situation or problem questions, do not move directly into your sales presentation. Continue with the next two steps to increase your chances of making the sale. A prospect may sometimes not appreciate all the ramifications of a problem.

Step 3

*I*mplication questions. Ask about the implications of the prospect's problems or how a problem affects various related operational aspects of a home, life, or business.

Industrial examples: Dyno Electric Cart salesperson to purchasing agent: "It sounds as if your executives would have an interest in reducing their travel time and not having to exert so much energy in transit. Doesn't it seem that if they could do so, they would get to the plant as quickly as they need to, saving themselves time and energy, and saving the company money?"

IBM computer salesperson to purchasing agent: "Does this problem mean your secretaries are not as efficient as they should be, thus increasing your costs per page typed?"

Consumer examples: Real estate salesperson to prospect: "So with the new baby and your needing a room as an office in your home, what problems does your present residence create for you?"

Appliance salesperson to prospect: "With both of you working, does your present kitchen oven mean . . . inconvenience for you? . . . that you have to eat out more than you want to? . . . that you have to eat junk foods instead of well-balanced meals?"

Implication questions seek to help the prospect realize the true dimensions of a problem. The phrasing of the question is important in getting the prospect to discuss problems or areas for improvement, and it fixes them in the prospect's mind. In this situation, the prospect is motivated to fulfill this need or solve this problem.

If possible, attach a bottom-line figure to the implication question. You want the prospect to state, or agree with you, that the implications of the problem are causing such things as: production slowdowns of 1 percent resulting in increased cost of 25 cents per unit; increased reproduction costs of 1 cent per copy; loss of customers; or hiring added personnel to make service calls costing an extra $500 per week.

Use this hard data later in your discussion of the business proposition. Using the prospect's data, you can show how your product can influence the prospect's costs, productivity, or customers.

S-P-I questions do not have to be asked in order, and you can ask more than one of each type. You will generally begin with a situation question and follow with a problem question. However, you could ask a situation question, a problem question, and another situation question, for example. The need–payoff question is always last.

Step 4

*N*eed–payoff questions. Ask if the prospect has an important, explicit need.

> *Industrial examples:* Dyno Electric Cart salesperson to purchasing agent: "If I could show you how you can solve your executives' problems in getting to and from your plant, and at the same time save your company money, would you have an interest?"
>
> IBM computer salesperson to purchasing agent: "Would you be interested in a method to improve your secretaries' efficiency at a lower cost than you now incur?"
>
> *Consumer examples:* Real estate salesperson to prospect: "If I could show you how to cover your space problems at the same cost per square foot, would you be interested?"
>
> Appliance salesperson to prospect: "Do you need a convenient way to prepare well-balanced, nutritious meals at home?"

Phrasing the need–payoff question is the same as opening with a benefit statement. However, in using the SPIN approach, the prospect defines the need. If the prospect responds positively to the need–payoff questions, you know this is an important (explicit) need. You may have to repeat the P-I-N questions to fully develop all of the prospect's important needs.

The Procter & Gamble and Tide sales presentation in Exhibit 8–6 is an example of using the P-I-N approach for a customer with whom you are familiar. Let's say your customer says yes to the need–payoff question: "If we could determine how much volume you're missing, I think you'd be willing to make space for the larger size, wouldn't you?" Then, you move directly into a brief sales presentation.

If the answer is no, this is not an important need. Start over again by asking *P*roblem, *I*mplication, and *N*eed–payoff questions to determine important needs.

Product Not Mentioned in SPIN Approach

As you see from SPIN examples, the product is not mentioned in the approach. This allows you to develop the prospect's need without revealing exactly what you are selling.

When a salesperson first walks into the buyer's office and says, "I want to talk about Product X," the chances of a negative response greatly increase because the buyer does not perceive a need for the product. SPIN questions allow you to better determine the buyer's needs before starting the presentation.

TECHNOLOGY IN THE APPROACH

How can a salesperson quickly capture a prospect's attention and interest? If technology could be incorporated into the approach, it can be a powerful attention-grabber!

Imagine a salesperson asking an organization's purchasing agent to follow her to the parking lot to "see something." She doesn't discuss the product until after the prospect has entered her mobile office, as discussed in Chapter 5.

A salesperson could hand the buyer a new pager or place a new laptop computer on his desk without saying anything. Or using a palm-top computer, a salesperson could open with a demonstration of her new presentation software and hardware.

Technology can be a wonderful way to creatively and professionally begin a sales presentation. Sounds, visuals, and touch cause the prospect's mind to instantly focus on the salesperson's words and action.

USING QUESTIONS RESULTS IN SALES SUCCESS

Since this chapter introduces questioning techniques, and since properly questioning a prospect or customer is important to sales success, you are ready for the many uses and types of questions.

Asking questions, sometimes called *probes,* is an excellent technique for (1) obtaining information from the prospect, (2) developing two-way communication, and (3) increasing prospect participation.

When using questions in selling, you need to know or anticipate the answer you want for a question. Once you know the answer wanted, you can develop the question. This procedure can be used to request information you do not have, and to confirm information you already know.

An ideal question is one a prospect is willing and able to answer. Only questions that help make the sale should be asked, so use questions sparingly and wisely.

Why would asking a question get the prospect's attention? To give an answer, a prospect must think about the topic. You can use four basic categories of questions at any point during the presentation. These categories are (1) direct, (2) nondirective, (3) rephrasing, and (4) redirect questions.

The Direct Question

The **direct question** or closed-ended question is answered with very few words. A simple yes or no answers most direct questions. They are especially useful in moving a customer toward a specific topic. Examples the salesperson might use are: "Mr. Berger, are you interested in saving 20 percent on your manufacturing costs?" or, "Reducing manufacturing costs are important, aren't they?" You can anticipate a yes response to these questions.

Never phrase the direct question as a direct negative–no question. A *direct negative–no question* is any question that can be answered in a manner that cuts you off completely. The retail salesperson says, "May I help you?" and the reply usually is, "No, I'm just looking." It's like hanging up the telephone on you. You are completely cut off.

Other types of direct questions ask "What kind?" or "How many?" The questions also ask for a limited, short answer from the prospect. The implication and need–payoff questions used in SPIN are examples of direct questions used for the approach.

However, the answer to a direct question does not really tell you much, because there is little feedback involved. You may need more information to determine the buyer's needs and problems, especially if you could not determine them before the sales call. Nondirective questioning aids you in the quest for information.

The Nondirective Question

To open up two-way communication, the salesperson can use an open-ended or **nondirective question** by beginning the question with one of six words: Who, what, where, when, how, and why. Examples include:

- Who will use this product?
- What features are you looking for in a product like this?
- Where will you use this product?
- When will you need the product?
- How often will you use the product?
- Why do you need or want to buy this type of product?

One-word questions such as Oh? or Really? also can be useful in some situations. One-word questions should be said so that the tone increases or is emphasized: Oh?! This prompts the customer to continue talking. Try it—it works.

To practice using the open-ended questioning technique, ask a friend a question—any question—beginning with one of these six words, or use a one-word question, and see what answer you get. Chances are, the response will consist of several sentences. In a selling situation, this type of response allows the salesperson to better determine the prospect's needs.

The purpose of using a nondirective question is to obtain unknown or additional information, to draw out clues to hidden or future needs and problems, and to leave the situation open for free discussion of what is on the customer's mind. Situation and implication questions are examples of the nondirective question.

The Rephrasing Question

The third type of question is called the **rephrasing question.** At times, the prospect's meaning is not clearly stated. In this situation, if appropriate, the salesperson might say:

- Are you saying that price is the most important thing you are interested in? [sincerely, not too aggressively]
- Then what you are saying is, if I can improve the delivery time, you would be interested in buying?

This form of restatement allows you to clarify meaning and determine the prospect's needs. If the prospect answers yes to the second question, you would find a way to improve delivery. If no is the answer to the delivery question, you know delivery time is not an important buying motive; continue to probe for the true problem.

The Redirect Question

The fourth type of question is the **redirect question.** This is used to redirect the prospect to selling points that both parties agree on. There are always areas of agreement between buyer and seller even if the prospect is opposed to purchasing the product. The redirect question is an excellent alternative or backup opener. This example clarifies the concept of redirective questioning:

MAKING THE SALE

Keep Quiet and Get the Order

Dennis DeMaria, a branch manager for Westvaco from Folcroft, Pennsylvania, says, "One of the biggest single weapons you as a salesperson can use in getting an order from a customer or prospect is keeping quiet and patiently waiting for the buyer to answer your questions. A general rule in the selling profession is that the person who asks the questions is the person who has control of the interview. The information obtained from asking questions is the necessary ammunition you use to find the buyer's likes, dislikes, hot buttons, and areas to avoid. This valuable information also informs the salesperson whether the customer is ready to buy or whether he or she could continue selling.

"Experience has shown that salespeople *do* ask questions but they forget the most important part of this sales principle: *After you ask a question, you must be patient, don't talk, and let the buyer answer.* It does not matter how long it takes for the buyer to respond; keep quiet and wait for the answer. Remember, the first person to speak after a question has been asked, loses."[2]

Imagine you walk into a prospect's office, introduce yourself, and get this response, "I'm sorry, but there is no use in talking. We are satisfied with our present suppliers. Thanks for coming by." Respond by replacing your planned opener with a redirecting question. You might say:

- We agree that having a supplier who can reduce your costs is important.
- You would agree that manufacturers must use the most cost efficient equipment to stay competitive these days, wouldn't you?
- Wouldn't you agree that you continually need to find new ways to increase your company's sales?

Using a redirect question moves the conversation from a negative position to a positive or neutral one while reestablishing communication between two people. The ability to redirect a seemingly terminated conversation through a well-placed question may impress the prospect simply by showing that you are not a run-of-the-mill order-taker, but a professional salesperson who sincerely believes in the beneficial qualities of your product.

Three Rules for Using Questions

The first rule is to use only questions that you can anticipate the answer to or that will not lead you into a situation from which you cannot escape. While questions are a powerful selling technique, they can easily backfire.

The second rule in using a question is to pause or wait after submitting a question to allow the prospect time to respond to it. Waiting for an answer to a well-planned question is sometimes an excruciating process—seconds may seem like minutes. A salesperson must allow the prospect time to consider the question, and hope for a response. Failing to allow a prospect enough time defeats the major purpose of questioning, which is to establish two-way communication between the prospect and the salesperson.

The third rule is to listen. Many salespeople are so intent on talking that they forget to listen to what the prospect says (or disregard nonverbal signals). Salespeople need to listen consciously to prospects so that they can ask intelligent, meaningful questions that aid both themselves and their prospects in determining what needs and problems exist and how to solve them. Prospects appreciate a good listener and view a willingness to listen as an indication that the salesperson is truly interested in their situation.

IS THE PROSPECT STILL NOT LISTENING?

What happens when, using your best opening approach, you realize that the prospect is not listening? What about prospects who open mail, who fold their arms while looking at the wall or seem to be looking beyond you into the hallway, who make telephone calls in your presence, or who may even doze off?

This is the time to use one of your alternative openers that tunes the prospect in to your message. The prospect must be forced to participate in the talk by using either the question or demonstration approach. By handing the person something, showing something, or asking a question, attention can be briefly recaptured, no matter how indifferent a prospect is to your presence.

If you can overcome such preoccupation or indifference in the early minutes of your interview by quickly capturing the prospect's attention and interest, the probability of your making a sale will greatly improve. This is why the approach is so important to the success of a sales call.

It is crucial to never become flustered or confused when a communication problem arises during your approach. As mentioned earlier, the salesperson who can deftly capture another person's imagination earns the right to a prospect's full attention and interest. Your prospect should not be handled as an adversary, for in that type of situation you seldom gain the sale.

BE FLEXIBLE IN YOUR APPROACH

Picture yourself as a salesperson getting ready for coming face-to-face with an important prospect, Ellen Myerson. You have planned exactly what you are to say in the sales presentation: but how can you be sure Myerson will listen to your sales presentation? You realize she is busy and may be indifferent to your being in the office; she probably is preoccupied with her own business-related situation and several of your competitors already may have seen her today.

You have planned to open your presentation with a statement on how successful your memory typewriter has been in helping secretaries save time and eliminate errors in their typing. When you enter the office, Myerson comments on how efficient her secretaries are and how they produce error-free work. From her remarks, you quickly determine that your planned statement approach is inappropriate. What do you do now?

You might begin by remarking how lucky she is to have such conscientious secretaries, and then proceed into the SPIN question approach, first asking questions to determine general problems that she may have, and second using further questions to uncover specific problem areas she might like to solve. Once you have determined specific problems, you could ascertain whether they are important enough for her to want to solve them in the near future. If so, you can make a statement that summarizes how your product's benefits will solve her critical needs, and test for a positive response. A positive response allows you to conditionally move into the sales presentation.

ETHICAL DILEMMA

Oh, How You'd Love to Know!

Selling has always been fun for you, maybe because of your success in selling high-priced products to the automotive industry. The only thing you do not like is the length of time it takes to sell someone. Your average sale takes an average of eight sales calls, 30 to 40 hours analyzing the prospect's operation, and submitting a bid in competition with six to eight other suppliers. Your average sale last year was $425,000.

During prolonged negotiation with a large customer, it becomes apparent that the purchasing agent wants to do business with you. For example, he has indicated in subtle ways that he wants to work with your firm and has offered to share bid prices from your competitors with you. If you accept the list of your competitors' bid prices, you will not have to spend so much time compiling the bid, plus you will be guaranteed business that will produce 20 percent more sales than expected. You also realize that this explicitly breaks the confidentiality of your competitors, and your business could suffer if word got out about your transaction.

What would you do?

SUMMARY OF MAJOR SELLING ISSUES

As the first step in your sales presentation, the approach is a critical factor. To assure your prospects' attention and interest during a memorized or formula mode of presentation, you may want to use a statement or demonstration approach. In more technically oriented situations where you and the prospects must agree on needs and problems, a questioning approach (SPIN, for instance) is in order. Generally, in developing your approach, imagine your prospects asking themselves, "Do I have time to listen to, talk with, or devote to this person? What's in it for me?"

Words alone will not assure that you are heard. The first impression that you make on a prospect can negate your otherwise positive and sincere opening. To assure a favorable impression in most selling situations, dress conservatively, be well groomed, and act as though you are truly glad to meet the prospect.

Your approach statement should be especially designed for each prospect. You can choose to open with a statement, question, or demonstration by using any one of the techniques. Several alternative approaches should be read in case you need to alter your plans for a specific situation.

Carefully phrased questions are useful at any point in a sales presentation. Questions should display a sincere interest in prospects and their situations. Skillfully handled questions employed in a sales approach can wrest a prospect's attention from distractions and center it on you and your presentations. Questions are generally used to determine prospect wants and needs, thereby increasing prospect participation in the sales presentation. Four basic types of questions discussed in this chapter are direct, nondirective, rephrasing, and redirect questions.

In using questions, ask the type of questions that you can anticipate the answer to. Also, remember to allow prospects time to completely answer the question. Listen carefully to their answers for a guide as to how well you are progressing toward selling to them. Should you determine that your prospect is not listening, do something to regain attention. Techniques such as offering something or asking questions can refocus the prospect's attention long enough for your return to the presentation.

<table>
<tr><td>

MEETING A SALES CHALLENGE

</td><td>

Questions are important tools for salespeople. They help uncover needs and problems, obtain valuable selling information, and qualify the prospect's interest and buying authority. So it pays to ask good ones.

Since you may need to first develop an analysis of the bank's operation, the need-satisfaction or problem-solving presentation methods would work well for this situation. Begin with questions that are direct, well aimed, and most importantly, force the prospect to talk about a specific problem. Questions that cannot be answered *yes* or *no* provide the most information. A multiple-question approach, such as SPIN, would be appropriate for this situation.

</td></tr>
</table>

KEY TERMS FOR SELLING

creative imagery 250	curiosity approach 258
introductory approach 254	opinion approach 259
complimentary approach 254	shock approach 259
referral approach 254	multiple question approach (SPIN) 260
premium approach 255	direct question 263
product approach 256	nondirective question 264
showmanship approach 256	rephrasing question 264
customer benefit approach 257	redirect question 264

SALES APPLICATION QUESTIONS

1. Explain the reasons for using questions when making a sales presentation. Discuss the rules for questioning that should be followed by the salesperson.
2. What are three general categories of the approach? Give an example of each.
3. What is SPIN? Give an example of a salesperson using SPIN.
4. In each of the following instances, determine if a direct, nondirective, rephrasing, or redirect question is being used. Also, discuss each of the four types of questions.
   a. "Now let's see if I have this right; you are looking for a high-quality product and price is no object?"
   b. "What type of clothes are you looking for?"
   c. "Are you interested in Model 101 or Model 921?"
   d. "Well, I can appreciate your beliefs, but you would agree that price is not the only thing to consider when buying a copier, wouldn't you?"
   e. "When would you like to have your new Xerox 9000 installed?"
   f. "Are you saying that *where* you go for vacation is more important than the cost of getting there?"
   g. "You would agree that saving time is important to a busy executive like yourself, wouldn't you?"
5. Which of the following approaches do you think is the best? Why?
   a. "Ms. Jones, in the past, you've made it a practice to reduce the facings on heavy-duty household detergents in the winter months because of slower movement."
   b. Mr. Brown, you'll recall that last time I was in, you expressed concern over the fact that your store labor was running higher than the industry average of 8 percent of sales."
   c. "Hi! I'm Jeanette Smith of Procter & Gamble, and I'd like to talk to you about Cheer. How's it selling?"

6. Assume you are a salesperson for NCR (National Cash Register Corporation) and you want to sell Mr. Johnson, the owner/manager of a large independent supermarket, your computerized customer checkout system. You have just met Mr. Johnson inside the front door of the supermarket, and after your initial introduction, the conversation continues:

> **Salesperson:** Mr. Johnson, your customers are really backed up at your cash registers, aren't they?
>
> **Buyer:** Yeah, it's a real problem.
>
> **Salesperson:** Do your checkers ever make mistakes when they are in a rush?
>
> **Buyer:** They sure do!
>
> **Salesperson:** Have you ever thought about shortening checkout time while reducing checker errors?
>
> **Buyer:** Yes, but those methods are too expensive!
>
> **Salesperson:** Does your supermarket generate over $1 million in sales each month?
>
> **Buyer:** Oh, yes—why?
>
> **Salesperson:** Would you be interested in discussing a method of decreasing customer checkout time 100 percent and greatly lessening the number of errors made by your checkers, if I can show you that the costs of solving your problems will be more than offset by your savings?

   a. Using the framework of the SPIN approach technique, determine whether each of the above questions asked by the salesperson is a *Situation*, *Problem*, *Implication*, or *Need–payoff* question.
   b. If Mr. Johnson says yes to your last question, what should you do next?
   c. If Mr. Johnson says no to your last question, what should you do next?

7. As a salesperson for Gatti's Electric Company, Cliff Defee is interested in selling John Bonham more of his portable electric generators. John is a construction supervisor for a firm specializing in constructing large buildings such as shopping centers, office buildings, and manufacturing plants. He currently uses three of Cliff's newest models. Cliff just learned that John will be building a new manufacturing plant. As Cliff examines the specifications for the new plant, he feels John will require several additional generators. Two types of approaches Cliff might make are depicted in the following situations:

Situation A:

> **Salesperson:** I see you got the Jonesville job.
>
> **Buyer:** Sure did.
>
> **Salesperson:** Are the specs OK?
>
> **Buyer:** Yes.
>
> **Salesperson:** Will you need more machines?
>
> **Buyer:** Yes, but not yours!

Situation B:

Salesperson: I understand you have three of our electric sets.

Buyer: Yes, I do.

Salesperson: I'm sure you'll need additional units on your next job.

Buyer: You're right, I will.

Salesperson: Well, I've gone over your plant specifications and put together products just like you need.

Buyer: What I don't *need* are any of your lousy generators.

Salesperson: Well, that's impossible. It's a brand new design.

Buyer: Sorry, I've got to go.

   a. Briefly describe both approaches in situations A and B. In both situations, Cliff is in a tough spot. What should he do now?

   b. What type of approach could Cliff have made that would have allowed him to uncover John's dissatisfaction? Would the approach you are suggesting also be appropriate if John was satisfied with the generators?

8. This is a cold call on the warehouse manager for Coats Western Wear, a retailer with four stores. You know most of the manager's work consists of deliveries from the warehouse to the four stores. Based on your experience, you suspect that the volume of shipments to the warehouse fluctuates; certain seasons of the year are extremely busy.

As a salesperson for Hercules Shelving, you want to sell the manager your heavy-duty gauge steel shelving for use in the warehouse. Since this is a relatively small sale, you decide to go in cold, relying only on your questioning ability to uncover potential problems and make the prospect aware of them.

You are now face-to-face with the warehouse manager. You have introduced yourself and after some small talk it is time to begin your approach. Which of the following questions would be best?

   a. "Have you had any recent storage problems?"

   b. "How do you take care of your extra storage needs during busy seasons such as Christmas?"

   c. "Can you tell me a little about your storage problems?"

SALES WORLD WIDE WEB EXERCISES

Can the World Wide Web Help Build Relationships?

The ultimate outcome of relationship selling is the building of a partnership between the seller and the buyer. More and more companies are using the Web to stay in touch with customers. Pick several organizations listed in the Sales World Wide Web Directory found at the end of the book to see what information they provide to people.

Look for documents, such as annual reports that describe their sales, profits, markets, and customers. Check to see if they are collecting information from you, such as having you complete a questionnaire. Then write a report to your boss discussing your findings. Include your suggestions on how an organization can use the Web to build long-term relationships with their customers and attract new customers.

FURTHER EXPLORING THE SALES WORLD

1. Television advertisements are constructed to capture the viewer's attention and interest to sell a product or service quickly. Examine at least five commercials and report on the method each one used to get your attention, stimulate your interest, and move you from this attention–interest phase into discussing the product. Determine whether the first few seconds of the commercial related to the product's features, advantages, or benefits, and if so, how? Using a tape recorder may help you.

2. Assume that you have a 30-minute job interview next week with a representative of a company you are really interested in. How would you prepare for the interview, and what could you do during the first few minutes of the interview to get the recruiter interested in hiring you? Can you see any differences between this interview situation and the environment of a salesperson making a sales call?

STUDENT APPLICATION LEARNING EXERCISES (SALES)

(Part 4 of 7)

To make **Sale 4** first select the method you will use for your presentation. See pages 226–241. Next, write down the name of the approach technique you will use for this presentation method. See pages 254–261.

Presentation method: ───────────────────────────────

Approach technique: ───────────────────────────────

Now write out what you will actually say in your approach, including what the buyer should say. Relate your approach to your **FABs** developed in **Sale 1** so you have a smooth transition into discussing your product.

Seller:

Buyer:

Imagine you have now finished the approach. Write out the buyer–seller dialogue for the first two **SELL Sequences.** Refer back to **Sale 1.** Create an imagery response by the buyer to each of your trial closes.

SELL 1
Seller:

Buyer:

SELL 2
Seller:

Buyer:

Role-play your approach and **SELL Sequences** with someone to see if you are satisfied. If available, use a tape recorder to listen to your speed, voice inflections, phrases and any unwanted mannerisms, such as frequently repeating "uh" or "I see."

CASE 9–1
The Thompson Company

Before making a cold call on the Thompson Company, you did some research on the account. Barbara Thompson is both president and chief purchasing officer. In this dual capacity, she often is so rushed that she is impatient with salespeople. She is known for her habit of quickly turning down the salesperson and shutting off the discussing by turning and walking away. In looking over Thompson's operation, you notice that the inefficient metal shelving she uses in her warehouse is starting to collapse. Warehouse employees have attempted to remedy the situation by building wooden shelves and reinforcing the weakened metal shelves with lumber. They also have begun stacking boxes on the floor requiring much more space.

You recognize the importance of getting off to a fast start with Thompson. You must capture her attention and interest quickly or she may not talk with you.

Question

Which of the following attention-getters would you choose:
1. Ms. Thompson, I'd like to show you how Hercules shelving can save you both time and money.
2. Ms. Thompson, can you spare a few minutes of your time to talk about new shelving for your warehouse?
3. Ms. Thompson, how would you like to double your storage space?

CASE 9–2
The Copy Corporation

Assume you are contacting the purchasing agent for office supplies of a large chain of retail department stores. After hearing that the company is opening 10 new stores, you determine that they will need a copier for each store. Three months earlier, you had sold this purchasing agent a lease agreement on two large machines. The buyer wanted to try your machines in the company's new stores. If they liked them, you would get the account. Unknown to you, one of the machines was broken, which cause the purchasing agent to be pressured by a store manager to replace it immediately. As you walk into the purchasing agent's office, you say:

Salesperson: I understand you are opening 10 new stores in the next six months.

Buyer: I don't know who told you, but you seem to know!

Salesperson: If you'll let me know when you want a copier at each store, I'll arrange for it to be there!

Buyer: Look, I don't want any more of your lousy copiers! When the leases expire, I want you here to pick them up, or I'll throw them out in the street! I've got a meeting now. I want to see you in three months.

Questions

1. Describe this situation, commenting on what the salesperson did correctly and incorrectly.

2. Develop another approach the salesperson could use to uncover the problems experienced by the purchasing agent.

Ann Saroyan is a salesperson for the Electronic Office Security Corporation. She sells industrial security systems that detect intruders and activate an alarm. When Ann first began selling, she used to make brief opening remarks to her prospects and then move quickly into her presentation. While this resulted in selling many of her security systems, she felt there must be a better method.

Ann began to analyze the reasons prospects would not buy. Her conclusion was that even after her presentation, prospects still did not believe they needed a security alarm system. She decided to develop a multiple-question approach that would allow her to determine the prospect's attitude toward a need for a security system. If the prospect does not initially feel a need for her product, she wants her approach to help convince the prospect of a need for a security system.

Ann developed and carefully rehearsed her new sales presentation. Her first sales call using her multiple-question approach was with a large accounting firm. She asked the receptionist who she should see and was referred to Joe Bell. After she waited 20 minutes, Bell asked her to come into his office. The conversation went like this:

1. **Salesperson:** This is a beautiful old building, Mr. Bell. Have you been here long?
   Buyer: About 10 years. Before we moved here, we were in one of those ugly glass and concrete towers. Now, you wanted to talk to me about office security.

2. **Salesperson:** Yes, Mr. Bell. Tell me, do you have a burglar alarm system at present?
   Buyer: No, we don't. We've never had a break-in here.

3. **Salesperson:** I see. Could you tell me what's the most valuable item in your building?
   Buyer: Probably the computer.

4. **Salesperson:** And is it fairly small?
   Buyer: Yes, amazingly, it's not much bigger than a typewriter.

5. **Salesperson:** Would it be difficult to run your business without it—if it were stolen for example?
   Buyer: Oh, yes, that would be quite awkward.

6. **Salesperson:** Could you tell me a bit more about the problem you would face without your computer?
   Buyer: It would be inconvenient in the short term for our accounts and records people, but I suppose we could manage until our insurance gave us a replacement.

7. **Salesperson:** But without a computer, wouldn't your billing to customers suffer?
   Buyer: Not if we got the replacement quickly.

8. **Salesperson:** You said the computer itself is insured. Do you happen to know if the software—the programs, your customer files— is also insured?
   Buyer: I don't believe so; our insurance covers the equipment only.

9. **Salesperson:** And do you keep backup records somewhere else—in the bank, for example?
Buyer: No, we don't.

10. **Salesperson:** Mr. Bell, in my experience, software isn't left behind after a theft. Wouldn't it be a serious problem to you if that software was taken?
Buyer: Yes, you're right, I suppose. Redevelopment would certainly cost a lot. The original programs were expensive.

11. **Salesperson:** And even worse, because software development can take a long time, wouldn't that hold up your billings to customers?
Buyer: We could always do that manually.

12. **Salesperson:** What effect would that have on your processing costs?
Buyer: I see your point. It would certainly be expensive to run a manual system as well as being inconvenient.

13. **Salesperson:** And if you lost your software, wouldn't it also make it harder to process customer orders?
Buyer: Yes. I don't have much contact with that part of the business, but without order processing and stock control I'm sure we would grind to a halt in a matter of days.

14. **Salesperson:** Are there any other items in the building that would be hard to replace if stolen?
Buyer: Some of the furnishings. I would hate to lose this antique clock, for example. In fact, most of our furnishings would be very hard to replace in the same style.

15. **Salesperson:** So, if you lost them, wouldn't it hurt the character of your office?
Buyer: Yes, it would be damaging. We've built a gracious, civilized image here, and without it we would be like dozens of other people in our business—the glass and concrete image.

16. **Salesperson:** This may sound like an odd question, but how many doors do you have at ground level?
Buyer: Let me see . . . uh . . . six.

17. **Salesperson:** And ground-level windows?
Buyer: About 10 or a dozen.

18. **Salesperson:** So there are 16 or 18 points where a thief could break in, compared with 1 or 2 points in the average glass and concrete office. Doesn't that concern you?
Buyer: Put that way, it does. I suppose we're not very secure.

Questions

1. Did the dialogue between buyer and seller seem natural to you?
2. Did the salesperson use too many questions in her approach?
3. Analyze each of the salesperson's questions and state whether it is a situation, problem, implication, or need–payoff type of question.

4. Analyze each of the buyer's responses to the salesperson's questions and state what type of need the salesperson's question uncovered. Was it an implied or minor need response or was it an explicit or important need response? Why?

5. How would you improve on this salesperson's approach?

6. After the buyer's last statement, which of the following would you do?

   a. Move into the presentation.

   b. Ask a problem question.

   c. Ask a need–payoff question.

   d. Ask for an appointment to fully discuss your system.

10

Elements of a Great Sales Presentation

MAIN TOPICS

The Purpose of the Presentation

Three Essential Steps within the Presentation

The Sales Presentation Mix

Visual Aids Help Tell the Story

Dramatization Improves Your Chances

Demonstrations Prove It

Technology Can Help!

The Ideal Presentation

Be Prepared for Presentation Difficulties

LEARNING OBJECTIVES

The fourth step in the sales process is the presentation. Here, you discuss with the buyer the product's features, advantages, and benefits, your marketing plan, and the business proposition. After studying this chapter, you should be able to:

- Discuss the purpose and essential steps of the sales presentation.

- Give examples of the six sales presentation mix elements.

- Describe difficulties that may arise during the sales presentation and explain how to handle them.

- State how to handle discussion of the competition.

- Explain the need to properly diagnose the prospect's personality to determine the design of the sales presentation.

You are a mill salesperson for Superior Carpets. You have been talking about several of your new carpet's features, advantages, and benefits to a retailer. You have just told your customer that because of Superior's new technology, the synthetic fibers in your new product will not fade even if exposed to direct sunlight. Your customer then says, "That sounds great, but I don't know. I've had too many customers complain about fading."

What do you do in this situation? As you see, the customer doubts whether your carpet will resist fading. How do you prove the carpet will not fade? What if the customer will not take your word?

The presentation part of the selling process is a persuasive vocal and visual explanation of a proposition. In developing your presentation, consider the elements you will use to provide the information a buyer needs to make a buying decision. At any time a customer may mention a concern, as in "Facing a Sales Challenge" above. A proper response is needed to make the sale.

This chapter discusses the elements of the presentation—the fourth step in the sales process (see Exhibit 10–1). We begin by examining the purpose and essential steps in the presentation. Next, we review and expand on the presentation techniques

EXHIBIT 10–1

The presentation is the heart of the sale. An effective approach allows a smooth transition into discussing your product's features, advantages, and benefits.

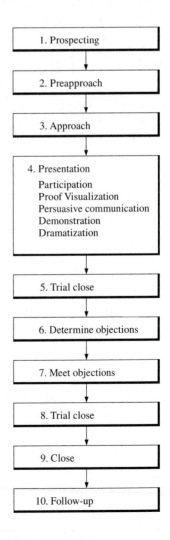

used by salespeople and how to handle the customer in the sales challenge. The chapter ends by discussing the importance of the proper use of trial closes and difficulties that may arise in the presentation along with the need to design your presentation around an individual situation and buyer.

THE PURPOSE OF THE PRESENTATION

The main goal of your presentation is to sell your product to your customer. However, we know that a prospective buyer considers many things before making a decision about what product to buy. As we have seen, the approach or first few minutes of the interview should be constructed to determine the prospect's need, capture attention and interest, and allow for a smooth transition into the presentation.

The presentation is a continuation of the approach. What is the purpose of the presentation? It provides *knowledge* via the features, advantages, and benefits of your product, marketing plan, and business proposal. This allows the buyer to develop positive personal *beliefs* toward your product. The beliefs result in *desire* (or *need*) for the type of product you sell. Your job, as a salesperson, is to convert that need into a want and into the *attitude* that your product is the best product to fulfill a certain need. Furthermore, you must convince the buyer that not only is your product the best but that you are the best source to buy from. When this occurs, your prospect has moved into the *conviction* stage of the mental buying process.

A real need is established, the buyer wants to fulfill that need, and there is a high probability that your product is best. This results in you making a sale, as shown in Exhibit 10–2. Whether to buy or not is a choice decision, and you have provided the necessary information so that the customer chooses to buy from you.

Assume, for example, that you are a salesperson for IBM and you wish to sell 10 of your new personal computers costing $5,000 each to a company. The prospect's company uses your competitor's products which cost $3,000 each. How should you conceptualize the prospect's thought processes regarding whether to buy or not buy from you (as shown in Exhibit 10–1) to develop your presentation?

Begin by realizing that the prospect has certain attitudes toward the present personal computers. The prospect's job performance is judged by her management of certain responsibilities. Thus, improving the performance of company employees is important. However, the prospect knows nothing about you, your product, or your product's benefits. The prospect may feel that IBM products are good, high-quality, expensive products. However, you cannot be sure about the buyer's present attitudes.

Develop a SPIN approach to determine the buyer's attitudes toward personal computers in general and your personal computer specifically. Once you have addressed

EXHIBIT 10–2

The five purposes of the presentation

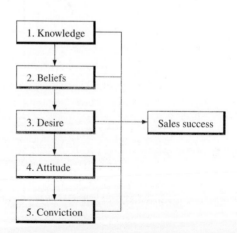

each of the four SPIN questions, and you feel more information about your product is needed, begin the presentation.

Present the product information that allows the buyer to develop a positive attitude toward your product. Next, possibly using a value-analysis proposal, show how your product can increase efficiency, reduce costs, and pay for itself in one year, using a return-on-investment (ROI) technique. A positive reaction from your prospect indicates that the desire stage of the mental buying process has been reached. There is a need for some brand of personal computer.

Now, show why your IBM personal computer is the best solution to the buyer's need and show that you will provide service after the sale. A positive response on these two items indicates that the prospect believes your product is best and that the conviction stage has been reached. The prospect wants to buy the IBM personal computer.

Up to this point, you have discussed your product's features, advantages, and benefits, your marketing plan, and your business proposition. You have *not* asked the prospect to buy. Rather, you have developed a presentation to lead the prospect through four of the five mental buying steps: the attention, interest, desire, and conviction steps. It may take you five minutes, two hours, or several weeks of repeat calls to move the prospect into the conviction stage.

You must move the prospect into the conviction stage before a sale is made. So hold off asking the prospect to buy until the conviction stage. Otherwise, this usually results in objections and failure to listen to your whole story and fewer sales. The sales presentation has seven major steps. Each step is taken in order to logically and sequentially move the prospect into the conviction stage of the buying process.

When a person buys something, did you ever stop to think about what is actually purchased? Is the customer really buying your product? No. What is actually bought is a mental picture of the future in which your product helps to fulfill some expectation. The buyer has mentally conceived certain needs. Your presentation must create mental images that move your prospect into the conviction stage.

THREE ESSENTIAL STEPS WITHIN THE PRESENTATION

No matter which of the four sales presentation methods used, your presentation must follow these three essential steps, also shown in Exhibit 10–3.*

Step 1:

Fully discuss the *features, advantages,* and *benefits* of your product. Tell the whole story.

Step 2:

Present your marketing plan. For wholesalers and retailers, this is your suggestion on how they should *resell* the product. For end users, it is your suggestion on how they can *use* the product.

Step 3:

Explain your business proposition. This step relates the *value* of your product to its *cost.* It should be discussed last, since you always want to present your product's benefits and marketing plan relative to your product's price.

* The three steps are discussed in Chapter 7 under "Customer Benefit Plan."

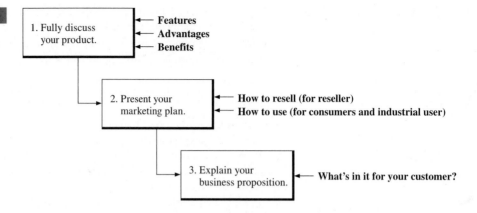

Three essential steps within the presentation

Remember Your FABs!

It is extremely important to emphasize benefits throughout the presentation. Using the SELL Sequence communication technique when discussing the product, marketing plan, and business proposition greatly improves your chances of making the sale.

Jeff Lucas of the Restaurant Supply Corporation—a $400 million distributor—preaches this to his salespeople. Exhibit 10–4 is a table used in his training program. This product is a pancake mix sold to hotels and food retail chains. Notice the FABs for each of the three essential steps within the presentation. "It is extremely important our salespeople emphasize benefits when talking with our customers," says Jeff. "Even for a product like pancake mix, salespeople must use benefits to paint a visual picture in the mind of the buyers on how this product will fulfill their needs. This is what consultative selling is all about—relating our product's benefits to their needs."

Ideally, information in each of these steps shown in Exhibit 10–3 should be presented to create a visual picture in the prospect's mind of the benefits of the purchase. To do this, use persuasive communication and participation techniques, proof statements, visual aids, dramatization, and demonstrations as you move through each of the three steps during the presentation.

THE SALES PRESENTATION MIX

Salespeople sell different products in different ways, but all salespeople use six classes of presentation elements to some degree in their presentations to provide meaningful information to the customer. These elements are called the *presentation mix.*

The **sales presentation mix** refers to the elements the salesperson assembles to sell to prospects and customers. While all elements should be part of the presentation, it is up to the individual to determine how much each element is emphasized. This determination is primarily based on the sales call objective, customer profile, and customer benefit plan. Let's examine each of the six elements, as shown in Exhibit 10–5.

Persuasive Communication

To be a successful salesperson, do you need to be a smooth talker? No, but you do need to consider and use factors that aid clear communication of your messages. In Chapter 4, we discussed seven factors that help you be a better communicator. They are:

1. Using questions.
2. Being empathic.

EXHIBIT 10–4

Salespeople use these FABs in their presentations

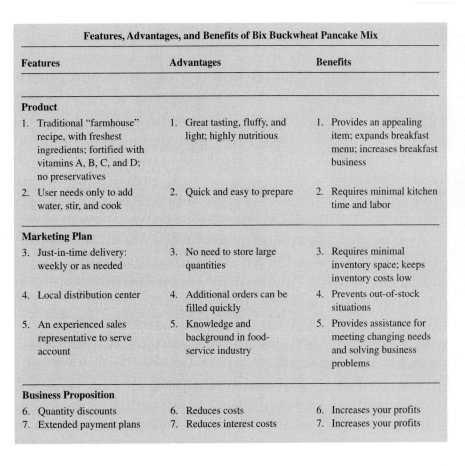

Features, Advantages, and Benefits of Bix Buckwheat Pancake Mix

Features	Advantages	Benefits
Product		
1. Traditional "farmhouse" recipe, with freshest ingredients; fortified with vitamins A, B, C, and D; no preservatives	1. Great tasting, fluffy, and light; highly nutritious	1. Provides an appealing item; expands breakfast menu; increases breakfast business
2. User needs only to add water, stir, and cook	2. Quick and easy to prepare	2. Requires minimal kitchen time and labor
Marketing Plan		
3. Just-in-time delivery: weekly or as needed	3. No need to store large quantities	3. Requires minimal inventory space; keeps inventory costs low
4. Local distribution center	4. Additional orders can be filled quickly	4. Prevents out-of-stock situations
5. An experienced sales representative to serve account	5. Knowledge and background in food-service industry	5. Provides assistance for meeting changing needs and solving business problems
Business Proposition		
6. Quantity discounts	6. Reduces costs	6. Increases your profits
7. Extended payment plans	7. Reduces interest costs	7. Increases your profits

EXHIBIT 10–5

The salesperson's presentation mix

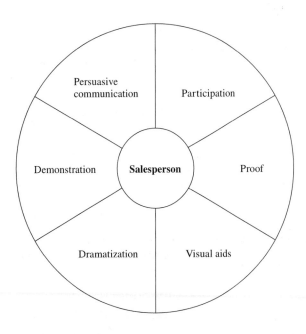

3. Keeping the message simple.
4. Creating mutual trust.
5. Listening.[1]
6. Having a positive attitude and enthusiasm.
7. Being believable.

The SELL Sequence and Trial Close

The use of a question to induce feedback is an excellent persuasive communication technique. As illustrated in Exhibit 10–1, the trial close should be used after making a strong selling point in the presentation, after the presentation itself, after answering an objection, and immediately before you move to close the sale.

When a question is coupled with discussing a product's feature, advantage, and benefit it forms the SELL Sequence. The SELL Sequence is a great method of determining if the FAB is of interest to the buyer. Thus, the SELL Sequence is an effective form of persuasive communication.

Additional persuasive factors to consider in the presentation are logical reasoning, persuasive suggestions, a sense of fun, personalized relationships, trust, body language, a controlled presentation, diplomacy, the Paul Harvey dialogue or conversation style, and using words as selling tools.

Logical Reasoning

The application of logic through reasoning is an effective persuasive technique that appeals to prospects' common sense by requiring them to think about the proposition and to compare alternative solutions to problems. It can have excellent results when applied to selling computers, heavy equipment, and communication systems. This is especially true when selling complicated proposals involving comparative cost data, when price versus benefits must be judged, and when the product is a radically new concept.

Logical reasoning involves a presentation constructed around three parts: a major premise, a minor premise, and a conclusion. Here is an example:

1. *Major premise:* All manufacturers wish to reduce costs and increase efficiency.
2. *Minor premise:* My equipment will reduce your costs and increase your efficiency.
3. *Conclusion:* Therefore, you should buy my equipment.

If presented exactly in this straightforward manner, the logical formula may be too blunt; the prospect may raise defenses. However, you can develop the framework or presentation outline to determine if the prospect is interested in reducing costs and increasing manufacturing efficiency. If so, then present a value analysis that shows the benefits of your product over alternatives. Information such as performance data, costs, service, and delivery information can be presented in a persuasive manner using various elements of the presentation mix.

Persuasion through Suggestion

Suggestion, like logical reasoning, is used effectively to persuade prospects. The skilled use of suggestions can arouse attention, interest, desire, conviction, and action. Types of suggestions that may be considered for the presentation are

1. **Suggestive propositions** imply that the prospect should act now, such as, "Shouldn't you go ahead and buy now before the price goes up next month?" Prospects often like to postpone their buying decisions, so the suggestive approach can help overcome this problem.

2. **Prestige suggestions** ask the prospect to visualize using products that famous people, companies, or persons the prospect trusts use, such as, "The National Professional Engineers Association has endorsed our equipment. That's the reason several hundred Fortune 500 manufacturers are using our products. This elite group of manufacturers finds the equipment helps increase their profits, sales, and market share. Is this of interest to you?"

3. **Autosuggestion** attempts to have prospects imagine themselves using the product. Television advertisements frequently use this form of suggestion. The sales person visualizes the product saying, "Just imagine how this equipment will look and operate in your store. Your employees will perform much better and they will thank you."

4. The **direct suggestion** is used widely by professional salespeople in all industries because it does not "tell" but suggests buying, which does not offend the buyer. Such a suggestion might state: "Based on our survey of your needs, I suggest you purchase . . ." or "Let's consider this: We ship you three train carloads of Whirlpool washers and dryers in the following colors and models . . ."

5. The **indirect suggestion** is used at times for some prospects when it is best to be indirect in suggesting a recommended course of action. Indirect suggestions help instill in prospects' minds factors such as doubt about a competitor's products or desire for your product, which makes it seem as if it is their idea: "Should you buy 50 or 75 dozen 12-oz. cans of Revlon hairspray for your promotion?" or "Have you talked with anyone who has used that product?"

6. The **counter suggestion** evokes an opposite response from the prospect: "Do you really want such a high-quality product?" Often, the buyer will begin expanding on why a high-quality product is needed. This is an especially effective technique to include in the presentation if you have already determined that the prospect wants a high-quality product.

Make the Presentation Fun

Selling is fun, not a battle between the prospect and salesperson, so loosen up and enjoy the presentation. This is easy to do once you believe in yourself and what you are selling—so sound like it! Have the *right mental attitude* and you will be successful.

Personalize Your Relationship

When I worked for a large national industrial manufacturer, my sales manager taught me to personalize the presentation. He would say, "Charles, you are enthusiastic; you believe in yourself, your products, your company; and you give a very good presentation. To improve, however, you need to personalize your relationship with each of your customers. In some manner, let them know during your presentation that you have their best interests at heart." He would always say, "Show 'em that you love 'em."

I came up with the short phrase, "You have me." Once I incorporated this into my presentation at the appropriate time, I saw a significant increase in my total sales and sales-to-customer call ratio by saying something like: "You are not only buying my products but me as well. You have me on call 24 hours a day to help you in any way I can."

Yes, it sounds corny, but it helped show customers that I cared for them and that they could believe in me. This helped build trust between us. You might choose a different way, yet be sure to demonstrate that you look out for their interests.

Build Trust

Two of the best and easiest ways to build your persuasive powers with prospects are *being honest* and *doing what you say you will do.* This builds trust, which increases sales. Most professional buyers have elephantlike memories that can be used to your advantage if you follow through after the sale as you said you would when presenting the proposal.

Honesty is always the best policy, and it is an effective way to build trust. The salesperson should never claim more than the product can accomplish. If the product does not live up to expectations, apologize, return the product for credit, or trade for another product. This action is important in obtaining repeat sales. It builds trust; the next time the prospect is reluctant to buy, you say, "Haven't I always taken care of you? Trust me, this product is what you need. I guarantee it!"[2]

Use Body Language

Just as you watch for buying signals from a prospect, the prospect watches your facial expressions and body movements. The salesperson's nonverbal communication must project a positive image to the prospect, one that shows you know what you are taking about and understand the buyer's needs. Your customer will think, "I can trust this person."

The best nonverbal selling technique is the smile. As a sales manager once said, "It's often not what you say but how you say it, and you can say almost anything to anyone if you do it with a smile. So, practice your facial expressions and smile—always smile."

Control the Presentation

In making the presentation, direct the conversation to lead the prospect through the presentation and proposal. The salesperson often faces how to maintain control and what to do if the prospect takes control of the conversation. For example, what do you do if the prospect likes to talk about hobbies, attacks your company or products for poor service or credit mix-ups, or is a kidder and likes to poke fun at your products?

When this happens, the salesperson should stay with a planned presentation if possible. If there is some complaint, this should be addressed first. If the prospect likes to talk about other things, do so briefly. When the prospect's attention and interest are hard to maintain, questions or some manner of eliciting participation in the presentation are the two best methods to rechannel the conversation.

Be sure to control the visual aids and any materials you use in the presentation. New salespeople often make the mistake of handing prospects their catalog, price list, or brochures showing several products. When buyers are looking through these items, chances are that they are not listening. Too much information can cause frustration and they will not buy. So, keep your product materials and discuss the information you wish to present while prospects look at and listen to you.

Be a Diplomat

All salespeople face the situation where the prospects feel they are right or know it all, and the salesperson has different opinions. For example, the salesperson previously may have sold the prospect's company a machine that always breaks down due to its operator, not the equipment, yet the salesperson's company is blamed. What to do?

The salesperson has to be a diplomat in cases where tempers rise and prospects are wrong but feel they are correct and will not change their opinions. Retreat may be the best option; otherwise, you risk destroying the relationship. If you challenge the prospect, you could win the battle only to lose the war. This is a decision that the salesperson must make based on individual situations.

Use the Paul Harvey Dialogue

Paul Harvey has the most listened-to radio news broadcast in America because of what he says and how he says it. Listen to his unique conversation style yourself. (His broadcast is syndicated; you may have to search to find it.) Then use the **Paul Harvey dialogue.** Construct your presentation to incorporate his excellent methods of speech, delivery, and particularly how he builds suspense into his stories. With these techniques, your talk comes alive rather than sounding like a dull, memorized presentation spoken in a monotone voice.

Simile, Metaphor, and Analogy

Words are selling tools. Similes, metaphors, analogies, pauses, silence, and changes in the rate of speaking, tone, and pitch are effective methods of gaining prospects' attention and capturing their interest in a proposal.

A **simile** is a direct comparison statement using the words *like* or *as:* A poorly manicured lawn is *like* a bad haircut. Our Sylvania Safeline bulbs are *like* a car's shatterproof windshield. Shaklee diet drinks are *like* a chocolate milkshake. The carton folds *as flat* as a pancake for storage.

A **metaphor** is an *implied* comparison that uses a contrasting word or phrase to evoke a vivid image: Our power mowers *sculpt* your lawn. Our cabin cruiser *plows* the waves smoothly. The computer's *memory* stores your data. The components *telescope* into a two-inch-thick disk.

The **analogy** compares two different situations that have something in common such as, "Our sun screen for your home will stop the sun's heat and glare before it hits your window. It's like having a shade tree in front of your window without blocking the view." Remember to talk the prospect's language by using familiar terminology and buzzwords in a conversational tone.

Participation Is Essential to Success

The second major part of the presentation involves techniques for motivating the prospect to participate in the presentation. Four ways to induce participation are

1. Questions.
2. Product use.

3. Visuals.

4. Demonstrations.

We have already discussed the use of questions and will discuss the use of visuals and demonstrations later, so let's briefly consider having prospects use the product:

- If you sell stereos, let them see, hear, and touch them!
- If you sell food, let them see, smell, and taste it!
- If you sell clothes, let them touch and wear them!

By letting prospects use the product, you can appeal to their senses: sight, sound, touch, smell, and taste. The presentation should be developed with appeals to the senses, since people often buy because of emotional needs and the senses are keys to developing emotional appeals.

Proof Statements Build Believability

Prospects often say to themselves, before I buy, you must *prove* it. "Prove it" is a thought everyone has at times. Salespeople must prove that they will do what they promise, such as helping to make product displays when the merchandise arrives. Usually, prove it means proving to a prospect during a presentation that the product's benefits and salesperson's proposal are legitimate.

Because salespeople often have a reputation for exaggeration, at times prospects are skeptical of the salesperson's claims. By incorporating **proof statements** into the presentation, the salesperson can increase the prospect's confidence and trust that product claims are accurate. Several useful proof techniques are the customer's past sales figures, the guarantee, testimonials, company proof results, and independent research results.

Past Sales Help Predict the Future

Customers' past sales proof statements are frequently used by salespersons when contacting present customers. Customers keep records of their past purchases from each of their suppliers; the salesperson can use these to suggest what quantities of each product to purchase. For example, the Colgate salesperson checks a customer's present inventory of all products carried, determines the number of products sold in a month, subtracts inventory from forecasted sales, and suggests the customer purchase that amount. It is difficult for buyers to refuse when presentations are based on their sales records. If they are offered a price discount and promotional allowances, they might purchase three to ten times the normal amount (a promotional purchase).

Assume, for example, that a food store normally carries 10 dozen of the king-size Colgate toothpaste in inventory with 3 dozen on the shelf, and sells approximately 20 dozen a month. The salesperson produces the buyer's past sales record and says, "You should buy 7 to 10 dozen king-size Colgate toothpaste." If offering promotional allowances, the salesperson might say:

> The Colgate king-size is your most profitable and best-selling item. You normally sell 20 dozen Colgate king-size each month with a 30 percent gross profit. With our 15 percent price reduction this month only, and our advertising allowances, I suggest, based on your normal sales, that you buy 80 to 100 dozen, reduce the price 15 percent, display it, and advertise the discount in your newspaper specials. This will attract people to your store, increase store sales, and make your normal profit.

The salesperson stops talking to see the buyer's reaction. A suggested order plus an alternative on the quantity to purchase have been proposed. Does the quantity seem high? It may be high, just right, or low, but it is the buyer's decision. The salesperson is saying that, given your past sales and with my customer benefit plan, I believe you can sell *X* amount.

Be realistic about your suggested increase in order size. Some salespeople double the size of the order expecting the prospect to cut it in half. Your honesty builds credibility with the buyer.

The Colgate salesperson might suggest purchases not only of toothpaste but of all Colgate products. That same sales call could involve multiple presentations of several products that have promotional allowances plus the recommended purchase of 10 or more items based on present inventories and the previous month's sales.

The Guarantee

The guarantee is a powerful proof technique. It assures prospects that if they are dissatisfied with their purchase, the salesperson or the company will stand behind a product. The manufacturer has certain product warranties that the retail salesperson can use in a presentation.

Furthermore, the consumer goods salesperson selling to retailers might say, "I'll guarantee this product will sell for you. If not, we can return what you do not sell." The industrial salesperson may explain the equipment's warranties, service policies, and state, "This is the best equipment for your situation that you can buy. If you are not 100-percent satisfied after you have used it for three months, I will return it for you."

Testimonials

Testimonials in the presentation as proof of the product's features, advantages, and benefits are an excellent method to build trust and confidence. Today, manufacturers effectively advertise their consumer products using testimonials. Professional buyers are impressed by testimonials from prominent people, experts, and satisfied customers about a product's features, advantages, and benefits.

Company Proof Results

Companies routinely furnish data concerning their products. Consumer goods salespeople can use sales data such as test market information and current sales data. Industrial salespeople use performance data and facts based on company research as proof of their product's performance.

A consumer goods manufacturer gave its salespeople test market sales information to use in their presentations on a new product being introduced nationally. Using this information, a salesperson might say:

> Our new product will sell as soon as you put it on your shelf. The product was a success in our Eastern test market. It had 9.8 percent market share only nine months after the start of advertising. Laboratory tests proved our formula superior to that of the leading competition in our consumer product tests. There was a high repurchase rate of 50 percent after sampling. This means increased sales and profits for you.

Independent Research Results

Proof furnished by reputable sources outside the company usually have more credibility than company-generated data. Pharmaceutical salespeople frequently tell physicians about medical research findings on their products published in leading medical journals by medical research authorities.

"On a typical day selling pharmaceuticals," says Sandra Snow of The Upjohn Company,

> I see as many physicians as possible and initiate a discussion with them about one of our products that will have importance to them in medicine. I attempt to point out advantages that our drugs have in various states by using third-party documentation published in current medical journals and texts. The information has much more meaning to a physician who knows that it is not me or The Upjohn Company that has shown our drug to have an advantage, but rather a group of researchers who have conducted a scientific study. All of the material that we give to the physicians has been approved for our use by the Food and Drug Administration.

Publications such as *Road Test Magazine, Consumer Reports,* newspaper stories, and government reports such as Environmental Protection Agency publications, may contain information the salesperson can use in the presentation. For a proof statement referring to independent research results to be most effective, it should contain (1) a restatement of the benefit before proving it, (2) the proof source and relevant facts or figures about the product, and (3) expansion of the benefit. Consider the following example of a salesperson's proof statement:

> I'm sure that you want a radio that's going to sell and be profitable for you (benefit restatement). Figures in *Consumer Guide* and *Consumer Sales* magazines indicate that the Sony XL-100 radios, although the newest on the market, are the third largest in sales (source and facts). Therefore, when you handle the Sony XL line, you'll find that radio sales and profits will increase, and more customers will come into your store (benefit expansion).

Proof statements must be incorporated into the presentation. They provide a logical answer to the buyer's challenge of "prove it!"

Exhibit 10–6 shows four examples of using proof to support what is said about FABs—features, advantages, benefits. Proof statements are a great way to help prove what you have said is true. Often, proof statements are presented through visual aids.

The Visual Presentation— Show and Tell

In giving a sales presentation, as a salesperson you do two things: You *show* and *tell* the prospect about a proposal. You *tell* using persuasive communications, participation techniques, and proof statements. You *show* by using visual aids.

People retain approximately 10 percent of what they hear but 50 percent of what they see. Consequently, you have five times the chance of making a lasting impression with an illustrated sales presentation rather than with words alone.

EXHIBIT 10–6

Proof statements help prove what you say.

Feature	Advantage	Benefit	Proof
New consumer product	Will be big seller	Excellent profits	Test-market results
High energy efficiency rating	Uses less electricity	Saves 10% on energy costs	*Consumer Reports* magazine
Electronic mail software	Gets information to sales force instantly	Reduces mailing and telephone costs	Testimonials
Buy 100 cases	Reduces out-of-stocks	Increases sales, profits, customer satisfaction	Customer's past sales or personal guarantee

Visuals are most effective when you believe in them and have woven them into your sales presentation message. Use them to:

- Increase retention.
- Reinforce the message.
- Reduce misunderstanding.
- Create a unique and lasting impression.
- Show the buyer that you are a professional.

The visual presentation (showing) incorporates the three remaining elements of the presentation mix: visual aids, dramatization, and demonstration. There is some overlap between the three; for example, a demonstration uses visuals and has some dramatics. Let's examine each of the elements to consider how they can be used in a sales presentation.

VISUAL AIDS HELP TELL THE STORY

Visuals, or visual aids, are devices that chiefly appeal to the prospect's vision with the intent of producing mental images of the product's features, advantages, and benefits. Many companies routinely supply salespeople with visuals for their products. Some common visuals are

- The product.
- Charts and graphics illustrating product features and advantages such as performance and sales data.
- Photographs and videos of the product and its uses.
- Models or mock-ups of products, especially for large, bulky products.
- Equipment such as videos, slides, audiocassettes, and computers.
- Sales manuals and product catalogs.
- Order forms.
- Letters of testimony.
- A copy of the guarantee.
- Flip-boards and posters.
- Sample advertisements.

Most visual aids are carried in the salesperson's bag. See Exhibit 10–7. The sales bag should be checked before each sales call to ensure that all visuals necessary for the presentation are organized in a manner that allows the salesperson to easily access needed visuals. Only new, top-quality, professionally developed visuals should be used. Tattered, torn, or smudged visuals should be routinely discarded. The best visual aid is showing the actual product.

DRAMATIZATION IMPROVES YOUR CHANCES

Dramatics refers to talking or presenting the product in a striking, showy, or extravagant manner. Thus, sales expertise can involve **dramatization** or a theatrical presentation of products. However, dramatics should be incorporated into the presentation only when you are 100 percent sure that the dramatics will work effectively. This was not considered by the salesperson who set the buyer's trash can on fire. When the salesperson had difficulty extinguishing the fire with a new fire extinguisher, the buyer ran out of the room because of the extensive smoke. However, if

EXHIBIT 10–7

Visual aids are an important part of this salesperson's presentation.

1. She reviews the call plan before seeing buyer.

2. Products and visual aids are placed in her sales bag.

3. Some visual aids are furnished by her company.

4. She uses personally developed sales aids customized to her buyer.

implemented correctly, dramatics are effective. One of the best methods of developing ideas for the dramatization of a product is to watch television commercials. Products are presented using visuals, many products are demonstrated, and most products are dramatized. Take, for example, the following television advertisements:

■ "We challenged the competition . . . and they ran!" says the Heinz tomato ketchup advertisement. Two national brands of ketchup and Heinz ketchup are poured into paper coffee filters held up by tea strainers. The competition's ketchup begins to drip and then runs through the filter. The Heinz ketchup does not drip or run, which indicates the high quality of Heinz ketchup relative to the competition.

■ Bounty paper towel advertisements show coffee spilled and how quickly the product absorbs the coffee relative to the competitive paper towel.

■ The STP motor-oil additive advertisement shows a person dipping one screwdriver into STP motor-oil additive and another screwdriver into a plain motor oil. The person can hold with two fingers the end of the screwdriver covered with plain motor oil. The screwdriver covered with STP motor-oil additive slips out of the fingers—indicating STP provides better lubrication for an automobile engine.

Use a dramatic demonstration to set yourself apart from the many salespeople that buyers see each day. Buyers, such as industrial purchasing agents, like to see you as they know you will have an informative and often entertaining sales presentation. One salesperson known for his effective presentation was George Wynn. George was an industrial salesperson for Exxon, and he was responsible for sales of machine lubricating oils and greases in Dayton, Cincinnati, and Columbus, Ohio.

One group of products sold by Wynn were oils and greases sold to the food-processing industry. These lubricants had to be approved by the federal Food and Drug Administration for incidental food contact. One of the products was a lubricating grease, Carum 280. Wynn ordered a number of one-pound cans for customer samples. As Wynn started his sales presentation of these FDA-approved products, he would take one of the cans from his sample case, open it, and spread this grease on a slice of bread. After taking a bite of bread spread with the grease, he then offered a bite to the buyer. The buyer generally refused the offer. However, in the mind of the buyer, this dramatic demonstration set Wynn's presentation apart from others. It helped prove to the buyer the product was safe to use in a food-processing plant.

Another of Wynn's dramatic demonstrations involved lubricating greases used by the steel industry. Greases that resist high temperatures are desirable for most applications in the steel industry. Exxon developed a line of temperature-resistant greases that used a new thickener that held the oil in suspension better than competitive products. To demonstrate this product attribute, Wynn used a pie tin held at a 45° angle centered over a small lighted alcohol lamp. A small glob of the Exxon grease and globs of several better-known competitors were placed on the pie tin. As the pie tin was heated, the oil separated from each of the competitive greases and ran down the pie tin. The oil did not separate from the Exxon product, dramatically demonstrating the high temperature resistance of this steel-mill grease compared to leading competitive products.

DEMONSTRATIONS PROVE IT

One of the best ways to convince a prospect that a product is needed is to show the merits of the product through a **demonstration,** as did George Wynn. If a picture is worth a thousand words, then a demonstration is worth a thousand pictures. Therefore, it is best to show the product, if possible, and have the prospect use it. If this is not feasible, then pictures, models, videotapes, films, or slides are the best alternatives. Whatever the salesperson is attempting to sell, the prospect should be able to see it.

Psychological studies have shown that people receive 87 percent of their information on the outside world through their eyes and only 13 percent through the other four senses. What this says to the salesperson is to make a product visible. Also let the prospect feel, see, hear, smell, and use the product. The dynamic demonstration appeals to human senses by telling, showing, and creating buyer–seller interaction. See Exhibit 10–8.

Demonstrations are part of the dramatization and fun of your presentation. Do not underestimate their ability to make sales for you, no matter how simple they may appear. For example, a glass company once designed a shatterproof glass. This was not standard equipment in automobiles then, as it is now. They had their salespeople going around the country trying to sell shatterproof glass. One of the salespeople completely outsold the rest of the sales force. When they had their convention, they said, "Joe, how come you sell so much glass?" He replied, "Well, what I've been doing is taking little chunks of glass and a ball peen hammer along with me on my sales calls.

Software demonstration

This systems analyst demonstrates the benefits of a software package to a group of buyers. A demonstration is worth a thousand pictures in helping to make a sale.

I take the little chunk of glass and I hit it with the hammer. This shows that it's shatterproof. It splinters, but doesn't shatter and fall all over the ground. This has helped me sell a lot of glass."

So, the next year they equipped every salesperson with a ball peen hammer and little chunks of glass. But an interesting thing happened. Joe still far outsold the rest of the sales force. So, when the convention occurred the next year, they asked, "Joe, how is it you're selling so much? You told us what you did last year. What are you doing differently?" He replied, "Well, this year, I gave the glass *and* the hammer to the customer to let *him* hit it." You see, the first year he had dramatization in his demonstration. The second year, Joe had dramatization and participation in his demonstration. Again, it's often not what you say but how you say it that makes the sale.

A Demonstration Checklist

There are seven points to remember as you prepare your demonstration. These points are shown in Exhibit 10–9. Ask yourself if the demonstration is really needed and appropriate for your prospects. Every sale does not need a demonstration nor will all products lend themselves to a demonstration.

If the demonstration is appropriate, what is its objective? What should the demonstration accomplish? Next, be sure you have properly planned and organized the demonstration; rehearse it so the demonstration flows smoothly and appears natural. Take your time in talking and going through your demonstration; make it look easy. Remember, if you, the expert, cannot operate a machine, for example, imagine how difficult it will be for the prospect.

The only way to ensure a smooth demonstration is to practice. Yet, there is always the possibility that the demonstration will not go as planned or will backfire no matter how simple. Be prepared. An example was a former student who was

EXHIBIT 10–9

Seven points to remember about demonstrations

☑ Is the demonstration *needed* and *appropriate?*
☑ Have I developed a specific demonstration *objective?*
☑ Have I properly *planned* and *organized* the demonstration?
☑ Have I rehearsed to the point that the demonstration *flows smoothly* and appears to be *natural?*
☑ What is the probability that the demonstration will go as *planned?*
☑ What is the probability that the demonstration will *backfire?*
☑ Does my demonstration present my product in an *ethical* and *professional* manner?

demonstrating his new Kodak slide projector. Two bulbs in a row burned out as he demonstrated the product to a buyer for a large discount chain. He anticipated what could go wrong and always carried extra parts in his sales bag. When the first bulb went out, he talked of how easy it was to change bulbs, and when the second one blew, he said, "I want to show you that again," with a smile. He always carried two spare bulbs, but now he carries three.

Finally, make sure your demonstration presents the product in an ethical and professional manner. You do not want to misrepresent the product or proposal. A complex product, such as a large computer system, can be presented as simple to install with few start-up problems, yet the buyer may find the computer system difficult to operate.

Use Participation in Your Demonstration

By having the prospect participate in the demonstration, you obtain a buyer's attention and direct it where you want it. It also helps the prospect visualize owning and operating the product. The successful demonstration aids in reducing buying uncertainties and resistance to purchase. The salesperson has the prospect do four things in a successful demonstration.

1. Let the prospect do something simple.
2. Let the prospect work an important feature.
3. Let the prospect do something routine or frequently repeated.
4. Have the prospect answer questions throughout the demonstration.

First, ask the prospect to do something simple with a low probability of foul-ups. Second, in planning the demonstration, select the main features that you will stress in the interview and allow the prospect to participate on the feature that relates most to an important buying motive. Again, keep it simple.

A third way to have a successful demonstration is by having the prospect do something with the product that is done frequently. Finally, receive feedback from the prospect throughout the demonstration by asking questions or pausing in your conversation. This is extremely important, as it will:

■ Determine the prospect's attitude toward the product.
■ Allow you to progress in the demonstration or wait and answer any questions or address any objections.
■ Aid in moving the prospect into the positive yes mood.
■ Set the stage for closing the sale.

Little agreements lead to the big agreement and saying yes. Phrase questions in a positive manner such as "That is really easy to operate, isn't it?" instead of, "This isn't hard to operate, is it?" They ask the same thing, yet the response to the first question is positive instead of negative. The best questions force the prospect to place the product in use mentally, such as the question phrased, Do you feel this feature could increase your employees' production? This yes answer commits the buyer to the idea that the feature will increase employee production. Remember, it is often not what you say but how you say it.

Reasons for Using Visual Aids, Dramatics, and Demonstrations

As we have seen, visual aids, dramatics, and demonstrations are important to the salesperson's success in selling a prospect. The reasons to use them include wanting to:

- Capture attention and interest.
- Create two-way communication.
- Involve the prospect through participation.
- Afford a more complete, clear explanation of products.
- Increase a salesperson's persuasive powers by obtaining positive commitments on a product's single feature, advantage, or benefit.

Guidelines for Using Visual Aids, Dramatics, and Demonstrations

While visual aids, dramatics, and demonstrations are important, their proper use is critical to be effective. When using them, consider:

- Rehearsing by practicing in front of a mirror, on a tape recorder, and/or videotape yourself selling to a friend. Once you are ready to make the presentation, begin using it with less important prospects. This allows you time to refine the presentation before contacting more important accounts.
- Customizing them to the sales call objective—the prospect's customer profile; the customer benefit plan—and concentrating on the prospect's important buying motives and using appropriate multiple appeals to sight, touch, hearing, smell, and taste. See Exhibit 10–10.
- Making them *simple, clear,* and *straightforward.*
- Being sure you control the demonstration by not letting the prospect divert you from selling. It can be disastrous to have the prospect not listen or pass up major selling points you wished to present.

Which buyer senses are being appealed to by the seller?

- Making them *true to life.*
- Encouraging *prospect participation.*
- Incorporating *trial closes* (questions) after showing or demonstrating a major feature, advantage, or benefit to determine if it is believed and important to the prospect.

TECHNOLOGY CAN HELP!

Technology can provide excellent methods of presenting information to the buyer in a visually attractive and dramatic manner. Using a computer in front of the buyer can be impressive. That's one of the reasons Bob Boyland, vice president of sales for Owens-Corning's insulation division, invested in 67 laptops with relatively expensive active-matrix color screens. Today, multimedia computers present video clips, play sound bites, show beautifully illustrated graphics, and can be connected to projection equipment for great presentations. Computer software can quickly crunch data—providing instant solutions to buyers' questions. Salespeople selling products such as service, real estate, and industrial equipment can quickly show buyers a product's cost when considering different installment payment schedules at various interest rates. Here are several examples of creating high-tech presentations.

- Xerox employs multimedia sales demonstrations with sophisticated graphics and animation to explain the features, advantages and benefits of its printers and fax machines. It's a lot easier and more economical to hand a prospective customer a disk than it is to wheel in a large piece of equipment for a demonstration.
- When GTE introduced GenStar, its new digital Airfone system, the company spent six months working on a multimedia sales presentation that would deliver a wealth of information in an entertaining format. The program, which runs on a laptop computer, combines an overview of digital communications for nontechnical buyers with demonstrations of a host of GenStar services, from in-flight e-mail and videoconferencing to on-line shopping. Sales reps can customize a presentation on the spot while gauging customer interest by skipping sections or pursuing particular topics in depth. If a prospect wants to know about on-line shopping, the salesperson can demonstrate a transaction. If the customer is more interested in airborne office services, the rep can go directly to e-mail or videoconferencing information.
- Dun & Bradstreet developed a well-conceived multimedia program that helps salespeople qualify leads by prompting prospective customers through a series of questions, with each consecutive question based on the person's previous response. Prospects work their way through the self-guided program and then fax or mail their responses, which allows sales reps to qualify prospects quickly and tailor their follow-ups to specific needs. Dun & Bradstreet used this type of interactive multimedia disk for direct marketing to Fortune 1000 companies. Prospects answered a series of questions and faxed their responses to Dun & Bradstreet salespeople, who followed up with a recommended information systems plan.[3]
- It can be difficult, for example, to illustrate a complex project without losing a customer's attention due to jargon and diagrams. But when sales reps from McDevitt Street Bovis, a North Carolina construction company, used a computer-based, 3-D interactive multimedia presentation to win a multimillion-dollar hospital renovation contract, it was as easily as graphically lifting the

roof off the hospital and taking the administrators on a step-by-step tour. "It helped us from a professional perspective, because it showed our client that we knew his job as well as or better than his competitors," Senior Vice President Jeff Thompson says.

Overhead transparencies, 35mm slides, and black-and-white handouts are being replaced by dynamic software packages, interactive multimedia programs, active-matrix color screens, and multimedia projectors that bring computer images to life. Remember, it's often not what you say but how you say it that makes the sale.[4]

THE IDEAL PRESENTATION

In the ideal presentation, your approach technique quickly captures your prospect's interest and immediately finds signals that the prospect has a need for your product and is ready to listen. The ideal prospect is friendly, polite, relaxed, will not allow anyone to interrupt you, asks questions, and participates in your demonstration as planned. This allows you to move through the presentation skillfully.

The ideal customer cheerfully and positively answers each of your questions, allowing you to anticipate the correct moment to ask for the order. You are completely relaxed and sure of yourself when you come to the close. The customer says yes, and enthusiastically thanks you for your valuable time. Several weeks later, you receive a copy of the letter your customer wrote to your company's president glowing with praise for your professionalism and sincere concern for the customer.

BE PREPARED FOR PRESENTATION DIFFICULTIES

Yes, a few sales presentations are like the previous example; most presentations have one or more hurdles you should prepare for. While all of the difficulties you might face cannot be discussed here, three main problems that are encountered during sales presentations are handling an interruption, discussing your competition, and making the presentation in a less-than-ideal situation.

How to Handle Interruptions

It is common for interruptions to occur during the presentation. The secretary comes into the office or the telephone rings, distracting the prospect. What should you do?

First, determine if the discussion that interrupted your presentation is personal or confidential. If so, by gesture or voice you can offer to leave the room—this is always appreciated by the prospect. Second, while waiting, regroup your thoughts and mentally review how to return to the presentation. Once the discussion is over, you can:

1. Wait quietly and patiently until you have regained the prospect's attention completely.
2. Briefly restate the selling points that had interested the prospect, for example: "We were discussing your needs for a product such as ours and you seemed especially interested in knowing about our service, delivery, and installation. Is that right?"
3. Do something to increase the prospect's participation, such as showing the product, using other visuals, or asking questions. Closely watch to determine if you have regained the prospect's interest.
4. If interest is regained, move deeper into the presentation.

SELLING GLOBALLY

Salespeople Are Making It Happen in China

Today thousands of American companies are competing to take advantage of the booming market in China. Avon is selling cosmetics door to door. Texaco opened gas stations. Xerox has captured 45 percent of the copier market. AST computers hum away in schools and factories while Keystone valves are finding their way into infrastructure projects. Boeing keeps its assembly lines at peak capacity through lucrative aircraft sales to China. Experts estimate that China will purchase 50 to 60 large aircraft per year for the next three years to meet the rapidly growing demand. Motorola built a plant in China that produces 10,000 pagers a week that retail for $200 with a one-year service contract. The market for pagers is estimated at 4 million a year.

AT&T has publicly stated its Chinese business may eclipse its U.S. business after the turn of the century. While most of the country's 400,000 entrepreneurs view cellular telephones as a necessity, 95 percent of the people in China look with envy at the communication toys used by their rich cousins.

The insurance giant AIG has hired 140 salespeople who are knocking on doors in Shanghai. According to *The Wall Street Journal,* in eight months they sold more than 12,000 policies.

A few years ago, Diebold Inc., an Ohio-based manufacturer of banking equipment, learned that China was in the process of upgrading 100,000 bank branches. The company sent a lone sales representative, Edgar Petersen, on a two-week trip to China. He visited a number of banks, found a need for safe-deposit boxes, and returned with orders for safe-deposit boxes equal to a year's worth of Diebold's manufacturing capacity. Today, Diebold has captured 60 percent of China's ATM market. Diebold's chairman, Robert W. Mahoney, estimates the Chinese market for ATMs will grow to 5,000 units per year within a short time. (That's about one-half the size of the U.S. market.)[5]

Should You Discuss the Competition?

Competition is something all salespeople must contend with every day. If you sell a product, you must compete with others selling comparable products. How should you handle competition? Basically, remember three considerations: (1) do not refer to a competitor unless absolutely necessary; (2) acknowledge your competitor only briefly; and (3) make a detailed comparison of your product and the competition's product.

Do Not Refer to Competition

First of all, lessen any surprises the buyer may present by properly planning for the sales call. In developing your customer profile, chances are that you will learn what competing products are used and your prospect's attitude toward your products and competitors' products. Based on your findings, the presentation can be developed without specifically referring to competition.

Acknowledge Competition and Drop It

Many salespeople feel their competition should not be discussed unless the prospect discusses it. Then, acknowledge competition briefly and return to your product. "Yes, I am familiar with that product's features. In fact, the last three of my customers were using that product and have switched over to ours. May I tell you why?"

Here, you do not knock competition, but acknowledge it and in a positive manner move the prospect's attention back to your products. If the prospect continues to discuss a competing product, you should determine the prospect's attitude toward it. You might ask, "What do you think about the IBM 6000 computer system?" The answer will help you mentally determine how you can prove that your product offers the prospect more benefits than your competitor's product.

Make a Detailed Comparison

At times, it is appropriate to make a detailed comparison of your product to a competing one, especially for industrial products. If products are similar, emphasize your company's service, guarantees, and what you do personally for customers.

If your product has features that are lacking in a competitor's product, refer to these advantages. "Our product is the only one on the market with this feature! Is this important to you?" Ask the question and wait for the response. A yes answer takes you one step closer to the sale.

Often the prospect can use both your product and a competitor's product. For example, a pharmaceutical salesperson is selling an antibiotic that functions like penicillin and kills bacteria resistant to penicillin. However, it costs 20 times more than penicillin. This salesperson would say, "Yes, Dr. Jones, penicillin is the drug of choice for . . . disease. But, do you have patients for whom penicillin is ineffective?" "Yes, I do," says the doctor. "Then, for those patients, I want you to consider my product because . . ."

Competition Discussion Based on the Situation. Whether or not you discuss competition depends on the prospect. Based on your selling philosophy and your knowledge of the prospect, you can choose how to deal with competition. If you are in doubt due to insufficient prospect knowledge, it is best not to discuss competition.

Be Professional

No matter how you discuss competition with your prospect, always act professionally. If you discuss competition, talk only about information that you know is accurate, and be straightforward and honest—not belittling and discourteous.

Your prospect may like both your products and the competitor's products. A loyalty to the competitor may have been built over the years; by knocking competition, you may insult and alienate your prospect. However, the advantages and disadvantages of a competitive product can be demonstrated acceptably if done professionally. One salesperson relates this story:

> Several customers I called on were loyal to my competitors; however, just as many were loyal to my company. I will always remember the president of a chain of retail stores who flew 500 miles to be at one of our salesperson's retirement dinners. In his talk, he noted how 30 years ago, when he opened his first store, this salesperson extended him company credit and made him a personal loan that helped him get started.

It would be difficult for a competing salesperson to sell to this loyal customer. When contacting customers, especially ones buying competitive products, it is important to uncover why they use competitive products before discussing competition in the presentation.

Where the Presentation Takes Place

The ideal presentation happens in a quiet room with only the salesperson, the prospect, and no interruptions. However, at times the salesperson may meet the prospect somewhere other than a private office and need to make the presentation under less than ideal conditions.

ETHICAL DILEMMA

Lying Like a Dog

You are in the competitive business of selling office machines. You have an appointment with the senior partner of a large medical center. She has already studied several competitive products. Her hot buttons are low operating costs and low maintenance. You know that four competitors have demonstrated their products to your prospect.

After you have shown her the benefits of your product, she asks you, "Tell me, what makes your machine better than Brand X?" You restate some of your obvious product benefits and she comes back with: "The salesperson with company X told me that they use a special kind of toner that is far superior to what you use for your machine and that it will increase the lifetime of their machine by 20 percent." You know that this is an obvious lie, so you ask, "What evidence did this salesperson give you to prove the claim?" She shows you a customer testimonial letter that talks about how satisfied they were with their machine, but it says nothing about a longer lifetime. You reply carefully, "That's the first time I have ever seen a letter praising a brand X machine."

Next, she shows you another piece of paper, a chart that graphically illustrates the operating costs of five different brands. The chart says on the bottom, "Marketing Research Brand X, 1995." It shows your machine with the highest operating costs over a five-year period, and it shows brand X in the leading position with 50 percent lower operating costs. You are stunned by this unfair competitive comparison. You try to control your temper.

What do you do?

For short presentations, a stand-up situation may be adequate; however, when making a longer presentation, you may want to ask the prospect, "Could we go back to your office?" or make another appointment.

Diagnose the Prospect to Determine Your Sales Presentation

You have seen that in contacting prospects you must prepare for various situations. That is why selling is so challenging and why companies reward their salespeople so well. A major challenge is adapting your sales presentation to each potential buyer. In Chapter 3, you read about selling based on personality. Reexamine that discussion to better understand how and why you should be prepared to adapt your presentation.

SUMMARY OF MAJOR SELLING ISSUES

The sales presentation is a persuasive vocal and visual explanation of a proposition. While there are numerous methods for making a sales presentation, the four common ones are the memorized, formula, need-satisfaction, and problem–solution selling methods. Each method is effective if used for the proper situation.

In developing your presentation, consider the elements of the sales presentation mix that you will use for each prospect. The proper use of persuasive communication techniques, methods to develop prospect participation, proof statements, visual aids, dramatization, and demonstrations increase your chance of illustrating how your products will satisfy your prospect's needs.

It is often not what we say but how we say it that results in the sale. Persuasive communication techniques (questioning, listening, logical reasoning, suggestion, and the use of trial closes) help to uncover needs, to communicate effectively, and to pull the prospect into the conversation.

Proof statements are especially useful in showing your prospect that what you say is true and that you can be trusted. When challenged, prove it by incorporating facts in your presentation on a customer's past sales—guaranteeing the product will work or sell, testimonials, and company and independent research results.

To both show and tell, visuals must be properly designed to illustrate features, advantages, and benefits of your products through graphics, dramatization, and demonstration. This allows you to capture the prospect's attention and interest; to create two-way communication and participation; to express your proposition in a clearer, more complete manner; and to make more sales. Careful attention to development and rehearsal of the presentation is needed to ensure it occurs smoothly and naturally.

Always prepare for the unexpected, such as a demonstration that falls apart, interruptions, the prospect's questions about the competition, or the necessity to make your presentation in a less than ideal place, such as the aisle of a retail store or in the warehouse.

The presentation part of the overall sales presentation is the heart of the sale. It is where you develop the desire, conviction, and action. By giving an effective presentation, you have fewer objections to your proposition, which makes for an easier sale close.

If you want to be a real professional in selling, acquire or create materials that convey your message and convince others to believe it. If you try to sell without using the components of the sales presentation mix, you are losing sales not because of what you say but how you say it. Exhibits, facts, statistics, examples, analogies, testimonials, and samples should be part of your repertoire. Without them, you are not equipped to do a professional job of selling.

MEETING A SALES CHALLENGE

The carpet's ability to resist fading is important to the customer who needs proof your carpet will not fade. In this situation, the proof statement should be authoritative, using independent research results, if possible. Here is an example of an effective proof statement:

"Mr. Jones, a carpet made of our new XT-15 synthetic fibers will not fade." (Restatement of the benefit.) "A recent study conducted by the Home Research Institute and reported in the *Home Digest* proves that our fibers hold their colors much better than natural fibers." (A proof of the benefit.) "And since Superior's carpets are made with synthetic fibers, you'll never hear any complaints about these carpets fading." (An expansion of the benefit.) "What do you think?" (Trial close.)

KEY TERMS FOR SELLING

sales presentation mix   280
logical reasoning   282
suggestive propositions   283
prestige suggestions   283
autosuggestion   283
direct suggestion   283
indirect suggestion   283
counter suggestion   283

Paul Harvey dialogue   285
simile   285
metaphor   285
analogy   285
proof statements   286
visuals   289
dramatization   289
demonstration   291

SALES APPLICATION QUESTIONS

1. You plan to give a demonstration of the Dyno Electric Cart to the purchasing agent of a company having a manufacturing plant that covers 200 acres. Which of the following is the best technique for your demonstration? Why?

    a. Let your prospect drive the cart.

    b. You drive the cart and ask the prospect to ride so that you can discuss the cart's benefits.

    c. Leave a demonstrator and return a week later to see how many the prospect will buy.

2. When contracting a purchasing agent for your Dyno Electric Carts, you plan to use your 10-page visual presenter to guide the prospect through your benefit story. This selling aid is a binder containing photographs of your cart in action along with its various color options, a guarantee, and a testimonial. Should you:

    a. Hand over the binder? Why?

    b. Hold on to it? Why?

3. Assume you were halfway through your presentation when your prospect had to answer the telephone. The call lasted five minutes. What would you do?

4. Discuss the various elements of the sales presentation mix and indicate why you need to use visuals during your presentation.

5. In your proof statement of the benefit, cite your proof source, in addition to relevant facts or figures about your product. Which of the following is a correct proof of a benefit?

    a. Well, an article in last month's *Appliance Report* stated that the Williams blender is more durable than the other top 10 brands.

    b. You'll get 10 percent more use from the Hanig razor.

    c. *Marathon* is the most widely read magazine among persons with incomes over $25,000 per year.

    d. Figures in *Marathon* magazine indicate that your sales will increase if you stock Majestic housewares in your store.

6. Examine the following conversation:

Customer: What you say is important, all right, but how do I know that these chairs will take wear and tear the way you say they will?

Salesperson: The durability of a chair is an important factor to consider. That's why all Crest chairs have reinforced plastic webbing seats. *Furniture Dealer's Weekly* states that the plastic webbing used in Crest chairs is 32 percent more effective in preventing sagging chair seats than fabric webbing. This means that your chairs will last longer and will take the wear and tear that your customers are concerned about.

Look at each sentence in this conversation and state if it is:

    a. An expansion of the benefit.

    b. A restatement of the benefit.

    c. A proof of the benefit.

7. After a two-hour drive to see an important new prospect, you stop at a local coffee shop for a bite to eat. As you look over your presentation charts, you spill coffee on half a dozen of them. You don't have substitute presentation charts with you. What should you do?

    a. Phone the prospect and say that you'd like to make another appointment. Say that something came up.

    b. Keep the appointment. At the start of your presentation, tell the prospect about the coffee spill and apologize for it.

c. Go ahead with your presentation, but don't make excuses. The coffee stains are barely noticeable if you're not on the lookout for them.

SALES WORLD WIDE WEB EXERCISES

High-Tech Presentations!

The sales presentation is a persuasive vocal and visual explanation of a proposition. It is often not what we say but how we say it that results in the sale. Search the following URLs to find information to help you create a presentation enhanced by the use of technology:

Sales and Marketing Management Magazine
www.salesandmarketing.com

Selling Power Magazine   Videoconferencing
www.sellingpower.com   www.cuseeme.com/pub/cu-sales.html

Use your search engines for sales or presentation technology.

It is often not what you say but how you say it that influences someone to buy from you. Salespeople are using more multimedia presentations to convey their message. See what you can find out about methods, equipment, and the effectiveness of using multimedia in a sales presentation.

FURTHER EXPLORING THE SALES WORLD

1. What is one thing in this world on which you are an expert? Yourself! Develop a presentation on yourself for a sales job with a company of your choice. Relate this assignment to each of the 10 steps of the selling process.

2. Visit several retail stores in your community such as an appliance, bicycle, or sporting goods store and report on the demonstration techniques, if any, that were used in selling a product. Suggest ways that you would have presented the product.

3. Report on one television advertisement that used each of the following: a proof statement, a demonstration, unusual visual aids, and a dramatization.

4. In your library are magazines where companies advertise their products to retail and wholesaler customers, along with information about current price discounts. Find at least three advertisements containing current price discounts offered by manufacturers to wholesalers and/or retailers. How might you use this information in a sales presentation?

STUDENT APPLICATION LEARNING EXERCISES (SALES) (Part 5 of 7)

An important part of consultative selling is the use of questions to uncover the customer's needs. You have planned some of your questions in constructing your **SELL Sequences. SELL Sequences** should be contained in your discussion of the product, marketing plan, and business proposition.

Every important sales presentation should contain most—if not all—of the presentation mix ingredients shown in Exhibit 10–5 on page 281. To make **Sale 5:**

1. Construct and write out one **SELL Sequence.** After your trial close, the buyer questions what you have just said. The buyer sounds as if unsure what you

are saying is true. Create a proof statement that shows your claim is true. See pages 286–288.

SELL Sequence:

Buyer's skeptical remark:

Proof statement:

2. Create one analogy, simile, and metaphor to use in your role-play. See page 285.

   Analogy:

   Simile:

   Metaphor:

3. Describe a demonstration you could do of one of your product's benefit. If possible, add dramatization. Remember, simply showing the product is not a demonstration.
4. Describe three visual aids you could use in your presentation. Flip charts and notebooks are easy to develop, or you can place your visuals in a folder and pull one at a time out as you discuss it.

   Visual 1:

   Visual 2:

   Visual 3:

CASE 10–1
Dyno Electric Cart Company

You plan a call-back on Conway Pride and the president of his company to sell them several of your electric carts. (See Exhibit 8–4 in Chapter 8.) The company's manufacturing plant covers some 200 acres and you have sold up to 10 carts to many companies smaller than this one. Since Pride allows you to meet with his company's president and maybe other executives, you know he is interested in your carts.

You are determined to make a spellbinding presentation of your product's benefits using visual aids and a cart demonstration. Mr. Pride raised several objections on your last presentation that may be restated by other executives. Your challenge is to develop a dramatic, convincing presentation.

Questions

1. You plan to give a cart demonstration to show how effective it is in traveling around the plant. Which of the following is the best technique for the demonstration?

   a. Get Pride and the president involved by letting them drive the cart.

   b. You drive, letting them ride so they will listen more carefully to you.

c. Leave a demonstrator and check back the next week to see how many they will buy.

2. You also plan to use a 10-page visual presenter to guide them through your benefit story. This selling aid is in a binder and contains photographs of your cart in action, along with its various color options, guarantee, and testimonials. Should you:

    a. Get Pride to participate by letting him hold it?

    b. Handle it yourself, allowing him to watch and listen while you turn the pages and tell your story?

CASE 10–2

Major Oil, Inc.*

Tim Christensen sells industrial lubricants to manufacturing plants. The lubricants are used for the plants' machinery. He is calling on Ben Campbell, a purchasing agent for Acme Manufacturing Company. Ben presently buys Tim's Hydraulic Oil 65 in drums. Tim's sales call objective is to persuade Ben to switch from purchasing his oil in drums to a bulk oil system. The secretary has just admitted him to Ben's office.

Salesperson: Hello, Ben.

Customer: Well, if it isn't Tim Christensen, my lube oil salesperson! How is everything over at Major Oil these days?

Salesperson: Fine! We're adding to our warehouse, so we won't be quite as crowded. Say, I know you like to fly. I was just reading in a magazine about the old Piper Tri-Pacer.

Customer: Yeah! I do enjoy flying and fooling with old airplanes. I just got back this weekend from a fly-in over at Houston.

Salesperson: You don't say! What type of planes did they have?

Customer: They had a bunch of homebuilts. You know, many pilots spend from 5 to 15 years just building their own planes.

Salesperson: Would you like to build your own plane someday?

Customer: Yes, I would. But you know, this job takes so much time—and with my schedule here and some travel, I don't know if I'll ever get time to start on a plane, much less finish one.

Salesperson: Well, I don't know that I can save you that much time, but I can save the people in the plant time and reduce your cost of Hydraulic Oil 65. Also, I may even save your office some time and expense by not having to place so many orders.

You know, we talked a couple of weeks ago about the possibility of Acme buying Hydraulic Oil 65 in bulk and thus reducing the cost per gallon by buying larger quantities each time you order. In addition, you will save tying your money up in the $20 drum deposit or even losing the deposit by losing or damaging the empty drum.

*Case developed by George Wynn, Professor of Marketing, James Madison University, © 1998.

Customer: Sounds like this is fixing to cost us some money.

Salesperson: Well, we might have to spend a little money to save a larger amount, plus make it easier and quicker in the plant. Do you know exactly what you are paying for Hydraulic Oil 65 now?

Customer: I think it's about $1.40 a gallon.

Salesperson: That's close. Your delivery cost is $1.39 per gallon, not counting drum deposit. You used approximately 20,000 gallons of Hydraulic Oil 65 last year at a total cost of $27,800.

Customer: Between what I pay at the gas station and what we pay here, I see why Major Oil is getting bigger and richer all the time. How much money *can* you save us?

Salesperson: Well, we try to get by and make ends meet. However, I can save your company more than $2,800 per year on oil costs alone.

Customer: That sounds awful big. How are you going to do that?

Salesperson: I am going to show you how you can purchase oil in bulk, save 14¢ per gallon on each gallon you buy (14¢ times 20,000 gallons equals $2,800), and eliminate handling those drums and having your money tied up in deposits. Last year, you purchased about 364 drums—and I'll bet you did not return all the drums to us.

Customer: I know we damaged some drums, and I imagine we furnished some trash barrels for our employees. I wonder how much of a total deposit we pay?

Salesperson: The total deposit on those drums was $7,280. Are you and your company totally satisfied with the performance of Hydraulic Oil 65?

Customer: It seems so. I have heard nothing to the contrary; and our bearing supplier, Timken, says that the oil is doing a first-class job. You know, this savings sounds good in theory; but will it really work? Besides, where will we put a big bulk system?

Salesperson: Ben, I've already thoroughly checked into what the total equipment and installation will cost. Here's a picture of the installation we made over at the Foundry and Machine Shop. We put the installation above ground to save the expense of digging holes for the tanks. The cover shown here in the picture protects the pump and motor from the weather, and the pipe into the shop goes underground. There's a control switch for the pump motor mounted inside the building next to the nozzle outlet. It looks good, doesn't it?

Customer: It certainly does, Tim, but what about the cost?

Salesperson: We can get two new 3,000-gallon tanks delivered here for a cost of $1,700 from our tank supplier. This is about $120 less than what you could buy them for. Our quantity purchases of tanks give us a little better price—and we'll be glad to pass these savings on to you. I have checked with Pump Supply Company, and they have in stock the pump and motor with flexible coupling and built-in pump relief valve, just what we need for handling this oil. The cost is $475. The control switch, pipe, pipe fittings, inside hose, and nozzle come to $120, and the person who does our installation work has given me a commitment to do all the installation work for $500, including furnishing the blocks to make the tank supports.

This totals $2,795, so let's round off to $2,800. And at a savings of 14¢ per gallon, based on your present usage of 20,000 gallons per year, this would be paid off in about 12 months, during which time you'd pay $1.25 per gallon for your oil rather than the $1.39 you now pay. How does that sound to you, Ben?

Customer: That sounds pretty good to me, Tim. Didn't you have an article about this in a recent issue of your company magazine?

Salesperson: We sure did. It was in the March issue. Here it is, right here. The situation was a little different, but the basic idea is the same. Our company has used this idea to considerable advantage; and over the past three years, I have set up six installations of this type. Do you have any questions regarding the plan I've outlined?

Customer: Just one thing—you know we're short on space behind the warehouse. Have you thought about where we might locate an installation of this type?

Salesperson: Yes, I have, Ben. Recall one of our earlier conversations where you told me about your plans to clean up that old scrap pile near the corner of the warehouse. That would be an ideal location. We could then locate the control switch, filling hose, and nozzle right on the inside at the end of the assembly line so the units could have their initial oil fill just before they come off the assembly line. How would that fit into your plans?

Customer: That's a good idea, Tim. That way we can get that junk pile cleaned up, replace it with a decent looking installation, and then make our initial oil fill the last step in our assembly procedure.

Salesperson: Do you have any other questions, Ben?

Customer: No, I believe I've got the whole picture now.

Salesperson: Good. Now, to sum up our thinking, Ben, the total cost of installation will be about $3,000. Immediately on completion of the installation, and when you receive your first transport truckload shipment of Hydraulic Oil 65, instead of being billed at $1.39 per gallon, as you are now paying for barrel deliveries, you will be billed $1.25 per gallon. I'll work with Bill Smith, the plant superintendent, and I'll handle all the outside contacts so that we can make the installation with little turmoil.

Customer: That sounds good to me. When can we start the installation?

Salesperson: Tomorrow. I'll bring a contract for you to have your people sign. It should take about three to four weeks after the contract is signed.

Customer: Good. What do I need to do right now?

Salesperson: If you'll arrange to clean the junk out of the corner, then we'll be ready. I'll order the equipment and have it moving so that we can be ready in about four weeks. What would be the best time to see you tomorrow?

Customer: Anytime will be OK with me, Tim.

Salesperson: Swell, Ben. Thanks for your help. I know you will be pleased with this new installation and also save money. See you tomorrow.

Questions

1. Evaluate Tim's sales presentation. Include in your answer comments on his approach, presentation, use of trial closes, handling of objections, and his close.
2. How would you develop visual materials to illustrate Tim's sales presentation, including the arithmetic?
3. Now that Tim has sold to Ben, what should Tim do next?

11

Welcome Your Prospect's Objections

LEARNING OBJECTIVES

When you learn how to skillfully handle your prospect's questions, resistance, and objections, you are a professional. After studying this chapter, you should be able to:

- Explain why you should welcome a prospect's objections.

- Describe what to do when objections arise.

- Discuss seven basic points to consider in meeting a prospect's objections.

- Explain six major categories of prospect objections and give an example of how to handle each of them.

- Present, illustrate, and use in your presentation several techniques for meeting prospect obligations.

- Describe what to do after meeting an objection.

As you drive up into the parking lot of a top distributor of your home building supplies, you recall how only two years ago they purchased the largest opening order you ever sold. Last year, their sales doubled and this year you hope to sell them over $100,000 worth.

As you wait, the receptionist informs you that since your last visit, your buyer, Mary Smalley, was fired and another buyer, Nonnie Young, was transferred to her place. Mary and you had become good friends over the past two years and you hated to see her go.

As you enter the new buyer's office, Young asks you to have a seat and then says: "I've got some bad news for you. I'm considering switching suppliers. Your prices are too high."

What would you do in this situation? What would you say to the buyer? Salespeople commonly face challenges; in most presentations, they experience objections. How does a professional salesperson handle a possible difficult situation?

This chapter examines objections. It discusses how to meet objections, techniques to use in overcoming objections, and how to proceed after addressing an objection. Professionals welcome objections!

WELCOME OBJECTIONS!

When a prospect first gives an objection, *smile,* because that's when you start earning your salary. You want to receive personal satisfaction from your job and at the same time increase your salary—right? Well, both occur when you accept objections as a challenge that, handled correctly, benefit both your prospect and you. The more effectively you meet customers' needs and solve their problems, the more successful you will be in sales. If you *fear* objections, you will *fumble* your response, which often causes *failure.*

Remember, while people want to buy, they do not want to be taken advantage of. Buyers who cannot see how your offering will fulfill their needs ask questions and raise objections. If you cannot effectively answer the questions or meet the objections, you will not make the sale. It is *your* fault, not the buyer's fault, that the sale was not made if you sincerely believe your offering fulfills a need but the prospect still will not buy. The salesperson who can overcome objections when they are raised and smoothly return to a presentation will succeed.

WHAT ARE OBJECTIONS?

Interestingly, prospects who present objections often are easily sold on your product. They are interested enough to object; they want to know what you have to offer.

Opposition or resistance to information or to the salesperson's request is labeled a **sales objection.** Sales objections must be welcomed because they show prospect interest and help determine what stage the prospect has reached in the buying cycle—attention, interest, desire, conviction, or readiness to close.

WHEN DO PROSPECTS OBJECT?

The prospect may object at any time during your sales call—from introduction to close. Imagine walking into a retail store, carrying a sales bag, and the buyer yells out, "Oh no, not another salesman. I don't even want to see you, let alone buy from you!" What do you say?

I said, "I understand. I'm not here to sell you anything, only to check your stock, help stock your shelves, and return any old or damaged merchandise for a refund." As I turned to walk away, the buyer said, "Come on back here; I want to talk to you."

If I had simply said OK, I would not have made that sale. I knew that I could benefit that customer, and my response and attitude showed it. The point is always be ready to handle a prospect's objections, whether at the approach, during the presentation, after a trial close, after you have already met a previous objection, or during the close of the sale.

OBJECTIONS AND THE SALES PROCESS

Objections can occur at any time. Many times, however, the prospect allows you to make a presentation, often asking questions along the way. Inexperienced salespeople traditionally finish their presentation and wait for the prospect's response.

Experienced, successful salespeople have learned to use the system shown in Exhibit 11–1. After the presentation, they use a trial close to determine the prospect's attitude toward the product and if it is time to close.

Remember, the *trial close* asks for the prospect's opinion, not a decision to buy. The trial close asks about what was said in the presentation. Since you may not know the prospect's opinion, it is too early to close. Typically, the trial close causes the prospect to ask questions and/or state objections. The salespeople should be prepared to respond in one of four ways:

1. If there is a positive response to the trial close immediately after the presentation, move to the close as shown on the right side of Exhibit 11–1, moving from Step 5 to Step 9.
2. If an objection is raised, understand or clarify it, respond to it, and ask another trial close to see if you have met the objection. If you have, then move to the close.
3. After meeting one objection, be prepared to determine if there are other objections. You may have to move from Step 8 back to Step 6.
4. If, after responding to the objection and asking a trial close, you have not overcome the objection, return to your presentation (Step 4) and further discuss the product relative to the objection.

Thus, there are several strategies that a salesperson needs to handle objections. It is important to adapt to the situation. A big help to successfully handling objections is to thoroughly understand several points.

BASIC POINTS TO CONSIDER IN MEETING OBJECTIONS

No matter what type of objections are raised by the prospect, there are certain basic points to consider in meeting objections. They are to:

- Plan for objections.
- Anticipate and forestall.
- Handle as they arise.
- Be positive.
- Listen—hear them out.
- Understand objections.
- Meet the objection.

EXHIBIT 11–1

When objections occur, quickly
determine what to do

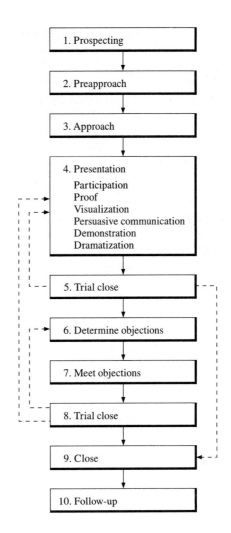

Each of these basic points for meeting objections can be planned for by the salesperson.

**Plan for
Objections**

Plan for objections that might be raised by your presentation. Consider not only the
reasons that prospects should buy but why they should *not* buy. Structure your presentation to minimize the disadvantages of your product. Do not discuss disadvantages unless prospects raise them in the conversation.

After each sales call, review the prospect's objections. Divide them into major and
minor objections. Then, develop ways to overcome them. Your planning for and rehearsal of overcoming objections allows you to respond in a natural and positive
manner. Planning for and review of the sales call allows you to anticipate and forestall objections.

**Anticipate and
Forestall**

Forestalling the objection has the salesperson discussing an objection before it is
raised by the prospect. It often is better to forestall or discuss objections before they
arise. The sales presentation can be developed to address anticipated objections
directly.

For example, take an exterior house paint manufacturer's salesperson who learns
that an unethical competitor is telling retail dealers that his paint starts to chip and

SELLING GLOBALLY

Watch out in Russia and China— They May Bug Your Room to Find out Your Secrets

Computerized banking services are, at long last, coming to Russia and China—thanks in no small part to Hurston Anderson at Arkansas Systems Inc. in Little Rock. Over the course of several months Anderson, vice president of sales and marketing, and his colleagues worked out deals to supply the Central Bank of Russia and the People's Bank of China with software that will help bring their banking systems into the 20th century. Arkansas Systems beat out a number of competitors, mostly foreign. In Russia and China, says Anderson, there's still "this idea that because it's American, it's the best."

Negotiating in these countries can be dicey, says Anderson. "They bug your hotel rooms, for one thing," he says. But then again, the stakes are huge. While the initial deals have been in six figures, the long-term payoff could reach into the tens of millions.

One new deal is for automated teller machine software and a check-clearing system in Siberia. In an earlier ATM deal in Moscow, recalls Anderson, "the guy from Central Bank pulled $130,000 out of a valise and wanted to pay us that way!"

The Chinese project includes check-clearing systems at 10,000 branch banks in three Chinese banking regions. Though the initial contract is for $500,000, Anderson notes that there are no fewer than 77 banking regions in China. "And 77 times $500,000 is what? About $40 million, I'd say. Boy, I hope they don't try delivering all that in a valise."[1]

peel after six months. Realizing the predicament, this salesperson develops a presentation that states, "Three independent testing laboratories have shown that this paint will not chip or peel for eight years after application." The salesperson has forestalled or answered the objection before it is raised by using a proof statement. This technique also can prevent a negative mood from entering the buyer–seller dialogue.

Another way to anticipate objections is to discuss disadvantages before the prospect does. Many products have flaws, and they sometimes surface as you try to make a sale. If you know of an objection that arises consistently, discuss it. If you acknowledge it first, you don't have to defend it.

On the other hand, a customer who has an objection feels compelled to defend that objection. For example, you might be showing real estate property. En route to the location you say, "You know, before we get out there, I just want to mention a couple of things. You're going to notice that it needs a little paint in a few places, and I noticed a couple of shingles on the roof the other day that you may have to replace." When you arrive, your customer may take a look and say, "Well, those shingles aren't so bad and we're going to paint it anyway." Yet, if you reached the house without a little prior warning of small defects, those items are often what a customer first notices.

A third way of using an anticipated objection is to brag about it and turn it into a sales benefit. A salesperson might say, "I want to mention something important before we go any further. Our price is a high one because our new computerized electronics provide technology found in no other equipment. It will improve your operation and eliminate the costly repairs you are now experiencing. In just a minute, I want to fully discuss your investment. Let's first discuss the improvements we can provide. Take a look at this."

This takes the sting out of the price objection because you have discussed it. It is difficult for a buyer to come back and say, "It's too high," because you have mentioned that already. So, there are times when you can anticipate objections and use them advantageously.

Handle Objections As They Arise

At times, situations arise where it is best to postpone your answer to an objection. When the objection raised will be covered later in your presentation, or when you build to that point, pass over it for a while. However, it is best to meet objections as they arise; postponement may cause a negative mental picture or reaction such as:

- The prospect may stop listening until you address the objection.
- The prospect may feel you are trying to hide something.
- You also feel it's a problem.
- You cannot answer because you do not know the answer or how to deal with this objection.
- It may appear that you are not interested in the prospect's opinion.

The objection could be the only item left before closing the sale. So, meet the objection, determine if you have satisfied the prospect, use another trial close to uncover other objections, and if there are no more objections, move toward closing the sale.

Be Positive

When responding to an objection, use positive body language such as a smile. Strive to respond in a manner that keeps your prospect friendly and in a positive mood. Do not take the objection personally. Never treat the objection with hostility. Take the objection in stride by responding respectfully and showing sincere interest in your prospect's opinion.

At times, the prospect may raise objections based on incorrect information. Politely deny false objections. Be realistic; all products have drawbacks, even yours. If a competitor's product has a feature your product lacks, demonstrate the overriding benefits of your product.

Listen—Hear Them Out

Many salespeople leap on an objection before the other person has a chance to finish. The prospect barely says five words—and already the salesperson is hammering away as though the evil thing will multiply unless it's stomped out. "I have to prove he is mistaken, or he won't take the product," is a panicky reaction to the first hint of any objection.

Not only does the prospect feel irritated at being interrupted, but the prospect also feels pushed and uneasy. Your prospect will ask, "Why's he jumping on that so fast and so hard? I smell a rat." Suppose you run south when the prospect hits north, and you answer the wrong objection or even raise one that the prospect hadn't thought of? Review the listening guidelines discussed in Chapter 4; they apply.[2]

Understand Objections

When customers object, they do one of several things, as shown in Exhibit 11–2. They are either requesting more information, setting a condition, or giving a genuine objection. The objection can be hopeless or true.

Request for Information

Many times, prospects appear to make objections when they are requesting more information. That is why it is important to listen. If prospects request more information, chances are that they are in the conviction stage. You have created a desire; they want the product, but they are not convinced that you have the best product or you

EXHIBIT 11–2

What does a prospect mean by
an objection?

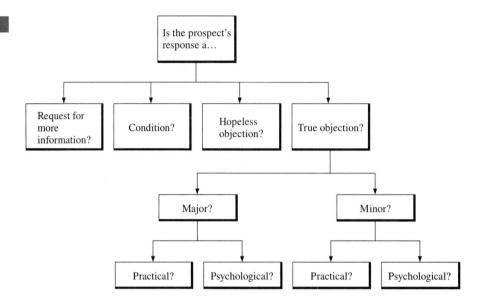

are the best supplier. If you feel this may be the case—supply the requested information indirectly.

A Condition

At times, prospects may raise an objection that turns into a **condition of the sale.**
They are saying, "If you can meet my request, I'll buy," or "Under certain conditions,
I will buy from you."

If you sense that the objection is a condition, quickly determine if you can help the
prospect meet it. If you cannot, close the interview politely. Take the following real
estate example:

> **Prospect:** It's a nice house, but the price is too high. I can't afford a $1,000 a
> month house payment. [You do not know if this is an objection or a condition.]

> **Salesperson:** I know what you mean [acknowledging the prospect's viewpoint].
> If you don't mind my asking, what is your monthly salary?

> **Prospect:** My take-home pay is $1,400 a month.

In this case, the prospect has set a condition on the purchase that cannot be met by
the salesperson realistically; it is not an objection. Continuing the exchange by bargaining would waste time and possibly anger the prospect. Now that the prospect's
income is known, the salesperson can show a house in the prospect's price range.

Negotiation Can Overcome a Condition. Often, conditions stated by the prospect
are overcome through negotiation between buyer and seller. **Negotiation** refers to
reaching an agreement mutually satisfactory to both buyer and seller. Prospects may
say things like, "I'll buy your equipment if you can deliver it in one month instead of
three," or "If you'll reduce your price by 10 percent, I'll buy."

If you determine that this type of statement is a condition rather than an objection,
through negotiation you may make the sale with further discussion and an eventual
compromise between you and the buyer. In the example above, you might ask the
manufacturing plant if equipment can be shipped to the prospect in two months

instead of three. This arrangement may be acceptable to the prospect. You may have a present customer who has that piece of equipment but is not using it. You might arrange for the prospect to lease it from your customer for three months.

If the prospect sets a price condition saying, "I will buy your computer only if you reduce your price by 10 percent," determine if your company will reduce the price if the buyer will purchase a larger quantity of computers. Consider this example. As a state agency, Texas A & M University purchases much of its office equipment on a bid system. The IBM salesperson could not sell the Texas A & M Marketing Department a computer because the cost of a single machine was too high for that department's budget. The department wanted the machine; however, they could not afford it. Instead of giving up, the salesperson went to other departments in the university and found a need for a total of 16 machines (at a price of $2,400 per computer, less than the price of one machine). IBM could lower the price substantially because of the large number of machines purchased. The salesperson determined that price was a condition, found a way to overcome the condition, and made the sale. Through initiation and inquiry, a potentially lost sale became a multiple victory beneficial to all parties.

There are two broad categories of objections. One of them is called *hopeless.* A hopeless objection is one that cannot be solved or answered. Examples of hopeless objections are I already have one, I'm bankrupt, and I'd like to buy your life insurance, but the doctor only gives me 30 days to live. So, hopeless objections cannot be overcome.

If your prospect does not buy, and no condition exists or the objection is not hopeless, it is your fault if you did not make the sale because you could not provide information to show how your offering would suit the buyer's needs.

The second category is the objection that can be answered. Called a true objection, it has two types: major and minor.

Major or Minor Objections

Once you determine that the prospect has raised a true objection, determine its importance. If it is of little or no importance, quickly address it and return to selling. Do not provide a long response or turn a minor objection into a major discussion item. The minor objection is often a defense mechanism of little importance to the prospect. Concentrate on objections directly related to the prospect's important buying motives.

Practical or Psychological Objection

Objections, minor or major, can be **practical** (overt) or **psychological** (hidden) in nature. Exhibit 11–3 gives some examples. A real objection is tangible, such as a high price. If this is a real objection, and the prospect says so, you can show that your product is of high quality and worth the price, or you might suggest removing some optional features and reducing the price. As long as the prospect states the real objection to purchasing the product clearly, you should be able to answer the objection.

However, prospects do not always clearly state their objections. Rather, they often give some excuse why they are not ready to make a purchase, which conceals real objections. Usually, the prospect cannot purchase the product until hidden objections are rectified. You must uncover a prospect's hidden objections and eliminate them.

EXHIBIT 11-3

EXHIBIT 11-3

Examples of objections

Practical	Psychological
■ Price	■ Resistance to spending money
■ Product is not needed	■ Resistance to domination
■ Prospect has an overstock of your or your competitor's products	■ Predetermined beliefs
■ Delivery schedules	■ Negative image of salespeople
	■ Dislikes making a buying decision

Meet the Objection

Once you fully understand the objection, you are ready to respond to the prospect. How to respond depends on the objection. During the year, a salesperson will hear hundreds of objections. Prospects object to various items in different ways.

Generally, objections fall into six categories. By grouping objections, you can better plan how to respond. Let's examine these six categories and discuss specific techniques for meeting objections.

SIX MAJOR CATEGORIES OF OBJECTIONS

Most objections that salespeople encounter are placed into the six categories shown in Exhibit 11–4. Know how you will handle each situation before it occurs. An advance idea about how you handle these objections will help you become a better salesperson by improving your image as a problem solver.

The Hidden Objection

Prospects who ask trivial, unimportant questions or conceal their feelings beneath a veil of silence have **hidden objections.** They do not discuss their true objections to a product because they may feel they are not your business, they are afraid objections will offend you, or they may not feel your sales call is worthy of full attention.

Such prospects may have a good conversation with you without revealing their true feelings. You have to ask questions and carefully listen to know the questions to ask that reveal their real objections to your product. Learning how to determine what questions to ask a prospect and how to ask them are skills developed by conscious effort over time. Your ability to ask probing questions improves with each sales call if you try to develop this ability.

Smoke Out Hidden Objections

With prospects who are unwilling to discuss their objections or who may not know why they are reluctant to buy, be prepared to smoke out objections by asking questions. Do what you can to reveal the objections. Consider the following questions:

- What would it take to convince you?
- What causes you to say that?
- Let's consider this, suppose my product would [do what prospect wants] . . . then you would want to consider it, wouldn't you?
- Tell me, what's really on your mind?

Uncovering hidden objections is not always easy. Observe the prospect's tone of voice, facial expressions, and physical movements. Pay close attention to what the prospect is saying. You may have to read between the lines occasionally to find the

Six major categories of
objections

1. Hidden objections	2. Stalling objections	3. No-need objections	4. Money objections	5. Product objections	6. Source objections

buyer's true objections. All of these factors will help you discover whether objections are real or simply an excuse to cover a hidden objection.

Prospects may now know consciously what their real objections are. Sometimes they claim that the price of a product is too high. In reality, they may be reluctant to spend money on anything. If you attempt to show that your price is competitive, the real objection remains unanswered and no sale results. Remember, you cannot convince anyone to buy until you understand what a prospect needs to be convinced of.

If, after answering all apparent questions, the prospect is still not sold, you might subtly attempt to uncover the hidden objection. You might ask the prospect what the real objection is. Direct inquiry should be used as a last resort because it indirectly may amount to calling the prospect a liar, but if it is used carefully, it may enable the salesperson to reveal the prospect's true objection. Smoking out hidden objections is an art form developed over time by skillful salespeople. Its successful use can greatly increase sales. This approach should be used carefully, but if it enables the salesperson to uncover a hidden objection, then it has served its purpose.

The Stalling Objection

When your prospect says, "I'll think it over," or "I'll be ready to buy on your next visit," you must determine if the statement is the truth or if it is a smoke screen designed to get rid of you. The **stalling objection** is a common tactic.

What you discovered in developing your customer profile and customer benefit plan can aid you in determining how to handle this type of objection. Suppose that before seeing a certain retail customer, you checked the supply of your merchandise in both the store's stockroom and on the retail shelf and this occurs:

Buyer: I have enough merchandise for now. Thanks for coming by.

Salesperson: Ms. Marcher, you have 50 cases in the warehouse and on display. You sell 50 cases each month, right?

You have forced her hand. This buyer either has to order more merchandise from you or tell you why she is allowing her product supply to dwindle. An easily handled stall is illustrated in Exhibit 11–5. When the prospect says, "I'm too busy to see you now," you might ask, "When would be a good time to come back today?"

One of the toughest stalls to overcome arises in selling a new consumer product. Retail buyers are reluctant to stock consumer goods that customers have not yet asked for, even new goods produced by large, established consumer product manufacturers. The following excerpt is from a sales call made by an experienced consumer goods salesperson on a reluctant retail buyer. This excerpt begins with an interruption made by the buyer during a presentation of a new brand of toothpaste:

Buyer: Well, it sounds good, but I have 7 brands and 21 different sizes of toothpaste now. There is no place to put it. [A false objection—smoke screen.]

Salesperson: Suppose you had 100 customers walk down the aisle and ask for Colgate 100 Toothpaste. Could you find room then?

Buyer: Well, maybe. But I'll wait until then. [The real objection.]

Salesperson: If this were a barbershop and you did not have your barber pole outside, people wouldn't come in because they wouldn't know it was a barbershop, would they?

Imagine walking up to your prospect, who says, "I'm too busy to see you now." What would you say?

Buyer: Probably not.

Salesperson: The same logic applies to Colgate 100. When people see it, they will buy it. You would agree that our other heavily advertised products sell for you, right? [Trial close.]

Buyer: Yeah, they do. [Positive response; now reenter your selling sequence.]

The salesperson eliminated the stall in this case through a logical analogy.

A third common stall is the alibi that your prospect must have approval from someone else, such as a boss, buying committee, purchasing agent, or home office. Since the buyer's attitude toward purchasing your product influences the firm's buying decision, it is important that you determine the buyer's attitude toward your product.

When the buyer stalls by saying, "I will have to get approval from my boss," you can counter by saying, "If you had the authority, you would go ahead with the purchase, wouldn't you?" If the answer is yes, chances are that the buyer will positively influence the firm's buying decision. If not, you must uncover the real objections. Otherwise, you will not make the sale.

An additional response to the "I've got to think it over" stall is, "What are some of the issues you have to think about?" Or you may focus directly on the prospect's stall by saying, "Would you share with me some things that hold you back?"

Another effective response to "I've got to talk to my boss" is, "Of course you do. What are some things that you would talk about?" This allows you to agree with the reluctant prospect. You are now on the buyer's side. It helps encourage the buyer to talk and to trust you. This empathic response ("Of course you do.") puts you in the other person's position.

Sometimes, the prospect will not answer the question. Instead, the response is, "Oh, I just need to get an opinion." You can follow up with a multiple-choice question such as, "Would you explore whether this is a good purchase in comparison with a competitor's product or would you wonder about the financing?" This helps display an attitude of genuine caring.

As with any response to an objection, communicate a positive attitude. Do not get demanding, defensive, or hostile. Otherwise, your nonverbal expressions may signal a defensive attitude—reinforcing the prospect's defenses.

Your goal in dealing with a stall is to help prospects realistically examine reasons for and against buying now. If you are absolutely sure it is not in their best interest to

---

SELLING TIPS

Stalling Objections

A. I have to think this over.

 1. Let's think about it now while it is fresh in your mind. What are some of the items you need to know more about?

 2. I understand that you want more time to think. I would be interested in hearing your thoughts about the reasons for and the reasons against buying now.

 3. You and I have been thinking this over since the time we first met. You know that this is a terrific opportunity, you like the product, and you know it will save you money. Right? [If prospect says yes:] Let's go ahead now!

B. I'm too busy.

 1. I appreciate how busy you are. When could we visit for just a few minutes? [Stop, or add a benefit for seeing you.]

C. I'm too busy. Talk to _____ first.

 1. Does he/she have the authority to approve the purchase? [If prospect says yes:] Thank you. I'll tell him/her you sent me. [If prospect says no:] Well, then, why should I talk with him/her?

 2. We almost never deal with purchasing managers. This is an executive-level decision. I need to talk with you.

D. I plan to wait until next fall.

 1. Why?

 2. Some of my best customers said that. Once they bought, they were sorry they waited.

 3. You promise me you will buy this fall? [If prospect says yes, then:]

    a. OK, let's finalize the order today and I'll have it ready to arrive October 1.

    b. Great! Should I call you in September or October so we can set it up?

 4. What if I could arrange for it to be shipped to you now, but you didn't have to pay for it until the fall?

---

buy now, tell them so. They will respect you for it. You will feel good about yourself. The next time you see these customers, they will be more trusting and open with you.

However, the main thing to remember is to not be satisfied with a false objection or a stall; see "Selling Tips, Stalling Objections." Tactfully pursue the issue until you have unearthed the buyer's true feelings about your product. If this does not work (1) present the benefits of using your product now; (2) if there is a special price deal, mention it; and (3) if there is a penalty for delay, mention it. Bring out any or all of your main selling benefits and keep on selling!

The No-Need Objection

The prospect says, "Sounds good. I really like what you had to say, and I know you have a good product, but I'm not interested now. Our present product [or supply or merchandise] works well. We will stay with it." Standing up to conclude the interview, the prospect says, "Thanks very much for coming by." This type of objection can disarm an unwary salesperson.

The **no-need objection** is used widely because it politely gets rid of the salesperson. Some salespeople actually encourage it by making a poor sales presentation. They allow prospects to sit and listen to a sales pitch without motivating them to participate by showing true concern and asking questions. Therefore, when the presentation is over, prospects can say quickly, "Sounds good, but . . ." In essence, they say no, making it difficult for the salesperson to continue the call. While not always a valid objection, the no-need response strongly implies the end of a sales call.

The no-need objection is especially tricky because it also may include a hidden objection and/or a stall. If your presentation was a solo performance or a monologue,

No-Need Objections

A. I'm not interested.

1. May I ask why?

2. You are not interested now or forever?

3. I wouldn't be interested if I were you, either. However, I know you'll be interested when you hear about . . . It is very exciting! [If prospect still says no:] What would be a better time to talk?

4. Some of my best customers first said that until they discovered . . . [state benefits].

5. You are not interested? Then who should I talk to who would be interested in . . . [state benefits].

B. The . . . we have is still good.

1. Good compared to what?

2. I understand how you feel. Many of my customers said that before they switched over. However, they saw that this product would . . . [discuss benefits of present product or service versus what you are selling].

3. That's exactly why you should buy—to get a good trade now.

4. What stops you from buying?

C. We are satisfied with what we have now.

1. Satisfied in what way?

2. What do you like most about what you have right now? [then compare to your product].

3. I know how you feel. Often we're satisfied with something because we have no chance [or don't have the time] to compare it with something better. I've studied what you are using and would like a few minutes to compare products and show you how to . . . [state benefits].

4. Many of our customers were happy with what they had before they saw our product. There are three reasons they switched . . . [state three product benefits].

your prospect might be indifferent to you and your product, having tuned out halfway through the second act. Aside from departing with a "Thanks for your time," you might resurrect your presentation by asking questions. See "Selling Tips, No-Need Objections" for ways to respond to the no-need objections.

The Money Objection

The **money objection** encompasses several forms of economic excuses: I have no money, I don't have that much money, It costs too much, or Your price is too high. These objections are simple for the buyer to say, especially in a recessionary economy.

Often, prospects want to know the product's price before the presentation, and they will not want you to explain how the product's benefits outweigh its costs. Price is a real consideration and must be discussed, but it is risky to discuss product price until it can be compared to product benefits. If you successfully postpone the price discussion, you must eventually return to it because your prospect seldom forgets it. Some prospects are so preoccupied with price that they give minimal attention to your presentation until the topic reemerges. Other prospects falsely present price as their main objection to your product, which conceals the true objection.

By observing nonverbal signals, asking questions, listening, and positively responding to the price question when it arises, you can easily handle price-oriented objections.

Many salespeople think that offering the lowest price gives them a greater chance of sales success. Generally, this is not the case. Once you realize this, you can become even more successful. You might even state that your product is not the least expensive one available because of its benefits and advantages, and the satisfaction

SELLING TIPS

Money Objections

A. Your price is too high.
   1. Compared to what?
   2. How much did you think it would cost?
   3. We can lower the price right now, but we need to decide what options to cut from our proposal. Is that what you really want to do?
   4. Our price is higher than the competition. However, we have the best value (now explain).
   5. How high is too high?
   6. If it were cheaper, would you want it?

B. I can't afford it.
   1. Why?
   2. If I could show you a way to afford this purchase, would you be interested?
   3. I sincerely believe that you cannot afford *not* to buy this. The benefits of . . . far outweigh the price. Right?
   4. You cannot afford to be without it! The cost of not having it is greater than the cost of having it. Think of all the business you can lose, the productivity you can lose, that lost income from not having the latest, best,

and most reliable technology. You'll love it! You'll wonder how you've gone without it! Let's discuss how you can afford it—OK?
   5. Do you mean you can't afford it now or forever?

C. Give me a 10 percent discount and I'll give you an order today.
   1. I always quote my best price.
   2. If you give me an order for 10, I can give you a 10 percent discount. Would you like to order 10?
   3. [Prospect's name], we build your product up to a certain quality and service standard—not down to a certain price. We could produce a lower-priced item, but our experience shows it isn't worth it. This is a proven product that gives 100 percent satisfaction—not 90 percent.

D. You've got to do better than that.
   1. Why?
   2. What do you mean by better?
   3. Do you mean a longer service warranty? A lower price? Extended delivery? Tell me exactly what you want.

---

it provides. Once you convey this concept to your buyer, price becomes a secondary factor that usually can be handled successfully.

Do not be afraid of price as an objection; be ready for it and welcome it. Quote the price and keep on selling. It is usually the inexperienced salesperson who blows this often minor objection into a major one. If the price objection becomes major, prospects can become excited and overreact to your price. The end result is losing the sale. If prospects overreact, slow down the conversation; let them talk it out and slowly present product benefits as related to cost.

See "Selling Tips, Money Objections" for ways to respond to the money objection. One way to view the money objection concerns the price/value formula.

The Price/Value Formula

The price objection is a bargaining tool for a savvy buyer who wants to ensure the best, absolutely lowest price. But, often there is more to it than shrewd bargaining.

If the buyer is merely testing to be sure the best possible price is on the table, it's a strong buying signal. But perhaps the prospect sincerely believes the price is too high.

Let's define why one buyer might already be convinced the product is a good deal—fair price—but is just testing to make sure it's the best price, while another buyer may sincerely believe the asking price is more than the goods are worth.

Remember that cost is what concerns the buyer, not just the price. Cost is arrived at in the buyer's mind by considering what is received compared to the money paid.

In other words, price divided by value equals cost:

$$\frac{Price}{Value} = Cost$$

In this price/value formula, the value is what the prospect sees the product doing for them and/or their company. *Value* is the total package of benefits you have built for the prospect. Value is the solution you provide to the buyer's problems.

The price will not change. The company sets that price at headquarters. The company has arrived at the price scientifically—computers were used—based on costs, competition, and other salient factors. It is a fair price, and it's not going to change. So, the only thing to change is the prospect's perception of the value. For example, assume the buyer viewed the cost as follows:

$$\frac{Price\ 100.}{Value\ 90.} = Cost\ 1.11$$

The price is too high. You have to solve the prospect's problem with the product by translating product benefits into what it will do for the buyer. You have to build up the value:

$$\frac{Price\ 100.}{Value\ 110.} = Cost\ .90$$

Now that is more like it. The cost went down because the value went up.

The price/value formula is not the answer to "Your price is too high." It is only a description of the buyer's thinking process and an explanation of why the so-called price objection is heard so often. It tells us what we must do to answer the price objection.

The salesperson is usually the one who identifies a statement or question from the prospect as an objection. Rarely does the prospect say, "This is my objection." So, you need to ask, "Why did the buyer say that?" If you ask that question, you can ask the prospect to say more about why he or she made that objection.

Remember, at one extreme, the buyer may be sold on the product and simply testing to see if there is an extra discount. At the other extreme, the buyer may not see any benefit in the product or service but only see the price. When this is the case, "it costs too much" is a legitimate objection to be overcome by translating features into advantages into benefits for the buyer. Use the SELL sequence technique.

The Product Objection

All salespeople encounter **product objections** that relate directly to the product. Everyone does not like the best-selling product on the market. At times, most buyers have fears over risks associated with buying a product—they are afraid that the product will not do what the salesperson says it will do, or that the product is not worth either the time and energy required to use it or the actual cost.

You also sell against competition. The prospect either already uses a competitive product, has used one, would like to use one, has heard of one, or knows people who have used one. Your reaction to a product must use a positive tone. The use of a guarantee, testimonial, independent research results, and demonstrations helps counter the product objection. See "Selling Tips, Handling Product Objections" for ways to respond to the product objection.

The Source Objection

The **source objection** is the last major category of objections typically faced by salespeople. Source objections relate loyalty to a present supplier or salesperson. Also, the prospect may not like you or your company.

SELLING TIPS

Handling Product Objections

A. Your competitor's product is better.

  1. You're kidding! [Act surprised.]

  2. Better in what way? [Have customer list features liked in the other product; then show how your product has the same or better features.]

  3. I'm interested in hearing your unbiased opinion of the two products.

  4. You've had a chance to look at their product. What did you see that impressed you?

  5. Are you referring to quality, service, features, or the product's value after five years of use?

B. The machine we have is still good.

  1. I understand how you feel. Many of my customers have said that before they switched over. However, they found that the reason a new model makes an old model obsolete is not that the old one is bad, but that the new one is so much more efficient and productive. Would you like to take a look at what these businesses found?

  2. That's exactly why you should trade now. Since your machine is still good, you still have a high trade-in value. When it breaks down, your trade-in value will go down, too. It's less expensive to trade in a workable machine than to wait for it to fail.

C. I'll buy a used one.

  1. When you buy a used product, you take a high risk. You buy something that someone else has used and prob-

ably abused. Do you want to pay for other people's mistakes?

  2. You may save a few dollars on your monthly payments, but you'll have to pay much more in extra service, more repairs, and downtime. Which price would you rather pay?

  3. Many of our customers thought about a used product before they decided to buy a new one. Let me show you why they decided that new equipment is the best buy. The cost comparisons will make it clear.

  4. I understand you want to save money. I like to save money. But, you have to draw the line somewhere. Buying a used product in this field is like shopping for a headache. Perhaps you should consider the smaller model for starters. At least you won't have any worries about its reliability!

D. I don't want to take risks.

  1. You feel it's too risky? We rarely hear that. What do you mean by risky?

  2. "Risky" compared to what?

  3. What could we do to make you feel more secure?

  4. [Prospect's name], it may be more risky for you not to buy. What is the price you may pay for low productivity in your plant?

Prospects often discuss their like for a present supplier or salesperson. They may tell you that they do not like your company. Seldom, however, will someone directly say, "I don't want to do business with you."

Usually, handling a source objection requires calling on the prospect routinely over a period. It takes time to break this resistance barrier. Get to know the prospect and the prospect's needs. Show your true interest. Do not try to get all of the business at once—go for a trial run, a small order. It is important to learn exactly what bothers the prospect. Some examples are shown in the "Selling Tips, The Source Objection." Choose one of these responses to handle the objection illustrated in Exhibit 11–6.

TECHNIQUES FOR MEETING OBJECTIONS   Having uncovered all objections, a salesperson must answer them to the prospect's satisfaction. Naturally, different situations require different techniques; several techniques shown in Exhibit 11–7 apply in most situations. You can:

SELLING TIPS

The Source Objection

A. I'm sorry; we won't buy from you.

1. Why?

2. You must have a reason for feeling that way. May I ask what it is?

3. Are you not going to buy from us now or forever?

4. What could we do to win your business in the future?

5. Is there anyone else in your company who might be interested in buying our cost-saving products? Who?

6. I respect the fact you aren't buying from us this one time. However, I suspect that as you hear more about our fantastic products in the news and from customers, you will buy something from us in the future. Do you mind if I stop by periodically to update you on our new products?

7. Would you like to work with someone else in our company?

8. Is there anything about me that prevents you from doing business with our company?

B. I want to work with a more established company. We've done business with . . . for five years. Why should I change?

1. I understand how safe you feel about a relationship that goes back five years. And yet, I saw your eyes light up when you looked at our products. I can see that you're giving serious consideration to diversity. Just out of curiosity, could we compare the pros and cons of the two choices? Let's take a piece of paper and list the reasons for and against buying from us. The first reason against us is that we haven't worked with you for the past five years. What are some reasons for giving us a chance to prove ourselves?

2. I can only say good things about my competitor and if I were you, I would go with him or her—unless, of course, you want a better product at a better price.

- Dodge.
- Pass up the objection.
- Rephrase an objection as a question.
- Postpone the objection.
- Boomerang the objection.
- Ask questions regarding the objection.
- Directly deny the objection.
- Indirectly deny the objection.
- Anticipate the objection.
- Compensate for the objection.
- Obtain a third-party answer to the objection.

The Dodge Neither Denies, Answers, nor Ignores   Central Michigan University students in Professor Dean Kortge's personal selling class created a new communication technique for handling a sales objection. Here's how. When the buyer said, "I think your price is a little high," Scott Dodge replied, "Before you decide to buy let me tell you about the value that goes with this product." It is called the **dodge** because the salesperson neither denies, answers, nor ignores the objection, but simply temporarily dodges the objection.

Notice how the phrase is structured in a positive manner: "Before you decide to buy . . ." This positive communication technique now allows the seller to effectively make a smooth transition into a proper response to the buyer. Done in a calm, natural manner it is a very professional technique.

EXHIBIT 11–6

Imagine that this customer says, "I like your car but I'm concerned about buying it from your dealership. I'm going to shop around." What would you say?

EXHIBIT 11–7

Techniques for meeting objections

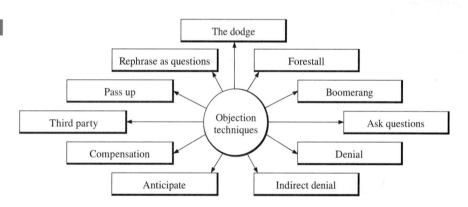

We discuss the *dodge* as the first objection handling technique because you could use it by itself or in combination with one of the other techniques, such as the pass up, rephrase, postpone, boomerang, or third-party. As you study the following objection handling techniques, see if you could first use the phrase, "Before you decide to buy . . ." You would use it only once in a presentation.

Don't Be Afraid to Pass up an Objection

Occasionally, you may have a prospect raise an objection or make a statement that requires not addressing it. After introducing yourself, for example, a prospect may say, "I'm really not interested in a service such as yours."

You have two options. First, you can say, "Well, if you ever do, here is my card. Give me a call." Or second, you could take the **pass up** approach used by top salespeople and say something that allows you to move into your presentation, such as immediately using the customer benefit approach or simply asking "Why?"

As you gain selling experience, you will be confident in knowing when to pass or to stop and respond to the objection. If you pass up an objection and the prospect raises it again, then treat this as an important objection. Use your questioning skills to uncover the prospect's concerns.

Rephrase an Objection As a Question

Since it is easier to answer a question than to overcome an objection, **rephrase** an objection **as a question** when you can do so naturally. Most objections are easily rephrased. Exhibit 11–8 presents examples of several procedures for rephrasing an objection as a question. Each procedure, except the objection based on a bad previous experience with the product by the prospect, has the same first three steps: (1) acknowledging the prospect's viewpoint, (2) rephrasing the objection into a question, and (3) obtaining agreement on the question. Here is an example:

Buyer: I don't know—your price is higher than your competitors'.

Salesperson: I can appreciate that. You want to know what particular benefits my product has that make it worth its slightly higher price. [Or, What you're saying is that you want to get the best product for your money.] Is that correct?

Buyer: Yes, that's right.

Now discuss product benefits versus price. After doing so, attempt a trial close by asking for the prospect's viewpoint to see if you have overcome the objection.

Salesperson: Do you see how the benefits of this product make it worth the price? [Trial close.]

A variation of this sequence is sales training consultant Bruce Scagel's Feel-Felt-Found method, where he first acknowledges the prospect's viewpoint, saying, "John, I understand how you *feel*. Bill at XYZ store *felt* the same way, but he *found*, after reviewing our total program of products and services, that he would profit by buying now."

Scagel refers to rephrasing the objection to a question as his Isolate and Gain Commitment method. He gives as an example: "Mary, as I understand it, your only objection to our program is the following. . . . If I can solve this problem, then I'll assume that you will be prepared to accept our program."

EXHIBIT 11–8

Examples of rephrasing objections as a question

Facts Are Incorrect	Facts Are Incomplete	Facts Are Correct	Based on Bad Personal Experience
■ Acknowledge viewpoint.	■ Acknowledge their viewpoint.	■ Acknowledge their viewpoint.	■ Thank the prospect for telling you.
■ Rephrase objection.	■ Rephrase the objection.	■ Rephrase the objection.	■ Acknowledge their viewpoint.
■ Obtain agreement.	■ Obtain an agreement.	■ Obtain an agreement.	■ Rephrase the objection.
■ Answer question providing information supported by proof— a third party.	■ Answer the question by providing the complete facts.	■ Answer the question, outweigh it with benefits.	■ Obtain an agreement.
■ Ask for their present viewpoint.	■ Ask for a present viewpoint.	■ Ask for a present viewpoint.	■ Answer the question.
■ Return to the selling sequence.	■ Return to the selling sequence.	■ Return to the selling sequence.	■ Return to the selling sequence.

Scagel knows that he can solve the problem or he would not have asked the question. When Mary says yes, he has isolated the main problem. He is not handling an objection; he is answering a question. He now shows her how to overcome the problem and then continues selling. If Mary says no, Bruce knows he has not isolated her main objection. He must start over in uncovering her objections. He might say, "Well, I guess I misunderstood. Exactly what is the question?" And now, when Mary responds, it usually will be a question. "Well, the question was about . . ." Involve the customer and find out what is happening internally. You can do this with the proper use of questions.

Postponing Objections Is Sometimes Necessary

Often, the prospect may skip ahead of you in the sales presentation by asking questions that you address later in the presentation. (See Exhibit 11–9.) If you judge that the objection will be handled to your prospect's satisfaction by your customary method, and that the prospect is willing to wait until later in the presentation, you politely **postpone the objection.** Five examples of postponing objections are

Prospect: Your price is too high.

Salesperson: In just a minute, I'll show you why this product is reasonably priced, based on the savings you will receive compared to what you presently do. That's what you're interested in, savings, right? [Trial close.]

or

Salesperson: Well, it may sound like a lot of money. But let's consider the final price when we know the model you need. OK? [Trial close.]

or

Salesperson: There are several ways we can handle your costs. If it's all right, let's discuss them in just a minute. [Pause. This has the same effect as the trial close. If there is no response, continue.] First, I want to show you . . .

or

Salesperson: I'm glad you brought that up [or, I was hoping you would want to know that.] because we want to carefully examine the cost in just a minute. OK? [Trial close.]

or

EXHIBIT 11-9

Suppose you show your prospect computer software, and the prospect says, "How much does this software cost?" What would you say?

Salesperson: High? Why, in a minute I'll show you why it's the best buy on the market. In fact, I'll bet you a Coke that you will believe it's a great deal for your company! Is it a deal? [Trial close.]

Tactfully used, postponing can leave you in control of the presentation. Normally, respond to the objection immediately. However, occasionally it is not appropriate to address the objection. This is usually true for the price objection. Price is the primary objection to postpone if you have not had the opportunity to discuss product benefits. If you have discussed the product fully, then respond to the price objection immediately.

Send It Back with the Boomerang Method

Always be ready to turn an objection into a reason to buy. By convincing the prospect that an objection is a benefit, you have turned the buyer immediately in favor of your product. This is the heart of the **boomerang method.** Take, for example, the wholesale drug salesperson working for a firm like McKesson and Robbins, who is selling a pharmacist a new container for prescription medicines. Handling the container, the prospect says:

Prospect: They look nice, but I don't like them as well as my others. The tops seem hard to remove.

Salesperson: Yes, they are hard to remove. We designed them so that children couldn't get into the medicine. Isn't that a great safety measure? [Trial close.]

Or, consider the industrial equipment salesperson who is unaware that a customer is extremely dissatisfied with a present product:

Prospect: I have been using your portable generators and do not want to use them anymore.

Salesperson: Why?

Prospect: Well, the fuses kept blowing out and causing delays in completing this project! So get out of here and take your worthless generators with you.

Salesperson: [with a smile] Thank you for telling me. Say, you and our company's design engineers have a lot in common.

Prospect: Oh yeah? I'll bet! [Sarcastically.]

Salesperson: Suppose you were chief engineer in charge of manufacturing our generators. What would you do if valued customers—like yourself—said your generators had problems?

Prospect: I'd throw them in the trash.

Salesperson: Come on, what would you really do? [With a smile.]

Prospect: Well, I would fix it.

Salesperson: That's why I said you and our design engineers have a lot in common. They acted on your suggestion—don't you think? [Trial close.]

You have used reverse psychology. Now, the prospect is listening, giving you time to explain your product's new features and to make an offer to repair the old units. You are ready to sell more products, if possible.

Another example is the industrial salesperson who responded to the prospect's high price objection by saying, "Well, that's the very reason you should buy it." The prospect was caught off guard and quickly asked, "What do you mean?" "Well," said

Be Positive in Discussing Price

All prospects are sensitive to how price is presented. This is a typical list of negative and positive ways to deal with price issues during the business proposition phase:

Negative Words	Positive Words
■ This costs $2,300.	■ This is only $2,300.
■ Your down payment . . .	■ Your initial investment . . .
■ Your monthly payment . . .	■ Your monthly investment . . .
■ You can pay the purchase price over a series of months.	■ We would be happy to divide this investment into small monthly shares.
■ How much would you like to pay us every month?	■ What monthly investment would you feel comfortable with?
■ We'll charge you two points above the prime rate.	■ Your rate will be only prime plus two.
■ We'll take off $6,700 to trade in your used car.	■ We are offering you $6,700 to trade your existing model.

the salesperson, "for just 10 percent more, you can buy the type of equipment you really want and need. It is dependable, safe, and simple to operate. Your production will increase so that you will pay back the price differential quickly." The prospect said, "Well, I hadn't thought of it quite like that. I guess I'll buy it after all."

Boomeranging an objection requires good timing and quick thinking. Experience in a particular selling field, knowledge of your prospect's needs, a positive attitude, and a willingness to stand up to the objection are necessary attributes for successful use of this technique.

Ask Questions to Smoke out Objections

Intelligent questioning impresses a prospect in several ways. Technical questions show a prospect that a salesperson knows the business. Questions relating to a prospect's particular business show that a salesperson is concerned more with the prospect's needs than with just making a sale. Finally, people who ask **intelligent questions,** whether they know much about the product, the prospect's business, or life in general, often receive admiration. Buyers are impressed with the sales professional who knows what to ask and when to ask it. Examples of questions are

Prospect: This house is not as nice as the one someone else showed us yesterday.

Salesperson: Would you tell me why?

or

Prospect: This product does not have the [feature].

Salesperson: If it did have [feature], would you be interested?

[This example is an excellent questioning technique to determine if the objection is a smoke screen, a major or minor objection, or a practical or psychological objection. If the prospect says no to the response, you know the feature was not important.]

or

Prospect: I don't like your price.

Salesperson: Will you base your decision on price or on the product offered you . . . at a fair price?

[If the prospect says "Price," show how benefits outweigh costs. If the decision is based on the product, you have eliminated the price objection.]

Five-Question Sequence Method of Overcoming Objections

Buyers state objections for numerous reasons. From time to time, all salespeople sense that a buyer will not buy. As you gain sales experience, you will be able to feel it. It may be the buyer's facial expressions or a tone of voice that tips you off. When this occurs, find out quickly why a prospect doesn't want to buy. To do this, consider using a preplanned series of questions as shown in Exhibit 11–10.

Let's assume you have finished the presentation. You try to close the sale and see that the buyer will not go further in the conversation. What do you do? Consider using the following **five-question sequence.**

First, use this question: "There must be some good reason why you're hesitating to go ahead now; do you mind if I ask what it is?" When the reason is stated, or if it is an objection, immediately double-check the objection with one more question by using question number two: "In addition to that, is there any other reason for not going ahead?" The buyer may give the real reason for not buying, or the buyer may give the original objection. No matter what is said, you have created a condition for buying.

Now, use question number three, a just supposing question: "Just suppose you could . . . then you'd want to go ahead?" If the answer is yes, discuss how you can do what is needed. If you receive a negative response, use question number four: "Then there must be some other reason. May I ask what it is?" Respond with question number two again. Then ask, "Just supposing . . . you'd want to go ahead?" If you receive another negative response, use question number five by saying, "What would it take to convince you?"

What often happens will surprise you. The buyer often will say, "Oh, I don't know. I guess I'm convinced. Go ahead and ship it to me." Or, you might be asked to go back over some part of your presentation. The important point is that this series of questions keeps the conversation going and reveals the real objections, which increases your sales. Imagine you are the salesperson in this example:

Salesperson: Should we ship the product to you this week or next?

Buyer: Neither; see me on your next trip. I'll have to think about it.

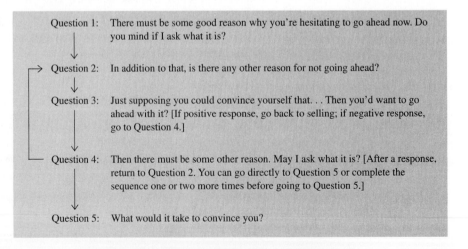

EXHIBIT 11–10

Five-question sequence method of overcoming objections

Question 1:   There must be some good reason why you're hesitating to go ahead now. Do you mind if I ask what it is?

Question 2:   In addition to that, is there any other reason for not going ahead?

Question 3:   Just supposing you could convince yourself that. . . Then you'd want to go ahead with it? [If positive response, go back to selling; if negative response, go to Question 4.]

Question 4:   Then there must be some other reason. May I ask what it is? [After a response, return to Question 2. You can go directly to Question 5 or complete the sequence one or two more times before going to Question 5.]

Question 5:   What would it take to convince you?

Salesperson: You know, there must be some good reason why you're hesitating to go ahead now. Would you mind if I asked what it is? [Question 1]

Buyer: Too much money.

Salesperson: Too much money. Well, you know, I appreciate the fact that you want to get the most for your money. In addition to the money, is there any other reason for not going ahead? [Question 2]

Buyer: No.

Salesperson: Well, suppose that you could convince yourself that the savings from this machine would pay for itself in just a few months, and that we could fit it into your budget. Then you'd want to go ahead with it? [Question 3]

Buyer: Yes, I would.

Now, return to selling by discussing the return on investment and affordable payment terms. You went from the first objection to the double-check question. ("In addition to the money, is there any other reason for not going ahead?") Then, you used the just supposing question. You met the condition, the machine's cost. Then, you used the convince question. The buyer said yes, so you can keep selling. Now, let's role-play as if the buyer had said no. (Again, you are the salesperson.)

Buyer: No, I wouldn't go ahead.

Salesperson: Well, then there must be some other reason why you're hesitating to go ahead now. Do you mind if I ask what it is? [Question 4]

Buyer: It takes too much time to train my employees in using the machine.

Salesperson: Well, you know, I appreciate that. Time is money. In addition to the time, is there any other reason for not going ahead? [Question 2]

Buyer: Not really.

Salesperson: Suppose that you could convince yourself that this machine would save employees time so that they could do other things. You'd find the money then, wouldn't you? [Question 3]

Buyer: I'm not sure. [Another potential negative response]

Salesperson: Money and time are important to you, right?

Buyer: Yes, they are.

Salesperson: What would it take for me to convince you that this machine will save you time and money? [Question 5]

Now you have to get a response. The buyer has to set the condition. You, as the salesperson, are in control. The buyer is answering the questions. Remember, you want to help the person buy. When you get an objection, you are told what you must do to make the sale happen. So do not fear objections; welcome them!

Use Direct Denial Tactfully

You will face objections that are often incomplete or incorrect. Acknowledge the prospect's viewpoint; then answer the question by providing the complete or correct facts:

Prospect: No, I'm not going to buy any of your lawn mowers for my store. The Bigs-Weaver salesperson said they break down after a few months.

Salesperson: Well, I can understand. No one would buy mowers that don't hold up. Is that the only reason you won't buy?

Prospect: Yes, it is, and that's enough!

Salesperson: The BW salesperson was not aware of the facts, I'm afraid. My company produces the finest lawn mowers in the industry. In fact, we are so sure of our quality that we have a new three-year guarantee on all parts and labor. [Pause]

Prospect: I didn't know that. [Positive buying signal]

Salesperson: Are you interested in selling your customers quality lawn mowers like these? [Trial close]

Prospect: Yes, I am. [Appears that you have overcome the objection]

Salesperson: Well, I'd like to sell you 100 lawn mowers. If even one breaks down, call me and I'll come over and repair it. [Close]

As you see by this example, you do not say, "Well, you so-and-so, why do you say a thing like that?" Tact is critical in using a direct denial. A sarcastic or arrogant response can alienate a prospect. However, a **direct denial** based on facts, logic, and politeness can effectively overcome the objection.

If I say to you, "You're wrong. Let me tell you why," what happens to your mind? It closes! So, if I tell you that you are wrong and this closes your mind, what would I have to tell you to open your mind? That you are right! But, if what you said was wrong, do I tell you it was right? No, instead, do what the example illustrated by saying, "You know, you're right to be concerned about this. Let me explain." You have made the buyer right and kept the buyer's mind open. Also, you could say, "You know, my best customer had those same feelings until I explained that . . ." You have made the customer right.

The Indirect Denial Works

An **indirect denial** is different from a direct denial in that it initially appears as agreement with the customer's objection but then moves into a denial of the fundamental issue in the objection. The difference between the direct denial and the indirect denial is that the indirect denial is softer, more tactful, and more courteous. Use the direct denial judiciously, only to disconfirm especially damaging misinformation.

The typical example of indirect denial is the yes, but phrase. Here are several examples:

- Yes, but would you agree that it takes information, not time, to make a decision? What kind of information are you really looking for to make a good decision?
- I agree. Our price is a little higher, but so is our quality. Are you interested in saving $1,200 a year on maintenance?
- Sure, it costs a little more. However, you will have the assurance that it will cost much less over its lifetime. Isn't that the way your own products are made?
- Your point is well taken. It does cost more than any other product on the market. But why do you think we sell millions of them at this price?
- I appreciate how you feel. Many of our customers made similar comments prior to buying from me. However, they all asked themselves: "Can I afford not to have the best? Won't it cost me more in the long run?"

The indirect denial begins with an agreement or an acknowledgment of the prospect's position: Yes, but, I agree, Sure, Your point is well taken, and I appreciate how you feel. These phrases allow the salesperson to tactfully respond to the objection. Done in a natural, conversational way, the salesperson will not offend the prospect.

Try this yourself: when a friend says something you disagree with, instead of saying, "I don't agree," say something like "I see what you mean. However, there's another way to look at it." See if this, as well as the other communication skills you have studied, helps you to better sell yourself—and your product.

Compensation or Counterbalance Method

Sometimes a prospect's objection is valid and calls for the **compensation method.** Several reasons for buying must exist to justify or compensate for a negative aspect of making a purchase. For example, a higher product price is justified by benefits such as better service or higher performance. In the following example, it is true that the prospect can make more profit on each unit of a competing product. You must develop a technique to show how your product has benefits that will bring the prospect more profit in the long run.

Prospect: I can make 5 percent more profit with the Stainless line of cookware, and it is quality merchandise.

Salesperson: Yes, you are right. The Stainless cookware is quality merchandise. However, you can have an exclusive distributorship on the Supreme cookware line, and still have high-quality merchandise. You don't have to worry about Supreme being discounted by nearby competitors as you do with Stainless. This will be the only store in town carrying Supreme. What do you think? [Trial close.]

If the advantages presented to counterbalance the objection are important to the buyer, you have an opportunity to make the sale.

Let a Third Party Answer

An effective technique for responding to an objection is to answer it by letting a **third party answer** and using someone else's experience as your proof of testimony. A wide range of proof statements are used by salespeople today. You might respond to a question in this way: "I'm glad you asked. Here is what our research has shown," or, "EPA tests have shown," or, "You know, my best customer brought that point up before making the purchase . . . but was completely satisfied." These are examples of proof statement formats. If you use a person or a company's name, be sure to obtain their approval first.

Secondary data or experience, especially from a reliable or reputable source, is successful with the expert or skeptical prospect. If, after hearing secondary testimony, the prospect is still unsure about the product, one successful equipment salesperson asks the buyer to contact a current user directly:

Salesperson: I still haven't answered your entire question, have I?

Buyer: Not really.

Salesperson: Let's do this. Here is a list of several people presently using our product. I want you to call them up *right now* and ask them that same question. I'll pay for the calls.

A salesperson should use this version of the third-party technique only when certain that the prospect is still unsatisfied with how an objection has been handled, and that positive proof will probably clinch the sale. This dramatic technique allows the salesperson to impress a prospect. It also shows a flattering willingness to go to great lengths to validate a claim.

TECHNOLOGY CAN EFFECTIVELY HELP RESPOND TO OBJECTIONS!

Providing buyers the necessary information to make a decision can frequently overcome objections. Data stored in handheld computers or laptops, or obtained using a telephone modem or satellite transmission, can provide information to overcome buyers' objections.

Frito-Lay salesperson June Steward frequently uses her computer to show buyers their past purchases of products and to project future sales. Using his laptop computer while in the buyer's office, Fisher Electronics's salesperson John Berry checks with his warehouse daily on available products and shipment schedules. Merrill Lynch salesperson Sandy Lopez uses Lotus software to display her client's present investments, past earnings, and recommendations on how much money should be put into stock and bond mutual funds.

Technology can be incorporated easily into most, if not all, of the techniques for meeting objections. Anytime you need to provide information to buyers, you can create a technological method of presenting data in an accurate and dramatic manner.

AFTER MEETING THE OBJECTION— WHAT TO DO?

As shown in Exhibit 11–11, your prospect has raised an objection that you have answered and overcome; now what? First, as shown in Exhibit 11–12, use a trial close, then either return to your presentation or close the sale.

First, Use a Trial Close—Ask for Opinion

After meeting an objection at any time during the interview, you need to know if you have overcome the objection. If you have not overcome it, your prospect may raise it again. Whether it resurfaces or not, if your prospect believes that an objection was important, your failure to handle it, or your mishandling of it, will probably cost you the sale. Ideally, all objections raised should be met before closing the sale. So, after responding to the objection, use a trial close to determine if you have overcome the objection. Ask questions such as:

- That clarifies this point entirely, don't you agree?
- That's the answer you're looking for, isn't it?
- With that question out of the way, we can go ahead—don't you think?
- Do you agree with me that we've covered the question you raised, and given you a way to handle it?
- Now that's settled entirely, isn't it?
- That solves your problem, doesn't it?

Once you have confirmed overcoming an objection, immediately go to the next SELL sequence step. To signal that the last step is over, and that you are moving on, use body language as you speak. That is, make an appropriate gesture, look in a new direction, turn the page of your proposal, or shift in your chair—make some physical movement. Now, do one of two things (assuming you have handled the objection): either return to your presentation or close the sale.

Move Back into Your Presentation

When you have answered and overcome an objection, make a smooth transition back into your presentation. As you nonverbally signal that the last step is over, let the prospect know you are returning to your presentation with a phrase such as, "As we were discussing earlier." Now, you can continue the presentation.

EXHIBIT 11–11

Imagine you are this bank loan officer and you just answered this person's objection. What should you do now?

EXHIBIT 11–12

The procedure to follow when an objection is raised by a prospect

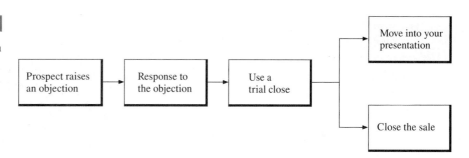

Move to Close Your Sale

If you have finished your presentation when the prospect raised an objection, and the prospect's response to your trial close indicates that you overcame an objection, your next move is to close the sale. If the objection was raised during your close, then it is time to close again.

As you move on to the close with a gesture, you might summarize benefits discussed previously with a phrase such as, "Well, as we have discussed, you really like . . ." Then, again ask the prospect for the order. Chapter 12 gives you other ideas on how to ask for the order.

If You Cannot Overcome the Objection

If you cannot overcome an objection or close a sale because of an objection, be prepared to return to your presentation and concentrate on new or previously discussed features, advantages, and benefits of your product. If you determine that the objection raised by your prospect is a major one that cannot be overcome, admit it, and show how your product's benefits outweigh this disadvantage.

If you are 100 percent sure that you cannot overcome the objection and that the prospect will not buy, go ahead and close. *Always ask for the order.* Never be afraid to ask your prospect to buy. The buyer says no to the product—not you. Someone else may walk into the prospect's office after you with a product similar to yours. Your competitor also may be able to overcome this person's objection, but he or she may get the sale nonetheless just by asking for it!

SELLING TIPS

A Strategy for Handling Objections

One of the biggest hurdles to success for salespeople is how to handle objections. Here is a strategy top salespeople use to draw out, understand, and overcome objections:

1. Plan for objections.
2. Anticipate and forestall objections when needed.
3. Handle objections as they arise.
4. Be positive.
5. Listen to objections—hear them out.
6. Understand objections—ask questions to clarify.
7. Meet the objection by selecting methods or techniques to use in responding to the objection.
8. Confirm that you have met the objection—use a trial close.
9. Where am I? Decide if you need to keep selling, handle another objection, or close the sale.

ETHICAL DILEMMA

A University Sets a Condition

You are a salesperson for a large, national company that publishes and sells college textbooks. Three days ago you talked with Dr. Bush, the department head, about adopting one of your books in a sophomore course of 2,000 students. He said the book is a good one but there were three others just as good.

Before leaving, Dr. Bush said the department will use your book if the publisher donates $1,000 and provides a new computer and printer to the English department. You tell your boss about this and she says, "Do it, but keep it quiet so none of your other schools hear of it. This will be a $100,000 sale. The home office will approve this expense if we don't do it for too many schools."

What do you do?

SUMMARY OF MAJOR SELLING ISSUES

People want to buy, but they do not want to be misled, so they often ask questions or raise objections during a sales presentation. Your responsibility is to be prepared to logically and clearly respond to your prospect's objections whenever they arise.

Sales objections indicate a prospect's opposition or resistance to the information or request of the salesperson. Basic points to consider in meeting objections are to (1) plan for them, (2) anticipate and forestall them, (3) handle them as they arise, (4) listen to what is said, (5) respond warmly and positively, (6) make sure you understand, and (7) respond using an effective communication technique.

Before you can successfully meet objections, determine if the prospect's response to your statement or close is a request for more information, a condition of the sale, or an objection. If it is a real objection, determine whether it is minor or major. Respond to it using a trial close, and if you have answered it successfully, continue your presentation based on where you are in the sales presentation. For example, if you are still in the presentation, then return to your selling sequence. If you have completed the presentation, move to your close. If you are in the close and the prospect voices an objection, then you must decide whether to use another close or return to the presentation and discuss additional benefits.

Be aware of and plan for objection. Objections are classified as hidden, stalling, no-need, money, product, and source objections. Develop several techniques to help overcome each type of objection, such as stalling the objection, turning the objection into a benefit, asking questions to smoke out hidden objections, denying the objection if appropriate, illustrating how product benefits outweigh the objection drawbacks, or developing proof statements that answer the objection.

Welcome your prospect's objections. They help you determine if you are on the right track to uncover prospects' needs and if they believe your product will fulfill those needs. Valid objections are beneficial for you and the customer. A true objection reveals the customer's need, which allows a salesperson to demonstrate how a product can meet that need. Objections also show inadequacies in a salesperson's presentation or product knowledge. Finally, objections make selling a skill that a person can improve constantly. Over time, a dedicated salesperson can learn how to handle every conceivable product objection—tactfully, honestly, and to the customer's benefit.

MEETING A SALES CHALLENGE

Before handling an objection, it's important to find out what the **exact** objection is. Is price a stall or bona fide reason for changing suppliers? Is the competitor's cheaper price attractive, or does the problem exist with the salesperson and the possible inability to sell a high-priced line? There could be many problems, so before you answer the objection, do some probing and find out what the real one is. A good question would be, "Would you mind telling me exactly why you're considering this move?" Then continue to probe until you totally understand the buyer's reasoning for wanting to change suppliers.

Listen carefully to what the buyer says. This person may be a tough negotiator wanting to see if you will lower your prices. Nonnie Young may be happy with your prices.

KEY TERMS FOR SELLING

sales objection 309	dodge 324
condition of the sale 314	pass up 325
negotiation 314	rephrase as a question 326
practical objection 315	postpone the objection 327
psychological objection 315	boomerang method 328
hidden objection 316	intelligent questions 329
stalling objection 317	five-question sequence 330
no-need objection 319	direct denial 332
money objection 320	indirect denial 332
product objection 322	compensation method 333
source objection 322	third-party answer 333

SALES APPLICATION QUESTIONS

1. Halfway through your sales presentation, your prospect stops you and says, "That sounds like a great deal and you certainly have a good product, but I'm not interested now; maybe later." What should you do?

2. Assume you are a salesperson for the Japan Computer Corporation. You have finished your computer presentation, and the purchasing agent for Gulf Oil says, "Well, that sounds real good and you do have the lowest price I have ever heard of for a computer system. In fact, it's $200,000 less than the other bids. But we

have decided to stay with IBM, mainly because $200,000 on a $1 million computer system is not that much money to us." Let's further assume that you also know that other than price, IBM has significant advantages in all areas over your product. What would you do?

3. When a customer is not receptive to your product, there is some objection. In each of the following situations, the customer has an objection to a product:

    a. The customer assumes she must buy the whole set of books. However, partial purchases are permitted.

    b. The customer does not like the color and it's the only color your product comes in.

    c. The customer doesn't want to invest in a new set of books because she doesn't want to lose money on her old set. You have not told her yet about your trade-in deal.

    In which of these situations does the objection arise from a misunderstanding or lack of knowledge on the customer's part? In which situation(s) does the product fail to offer a benefit that the customer considers important?

4. Which response is best when you hear the customer reply, "I'd like to think it over"? Why?

    a. Give all the benefits of using the product now.

    b. If there is a penalty for delaying, mention it now.

    c. If there is a special-price deal available, mention it now.

    d. None of the above is appropriate.

    e. Depending on the circumstances, the first three choices are appropriate.

5. Cliff Jamison sells business forms and he's regarded as a top-notch salesperson. He works hard, plans ahead, and exhibits self-confidence. One day, he made his first presentation to a prospective new client, the California Steel Company.

    "Ladies and gentlemen," said Jamison, "our forms are of the highest quality, yet they are priced below our competitor's forms. I know that you are a large user of business forms and that you use a wide variety. Whatever your need for business forms, I assure you that we can supply them. Our forms are noted for their durability. They can run through your machines at 60 per minute and they'll perform perfectly."

    "Perfectly, Mr. Jamison?" asked the California Steel executive. "Didn't you have some trouble at Ogden's last year?"

    "Oh," replied Jamison, "that wasn't the fault of our forms. They had a stupid operator who didn't follow instructions. I assure you that if our instructions are followed precisely you will have no trouble.

    "Furthermore, we keep a large inventory of our forms so that you need never worry about delays. A phone call to our office is all that is necessary to ensure prompt delivery of the needed forms to your plant. I hope, therefore, that I can be favored with your order." Did Jamison handle this situation correctly? Why?

6. One of your customers, Margaret Port, has referred you to a friend who needs your Hercules Shelving for a storage warehouse. Port recently purchased your heavy-duty, 18-gauge steel shelving and is pleased with it. She said, "This will be an easy sale for you. My friend really needs shelving and I told him about yours."

    Port's information is correct and your presentation to her friend goes smoothly. The customer has asked numerous questions and seems ready to buy. Just before you ask for the order, the customer says, "Looks like your product is exactly what I need. I'd like to think this over. Could you call me next week?" Which of the following would you do? Why?

    a. Follow the suggestion and call next week.

    b. Go ahead and ask for the order.

    c. Ask questions about the reason for the delay.

SALES WORLD WIDE WEB EXERCISES

Finding People, Organizations, Maps, Areas, Phone, and Address

Opposition or resistance to information or to the salesperson's request is labeled a sales objection. Objections often arise because the salesperson has not researched the individual or organization. Some types of selling require a tremendous amount of research to create a sales presentation. The better your research, the fewer objections, and thus the more likely you are to make the sale. The following are URLs, which can help you in your research:

People Finders:

www.four11.com   www.bigyellow.com

www.switchboard.com

Organization Finders:

www.bigyellow.com   www.mfginfo.com

www.bigbook.com   www.bnet.att.com

www.companiesonline.com   www.industry.net

Maps:

www.lookupusa.com   www.mapquest.com

Geographic–Market Areas:

www.census.gov

E-Mail:

www.el.com (see phone/address)

Of course, also use your favorite search engines to find out more about people, organizations, markets, and geographical areas.

FURTHER EXPLORING THE SALES WORLD

1. A national sales company is at your school wishing to hire salespeople. What are some objections that such a school might have toward hiring you? How would you overcome them during a job interview?

2. Visit three different types of business (such as a grocery store, a hardware store, and a stereo shop), and pick out one product from each business. If you were that store's buyer, think of the major objections or questions you would ask a product salesperson if you were asked to buy a large quantity and promote it. Now, as that salesperson, how would you overcome those objections?

STUDENT APPLICATION LEARNING EXERCISES (SALES) (Part 6 of 7)

Sales objections are defined as opposition or resistance from the buyer. To make **Sale 6**

1. List three objections a buyer might give you. See example of various types of objections on pages 316–323. Make certain you use objections that relate to your product. Do not use general objections, such as "I do not like it." The objection should be specific, such as "I do not like the color."

Objection 1:

Objection 2:

Objection 3:

2. Select a different technique for handling each of the above objections. Write the technique's name below. See pages 323–333.

Technique 1: _____

Technique 2: _____

Technique 3: _____

3. Write the buyer–seller dialogue for each objection. State the buyer's objection and then your response to it. Each time you respond to an objection use a trial close, see pages 74–77, to determine if you have overcome the objection or correctly answered the buyer's concern or question. After your trial close, label it using parentheses (Trial Close). See examples on page 327.

Buyer's objection 1:

Your response:

Buyer's objection 2:

Your response:

Buyer's objection 3:

Your response:

Role-play the buyer giving you the above objections and your response. If possible, use a tape recorder to play back the dialogue. Does what you say sound natural and conversational to you? If not, adjust it. If it does, go with it.

CASE 11–1
Ace Building Supplies

This is your fourth call on Ace Building Supplies to motivate them to sell your home building supplies to local builders. Joe Newland, the buyer, gives every indication that he likes your products.

During the call, Joe reaffirms his liking for your products and attempts to end the interview by saying: "We'll be ready to do business with you in three months—right after this slow season ends. Stop by then and we'll place an order with you."

Questions

1. Which one of the following steps would you take? Why?
   a. Call back in three months to get the order as suggested.
   b. Try to get a firm commitment or order now.

    c. Telephone Joe in a month (rather than make a personal visit) and try to get the order.

2. Why did you not choose the other two alternatives?

CASE 11–2

Electric Generator Corporation (B)

George Wynn is a salesperson for EGC whose primary responsibility is to contact engineers in charge of constructing commercial buildings. One such engineer is Don Snyder, who is in charge of building the new Texas A & M College of Business Administration facility. Don's Houston-based engineering firm purchased three new EGI portable generators for this project. George learned that Don's company will build four more buildings on the Texas A & M campus, and he felt that Don might buy more machines.

Salesperson: Don, I understand you have three of our new model electric generators.

Buyer: Yeah, you're not kidding.

Salesperson: I'm sure you'll need additional units on these new jobs.

Buyer: Yeah, we sure will.

Salesperson: I've gone over the building's proposed floor plans and put together the type of products you need.

Buyer: They buy down in Houston; you need to see them!

Salesperson: I was just in there yesterday and they said it was up to you.

Buyer: Well, I'm busy today.

Salesperson: Can I see you tomorrow?

Buyer: No need; I don't want any more of your lousy generators!

Salesperson: What do you mean? That is our most modern design!

Buyer: Those so-called new fuses of yours are exploding after five minutes' use. The autotransformer starter won't start. . . Did you see the lights dim? That's another fuse blowing.

Question

George Wynn feels pressured to sell the new EGI. Don Snyder's business represents an important sale both now and in the future. If you were George, what would you do?

a. Have EGC's best engineer contact Don to explain the generator's capabilities.

b. Come back after Don has cooled down.

c. Get Don to talk about problems and then solve them.

12

Closing Begins the Relationship

LEARNING OBJECTIVES

If everything has been done to properly develop and give a sales presentation, then closing the sale is the easiest step in the presentation. After studying this chapter, you should be able to:

- Explain when to close.

- Describe what to do if when you ask for the order, your prospect asks for more information, gives an objection, or says no.

- Explain why you must prepare to close more than once.

- Discuss the 12 keys to a successful close.

- Present, illustrate, and use several techniques for closing the sale in your presentation.

- Construct a multiple-close sequence.

John made his presentation for in-office coffee service to the office manager. As he neared the end of it, the office manager asked, "What's your price?" John quoted the standard price, and immediately the manager said, "Way out—your competitor's price is $10 cheaper!"

As Lisa, who represented a medical laboratory equipment company, finished her presentation, the pathologist asked her about the cost. She stated the list price and heard, "Your price is too high. I can get the same type of equipment for a lot less."

Ralph, selling a line of office copying machines, was only halfway through his presentation when the director of administration asked for the cost. When Ralph quoted the price on the top-of-the-line model the administrator closed off the interview with the familiar phase, "Your price is too high."

John, Lisa, and Ralph are facing a real challenge. Their buyers said, "Your price is too high," indirectly saying, "No, I'm not interested." In each situation, what would you do now?

Successful salespeople do not give a presentation and then ask for the order. Successful salespeople cultivate selling techniques that help develop a natural instinct, sensitivity, and timing for when and how to close with each buyer. This chapter wraps up our discussion of the main sales presentation elements. We begin by discussing when to close, showing examples of buying signals, and discussing what makes a good closer. Next we discuss the number of times you should attempt to close a sale, along with some problems associated with closing. Eleven closing techniques are presented followed by an explanation of the importance of being prepared to close several times based on the situation.

To be a good closer, you must be able to handle objections. Objections frequently arise as the salesperson nears the end of the presentation, as in the case of John, and after the close, as experienced by Lisa. However, as Ralph found out, price objection can pop up anytime. This chapter and the previous chapters on objection will help you solve the "Sales Challenge" above.

WHEN SHOULD I POP THE QUESTION?

Closing is the process of helping people make a decision that will benefit them. You help people make the decision by asking them to buy. As successful salespeople know, there are no magic phrases and techniques to use in closing a sale. It is the end result of your presentation. If everything has been done to properly develop a sales presentation, closing the sale is the next step in a logical sequence.

Although it seems obvious, some salespeople forget that prospects know that the salesperson is there to sell them something. So, as soon as they meet, the prospect's mind already may have progressed beyond the major portion of the salesperson's presentation. At times, the prospect may be ready to make the buying decision early in the interview.

So when should you attempt to close a sale? Simply, *when the prospect is ready!* More specifically, when the prospect is in the conviction stage of the mental buying process. A buyer can enter the conviction stage at any time during the sales presentation. As shown in Exhibit 12–1, you might ask someone to buy as early as the approach stage or as late as another day. Much of the time, however, the close comes after the presentation. An ability to read a prospect's buying signals correctly helps a salesperson decide when and how to close a sale.

EXHIBIT 12–1

Close when the prospect is ready

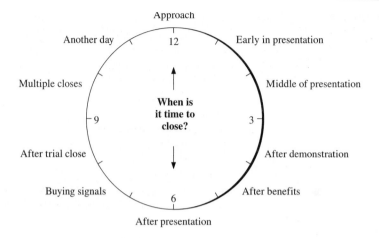

READING BUYING SIGNALS

After prospects negotiate each stage of the mental buying process and are ready to buy, they often give you a signal. A **buying signal** refers to anything that prospects say or do indicating they are ready to buy. Buying signals hint that prospects are in the conviction stage of the buying process. Here are several ways a prospective buyer signals readiness to buy:

- **Asks questions**—"How much is it?" "What is the earliest time that I can receive it?" "What are your service and returned goods policies?" At times, you may respond to a buying signal question with another question, as shown in Exhibit 12–2. This helps determine your prospect's thoughts and needs. If your question is answered positively, the prospect is showing a high interest level and you are nearing the close.

- **Asks another person's opinion**—The executive calls someone on the telephone and says, "Come in here a minute; I have something to ask you." Or the husband turns to his wife and says, "What do you think about it?"

- **Relaxes and becomes friendly**—Once the prospect decides to purchase a product, the pressure of the buying situation is eliminated. A state of visible anxiety changes to relaxation because your new customer believes that you are a friend.

- **Pulls out a purchase order form**—If, as you talk, your prospect pulls out an order form, it is time to move toward the close.

- **Carefully examines merchandise**—When a prospect carefully scrutinizes your product or seems to contemplate the purchase, this may be an indirect request for prompting. Given these indications, attempt a trial close: "What do you think about . . . ?" If you obtain a positive response to this question, move on to close the sale.

A buyer may send verbal or nonverbal buying signals at any time before or during your sales presentation (remember Exhibit 12–1). The accurate interpretation of buying signals should prompt you to attempt a trial close. In beginning a trial close, summarize the major selling points desired by your prospect. If you receive a positive response to the trial close, you can move to Step 9 and wrap up the sale. See Exhibit 12–3. A negative response should result in a return to your presentation, Step 4, or to determine objections, Step 6. This is illustrated in Exhibit 12–3. In any case, a successful trial close can save you and your prospect valuable time, while a thwarted trial close allows you to assess the selling situation.

EXHIBIT 12–2

Answering a prospect's buying
signal question with a question

Buyer Says:	Salesperson Replies:
■ What's your price?	■ In what quantity?
■ What kind of terms do you offer?	■ What kind of terms do you want?
■ When can you make delivery?	■ When do you want delivery?
■ What size copier should I buy?	■ What size do you need?
■ Can I get this special price on orders placed now and next month?	■ Would you like to split your shipment?
■ Do you carry 8-, 12-, 36-, and 54-foot pipe?	■ Are those the sizes you commonly use?
■ How large an order must I place to receive your best price?	■ What size order do you have in mind?
■ Do you have Model 6400 in stock?	■ Is that the one you like best?

EXHIBIT 12–3

A positive response to the trial
close indicates a move toward
the close; a negative response
means return to your
presentation or determine
the prospect's objections.

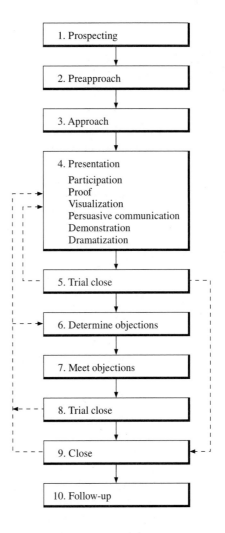

1. Prospecting
2. Preapproach
3. Approach
4. Presentation
   Participation
   Proof
   Visualization
   Persuasive communication
   Demonstration
   Dramatization
5. Trial close
6. Determine objections
7. Meet objections
8. Trial close
9. Close
10. Follow-up

WHAT MAKES A GOOD CLOSER?

In every sales force, some individuals are better than others at closing sales. Some persons rationalize this difference of abilities by saying, "It comes naturally to some people," or, "They've just got what it takes." Well, what does it take to be a good closer?

Good closers have a strong desire to close each sale. They have a positive attitude about their product's ability to benefit the prospect. They know their customers and tailor their presentations to meet each person's specific needs.

Good closers prepare for each sales call. They take the time to carefully ascertain the needs of their prospects and customers by observing, by asking intelligent questions, and most of all, by earnestly listening to them. To be successful, salespeople should know their ABCs. ABC stands for *Always Be Closing.* Be alert for closing signals and close when the prospect is ready to buy.

The successful salesperson does not stop with the prospect's first no. If a customer says no, determine the nature of the objection and then return to the presentation. After discussing information relative to overcoming the objection, use a trial close to determine if you have overcome the objection, and then determine if there are other objections. If resistance continues, remain positive and remember that every time you attempt to close, you are closer to the sale. Additionally, always ask for the order and then be silent.

Ask for the Order and Be Quiet

No matter when or how you close, remember that when you ask for the order, it is important to be silent. Do not say a word. If you say something—anything—you increase the probability of losing the sale.

You must put the prospect in a position of having to make a decision, speak first, and respond to the close. If you say anything after your close, you take the pressure off the prospect to make that decision.

Imagine this situation: The salesperson has finished the presentation and says, "Would you want this delivery in two or four weeks?" The average salesperson cannot wait more than two seconds for the prospect's reply without saying something like, "I can deliver it anytime," or starting to talk again about the product. This destroys the closing moment. The prospect does not have to make the decision. There is time to think of reasons not to buy. By keeping quiet for a few seconds, the prospect can escape making the decision.

All individuals experience the urge to say no, even when they are not sure of what you are selling, or they may want what you propose. At times, everyone is hesitant in making a decision. To help the prospect make the decision, you must maintain silence after the close.

The professional salesperson can stay quiet all day, if necessary. Rarely will the silence last over 30 seconds. During that time, do not say anything or make a distracting gesture; merely project positive nonverbal signs. Otherwise, you will lessen your chances of making the sale. This is the time to mentally prepare your responses to the prospect's reaction.

It sounds simple, yet it is not. Your stomach may churn. Your nerves make you want to move. You may display a serious look on your face instead of a positive one. You may look away from the buyer. Most of all, you may want to talk to relieve the uncomfortable feeling that grows as silence continues. Finally, the prospect will say something. Now, you can respond based on the reaction to your close.

Constantly practice asking your closing question, staying silent for 30 seconds, and then responding. This will develop your skill and courage to close.

Get the Order— Then Move On!

Talking also can stop the sale after the prospect has said yes. An exception would be if you ask the customer for names of other prospects. Once this is done, it is best to take the order and move on.

In continuing to talk, you may give information that changes the buyer's mind. So, ask for the order and remain silent until the buyer responds. If you succeed, finalize the sale and leave.

A Mark Twain Story

Mark Twain attended a meeting where a missionary had been invited to speak. Twain was deeply impressed. Later he said, "The preacher's voice was beautiful. He told us about the sufferings of the natives and pleaded for help with such moving simplicity that I mentally doubled the fifty cents I had intended to put in the plate. He described the pitiful misery of those savages so vividly that the dollar I had in mind gradually rose to five. Then that preacher continued.

I felt that all the cash I carried on me would be insufficient. I decided to write a large check. Then he went on," added Twain, "and on and on about the dreadful state of those natives. I abandoned the idea of the check. Again, he went on, and I was back to five dollars. As he continued, I went to four, two, and then one dollar. Still, he persisted to preach. When the plate finally came around, I took ten cents out of it."[1]

HOW MANY TIMES SHOULD YOU CLOSE?

Courtesy and common sense imply a reasonable limit to the number of closes attempted by a salesperson at any one sitting. However, salespeople call on customers and prospects to sell their products.

To sell, you must be able to use multiple closes. Keep in mind that three closes is a minimum for successful salespeople. Three to five well-executed closes should not offend a prospect. Attempting several closes in one call challenges a salesperson to employ wit, charm, and personality in a creative manner. So, always take at least three strikes before you count yourself out of the sale.

CLOSING UNDER FIRE

To close more sales effectively, never take the first no from the prospect to mean an absolute refusal to buy. Instead, you must be able to close under fire. See Exhibit 12–4. In other words, you must be able to ask a prospect who may be in a bad mood or even hostile toward you to buy.

Take the experience of a consumer goods salesperson who suggested that a large drug wholesaler should buy a six-month supply of the company's entire line of merchandise. Outraged, the purchasing agent threw the order book across the room. The salesperson explained to the furious buyer that the company had doubled its promotional spending in the buyer's area and that it would be wise to stock up because of an upcoming increase in sales. The salesperson calmly picked up the order book, smiled, and handed it to the buyer saying, "Did you want to buy more?"

The buyer laughed and said, "What do you honestly believe is a reasonable amount to buy?" This was a buying signal that the prospect would buy, but in a lesser quantity. They settled on an increased order of a two-month supply over the amount of merchandise normally purchased. This example illustrates why it is important for the salesperson to react calmly to an occasional hostile situation. That salesperson was your author. I will never forget that day!

DIFFICULTIES WITH CLOSING

Closing the sale is the easiest part of the presentation. It is a natural wrap-up to your sales presentation because you solidify details of the purchase agreement. Yet, salespeople sometimes have difficulty closing the sale for several reasons.

One reason salespeople may fail to close a sale and take an order is that they are not confident of their ability to close. Perhaps some earlier failure to make a sale has

EXHIBIT 12–4

Closing under fire

You can tell this customer is unhappy with your product or you. How do you save the sale and close her?

caused this mental block. They may give the presentation and stop short of asking for the order. The seller must overcome this fear of closing to become successful.

Second, salespeople often determine that the prospect does not need the quantity or type of merchandise, or that the prospect should not buy. So, they do not ask the prospect to buy. The salesperson should remember that "it is the prospect's decision and responsibility whether or not to buy." Do not make the decision for the prospect.

Finally, the salesperson may not have worked hard enough in developing a customer profile and customer benefit plan—resulting in a poor presentation. Many times, a poorly prepared presentation falls apart. Be prepared and develop a well-planned, well-rehearsed presentation.

ESSENTIALS OF CLOSING SALES

While there are many factors to consider in closing the sale, the following items are essential if you wish to improve your chances:

- Be sure your prospect understands what you say.
- Always present a complete story to ensure understanding.
- Tailor your close to each prospect. Eighty percent of your customers will respond to a standard close. It is the other 20 percent of customers that you need to prepare for. Prepare to give the expert customer all facts requested, to give the egotistical customer praise, to lead the indecisive customer, and to slow down for a slow thinker.
- Everything you do and say should consider the customer's point of view.
- Never stop at the first no.
- Learn to recognize buying signals.
- Before you close, attempt a trial close.

MAKING THE SALE

Closing Is Not One Giant Step

Too many salespeople regard the close as a separate and distinct part of the sales call. "I've discussed benefits and features, answered some objections, handled price, and now it's time to close."

Chronologically, of course, the close does come at the end. However, you must close all along. Closing is the natural outgrowth of the sales presentation. If the rest of the sales call has been a success, closing simply means working out terms and signing the order.

What about the salesperson who says, "I always have trouble closing. Everything's fine until it's time to close the sale." Chances are, there's no basis for the sale. "Everything's fine . . . " may merely be a way of saying, "I stated my case and the prospect listened. At least she never told me to pack up and go."

- After asking for the order—be silent.
- Set high goals for yourself and develop a personal commitment to reach your goals.
- Develop and maintain a positive, confident, and enthusiastic attitude toward yourself, your products, your prospects, and your close.

Before we discuss specific techniques on how to ask for the order or close the sale, remember that you will increase your sales closings by following 12 simple keys to success. The keys are shown in Exhibit 12–5.

As you see from these 12 keys, a successful close results from a series of actions that you have followed before asking for the order. Closing is not one giant step.

Should you not make the sale, always remember to act as a professional salesperson and be courteous and appreciative of the opportunity to present your product to the prospect. This allows the door to be open another time. Thus, Key 12 cannot be overlooked—always remember to leave the door open!

Often, salespeople believe that there is some mystical art to closing a sale. If they say the right words in the appropriate manner, the prospect will buy. They concentrate on developing tricky closing techniques and are often pushy with prospects in hopes of pressuring them into purchasing. Certainly, salespeople need to learn alternative closing techniques. However, what is most needed is a thorough understanding of the entire selling process and of the critical role that closing plays in that process.

A memorized presentation and a hurriedly presented product will not be as successful as the skillful use of the 12 keys to a successful close. A close look at the 12 keys illustrates that a lot of hard work, planning, and skillful execution of your plan occurs before you reach number 11 and ask for the order. The point is that if salespeople understand how each of the 12 applies to them and their customers, and if they perform each successfully, they earn the right to close.

In fact, many times the close occurs automatically because it has become the easiest part of the sales presentation. Often, the prospect will close for the salesperson, saying: "That sounds great! I'd like to buy that." See Exhibit 12–6. All the salesperson has to do is finalize the details and write up the order. Often, though, the prospect is undecided on the product after the presentation, so the skillful salesperson develops multiple closing techniques.

EXHIBIT 12–5

Twelve keys to a successful closing

1. Think *success!* Be enthusiastic.
2. *Plan* your sales call.
3. Confirm your prospect's *needs* in the approach.
4. Give a *great* presentation.
5. Use *trial closes* during and after your presentation.
6. Smoke out a prospect's *real* objections.
7. *Overcome* real objections.
8. Use a *trial close* after overcoming each objection.
9. Summarize *benefits* as related to buyer's *needs.*
10. Use a *trial close* to confirm Step 9.
11. Ask for the *order* and then *be quiet.*
12. Leave the door *open.* Act as a professional.

EXHIBIT 12–6

Often the seller does not have to close

In this case, the product sold itself. After trying the product, the prospect bought without the salesperson asking for an order.

PREPARE SEVERAL CLOSING TECHNIQUES

To successfully close more sales, you must determine your prospect's situation, understand the prospect's attitude toward your presentation, and be prepared to select instantly a closing technique from several techniques based on your prospect. For example, suppose you profiled the prospect as having a big ego, so you planned to use the compliment closing technique. You find the prospect is eager to buy but undecided about the model or the number of products to buy, so you switch to using your standing-room-only closing technique. By changing to a closing technique that fits the situation, you can speed the sale and keep your customer satisfied.

Successful salespeople adapt a planned presentation to any prospect or situation that may arise. Some salespeople have up to 11 closing techniques, each designed for a specific situation. Following are 11 common closing techniques:

- Alternative-choice close.
- Assumptive close.
- Continuous-yes close.
- Minor-points close.
- T-account or balance-sheet close.
- Standing-room-only close.

- Compliment close.
- Summary-of-benefits close.
- Probability close.
- Negotiation close.
- Technology close.

Whatever product is sold, whether an industrial or consumer product, these closing techniques are used to ask a prospect for the order. See Exhibit 12–7.

The Alternative-Choice Close Is an Old Favorite

The **alternative-choice close** was popularized in the 1930s as the story spread of the Walgreen Drug Company's purchase of 800 dozen eggs at a special price. A sales trainer named Elmer Wheeler suggested to the Walgreen clerks that when a customer asked for a malted milk at a Walgreen fountain, the clerk should say, "Do you want one egg or two?" Customers had not even thought of eggs in their malteds. Now, they were faced with the choice of *how many eggs*—not whether or not they wanted an egg. Within one week, all 800 dozen of the eggs were sold at a profit. Two examples of the alternative close are

- Which do you prefer—one or two neckties to go with your suit?
- Would you prefer the Xerox 6200 or 6400 copier?

As you see, the alternative choice does not give prospects a choice of buying or not buying, but asks which one or how many items they want to buy. It says, "You are going to buy, so let's settle the details on what you will purchase." Buying nothing at all is not an option.

Take, for example, the salesperson who says: "Would you prefer the Xerox 6200 or 6400?" This question: (1) assumes the customer has a desire to buy one of the copiers; (2) assumes the customer will buy; and (3) allows the customer a preference. If the customer prefers the Xerox 6400, you know the prospect is ready to buy, so you begin the close. A customer who says, "I'm not sure," is still in the desire stage, so you continue to discuss each product's benefits. However, you see that the customer likes both machines. Should the prospect appear indecisive, you can ask: "Is there something you are unsure of?" This question probes to find out why your prospect is not ready to choose.

EXHIBIT 12-7

Techniques for closing the sale: Which close should be used?

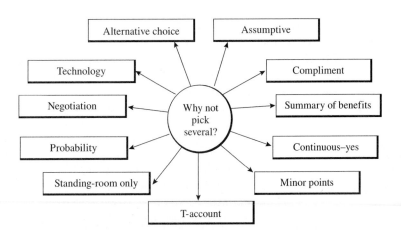

EXHIBIT 12–8

Ask for the order in a natural, low-key manner

This sales representative has begun to fill out the Customer Agreement form. What type of close is he using?

If used correctly, the alternative-choice close is an effective closing technique. It provides a choice between items, never between something and nothing. By presenting a choice, you either receive a yes decision or uncover objections, which if successfully met, allow you to come closer to making the sale.

The Assumptive Close

With the **assumptive close,** the salesperson assumes the prospect will buy (see Exhibit 12–8). Statements can be made such as, "I'll call your order in tonight," or, "I'll have this shipped to you tomorrow." If the prospect does not say anything, assume the suggested order has been accepted.

Many times the salesperson who has called on a customer for a long time can fill out the order form, hand it to the customer, and say, "This is what I'm going to send you," or, "This is what I believe you need this month." Many salespeople have earned customer trust to such an extent that the salesperson orders for them. Here, the assumptive close is especially effective.

The Compliment Close Inflates the Ego

Everyone likes to receive compliments. The **compliment close** is especially effective when you talk with a prospect who is a self-styled expert, who has a big ego, or who is in a bad mood. Would-be experts and egotistical prospects value their own opinions. By complimenting them, they listen and respond favorably to your presentation. The prospect with low self-esteem or one who finds it difficult to decide also responds favorably to a compliment. Here is an example of a housewares salesperson closing a sale with a grocery retail buyer.

> **Salesperson:** Obviously, you know a great deal about the grocery business. You have every square foot of your store making a good profit. Ms. Stevenson, our products also will provide you with a good profit margin. In fact, our profit will exceed your store's average profit-per-square-foot. And, they sell like hotcakes. This added benefit of high turnover will further increase your profits—which you have said is important to you. [He pauses, and when there is no response, he continues.] Given the number of customers coming into your store, and our expected

sales of these products due to normal turnover, along with our marketing plan, *I suggest you buy* [he states the products and their quantities]. This will provide you with sufficient quantities to meet your customers' demands for the next two months, plus provide you with the expected profit from your products. [Now he waits for the response or again asks for the order using the alternative choice or assumptive close.]

All buyers appreciate your recognition of their better points. Conscientious merchants take pride in how they do business; customers entering the retail clothing store take pride in their appearance; people considering life insurance take pride in looking after their families. So compliment prospects relative to something that will benefit them as you attempt to close the sale. Remember, always make honest compliments. No matter how trusting you may think people are, nearly anyone can detect insincerity in a compliment. When a compliment is not in order, summarize the benefits of your product for a specific customer.

The Summary-of-Benefits Close Is Most Popular

During the sales presentation, remember the main features, advantages, and benefits of interest for the prospect and use them successfully during the close. Summarize these benefits in a positive manner so that the prospect agrees with what you say; then ask for the order.

Here is an example of using the **summary-of-benefits close** on a prospect. Assume that the prospect indicates during your sales presentation that she likes your profit margin, delivery schedule, and credit terms.

Salesperson: Ms. Stevenson, you say you like our profit margin, fast delivery, and credit policy. Is that right? [Summary and trial close.]

Prospect: Yes, I do.

Salesperson: With the number of customers in your store and our expected sales of the products due to normal turnover, along with our marketing plan, *I suggest you buy* [state the products and their quantities]. This will provide you with sufficient quantities to meet customer demand for the next two months, plus provide you with the profit you expect from your products. I can have the order to you early next week. [Now wait for her response.]

You can easily adapt the FAB statements and SELL Sequence for your summary close. The vacuum cleaner salesperson might say, "As we have discussed, this vacuum cleaner's high speed motor [feature] works twice as fast [advantage] with less effort [advantage], saving you 15 to 30 minutes in cleaning time [benefit] and the aches and pains of pushing a heavy machine [benefit of benefit]. Right? [trial close. If positive response, say] Would you want the Deluxe or the Ambassador model?"

The sporting goods salesperson might say, "As we have said, this ball will give you an extra 10 to 20 yards on your drive [advantage], helping to reduce your score [benefit] because of its new solid core [feature]. That's great—isn't it? [trial close. If positive response, say] Will a dozen be enough?"

The air-conditioning salesperson could say, "This air conditioner has a high efficiency rating [feature] that will save you 10 percent on your energy costs [benefit] because it uses less electricity [advantage]. What do you think of that? [trial close. If positive response, say] Would you want it delivered this week or do you prefer next week?"

The summary close is possibly the most popular method to ask for the order. Emmett Reagan, sales trainer at the Xerox Training Center, says the major closing technique taught consists of these three basic steps of the summary close: (1) determine the key product benefits that interest the prospect during the presentation, (2) summarize these benefits, and (3) make a proposal. The summary-of-benefits technique is useful when you need a simple, straightforward close rather than a close aimed at a specific prospect's personality.

The Continuous-Yes Close Generates Positive Responses

The **continuous-yes close** is like the summary close. However, instead of summarizing product benefits, the salesperson develops a series of benefit questions that the prospect must answer.

Salesperson: Ms. Stevenson, you have said you like our quality products, right?

Prospect: Yes, that's right.

Salesperson: And you like our fast delivery?

Prospect: Yes, I do.

Salesperson: You also like our profit margin and credit terms?

Prospect: That's correct.

Salesperson: Ms. Stevenson, our quality products, fast delivery, profit margin, and good credit terms will provide you with an excellent profit. With the large number of customers you have coming into your store [salesperson completes the close as done in the summary-of-benefits close].

In this example of the continuous-yes close, the salesperson recognized four product benefits that the prospect liked: (1) the product's quality, (2) fast delivery, (3) profit margin, and (4) favorable credit terms. After the presentation, three questions were used to give the prospect the opportunity to agree that she was impressed with each of the four product benefits. By stacking these positive questions, the salesperson kept the prospect continually saying, "Yes, I like that benefit."

The prospect has placed herself in a positive frame of mind. Her positive stance toward the product makes it likely that she will continue to say "yes" when asked to buy.

Realize, of course, that some prospects may want to be cute and relish the thought of seeing the look of surprise on your face when, after they agree to all of your product benefit statements (yes . . . yes . . . yes), they respond to your order request with an unexpected no. Also, suspicious prospects may view your continuous-yes close as trickery or as an insult to their intelligence rather than aiding a purchase decision. In either case, calmly handling the situation reflects a sales professionalism that both surprises the trickster and impresses the suspicious person.

The Minor-Points Close Is Not Threatening

It is sometimes easier for a prospect to concede several minor points about a product than to make a sweeping decision on whether to buy or not to buy. Big decisions are often difficult for some buyers. By having the prospect make decisions on a product's minor points, you can subtly lead into the decision to buy.

The **minor-points close** is similar to the alternative-choice close. Both methods involve giving the buyer a choice between two options. The alternative-choice close asks the prospect to make a choice between *two* products, which represents a high-risk decision to some people that they may prefer not to make. However, the minor-points close asks the prospect to make a low-risk decision on a minor, usually low-cost element of a *single* product such as delivery dates, optimal features, color, size, payment terms, or order quantity.

SELLING GLOBALLY

French versus American Salespeople

Gerhard Gschwandtner, editor of *Personal Selling Power* (PSP) magazine interviewed Jean-Pierre Tricard, a French sales trainer. The following excerpts from this interview discuss three important areas of a salesperson's job:

1. Differences between French and American salespeople

PSP: How do you see the differences between French salespeople and American salespeople?

Jean-Pierre Tricard: As you know, there are significant cultural differences between our two countries. For example, in our culture, the one thing that we tend to be afraid of is to talk about money. While the French are embarrassed to talk about how much money they make, Americans consider money as a concrete measure of success. In France, people who brag about how much money they make are looked on as thieves.

PSP: How does this impact a sales negotiation?

Tricard: When French salespeople get to the point of discussing the price, they start to panic. They literally don't know how to deal with that because they have not been trained to talk about money. In my opinion, American salespeople are better equipped to talk about price.

2. French salespeople focus on solving customer problems

PSP: Let's talk about the strong points of French salespeople.

Tricard: First, most French salespeople love their company. They tend to love their product more than their bosses give them credit for. They tend to work hard for their company. Also, they have a great desire to be well thought of by their clients.

PSP: How would you describe their relationship with their clients?

Tricard: They go out of their way to help a customer solve a problem even when the problem has nothing to do with the sale. In other words, their aim is to be of service. Salespeople in France see themselves more as the client's team. For example, if a reseller has an in-

ventory problem, the salesperson will help the customer move the inventory.

3. How Americans appear to the French

PSP: What is a difference in selling between the two countries?

Tricard: One difference would be that American salespeople are very direct. When you want something, you ask for it directly. In France, we're following different customs. We don't want to risk offending someone and we're afraid to show bad manners. As a result, we skirt the issues—we beat around the bush and it takes us much longer to make a request. Therefore, French salespeople tend to make more sales calls than necessary. They're often afraid of leading the prospect to the close.

PSP: So you are saying that American salespeople who sell to a French prospect should plan on spending more time . . .

Tricard: Yes, more time to listen to their clients, encouraging them to talk more, trying to get them relaxed and comfortable. French customers don't like to be pushed to a conclusion.[2]

Single- or multiple-product element choices may be presented to the prospect. The stereo salesperson says, "Would you prefer the single or multiple disc player for your car stereo system?" The Xerox Business Products salesperson asks, "Are you interested in buying or leasing our equipment?" The automobile salesperson asks, "Would you like to install a cellular telephone?"

This close is used widely when prospects have difficulty in making a decision or when they are not in the mood to buy. It is also effective as a second close. If, for example, the prospect says no to your first close because of difficulty in deciding whether or not to buy, you can close on minor points.

The T-Account or Balance-Sheet Close Was Ben Franklin's Favorite

The **T-account close** is based on the process that people use when they make a decision. Some sales trainers refer to it as the Benjamin Franklin close. In his *Poor Richard's Almanac,* Franklin said, "You know, I believe most of my life is going to be made up of making decisions about things. I want to make as many good ones as I possibly can." So, in deciding on a course of action, his technique was to take pencil and paper and draw a line down the center of the paper. On one side, he put all the pros and on the other side he put all the cons. If there were more cons than pros, he would not do something. If the pros outweighed the cons, then he felt it was a good thing to do; this was the correct decision.

This is the process a customer uses in making a buying decision, weighing the cons against the pros. At times, it may be a good idea to use this technique. Pros and cons, debits and credits, or to act and not to act are common column headings. For example, on a sheet of paper, the salesperson draws a large T, placing *to act* (asset) on the left side and *not to act* (liability) on the right side (debit and credit, in accounting terms). The salesperson reviews the presentation with the prospect, listing the positive features, advantages, and benefits the prospect likes on the left side and all negative points on the right. This shows that the product's benefits outweigh its liabilities, and it leads the prospect to conclude that now is the time to buy. If prospects make their own lists, the balance-sheet close is convincing. Here is an example:

Salesperson: Ms. Stevenson, here's a pad of paper and a pencil. Bear with me a minute and let's review what we have just talked about. Could you please draw a large T on the page and write "To Act" at the top on the left and "Not to Act" on the right? Now, you said you liked our fast delivery. Is that right?

To Act	Not to Act
Fast delivery	Narrow assortment
Good profit	
Good credit	

Prospect: Yes.

Salesperson: OK, please write down "fast delivery" in the To Act column. Great! You were impressed with our profit margin and credit terms. Is that right?

Prospect: Yes

Salesperson: OK, how about writing that down in the left-hand column? Now is there anything that could be improved?

Prospect: Yes, don't you remember? I feel you have a narrow assortment with only one style of broom and one style of mop. [Objection.]

Salesperson: Well, write that down in the right-hand column. Is that everything?

Prospect: Yes.

Salesperson: Ms. Stevenson, what in your opinion outweighs the other—the reason to act or not to act? [A trial close.]

Prospect: Well, the To Act column does. But it seems I need a better assortment of products. [Same objection again.]

Salesperson: We have found that assortment is not important to most people. A broom and mop are pretty much a broom and mop. They want a good quality product that looks good and that holds up continuously. Customers like our products' looks and quality. Aren't those good-looking products? [Trial close showing broom and mop.]

Prospect: They look OK to me. [Positive response—she didn't bring up assortment so assume you have overcome objection.]

Salesperson: Ms. Stevenson, I can offer you a quality product, fast delivery, excellent profit, and good credit terms. I'd like to suggest this: Buy one dozen mops and one dozen brooms for each of your 210 stores. However, let's consider this first: The XYZ chain found that our mops had excellent drawing power when advertised. Their sales of buckets and floor wax doubled. Each store sold an average of 12 mops. [He pauses, listens, and notices her reaction.] You can do the same thing.

Prospect: I'd have to contact the Johnson Wax salesperson and I really don't have the time. [A positive buying signal.]

Salesperson: Ms. Stevenson, let me help. I'll call Johnson's and get them to contact you. Also, I'll go see your advertising manager to schedule the ads. OK? [Assumptive close.]

Prospect: OK, go ahead, but this stuff had better sell.

Salesperson: [Smiling] Customers will flock to your stores [he's building a picture in her mind] looking for mops, polish, and buckets. Say, that reminds me, you will need a dozen buckets for each store. [Continuous-yes, keep talking.] I'll write up the order. [Assumptive.]

Some salespeople recommend that the columns of the T-account be reversed so that the Not to Act column is on the left and the To Act column is on the right. This allows the salesperson to discuss the reasons not to buy first, followed by the reasons to buy, ending the presentation on the positive side. This decision depends on a salesperson's preference.

Modified T-Account or Balance-Sheet Close

Some salespeople modify the T-account close by only listing reasons to act in one column. They do not want to remind the prospect of any negative reasons not to buy as they attempt to close the sale. This is similar to the continuous-yes close. The only difference is that the product benefits are written on a piece of paper.

This is a powerful sales tool because the prospects are mentally considering reasons to buy and not to buy anyway. Put the reasons out in the open so that you can participate in the decision-making process.

While this close can be used anytime, it is especially useful as a secondary or backup close. For example, if the summary close did not make the sale, use the T-account close. A contrary idea in the prospect's mind is like steam under pressure—explosive. So, when you remove the pressure by openly stating an objection, opposition vaporizes. An objection often becomes minor or disappears. Remember, however, if the customer says, "Well, I'm going to buy it," do not say, "Well, let's first look at the reasons not to buy." Instead, finalize the sale.

The Standing-Room-Only Close Gets Action

What happens if someone tells you that you cannot have something that you would like to have? You instantly want it! When you face an indecisive prospect or if you want to have the prospect purchase a larger quantity, indicate that if they do not act now they may *not* be able to buy in the future. Motivate the prospect to act immediately by using the **standing-room-only close:**

- I'm not sure if I have your size. Would you want them if I have them in stock?
- My customers have been buying all we can produce. I'm not sure if I have any left to sell you.
- Well, I know you are thinking of ordering *X* amount, but we really need to order (a larger amount) because we now have it in stock and I don't think we will be able to keep up with demand and fill your summer order.
- The cost of this equipment will increase 10 percent next week. Can I ship it today, or do you want to pay the higher price?

For the right product, person, and situation, this is an excellent close. Both retail and industrial salespeople can use this technique to get the prospects so excited that they cannot wait to buy. However, it should be used honestly. Prospects realize that factors such as labor strikes, weather, transportation, inflation, and inventory shortages could make it difficult to buy in the future. Do them a favor by encouraging them to buy now using the standing-room-only close.

The Probability Close

When the prospect gives the famous, I want to think it over objection, or some variation, try saying, "Ms. Prospect, that would be fine. I understand your desire to think it over, but let me ask you this—when I call you back next week, what is the probability, in percentage terms out of a total of 100, that you and I will be doing business?" Then pause, and don't say another word until the prospect speaks.

The prospect's response will be from three possible categories:

1. *More than 50 percent but less than 85 percent for buying.* If your prospects respond in this range, ask what the remaining percent is against buying, then pause and be silent. When you become skilled in this technique, you will see prospects blink as they focus on their real objections.

Many times, we hear that prospects want to think it over. It is not because they want to delay the decision; it is because they don't fully understand what bothers them. The **probability close** permits your prospects to focus on their real objections. Once you have a real objection, convert that objection with a persuasive sales argument.

2. *Above 85 percent but not 100 percent for buying.* If they're in this range, recognize that there is a minor probability against you. You might want to say, "As it is almost certain that we'll do business together, why wait until next week? Let's go ahead now; and if you decide in the next couple of days that you want to change your mind, I'll gladly tear up your order. Let's get a running start on this project together."

Your Prospect's Name Is a Powerful Closing Tool

Dale Carnegie, author of *How to Win Friends and Influence People,* taught his students, "If you remember my name, you pay me a subtle compliment; you indicate that I have made an impression on you." Your prospect's name is one of the most powerful closing tools because most of us are more interested in ourselves than anyone else.

Repeat your prospect's name several times—but don't overdo it—during your sales call. *Connect your prospect's name with the major benefit statements:*

■ "This automatic dialing feature, Jim, will save you a lot of time."

■ "Our warranty is designed to give you peace of mind, Susan."

Your prospect will not know that you are using a powerful psychological strategy referred to as *learned association* or *positive pairing.* If you have connected your prospect's name with three or four prominent product benefits, your customer will expect to hear something positive when you merely mention his or her name. When you approach the close, remember to use your prospect's name. Chances are that the sound of her or his name will again evoke positive feelings. By using this little-known secret of master sales closers, you will close any sale quickly.

When prospects indicate a high percentage of probability, you can use their statements as a lever to push them over the top.

3. *Less than 50 percent for buying.* This is a signal that there is little, if any, chance that you will ever close this particular sale. The only appropriate tactic is returning to square one and starting the reselling process. It is amazing how many professional salespeople in a closing situation expect the prospect to say 80–20 as a probability in their favor, and instead they hear "80–20 against."

The probability close permits prospects to focus on their objections. It allows the true or hidden objections to surface. The more prospects fight you and the less candid they are about the probability of closing, the less likely they will buy anything.

The Negotiation Close

Every sale is a negotiation. Most sales negotiations focus on two major themes: value and price. Customers often demand more value and lower prices. In their quest for more value at a lower cost, prospects often resort to unfair tactics and put heavy pressure on the salesperson. The purpose of a good sales **negotiation close** is not to haggle over who gets the larger slice of pie, but to find ways for everyone to have a fair deal. Both the buyer and seller should win. Here are two examples of a salesperson using a negotiation close:

■ If we could find a way in which we would eliminate the need for a backup machine and guarantee availability, would you be happy with this arrangement?

■ Why don't we compromise? You know I can't give you a discount, but I could defer billing until the end of the month. That's the best I can do. How does that sound?

When you hit a tennis ball over the net, the kind of spin put on the ball determines the type of return shot received. In a negotiation, the attitude that you project determines the attitude you receive. Be positive! Be helpful! Be concerned! Show your interest in helping the prospect.

The Technology Close

Picture this! You have just completed the discussion of your product, marketing plan, and business proposition. You summarize your product's main benefits to your customer. Now you bring out your laptop computer, placing it on the buyer's desk so she can see the screen or you prepare to project the computer screen onto the wall. Using graphs and bar charts, you show the buyer past purchases and sales trends. Then you call up your recommended purchase suggestion. If appropriate, you can show payment schedules considering different quantity discounts. This **technology close** is very impressive to buyers.

The exact use of technology in closing a sale depends on the type of product and customer you're selling. Without a doubt, incorporating technology into your presentation will help you close more prospects and customers.

PREPARE A MULTIPLE-CLOSE SEQUENCE

By keeping several difficult closes ready in any situation, you are in a better position to close more sales. Also, the use of a multiple-close sequence, combined with methods to overcome objections, enhances your chance of making a sale.

For example, you could begin with a summary close. Assuming the buyer says no, you could rephrase the objection and then use an alternative close. If again the buyer says no and would not give a reason, you could use the five-question sequence method for overcoming objections, repeating it two or three times.*

Exhibit 12–9 gives an example of a multiple-close sequence that was developed by Jane Martin, who works for an electrical wholesaler. Notice that she uses both methods to overcome objections and closing techniques. First, she uses the summary of benefits close and then waits for a response. Martin does not rush. She realizes it is a big decision and is prepared to handle resistance and ask for the order several times. The buyer is sending out green signals, so Martin does not stop; she continues to respond to the buyer.

Notice that the buyer finally gave the real reason for not buying when he said, "No. My supervisor will not let me buy anything." By professionally handling John's objections and politely continuing to close, Jane is in a position to talk with the real decision maker—John's boss.

CLOSE BASED ON THE SITUATION

Since different closing techniques work best for certain situations, salespeople often identify the common objections they encounter and develop specific closing approaches designed to overcome these objections. Exhibit 12–10 shows how different closing techniques are used to meet objections.

Assume, for example, that a buyer has a predetermined belief that a competitor's product is needed. The salesperson could use the T-account approach to show how a product's benefits are greater than a competitor's product. In developing the sales presentation, review your customer profile and develop your main closing technique and several alternatives. By being prepared for each sales call, you experience increased confidence and enthusiasm, which results in a more positive selling attitude. You can both help the customer and reach your goals.

*See Chapter 11 for correct procedures on overcoming objections.

EXHIBIT 12–9

Multiple closes incorporating
techniques for overcoming
objections

Salesperson: John, we have found that the Octron bulb will reduce your storage space
requirements for your replacement stock. It offers a higher color output for your designers, which
reduces their eye fatigue and shadowing. Should I arrange for delivery this week or next week?
[Close 1—Summary-of-benefits close.]

Buyer: Well, those are all good points, but I'm still not prepared to buy. It's too costly.

Salesperson: What you're saying is, "You want to know what particular benefits my product has
that make it worth its slightly higher price." Is that correct? [Rephrase as question.]

Buyer: Yes, I guess so.

Salesperson: Earlier, we saw that considering the extended life of the lamps and their energy
savings, you can save $375 each year by replacing your present lamps with GE Watt-Misers. This
shows, John, that you save money using our product. Right? [Trial close.]

Buyer: Yes, I guess you're right.

Salesperson: Great! Do you prefer installation this weekend or after regular business hours next
week? [Close 2—Alternative close.]

Buyer: Neither, I need to think about it more.

Salesperson: There must be some good reason why you're hesitating to go ahead now. Do you
mind if I ask what it is? [Question 1 in sequence.]

Buyer: I don't think I can afford new lighting all at one time.

Salesperson: In addition to that, is there another reason for not going ahead? [Question 2 in
sequence.]

Buyer: No.

Salesperson: Just supposing you could convince yourself that group replacement is less expensive
than spot replacement . . . then you'd want to go ahead with it? [Question 3.]

Buyer: I guess so.

Salesperson: Group replacement is not a necessity; however, it does allow you to realize
immediate energy savings on all of your fixtures. It saves you much of the labor costs of spot
replacement because the lamps are installed with production-line efficiency. See what I mean?
[Trial close.]

Buyer: Yes, I do.

Salesperson: Do you feel that installation would be better at night or on the weekend? [Close
3—Minor-points close.]

Buyer: I'd still like to think about it.

Salesperson: There must be another reason why you're hesitating to go ahead now. Do you mind if
I ask what it is? [Question 1.]

Buyer: We just don't have the money now to make that kind of investment.

Salesperson: In addition to that, is there any other reason for not going ahead? [Question 2.]

Buyer: No. My supervisor will not let me buy anything.

Salesperson: You agree you could save money for your company on this purchase—right?

Buyer: Yes.

Salesperson: Well, John, how about calling your supervisor now and telling her about how much
money we can save in addition to reducing your storage space and the eye fatigue of your
employees? Maybe both of us could visit your supervisor. [Close 4—Summary-of-benefits close.]

EXHIBIT 12-10

EXHIBIT 12-10

Examples of closing techniques based on situations

Situation \ Closing approach	Alternative	Compliment	Summary	Continuous-yes	Minor-points	Assumptive	T-account	Standing-room-only	Probability	Negotiation	Reason why
Customer is indecisive	X		X	X	X		X	X	X	X	Forces a decision
Customer is expert or egotistical		X					X		X	X	Lets expert make the decision
Customer is hostile		X		X					X	X	Positive strokes
Customer is a friend						X			X	X	You can take care of the small things
Customer has predetermined beliefs							X		X	X	Benefits outweigh disbeliefs
Customer is greedy, wants a deal								X	X	X	Buy now

RESEARCH REINFORCES THESE SALES SUCCESS STRATEGIES

While it is difficult to summarize all sales success strategies discussed throughout this book, one research report reinforces several key procedures that improve sales performance. This research sought to examine two key questions all salespeople frequently ask themselves: What makes one sales call a success and another a failure? Do salespeople make common mistakes that prevent success?

To answer questions such as these, Xerox Learning Systems enlisted a team of observers to monitor and analyze more than 500 personal sales calls of 24 different sales organizations. The products and services sold ranged from computers to industrial refuse disposal.

Mike Radick, the Xerox senior development specialist overseeing the study, stated that the average successful sales call was 33 minutes long. During that call, the salesperson asked an average of 13.6 questions and described 6.4 product benefits and 7.7 product features. Meanwhile, the customer described an average of 2.2 different needs, raised 1.0 objections, made 2.8 statements of acceptance, and asked 7.7 questions.

The observers noted that it does not seem to matter whether the salesperson is 28 or 48 years old, male or female, or has 2 or 20 years of experience. What matters is the ability to use certain skills and avoid common errors. These six common mistakes have prevented successful sales calls:

■ **Tells instead of sells; doesn't ask enough questions.** The salesperson does most of the talking. Instead of asking questions to determine a customer's interest, the salesperson charges ahead and rattles off product benefits. This forces the customer into the passive role of listening to details that may not be of interest. As a result, the customer becomes increasingly irritated.

For example, a person selling a computerized payroll system may tell a customer how much clerical time could be saved by using this service. However, if clerical time is not a concern, then the customer has no interest in learning how to reduce payroll processing time. On the other hand, the same customer may have a high need for more accurate recordkeeping and be extremely interested in the computerized reports generated by the system.

■ **Over-controls the call; asks too many closed-end questions.** This sales dialogue resembles an interrogation, and the customer has limited opportunities to express needs. The over-controlling salesperson steers the conversation to subjects the salesperson wants to talk about without regarding the customer. When the customer does talk, the salesperson often fails to listen or respond, or doesn't acknowledge the importance of what the customer says. As a result, the customer is alienated and the sales call fails.

■ **Doesn't respond to customer needs with benefits.** Instead, the salesperson lets the customer infer how the features will satisfy his or her needs. Consider the customer who needs a high-speed machine. The salesperson responds with information about heat tolerance, but doesn't link that to how fast the equipment manufactures the customer's product. As a result, the customer becomes confused, loses interest, and the call fails.

Research shows a direct relationship between the result of a call and the number of different benefits given in response to customer needs; the more need-related benefits cited, the greater the probability of success.

■ **Doesn't recognize needs; gives benefits prematurely.** For example, a customer discussing telephone equipment mentions that some clients complain that the line is always busy. The salesperson demonstrates the benefits of his answering service, but the customer responds that busy lines are not important since people will call back. In this case, the customer is not concerned enough to want to solve the problem.

■ **Doesn't recognize or handle negative attitudes effectively.** The salesperson fails to recognize customer statements of objection (opposition), indifference (no need), or skepticism (doubts). What isn't dealt with effectively remains on the customer's mind, and left with a negative attitude, the customer will not make a commitment. The research also shows that customer skepticism, indifference, and objection are three different attitudes. Each attitude affects the call differently; each one requires a different strategy for selling success.

■ **Makes weak closing statements; doesn't recognize when or how to close.** In one extreme case, the customer tried to close the sale on a positive note, but the salesperson failed to recognize the cue and continued selling until the customer lost interest. The lesson is that successful salespeople are alert to closing opportunities throughout the call.

The most powerful way to close a sales call involves a summary of benefits that interest the customer. Success was achieved in three out of four calls that included this closing technique in Radick's study.

KEYS TO IMPROVED SELLING

How is the bridge from average to successful salesperson made? Xerox found it involves learning and using each of the following skills:

■ Ask questions to gather information and uncover needs.

■ Recognize when a customer has a real need and how the benefits of the product or service can satisfy it.

■ Establish a balanced dialogue with customers.

■ Recognize and handle negative customer attitudes promptly and directly.

■ Use a benefit summary and an action plan requiring commitment when closing.[3]

Learn and use these five selling skills, use the other skills emphasized throughout the book, and develop your natural ability and a positive mental attitude to become a successful, professional salesperson.

THE BUSINESS PROPOSITION AND THE CLOSE

For some salespeople, the discussion of the business proposition provides an excellent opportunity to close. The business proposition, as discussed in Chapter 5, is the discussion of costs, markups, value analysis, or a return-on-investment (ROI) profit forecast. It follows the discussion of a product's FABs and marketing plan. Remember, the marketing plan explains:

1. For wholesalers or retailers, how they should resell the product.
2. For end users, how they can use the product.

The product's FABs and marketing plan justify your suggested order. The business proposition is the third step within the presentation and very important to closing the sale.*

Use a Visual Aid to Close

The use of the visual aid works well in discussing the business proposition and when closing. Immediately after discussing the marketing plan for Cap'n Crunch cereal, the salesperson pulls out the profit forecaster shown in Exhibit 12–11. Notice it is personalized by writing the account's name at the top.

The salesperson discusses each item on the profit forecaster. Then the salesperson says, "Based on your past sales, the profits you will earn, and our marketing plan, I suggest you buy 100 cases for your three stores." The suggested order is written on the profit forecaster.

Now the salesperson remains silent. The buyer will respond with either yes, no, or that is too much to buy. While waiting, the salesperson should mentally go over what to say for each response that can be made by the buyer.

WHEN YOU DO NOT MAKE THE SALE

A group of purchasing agents were asked their biggest gripes about poor sales procedure. One item on their list was this: "They [salespeople] seem to take it personally if they don't get the business, as though you owe them something because they are constantly calling on you."[4]

Although you should try, you cannot always sell everyone. When you have done the best you can to persuade prospects or customers to make a purchase, and they still will not buy or do what you wish, remember there is always tomorrow. Act as a professional, adult salesperson, and do not take the buyer's denial personally, but recognize it as a business decision that the buyer must make given the circumstances. Be courteous and cheerful; be grateful for the opportunity to discuss your product. See Exhibit 12–12.

The proper handling of a no-sale situation actually helps build a sound business relationship with your customers by developing a spirit of cooperation. Ask why you

*The three steps are discussed in Chapters 6 and 10.

EXHIBIT 12–11

Example of a personalized visual

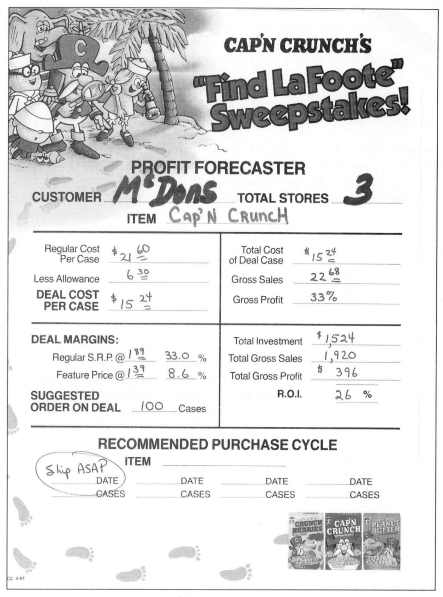

Using a visual is an excellent way to close. After discussing the financial information on the visual, close by suggesting what and how much should be ordered.

lost out. At the end of each day, review why you did or did not close the sale. Use this information to strengthen your presentation. Learn from your successes and your no-sales.

SUMMARY OF MAJOR SELLING ISSUES

Closing is the process of helping people make decisions that will benefit them. You help people make those decisions by asking them to buy. The close of the sale is the next logical sequence after your presentation. At this time, you finalize details of the sale (earlier, your prospect was convinced to buy). Constantly look and listen for

ETHICAL DILEMMA

I'll Buy If . . .

You have been seated in the president's office of a large bank in your town for an appointment you had worked six months to obtain.* The president begins your meeting by saying that he is in the market for more insurance and that he had spoken with one of your competitors earlier in the day.

After your presentation and proposal, you begin to close, and he tells you that he is convinced and you get the sale. But there is one condition. He will only accept a policy with preferred-nonsmoker rates. A dirty ashtray is on his desk, and he is obviously at least 25 pounds overweight. You know it is impossible to obtain preferred-nonsmoker rates for him if you complete the application truthfully. You also know your company relies on the information you send them when it underwrites the policy.

Purposely submitting false information on an application is grounds for agent termination. If the client dies during the policy's two-year contestable period, death benefits are reduced to the amount of premiums paid if the application had been submitted falsely.

However, if he dies you can say he told you he did not smoke. He also has to take a physical, so you can blame it on the doctor. This is a big sale, with high commissions. You know he will buy and that you can get away with falsifying the application. If you do not do it, someone else will.

What do you do?

*Developed by Richard T. Brown.

EXHIBIT 12–12

Sometimes the salesperson will not make the sale.

If this restaurant supplier had not made a sale, she would have left the door open for a return sales call by being just as friendly leaving as when she came.

buying signals from your prospect to know when to close. It is time to close the sale any time the prospect is ready, whether at the beginning or end of your presentation.

As you prepare to close the sale, be sure you have presented a complete story on your proposition and that your prospect completely understands your presentation. Tailor your close to each prospect's personality and see the situation from the prospect's viewpoint. Remember that you may make your presentation and close too early, which causes a prospect to say no instead of "I don't understand your proposition and I don't want to be taken advantage of." This is why you should never take the first no. It is another reason to use a trial close immediately before the close. But, no matter when or how you close, do so in a positive, confident, and enthusiastic manner to better serve your prospect and help reach your goals. Learn and abide by the 12 steps to a successful closing.

Plan and rehearse closing techniques for each prospect. Develop natural closing techniques or consider using closes such as the alternative, compliment, summary, continuous-yes, minor-decision, assumption, T-account, or the standing-room-only close. Consider the situation and switch from your planned close if your prospect's situation is different than anticipated.

A good closer has a strong desire to close each sale. Rarely should you accept the first no as the final answer. If you are professional, you should be able to close a minimum of three to five times.

Do not become upset or unnerved if a problem occurs when you are ready to close. Keep cool, determine any objections, overcome them, and try to close again— you can't make a sale until you ask for the order!

MEETING A SALES CHALLENGE

Lisa had finished her presentation. John and Ralph had not. At least Lisa was able to tell her whole story. John and Ralph should have postponed discussing price. They may have lost all hope of making the sale.

In all three cases, the prospect said, "Your price is too high." Many buyers learn or are trained to say this to see if the seller will decrease the price.

When the buyer said, "What's your price?" John could have said, "It will depend on the type of service you need and the quantity purchased. Let's discuss that in just a minute." When the buyer said, "Way out—your competitor's price is $10 cheaper!" John could say, "I quoted you our base price. Your actual price will depend upon the quantity purchased. We can meet and beat that price (the competitor's price)."

Lisa needs to find out more, such as what specific equipment and from whom. Equipment is different. So are service, terms, and delivery.

When Ralph's buyer says, "Your price is too high," he needs to find out, compared to what. Ralph's buyer may not need his top-of-the-line model. So he must get back to a discussion of the buyer's needs before determining the model and price.

KEY TERMS FOR SELLING

closing 343	minor-points close 354
buying signal 344	T-account close 356
alternative-choice close 351	standing-room-only close 358
assumptive close 352	probability close 358
compliment close 352	negotiation close 359
summary-of-benefits close 353	technology close 360
continuous-yes close 354	

SALES APPLICATION QUESTIONS

1. A salesperson must use a closing technique that is simple and straightforward, and ask the prospect only to buy rather than something in addition to buying. In which of the following examples, if any, is the salesperson suggesting something to the buyer that is a close, rather than something the buyer must do in addition to buying?

   a. If you have no objection, I'll go out to the warehouse now to see about reserving space for this new item.

       b. To get this promotion off right, we should notify each of your store managers. I've already prepared a bulletin for them. Should *I* arrange to have a copy sent to each manager, or do *you* want to do it?

       c. To start this promotion, we should notify each of your store managers. I've already prepared a bulletin for them. On my way out, I can drop it off with the secretary.

       d. We should contact the warehouse manager about reserving a space for this new item. Do you want to do it now or after I've left?

2. Buying signals have numerous forms. When you receive a buying signal, stop the presentation and move in to close the sale. For each of the following seven situations, choose the appropriate response to your prospect's buying signal that leads most directly to a close.

    a. "Can I get it in blue?" Your best answer is:
      (1) Yes.
      (2) Do you want it in blue?
      (3) It comes in three colors, including blue.

    b. "What's your price?" Your best answer is:
      (1) In what quantity?
      (2) To quote a specific price.
      (3) In which grade?

    c. "What kind of terms do you offer?" Your best answer is:
      (1) To provide specific terms.
      (2) Terms would have to be arranged.
      (3) What kind of terms do you want?

    d. "How big an order do I have to place to get your best price?" Your best answer is:
      (1) A schedule of quantity prices.
      (2) A specific-size order.
      (3) What size order do you want to place?

    e. "When will you have a new model?" Your best answer is:
      (1) A specific date.
      (2) Do you want our newest model?
      (3) This is our newest model.

    f. "What is the smallest trial order I can place with you?" Your best answer is:
      (1) A specific quantity.
      (2) How small an order do you want?
      (3) A variety of order sizes.

    g. "When can you deliver?" Your best answer is:
      (1) That depends on the size of your order. What order size do you have in mind?
      (2) A specific delivery date.
      (3) When do you want delivery?

3. Which of the following is the most frequently committed sin in closing? Why?
    a. Asking for the order too early.
    b. Not structuring the presentation toward a closing.
    c. Not asking for the order.

4. Is a good closing technique to ask the customer outright (but at the right time), "Well, how about it? May I have the factory ship you a carload?" Why do you agree or disagree?

5. After completing a presentation that has included all of your product's features, advantages, and benefits, do not delay in asking the customer, "How much of the product do you wish to order?" Is this statement true or false? Why?

6. Each visual aid used during your presentation is designed to allow the customer to say yes to your main selling points. What should your visual aids include that allows you to gauge customer interest and help move to the close? What are several examples?

7. "Now, let's review what we've talked about. We've agreed that the Mohawk's secondary backing and special latex glue make the carpet more durable and contribute to better appearance. In addition, you felt that our direct-to-customer delivery system would save a lot of money and time. Shall I send our wall-sample display or would you be interested in stocking some 9 by 12's?"

   a. The salesperson's closing statement helps ensure customer acceptance by doing which of the following:
      (1) Summarizing benefits that the customer agreed were important.
      (2) Giving an alternative.
      (3) Assuming that agreement has been reached.

   b. The salesperson ends the closing statement by:
      (1) Asking if the customer has any other questions.
      (2) Asking if the product will meet the customer's requirements.
      (3) Requesting a commitment from the customer.

8. "Assuming agreement has been reached" reflects the kind of attitude you should project when making a closing statement. When you make a close, nothing you say should reflect doubt, hesitation, or uncertainty. Which of the following salesperson's remarks assume agreement?

   a. If you feel that Munson is really what you want.
   b. Let me leave you two today and deliver the rest next week.
   c. Well, if you purchase.
   d. Well, it looks as if maybe.
   e. We've agreed that.
   f. When you purchase the X-7100.
   g. Why don't you try a couple, if you like.

9. A good rule is, "Get the order and get out." Do you agree? Why?

10. The real estate salesperson is showing property to a couple who look at the house and say, "Gee, this is great. They've taken good care of this place and the rugs and drapes are perfect. Do you think they'd be willing to leave the rugs and drapes?" What should the salesperson do or say? Why?

SALES WORLD WIDE WEB EXERCISES

Research Helps You Be a Better Closer!

Pick a good or service of your schools to sell to someone or an organization. Selling advertisements or tickets to events on campus, or getting contributions are examples of products to sell. Choose a prospect—someone or some organization that might buy what you are selling. Using the appropriate URLs and your school's library, research the prospect. Begin your research by reviewing the Sales World Wide Web Directory for appropriate URLs.

Write a report to your boss on the sources and URLs you found useful in planning your sales presentation. Be sure and include how you would ask for the order, including what to buy and the quantity.

FURTHER EXPLORING THE SALES WORLD

1. Assume you are interviewing for a sales job and there are only five minutes remaining. You are interested in the job and know if the company is interested, they will invite you for a visit to their local distribution center and have you work with

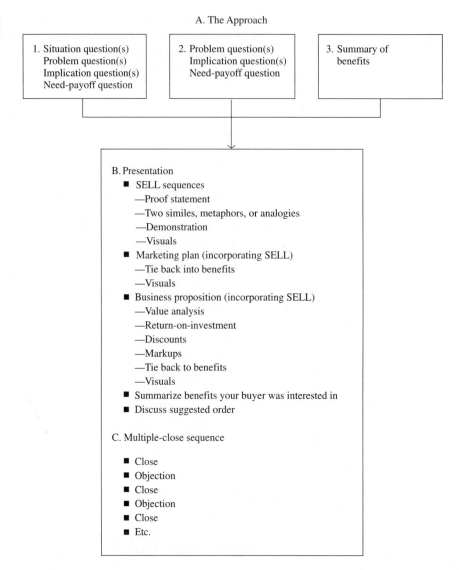

EXHIBIT A

Format of your sales
presentation

A. The Approach

1. Situation question(s)
   Problem question(s)
   Implication question(s)
   Need-payoff question

2. Problem question(s)
   Implication question(s)
   Need-payoff question

3. Summary of
   benefits

B. Presentation
- SELL sequences
  —Proof statement
  —Two similes, metaphors, or analogies
  —Demonstration
  —Visuals
- Marketing plan (incorporating SELL)
  —Tie back into benefits
  —Visuals
- Business proposition (incorporating SELL)
  —Value analysis
  —Return-on-investment
  —Discounts
  —Markups
  —Tie back to benefits
  —Visuals
- Summarize benefits your buyer was interested in
- Discuss suggested order

C. Multiple-close sequence

- Close
- Objection
- Close
- Objection
- Close
- Etc.

one of their salespeople for a day. What are several closing techniques you could use to ask for the visit?

2. Visit several retail stores or manufacturing plants in your local area and ask their purchasing agents what they like and do not like about the closing when they are contacted by salespeople. See if they have already decided to buy or not to buy before the salesperson closes. Ask how a salesperson should ask for their business.

3. Develop a complete sales presentation that can be given in eight minutes. Include the buyer-seller dialogue. Make sure the appropriate components in Exhibit A are contained in the presentation. Use one of the three approaches shown in Exhibit A depending on your situation. For example, use the SPIN approach if this is the first time you have called this prospect. Use the SPIN or summary-of-benefits approach if this is a repeat sales call on a prospect or customer.

Your presentation must use several SELL sequences and should contain a minimum of one proof statement; two similes, metaphors, or analogies; and a demonstration of important benefits. The marketing plan also must incorporate one or more SELL sequences that tie the marketing plan back to the information uncovered in the approach and the first SELL sequence.

The business proposition is last and contains the appropriate discussion on price and value. Relate the business proposition to the information uncovered earlier in the presentation. Develop visuals for presenting your benefits, marketing plan, and business proposition. Anywhere within the presentation prior to the close, use a minimum of one objection and answer one of the buyer's questions with a question.

Now, ask for the order using a summary-of-benefits close that includes a suggested order if appropriate for your product or service. Use a minimum of three closes. This requires you to develop a *multiple-close sequence* since the buyer has raised an objection or asked for more information after each close. Use three different closes, the first being the summary-of-benefits close. Also, use different methods of handling objections. In the presentation, be sure to: (1) have a professional appearance; (2) firmly shake hands and use direct eye contact before and after the presentation; (3) project positive nonverbal signs; and (4) use a natural level of enthusiasm and excitement in conversation.

STUDENT APPLICATION LEARNING EXERCISES (SALES)

(Part 7 of 7)

Now it's time to ask for the order! Frequently, questions and objections arise when you ask someone to buy. Thus, you should anticipate questions and/or objections and be prepared to use several different closing and objections-handling techniques. To make **Sale 7**

1. List the main benefits discussed in your presentation.

2. Select a closing technique, such as the summary-of-benefits close on pages 353–354. Write out your close and label it with the name of the closing technique in parentheses. Use a trial close after completing the close to verify these are important benefits to the buyer. Write out your trial close and label it using parentheses as shown on page 353 (trial close).

3. Create a visual aid showing your suggested order. See page 365 for an example. This visual aid may be similar to the same one you developed for discussing your price(s).

4. Now you are ready to construct your multiple-closing sequence. First carefully study Exhibit 12–3 on page 345. Now look at the example of a multiple-closing sequence on page 361. The multiple-closing sequence should be composed of the following:

   a. Your summary-of-benefits close.

   b. Your trial close.

   c. Your suggested order.

   d. Use the assumptive or alternative close.

   e. Have the buyer ask a question or give an objection.

   f. Respond using another objection-handling technique.

   g. Ask a trial close to see if you successfully handled the objection.

      h. Ask for the order again using an unused closing technique. Don't be pushy. Use a calm, laid-back, friendly conversational style.

      i. The close–objection–close–objection sequence can be repeated if appropriate.

5. To complete **Sale 7,** write up the above *a–i* in a script format. Role-play this dialogue until it sounds natural to you. This may require replacing the used techniques with new ones. Once the manuscript is finalized, type it and turn it in to your instructor.

CASE 12–1

Skaggs Omega

Skaggs Omega, a large chain of supermarkets, has mailed you an inquiry on hardware items. They want to know about your hammers, screwdrivers, and nails. On arrival, you make a presentation to the purchasing agent, Linda Johnson. You state that you had visited several of their stores. You discuss your revolving retail display, which contains an assortment of the three items Johnson had mentioned in her inquiry, and relate the display's advantages and features to benefits for Skaggs.

During your presentation, Johnson has listened but has said little and has not given you any buying signals. However, it appears she is interested. She did not object to your price nor did she raise any other objections.

You approach the end of the presentation and it is time to close. Actually, you have said everything you can think of.

Questions

1. What is the best way to ask Johnson for the order?

    a. How do you like our products, Ms. Johnson?

    b. What assortment do you prefer, the A or B assortment?

    c. Can we go ahead with the order?

    d. If you'll just OK this order form, Ms. Johnson, we'll have each of your stores receive a display within two weeks.

2. Discuss the remaining alternatives from Question 1, ranking them from good to bad, and state what would happen if a salesperson responded in that manner.

CASE 12–2

Central Hardware Supply

Sam Gillespie, owner of Central Hardware Supply, was referred to you by a mutual friend. Gillespie was thinking of dropping two of their product suppliers of home-building supplies. "The sale should be guaranteed," your friend had stated.

Your friend's information was correct and your presentation to Gillespie convinces you that he will benefit from buying from you. He comments as you conclude the presentation: "Looks like your product will solve our problem. I'd like to think this over, however. Could you call me tomorrow or the next day?"

Questions

1. The best way to handle this is to:

    a. Follow his suggestion.

    b. Ignore his request and try a second close.

c. Probe further. You might ask: "The fact that you have to think this over suggests that I haven't convinced you. Is there something I've omitted or failed to satisfy you with?"

2. What would be your second and third choices? Why?

CASE 12–3

Furmanite Service Company—A Multiple-Close Sequence

Chris Henry sells industrial valves and flanges, plus tapes and sealants. He is calling on Gary Maslow, a buyer from Shell Oil, to sell him on using Furmanite to seal all of his plant's valve and flange leaks. Chris has completed the discussion of the product's features, advantages, and benefits, plus the marketing plan and the business proposition. Chris feels it is time to close. Chris says:

Salesperson: Let me summarize what we have talked about. You have said that you like the money you will save by doing the repairs. You also like our response time in saving the flanges so that they can be rebuilt when needed. Finally, you like our three-year warranty on service. Is that right?

Buyer: Yes, that is about it.

Salesperson: Gary, I suggest we get a crew in here and start repairing the leaks. What time do you want the crew here Monday?

Buyer: Not so fast—how reliable is the compound?

Salesperson: Gary, it's very reliable. I did the same service for Mobil last year and we have not been back for warranty work. Does that sound reliable to you?

Buyer: Yeah, I guess so.

Salesperson: I know you always make experienced, professional decisions, and I know that you think this is a sound and profitable service for your plant. Let me schedule a crew to be here next week or maybe in two weeks.

Buyer: Chris, I am still hesitant.

Salesperson: There must be a reason why you are hesitating to go ahead now. Do you mind if I ask what it is?

Buyer: I just don't know if it is a sound decision.

Salesperson: Is that the only thing bothering you?

Buyer: Yes, it is.

Salesperson: Just suppose you could convince yourself that it's a good decision. Would you then want to go ahead with the service?

Buyer: Yes, I would.

Salesperson: Gary, let me tell you what we have agreed on so far. You like our online repair because of the cost you would save, you like our response time and the savings you would receive from the timely repair of the leaks, and you like our highly trained personnel and our warranty. Right?

Buyer: Yes, that's true.

Salesperson: When would you like to have the work done?

Buyer: Chris, the proposition looks good, but I don't have the funds this month. Maybe we can do it next month.

Salesperson: No problem at all, Gary; I appreciate your time, and I will return on the fifth of next month to set a time for a crew to start.

Questions

1. Label each of the selling techniques used by Chris.
2. What were the strengths and weaknesses of this multiple-closing sequence?
3. Should Chris have closed again? Why?
4. Assume Chris felt he could make one more close. What could he do?

13

Service and Follow-up for Customer Retention

LEARNING OBJECTIVES

Providing service to the customer is extremely important in today's competitive marketplace. After studying this chapter, you should be able to:

■ State why service and follow-up are important to increasing sales.

■ Discuss how follow-up and service result in account penetration and improved sales.

■ List the eight steps involved in increasing sales to your customer.

■ Explain the importance of properly handling customers' returned goods requests and complaints in a professional manner.

As a construction machinery salesperson, you know that equipment malfunctions and breakdowns are costly to customers. Your firm, however, has an excellent warranty that allows you to replace a broken piece of equipment with one of your demonstrators for a few days while the equipment is repaired. King Masonry has called you four times in the past three months because the mixer you sold them has broken down. Each time you have cheerfully handled the problem, and in less than two hours they have been back at work. Your company's mixer has traditionally been one of the most dependable on the market, so after the last breakdown, you let King Masonry keep the new replacement in hopes of solving any future problems.

The owner, Eldon King, has just called to tell you the newest mixer has broken down. He is angry and says he may go to another supplier if you cannot get him a replacement immediately.

If you were the salesperson, how would you handle this situation?

The last but not least cliché applies to this chapter, which ends our discussion of the elements of the selling process. Customer retention, service, and follow-up are important to the success of a salesperson in today's competitive markets. This chapter discusses the importance of follow-up and service, ways of keeping customers, methods of helping them increase sales, and how to handle customer complaints. It ends by emphasizing the need to act as a professional when servicing accounts.

SUPER SALESPEOPLE DISCUSS SERVICE

Providing service after the sale to customers is important, no matter what type of company, product, or service you represent. To illustrate the importance of service to the professional salesperson, three of America's greatest salespeople discuss the importance of service in selling real estate, steel, and information systems.

Rich Port built a successful real estate business in Chicago on service. As he explains:

> In most fields, a salesperson can offer the customer a product that has some differences from competitive products. But when we sell a residential property, we're often selling the same product that the buyer can purchase from the real estate office down the street. So, for us to offer something better, we must give more service. The key to success in the real estate business is service.[1]

In discussing service, Mike Curto, a retired group vice president of a large steel company, says:

> You're got to realize that what we're selling isn't a whole lot different from what our competitor can produce. In steel, we take some iron ore, refine it, and eventually end up with a product of a semifinished nature . . . we have to sell *service*. Our salesperson must convince the customer that we're the best in our industry, and that over the long run, the customer is better off doing business with us.
>
> A salesperson has to develop a customer's confidence; the customer must believe that U.S. Steel products are not only equal to what the competition sells, but are the best that can be produced in that particular line. And the salesperson better be sure that the products are as good as stated, because the salesperson will be calling on that customer many times throughout the year.[2]

These men stated that their service or product is similar to ones offered by the competition. What about a product like computers, sold by companies such as IBM and Apple? Francis G. "Buck" Rogers, a recent vice president of marketing for IBM, believes one of the keys to success at IBM is service. He says:

> IBM means service. With IBM, nothing is successfully sold until it's successfully installed. Now, the salesperson goes through the installation phase, including educating the customer, teaching people how the products will actually perform, and showing them how to properly apply the product. Finally, the equipment is delivered; this can be almost a year later. At any rate, that's the installation phase of the sale.
>
> Beyond that, we take it much further. We're dealing with customers on a continual basis, for example, trying to find new applications to further justify the equipment. At IBM, we're often leasing a fairly expensive piece of equipment, and unless we continue to give customers the best possible service, always looking out for their best interests, we're taking the risk of losing them.[3]

Based on statements from these successful sales-oriented individuals alone, it is easy to see the importance of customer service before, after, and between sales. Providing excellent service is an important part of building relationships. Before discussing how to build relationships, let's review.

RELATIONSHIP MARKETING AND CUSTOMER RETENTION

Chapter 1 discussed these three levels of customer relationship marketing:

- *Transaction selling:* a customer is sold and not contacted again.
- *Relationship selling:* after the purchase the seller finds out if the customer is satisfied and has future needs.
- *Partnering:* the seller works continually to improve the customer's operations, sales, and profits.

Relationship marketing is a creation of customer loyalty and retention. Organizations use combinations of products, prices, distribution, promotions, and service to achieve this goal. Relationship marketing is based on the idea that important customers need continuous attention.

An organization using relationship marketing is not seeking simply a sale or a transaction. It has targeted a major customer that it would like to sell now and in the future. The company would like to demonstrate to the customer that it has the capabilities to serve the account's needs in a superior way, particularly if a *committed relationship* can be formed. The company's goal is to get customers and more important, to retain customers. Customer relationship marketing provides the key to retaining customers.

THE PRODUCT AND ITS SERVICE COMPONENT

When a customer buys a product, what is being purchased? A **product** (good or service) is a bundle of tangible and intangible attributes, including packaging, color, and brand, plus the services and even the reputation of the seller. People buy more than a set of physical attributes. They buy want-satisfaction such as what the product does, its quality, and the image of owning the product.

Please note the phrase *plus the services.* Buyers usually believe an organization ought to deliver a certain level of service to the customers when they purchase something. Here are several expected services:

Israel—The Home Court Advantage

Rita Hunter was sent to Israel during the 1994 peace process to establish a beachhead for her company in a region that finally seemed prepared to live up to its market potential.

After two weeks and three broken appointments at one company, she had begun to wonder if she would ever get her foot in the door. The next day she mentioned the problem to a local friend of hers, Sarit; she was surprised when Sarit called back to say that the appointment was set up for the following week. Hunter asked Sarit how she had arranged the appointment; Sarit explained her husband served in the same reserve unit as a manager at her target company. This manager set up the appointment for Hunter; and because the request came from in-house, the appointment was kept.

Getting an appointment in Israel is not always this easy. However, given the geographical density, close family ties, local friendliness, military reserve duty, and work force mobility, sometimes it is not too difficult to find somebody to act as a contact in an organization, either to set up an appointment or to find out who can set up the appointment.

Most Israelis are very social and friendly people. Their desire to be helpful enables them to assist others just for the intrinsic satisfaction of being able to help. They tend to make everybody's business their own, so that they can offer a solution. Perhaps one of the key reasons for this is the feeling that all Israelis face the same problems, and if they can't help each other, who else will help? On the other hand, their generosity and courtesy are not always extended to foreigners; thus a local contact can ease the difficulty.

Not everyone, however, is willing to act as a go-between because this implicitly suggests an obligation. Although Israelis will usually go out of their way for friends, making friends locally is not always easy for a foreigner. Finding the right contact can sometimes consume more time than it is worth, and salespeople are encouraged to try the frontal approach as well.[4]

- Product—the product purchased has no defects.
- Price—fair value for the price.
- Place—the product is available when and where needed and promised.
- Promotion—correct, honest information in advertisements, from salespeople, and on product labels.
- Exchange transaction—handled correctly, quickly, and professionally the first time.
- After the sale—warranty honored, repairs or exchanges made cheerfully; written information or company representative available to discuss how to put together, hook-up, or use the product.

When buying something, you have certain expectations of what you are receiving for your money. So do organizations. Did the customer receive what was expected? The answer to this question determines the level of service quality perceived by the buyer.

Customer service refers to the activities and programs provided by the seller to make the relationship satisfying for the customer. The activities and programs add value to the customer's relationship with the seller. Warranties, credit, speedy delivery, invoices, financial statements, computer-to-computer ordering, parking, gift wrapping, and not being out of stock are services designed to satisfy customers.

Expectations Determine Service Quality

The quality of service provided by an organization and its salespeople must be based on its customers' expectations. Customers expect a certain level of service from the seller. Their expectations frequently are based on information provided by the salesperson, past experiences, word of mouth, and personal needs.

EXHIBIT 13-1

Customer retention: when the buyer is satisfied with purchases over time

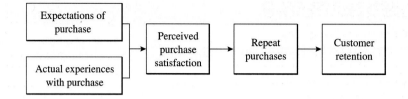

When buyers perceive service received as what they expected, they are satisfied. Thus, service quality must match the customers' perception of how well the service provided meets their expectations.

CUSTOMER SATISFACTION AND RETENTION

Customer satisfaction also relates to met expectations. **Customer satisfaction** refers to feelings toward the purchase. As illustrated in Exhibit 13–1, perceived purchase satisfaction is the customer's feelings about any differences between what is expected and actual experiences with the purchase. If satisfied, chances of selling the customer in the future increase. If satisfied with repeat purchases, customers tend to continue to buy from the salesperson.

Satisfaction can result in a customer so loyal that it is very difficult for another seller to get the business. Thus, customer retention is critical to a salesperson's long-run success.

EXCELLENT CUSTOMER SERVICE AND SATISFACTION REQUIRE TECHNOLOGY

Providing good service to customers in today's competitive marketplace is not enough—service must be excellent. To do this often requires technology and automation. Here is an example of how companies are improving customer service.[5]

For the Livingston Group, a Toronto-based logistics company that sells such services as freight-forwarding and distribution to importers and exporters, the question was how to spend no more than $80,000 to make their eight salespeople more effective in working with their customers. The division's goals were (1) to make account executives accessible to customers and each other no matter where they were; (2) to create presentations on the road that could be shared internally; and (3) to be sure account executives could manage their accounts effortlessly and easily while eliminating the administrative tasks that take up considerable selling time.

InteGain set up the following integrated application for Livingston Group: Each account executive received an IBM Thinkpad, loaded by GoldMine for Windows Software (produced by ELAN Software Corporation of Pacific Palisades, California), Microsoft Windows for WorkGroups 3.11, WinFax Pro 4.0, and WinCIM (which allows access to CompuServe). They each also received a Hewlett-Packard DeskJet portable printer and a Nokia portable telephone. Each account executive was equipped with the MyLine telephone service from Call America Business Communications based in San Luis Obispo, California. This service provides account executives with their own 800 numbers and directly connects inbound calls to them wherever they are via their portable or home office phones.

The program works like this: At the end of each business day, account executives use their laptops to send new data or presentations collected and created during the day to a CompuServe mailbox. As part of an automated process, a system at Livingston Trade Technologies' home office automatically dials into this CompuServe

EXHIBIT 13-2

Sales come from present and new customers. Salespeople are constantly involved in follow-up and service, plus planning their next sales call on the customer: they also spend time prospecting.

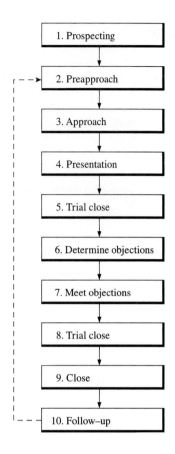

mailbox, retrieves the uploaded information, consolidates it, prepares reports, and redistributes the consolidated information to each of the executives in several minutes. InteGain's integrated application is called TARGET.

Automating allows salespeople to work independently out of their cars and to spend less time on administrative tasks. And, because management is kept informed, it can make quick decisions on facts relating to customer service.

SO, HOW DOES SERVICE INCREASE YOUR SALES?

Take a look at Exhibit 13–2. By now you are very familiar with it! Now what's the answer to the heading question?

You—the salesperson—increase sales by obtaining new customers and selling more products to present customers. What is the best method for obtaining new customers? For many types of sales, customer referrals are best! Customers provide referrals when they are satisfied with the salesperson. So how important is it to your success and livelihood to take care of your customers? Even though it is last in the selling process, step 10 is extremely important to a salesperson's success.

As illustrated in Exhibit 13–2, after step 10 of the selling process the salesperson moves back to the second step, or preapproach, when it's time to plan the next sales call on a customer. Meanwhile, the salesperson also is prospecting, as discussed in Chapter 6. Thus, the salesperson is involved in the ongoing process of finding new customers and taking care of present customers. With this review in mind, let's discuss service and follow-up techniques next.

Follow-up calls can be productive.

Here, a sales rep follows up his sale with tips for additional uses for the product, and also answers questions.

TURN FOLLOW-UP AND SERVICE INTO A SALE

High-performing salespeople can convert follow-up and service situations into sales (see Exhibit 13–3). Jack Pruett of Bailey, Banks & Biddle, a jewelry retailer, gives several examples:

I send customers a thank-you card immediately after the sale, and after two weeks, I call again to thank them and see if they are pleased with their purchase. If the purchase is a gift, I wait on contacting the customer or contact the spouse. This has been a key to my success in building a relationship and in farming or prospecting. Very often I get a lead.

Here is how it works. In two weeks they have shown it around to someone who has made a comment. I start with, "Is everything OK?" Then I say, "Well, I know Judy [or Jack] is real proud of it, and I'm sure she's [he's] shown it to someone—parents, family, friends. I was curious if there is anyone I could help who is interested in something. I'd like to talk to them or have you call and see if they'd like me to call them." If I've done a good job, the customer feels good about letting me call this individual and will help me. If I wait too long to call, they say, "Well, someone was asking about it, but I've forgotten who it was."

My biggest sale to a single customer was $120,000. It took about two weeks. A man initially called asking for 12 diamonds to give 2 stones to each of his children. In handling this, I found some other pieces I felt were good for him—a ruby ring, a 4.62 sapphire ring, a gold and diamond bracelet, and two other rings. He bought everything. Thus, much of my success comes from follow-ups, suggestion selling [when someone comes in for something and they buy other things], or service situations. Once you realize you can turn routine situations into sales, retail selling becomes exciting and challenging.[6]

Pruett realizes follow-up and service help satisfy the needs of his customers. Another way to help customers involves account penetration.

ACCOUNT PENETRATION IS A SECRET TO SUCCESS

Follow-up and service create goodwill between a salesperson and the customer, which increases sales faster than a salesperson who does not provide such service. By contacting the customer after the sale to see that the maximum benefit is derived from the purchase, a salesperson lays the foundation for a positive business relationship. Emmett Reagan of Xerox says:

Remember that there is still much work to be done after making the sale. Deliveries must be scheduled, installation planned, and once the system is operational, we must monitor to assure that our product is doing what is represented. This activity gives us virtually

SELLING TIPS

Can Someone Please Help Me?

Customer: May I speak to Frank, please? I want to reorder.

Supplier: Frank isn't with us anymore. May someone else help you?

Customer: What happened to Frank? He has all my specs; I didn't keep a record.

Supplier: Let me give you Roger; he's taken over Frank's accounts.

Customer: Roger, you don't know me, but maybe Frank filled you in. I want to reorder.

Salesperson: You want to reorder what?

Customer: I want to repeat the last order, but increase your number 067 to 48.

Salesperson: What else was in the order?

Customer: Frank had a record of it. It's got to be in his file.

Salesperson: Frank isn't here anymore, and I don't have his records.

Customer: Who does?

Salesperson: I don't know. I'm new here, so you'll have to fill me in on your requirements. Are you a new customer?

Customer: Does four years make me new?

Salesperson: Well, sir, you are new to me. How long ago did you place your order?

Customer: Last month.

Salesperson: What day last month?

Customer: I don't remember; Frank always kept track of it. Maybe I could speak to the sales manager?

Salesperson: You mean Mort?

Customer: No, I think his name is Sam.

Salesperson: Sam left us about the same time as Frank. I can ask Mort to call you, but I'm sure he doesn't have your file either.

Customer: Roger, have you ever heard that your best prospect is your present customer?

Salesperson: Is that true?

Customer: I don't think so.

Multiply this conversation by the millions of times it happens each year, and you have the biggest deterrent to sales in America.

unlimited access to the account, which moves us automatically back to the first phase of the cycle. We now have the opportunity to seek out new needs, develop them, and find new problems that require solutions. Only this time, it's a lot easier because, by now, we have the most competitive edge of all, a satisfied customer.[7]

The ability to work and contact people throughout the account, discussing your products, is referred to as *account penetration.* Successful penetration of an account allows you to properly service that account by uncovering its needs and problems. Achieving successful account penetration is dependent on knowledge of that account's key personnel and their situation. If you do not have a feel for an account's situation, you reduce chances of maximizing sales in that account.

Tailor the presentation to meet buyers' objectives and benefit them. By knowing your buyers, their firms, and other key personnel, you uncover their needs or problems and develop a presentation that fulfills the needs or solves the problems. Account penetration is determined by:

- Your total and major-brand sales growth in an account.
- Distribution of the number of products in a product line, including sizes used or merchandised by an account.
- Level of cooperation obtained, such as reduced resale prices, shelf space, advertising and display activity, discussion with their salespeople, and freedom to visit with various people in the account.
- Your reputation as the authority on your type of merchandise for the buyer.

As a general rule, the greater your account penetration, the greater your chances of maximizing sales within the account. Earning the privilege to move around the account freely allows you to better uncover prospect needs and to discuss your products with people throughout the firm. As people begin to know you and believe that you are there to help, they allow you to take action that ultimately increases sales, such as increasing shelf space or talking with the users of your industrial equipment in the account's manufacturing facilities. A good sign that you have successfully penetrated an account is when a competitor dismally says, "Forget that account; it's already sewn up." You have created true customer loyalty.

SERVICE CAN KEEP YOUR CUSTOMERS

You work days, weeks, and sometimes months to convert prospects into customers. What can you do to ensure that they buy from you in the future? After landing a major account, consider these six factors:

1. Concentrate on improving your account penetration. As discussed earlier, account penetration is critical in uncovering prospect needs or problems and consistently recommending effective solutions through purchasing your products. This allows you to demonstrate that you have a customer's best interests at heart and are there to help.

2. Contact new accounts frequently on a regular schedule. In determining the frequency of calls, consider:

- Present sales and/or potential future sales to the account.
- Number of orders expected in a year.
- Number of product lines sold to the account.
- Complexity, servicing, and redesign requirements of the products purchased by the account.

Since the amount of time spent servicing an account may vary from minutes to days, be flexible in developing a call frequency for each customer. Typically, invest sales time in direct proportion to the actual or potential sales represented by each account. The most productive number of calls is reached at the point where additional calls do not increase sales to the customer. This relationship of sales volume to sales calls is referred to as the *response function* of the customer to the salesperson's calls.

3. Handle customers' complaints promptly. This is an excellent opportunity to prove to customers that they and their businesses are important, and that you sincerely care about them. The speed with which you handle even the most trivial complaint shows the value you place on that customer.

4. Always do what you say you will do. Nothing destroys a relationship with a customer faster than not following through on promises. Promises made and subsequently broken are not tolerated by professional buyers. They have placed their faith (and sometimes reputation) in you by purchasing your products, so you must be faithful to them to ensure future support.

5. Provide service as you would to royalty. By providing your client with money-saving products and problem-solving ideas, you can become almost indispensable. You are an advisor to listen to rather than an adversary to haggle with. Provide all possible assistance. As State Farm insurance agent Catherine Irons says in Exhibit 13–4, "We're there to help."

EXHIBIT 13–4

Advertising helps inform customers of the service provided by salespeople.

COMMON QUESTION. UNCOMMON ANSWER.

Q
Where can you find an insurance agent who delivers personal service?

A
"State Farm agents back everything they sell with personal service. We help you get your coverages up-to-date with our Family Insurance Checkup. As your needs change, we help keep you up-to-date with the checkup. All the advice is free, any decisions are yours. And when you have a claim, you call us. One-to-one service is what we're all about."
—Agent Catherine Irons

Like a good neighbor, State Farm is there.®

State Farm Insurance Companies
Home Offices: Bloomington, Il.

6. Show your appreciation. A buyer once said to a salesperson, "I'm responsible for putting the meat and potatoes on your table." Customers contribute to your success, and in return, you must show appreciation. Thank them for their business and do them favors. Here are several suggestions:

- Although you may be hundreds of miles away, phone immediately whenever you've thought of something or seen something that may solve one of your customer's problems. See Exhibit 13–5.
- Mail clippings that may interest your customers even if the material has no bearing on what you're selling. They could be items from trade journals, magazines, newspapers, or newsletters.
- Write congratulatory notes to customers who have been elected to office, promoted to higher positions, given awards, and so on.
- Send newspaper clippings about your customers' families such as marriages, births, and activities.
- Send holiday or special-occasion cards. If you limit yourself to just one card for the entire year, send an Easter card, Fourth of July card, or a Thanksgiving card. This makes a big impression on customers.
- Send annual birthday cards. To start this process, subtly discover when your prospects were born.
- Prepare and mail a brief newsletter, perhaps quarterly, that keeps customers informed on important matters.
- Fax information to prospects and buyers. See Exhibit 13–5.

EXHIBIT 13–5

Two fast and inexpensive tools for customer follow-up and service are the fax machine and the telephone.

These are just a few of the many practical, down-to-earth ways you can remember customers. The important point is to personalize whatever you send.

Specifically, it doesn't take much thought, energy, or time to send a card, newspaper clipping, or copy of an article. The secret of impressing customers is to personalize the material with a couple of sentences in your handwriting. Be sure it's legible!

YOU LOSE A CUSTOMER—KEEP ON TRUCKING

All salespeople suffer losses, either through the loss of a sale or an entire account to a competitor. Four things can win back a customer.

1. Visit and investigate. Contact the buyer and your friends within the account to determine why the customer did not buy from you. Find out the real reason.

2. Be professional. If you have lost the customer to a competitor completely, let the customer know you have appreciated past business, that you still value the customer's friendship, and that you are still friendly. Remember to assure this lost account that you are ready to earn future business.

3. Don't be unfriendly. Never criticize the competing product that your customer has purchased. If it was a bad decision, let the customer discover it. Sales is never having to say, "I told you so!"

4. Keep calling. Treat a former customer like a prospect. Continue to make calls normally; present your product's benefits without directly comparing them to the competition.

Like a professional athlete, a professional salesperson takes defeat gracefully, moves on to the next contest, and performs so well that victories overshadow losses. One method of compensating for the loss of an account is to increase sales to existing accounts.

INCREASING YOUR CUSTOMER'S SALES

To maximize your sales to a customer, develop a customer benefit program. This means the account uses in business, or sells to customers, a level of merchandise equal to its maximum sales potential. The salesperson has only two methods to do this:

1. Have present customers buy *more* of a product than they currently use.
2. Have present customers buy the same products to use for different purposes. A Johnson & Johnson retail sales representative may encourage accounts to stock the firm's baby shampoo in both the infant care and adult toiletries sections of their establishments.

It is often not difficult to sell repeat orders; however, to maximize sales in an account with a retailer, for example, you must persuade the customer to consistently promote your product through advertisements, displays, and reduced prices. To increase sales with a customer, the following steps can be taken. Each step cannot be used in all situations, but using some can increase sales:

Step 1:

Develop an account penetration program. Develop a master plan for each account consisting of specific actions to take toward developing friends within the account and increasing sales.

Step 2:

Examine your distribution. Review the merchandise currently used or carried in inventory. If the account is not using or carrying some of your merchandise, concentrate on improving your distribution. For example, if you have four sizes of a product and the account only carries one or two of them, develop a plan to persuade the customer to carry all four sizes. A general goal may be having each account carry all sizes of your products.

Step 3:

Keep merchandise in the warehouse and on the shelf. Never allow the account to run out of stock. Stockouts result in lost sales for your firm and account. Routine calls on customers help to avoid stockouts. If the account is critically low on merchandise, telephone in an emergency order. Quick service can maintain, or even increase, your credibility as a sales professional.

Step 4:

Fight for shelf space and shelf positioning. If you are selling consumer goods, constantly seek the best shelf space and aisle position. On each sales call, stock the shelf, keep your merchandise clean, and develop merchandising ideas. For example, during a routine visit to a client's store, a consumer-goods salesperson found that one of his products with a list price of $2 was being sold for $1.79. This enterprising salesperson taped a small sign to the shelf showing both prices and later discovered that sales of the product increased. This device is now routine for all of this salesperson's products.

Step 5:

Assist the product's users. If you sell business products, help users learn to operate products properly. Make users aware of product accessories that might aid them in performing a function in a safer, better, or more profitable manner. This type of account servicing can increase both account penetration and sales.

Step 6:

Assist reseller's salespeople. To ensure enthusiastic promotion of your firm's products, work closely with your account's sales force. Experience indicates that manufacturer's salespeople who cultivate the friendship of the reseller's salespeople and provide them with product knowledge and selling tips are more successful than the salespersons who call only on buyers.

A successful pharmaceutical salesperson suggested to all retail salespeople involved in a certain account that as they hand a customer a prescription for an antibiotic they say, "When taking these antibiotics, you also should double up on taking your vitamins." Well, most customers were not taking vitamins, so when they said, "I don't have any vitamins," the salesperson would hand them a bottle of vitamins, saying, "I take these myself and highly recommend them to you." Of course, this manufacturer's salesperson previously gave the retail salesperson a sample bottle of vitamins. This sales tip accounted for an increase of more than 300 percent in vitamin sales for this reseller.

Step 7:

Demonstrate your willingness to help. On each sales call, demonstrate your willingness to help the account through your actions. Your actions—not just words—are what build respect or distaste for you. Pull off your coat and dust, mark, stack, and build displays of your merchandise, and return damaged merchandise for credit. Let the buyer know that you are there to help increase retail sales.

Step 8:

Obtain customer support. By working hard to help your customers reach their goals through doing the items just discussed, you will find they help and support you. You help them; they help you. This type of relationship benefits you and the customer.

Again, there is no guarantee that doing everything suggested in this text will always result in a sale. Conscientious use of sound selling principles *will* increase your likelihood of overall success, though.

Vincent Norris of Scientific Equipment Corporation sent us a copy of his secret to sales success. While follow-up is at the bottom of his list of secrets shown in Exhibit 13–6, it is extremely important, as you can see.

As mentioned earlier in this chapter, a key characteristic of a sales professional is the ability to accept failure or rejection gracefully and to then quickly move to the next objective.

RETURNED GOODS MAKE YOU A HERO	One of the best ways to help customers is through careful examination of merchandise you have sold in the past to see if it is old, out-of-date, or unsalable due to damage. If any of these conditions exist, the salesperson should cheerfully return the merchandise following the company's returned goods policies.

Some companies allow you to return any amount of merchandise, whereas other firms have limits on unauthorized returns. A firm may allow no more than $100 of merchandise to be returned at a time without the company's approval. Some companies require a reciprocal replacement order. Thus, if $100 worth of merchandise is returned, the customer must place an order for $100 of new merchandise. You do not

EXHIBIT 13-6

A super sales success secret

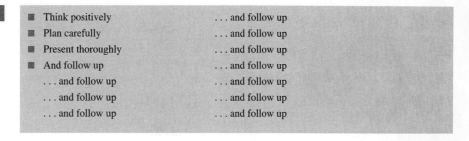

■ Think positively	. . . and follow up
■ Plan carefully	. . . and follow up
■ Present thoroughly	. . . and follow up
■ And follow up	. . . and follow up
. . . and follow up	. . . and follow up
. . . and follow up	. . . and follow up
. . . and follow up	. . . and follow up

want the customer to display or sell damaged goods, so it is in your best interest to return faulty merchandise, an action that builds friendship with each customer.

HANDLE COMPLAINTS FAIRLY

Customers may be dissatisfied with products for any number of reasons:

■ The product delivered is a different size, color, or model than the one ordered.

■ The quantity delivered is less than the quantity ordered—the balance is back-ordered (to be delivered when available).

■ The product does not arrive by the specified date.

■ Discounts (trade or promotional payment, see Chapter 6) agreed on are not rendered by the manufacturer.

■ The product does not have a feature or perform a function that the customer believed it would.

■ The product is not of the specified grade or quality (does not meet agreed-on specifications).

Whenever you determine that the customer's complaint is honest, make a settlement that is fair to the customer. "The customer is always right" is a wise adage to follow. Customers actually may be wrong, but if they honestly believe they are right, no amount of haggling or arguing will convince them otherwise. A valued account can be lost through temperamental outbursts.

Occasionally, a dishonest customer may require you and your company not to honor a request. Retailer A once purchased some of my firm's merchandise from Retailer B, who had a fire sale and eventually went out of business. Retailer A insisted he purchased it from me and that I return close to $1,000 of damaged goods to my company for full credit. He actually had paid ten cents on the dollar for it at the fire sale. I told Retailer A that I would have to obtain permission from the company to return such a large amount of damaged goods.

That afternoon, a competitive salesperson told me that Retailer A had asked him to do the same thing. I informed my sales manager of the situation. He investigated the matter and found out about Retailer B, who sold most of his merchandise to Retailer A—who happened to be my customer. I went back and confronted Retailer A with this and said it was company policy only to return merchandise that was purchased directly from me. This was a rare situation; yet, you must occasionally make similar judgments considering company policy and customer satisfaction.

Customers should get the benefit of the doubt. Always have a plan for problem solving. Some procedures you can use include:

■ Obtain as much relevant information from your customer as possible.

■ Express sincere regret for the problem.

- Display a service attitude (a true desire to help).
- Review your sales records to make sure the customer purchased the merchandise.
- If the customer is right, quickly and cheerfully handle the complaint.
- Follow up to make sure the customer is satisfied.

Take care of your customers—especially large accounts. They are difficult to replace and are critical to success. When you take care of accounts, they take care of you.

BUILD A PROFESSIONAL REPUTATION

Your text stresses the concept of sales professionalism. Sales professionalism directly implies that you are a professional person—due the respect and ready for the responsibilities that accompany the title. In speaking before a large class of marketing students, one sales manager for a large college textbook publishing company continually emphasized the concept of sales professionalism. This man stated that a professional sales position is not just an 8-to-5 job. It is a professional and responsible position promising both unlimited opportunity and numerous duties. This veteran sales manager emphasized that a sales job is an especially good vocational opportunity because people are looking for "someone we can believe in; someone who will do what she says—a sales professional."

To be viewed as a professional and respected by your customers and competitors, consider these eight important points:

- First, be truthful and follow through on what you tell the customer. Do not dispose of your conscience when you start work each day.
- Second, maintain an intimate knowledge of your firm, its products, and your industry. Participate in your company's sales training and take continuing education courses.
- Third, speak well of others, including your company and competitors.
- Fourth, keep customer information confidential; maintain a professional relationship with each account.
- Fifth, never take advantage of a customer by using unfair, high-pressure techniques.
- Sixth, be active in community affairs and help better your community. For example, live in your territory, be active in public schools, and join worthwhile organizations such as the Lions Club, the Chamber of Commerce, environmental organizations, and so forth.
- Seventh, think of yourself as a professional and always act like one. Have a professional attitude about yourself and your customers.
- Eighth, provide service "above and beyond the call of duty." Remember that it is easier to maintain a relationship than to begin one. What was worth attaining is worth preserving. Remember, when you do not pay attention to customers, they find someone who will. The professional salesperson never forgets a customer after the sale.

DOS AND DON'TS FOR BUSINESS SALESPEOPLE

What do purchasing agents expect of business salespeople? A survey of purchasing agents showed that they expect results. The following list shows the most important traits that purchasing agents found in their top business salespeople:

EXHIBIT 13–7

The seven deadly sins of business selling

1. *Lack of product knowledge.* Salespeople must know their product line as well as the buyer's line or nothing productive can occur.

2. *Time wasting.* Unannounced sales visits are a nuisance. When salespeople start droning about golf or grandchildren, more time is wasted.

3. *Poor planning.* A routine sales call must be preceded by some homework—see if it's necessary.

4. *Pushiness.* This includes prying to find out a competitor's prices, an overwhelming attitude, and backdoor selling.

5. *Lack of dependability.* Failure to stand behind the product, keep communications clear, and honor promises.

6. *Unprofessional conduct.* Knocking competitors, drinking excessively at a business lunch, sloppy dress, and poor taste aren't professional.

7. *Unlimited optimism.* Honesty is preferred to the hallmark of the good news bearers who promise anything to get an order. Never promise more than you can deliver.

Here are a few comments purchasing agents made on these deadly sins:

- They take it personally if they don't get the business; it's as though you owe them something because they constantly call on you.

- I don't like it when they blast through the front door like know-it-alls and put on an unsolicited dog-and-pony show that will guarantee cost saving off in limbo somewhere.

- Many salespeople will give you any delivery you want, book an order, and then let you face the results of their "short quote."

- They try to sell *you*, rather than the product.

- After the order is won, the honeymoon is over.

- Beware the humble pest who is too nice to insult, won't take a hint, won't listen to blunt advice, and is selling a product you neither use nor want to use, yet won't go away.

- Willingness to go to bat for the buyer within the supplier's firm.
- Thoroughness and follow-through after the sale.
- Knowledge of the firm's product line.
- Market knowledge and willingness to "keep the buyer posted."
- Imagination in applying one's products to the buyer's needs.
- Knowledge of the buyer's product line.
- Preparation for sales calls.
- Regularity of sales calls.
- Diplomacy in dealing with operating departments.
- Technical education—knowledge of specifications and applications.

The survey also asked purchasing agents what they did not like salespeople to do in sales calls. The results, shown in Exhibit 13–7, are "The Seven Deadly Sins of Industrial Selling."[8] Purchasing agents want salespeople to act professionally, to be well trained, to be prepared for each sales call, and to keep the sales call related to *how the salesperson can help the buyer.*

Professional selling starts in the manufacturer's firm. A professional attitude from the manufacturer reinforces professionalism among the sales force. One such company is B. J. Hughes, a division of the Hughes Tool Company. B. J. Hughes manufactures and sells oil-field equipment and services to companies in the oil

ETHICAL DILEMMA

I Appreciate Your Business

People buy from you for many reasons but primarily because of your excellent products and the service you and your company provide to customers. You follow the Golden Rule: "Do unto others as you would have them do unto you." You feel customers put the meat and potatoes on your table. They are responsible for the good income you earn. You appreciate that and always try to show how much you thank them for their trust and business.

You have been taking one of your customers, whom you like personally, out to lunch on infrequent occasions.

Recently, this customer's purchases have increased from $50,000 to $650,000 a year. You want to show your appreciation by buying two season tickets for the local professional basketball team. The buyer and spouse are great basketball fans. However, you are unsure if your other clients and co-workers will think it is unprofessional if they found out.

What would you do?

and gas industry. Exhibit 13–8 presents Hughes' checklists of *dos* and *don'ts* for their salespeople. By providing these checklists, the company encourages them to act professionally.[9]

| SUMMARY OF MAJOR SELLING ISSUES | Salespeople increase sales by obtaining new customers and selling more product to present customers. Customer referrals are the best way to find new prospects. Thus, it's important to provide excellent service and follow-up to customers. By building a relationship and partnership, you can provide a high level of customer service. |

Customers expect service. When you deliver service, customers are satisfied and continue to buy; this results in retention and loyalty. Providing service to customers is important in all types of selling. Follow-up and service create goodwill between salesperson and customer that allows the salesperson to penetrate or work throughout the customer's organization. Account penetration helps the salesperson to better service the account and uncover its needs and problems. A service relationship with an account leads to increases in total and major brand sales, better distribution on all product sizes, and customer cooperation in promoting your products.

To serve customers best, improve account penetration. Contact each customer frequently and regularly; promptly handle all complaints. Always do what you say you will do, and remember to serve customers as if they were royalty. Finally, remember to sincerely thank all customers for their business, no matter how large or small, to show you appreciate them.

Should customers begin to buy from a competitor or reduce their level of cooperation, continue to call on them in your normal professional manner. In a friendly way, determine why they did not buy from you, and develop new customer benefit plans to recapture their business.

Always strive to help your customers increase their sales of your product or to get the best use from products that you have sold to them. To persuade a customer to purchase more of your products or use your products in a different manner, develop a sales program to help maximize sales to that customer. This involves developing an account penetration program; increasing the number and sizes of products purchased by the customer; maintaining proper inventory levels in the customer's warehouse

EXHIBIT 13-8

B. J. Hughes' checklists of dos and don'ts help it to be a customer-oriented company.

Salesperson's Checklist of Dos	Salesperson's Checklist of Don'ts
1. Know the current products/services and their applications in your area. Look for the new techniques/services your customers want.	1. Never bluff; if you don't know, find out.
2. Maintain an up-to-date personal call list.	2. Never compromise your, or anyone else's, morals or principles.
3. Listen attentively to the customers.	3. Don't be presumptuous—never with friends.
4. Seek out specific problems and the improvements your customers want.	4. Never criticize a competitor—especially to a customer.
5. Keep calls under five minutes unless invited to stay.	5. Do not take criticisms or turndowns personally—they're seldom meant that way.
6. Leave a calling card if the customer is not in.	6. Do not worry or agonize over what you cannot control or influence. Be concerned about what you *can* affect.
7. Identify the individual who makes or influences decisions, and concentrate on that person.	7. Do not offend others with profanity.
8. Entertain selectively; your time and your expense account are investments.	8. Do not allow idle conversation to dominate your sales call. Concentrate on your purpose.
9. Make written notes as reminders.	9. Don't try to match the customer drink-for-drink when entertaining. Drink only if you want to and in moderation.
10. Plan work by the week, not by the clock. Plan use of available time. Plan sales presentations. Have a purpose.	10. Don't be so gung ho that you use high-pressure tactics.
11. Ask for business on every sales call.	11. Never talk your company down—especially to customers. Be proud of it and yourself.
12. Follow through with appropriate action.	12. If you smoke, never do so in the customer's office unless invited to smoke.

and on the shelf; achieving good shelf space and shelf positioning; clear communication with persons who directly sell or use a product; a willingness to assist wholesale and retail customers' salespeople in any way possible; a willingness to help customers; and an overall effort to develop a positive, friendly business relationship with each customer. By doing these eight things, your ability to help and properly service each customer increases.

Today's professional salesperson is oriented to service. Follow-up and service after the sale maximize your territory's sales and help attain personal goals.

MEETING A SALES CHALLENGE

What a tough situation! You have to keep servicing the equipment if you want to keep King Masonry as a customer. If the customer is misusing the mixer, causing it to break down, you must train the operators of the mixer and explain to Eldon King what is happening. Before saying anything to King, get his permission to talk with the mixer operators. Find out why the machine is breaking down.

KEY TERMS FOR SELLING

SALES APPLICATION QUESTIONS

1. Rich Port, Mike Curto, and Francis Rogers all discussed service in this chapter. What do they feel is important for salespeople to understand about service?

2. What is account penetration? What benefits can a salesperson derive from it?

3. List and briefly explain the factors salespeople must consider to ensure that customers buy from them in the future.

4. What must a salesperson do after losing a customer?

5. A good way for a salesperson to create goodwill is by helping customers increase their sales. What are the steps for the salesperson who attempts to increase customer sales?

6. This chapter discussed several reasons why a salesperson must project a professional image. Why is being a sales professional so important?

7. Return to Exhibit 13–7, the seven deadly sins of business selling. Think of an experience you had with a salesperson who displayed a poor sales image. How did the salesperson's attitude affect your purchase decision?

8. You have just learned that one of your customers, Tom's Discount Store, has received a shipment of faulty goods from your warehouse. The total cost of the merchandise is $2,500. Your company has a returned-goods policy that only allows you to return $500 worth of your product at one time unless a reciprocal order is placed. What would you do?

   a. Call Tom's and tell them you will be out to inspect the shipment in a couple of days.

   b. Ask Tom's to patch up what they can and sell it at a reduced cost in an upcoming clearance sale.

   c. Send the merchandise back to your warehouse and credit Tom's account for the price of the damaged goods.

   d. Go to Tom's as soon as possible that day, check the shipment to see if there are any undamaged goods that can be put on the shelf, take a replacement order from Tom's manager, and phone in the order immediately.

   e. Call your regional sales manager and ask what to do.

SALES WORLD WIDE WEB EXERCISES

What Is the Best Method to Determine Feedback?

Providing service after the sale to customers is important, no matter what type of company, product, or service you represent. Customer service refers to the activities and programs provided by the seller to make the relationship satisfying for the customer.

Some organizations specialize in analyzing a company's customer's satisfaction, such as J. D. Power in the automobile industry. Their URL is www.jdpower.com.

For this assignment, determine how one or more companies determine the satisfaction of their customers with their product(s) and service. Find a company who has people answer a satisfaction questionnaire over the Internet.

One place to begin is using your favorite search engine. Input "customer satisfaction" and if possible add selling to the search.

Write a brief report to your boss on your findings. State what you feel would be the best way for a company of your choice to determine their customer's satisfaction.

FURTHER EXPLORING THE SALES WORLD

1. Contact the person in charge of the health and beauty aids department of a local supermarket. In an interview with this person, ask questions to determine what service activities salespeople perform in the department. For example, do they build product displays, put merchandise on the shelves, straighten products on the shelves, and keep a record of how much product is in the store? Also, determine how the department head feels salespeople can provide the best service.
2. Contact the person in charge of marketing in a local bank. Report on the role that service plays in attracting and retaining bank customers.

SELLING EXPERIENTIAL EXERCISE

What's Your Attitude Toward Customer Service?

Providing excellent customer service often requires a special person—someone who quietly enjoys interacting with people even when they are upset. To help you better understand yourself, respond to each statement by placing the number that best describes your answer on a separate sheet of paper.

1 Never   2 Rarely   3 Sometimes   4 Usually   5 Often

1. I accept people without judging them.
2. I show patience, courtesy, and respect to people regardless of their behavior toward me.
3. I maintain my composure and refuse to become irritated or frustrated when coping with an angry or irate person.
4. I treat people as I would want them to treat me.
5. I help others maintain their self-esteem, even when the situation requires negative or critical feedback.
6. I do not get defensive when interacting with other persons, even if their comments are directed at me.
7. I realize that my attitude toward myself and others affects the way I respond in any given situation.
8. I realize that each person believes his or her problem is the most important and urgent thing in the world at this time, and I attempt to help each one resolve it immediately.
9. I treat everyone in a positive manner, regardless of how they look, dress, or speak.
10. I view every interaction with another person as a golden moment, and I do everything in my power to make it a satisfactory win–win situation for both of us.

Total Score _____

Total your score: If your score is more than 40 you have an excellent service attitude; if it is 30–40, you could use improvement; and if you scored less than 30, you need an attitude adjustment.[10]

CASE 13–1
California Adhesives Corporation

Marilyn Fowler recently became a sales representative for the California Adhesives Corporation and covers the states of Oregon and Washington. After completing a three-week training program, Marilyn was excited about the responsibility of reversing a downward sales trend in her territory, which had been without a salesperson for several months.

The previous salesperson was fired due to poor sales performance and had not left behind any information regarding accounts. After contacting her first 20 or so customers, Marilyn came to a major conclusion: none of these customers had seen a CAC salesperson for six to nine months; they had CAC merchandise, which was not selling, and they had damaged merchandise to return. These customers were hostile toward Marilyn because the previous salesperson had used high-pressure tactics to force them to buy, and as one person said, "Your predecessor killed your sales in my business. You said you would provide service and call on me regularly, but I don't care about service. In fact, it's OK with me if I never see anyone from your company again. Your competition's products are much better than yours, and their salespeople have been calling in this area for years trying to get my business." Marilyn was wondering if she had gone to work for the right company.

Questions

1. If you were Marilyn, what would you do to improve the sales in your territory?
2. How long would your effort take to improve sales and would you *sell* it to your sales manager?

CASE 13–2
Sport Shoe Corporation

You are a salesperson for the Sport Shoe Corporation. At the office, there is a letter marked urgent on your desk. This letter is from the athletic director of Ball State University, and it pertains to the poor quality of basketball shoes that you sold to him. The director cited several examples of split soles and poor overall quality as his main complaints. In closing, he mentioned that since the season was nearing, he would be forced to contact the ACME Sport Shoe Company if the situation could not be rectified.

Question

What actions would be appropriate for you? Why?

a. Place a call to the athletic director assuring him of your commitment to service. Promise to be at Ball State at his convenience to rectify the problem.

b. Go by the warehouse and take the athletic director a new shipment of shoes and apologize for the delay and poor quality of the merchandise.

c. Write a letter to the athletic director assuring him that SSC sells only high-quality shoes and that this type of problem rarely occurs. Assure him you'll come to his office as soon as possible but if he feels ACME would be a better choice than Sport Shoe he should contact them.

d. Don't worry about the letter because the athletic director seems to have the attitude that he can put pressure on you by threatening to switch companies. Also, the loss in sales of 20 to 40 pairs of basketball shoes will be a drop in the bucket compared to the valuable sales time you would waste on a small account like Ball State.

PART IV

CAREERS IN SELLING

Sales personnel are managers of themselves, their time, and their customers. They work in a variety of industries. Yet most of the basics of selling remain the same no matter what is being sold. Selling skills frequently need to be adapted to certain situations. Retail, organizational, and nonprofit sales are similar in that they each have an opening, a presentation, and a close. Yet in other ways they are very different. Included in this part are:

14. Time, Territory, and Self-Management: Keys to Success

15. Retail, Business, Services, and Nonprofit Selling

14

Time, Territory, and Self-Management: Keys to Success

MAIN TOPICS

Customers Form Sales Territories

Elements of Time and Territory Management

LEARNING OBJECTIVES

A salesperson's ability to manage time and territory is important to success. After studying this chapter, you should be able to:

- Discuss the importance of the sales territory.

- Explain the major elements involved in managing the sales territory.

- Explain why salespeople need to segment their accounts by size.

- Calculate a saleperson's break-even point per day, hour, and year.

How can I manage my time to take better care of my customers? thought Alice Jenson. It seems each day I work I get further and further behind.

Alice had recently taken over the sales territory of Mike Batemen, who retired and moved across the country after 35 years of calling on customers. He kept all records in his head. Alice had to contact the 200 customers in the sales territory with no information other than their past sales. After several weeks, Alice had seen 95 percent of the customers once and 25 percent of them a second time. Two weeks ago, complaints started coming in that Alice had not followed up on her last calls or that she had not been back to see them.

Alice started telephoning people. That helped some, but customers wanted to see her. She almost stopped prospecting for new customers because she felt it was easier to keep a customer than get a new one. However, as sales started to decline, Alice realized customers were beginning to buy from her competitors.

Alice is in trouble and it is getting worse. What can you suggest Alice do to keep customers, have time to prospect, and increase sales?

Planning your workday and managing your time and customers are key to your success. According to a national survey of thousands of salespeople across the nation, managing time and territory is the most important factor in selling. Because of such things as the rapidly increasing cost of direct selling, decreasing time for face-to-face customer contact, continued emphasis on profitable sales, and the fact that time is always limited, it is no wonder that many companies are concentrating on improving how salespeople manage time and territory.[1]

Time is important for salespeople. Yesterday's the past, tomorrow's the future, but today is a *gift*. That's why it's called the *present*.

CUSTOMERS FORM SALES TERRITORIES

A **sales territory** comprises a group of customers or a geographical area assigned to a salesperson. The territory may or may not have geographical boundaries. Typically, however, a salesperson is assigned to a geographical area containing present and potential customers.

Why Establish Sales Territories?

Companies develop and use sales territories for numerous reasons. Next, we discuss the seven important reasons listed in Exhibit 14–1.

EXHIBIT 14-1

Reasons companies develop and use sales territories

- To obtain thorough coverage of the market.
- To establish each salesperson's responsibilities.
- To evaluate performance.
- To improve customer relations.
- To reduce sales expense.
- To allow better matching of salesperson to customer's needs.
- To benefit both salespeople and the company.

To Obtain Thorough Coverage of the Market

With proper coverage of territories, a company will reach the sales potential of its markets. The salesperson analyzes the territory and identifies customers. At the individual territory level, the salesperson better meets customers' needs. Division into territories also allows management to easily realign territories as customers and sales increase or decrease.

To Establish Each Salesperson's Responsibilities

Salespeople act as business managers for their territories. They are responsible for maintaining and generating sales volume. Salespeople's tasks are defined clearly. They know where customers are located and how often to call on them. They also know what performance goals are expected. This can raise the salesperson's performance and morale.

To Evaluate Performance

Performance is monitored for each territory. Actual performance data are collected, analyzed, and compared to expected performance goals. Individual territory performance is compared to district performance, district performance compared to regional performance, and regional performance compared to the performance of the entire sales force. With computerized reporting systems, the salesperson and a manager can monitor individual territory and customer sales to determine the success of selling efforts.

To Improve Customer Relations

Customer goodwill and increased sales are expected when customers receive regular calls. From the customer's viewpoint, the salesperson *is,* for example, Procter & Gamble. The customer looks to the salesperson, not to Procter & Gamble's corporate office, when making purchases. Over the years, some salespeople build such goodwill with customers that prospects will delay placing orders because they know the salesperson will be at their business on a certain day or at a specific time of the month. Some salespeople even earn the right to order merchandise for certain customers.

To Reduce Sales Expense

Sales territories are designed to avoid duplicating efforts so that two salespeople do not travel in the same area. This lowers selling cost and increases company profits. Such benefits as fewer travel miles and fewer overnight trips, plus regular contact of productive customers by the same salesperson, can improve the firm's sales–cost ratio.

To Allow Better Matching of Salesperson to Customer's Needs

Salespeople are hired and trained to meet the requirements of the customers in a territory. Often, the more similar the customer and the salesperson, the more likely the sales effort will succeed.

To Benefit Both Salespeople and the Company

Proper territory design aids in reaching the firm's sales objectives. Thus, the company can maximize its sales effort, while the sales force can work in territories that allow them to satisfy personal needs, such as a good salary.

Why Sales Territories May Not Be Developed

In spite of advantages, there are disadvantages to developing sales territories for some companies, such as in the real estate or insurance industries. First, salespeople may be more motivated if not restricted by a particular territory; they can develop customers anywhere. In the chemical industry, for example, salespeople may sell to any potential customer. However, after the sale is made, other company salespeople are not allowed to contact that client.

Second, the company may be too small to be concerned with segmenting the market into sales areas. Third, management may not want to take the time, or may not have the know-how for territory development. Fourth, personal friendships may be the basis for attracting customers. For example, life insurance salespeople may first sell policies to their families and friends. However, most companies establish sales territories such as the one assigned to Alice Jenson in "Facing a Sales Challenge."

ELEMENTS OF TIME AND TERRITORY MANAGEMENT

For the salesperson, time and territory management (TTM) is a continuous process of planning, executing, and evaluating. The seven key elements involved in time and territory management are shown in Exhibit 14–2.

Salesperson's Sales Quota

A salesperson is responsible for generating sales in a territory based on its sales potential. The salesperson's manager typically establishes the total sales quota that each salesperson is expected to reach.

Once this quota is set, it is the salesperson's responsibility to develop territorial sales plans for reaching the quota. While there is no best planning sequence to follow, Exhibit 14–2 presents seven factors to consider in properly managing the territory for reaching its sales quota.

Account Analysis

Once a sales goal is set, the salesperson must analyze each prospect and customer to maximize the chances of reaching that goal. First, a salesperson should identify all prospects and present customers. Second, a salesperson should estimate present customers' and prospects' sales potential. This makes it possible to allocate time between customers, to decide what products to emphasize for a specific customer, and how to better plan the sales presentation.

EXHIBIT 14–2

Elements of time and territory management for the salesperson

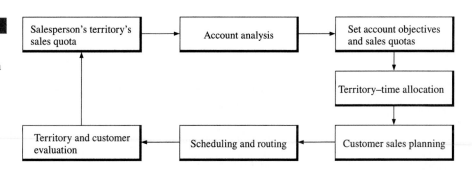

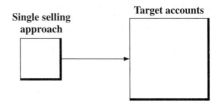

EXHIBIT 14–3

Undifferentiated selling
approach

Two general approaches to **account analysis**—identifying accounts and their varying levels of sales potential—are the undifferentiated selling approach and the account segmentation approach.

The Undifferentiated Selling Approach

An organization may see the accounts in its market as similar. When this happens and selling strategies are designed and applied equally to all accounts, the salesperson uses an **undifferentiated selling** approach. Notice in Exhibit 14–3 that the salesperson aims a single selling strategy at all accounts. The basic assumption underlying this approach is that the account needs for a specific product or group of products are similar. Salespeople call on all potential accounts, devoting equal selling time to each of them. The same sales presentation may be used in selling an entire product line. The salesperson feels it can satisfy most customers with a single selling strategy. For example, many door-to-door salespeople use the same selling strategies with each person they contact (a stimulus–response sales presentation).

Salespeople whose accounts have homogeneous needs and characteristics may find this approach useful. The undifferentiated selling approach was popular in the past, and some firms still use it. However, many salespeople feel that their accounts have different needs and represent different sales and profit potentials. This makes an account segmentation approach desirable.

The Account Segmentation Approach

Salespeople using the **account segmentation** approach recognize that their territories contain accounts with heterogeneous needs and differing characteristics that require different selling strategies. Consequently, they develop sales objectives based on overall sales and sales of each product for each customer and prospect. Past sales to the account, new accounts, competition, economic conditions, price and promotion offerings, new products, and personal selling are among key elements in the analysis of accounts and territories.

Salespeople classify customers to identify profitable ones. This classification determines where the salesperson's time is invested. One method of defining accounts is by:

1. Key account
   a. Buys over $200,000 from us annually.
   b. Loss of this customer would substantially affect the territory's sales and profits.
2. Unprofitable account.
   a. Buys less than $1,000 from us annually.
   b. Little potential to increase purchases to more than $1,000.
3. Regular account.
   a. All other customers.

EXHIBIT 14–4

Account segmentation based on yearly sales

Customer Size	Yearly Sales (actual or potential)	Number of Accounts	Percent
Extra large	over $200,000	100	3.3%
Large	$75,000–200,000	500	16.6
Medium	$25,000–75,000	1,000	33.3
Small	$1,000–25,000	1,400	46.6

EXHIBIT 14–5

Basic segmentation of accounts

	Customers		
Account Classification	Sales to Date	Potential Sales	Prospect Potential Sales
Extra large			
Large			
Medium			
Small			

The unprofitable accounts would not be called on. The **key accounts** and regular accounts become target customers.

Once the accounts are classified broadly, categories or types of accounts are defined in terms such as extra large (key), large, medium, and small, which we refer to as the **ELMS system.** For example, management may divide the 3,000 total accounts in the firm's marketing plan into these four basic sales categories, as shown in Exhibit 14–4. There are few extra large or large accounts, but they often account for 80 percent of a company's profitable sales even though they represent only 20 percent of total accounts. This is known as the **80/20 principle.** The number of key accounts in an individual territory varies, as does responsibility for them. Even though the key account is in another salesperson's territory, a key account salesperson may call on the extra-large customer. Typically, this is done because of the account's importance or because of an inexperienced local salesperson.

Accounts can be segmented whether or not the firms are actual customers or prospects. As shown in Exhibit 14–5, actual customers are further segmented based on sales to date and sales potential. Prospects also are segmented into the ELMS classification, and each account's potential sales are estimated.

Multiple Selling Strategies

Exhibit 14–6 illustrates how multiple selling strategies are used on various accounts. Salespeople know the importance of large accounts; in fact, meeting sales objectives often depends on how well products are sold to these customers. As a result, companies often develop their sales force organizational structure to service these accounts—incorporating elements such as a key-account salesperson.

As illustrated in Exhibit 14–6, selling strategies vary depending on the account. The bulk of sales force resources (such as personnel, time, samples, and entertainment expenses) should be invested in the key accounts, and the needs of these large accounts should receive top priority.

EXHIBIT 14–6

Account segmentation approach

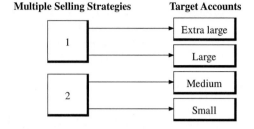

EXHIBIT 14–7

Multivariable account
segmentation

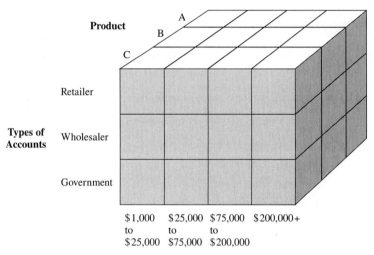

Company positioning relative to competition must receive careful consideration. Competitors also will direct a major selling effort toward these accounts. Thus, salespeople should strive to create the image that they, their company, and their products are uniquely better than the competition. One way to accomplish this is to spend more time on each sales call and to make more total sales calls during the year, thus providing a problem-solving approach to servicing accounts.

Selling larger accounts is different than selling medium and small accounts. However, these smaller accounts may generate 20 percent, and sometimes more, of a company's sales and must not be ignored.

Multivariable Account Segmentation

Multivariable account segmentation means using more than one criterion to characterize the organization's accounts. This is done because many sales organizations sell to several markets and use many channel members in these markets. Furthermore, different products, product sizes, or product lines may be emphasized to different channel members in various markets.

Exhibit 14–7 illustrates how firms might use several variables to segment their accounts. This allows sales personnel to develop plans for selling various products to specific segments of their accounts. For example, different selling strategies might be developed for the extra-large and large accounts. There might be different sales plans developed for retailers, wholesalers, and government accounts. These three types of accounts might be further segmented. Retailers, for instance, could be segmented into mass merchandisers and specialty stores. Furthermore, different products might be emphasized in each account segment. The type of market, environment, account sales potential, and sales volume are major variables for segmenting accounts.

Develop Account Objectives and Sales Quotas

The third element of time and territory management is developing objectives and sales quotas for individual products and for present and potential accounts. Objectives might include increasing product distribution to prospects in the territory or increasing the product assortment purchased by current customers.

Increasing the number of sales calls each day and the number of new accounts obtained for the year are other examples of objectives developed by the salesperson to help meet sales quotas. In recalling his early days as a salesperson, Shelby H. Carter, Jr., former Xerox senior vice president of sales of U.S. field operations, said, "I placed a sign on my car's visor that read, 'Calls are the guts of this business.' We lived in Baltimore," he recalls, "and I drove 40 miles every day to get to Annapolis. You've got to make extra calls," he told his salespeople, "because 1 more call a day is 5 a week, 20 a month, and 240 calls a year. If you close 10 percent of the people you contact, you have an extra 24 sales a year. You have to be tough on yourself to make that extra call."

Territory–Time Allocation

The fourth element of time and territory management is how salespeople's time is allocated within territories. Time allocation is the time spent by the salesperson traveling around the territory and in calling on accounts. These are seven basic factors to consider in time allocation:

1. Number of accounts in the territory.
2. Number of sales calls made on customers.
3. Time required for each sales call.
4. Frequency of customer sales calls.
5. Travel time around the territory.
6. Nonselling time.
7. Return on time invested.

Analysis of accounts in the territory has resulted in determining the total number of territory accounts and their classification in terms of actual or potential sales. Now, the number of yearly sales calls required, the time required for each call, and the intervals between calls can be determined. Usually, the frequency of calls increases as there are increases in (1) sales and/or potential future sales, (2) number of orders placed in a year, (3) number of product lines sold, and (4) complexity, servicing, and redesign requirements of products.

Since the time spent servicing an account varies from minutes to days, salespeople must be flexible in developing call frequencies. However, they can establish a minimum number of times each year they want to call on the various classes of accounts. For example, the salesperson determines the frequency of calls for each class of account in the territory, as shown in Exhibit 14–8, where all but the small accounts are contacted once a month.

Typically, the salesperson invests sales time in direct proportion to the actual or potential sales that the account represents. The most productive number of calls is reached at the point where additional calls do not increase sales. This relationship of sales volume to sales calls is the **sales response function** of the customer to the salesperson's calls.

Customer Size	Calls per Month	Calls per Year	Number of Account	=	Number of Calls per Year
Extra large	1	12	2		24
Large	1	12	28		336
Medium	1	12	56		672
Small	1*	4	78		312
Total			164		1,344

*every 3 months

Return on Time Invested

Time is a scarce resource. To be successful, the salesperson uses time effectively to improve territory productivity. In terms of time, costs also must be accounted for. That is, what is the cost both in time and money of an average sales call?

Break-even analysis determines how much sales volume a salesperson must generate to meet costs in a territory. The difference between cost of goods sold and sales is the gross profit on sales revenue. Gross profit should be large enough to cover selling expenses. **Break-even analysis** is a quantitative technique for determining the level of sales at which total revenues equal total costs. A territory's break-even point is computed in dollars with this formula:

$$\text{Break-even point (in dollar)} = \frac{\text{Salesperson's fixed costs}}{\text{Gross profit percentage}}$$

To illustrate the formula, let us use the values shown here for sales and costs, with gross profit being the difference between sales revenue of a salesperson and costs of goods sold in the territory, expressed as a ratio of gross profit to gross sales in percentage form:

Sales	$200,000
Cost of goods sold	− 140,000
Gross profit	$ 60,000
Gross profit (percentage)	(60,000 ÷ 200,000), or 30 percent

Assume the salesperson's direct costs are as follows:

Salary	$20,000
Transportation	4,000
Expenses	+ 5,000
Direct costs	$29,000

and substitute in the formula:

$$\text{BEP} = \frac{\$29,000}{.30} = \$96,667$$

If the salesperson sells $96,667 worth of merchandise, it exactly covers the territory's direct costs. A sales volume of $96,667 means that the salesperson produces a gross margin of 30 percent, or $29,000. Sales over $96,667 contribute to profit.

Assume that the salesperson works 46 out of 52 weeks (considering time off for vacations, holidays, and illness) for 230 days each year; also assume a five-day week and an eight-hour day in which six calls are made. There are 1,840 working hours per year and 1,380 sales calls (230 × 6 calls) made each year in the territory. To determine a salesperson's cost per hour, divide direct costs ($29,000) by yearly hours

EXHIBIT 14–9

This commission sales rep, knowing that time is money, works in this lobby while he waits for his next appointment.

worked (1,840 hours). The cost per hour equals $15.76. The break-even volume per hour is as follows:

$$\text{Break-even volume per hour} = \frac{\text{Cost per hour}}{\text{Gross profit percentage}} = \frac{\$15.76}{.30} = \$52.53$$

Thus, the salesperson must sell an average of $52.53 an hour in goods or services to break even in the territory. Carrying this logic further, the salesperson must sell an average of $420.24 each day or $70.04 each sales call to break even.

This simple arithmetic shows that a sales territory is a cost- and revenue-generating profit center, and because it is, priorities must be established on account calls to maximize territory profits.

The Management of Time

"Time is money" is a popular saying that applies to our discussion because of the costs and revenue generated by the individual salesperson. This is particularly evident with a commission salesperson. See Exhibit 14–9. This salesperson is a territory manager who has the responsibility of managing time wisely to maximize territorial profits. Thus, the effective salesperson consistently uses time well. How does the effective salesperson manage time?

Plan by the Day, Week, and Month. Many salespeople develop daily, weekly, and monthly call plans or general guidelines of customers and geographical areas to be covered. The salesperson may use them to make appointments with customers in advance, to arrange hotel accommodations, and so forth. Weekly plans are more specific, and they include the specific days that customers will be called on. Daily planning starts the night before, as the salesperson selects the next day's prospects, determines the time to contact the customer, organizes facts and data, and prepares sales presentation materials. Exhibit 14–10 is an illustration of a daily plan, and Exhibit 14–11 shows the location of each account and the sequence of calls.

"It's been said," says Tupperware's Terry Fingerhut, "21 days make a habit—good or bad. In three weeks, the results of the work I did or didn't do today will show up. If I spent my time well, three weeks from today I'll have positive results. If I wasted my time, three weeks from today, I'll have negative results. The conclusion—each

EXHIBIT 14–10

Daily customer plan

Hours	Customers	Prospects	Service Customers
	Sales Calls		
7:00–8:00 A.M.	Stop by office; pick up Jones Hardware order		
8:00–9:00	Travel		
9:00–10:00	Zip Grocery		
10:00–11:00	Ling Television Corp.		
11:00–12:00	Ling Television Corp.		
12:00–1:00 P.M.	Lunch and delivery to Jones Hardware		
1:00–2:00	Texas Instruments		
2:00–3:00		Ace Equipment	
3:00–4:00	Travel		
4:00–5:00			Trailor Mfg.
5:00–6:00	Plan next day—do paperwork		

EXHIBIT 14–11

Location of accounts and sequence of calls

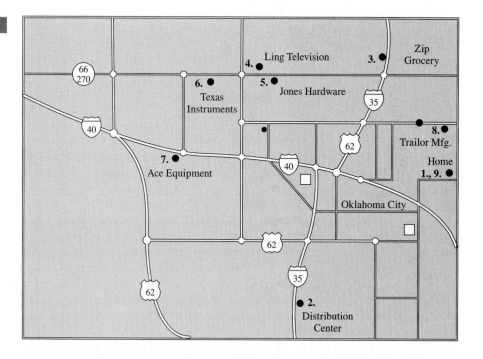

day, every day—is produce *now* at your best. In three weeks and every week thereafter you'll have a string of truly positive results."

Qualify the Prospect. Salespeople must be sure that their prospects are qualified to make the purchase decision, and they must determine whether sales to these accounts are large enough to allow for an adequate return on time invested. If not, they do not call on these prospects.

Use Waiting Time. Have you seen salespeople waiting to see buyers? Have you ever noticed their actions? Top salespeople do not read magazines. They work while

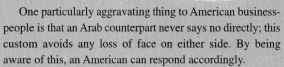

SELLING GLOBALLY

Working a Deal in the Arab World

Buyers in the Arab world are very hospitable and favorably disposed toward salespersons. Decisions there are frequently based on personal impressions supplemented by facts. The business climate and the tone of communication are very important. Arabs consider business transactions as social events; bargaining is an enjoyable and integral part of life.

Salespeople must respect all the religious and cultural customs of their Arab partners. They should remember that during the course of negotiations the Arabs may not be available at all times because of their religious customs.

One particularly aggravating thing to American businesspeople is that an Arab counterpart never says no directly; this custom avoids any loss of face on either side. By being aware of this, an American can respond accordingly.

At the end of the negotiation, an Arab counterpart signals agreement orally and commits himself firmly by giving his word. If circumstances change, however, an Arab buyer feels free to renegotiate a modification of the agreement.[2]

waiting: studying material about their products, completing call reports, or organizing material for the sales presentation. Also, they quickly determine whether buyers they wait for will be free in a reasonable time. If not, they contact other customers.

Have a Productive Lunchtime.   Salespeople often take prospects to lunch. However, the results of one study show that the business lunch does not lead directly to a sale, but to the buyer and seller knowing each other better, which builds confidence and trust. In turn, this may lead to sales in the long run.

During a business lunch, salespeople must keep an eye on the clock and not monopolize too much of the buyer's time. They should not have a lunchtime cocktail. While it is customary for some people to have a drink at lunch, the salesperson will be less alert in the afternoon as a result. In fact, in some companies, a luncheon cocktail or any use of alcohol or other drugs is against company policy. A salesperson's lunch is time to review activities and further plan the afternoon. It is a time to relax and start psyching up for a productive selling afternoon.

Records and Reports.   Records and reports are a written history of sales and of the salesperson's activities. Effective salespeople do paperwork during nonselling times; evenings are best. Many companies note these records and reports in performance evaluations of salespeople. However, paperwork should be held to a minimum by the company and kept current by the salesperson.

Customer Sales Planning   The fifth major element of time and territorial management is developing a sales-call objective, a customer profile, and a customer benefit program, including selling strategies for individual customers.* You have a quota to meet, have made your account analysis, have set account objectives and have established the time you will devote to each customer; now, develop a sales plan for each customer.

Scheduling and Routing   The sixth element of time and territory management is scheduling sales calls and planning movement around the sales territory.

Scheduling refers to establishing a fixed time (day and hour) for visiting a customer's business. **Routing** is the travel pattern used in working a territory. Some

---

*Refer to Chapter 6 for further discussion of customer sales planning.

sales organizations prefer to determine the formal path or route that their salespeople travel when covering their territory. In such cases, management must develop plans that are feasible, flexible, and profitable to the company and the individual salesperson, and satisfactory to the customer. In theory, strict formal route designs enable the company to (1) improve territory coverage; (2) minimize wasted time; and (3) establish communication between management and the sales force in terms of the location and activities of individual salespeople.

In developing route patterns, management needs to know the salesperson's exact day and time of sales calls for each account; approximate waiting time; sales time; miscellaneous time for contacting people such as the promotional manager, checking inventory, or handling returned merchandise; and travel time between accounts. This task is difficult unless territories are small and precisely defined. Most firms allow considerable latitude in routing.

Typically, after finishing a workweek, the salesperson fills out a routing report and sends it to the manager. The report states where the salesperson will work. See Exhibit 14–12. In the example, on Friday, December 16, she is based in Dallas and plans to call on accounts in Dallas for two days during the week of December 26. Then, she plans to work in Waco for a day, spend the night, drive to Fort Worth early the next morning and make calls, and be home Thursday night. The last day of the week, she plans to work in Dallas. The weekly route report is sent to her immediate supervisor. In this manner, management knows where she is and, if necessary, can contact her.

Some firms may ask the salesperson to specify the accounts to be called on and at what times. For example, on Monday, December 26, the salesperson may write, "Dallas, 9 A.M., Texas Instruments; Arlington, 2 P.M., General Motors." Thus, management knows where a salesperson will be and what accounts will be visited during a report period. If no overnight travel is necessary to cover a territory, the company may not require any route reports, because the salesperson can be contacted at home in the evening.

Carefully Plan Your Route

At times, routing is difficult for a salesperson. Customers do not locate themselves geographically for the seller's convenience. Also, there is the increasing difficulty of traveling throughout large cities. Another problem is accounts that see you only on certain days and hours.

In today's complex selling situation, the absence of a well-thought-out daily and weekly route plan is a recipe for disaster. It's impossible to operate successfully without it. How do you begin?

EXHIBIT 14–12

Weekly route report

Today's date: December 16		For week beginning December 26
Date	**City**	**Location**
December 26 (Monday)	Dallas	Home
December 27 (Tuesday)	Dallas	Home
December 28 (Wednesday)	Waco	Holiday Inn/South
December 29 (Thursday)	Fort Worth	Home
December 30 (Friday)	Dallas	Home

Start by locating your accounts on a large map. Mount the map on some corkboard or foamboard from an office supply store or picture-framing shop. Use a road map for large territories or a city map for densely populated areas. Also, purchase a supply of map pins with different colored heads. Place the pins on the map so that you can see where each account is located. For example, use:

- Red pins for extra large (**EL**) accounts.
- Yellow pins for large (**L**) accounts.
- Blue pins for medium (**M**) accounts.
- Green pins for small (**S**) accounts.
- Black pins for best prospects.

Once all pins are in place, stand back and take a look at the map. Notice first where the **EL** accounts are located. This helps determine your main routes or areas where you must go frequently.

Now, divide the map into sections, keeping the same number of **EL** accounts in each section. Each section should be a natural geographic division, that is, roads should be located in a way that allows you to drive from your home base to each section, as well as to travel easily once you are there. Generally, your **L, M,** and **S** accounts will fall into place near your **ELs,** with a few exceptions.

For example, if you work on a monthly or four-week call schedule for **ELs,** then divide your territory into four sections, working one section each week. In this way, you will reach all **ELs** while having the flexibility needed to reach your other accounts regularly.

Section 1	Section 2	Section 3	Section 4
7 **EL**	9 **EL**	5 **EL**	10 **EL**
15 **L**	12 **L**	15 **L**	15 **L**
35 **M**	25 **M**	35 **M**	25 **M**
40 **S**	35 **S**	49 **S**	36 **S**

By creating geographical routes this way, you could call on all **EL** accounts every four weeks, half of your **L** and **M** accounts (an 8-week call cycle) and 25 percent of your **S** accounts (a 16-week call cycle) in that period. Also, allow time for calls on prospective customers, too. Use the same procedure as for regular customers. The only difference is that in most cases prospects would be contacted less frequently than customers.

There is no right number of sections or routes for all salespersons. It depends on the size of your territory, the geographical layout of your area, and the call frequencies you want to establish. Design your travel route so that you can start from home in the morning and return in the evening—or, if you have a larger territory, make it a Monday to Friday route or a two-day (overnight) route. Remember that the critical factor is travel time—not miles. In some cases, by using major nonstop highways, your miles may increase but your total travel time may decrease.

The actual routes followed each day and within each section are important to maximize your prime selling hours each day. For this reason, make long drives early in the morning and in the late afternoon, if possible. For example, if most accounts are in a straight line from your home, leave early and drive to the far end of your territory before making your first call, then work your way back so that you end up near home at the end of the day, which is called the *straight-line method.* Exhibit 14–13 illustrates three ways to route yourself.

EXHIBIT 14–13

Three basic routing patterns

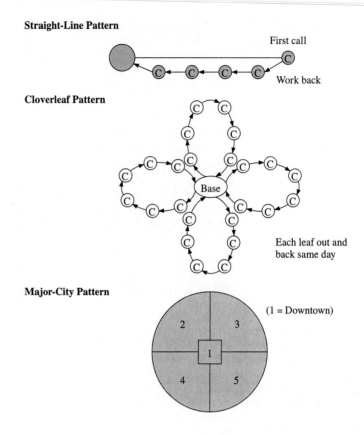

Straight-Line Pattern

First call

Work back

Cloverleaf Pattern

Base

Each leaf out and back same day

Major-City Pattern

(1 = Downtown)

Using the Telephone for Territorial Coverage

The telephone can be a great time-waster or time-saver, depending on how it is used. The increasing cost of a personal sales call, and the increasing amount of time spent traveling to make personal calls are reasons for the efficient territory manager to look to the telephone as a territory coverage tool.

With field sales costs still rising and no end in sight, more companies are developing telephone sales and marketing campaigns to supplement personal selling efforts. These campaigns utilize trained telephone communicators and well-developed telephone marketing techniques. Usually, they require a companywide effort.

Although each salesperson has to decide the types of calls and accounts that lend themselves to telephone applications, most people benefit from adopting the following practices as minimal territory coverage:

- Satisfy part of the service needs of accounts by telephone.
- Assign smaller accounts that contribute less than 5 percent of business to mostly telephone selling.
- Do prospecting, market data gathering, and call scheduling by telephone.
- Carefully schedule personal calls to distant accounts. If possible, replace some personal visits with telephone calls.

The telephone and the computer are important selling tools for salespeople. Many sales jobs require extensive travel. Even in airports, as shown in Exhibit 14–14, traveling salespeople can keep in contact with their offices, access computer files containing customer information, and record customer information.

EXHIBIT 14-14

The telephone is an effective aid that keeps salespeople connected to sales operations no matter where they travel.

EXHIBIT 14-15

Net sales by customer and call frequency: May 1, 1999

	Brown (GP, Houston)	Peterson (Pediatrics, Galveston)	Gilley (GP, Galveston)	Bruce (GP, Galveston)	Heaton (GP, Texas City)
Calls					
Month	2	1	1	0	2
Year-to-date	8	4	4	4	9
Last call	4/20	4/18	4/18	3/10	4/19
Net sales in dollars					
Current month	60	0	21	0	500
Year-to-date:					
This year	350	200	75	1,000	2,000
Last year	300	275	125	750	1,750
Entire last year	2,000	1,000	300	1,000	5,000

Territory and Customer Evaluation

Territorial evaluation is the establishment of performance standards for the individual territory in the form of qualitative and quantitative quotas or goals. Actual performance is compared to these goals for evaluation purposes. This allows the salesperson to see how well territory plans were executed in meeting performance quotas. If quotas were not met, new plans must be developed.

Many companies routinely furnish managers and individual salespeople with reports on how many times during the year salespeople have called on each account and the date of the last sales call. Management can monitor the frequency and time intervals between calls for each salesperson.

As an example, a national pharmaceutical company supplies its sales force with a net sales by customer and call report shown in Exhibit 14–15. The report lists each

ETHICAL DILEMMA

A Breakdown in Productivity

You are a hard worker, often putting in 60 hours a week. On your first sales job and with the company only five months, you realize the importance of getting off to a good start. You have sold an average of 30 percent over your sales quota for the last three months. One reason is your hard work. Another reason is the salesperson in this territory before you either neglected accounts or just renewed old orders, never striving to upgrade current accounts. Most customers complained they hadn't seen a salesperson from your company for months before you began to call on them.

Last month one of the older salespeople jokingly suggested to you to slow up. You were making everyone look bad. You have noticed a breakdown in productivity among your fellow salespeople who seem to be goofing off to extremes. While it doesn't affect you directly, it will ultimately have an adverse impact on the department's productivity. Your boss likes good news and frequently asks you for ideas on how to increase the sales in other territories. Since you are new and have not yet established yourself as a loyal employee, you have kept quiet in the past hoping to win the trust of your co-workers. Tomorrow you have a meeting with your boss about your territory's productivity, and you are sure that he is expecting input about the other territories.

What would you do?

customer's name, address, and medical specialty. The desired number of monthly calls on a given customer and the actual number of calls to date are noted. Net sales are broken down into last year's sales, the current month's sales, and year-to-date sales. Finally, the date the salesperson last called on each customer is reported.

Using the report, one can see that H. L. Brown is a Houston physician in a general practice. He should be called on twice a month, and for the past four months, he has been seen eight times. He purchased $60 worth of merchandise this month, and his purchases so far are $50 more than last year. He was last called on April 20 of the current year. Using this type of information, which might include 200 to 300 customers for each salesperson, management and salespeople can continually review sales-call patterns and customer sales to update call frequency and scheduling.

SUMMARY OF MAJOR SELLING ISSUES

How salespeople invest their sales time is a critical factor influencing territory sales. Due to the increasing cost of direct selling, high transportation costs, and the limited resource of time, salespeople have to focus on these factors. Proper time and territory management is an effective method for the salesperson for maximizing territorial sales and profits.

A sales territory comprises a group of customers or a geographical area assigned to a salesperson. It is a segment out of the company's total market. A salesperson within a territory has to analyze the various segments, estimate sales potential, and develop a marketing mix based on the needs and desires of the marketplace.

Companies develop and use sales territories for a number of reasons. One important reason is to obtain thorough coverage of the market to fully reach sales potential. Another reason is to establish salespeople's responsibilities as territory managers.

Performance can be monitored when territories are established. A territory may also be used to improve customer relations so that customers receive regular calls from the salesperson. This helps to reduce sales expenses by avoiding duplicated effort in traveling and customer contacts. Finally, they allow better matching of salespeople to customer needs and benefit salespeople and the company.

There also are disadvantages to developing sales territories. Some salespeople may not be motivated if they feel restricted by a particular territory. Also, a company may be too small to segment its market or management may not want to take time to develop territories.

Time and territory management is continuous for a salesperson; it involves seven key elements. The first major element is establishing the territory sales quota. The second element is account analysis, which involves identifying present and potential customers and estimating their sales potential. In analyzing these accounts, salespeople may use the undifferentiated-selling approach if they view accounts as similar; or, if accounts have different characteristics, they use the account-segmentation approach.

Developing objectives and sales quotas for individual accounts is the third element. How salespeople allocate time in their territories is another key element. Salespeople have to manage time, plan schedules, and use spare time effectively.

The fifth element of time and territorial management is developing the sales-call objective, profile, benefit program, and selling strategies for individual customers. Salespeople have to learn everything they can about customers and maintain records on each one. Once this is done, they can create the proper selling strategies to meet customers' needs.

Another major element is scheduling the sales calls at specific times and places and routing the salesperson's movement and travel pattern around the territory. Finally, objectives and quotas that were established are used to determine how effectively the salesperson performs. Actual performance is compared to these standards for evaluation purposes.

MEETING A SALES CHALLENGE

How Alice Jenson manages her time will determine her productivity. Alice should tell her boss the situation. Then she should analyze her accounts to classify them according to past sales and sales potential. Now she can allocate her time by concentrating on her extra-large and large accounts, contacting each as often as necessary. The medium-sized customers might be seen every one to two months, and the small ones less frequently or contacted by telephone. If needed, her boss could be asked to contact some customers. Alice's situation illustrates why companies require salespeople to do so much record-keeping. After each sales call, Alice needs to develop a customer profile, as shown in Chapter 7, to have up-to-date information on all customers.

KEY TERMS FOR SELLING

sales territory   399
account analysis   402
undifferentiated selling   402
account segmentation   402
key accounts   403
ELMS system   403

80/20 principle   403
sales response function   405
break-even analysis   406
scheduling   409
routing   409

SALES APPLICATION QUESTIONS

1. How could you use technology to better manage your customers and your territory? Explain how you could use technologies such as management software, e-mail, and cellular telephones to manage a sales territory.

2. What is a sales territory? Why do firms establish sales territories? Why might sales territories not be developed?

3. Briefly discuss each of the elements of time and territory management and indicate how these seven elements relate to one another.

4. What is the difference between the undifferentiated selling approach and the account segmentation approach for analyzing accounts? When might each approach be used?

5. Assume a sales manager determines that in a given territory each salesperson sells approximately $500,000 yearly. Also, assume that the firm's cost of goods sold are estimated to be 65 percent of sales and that a salesperson's direct costs are $35,000 a year. Each salesperson works 48 weeks a year, 8 hours a day, and averages 5 sales calls per day. Using this information, how much merchandise must each salesperson sell to break even?
   a. For the year?
   b. Each day?
   c. Each sales call?

6. What is a key account?

7. What are the factors to consider when a salesperson allocates time?

8. What is the purpose of customer sales planning?

9. Define *scheduling*. Define *routing*.

SALES WORLD WIDE WEB EXERCISES

Time Is Money, So Make Every Minute Count!

It is said that "time is money." Wasted time trying to find a prospect's address and location can cost a salesperson valuable time. For this assignment you are to imagine you work for an organization. Find three potential customers within a 50-mile radius of the city where you presently live. Choose another two potential customers who live in two states next to the state you live in. Using the following geographic information mapping tools found on the World Wide Web, create a travel schedule that would allow you to contact these five potential customers in a two-day period. The URLs are:

MapQuest

www.mapquest.com

Tiger Map Server

www.census.gov/main/www/access.html

Also look at the www.el.com search engine for maps and information on finding organizations and individuals. For example, under "references" click on "iTools!". See if the Phone/Address site has anything useful for you in this assignment. Finally, since time is money in sales, click on "USNO" under "Clock" to get the correct Naval Observatory time. You do not want to be late to your appointments!

Write a memo to your boss showing the addresses of each potential customer, plus the route and day you will be at that customer's business. Print out the appropriate maps showing locations of customers.

FURTHER EXPLORING THE SALES WORLD

1. Visit a large retailer in your community and ask a buyer or store manager what salespeople do when they make a sales call. Determine the number of times the retailer wants salespeople to visit each month. Are calls from some salespeople preferable to others? If so, why?

2. Contact a salesperson or sales manager and report on each one's philosophy toward managing time and territory. Ask each person to calculate how much it costs to contact one prospect, and on the average, what amount must be sold each day just to break even.

**SELLING
EXPERIENTIAL
EXERCISE**

Name_____ Week beginning_____
                                                                    (Date)

Make a chart similar to the one below and record the time you spend on various activities for one week. Each day, place codes on your chart to indicate the time spent
on each activity. Some codes are suggested here; add any codes you need. At the end
of the week, write your total hours in that column. If any activity takes up a great deal
of time—such as personal—subdivide it by assigning such additional activities as
television, phone, or partying. Now that you have a good idea of how you spend your
time, decide if you want to make some changes.

	Mon	Tue	Wed	Thur	Fri	Sat	Sun
7:00–7:30 A.M.							
7:30–8:00							
8:00–8:30							
8:30–9:00							
9:00–9:30							
9:30–10:00							
10:00–10:30							
10:30–11:00							
11:00–11:30							
11:30–12:00							
12:00–12:30 P.M.							
12:30–1:00							
1:00–1:30							
1:30–2:00							
2:00–2:30							
2:30–3:00							
3:00–3:30							
3:30–4:00							
4:00–4:30							
4:30–5:00							
5:00–5:30							
5:30–6:00							
6:00–6:30							
6:30–7:00							
7:00–7:30							
7:30–8:00							
After 8:00*							

Activity	Code	Total Hours
Class	CL	_____
Sleep	SL	_____
Study	SU	_____
Work	W	_____
Personal	P	_____
_____	_____	_____
_____	_____	_____

*Note: If you need to, make another sheet.

Your sales manager is working with you tomorrow only, and you want to call on customers with the greatest sales potential (see Exhibit A). Because you are on a straight commission, you will also have the opportunity to maximize your income for that day. The area of your territory that you want to cover contains 16 customers (see Exhibit B). To determine travel time, allow 15 minutes for each side of the square. Each

EXHIBIT A

Customers' sales potential

Customer	Sales Potential		Customer	Sales Potential
A	$4,000		I	$ 1,000
B	3,000		J	1,000
C	6,000		K	10,000
D	2,000		L	12,000
E	2,000		M	8,000
F	8,000		N	9,000
G	4,000		O	8,000
H	6,000		P	10,000

EXHIBIT B

A partial map of your sales territory

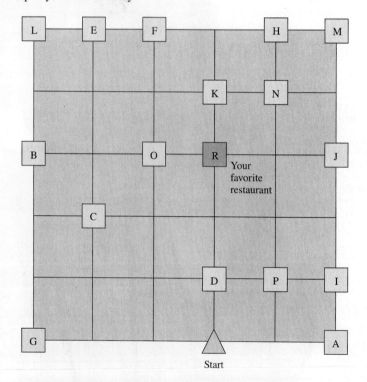

*Case copyright © 1997 by Charles M. Futrell.

sales call takes 30 minutes. You can leave your house at 8:00 A.M. or later. If you take time for lunch, it must be in 15-minute time blocks (15, 30, 45, or 60 minutes). Your last customer must be contacted by 4:30 P.M. to allow you enough sales time. Your customers do not see salespeople after 5:00 P.M. You travel home after 5:00 P.M.

Questions

1. Develop the route that gives the highest sales potential for the day your boss works with you.
2. For the next day, develop the route allowing you to contact the remaining customers in this part of the territory.

CASE 14–2

Sally Malone's District— Development of an Account Segmentation Plan

Sally Malone sat listening to her boss talk about the new time and territory management program being implemented by her company. Her boss was saying, "Since we wish eventually to establish priorities for our accounts in order to make time-investment decisions, we must classify the accounts into categories. A simple *A, B, C, D, E* designation of categories is the most commonly used approach, with *A* accounts the most valuable.

"The basis for setting the values or limits for each category is the distribution of sales or concentration patterns in most industries. In general, business in our company is distributed approximately as shown in Exhibit A. Generally, the top 10 percent of the accounts will generate 65 percent of sales, and the top 30 percent will generate 85 percent of the sales in any given territory. Salespeople may use this rule-of-thumb breakdown of accounts in determining the classification system for their accounts." Once the potential for all their accounts has been calculated, their territory should break down like this:

- *A* accounts = top 10 percent of the accounts
- *B* accounts = next 20 percent of the accounts
- *C* accounts = next 50 percent of the accounts
- *D* accounts = next 10 percent of the accounts
- *E* accounts = last 10 percent of the accounts

EXHIBIT A

Distribution of sales

Customer Classification	Percentage of Customers	Percentage of Total Sales Volume
A	10%	65%
B	20	20
C	50	10
D	10	3
E	10	2
	100%	100%

"Sally, I want you to have each of your salespeople take a close look at his or her sales-call cycles. As I have explained, a call cycle is a round of calls in which all *A* accounts are called on at least once and some, but not all, *B, C, D,* and *E* accounts are called on. When a salesperson has visited all of his or her *A* accounts, the cycle is completed. Then, a new cycle begins and the series of calls repeats. Since not all *B, C, D,* and *E* accounts are called on in every cycle, the specific accounts to be seen in these classifications differ from cycle to cycle. A call cycle, therefore, is established around the call frequency patterns of *A* accounts."

Suppose that a group of accounts is classified in this way:

Accounts	Expected Value
A	$100,000 and over
B	50,000–100,000
C	30,000–50,000
D	20,000–30,000
E	Under $20,000

The call frequency patterns, therefore, based on potential and return on time invested, may be as follows:

Accounts	Weeks Between Calls	Number of Accounts
A	2	10
B	4	20
C	6	45
D	8	12
E	10	10

Thus, a call cycle in this territory will cover two weeks. This means that in every two-week cycle the salesperson will call on these accounts:

- All of the *A*s.
- Half of the *B*s.
- One-third of the *C*s.
- One-fourth of the *D*s.
- One-fifth of the *E*s.

Questions

1. Develop a table showing a salesperson's call cycle using the call frequency patterns.
2. Discuss why this should be done.

15

Retail, Business, Services, and Nonprofit Selling

LEARNING OBJECTIVES

Retail selling is challenging and rewarding, depending on the particular retailer. Salespeople sell many types of goods and services in business, nonprofit, and consumer markets. After studying this chapter, you should be able to:

- Discuss the importance of personal selling in retailing.

- Describe the retail selling process.

- Discuss the differences between business and consumer products, as well as their markets.

- Describe the characteristics of business markets and products.

- Explain the steps business purchasing agents use in buying decisions.

- Explain the difference between services and nonprofit selling.

Barbara Coleman was very surprised to learn at least two people she worked with made more than $4,000 a month selling electronics and computers in a Kansas City retail store located in a mall. She felt lucky to earn $400 a month. Going to school only allowed her to work 50 hours a month, but Christmas was approaching and her manager said she could work 40 to 50 hours a week after finals.

Being paid the minimum wage, a commission, plus an occasional sales contest had not resulted in big bucks for Barbara. But if her co-workers were making 10 times her salary, she had room for improvement. In analyzing her procedures, Barbara waited for someone to enter the store and approached quickly asking, "May I help you?" Ten percent of the customers knew what they wanted, so Barbara showed it to them, asked questions, and let the prospects make up their own minds. About 15 percent of the people she waited on bought. Most people said no when Barbara asked, "May I help you?" Not wanting to seem pushy, she did not disturb shoppers as they looked around the store, but waited for them to ask for her help.

Can you suggest to Barbara how she might increase her sales and earn more money?

This chapter examines selling careers in four organizational settings—retail, business, services, and nonprofit. Since you are most familiar with retail selling, let's begin there.

WHAT IS RETAILING?

Many of us have worked retail, earning the minimum wage and not being challenged by the job. However, thousands of retail sales jobs are challenging and financially rewarding. Hard work, product knowledge, selling skills, and a good sales commission plan can make it very possible to earn $50,000 to more than $1,000,000 a year in retail sales. This chapter introduces you to the selling skills used by retail salespeople making big bucks.

Retailing refers to any individual or organization that sells its goods or services directly to final consumers for their personal, nonbusiness use. The distinguishing characteristic of a retail sale is that a retail transaction involves the final consumer—the retail customer. A retail sale may occur over the telephone, through the mail, on a street corner, in a private residence, or in a traditional retail store.

Goods and services sold to final consumers for their personal, nonbusiness use vary from items such as T-shirts and jogging shoes to stocks and bonds, legal services, Mary Kay cosmetics, cars, real estate, singing telegrams, and wedding cakes. A person selling panty hose to a department store shopper is engaged in retailing, as is a real estate agent selling a $90,000 house. This section focuses on retail transactions that occur in a retail store.

CAREER OPPORTUNITIES

Retail stores account for over $3 trillion in sales each year. The millions of salespeople associated with retailing are employed by firms as diverse as huge discount stores, upscale chain department stores, and mom-and-pop operations. By 2005, there are expected to be 6 million retail salespeople and 1.5 million retail managers.[1]

Financial Rewards Are Excellent

The financial rewards and promotional opportunities for the retail salesperson are excellent. Some retail firms pay only the minimum wage, but many pay excellent salaries to qualified people.

As in other forms of professional selling, the financial rewards and promotional opportunities for the retail salesperson are excellent. Earnings as a retail salesperson vary depending on the type of product sold, the compensation plan (straight salary, salary plus commission, or straight commission), and the organization. Salary ranges can be from $4.25 an hour to more than $1,000,000 a year. When you are in a store, ask salespeople if they are on an hourly salary or commission plan. Those on commissions could be making big bucks if they are (1) order-getters, (2) prospectors, and (3) able to obtain referrals.

Nonfinancial Rewards Are Many

Financial compensation is only one part of the reward received as a retail salesperson. Nonfinancial rewards offered by a retail career are numerous. They include excellent training programs, rapid assumption of responsibility, recognition, opportunity for personal growth and development, travel, and satisfaction from work.

RETAILERS SELL LIKE ORGANIZATIONAL SALESPEOPLE

Fundamental sales principles apply to all types of persuasive situations, including retailing. Of course, basic differences exist between retail and organizational sales; the main difference is that many retailers have customers enter their stores to purchase a good or service. However, retailers who sell products such as appliances, real estate, financial services, carpeting, and building supplies frequently send salespeople out to call on customers at home. Whether the retail salesperson is selling in the store, over the telephone, or outside the store, basic selling techniques can be used effectively when adapted to a particular retailing situation.

THE RETAIL SALESPERSON'S ROLE

The role requirements of retail salespersons vary greatly. Some jobs require the salesperson to act only as an order-taker. Other jobs require highly skilled people who can successfully identify and arouse the customers' needs and persuade them to purchase and satisfy those needs. Generally, a retail salesperson is involved, to some extent, in providing service, working stock, personal selling, and completing transactions. The following sections elaborate on each of these four retail sales functions.

Service Is the Key

To build clientele—and thus earn top money—retail salespeople need (1) to develop repeat sales from present customers; (2) to get new customers through referrals from customers, and (3) to sell prospects entering or calling the store. Salespersons do this by being able to close prospects and provide great service to customers.

Remember, we are not referring to transactional, McDonald's hamburger servers. We are describing relationship salespeople selling such products as cars, trucks, cosmetics, insurance, mutual funds, furniture, jewelry, clothes, travel services, and bank loans directly to people for their personal use.

Working and Knowing Stock Is Necessary

Maintaining a variety of neatly displayed items for sale to consumers and reordering or replacing stock items when depleted is a tedious, time-consuming, and important function of many retail salespeople. The appearance of a store, or a department within a large store, reflects on the retail salesperson and helps the consumer to develop a good first impression, thereby boosting the retailer's chance for making

MAKING THE SALE

Creative Suggestion Selling

"I witnessed an outstanding example of creative suggestion selling one day in a Neiman Marcus store," says Stanley Marcus. "A salesperson approached a young buyer and asked if she could help her by writing up the sale of a $50 necktie, so she could wait on another customer. She handed the buyer the $50 tie and quickly introduced the customer to another salesperson at the counter.

"As he began writing up the sale, he looked up and said, 'This is a beautiful tie you have selected. What is he going to wear with it?' The woman reached into her purse and pulled out a swatch of fabric. He looked at it a moment and said, 'There's an ancient madder pattern which comes in two color combinations that would go very well with this suit.' He pulled out the two ties as he was talking with her. She readily agreed and took both of them—at $100 each.

"He asked, 'Doesn't he need some new shirts to go with his new suit?' The customer replied, 'I'm glad you asked; he does need some, but I haven't been able to find any white ones with French cuffs. Do you have any size fifteen thirty-three?' He showed her two qualities, pointing out the difference in the cloths. She selected three shirts at $125 each. 'Doesn't he ever wear colored shirts?' he inquired. 'Yes; if you have this same shirt in blue, I'll take two.'

"The sale progressed from there to include gold-filled cuff links, a travel robe to match the ancient madder ties, pajamas, and slippers. The total sale was $1,500 versus the $50 the original salesperson was willing to settle for. Of even more importance, he made a new customer for the department. That is creative suggestion selling at its very best.

"Not once in the course of the sale did he oversell. He related to the customer's desires and wants and knew the content of the stock well enough to fulfill her requirements. Above all, he had the heart of a salesperson who not only thoroughly enjoys the excitement of meeting the expressed request of the customer but had the imagination to conceive of other things the buyer might find of interest. This type of selling technique can be taught; unfortunately, it doesn't happen very often. Americans have prided themselves on their selling ability, but lack of management attention to selling has dulled those skills."[2]

sales. Working stock also aids a retail salesperson in gaining knowledge of the company's products and their location within the store.

| **Personal Selling Is Where It's At** | Of the four functions of the retail salesperson, personal selling is most important. In most cases, the retail salesperson should consider using the same major parts of the sales presentation used by the business salesperson, beginning with the approach. Before going on, please read "Making the Sale" for an example of creative retail selling. |

Accurately Completing Transactions Is a Must

When a customer is ready to make a purchase, the salesperson must complete the transaction before the sale can be completed. A retail transaction should be handled smoothly and quickly with a great degree of accuracy to avoid frustrating the customer and possibly losing the sale. This is a good checklist to follow when transacting a sale:

- Prepare the sales slip clearly and accurately.
- Accept payment or arrange for credit.
- If change is required, count it accurately, and do not place the money received from the customer in the cash drawer until you have made change.
- When accepting a check or credit card, make sure all forms are signed by the customer.

Many retailing institutions encourage the use of charge accounts by qualified customers. In such an instance, you may encourage new customers to participate in your store's charge program by asking them to fill out a credit application. Later that day,

SELLING GLOBALLY

The Former Soviet Union, Eastern Europe, and the Third World

Despite essential differences between the former Soviet Union, its former satellites in Eastern Europe, and countries in the Third World, they share these similar business problems: low productivity, poor-quality products, and in many cases, a physically run-down manufacturing location with a poor—or nonexistent—infrastructure.

American retailers wanting to open stores in these countries should expect a bureaucratic tone to the negotiating process, the methods applied, and the goals to be achieved. Remember that your partners from the other side may have strong security concerns. Their jobs—even their careers—may still depend on the success of the individual negotiation.

Since red tape can be an obstacle, expect to waste a lot of time when dealing with the bureaucracy. Even if there are progressive, liberal laws and regulations, the bureaucrats continue to use discretion in approving key parts of foreign investment activities. A significant delay, however, shouldn't necessarily jeopardize the whole transaction.

Settlements are usually written in a highly detailed way; this applies to everything from feasibility studies to multi-million-dollar equipment and construction contracts. Also, don't expect the negotiation process to move quickly or smoothly. Negotiations are likely to continue right up to (and often through) the drafting of the final contract. Accept the possibility of a slow pace with a lot of attention given to what may seem like insignificant details.[3]

you could drop these customers a short thank-you card requesting their regular patronage. This type of retail service builds long-lasting relationships between salespeople and customers.

TECHNOLOGY BUILDS RELATIONSHIPS

Retailers are using technology to strengthen customer loyalties and build relationships. Here's an example. A chain of 30 fashion stores in five states created their Call Customer Program in which salespeople maintain ongoing relationships with their regular customers. All sales associates maintain personal *call books* that include detailed customer information such as size, color, and style preferences; previous purchases; names of family members; employment; and important dates to remember. The associate acts as a purchasing agent for customers, contacting them about special events or when appropriate merchandise arrives, or reminding them of important personal dates (e.g., the birthday of a spouse). They often act as personal shoppers selecting items throughout the store for customers.

Contact-management software—see Chapter 5—is great for recording customer information. Some retailers have salespeople view merchandise at their central warehouse showroom via satellite, make selections for specific customers, and then contact customers. Technology is rapidly becoming part of salespeople's basic retail selling process.

BASIC RETAIL SELLING PROCESS

Why do you shop at a particular retail store? Why do you buy from a particular salesperson? Your reasons will differ depending on the type of product you shop for, such as gasoline, a bank account, a wedding ring, or an automobile. Of the many basic reasons why people shop at a particular store, here are some of the most important:

- **The salesperson**—Is this the right salesperson for me to trust and from whom to buy? Does this salesperson have integrity, judgment, and knowledge concerning my situation?
- **Company**—Is this the store for me?
- **Product**—Will this product fulfill my needs?
- **Price**—Should I shop around for price? Will this store lower the price shortly? What about terms and returns?
- **Time to buy**—Should I buy now?
- **Service**—Will the company and salesperson help me if I need further help?
- **Trust**—Can I trust this salesperson, store, and product?

You probably have other reasons why you shop at various retailers to add to the list. However, consider these seven patronage motives when developing your basic retail selling process. Successful retail salespeople consider these patronage motives when using a selling process similar to these 10 steps:

1. Prospecting.
2. The approach.
   a. Attitude.
   b. Appearance.
   c. Manner.
3. Presentation.
   a. Agreement of need.
      (1) Bring sales presentations into focus on product needed.
   b. Selling the store.
      (1) Your reputation.
      (2) Company reputation.
   c. Fill the need.
      (1) Stress benefits of features and advantages of products and store using SELL sequence.
4. Use a trial close.
5. Respond to objection.
6. Use your trial close to determine if you've handled objection.
7. Close the primary sale.
8. Suggestion selling.
   a. Suggest other items to buy.
9. Wrap it up.
   a. Remove fears, uncertainties, doubts.
   b. Complete the transaction.
10. Follow-up and service after the sale.

Carefully orchestrated and executed, these 10 steps can bring you success and satisfied customers.

TWO PROS TELL YOU HOW TO BE SUCCESSFUL

In interviewing Jack Pruett and Richard Ciotti for this book, it quickly became apparent why they are so successful. Jack works for Bailey, Banks & Biddle Jewelers and Richard for JC Penney. Both earn over $100,000 a year. When asked for their secrets, here is what they said:

"Sales is a joy to me," says Jack Pruett. "I would really rather sell jewelry than anything in the world. It is both personally and financially rewarding. It takes hard work to earn serious money. Today, retailers recognize the importance of salespeople to their success and many are compensating on a commission basis, which allows good salespeople to make high salaries.

"I realize there are sales techniques, and many of us use parts of some techniques. But selling is a people business, and there are no two people with the same fingerprints or needs. So you can't treat people exactly the same. The most important factor to my success is my belief that I can do the best job taking care of a person's needs. I've studied hard, worked hard, and developed a selling process that works for me. It didn't happen over night—it was my second year in the business before I became comfortable in jewelry sales."

"Our customers don't have to buy from us, especially in my town," says Richard Ciotti. "We have many places to buy furniture. I need that customer; that customer doesn't need me. My job is to sell to the customer's wants and needs. I ask questions to determine the customer's needs, and then I provide what's necessary to make the customer happy. If they say they're looking for a living room set, I ask, 'Are you looking for a traditional or a country set? What style are you looking for? What size sofa are you looking for?' There are questions that you can ask to narrow the options so that you don't waste a lot of time—your time and the customer's time.

"It only takes one little thing to turn off a customer. Even if they wanted to buy it, they could just walk out of the store. So, it helps to know your products and how to approach people. You can't learn this overnight. Customers are smart. They shop around. They know if you know what you are talking about. I think after many years of dealing with people you get a sixth sense. You can tell how the customer is going to react to you.

"When the time is right, I move to close the sale. If the customer is looking at an item I'll say, 'We have a sale on and we've been selling quite a few of these. I can check the computer to see if we have it in stock.' Once I do this, I know I'm getting my foot in the door. What I'll ask them is, 'Do you have a JC Penney charge?' If they do I'll say, 'I can check the open-to-buy on your charge and see how much you can purchase,' or 'Would you like to open a Penney's charge?' I try to either use the computer as an excuse to check the stock for them, get their charge card, or anything like that so I can close the sale."

Ability, motivation, liking what they do, and a caring attitude toward helping customers have made Jack and Richard two of the top retail salespeople in America. If done correctly, retail selling can be challenging and rewarding.

WHAT'S DIFFERENT ABOUT THE BUSINESS MARKET?

The **business market,** sometimes called the *industrial, producer,* or *organizational market,* consists of all business users. Business users are profit and nonprofit organizations that buy goods and services for one of three purposes:

- **To make other goods and services.** Campbell's buys fresh vegetables to make soup, and American Airlines buys airplanes to transport people.
- **To sell to consumer or other industrial users.** Kroger's buys canned tuna to sell to consumers, and Boeing sells their airplanes to organizations such as American Airlines or the Air Force.

EXHIBIT 15-1

EXHIBIT 15-1

Classification of goods and
services in the business market

■ **Entering goods**

Raw materials:
- Farm products (wheat, cotton, livestock, fruits and vegetables)
- Natural products (fish, lumber, crude petroleum, iron ore)

Manufactured materials and parts:
- Component materials (steel, cement, wire, textiles)
- Component parts (small motors, tires, castings)

■ **Foundation goods**

Installations:
- Buildings and land rights (factories, offices)
- Fixed equipment (generators, drill presses, computers, elevators)

Accessory equipment:
- Portable or light factory equipment and tools (hand tools, lift trucks)
- Office equipment (calculators, desks)

■ **Facilitating goods**

Supplies:
- Operating supplies (lubricants, coal, paper, pencils)
- Maintenance and repair items (paint, nails, brooms)

Business services:
- Maintenance and repair services (window cleaning, calculator repair)
- Business advisory services (legal, management consulting, advertising)

■ **To conduct the organization's operation.** Texas A & M University buys office supplies and electronic office equipment for the registrar's office, and a dentist buys supplies to use in the office.

In the business market, salespeople can deal with both consumer products and business products. **Business marketing** is the marketing of goods and services to business users—as contrasted to ultimate consumers.

Because the business market is largely unknown, average consumers are apt to underrate its significance. Actually, this market is huge in total sales volume and the number of firms involved in it. About 50 percent of all manufactured products are sold to the business market. In addition, about 80 percent of all farm products and virtually all minerals, forests, and sea products are business goods. These are sold to firms for further processing. The U.S. government is the largest purchaser of goods and services in the world.[4]

The basic types of goods and services purchased by buyers in the producer market are shown in Exhibit 15–1. In addition to raw materials and components, producers purchase facilities (such as buildings), capital equipment, and a wide array of periodic services such as repairs, legal services, and advertising.

**CAREER
OPPORTUNITIES**

Sales career opportunities in the business, services, and nonprofit areas are excellent. The approximately 3 million salespeople and 1 million sales managers are expected to grow to 4 million and 1.3 million by 2005. Jobs may increase faster as nonprofit organizations discover the benefits of having a sales force.[5]

SELLING THE BUSINESS PRODUCT IS DIFFERENT

Selling products to businesses is often different than selling directly to customers. Let's examine the demand, types of purchases, and product characteristics of the business product.

Demand for Business Products

Three important factors distinguish the demand for business products from the demand for consumer goods. When selling in the business market, consider the influences on the demand for your products and services to properly plan a sales presentation. Customer demand is derived, inelastic, and joint.

Derived Demand

The demand for many business goods and services is linked to consumer demand for other products—it is a **derived demand.** For example, the Whirlpool Corporation buys small electric motors for its refrigerators because consumers purchase the refrigerator; the motor's demand is based on the demand for the refrigerator. People do not buy motors; they buy refrigerators. There would be little demand for refrigerator motors and other associated components, if no one bought refrigerators.

Other business sellers are affected by a change in demand for a particular product. If, for example, the demand for Whirlpool's refrigerators declined, the demand for production equipment would decline. Lower demands for steel would lead to a lower demand for iron ore. A change in a product's demand can set in motion a wave of changes affecting the demand for all firms involved in production.

Inelastic Demand

The demand for many business products is **inelastic demand.** An increase or decrease in the price of a product usually does not generate a proportionate increase or decrease in sales for the product. The Whirlpool refrigerator has many parts. The cost of each part represents a fraction of the total cost of producing the refrigerator. If there is an increase or decrease in the price of a single part, such as the motor, the demand for the appliance is not significantly influenced. Even if the cost of its motor doubled (assuming it did not represent a large proportion of production costs), and was passed along to the consumer, the refrigerator's sales price would increase by a small amount, having little effect on consumer demand.

Joint Demand

The demand for many business products also is affected by **joint demand.** Joint demand occurs when two or more products are used together to produce a single product. For example, a firm that manufactures automobiles needs numerous component parts—tires, batteries, steel, glass, and so on. These products are demanded jointly.

The salesperson selling products that are demanded jointly must understand the effect of joint demand on the market. When a customer purchases a product, there is an opportunity to sell companion products. An example is the grocery retailer who purchases computerized cash registers. It requires the purchase of associated items such as a small computer, cash registers, product scanners, and other supplies for operating the equipment in the grocery store.

Business goods have three types of demand—derived, inelastic, and joint. By understanding the demand for the product, a salesperson is better able to sell successfully.

Major Types of Business Purchases

Business purchases are usually one of three general types—new task purchases, straight rebuy purchases, or modified rebuy purchases.

The **new task purchase** is made when a product is bought in conjunction with a job or task newly performed by the purchaser. A long period is frequently needed for the salesperson to make this type of sale since the buyer is often cautious, especially when confronted with an expensive product or large quantities. This is the most challenging selling situation, since buyers want to consider all alternative suppliers and may need substantial information from each supplier. The salesperson may have to submit a prototype of the product, a price bid, and make several presentations over an extended period before the final purchase decision. New task purchases include buying capital equipment, construction materials for a new job site, and even an entire plant facility.

The **straight rebuy purchase** is a routine purchase of products bought regularly. This sale is normally casual order taking. Often, buyers negotiate a blanket purchase order (BPO) agreement, which establishes the price and terms of the sale for a set period. Buyers require little time and information to make a purchase decision. This type of purchase might include continually used raw materials, office supplies, or MRO (maintenance, repair, and operations items such as spare parts for machinery).

The **modified rebuy purchase** is somewhat like the straight rebuy purchase procedure. The buyer seeks a similar product, but wants or needs to negotiate different items. The buyer may want a lower price, faster delivery, or better quality. For example, a firm that buys oil field drilling bits from a supplier each month (straight rebuy situation) decides it needs a better-quality drilling bit. The firm goes to the same supplier and others to see whether a better-quality bit is available and at what price (modified rebuy situation). The drilling company still wants drill bits, but looks for a slightly different product to suit its present needs.

Product Characteristics

Business products, like business markets, have certain characteristics that a salesperson must consider when selling to buyers of these goods. These product characteristics differ from consumer product characteristics. Business products are (1) technical, (2) in need of specifications and bids, (3) complex in pricing, and (4) standardized.

Technical Products

Compared to consumer goods, business sales are more technical. The business salesperson must have more product knowledge training than a salesperson of consumer goods. Discussing complex production information with knowledgeable customers, which demands considerable expertise, is essential to success.

Specifications and Bids

Many business goods are bought based on specifications. These specifications may be determined by the customer, or they may be commonly accepted industry standards. They may be tremendously complex, such as the design of a specialized hydraulic pump, or as simple as stating a particular color to use.

Bids, based on stated specifications, usually are submitted by several selling firms to the purchasing firm. Each seller bids on a homogeneous, similar product. Depending on the buyer's wishes, bids may range from a similar oral quote given over the phone to a formalized written quotation or a sealed bid held in the buyer's office and opened on a specific closing date along with all other bids. If the purchasing agent does not want to accept any of the bids, suppliers may be asked to submit second bids. Purchasing firms typically use this system to identify the product's true market price.

If all other factors are equal, the company submitting the lowest bid wins the contract. However, other factors frequently affect the buying decision. The product's performance and quality level, for example, may be important considerations in the buying decision. Del Monte Corporation may pay a supplier several cents more per bushel for a higher grade of tomatoes so that they can charge a premium price for canned tomatoes at the retail level.

Complex Pricing

Because of the product's technical nature, its inelastic demand characteristic, the buyer's expertise, and the fact that competitive bidding often is involved in the purchase process, pricing is complex. Final price to the customer can be based on estimates of long-term agreements, present and future labor and material costs, availability of materials, expected salvage value of present equipment, product service agreements, cost effectiveness of production facilities, and return on investment.

A bid under complex pricing may include progressive payments whereby the buyer makes periodic payments to the supplier as a down payment, with the remainder paid when the product is delivered; escalator clauses, such as if the cost of manufacturing the product increases, the product's price also increases; specific foreign currency exchange rates; and letters of credit. In addition, the quote will probably include cash terms and delivery (discussed in Chapter 5).

In considering the many factors affecting the price of a business product, a sales manager may give the company's sales force a range of prices to use in negotiations. Avoid trying to use low price alone to make a sale. After all, your selling skills determine success in the long run.

Standardization

Many business products tend to be homogeneous. When compared to competing products, they show high similarity. See Exhibit 15–2. When a new product or product feature is introduced to the market, its initial advantage quickly may be lost. It is easy for competitors to improve a product slightly and market it as their own. Most of the time, the salesperson sells products that are similar to a competitor's products.

WHO MAKES THE DECISIONS AROUND HERE?

Business goods have market and product characteristics that differ from consumer goods. Therefore, the buying decision is somewhat different for business goods than for consumer goods. The business buying process, like the consumer buying process, is a series of steps. The eight steps involved in purchasing business products are (1) recognition of the problem or need; (2) determination of the characteristics of the needed product; (3) determination of product specifications; (4) search and qualification of potential sources; (5) acquisition and analysis of proposal; (6) selection of supplier(s); (7) establishment of an order routine; and (8) evaluation of product performance.

Exhibit 15–3 shows the steps in the business buying process, along with the three business buying situations. For the straight rebuy, Steps 2 through 7 can be eliminated. In this situation, a need is recognized, such as a low inventory of a product, and the order is automatically processed. The salesperson supplying a product on a

The characteristics of industrial products make selling them a challenge. How does the product shown on the left differ from the product on the right?

This product is built specifically for each missile.

These are standardized.

straight rebuy basis contacts the customer periodically to check inventory and to make sure that the order is processed quickly. This procedure strengthens a customer's loyalty to and reliance on a seller, indirectly warding off competition. Salespeople must continually watch for the possibility that present customers may reassess their needs and find some problem with a product, and thus seek another supplier. By routinely contacting the customer, the salesperson becomes aware of changes in the buyer's attitude.

In the new task and modified buying situations, several competing suppliers' salespeople may present the prospect with information. The salesperson helps determine the buyer's needs and shows the buyer how they are fulfilled by a product. The salesperson needs to work closely with everyone who has an influence on the buying decision. When no firm has an initial edge on an industrial order, the salesperson who spends the *right* amount of time with the *right* people often walks away with the

Business buying process and situations

Steps in Business Buying Process	Type of Buying Situation		
	New Task	Modified Rebuy	Straight Rebuy
1. Recognition of a problem or need	yes	yes	yes
2. Determination of characteristics of the needed product	yes	yes	no
3. Determination of product specifications	yes	yes	no
4. Search and qualification of potential sources	yes	yes	no
5. Acquisition and analysis of proposal	yes	yes	no
6. Selection of supplier(s)	yes	yes	no
7. Selection of an order routine	yes	yes	no
8. Evaluation of product performance	yes	yes	yes

order. This person probably spent some time learning *whom* to talk to. Knowing the right people in an organization is vital to a salesperson's existence. With experience, most good salespeople learn whom they need to contact. But how does the beginning salesperson find these influential people? The next section provides some answers.

WHOM SHOULD I TALK TO?

Many salespeople only contact the buyer or purchasing agent, who often only places the order. The purchasing agent may not actually decide what to buy. It is important to talk to anyone who might influence the purchase decision.

Gates Rubber Company's John Croley provides an excellent example of the many people he talks with in making a sale. Croley works out of his home in Mooresville, North Carolina. He makes sure the necessary product and sales materials are in his car before leaving. As Croley greets the receptionist, he presents his business card and asks to see the purchasing agent. While waiting, he reviews what will be discussed with the buyer.

The buyer arrives in the lobby and is greeted by Croley, who gets permission to talk with users of several Gates products. Croley inspects how his product is being used to make suggestions on improving its performance. He then demonstrates how a new product works to wholesaler salespeople so they feel comfortable discussing it with their customers.

In determining whom to see and how much time to spend with each person, the salesperson should learn who influences the purchase decision and the *strength of each person's influence.* People who may influence the purchase of a product include:

- **Initiator**—the person proposing to buy or replace the product.
- **Deciders**—the people involved in making the actual decision—such as the plant engineer, purchasing agent, and someone from top management.
- **Influencers**—plant engineer, plant workers, and research and development personnel who develop specifications needed for the product.
- **Buyers**—the purchasing agent.
- **Gatekeepers**—people who influence where information from salespeople goes and with whom salespeople talk. Receptionists, secretaries, and purchasing agents are gatekeepers.
- **Users**—those people who must work with or use the product; for example, plant workers or secretaries.

It is crucial that the salesperson get by the gatekeepers and talk to the initiators, users, influencers, buyers, and deciders. For example, users of a company's copy machine (initiators) may become dissatisfied with its quality of copies. A secretary (influencer) mentions that Xerox makes an excellent copier that the firm can afford. After a conference with several major users of the present duplicating machine, the office manager (decider) confers with the representatives of several competing copy machine firms and decides to lease the Xerox machine. A purchase order is forwarded to the corporate home office, where a purchasing agent (buyer) approves the machines. Which person should the Xerox salesperson have visited in selling the machine? In this example, each person who participates in the purchase decision should have been contacted—the secretary, major users, and office manager—and the salesperson should have explained the product's benefits to each person.

Often, a new salesperson is not allowed in the plant nor allowed to talk to people within the company other than the purchasing agent. Hundreds of other salespeople may have already called on the company wanting the same thing. Large manufacturers, like General Motors, have salespeople stop at the receptionist's desk. Whomever the salesperson has asked to see is telephoned. Purchasing agents and other influential individuals usually see only those salespeople who have appointments, or with whom they are well acquainted. A new salesperson calling on GM must plan ahead. It is essential to call ahead for an appointment, not just drop by.

If a buyer's secretary is reluctant to make an appointment, or if the buyer refuses to establish a meeting time, the salesperson must either give up or use creativity and charm. Sending a reluctant buyer a personalized novelty, such as a small figure of a salesperson holding a sample case along with a note saying, "This salesperson has something that will benefit you," is a creative way of gaining an appointment.

After being turned away by a head nurse (gatekeeper), a pharmaceutical salesperson put a stethoscope around his neck, obtained a small doctor's bag, and proceeded to the tenth floor of a large hospital to see the hospital's chief of surgery about a new drug. He told the doctor what he had done and why, and was asked not to do it again. All was not for naught, however, because he arranged to have future conferences with the surgeon in the doctor's lounge on request. This salesperson would not take no for an answer. While you do not want to offend any clients with persistence, you may open the door on a sale that a gatekeeper tried to keep closed.

Ask yourself, when you do something creative, how many others have been stopped by the gatekeeper? Buyers, like all of us, appreciate people who give them special attention or go out of their way for them, especially if they believe someone understands their needs, sincerely wants to help them, and acts professionally.

PURCHASING AGENTS ARE RATIONAL BUYERS

When selling to the producer market, the salesperson deals with well-trained, knowledgeable, and rational buyers. Purchasing agents in large corporations are often specialists. They are experts in dealing with salespeople. See Exhibit 15–4.

Purchasing agents carefully examine information presented to them. Quality sales presentations are expected from salespeople they see. Buying decisions are made based on practical, business reasons. Emotional reasons for buying play a less important role in purchasing decisions than in decisions made by a consumer. As a result, the time required to make a purchase decision is usually longer than in the consumer setting. This is because industrial buyers carefully compare their firm's needs with the features, advantages, and benefits of competing products—a process that takes time.

WHY DO PRODUCERS BUY?

Buyers in the producer market seek to buy for many reasons. Some common reasons usually evolve from an aspect of the product's cost and quality. Specific primary buying needs or motives include:

- Increasing profits.
- Increasing sales.
- Producing a quality product.
- Improving the operation's efficiency (resulting in cost reductions).
- Helpfulness of the salesperson.
- Service.
- Payment.
- Trade-in allowances.
- Delivery.
- Buying a product at the lowest price.

EXHIBIT 15–4

This purchasing agent is an expert on products used in manufacturing. The salesperson must know her product and how it can best be used by the customer.

To be a successful salesperson, determine each buyer's important buying needs. Then, develop a sales presentation emphasizing your product's features, advantages, and benefits, and how they can fulfill those needs. One of the best and most often used methods of presenting your product's benefits to the buyer is value analysis.

TECHNOLOGY HELPS SALESPEOPLE ON THE MOVE

Many business salespeople who work with customers in America and overseas are using technology to keep up with product and customer information. Take Doug Loewe, European sales manager for CompuServe. Based in New York, he acts as liaison between the company's two international offices (outside London and in Munich) and its corporate offices in Columbus, Ohio. "I live and die by my PC," he says. "When I'm not traveling to those locations I'm sending e-mail or project documents through CompuServe."

At home only 10 percent of the year, Loewe travels with his "virtual office"—a briefcase that carries his laptop. "In an airport lounge I'll find a phone plug-in, suck all my messages from the server [the brain of the company's computer network], then while I'm flying I'll respond to the message. Later I'll plug back in and upload the responses to their respective destinations." He receives, on average, some 40 e-mail messages a day, 10 of which require proactive responses. Now that the company is connected to the Internet, some of these put him in direct contact with his customers. "They can e-mail me now," he says, "so I have to be careful that my reply isn't as casual as one I might send to someone in-house."

SELLING SERVICES IS CHALLENGING

Most people think of selling physical products, such as candy, cars, or copiers. Yet one of the biggest recent trends has been the phenomenal growth of careers in selling services. The government sector with its schools, post office, and military services is in the service business. The private nonprofit sector with its charities, churches, colleges, and hospitals is in the service business. A good part of the business sector, with its airlines, banks, insurance companies, and law firms is in the service business.

EXHIBIT 15–5

A good-service continuum

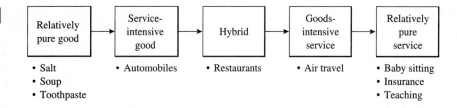

| Relatively pure good | → | Service-intensive good | → | Hybrid | → | Goods-intensive service | → | Relatively pure service |

- Salt
- Soup
- Toothpaste

- Automobiles

- Restaurants

- Air travel

- Baby sitting
- Insurance
- Teaching

A service is an action or activity done for others for a fee. Musical rock bands and barbers perform services. As you will see, the production of services may or may not be linked to a physical product.

Exhibit 15–5 shows a mix of goods and services on a continuum ranging from relatively pure goods to relatively pure services. There are few pure goods or services, since each usually requires the other. In taking a college course, for example, you may buy a textbook. Similarly, buying salt, soup, and toothpaste requires supporting services, such as totaling up what you owe and sacking the good(s) at the cashier's checkout.

Characteristics of Services

The special nature of services stems from several distinctive characteristics that create special selling challenges and opportunities. Services also result in sales techniques that are substantially different from those used to sell goods.

Intangibility. Because services are essentially intangible, customers cannot sample—taste, feel, see, hear, or smell—services *before* they buy them. This feature of services places some strain on a seller. Salespeople must concentrate on the *benefits* to be derived from the service, rather than emphasizing the service itself. An insurance salesperson thus may stress service benefits such as guaranteed payment of a child's college expenses, or a retirement income of so many dollars per month. AT&T salespersons discuss how business users can cut selling costs by using their long-distance calling system.

Inseparability. Services often cannot be separated from the person of the seller. Moreover some services must be created and dispensed simultaneously. For example, dentists create and dispense almost all their services at the same time.

From a sales standpoint, inseparability frequently means that direct sale is the only possible channel of distribution, and a seller's services cannot be sold in very many markets. This characteristic also limits the scale of operation in a firm. One person can repair only so many autos in a day or treat only so many medical patients.

As an exception to the inseparability feature, the service may be sold by a person representing the creator-seller. A travel agent, insurance broker, or rental agent, for instance, may represent and help promote the service that will be sold by the institution producing it.

Heterogeneity. A service industry, or even an individual seller of services, cannot standardize output. Each unit of the service is somewhat different from other units of the same service. For example, an airline does not give the same quality of service on each trip. All repair jobs a mechanic does on automobiles are not of equal quality. An added complication is the difficulty of judging the quality of a service. (Of course, we can say the same for some goods.) It is particularly difficult to forecast quality in advance of buying a service. For example, a person pays to see a ball game without knowing whether it will be an exciting one, well worth the price of admission, or a dull performance.

Perishability and Fluctuating Demand. Services are highly perishable, and they cannot be stored. Unused electric power, empty seats in a stadium, and idle mechanics in a garage all represent business lost forever. Furthermore, the market for services fluctuates considerably by season, by day of the week, and by hour of the day. Many ski lifts lie idle all summer, and in some areas golf courses go unused in the winter. The use of city buses fluctuates greatly during the day.

There are some notable exceptions to this generalization regarding the perishability and storage of services. In health and life insurance, for example, the service is purchased. Then it is held by the insurance company (the seller) until needed by the buyer or the beneficiary. This holding constitutes a type of storage.

The combination of perishability and fluctuating demand creates product-planning, pricing, and promotion challenges for service company executives. Some organizations have developed new uses for idle plant capacity during off-seasons. Thus, during the summer, several ski resorts operate their ski lifts for hikers and sightseers who want access to higher elevations. Advertising and creative pricing also stimulate demand during slack periods. Hotels offer lower prices and family packages for weekends. Telephone companies offer lower rates during nights and weekends. In some college towns, apartment rates are reduced in the summer.

Selling Services Is the Most Challenging

Selling services is the most challenging sales job you could have because of the characteristics of services. The salesperson, for example, cannot show and physically demonstrate services. Intangibles are often difficult for many prospects to understand—these include insurance, financial investments, car repairs, and health services such as surgery.

NONPROFIT SELLING—IT'S ABOUT TIME!

A **nonprofit organization** does not have profit as a goal; therefore, it neither intends nor tries to make a profit. Most of the nonprofit organizations sell services rather than tangible products. Here are examples:

- *Educational*—Private grade schools, high schools, colleges, universities.
- *Cultural*—Museums, zoos, symphony orchestras, opera and theater groups.
- *Religious*—Churches, synagogues, temples, mosques.
- *Charitable and philanthropic*—Welfare groups (Salvation Army, Red Cross), research foundations (American Cancer Society, Easter Seals), fund-raising groups (United Fund).
- *Social cause*—Organizations dealing with family planning, civil rights, stopping smoking, preventing heart disease, environmental concerns, those for or against abortion, or for or against nuclear energy.
- *Social*—Fraternal organizations, civic groups, clubs.
- *Health care*—Hospitals, nursing homes, health research organizations (American Cancer Society, American Health Association), HMOs (health maintenance organizations).
- *Political*—Political parties, individual politicians.

Business versus Nonprofit Selling

A major difference between business and nonprofit selling involves the groups that the particular organization must deal with. Business executives have traditionally defined their basic markets as being made up of their present and potential customers. They have thus directed their selling efforts primarily toward this one group. In contrast, most nonprofit organizations are involved with *two* major markets in their marketing effort. One of these groups consists of the **nonprofit contributors** (of money, labor, services, or materials) to the organization. Here the nonprofit organization's task is that of resource attraction.

The other major target market is the organization's **nonprofit clients**—the recipients of the organization's money and/or services. This recipient market is much like that of the customers of a business company. However, nonprofit organizations—such as churches, Girl Scout units, nursing homes, symphony orchestras, or universities—are unlikely to refer to their client-recipients as customers. Instead, these organizations use such terms as *parishioners, members, patients, audience,* or *students.*

This distinction between business and nonprofit selling based on the major markets involved is significant for this reason: A nonprofit organization must develop two separate sales programs—one looking back at its contributors, and the other looking forward at its clients.

Importance of Nonprofit Selling

The attention that is finally being devoted to nonprofit selling is long overdue and definitely needed. Thousands of these organizations handle billions of dollars and affect millions of people. Often the operation of these organizations is admittedly inefficient. Empty beds in hospitals and empty classrooms constitute a waste of resources we can ill afford. Often a large part of the money collected by a nonprofit organization goes to cover its administrative expenses, rather than to serve the intended customers. This creates a dual social and economic loss—donors' gifts are wasted and clients are not served efficiently.

The importance of selling shows up when nonprofit organizations fail to do an effective sales job. Then the result may be additional social and economic costs and wastes. If the death rate from smoking rises because the American Cancer Society and other organizations cannot persuade people of the harm of smoking, we all lose. When antilitter organizations fail to convince people to control their solid-waste disposal, we all lose. When good museums or good symphony orchestras must cease operating because of lack of contributions and/or lack of attendance, there again are social and economic losses.

By developing an effective sales program, a nonprofit organization can increase immeasurably its chances of (1) satisfactorily serving both its contributor and its client markets and (2) improving the overall efficiency of its operations.

Generally speaking, people in most nonprofit organizations do not realize that they are running a business and should employ business management techniques. It is true that making a profit is *not* the goal of these organizations. Yet only very recently have many nonprofit organizations started to employ salespeople.

How Selling Is Used

Personal selling is frequently used in fund-raising efforts. Sometimes a door-to-door campaign is used. At Christmastime, Salvation Army volunteers collect donations in the downtown area or malls of many cities. And potential large donors often are approached by salespeople.

Many nonprofit organizations also use personal selling to reach their client public. These personal representatives may not be called salespeople, but that is exactly what they are. For centuries, missionaries of countless religious organizations have recruited new members by personal contact—personal selling. Personal selling also is used to recruit new members for fraternal organizations (YMCA, Girl Scouts, Elks). Colleges send "salespeople" (admission officers, alumni, current students) to talk to high school students, their parents, and their counselors.

Using salespeople to reach either contributors or clients poses some management problems for a nonprofit organization. In effect, the organization has to manage a sales force—including recruiting, training, compensating, supervising, and evaluating performance. Unfortunately, not many nonprofit organizations think in these terms, nor are they as yet qualified to do this management job.

SELLING IS SELLING

No matter whether you are persuading someone to give you money for a copier, insurance policy, or charity—you are selling. Selling is selling. Personal selling refers to the personal communication of information to persuade a prospective customer to buy something—a good, service, idea, or something else—which satisfies the individual's needs. Anytime you are doing this, you are selling.

SUMMARY OF MAJOR SELLING ISSUES

The retailer is extremely important to the U.S. economy, accounting for trillions of dollars in sales each year. As a career, retailing offers excellent financial and personal rewards to people who are willing to work hard, have the ability to manage people, and understand the principles of selling.

The retail salesperson's job activities vary from store to store, yet they usually include making transactions, contacting customers, handling complaints, working stock, and personal selling. The fundamentals of selling discussed in earlier chapters and mentioned in this chapter are used by the retail salesperson just as they are used by the business salesperson.

Business products include the raw materials, supplies, equipment, and services used in production, as well as finished goods and services intended for the producer, reseller, and government markets. The producer market contains individuals and organizations that purchase products and services for the production of other goods or services. Characteristics of the producer market include derived demand, inelastic demand, and joint demand. Products are technical in nature and frequently require specifications and bids, complex pricing, and standardization.

The business buying decision may be a complex and lengthy process. It usually involves eight basic steps, depending on whether it is a new task, a modified rebuy, or a straight rebuy situation. It is important for the salesperson to locate individuals who influence the buying decision and determine the strength of each one's influence to allocate the right amount of time and effort needed to solve a customer's problems. Buyers are concerned about costs and product quality, which can result in increased profits and more efficient operations. A value analysis can be used to show the buyer that the salesperson's product is cost efficient.

A service is an action or activity done for others for a fee. Services can be characterized as intangible, inseparable, heterogeneous, perishable, and their demand fluctuates as compared to physical goods. Nonprofit organizations do sell others on contributing resources, such as money, labor, and materials. They also sell clients on using their services.

MEETING A SALES CHALLENGE

Many retail salespeople earn excellent incomes. It usually depends on what they sell, their store, compensation plan, product knowledge, and their selling skills. Assuming Barbara Coleman knows her products, she needs to develop a selling process to allow her to increase her sales. She should analyze how Jack Pruett and Richard Ciotti have become so successful.

Barbara needs to prospect, using customers plus people who come into the store but do not buy. She can keep a prospect file, take the names of people who are interested in

ETHICAL DILEMMA

Should You Mind Your Own Business?

You have been working part time for a large national department store chain for the past year. Your store, like others in the mall, has been experiencing a higher-than-normal amount of shoplifting. Store management has hired off-duty police wearing street clothes to walk around the store as if shopping and arrest thieves. The store manager strongly enforces the store policy that all people caught will be arrested and prosecuted.

For several months, you have suspected a fellow salesperson of taking office supplies home on a frequent basis. You have overlooked these discrepancies because she helped you learn the ropes when you started, and you believe that everyone takes a supply or two on occasion. Today, you saw the person take back a damaged jogging suit, give the customer credit, and then put it in a store bag and place the bag under the counter. That night, as you both were leaving, the person had the bag with something in it. It could be the jogging suit or just something that your co-worker purchased earlier. You want to know if the jogging suit is in the bag, but you also know that if it is the jogging suit, the store manager will prosecute her.

What would you do?

something, and telephone or mail something to them to see if they are interested in a new product or one that has gone on sale.

Barbara should be creative when someone enters the store. She should introduce herself and call the prospect by name, learn to remember names, and call them by name if they return. Ask questions to determine someone's needs and do not be afraid to positively handle objections. Barbara needs to use suggestion selling as recommended by Stanley Marcus.

If they buy, she should mail out a thank-you letter or call. Maybe she can uncover another prospect and have people ask for her when they need something. And Barbara must provide service after the sale.

It takes months, even years, to build a clientele. Yet using the 10-step retail selling process will help Barbara enjoy her work more and feel she is becoming a sales professional. She should certainly try to use selling skills to take advantage of people buying for Christmas and during the store's January sales.

KEY TERMS FOR SELLING		
retailing 423		initiator 434
business market 428		deciders 434
business marketing 429		influencers 434
derived demand 430		buyer 434
inelastic demand 430		gatekeepers 434
joint demand 430		users 434
new task purchase 431		nonprofit organization 438
straight rebuy purchase 431		nonprofit contributors 439
modified rebuy purchase 431		nonprofit clients 439

SALES APPLICATION QUESTIONS

1. Discuss the differences between selling for a retailer and selling for an industrial firm.

2. Suggestion selling is frequently used in retail selling. Explain suggestion selling and give an example of it.

3. Lynn Madden received four sweaters as holiday gifts. One was too small and she is now on her way to Feldman's Department Store to return it. As usual, the store is full of people with complaints about broken merchandise and wanting to return gifts that they can't use. Lynn spots a clerk in the clothing department and asks where to go for a refund. Annoyed, the busy clerk tells her to go to the window at the back of the store for a refund.

    a. Do you think the clerk did the proper thing?
    b. Analyze the situation and discuss what you believe the clerk could have done differently.
    c. Explain how Lynn Madden, the clerk, and the store may have been hurt in the situation.

4. John Black has been looking for a new sport coat for weeks. He has finally found one he really likes at Herb's Haberdashery.

    Buyer: I really like this coat.

    Salesperson: It's one of the best we carry. I think you've made an excellent choice.

    Buyer: I've been looking for quite awhile, but I'm not sure this is what I really need.

    Salesperson: I don't think you can go wrong with this coat, Mr. Black. You mentioned that you liked its quality, and it really does show off your good taste.

    Buyer: I am tired of shopping, and it is a good buy . . . OK, I'll take it.

    Salesperson: That's wonderful; I'm sure you'll be extremely happy with your decision. Will that be cash or charge?

    a. What did the salesperson do correctly in this situation?
    b. What opportunities were overlooked?

5. What three types of demand can affect business products? Describe each type with an example.

6. Assume you have been offered sales jobs with three different organizations. One sells computers, one sells insurance, and one gets medical doctors to use their nonprofit hospital. Describe the differences in the jobs.

SALES WORLD WIDE WEB EXERCISES

Comparing Places to Live for Your Salespeople

As a newly appointed sales manager, you are often hiring salespeople for different geographical locations within America. To help you better understand moving and living in other areas of the country, use the following URL to help you compare the city you live in with two other cities no less than 500 miles from you.

www.homefair.com

Click on all appropriate sites, such as The Salary Calculator and The Moving Calculator, to make a comparison between the city you presently live in and two other distant cities. Do not forget to also click on your favorite search engines for information on the three cities.

FURTHER EXPLORING THE SALES WORLD

1. Visit three different types of retailers in your community, pose as a customer, - and report on the selling techniques used by each salesperson you encounter. Comment on what each person could do to improve the sales presentation.

2. Visit a large retailer in your community that trains its employees in using selling techniques. Report on their reasons for sales training, how they train, and what they include in their sales training program.

3. Select a good, service, and a product sold by nonprofit organizations and compare their features, advantages, and benefits. How would you demonstrate a main benefit of each of the three?

SELLING EXPERIENTIAL EXERCISE

What Are Your People Skills?

How well do you understand people, observe their behavior, and address their personal and professional growth? This self-test can help you see your skills. On a separate sheet of paper, write your score for each question. Write 4 if you strongly agree, 1 if you strongly disagree, or 2 or 3 if your feelings are somewhat in between.[6]

Strongly Agree			Strongly Disagree
4	3	2	1

1. I think that people often are unaware of their true motivation.
2. Psychological factors often play more of a role in job performance than in the job's required skills.
3. I make a conscious effort to understand the basic needs of others.
4. I am able to empathize with other people, even when I don't share their viewpoints.
5. I consciously try to organize my thinking around others.
6. People often reveal themselves by small details of behavior.
7. I am usually aware of people's strengths and weaknesses.
8. Most people aren't easy to read.
9. I notice when someone gets a new haircut, eyeglasses, or clothes.
10. After a meeting, I can usually accurately report how others responded to the discussion.
11. People may present themselves in a certain way that doesn't show who they really are.
12. I try not to read my own attitudes into other people's behavior.
13. I often think about the implications of my past impressions of people on the job.
14. When dealing with others, I try to consider how different they may be from me.
15 I don't judge someone until I have enough information to form a sound judgment.
16. I often think about ways to foster other people's personal and professional growth.
17. I see people for their potential—not how they can be of use to me, but how they can fulfill their life goals.
18. You can't change someone else.
19. When making decisions about people, I deliberately consider a wide range of factors.
20. I consciously try to help people play to their strengths and address their weaknesses.

Total Score ————

What were your skills? If your score was:

- **75–80**—You're probably strong in solving people problems.
- **61–74**—You have potential strengths in this area.
- **40–60**—You have potential weaknesses in this area.
- **20–39**—You have weaknesses to work on in solving people problems.

Now relate what you've learned to your work experiences by setting goals and intermediate targets. Then adjust![7]

CASE 15–1
Plimpton's Tire Service

Beverly Williams put on the brakes to stop her car. It was a rainy day and the car seemed to slide a few extra feet. When she got home she checked her tires. Sure enough, they were worn almost bare. *Have I had these tires this long?* Beverly thought to herself. The answer to that question didn't matter. It was obviously time to buy new tires.

Beverly drove her 1966 Mustang to a nearby tire store she had heard advertised many times. She entered the store ready to buy a set of inexpensive, nylon, four-ply tires. She didn't feel she needed more expensive radial tires, because she drove the Mustang only in town, almost exclusively to and from work. While she didn't need a top-of-the-line tire, she did want whitewalls. She thought whitewalls really made her car look better. The conversation went like this:

Buyer: Hello, I'm looking for some new tires.

Salesperson: What type of car?

Buyer: A '66 Mustang. . . . I think the diameter is 14 inches. . . . Oh, I'm looking for an inexpensive tire.

Salesperson: [*Walking over to a display*] These are our cheapest tires.

Buyer: That's a little more than I wanted to spend. [*She pauses, waiting for a reply; getting none, she continues:*] Well, I guess I'll have to shop around.

Questions

1. Would this salesperson have sold you? Why or why not?
2. What did the salesperson do wrong in this case?
3. If you were the salesperson, what would you have done?

CASE 15–2
Competition Shoes, Inc.

The ad read, "Competition Shoes—We know what it takes to keep you running." Dave Wilson looked at his running shoes and knew they only had a couple of miles left in them.

Dave had only recently taken up running, but he was now addicted to his new hobby and generally ran 15 to 20 miles a week. He realized now that his running shoes were not high quality, and now that he was a serious runner, he wanted the proper equipment—and that meant better shoes. He decided to see if Competition Shoes had what he needed. That night, he went to the store:

Salesperson: Hello, what can I help you with this evening?

Buyer: I am looking for a new pair of running shoes.

Salesperson: Do you have a particular shoe you would like to try on?

Buyer: To be honest with you, I've only been running for three months and I don't know very much about running shoes.

Salesperson: How much do you run a week?

Buyer: I'm up to about 20 miles.

Salesperson: That's a lot of running for a beginner. Do you plan to compete in the future?

Buyer: Well, I started running for the exercise, like so many people do, but I really enjoy running and I would like to prove to myself that I can finish a marathon.

Salesperson: So you would like to compete.

Buyer: Come to think of it, I guess I would.

Salesperson: Where do you do most of your running—on a track, grass, or pavement?

Buyer: There is a high school track a few blocks from my house, but I have to run on street to get there and back.

Salesperson: Mr. Wilson, I have two shoes that I believe will work very well for you [*showing Dave two shoes from the display*]. This Nike shoe is very sturdy and generally holds up well for people who put in as many miles as you do each week. This Big Paw Olympian [*showing Dave the other shoe*] is just as sturdy and has this wide, vibration-reducing heel. This heel will save your feet and legs a lot of stress. It's especially made for running on hard surfaces.

Buyer: I'll try on the Olympian model. I'll probably need a size 10. [*The salesperson gets the shoes, and Dave tries them on.*]

Salesperson: How do they feel?

Buyer: Great [*realizing the difference between these shoes and his old pair*], I'll take them.

Salesperson: That's wonderful! I know they will suit your needs. Now come over here, I want to show you our new, thick, runners' socks. With your running schedule, I think you will need three pairs of new socks.

Questions

1. What did the salesperson do correctly in this situation? Do you think any errors were made?
2. If you were looking for a new pair of running shoes, would you have bought from this salesperson? Why?
3. What is the importance of sales professionalism in this retail situation? How did this salesperson differ from the one in Case 15–1?

Notes

Chapter 1

1. "Jobs for the Next Century," *Occupational Outlook Handbook* (Washington, D.C.: U.S. Department of Labor, Bureau of Labor Statistics, August 1997), p. 23.

2. "The Selling Power 200," *Selling Power,* November/December 1996, pp. 37–48 and "The Selling Power 300: Annual Ranking of America's Largest Sales Forces," *Selling Power,* September 1997, pp. 39–60.

3. For further discussion on direct selling, see Robert A. Peterson and Thomas R. Wotruba, "What is Direct Selling?—Definition, Perspectives, and Research Agenda," *The Journal of Personal Selling,* Fall 1996, pp. 1–16; and Richard C. Bartlett, *The Direct Option* (College Station, Tex.: Texas A & M University Press, 1994).

4. Adapted from "1997 Salesforce Compensation," *Dartnell's 30th Survey* (Chicago: Dartnell, 1994).

5. "Jobs for the Next Century," *Occupational Outlook Handbook* (Washington, D.C.: U.S. Department of Labor, Bureau of Labor Statistics, August 1997), pp. 18–31.

6. Ibid.

7. *1996 Census of Retail Trade,* Nonemployer Statistics Series—U.S. (Washington, D.C.: U.S. Bureau of the Census, 1997).

8. *1996 Census Wholesale Trade,* Nonemployer Statistics Series—U.S. (Washington, D.C.: U.S. Bureau of the Census, 1997).

9. Adapted from Susan Harte, "When in Rome, You Should Learn to Do What the Romans Do," *Atlanta Journal-Constitution,* January 22, 1996, pp. D1, D6. Also see Lufthansa's *Business Travel Guide/Europe,* 1995.

10. For more information, see *Sales & Marketing Management* magazine's yearly June special issue on selling costs, such as compensation. It is called the "Sales Manager's Budget Planner."

11. Excerpts from Xerox Corporation sales literature.

12. Adapted from Cynthia Barmun and Netasha Wolninsky, "Why Americans Fail at Overseas Negotiations," *Management Review,* October 1989, pp. 55–57.

Chapter 2

1. "NewsMakers," *Sales & Marketing Management,* February 1996, p. 16.

2. Weld F. Royal, "It's Not Easy Being Green," *Sales & Marketing Management,* July 1995, pp. 84–90.

3. Larry G. Mayewski, Michael L. Albanese, and Cynthia J. Crosson, "Market Conduct Emerges as Rating Issue," *Best Review,* November 1995, p. 30.

4. Amanda Richards, "Does Charity Pay?" *Marketing,* September 21, 1995, pp. 24–25.

5. Also see Thomas R. Wotruba, "A Comprehensive Framework for the Analysis of Ethical Behavior, with a Focus on Sales Organizations," *Journal of Personal Selling & Sales Management,* Spring 1990, pp. 29–42; and Michael A. Mayo and Lawrence J. Marks, "An Empirical Investigation of a General Theory of Marketing Ethics," *Journal of the Academy of Marketing Science,* Spring 1990, pp. 163–72.

6. Shay Sayre, Mary L. Joyce, and David R. Lambert, "Gender and Sales Ethics: Are Women Penalized Less Severely Than Their Male Counterparts?" *Journal of Personal Selling & Sales Management,* Fall 1991, pp. 50–65.

7. *Fair Employment Report,* August 2, 1996, p. 123.

8. Also see Leslie M. Fine and Janice R. Franke, "Legal Aspects of Salesperson Commission Payments: Implications for the Implementation of Commission Sales Programs," *Journal of Personal Selling & Sales Management,* Winter 1995, pp. 53–68.

9. Paula Champ, "How to Sell in Japan," *Selling,* December 1993, pp. 30–47.

10. Richard F. Beltramini, "Exploring the Effectiveness of Business Gifts: A Controlled Field Experiment," *Journal of the Academy of Marketing,* Winter 1992, pp. 87–91; and Bristol Voss, "Eat, Drink, and Be Wary," *Sales & Marketing Management,* January 1991, pp. 49–54.

11. Anne M. Phaneuf, "Is It Really Better to Give?" *Sales & Marketing Management,* September 1995, pp. 95–104.

12. Adapted from "Strange Tales of Sales," *Sales & Marketing Management,* June 3, 1995, p. 46.

13. John Jobs, "Watch Those Buyers," *Sales & Marketing Management,* October 1997, pp. 34–38.

14. Les Andrews, "Watch What You Say," *Distribution,* April 1997, p. 23.

15. Charles H. Schwepker, Jr., O. C. Ferrell, and Thomas N. Ingram, "The Influence of Ethical Climate and Ethical Conflict on Role Stress in the Sales Force," *Journal of the Academy of Marketing Science,* Spring 1997, pp. 99–108.

16. Based on Bart Victor and John B. Cullen, "The Organizational Bases of Ethical Work Climates," *Administrative Science Quarterly* 33 (1998), pp. 101–125.

Chapter 3

1. Developed by Professor John C. Hafer of the University of Nebraska at Omaha.

2. Developed by Pushkala Raman.

3. Carl Jung, *Psychological Types* (London, England: Routledge and Kegan Paul, 1923).

4. Adapted from I. Myers, *The Myers–Briggs Type Indicator* (Princeton, N.J.: Educational Testing Service, 1962).

5. Adapted from J. R. Schermerhorn, J. G. Hunt, and R. N. Osborn, *Managing Organizational Behavior* (New York: John Wiley, 1991), p. 123.

Chapter 4

1. Gerhard Gschwandtner, *Nonverbal Selling Power* (Englewood Cliffs, N.J.: Prentice Hall, 1995), p. 3.

2. Ibid.

3. Dorothea Johnson, "Five Tips for International Handshaking," *Sales & Marketing Management,* July 1997, p. 90.

4. Also see Dana Ray, "Every Guest Leaves Satisfied," *Selling Power,* April 1997, p. 37; and Robert A. Peterson, Michael P. Cannito, and Steven P. Brown, "An Exploratory Investigation of Voice Characteristics and Selling Effectiveness," *Journal of Personal Selling & Sales Management,* Winter 1995, pp. 1–16.

5. Text of figure reproduced from the sales training course, "The Languages of Selling," by Gerhard Gschwandtner & Associates (Falmouth, Va.). Photos by Professor Futrell.

6. Joann S. Lublin, "Companies Use Cross-Cultural Training to Help Their Employees Adjust Abroad," *The Wall Street Journal,* August 4, 1997.

7. Adapted from Ethel C. Glenn and Elliot A. Pood, "Listening Self-Inventory." Reprinted by permission of the publisher from *Supervisory Management,* January 1996, pp. 12–15.

Chapter 5

1. Based on the author's conversation with Jack Smith of the Colgate Company about his first month's selling.

2. Arne J. DeKeeijzer, "China: The Sales Doors Open," *Personal Selling Power,* January–February 1994, pp. 12–22.

3. Also see Sanjay K. Dhar and Stephen J. Hoch, "Price Discrimination Using In-Store Merchandising," *Journal of Marketing,* January 1996, pp. 17–30.

4. Karen Starr, "Blue Ribbon Training: DuPont Merck's Formula for Technology Training Win Awards," *Personal Selling Power,* October 1996, pp. 22–23.

5. Portions of this section were adapted from George W. Colombo, *Sales Force Automation* (New York: McGraw-Hill, 1994).

6. Kate Griffin, "Telephone-fax, Beeper—E-mail Address," *Marketing News,* September 1994, pp. 7–8.

7. Andy Cohen, "Going Mobile, Part 2," *Sales & Marketing Management,* June 1994, p. 5.

8. Adapted from Elwood N. Chapman, *Sales Training Basics* (Menlo Park, Calif.: Crisp Publications, 1992), p. 11.

Chapter 6

1. Also see Malcolm Fleschner, *Selling Power,* January/February 1997, p. 60.

2. Paula Champa, "How to Sell in Japan," *Selling,* December 1993, pp. 39–47.

3. Personal conversation with author.

4. Personal conversation with author.

5. Portions of this section adapted from Scott Krammick, *Expecting Referrals: The Resurrection of a Lost Art* (Fredericksburg, Va.: Associate Publishing, 1994).

6. Also see George W. Dudley and Shannon L. Goodson, *Earning What You're Worth? The Psychology of Sales Call Reluctance* (New York: Behavioral Sciences Research Press, 1992).

7. Ibid.

8. Adapted from William B. Martin, *Quality Customer Service* (Menlo Park, Calif.: Crisp Publications, 1993), p. 21.

Chapter 7

1. Adapted from Joseph P. Smith, *Dress for Business* (Menlo Park, Calif.: Crisp Publications, 1997), p. 23.

Chapter 8

1. Adapted from G. M. Grikscheit, H. C. Cash, and W. J. E. Crissy, *Handbook of Selling: Psychological, Managerial, and Marketing Bases* (New York: John Wiley & Sons, 1981).

2. Example provided by Professor Richard D. Nordstrom, California State University—Fresno.

3. Adapted from Grikscheit, Cash, and Crissy, *Handbook of Selling.*

4. Ibid.

5. Example provided by Professor Richard D. Nordstrom, California State University—Fresno.

6. Also see Tony Alessandra, Phil Wexler, and Rich Barrera, *Nonmanipulative Selling* (Englewood Cliffs, N.J.: Prentice Hall, 1997).

7. Adapted from Robert B. Maddux, *Successful Negotiation* (Menlo Park, Calif.: Crisp Publications, 1988), p. 19.

8. Arne J. DeKeijzer, "China: The Sales Doors Open," *Personal Selling Power,* January–February 1994, pp. 12–22.

9. For 18 concession strategies useful during sales negotiations, see Homer B. Smith, "How to Concede—Strategically," *Sales & Marketing Management,* May 1988, pp. 79–80.

10. Adapted from John A. Firestone, *Sales Fundamentals* (Menlo Park, Calif.: Crisp Publications, 1993), p. 12.

Chapter 9

1. For a complete discussion, see Neil Rackham, *SPIN Selling* (New York: McGraw-Hill, May 1988).

2. Dennis DeMaria, "Keep Quiet and Get the Order," *Personal Selling Power,* March–April 1993, p. 17.

Chapter 10

1. Rosemary P. Ramsey and Ravipreet S. Sohi, "Listening to Your Customers: The Impact of Perceived Salesperson Listening Behavior on Relationship Outcomes," *Journal of the Academy of Marketing Science,* Spring 1997, pp. 127–137.

2. Patricia M. Doney and Joseph P. Cannon, "An Examination of the Nature of Trust in Buyer–Seller Relationships," *Journal of Marketing,* April 1997, pp. 35–51.

3. Sam Lovejoy, "Technology Improves Communcations," *Sales & Marketing Management,* September 4, 1997, pp. 34–37.

4. Alice Graham, "Put Some Zip in Your Presentations," *Sales & Marketing Management,* August 14, 1997, pp. 26–29.

5. Arne J. DeKeijzer, "China: The Sales Doors Open," *Personal Selling Power,* January–February 1994, pp. 12–22.

Chapter 11

1. John Anderson, "Pulling Off a Six-Figure Bank Job," *Selling,* May 1994, p. 14.

2. Adapted from Tom Hopkins, *How to Master the Art of Selling* (New York: Warner Books, 1994), p. 191.

Chapter 12

1. Adapted from John L. Johnston, *Works of Mark Twain* (New York: Harper & Row, 1989), p. 133.

2. Gerhard Gschwandtner, "How to Sell in France," *Personal Selling Power,* July–August 1991, pp. 54–60.

3. Mike Radick, "Training Salespeople to Get Success on Their Side," *Sales & Marketing Management,* August 15, 1993. Also see Neil Rackham, *SPIN Selling* (New York: McGraw-Hill, 1988).

4. John C. Young, "When You Strike Out," *Journal of Purchasing,* December 1991, pp. 3–8.

Chapter 13

1. Robert L. Shook, *Ten Greatest Salespersons* (New York: Harper & Row, 1988), p. 95.

2. Ibid., p. 155.

3. Ibid., p. 67.

4. Written by Moshe Davidow.

5. Melissa Campanelli, "Starting from Scratch," *Sales & Marketing Management,* November 1994, p. 55.

6. Charles M. Futrell, *ABC's of Relationship Selling* (Burr Ridge, Ill.: Richard D. Irwin, Inc., 1997), p. 373.

7. Ibid.

8. James Lewis, "These Sins Will Kill a Sale," *Selling,* October 1997, p. 6.

9. Reprinted with permission of B. J. Hughes, Inc.

10. Adapted from Richard F. Gerson, *Beyond Customer Service: Keeping Customers for Life* (Menlo Park, Calif.: Crisp Publications, 1992), p. 79.

Chapter 14

1. Charles M. Futrell, "Survey of America's Top Sales Forces," private research project, 1998.

2. Adapted from Sergy Frank, "Global Negotiation," *Sales & Marketing Management,* May 1997, pp. 64–69.

Chapter 15

1. "Marketing and Sales Occupations," *Occupational Outlook Quarterly,* Spring 1996, p. 32.

2. Adapted from Stanley Marcus, "Fire a Buyer and Hire a Seller," *International Trends in Retailing,* Fall 1986, pp. 49–55.

3. Sergy Frank, "Global Negotiation," *Sales & Marketing Management,* May 1992, pp. 64–69.

4. *Occupational Outlook Quarterly,* Spring 1997, pp. 3–6.

5. Ibid.

6. Adapted from Wayne Rodgers, *People Management* (Menlo Park, Calif.: Crisp Publications, 1994), p. 25.

7. Aubrey Penny, "People Skills," *Personnel Skills,* February 1995, pp. 33–36.

Glossary

A

acceptance signals Signs that your buyer is favorably inclined toward you and your presentation. 112

account analysis The process of analyzing each prospect and customer to maximize the chances of reaching a sales goal. 402

account segmentation The process of applying different selling strategies to different territories 402

action The last of the prospect's mental steps—when the prospect buys your product.

advantage The performance characteristic of a product that describes how it can be used or will help the buyer. 69

advertising The nonpersonal communication of information paid for by an identified sponsor, for example, an individual or an organization.

alternative-choice close A type of close that does not give the prospect a choice of buying or not buying but instead asks which one or how many items he or she wishes to buy. 351

analogy A comparison between two different situations that have something in common. 285

assumptive close A type of close that assumes the prospect will buy. 352

attitudes A person's learned predispositions toward something. 80

autosuggestion A kind of suggestion that attempts to have prospects imagine themselves using the product. 283

B

belief A state of mind in which trust or confidence is placed in something or someone. 80

benefit A favorable result the buyer receives from the product because of a particular advantage that has the ability to satisfy a buyer's need. 70

benefit selling A method of selling whereby a salesperson relates a product's benefits to the customer's needs using the product's features and advantages as support. 69

black box The unobservable, internal process taking place within the mind of the prospect as he or she reaches a decision whether or not to buy. 67

boomerang method The process of turning an objection into a reason to buy. 328

breach of warranty A situation in which a product does not perform as promised by the company's representatives. 49

break-even analysis A quantitative technique for determining the level of sales at which total revenues equal total costs. 406

business market The market where all profit and nonprofit organizations buy goods and services for a specific purpose. 428

business marketing The marketing of goods and services to business users. 429

buyer The purchasing agent. 434

buying signal Anything that prospects say or do indicating they are ready to buy. 344

C

calendar management It forms a part of the electronic sales automation, which makes time management easier and less prone to errors or oversights. 145

call reluctance A feeling of not wanting to contact a prospect or customer. 191

career path The upward sequence of job movements during a sales career. 11

cash discounts Discounts earned by buyers who pay bills within a stated period. 157

caution signals Signs that a buyer is neutral or skeptical toward what the salesperson says. 112

CCC GOMES A stakeholder acronym: customers, creditors, community, government, owners, managers, employees, and suppliers. 38

center of influence method A method whereby the salesperson finds and cultivates people in a community or territory who are willing to cooperate in helping to find prospects. 182

Clayton Act An act that prohibits tie-in sales when they substantially lessen competition. This act also prohibits exclusive dealerships. 54

closing The process of helping people make a decision that will benefit them. 343

code of ethics A formal statement of the company's values concerning ethics and social issues. 56

cold canvas prospecting method A method whereby the salesperson contacts as many leads as possible with no knowledge of the business or individual called upon. 177

collect information The process by which buyers visit retail stores, contact potential suppliers, or talk with salespeople about a product's price, size, advantage, and warranty before making a decision regarding buying. 88

communication The act of transmitting verbal and nonverbal information and understanding between seller and buyer. 105

compensation method The method of offsetting negative product aspects with better benefit aspects. 333

compliment close A close wherein the salesperson ends with a compliment to the prospect. 352

complimentary approach An approach that opens with a compliment that is sincere and therefore effective. 254

computer-based presentations Dramatic and interactive presentations created with the help of sales force automation using a computer at relatively low costs. 146

condition of the sale A situation wherein an objection becomes a condition of the sale, such that if the condition is met the prospect will buy. 314

conscious need level A state of mind in which buyers are fully aware of their needs. 69

consultive selling The process of professionally providing information for helping customers make intelligent actions to achieve short- and long-term objectives.

consumer discounts One-time price reductions passed on from the manufacturer to channel members or directly to the customer. 157

consumer sales promotion A promotion that includes free samples, coupons, contests, and demonstrations to consumers. 138

contact management A listing of all the customer contacts that a salesperson makes in the course of conducting business. 145

contests and sweepstakes Premium offers offered to the public in the form of games.

continuous-yes close A kind of close whereby the salesperson develops a series of benefit questions that the prospect must answer. 354

conventional moral development level An individual conforms to the expectations of others, such as family, employer, boss, and society. Upholds moral and legal laws. 41

cooling-off laws Laws that provide a cooling-off period during which the buyer may cancel the contract, return any merchandise, and obtain a full refund. 54

cooperative acceptance The right of employees to be treated fairly and with respect regardless of race, sex, national origin, physical disability, age, or religion, while on the job. 45

cooperative (co-op) advertising Advertising conducted by the retailer with costs paid for by the manufacturer or shared by the manufacturer and the retailer. 137

counter suggestion A suggestion that evokes an opposite response from the prospect. 283

creative imagery A relaxation and concentration technique that aids in stress management in which a salesperson envisions successful coping in various sales situations. 250

creative problem solvers Individuals who have the ability to develop and combine nontraditional alternatives to meet the specific needs of the customer. 202

credibility A salesperson's believability, established through empathy, willingness to listen to specific needs, and continual enthusiasm toward his or her work and the customer's business. 124

cumulative quantity discounts Discounts received for buying a certain amount of a product over a stated period. 157

curiosity approach An approach whereby the salesperson asks a question or does something to make the prospect curious about the product or service. 258

customer benefit approach An approach whereby the salesperson asks a question that implies that the product will benefit the prospect. 257

customer benefit plan A plan that contains the nucleus of information used in the sales presentation. 207

customer profile An outline that gives relevant information regarding the firm, the buyer, and individuals who influence the buying decision. 206

customer satisfaction The feelings about any differences between what is expected and actual experiences with the purchase. 380

customer service The activities and programs provided by the seller to make the relationship a satisfying one for the customer. 190, 379

D

deciders Those persons actually involved in making the decision to buy. 434

decoding process Receipt and translation of information by the receiver. 106

demonstration The process of showing a product to a prospect and letting him or her use it, if possible. 291

derived demand Demand linked to consumer demand for other products. 430

direct denial The method of overcoming objections through the use of facts, logic, and tact. 332

direct mail A promotional medium whereby mailing is used to distribute messages.

direct-mail advertising Advertising that is mailed directly to the customer or industrial user. 138

direct mail prospecting The process of mailing advertisements to a large number of people over an extended geographical area. 182

direct marketing The method of using nonpersonal media to elicit a measurable response and/or transaction.

direct question A question that by and large can be answered with a yes or no response or at most by a very short response consisting of a few words. 263

direct question approach A question approach used to clarify customers' needs when they identify the product they wish to buy.

direct response Any kind of advertising that elicits an immediate response.

direct suggestion An approach that suggests prospects buy rather than telling them to buy. 283

disagreement signals Signs that the prospect does not agree with the presentation or does not think the product is beneficial. 113

discretionary responsibility Behaviors that are purely voluntary and guided by its desire to make social contributions not mandated by economics, law, or ethics. 39

dodge A technique used by seller that neither denies, answers, nor ignores the objection, but simply temporarily dodges the objection. 324

dramatization The theatrical presentation of products. 289

E

economic needs The buyer's need to purchase the most satisfying product for the money. 68

80/20 principle Eighty percent of sales often come from 20 percent of a company's customers. 27, 403

electronic mail (e-mail) Allows messages to be sent electronically through a computer system that delivers them immediately to any number of recipients. 147

ELMS system The process of dividing broad accounts into varying size accounts. 403

empathy The ability to identify and understand another person's feelings, ideas, and circumstances. 118

employee rights Rights desired by employees regarding their job security and the treatment administered by their employer while on the job 45

encoding process Conversion of ideas and concepts into information. 106

endless chain referral method A method whereby a salesperson asks each buyer for a list of friends who might also be interested in buying the product. 177

enthusiasm A state of mind wherein a person is filled with excitement toward something. 124

Equal Employment Opportunity Commission (EEOC) The principal governmental agency responsible for monitoring discriminatory practices.

ethical behavior Behavior demonstrating a willingness to treat others fairly and that shows one to be honest, trustworthy, and that exhibits loyalty to company, associates, and the work for which one is responsible. 41

ethical committee A group of executives appointed to oversee company ethics and provide rulings on questionable ethical issues. 57

ethical ombudsman An official given the responsibility of corporate conscience who hears and investigates ethical complaints and informs top management of potential ethical issues. 57

ethical responsibility Behaviors that are not necessarily codified into law and may not serve the corporation's direct economic interests, but relate to equity, fairness, impartiality, and the rights of individuals.

ethics Principles of right or good conduct, or a body of such principles, that affect good and bad business practices. 41

exhibitions and demonstrations A situation in which a firm operates a booth at a trade show or other special interest gathering staffed by salespeople. 181

extensive decision making Decision-making characteristic of buyers who are unfamiliar with a specific product and who must therefore become highly involved in the decision-making process. 86

F

FAB selling technique A technique stressing features, advantages, and benefits of a product. 69

feature Any physical characteristic of a product. 69

feedback Verbal or nonverbal reaction to communication as transmitted to the sender. 107

five-question sequence The five-step process of overcoming objections in which facts, logic, and tact are used. 330

FOB destination The point at which the seller pays all shipping costs. 155

FOB shipping point The shipping process in which the buyer pays transportation charges for goods the title for which passes to the customer when the goods are loaded onto the shipping vehicle. 155

forestalling the objection A technique whereby the salesperson discusses an objection before the prospect has stated it.

formula presentation A presentation by which the salesperson follows a general outline that allows more flexibility and tries to determine prospect needs. 229

G

gatekeepers People who influence where information from salespeople goes and with whom salespeople will be allowed to talk. 434

Green River ordinance These ordinances protect consumers and aid local firms by making it more difficult for outside competition to enter the market. 54

gross profit Money available to cover the costs of marketing the product, operating the business, and profit. 158

geographic information systems It allows salespeople to view and manipulate customer and/or prospect information on an electronic map. 146

H

hearing The ability to detect sounds. 119

hidden objection An objection that disguises the actual objection either with silence or triviality. 316

I

ideal self The person one would like to be. 81

indirect denial An apparent agreement with the prospect used by the salesperson to deny the fundamental issue of the objection. 332

indirect question approach A variation of the direct question approach that asks a question not related to the product.

indirect suggestion A statement by the salesperson recommending that the prospect undertake some action while making it seem that the idea to do so is the prospect's. 283

industrial advertising Advertising aimed at individuals and organizations who purchase products for manufacturing other products. 138

inelastic demand Demand that does not change in direct proportion to a change in price. 430

influencers People who influence the decision to buy a product. 434

information evaluation A process that determines what will be purchased as the buyer matches this information with needs, attitudes, and beliefs in making a decision. 88

initiator The person proposing to buy or replace a product. 434

intelligent questions Questions relating to a prospect's business that show the salesperson's concern for the prospect's needs. 329

Internet A global network of computers connected to one another. Also referred to as the Net. 149

intimate space A spatial zone up to two feet, about an arm's length from a person's body, that is reserved for close friends and loved ones. 108

introductory approach The most common but least powerful approach; it does little to capture the prospect's attention. 254

J

joint demand Demand that occurs when two or more products are used together to produce a single product. 430

K

key accounts Accounts that spend over $200,470 annually on a firm's products, the loss of which would greatly affect a territory's sales and profits. 403

KISS A memory device standing for Keep It Simple, Salesperson. 119

L

lead A person or organization who might be a prospect. 175

learning Acquiring knowledge or behavior based on past experiences. 79

limited decision making Decision-making characteristic of a buyer who invests a moderate level of energy in making the decision to buy because, although the buyer is not familiar with each brand's features, advantages, and benefits, the general quality of the good is known to him or her. 85

links Pointers which give the web its name. 149

list price A standard price charged to all customers. 155

listening Ability to derive meaning from sounds that are heard. 119

L-O-C-A-T-E An acronym for methods to uncover important needs: Listen, Observe, Combine, Ask questions, Talk to others, Empathize. 73

logical reasoning Persuasive techniques that appeal to the prospect's common sense by applying logic through reason. 282

looking-glass self The self that people think other people see them as. 81

M

manufacturer's sales representative A person who works for an organization that produces a product. 8

markup The dollar amount added to the product cost to determine its selling price. 158

medium The form of communication used in the sales presentation and discussion, most frequently words, visual materials, and body language. 106

memorized presentation A type of presentation in which the salesperson does 80 to 90 percent of the talking, focusing on the product and its benefits rather than attempting to determine the prospect's needs. 226

memory Ability to recall information over time. 123

merchandise approach An approach in which the salesperson waits until a browsing customer pauses to examine a product and then moves in to discuss its benefits.

message Information conveyed in the sales presentation. 106

metaphor An implied comparison that uses a contrasting word or phrase to evoke a vivid image. 285

minor-points close A close where the salesperson asks the prospect to make a low-risk decision on a minor element of a product. 354

misrepresentation Statements made by salespeople that exaggerate the capabilities of their products or services and false statements made to close a sale. 49

mobile offices Small offices installed or located in vehicles, such as a minivan. 148

modified rebuy purchases A type off purchase made when regular purchasing patterns are slightly changed to suit customers' present needs. 431

money objection A price-oriented objection. 320

multiple-question approach (SPIN) An approach where the salesperson uses four types of questions—situation, problem, implication, and need-payoff—to get a better understanding of the prospect's business. 260

N

national advertising Advertising designed to reach all users of the product, whether customers or industrial buyers. 136

need arousal A situation in which a salesperson triggers a psychological, social, or economic need in the buyer. 87

need awareness The stage in which the salesperson is aware of the buyer's needs and takes control of the situation by restating those needs to clarify the situation. 231

need development In a need-satisfaction sales presentation, a stage in which the discussion is devoted to the buyer's needs. 231

need fullfillment The last phase of a need-satisfaction sales presentation. Here, the salesperson shows how the product will satisfy mutual needs. 231

needs The desire for something a person feels is worthwhile. 68

need-satisfaction presentation A flexible, interactive type of presentation where a prospect's needs are thoroughly discussed. 230

negotiation The act of reaching an agreement mutually satisfactory to both buyer and seller. 314

negotiation close A close in which buyer and seller find ways for everyone to have a fair deal. 359

net price The price after allowance for all discounts. 155

net profit Money remaining after costs of marketing and operating the business are paid. 158

network An interconnecting group of people communicating and exchanging ideas and information.

networking The continuous prospecting method of making and utilizing contacts. 184

new task purchase A type of purchase made when a product is bought in conjunction with a job or task newly performed by the purchaser. 431

no-need objection An objection in which the prospect declares he or she does not need the product and implies the end of the selling effort, but which may actually be either a hidden or a stalling objection. 319

noise Factors that distort communication between buyer and seller, including barriers to communication. 107

noncumulative quantity discounts One-time price reductions. 157

nondirective question A question that opens up two-way communication by beginning the question with who, what, where, when, how, and why. 264

nonprofit clients The recipients of nonprofit organization's money and/or services. 439

nonprofit contributors A market that nonprofit organizations are involved in to gain resources. 439

nonprofit organization In this type of organization, profit is not a goal. Most sell services rather than tangible products. 438

nonverbal communication Unspoken communication such as physical space, appearance, handshake, and body movement. 107

O

observation method The process of finding prospects by a salesperson constantly watching what is happening in the sales area. 184

opinion approach An approach whereby a salesperson shows that the buyer's opinion is valued. 259

order-getter Individuals who get new and repeat business using a creative sales strategy and a well-executed sales presentation. 10

order-takers Individuals who ask what the customer wants or waiting for the customer to order. 10

orphaned customers Customers who are abandoned as a result of a salesperson leaving the company. 178

P

parallel referral sale A method of selling that makes the sale and gains referrals. 187

partnering The third level of selling where the seller works continually to improve the customer's operations, sales, and profits. 26

pass up the objection The option of a salesperson not to pursue a presentation or sale, or not to respond to an objection. 325

Paul Harvey dialogue The process of incorporating methods of speech and delivery to make talk come alive rather than sounding dull and memorized. 285

perception The process by which a person selects, organizes, and interprets information. 78

personal productivity Improvement of an individual's performance through more efficient data storage and retrieval, better time management, and enhanced presentations. 144

personal selling The personal communication of information to persuade a prospective customer to buy something that satisfies that individual's needs. 3

personal space An area two to four feet from a person; it is the closest zone a stranger or business acquaintance is normally allowed to enter. 108

personality A person's distinguishing character traits, attitudes, or habits. 81

persuasion Ability to change a person's belief, position, or course of action. 117

point-of-purchase (POP) displays Displays that allow a product to be easily seen and purchased. 139

postpone the objection The option of a salesperson to respond to an objection later during the sale presentation. 327

practical objection An overt objection based upon real or concrete causes. 315

preapproach Planning the sales call on a customer or prospect. 203

preconscious need level The level where needs are not fully developed in the conscious mind. 69

preconventional moral development level An individual acts in his or her own best interest and thus follows rules to avoid punishment or receive rewards. Will break moral and legal laws. 41

premium An article of merchandise offered as an incentive to the user to take some action. 140

premium approach An approach in which the salesperson offers a prospect something as an inducement to buy. 255

prestige suggestions A technique in which the salesperson has the prospect visualize using products that people whom the prospect trusts use.

price The value or worth of a product. 140

price discrimination The act of selling the same quantity of the same product to different buyers at different prices. 54

price lines The different price ranges of merchandise available to a customer.

principled moral development An individual lives by an internal set of morals, values, and ethics. These are upheld regardless of punishments or majority opinion. 41

probability close A close that permits the prospect to focus on his or her real objections, which a salesperson attempts to reverse with a persuasive sales argument. 358

probing The act of gathering information and uncovering customer needs using one or more questions. 118

problem–solution presentation A flexible, customized approach involving an in-depth study of a prospect's needs, requiring a well-planned presentation. 234

product Bundle of tangible and intangible attributes, including packaging, color, and brand, plus the services and even the reputation of the seller. 378

product approach An approach in which the salesperson places the product on the counter or hands it to the customer, saying nothing. 256

product objection An objection relating directly to the product. 322

proof statements Statements that substantiate claims made by the salesperson. 124, 286

prospect A qualified person or organization that has the potential to buy a salesperson's product or service. 175

prospect pool A group of names gathered from leads, referrals, orphans, or current customers. 186

prospecting The process of identifying potential customers. 175

psychological objection A hidden objection based on the prospect's attitudes. 315

public space Distances greater than 12 feet from a person. 108

purchase decision A buyer's decision to purchase something. 88

purchase dissonance Tension on the part of a buyer regarding whether the right decision was made in purchasing a product. 90

purchase satisfaction Gratification based upon a product that supplies expected, or greater than expected, benefits. 90

Q

qualified prospect A prospect who has the financial resources to pay, the authority to make the buying decision, and a desire for the product. 175

qualifier The verification that the person being called is a valid prospect.

R

real self People as they actually are. 81

receiver The person a communication is intended for. 107

reciprocity An agreement whereby a person or organization buys a product if the person or organization selling the product also buys a product from the first party. 54

redirect question A question that guides the prospect back to selling points that both parties agree on. 264

referral A person or organization recommended to you by someone who feels that this person could benefit from you or your product. 177

referral approach An approach that uses a third person's name as a reference to approach the buyer. 254

referral cycle The process that provides guidelines for a salesperson to ask for referrals. 187

relationship marketing The combination of products, prices, distributions, promotions, and service that organizations use to create customer loyalty. 25

relationship selling The second level of selling where customers are contacted after a purchase to determine future needs. 26

rephrasing question A question whereby the salesperson rephrases what the prospect has said in order to clarify meaning and determine the prospect's needs. 264, 326

retail advertising Advertising used by a retailer to reach customers within its geographic trading area. 137

retail salesperson An individual who sells goods or services to customers for their personal, nonbusiness use. 7

retailing Any individual or organization that sells its goods or services directly to final consumers for their personal, nonbusiness use. 423

return on investment (ROI) The additional sum of money expected from an investment over and above the original investment. 160

Robinson-Patman Act An act that allows sellers to grant quantity discounts to larger buyers based on savings in manufacturing costs. 54

routine decision-making The process of being in the habit of buying a particular product, so attitudes and beliefs toward the product are already formed and are usually positive. 85

routing The travel pattern used in working a sales territory. 409

S

sales-call objective The main purpose of a salesperson's call to a prospect. 205

sales objection The prospect's opposition or resistance to the salesperson's information or request. 309

sales planning The process of preparing to approach a prospect attempting to make a sale. 204

sales presentation The actual presentation of the sales pitch to the prospect. 209, 225

sales presentation mix The elements the salesperson assembles to sell to prospects. 280

sales process A sequential series of actions by the salesperson that leads toward the prospect taking a desired action and ends with a follow-up to ensure purchase satisfaction. 28, 173

sales response function The relationship between sales volume and sales calls. 405

sales territory A concept comprising a group of customers or a geographical area assigned to a salesperson. 399

sales training The effort put forth by an employer to provide the opportunity for the salesperson to acquire job-related attitudes, concepts, rules, and skills that result in improved performance in the selling environment. 131

scheduling The establishment of a fixed time for visiting a customer's business. 409

selective distortion The altering of information when it is inconsistent with a person's beliefs or attitudes. 79

selective exposure The process of allowing only a portion of the information revealed to be organized, interpreted, and permitted into awareness. 78

selective retention The act of remembering only the information that supports one's attitudes and beliefs. 79

self-concept A person's view of him- or herself. 81

self-image How a person sees him- or herself. 81

SELL sequence A sequence of things to do and say to stress benefits important to the customer: show the feature, explain the advantage, lead into the benefit, and let the customer talk by asking a question about the benefit. 76

selling The personal communication of information to persuade a prospective customer to buy something that satisfies that person's needs.

shelf facings The number of individual products placed beside each other on the shelf. 139

shelf positioning The physical placement of the product within the retailer's store. 139

shock approach An approach that uses a question designed to make the prospect think seriously about a subject related to the salesperson's product. 259

showmanship approach An approach that involves doing something unusual to catch the prospect's attention and interest. 256

simile A direct comparison statement using the words *like* or *as*. 285

social responsibility The responsibility to profitably serve employees and customers in an ethical and lawful manner. 37

social space A zone that is 4 to 12 feet from a person and is the area normally used for sales presentations. 108

source The origin of a communication. 106

source objection A loyalty-related objection by which the prospect states a preference for another company or salesperson, and may specify a dislike for the salesperson's company or self. 322

space invasion A situation in which one person enters another person's personal or intimate space. 108

space threat A situation in which a person threatens to invade another's spatial territory. 108

SPIN See *multiple question approach.* 260

stakeholder Any group within or outside the organization that has a stake in the organization's performance. 38

stalling objection An objection that delays the presentation or the sale. 317

standing-room-only close A close whereby a salesperson suggests that if a prospect does not act now he or she may not be able to buy in the future, thus motivating the prospect to act immediately. 358

stimulus–response model A model of behavior that describes the process of applying a stimulus (sales presentation) that results in a response (purchase decision). 67

strategic Programs, goals, and problems of great importance to customers. 201

strategic customer relationship Formal relationship with the customer, the purpose of which is joint pursuit of mutual goals. 201

straight rebuy purchase A routine purchase of products bought regularly. 431

suggestive propositions A proposition that implies that the prospect should act now. 283

summary-of-benefits close A close wherein the salesperson summarizes the benefits of the product in a positive manner so that the prospect agrees with what the salesperson says. 353

surfing the Internet Exploring the different web sites found within the web of links. 149

T

T-account close A close that is based on the process that people use when they make a decision by weighing the pros against the cons. 356

technology close A close in which the buyer is shown past purchases, sales trends, purchase suggestions, and payment schedules by graphs and bar charts. 360

telemarketing A marketing communication system using telecommunication technology and trained personnel to conduct planned, measurable marketing activities directed at targeted groups of consumers. 183

telephone prospecting The process of reaching potential customers over the phone. 183

telephone selling The use of a telephone in non-face-to-face selling.

termination-at-will rule A common law rule that allows a company to discharge employees at its discretion. 45

territorial space The area around oneself that a person will not allow another person to enter without consent. 107

territory manager A person who plans, organizes, and executes activities that increase sales and profits in a given territory. 22

third party answer The technique of responding to an objection with testimony from authoritative sources. 333

tie-in sale Sales in which a buyer is required to buy additional products not wanted when purchasing particular items. 54

trade advertising Advertising undertaken by the manufacturer and directed toward the wholesaler or retailer. 138

trade channel A group of firms acting together to move goods from the manufacturer to users.

trade discounts Discounts on the list retail price offered to channel members. 157

trade sales promotion A promotion that encourages resellers to purchase and aggressively sell a manufacturer's products by offering incentives like sales contests, displays, special purchase prices, and free merchandise. 138

transaction selling The first level of selling where customers are sold a product or service and not contacted again. 26

trial close A close that checks the attitude of your prospect toward the sales presentation. 74

U

unconscious need level The level at which people do not know why they buy a product. 69

undifferentiated selling The process of applying and designing selling strategies equally to all accounts. 402

unit cost Total cost of one unit of the product. 163

users People who must work with or use the product. 434

V

value analysis An investigation that determines the best product for the money. 161

visuals Illustrative material that aids a prospect in increasing memory retention of a presentation. 289

W

wants Needs that are learned by a person. 68

Web page A page site on the World Wide Web that contains information and usually a number of pointers to other pages of information. 149

wholesale salesperson A person who sells products to parties for resale, use in producing other goods or services, or operating an organization. 7

World Wide Web Part of the Internet that houses the "web sites" that provide text, graphics, video, and audio information on milllions of topics. 149

word processing Production of typewritten documents (as business letters) with automated and usually computerized typing and text-editing equipment. 147

Z

zone price The price based on geographical location or zone of customers. 155

Photo Credits and Acknowledgments

Chapter 1

Exhibit 1-4   Tim Brown/Tony Stone Images

Exhibit 1-9   Don Mason/The Stock Market

Exhibit 1-11   Gabe Palmer/Mugshots/ The Stock Market

Exhibit 1-21   J. McDermott/Tony Stone Images

Exhibit 1-25

(*top left*)   Jon Feingersh/The Stock Market

(*top right*)   Cindy Charles/Photo Edit

(*bottom left*)   Kaluzny/Thatcher/Tony Stone Images

(*bottom right*)   Andy Sachs/Tony Stone Images

Chapter 2

Exhibit 2-8   Jon Riley/Tony Stone Images

Exhibit 2-13   Gary A. Conner/Photo Edit

Exhibit 2-18   Pete Saloutos/The Stock Market

Exhibit 2-21   Pete Saloutos/The Stock Market

Chapter 3

Exhibit 3-4   Tom McCarthy/Photo Edit

Exhibit 3-7

(*left*)   Superstock

(*right*)   Dean Foods Company

Exhibit 3-14   Dana White/PhotoEdit

Exhibit 3-20

(*left*)   Robert Helfrick/The Picture Cube

(*right*)   Michael Newman/Photo Edit

Exhibit 3-22   Rob Nelson/Black Star

Exhibit 3-25

(*left*)   David J. Sams/Tony Stone Images

(*right*)   Jeff Zarauba/Tony Stone Images

Chapter 4

Exhibit 4-8

(*top left*)   Jose L. Pelaez/The Stock Market

(*top right*)   Tom & Degan McCarthy/ The Stock Market

(*bottom left*)   Jon Feingersh/The Stock Market

(*bottom right*)   Mug Shots/The Stock Market

Exhibit 4-10

(*left*)   Steve Niedorf/The Image Bank

(*right*)   Bruce Ayers/Tony Stone Images

Exhibit 4-12

(*left*)   Courtesy of Lucille Pointer/Charles Futrell

(*center*)   Courtesy of Jeffrey S. Conant/Charles Futrell

(*right*)   Courtesy of Larry Gersham/Charles Futrell

Exhibit 4-18   Frank Herholdt/Tony Stone Images

Exhibit 4-20   Mug Shots/The Stock Market

Chapter 5

Exhibit 5-5

(*left*)   David Young-Wolff/ PhotoEdit

(*right*)   Joseph Nettis/Stock Boston

Exhibit 5-10   Chris Jones/The Stock Market

Exhibit 5-12   Frank Siteman/Tony Stone Images

Exhibit 5-14   Gabe Palmer/The Stock Market

Exhibit 5-15   Bill Bachman/PhotoEdit

Exhibit 5-20   David Young-Wolff/ PhotoEdit

Exhibit 5-33   Steve Firebaugh/The Stock Market

Exhibit 5-35   Jose L. Pelaez/The Stock Market

Chapter 6

Exhibit 6-7   Courtesy Cindy Ramirez and Sonia Ramirez/ Charles Futrell

Box, page (6-9)   CIB Productions/The Stock Market

Exhibit 6-24   Superstock

Chapter 7

Exhibit 7-6   Charles Gupton/Stock Boston

Chapter 8

Box, page (8-17)   Ken Ross/FPG International

Chapter 9

Exhibit 9-9   Charles Futrell

Exhibit 9-12   Tony Freeman/PhotoEdit

Exhibit 9-14   Tom McCarthy/Photo Edit

Chapter 10

Exhibit 10-15   (all photos) Charles Futrell

Exhibit 10-17   Melanie Carr/Zephyr Pictures

Exhibit 10-19   Michael Newman/ PhotoEdit

Chapter 11

Exhibit 11-11   JPH Images/The Image Bank

Exhibit 11-17   Jeff Greenberg/PhotoEdit

Exhibit 11-20   Michael Newman/ PhotoEdit

Exhibit 11-28   Bruce Ayers/Tony Stone Images

Chapter 12

Exhibit 12-7   Stephen Frisch/Stock Boston

Exhibit 12-9   G+M David de Loosy/ The Image Bank

Exhibit 12-11   Ed Wheeler/The Stock Market

Index